BEITRÄGE ZUR EXPERIMENTELLEN WIRTSCHAFTSFORSCHUNG

Dritter Band

CONTRIBUTIONS TO EXPERIMENTAL ECONOMICS

Volume Three

Herausgegeben

von

HEINZ SAUERMANN

1972

J. C. B. MOHR (PAUL SIEBECK) TÜBINGEN

Printed in Germany
Offsetdruck: Gulde-Druck, Tübingen
Einband: Heinrich Koch, Großbuchbinderei, Tübingen

ISBN 3 16 333961 1 (brosch.)
ISBN 3 16 333962 X (Lw.)

CONTENTS

1. INTRODUCTION

HEINZ SAUERMANN*

This volume, the third of the "Contributions to Experimental Economics", contains the papers presented to the Conference on Experimental Economics in Kronberg im Taunus, 5. - 12. September 1971.
After approximately two decades of experimental economics at the University of Frankfurt a.M. our wish to meet with experimental researchers of other universities resp. other countries became more intensive, especially as in 1969 our macroeconomic experiment had begun to run successfully and first results were to be expected in the near future. When the financial means could be secured from the Kreutkniet-Stiftung, it became realistic to think of the organization of an international conference. At the end of 1969 we invited a group of scientists who were known to us by their experimental work in economics, sociology and psychology. The invitation was extended on the condition that an original paper be presented. First the conference was to take place in spring 1971; it had to be postponed until September 1971. The language of the conference was English.
The positive reaction to our invitation mirrowed the great interest in an international meeting, the interfacultative character of which playing no small part. The discussions have proved the experimental

method to be an ideal ground of cooperation in the social sciences. The same method of analysis of similar problems produced a fruitful basis of understanding.

The papers are printed in the sequence of presentation at the conference. Each paper was discussed independently and for that matter no other principle of order was necessary. Of course, preparing the program some affinities of topics were considered. Unfortunately Martin Shubik and Philip S. Gallo were unable to attend, which explains their papers being placed at the end. The authors were able to prepare their papers for publication after the conference; all papers were completed by October 1971.

The object of this first international conference on experimental economics was not only an appraisal of experimental economics to-day and the possibility of contacts between independently working scientists, but also to realize the present strategic position of this special field of research. In an opening address I tried to describe our common achievements and to evaluate the chances of development. Since September 1971 conditions have not changed, so that it seems justified to repeat some of my thoughts.

We realize that experimental economics cannot offer spectacular results. It began with the experimental investigation of some behavioral hypotheses, as the theories of important phenomena of economic reality did not produce a satisfactory explanation. Though the concepts of utility and profit maximization served to build up a complete microeconomic theory, these theories - while leaving out the large field of oligopoly and bilateral monopoly phenomena - were falsified by empirical investigations. In addition to the limited degree of explanation of so many theories, which differed in as much as their assumptions varied, there was not even the possibility to test their degree of quality. As in other sciences adopting mathematical methods we have also in the economic and social sciences used the experiment to test, step by step, the behavioral hypotheses to arrive at a more realistic theory via the decision behavior of human beings as observed in the experiment. The experimental research works - so to speak - in the brick laying manner, inasfar as all elements of a realistic theory of the economic world are treated experimentally one upon the other. The experiments of decisions on quantities and prices, of investment-, coalition- and reaction- behavior have produced the result that the process of decision is subject to the conditions of limited rationality and that gradual adaptation to certain realizable aspirations takes place. We have already seen an effect in the construction of more realistic economic models with relevance to aspiration levels under the conditions of limited rationality. This shows successful approaches in the construction of economic theories specially in connection with problems of the market and of the firm.

Not until experiments were actually tried in macroeconomics became it sufficiently possible to measure the value of experiments for the macroeconomic theory. Before macroeconomic experiments could be executed some special difficulties had to be delt with. In microeconomics we work with individual decisions on the ground of non-aggregated variables. To work with macroeconomic global quantities we use hypotheses of the average behavior with regard to aggregate variables. In an experiment the subjects decide, so to speak, as the representatives of a certain group. The difficulty for experimental macroeconomics was to develop an macroeconomic model with some characteristic parameters to mark the scope of decision without unduly endangering the existence of the system by one single decision. At the same time the experimental model had to be sufficiently complex to show the effects of decisions on the significant variables and to demonstrate the interdependence of the system. These complications required from the beginning the use of electronic simulation models.

Having successfully executed the first macroeconomic experiments we yet cannot foresee in which way experimental work will contribute towards the development of the economic theory. What we have learned from microeconomic experiments - the concept of adaptation of aspirations - we adopted in macroeconomic experiments, in my opinion with promising results. We have arrived at an elastic business cycle and growth model, in which the adaptive behavior produces a process with close relevance to reality. Already the first evaluations of our macroeconomic experiments justify the expectation that profound knowledge of the interdependence of an economic system is not only profitable to participants in experiment series. We hope that one day the economic process of business cycle and growth can be explained more exactly, more realistically and in more detail. It is justified to expect that experimental macroeconomics will be a useful instrument for preparation of and decision on rational actions in economic policy, as microeconomic experiments have led us to reasonable and practical decision rules.

To realize this aim it will be important that the experimental analysis of human decision behavior will be able to limit trial and error.

The path of rationalization of action in economics and economic policy will surely be a long one. Experimental economics, as a new approach in addition to empirical-statistical analysis and the construction of theoretical models, requires extensive material means for the laboratory experiments. The virtues of patience and perseverance are imperative for the evaluation of large quantities of material produced by the controlled experiments. Experimental work has always to accomplish four steps: the empirical-statistical analysis, the construction of a relevant decision model, the execution of the experiment and the evaluation of the experimental material with the aid of the modern means of mathematical statistics. Last not least the future of experimental economics depends on young qualified social scientists. Opposite the facts, that we observe a strong trend towards ideologies in the social sciences, that the postulate of democratization in education will necessarily lower the level, that so-called critical theories produce in the end but neo-nihilism or modernistic anarchism, that - at least in Germany - the introduction of the so-called "group-university" removes the principle of efficiency and the conditions of research - opposite these and other facts the future of all research, and also of experimental research in the social sciences, cannot be judged optimistically. However, just in the face of this pessimistic outlook the conference at Kronberg im Taunus, at which about thirty younger scientists reported on their research work, was at least a hopeful begin of international cooperation in experimental economics and social sciences.

That the conference could take place in best concentration and good spirit was the merit not only of the group of those presenting a paper but also of the group of those offering the necessary technical assistance: Sigrid Berg, Elisabeth Blochel, Denise Deissenberg, Ingeborg Sauermann, Elisabeth Selten, Michael Braulke, Christophe Deissenberg, Victor Menschow, Joachim Merz and Richard Zeiger. I owe thanks to each one of them.

2. ON ECONOMIC EXPERIMENTS IN ECONOMICS*

AUSTIN C. HOGGATT**

1. Experiments and Economics

With the rise to dominance of the large corporation, all of the major (and most minor) decisions which effect economic history are made in bureaucratic organizations. This is illustrative of a generally increasing social complexity and technological interdependence which has proceeded so far in the developed nations as to produce decision problems which are qualitatively different from those faced by past generations. Decision-makers at all levels of the bureaucratic order are increasingly confronted by problem situations for which their hard-won skills, experience, and values are ill-designed. Longrun viability of our institutions will require that new skills, new experience and perhaps new values be developed and accumulated, but if we come by these solely by trial and error methods, progress will be slow, short-run results might well be semi-disastrous, and we have no assurance that the world order is stable enough to bear the costs. In economics and organizations, applications of aids to decision-making for our crucial ill-structured problems are quite naturally falling behind applications to well-structured problems, however, we may have developed

* Research for this paper was supported, in part, by National Science Foundation Grant GS-2463. June 1971. Revised October 1971.

** Professor of Business Administration, University of California, Berkeley.

a methodology via man-machine laboratory experimentation with micro-economic models and computer simulation of macro-economic models which holds promise for success. We pursue these approaches because they offer the possibility of accumulating synthetic experience which may be used as guides to decision-making in novel situations for which actual experience is not available. Here we focus on laboratory experimentation and leave to a later paper the detailed linkage of this activity to simulation studies of macro-economic systems.

First, consider the universities: in these institutions, the lion's share of work on theoretical economics takes place.[1] All who are associated with these institutions know they are in crisis which seems to reflect a crisis in the world order. Our situation has been characterized by James Michener in his reviews of the Kent State riots in which he says,

> "Our age can best be understood if we compare it to European history in the year 1848. Then, great revolutionary movements swept the continent with crucial disturbances in France, Germany, and the Austro-Hungarian empire, and massive protests elsewhere. The old order established by Metternich and the Congress of Vienna was crumbling, and everyone knew this, but it still retained the power of self-defense. So, one after another of the revolutions was crushed."[2]

Those of us who believe that the current equilibrium, like that of 1848, will also be short-lived, also believe that when the inevitable changes occur in society, then the universities will be radically changed to reflect them. Each

---

1 Those who recall the fable will remember that the lion's share is all. This concentration has been documented, see George Stigler "Statistical Studies in the History of Economic Thought", Essays in the History of Economics, University of Chicago Press, 1965, pp. 31-50.

2 Kent State: What Happened and Why, Random House, 1971.

of the disciplines, if this comes to pass, will have to answer the basic questions of its own relevance, else its command over attention and resources will be brutally reduced in the adjustments which are to be made. If these choices are not made within the universities, they will be imposed from without with even less sensitivity, the blunt instrument of budget reduction being, perhaps, the least objectionable of these external devices.[1] As economists interested in the intrinsic value of our discipline, we should, in anticipation, take a look at our activities and ask ourselves the hard question as to whether the mix of our activities is the right one and whether the process by which the profession selects and rewards its practitioners will be adequate to meet the demands for answers which society must put to us. These requests cannot be put off - we have already experienced the leading disturbances of the last decade and these are but signals of the shocks which are to follow. Unfortunately, institutions of learning, government, and business proved to be illdesigned to withstand these leading transients. Faced with direct evidence of weak construction at a local level, we should be put well-advised to look to the state of our overall system architecture. Economic science is one of the means by which this investigation will be carried on. In the sequel, we shall be concerned with the contribution experimental economics can make to this vital activity with particular attention to changes in approach which may make it easier to apply theoretical economics to relevant problems.

---

1 For an example of how this external process works, consider the proposed U.S. Federal Budget support for science related activity in 1972, which, if viewed together with the state of California "disaster budget" for the University of California, implies drastic revision of our activities.

Economists have developed a deductive discipline in which we work out the logical implications of more or less plausible axioms of human behavior subject to principles based on natural law which we receive from physical science and engineering. Our sister discipline, in laying the groundwork for the psychology of man, has until very recently concentrated on experiments in extremely simple environments. Thus we have not had a body of knowledge based on direct evidence which could be used in the construction of Economic Man - the decisionmaker in our systems. Of late we have come to the realization that the currently employed model of Economic Man is an anachronism. This has been pointed up by recent experimental evidence, and we may briefly review a part of this development.

One of the first experiments in economics was directed at a key assumption of the model of Economic Man: the axiom of transitivity of choice in consumer decision-making. These experiments were performed in the late 1950's by a team of economists, including Papandreou, Hurwicz, Brownley, Boddy, and Sauerlander.[1] The results were hard to interpret but they did cast doubt ("perhaps we could reformulate transitivity stochastically") and if followed up could lead to the conclusion that whether or not man ought to be transitive, it is doubtful that many men are transitive in their individual consumer choices.

Another basic assumption about Economic Man is that individuals are essentially selfish and act as if their utility functions were independent of the rewards recei-

---

1 Papandreou, Andreas G., "A Test of a Stochastic Theory of Choice," University of California Publications in Economics, Vol. 16, No. 1, 1957.

ved by other actors in the system. This assumption is convenient for analytics but it may be unduly restrictive of the kinds of interaction which may take place. This assumption has not been borne out in the laboratory. In a series of experiments dealing with micro-economic decision-making,[1] subjects have consistently behaved as if they take pay-off of competitors into account when calculating the value of a given outcome from decisions involving substantial cash rewards. Thus were introduced elements of cooperation into situations which, in theory, are noncooperative.

Field studies of actual decision-making in organization units have led to models of administrative and bureaucratic man, which seriously question in other domains the accuracy and completeness of this con-

---

1 Hoggatt, A.C., "An Experimental Game," Behavioral Science, Vol. 4, No. 3, July 1959. Nine professors of Business Administration achieved Cournot solutions in three-firm oligopoly when playing each other for "points". In that situation they were not able to overcome their training in micro-economics. Similar results were obtained using robots programmed to play Cournot strategies in that technically trained economists reached Cournot equilibrium against them. See Hoggatt, A.C., "Measuring Cooperativeness of Behavior in Quantity Variation Duopoly Games," Behavioral Science, Vol. 12, 1967, pp. 109-121. Cooperation appears in studies of subjects who were paid substantial amounts of money - see Fouraker, L.E., and Sidney Siegel, Bargaining Behavior II, University Park: Pennsylvania State University, 1961; Friedman, James W., "Individual Behavior in Oligopolistic Markets: An Experimental Study," Yale Economic Essays, Vol. 3, No. 2, 1963; Hoggatt, A.C., "Response of Paid Student Subjects to Differential Behavior of Robots in Bifurcated Duopoly Games," Review of Economic Studies, Vol. XXXVI, October 1969, pp. 417-432; Friedman, James and A.C. Hoggatt, unpublished experiments in oligopoly at Berkeley Laboratory, Winter 1971.

struction.[1] It appears that in modern organizations the stringency of limited rationality and the welter of goal conflicts which necessarily attend bureaucratic choice assure that the necessary conditions for Economic Man to function do not obtain. The major decision-making units in our societies satisfice rather than optimize. The implications of this stubborn fact on questions of behavior of individual decision units and the optimality of the system of markets have not been studied in detail, but we can be sure that we do not have the necessary conditions for the great theorems of welfare economics which assert that economic equilibria are Pareto optimal. Unfortunately, it appears that these behavioral models, while they seem to be much closer to what actually takes place in organizational decision-making, give rise to mathematics which are formidable and our only path to deriving implications from them at this time is via computer simulation in which a computer program becomes a dynamic model of a system and is used to map points in the parameter space into response paths of the system. Analytic study of simulation models is a slow process and powerful generalizations are not yet forthcoming from these studies.

What these behavioral constructs call into question is the internal structure of models of the individual firm. Our view of the external environment of the firm is under attack from direct experience. Recall that micro-economics with regard to the firm and industry is directed at problems of efficiency of markets under the criterion of profit maximization with assumptions: (1) increasing

---

1 An example of these "strange" organizations may be sampled in Cyert, Richard and James March, A Behavioral Theory of the Firm, Prentice Hall, 1963.

returns to scale of operation are absent or that, in the few cases where they were significant, they may be artificially removed by public regulation, and (2) external costs are small relative to total costs and by argument based on continuity may be ignored since small departures from the antecedents would likely be associated with small changes in the consequences. This may have been a reasonable abstraction from turn-of-the-century conditions. Marshall has said that "Economics is a study of mankind in the ordinary business of life,"[1] implying that it took its materials from observations of economic practice, and abstracted from these to develop the models which guided the foundations of economic theory. The economic system has changed since that time and we face a radically different system in the 1970's as accumulating evidence indicates that the market environments of firms are diverging rapidly from these assumptions. For example, the electronic computer has broadened the effective span of control and spawned myriad cases with increasing returns to scale. And the technology of computer production itself is well on the way to creating single firm dominance of the supply of this essential factor of production. Great interdependence of economic activity in the developed economies has invalidated the second assumption (in fact, some reports from earlier times, i.e., smog over the English Midlands, indicate that it may never have had validity), and it is now clear that we urgently require institutional solutions to crucial problems of external costs for which modified laissez faire is not adequate.

---

1 Principles of Economics, Macmillan, 1890, 8th edition, 1949, p. 1.

We see that the main thrust of economics has been to develop a theory of a system with which we are not now confronted so that we operate under severe handicaps in using it to understand our current problems. How, then, are we to escape from the indictment that economics is a game played by a few experts to an audience of the same experts with results which have but slight social relevance? In a World of Public Utilities, instead of empty economic boxes, we may actually have empty economics.

This radical shift in economic "facts" should be a call to the creation of a radical economic theory to fit them, but in order to bring theoretical economics to bear on our problems, major revisions in ethics for economists will be required. Now we inhibit intervention to cases in which no actor in the system is made worse off, even in the short run, and this in turn leads us to prescriptions which are essentially conservative and we too often take an approach to "fix up" present solutions. Unless we are explicit about it, organized economics will line up in support of the status quo.[1] In our revolutionary times this is disfunctional. Most likely a good first step toward removing this bias would be for economists to pursue experimental observations of human decision-makers in the context of classical economic environments. That which Experimental Man may actually do in a "pure" economic environment may then be compared with the theoretical construct of Economic Man and relevant modifications to that model may arise out of this experience. Then at least

---

1 Stigler, in his "The Politics of Political Economists," loc cit., pp. 61-65, in great detail develops the theme that the study of economics introduces a conservative bias into the political thought of economists.

we can get our assumptions about decision-makers straightened out prior to studying more complex economic models.

Through population pressure and complex technology the developed societies are producing a life style in which each individual is increasingly dependent on many others. Whereas in "pure" economic systems self-interest was found to be socially desirable and cooperativeness often was thought to mitigate against social welfare, in highly interdependent systems the obverse may be the case. Inasmuch as we have already observed a wide variation between the poles of competitive and cooperative behavior in the laboratory and given that the intensity of other directedness may turn out to be a major determinant of economic productivity, I suggest that the measurement of the distribution of a disposition toward cooperativeness in economic decision-makers should have high priority. High priority should also be given to the study of individual rationality (or lack of it) in economic situations in which rational choice is possible. In order that we may build on the received body of economic thought rather than simply discard it, a natural way to proceed would be to use economic theory to construct the laboratory environments in which we test our human subjects. The work of McCrimmon (contained elsewhere in these proceedings) points the way to a further development of the measurement of individual rationality in a traditional economic setting which builds on the early experimental work in this area. The study of oligopoly behavior with firms which have simple mathematical cost and demand functions provides a laboratory environment for studying cooperativeness. Friedman and Hoggatt have a large experiment of this kind in the analysis stage in which approximately 100 subjects participated in several price-quantity variation markets containing 1 to 6 firms under varying information about other firm costs. For these situations the sharpness of market response and internal cost were systematically varied by parametric variation. Our experience in administering these games was very illuminating. Situations which we thought were simple proved too difficult for our subjects[1] and it took us over a year to learn how to structure games and instructions so that viable play obtained. Wide variation in the quality of internal decisions(production management) and market cooperation (price setting) were observed - actual behavior in oligopoly markets is much richer than the received body of theory would indicate. More detail about this work awaits the results of our analysis.[2]

Only after a thorough understanding of behavior in these simple situations do we propose to relax the simplifying structures we have employed. Then we may move in the direction of risk and uncertainty in choice theory and toward markets which are composed of firms which have the internal richness displayed by those of Cyert, March, Simon and their disciples. Real world firms face severe problems of external cost and increasing returns to scale of operation and competitive situations which lead them to be secretive. This domain is too rich; in the absence of direct knowledge the fruitful theorist may spin off a million original and interesting theories not one of which might be close to the actual case. In such a world a conservative experimental approach may be a useful guide to relevance.

---

1 In desparation we turned to our trained economist colleagues only to find they couldn't perform well in our initial games either.

2 We are encouraged to find that prices clustertyhtly about Cournot equilibria.

Unfortunately for the ready acceptance of such a scheme we find that observations in these experiments are very expensive. The data which were collected in the Friedman-Hoggatt experiments previously mentioned have a variable cost of approximately $60,000 and they were run in a laboratory with a capitalized value which is in the range of $250,000.[1] These costs had to be incurred in order to automate the process of data collection. Human behavior is inherently variable and large numbers of observations are required to permit data reduction to be effective. Our 1,000,000 observations were obtained at a (low) unit cost of 6¢ per observation, but as is usually the case in automation, setup costs are large and capital required is not small. Those who wish a more detailed discussion of computer controlled laboratory experiments may read the next section, others may choose to skip to the following section in which we propose a cooperative course of action among experimenters.

2. *Characterization of the Process of Experimentation with Human Decision-Makers*

In Figure 1, we have a schematic representation of experimentation in which learning by subjects and experimenters takes place. Pre-experimental analysis, design of experiments, and post-experimental analysis are represented with the processes of ex-

---

1 For a description of this prototype laboratory, see Hoggatt, A.C., J. Esherick, J. Wheeler, "A Laboratory to Facilitate Computer-controlled Behavioral Experiments," Administrative Science Quarterly, Vol. 14, No. 2, June, 1969.

periment and post-experimental analysis represented as joint activity for subjects and experimenters. The link of experiments to simulation studies is also shown to indicate the impact on the construction of economic models; its feedback loop to alter the design of experiments is also present. Note especially that we have shown prior information, values, and skills of both subjects and experimenters to be transformed as a consequence of experience in the experimental activity. People learn rapidly in these situations and one important thing that we have found from experiments to date is that values of participants change rapidly when they are exposed in this way. For example, we have seen the phenomena of value shift when professors step out of their usual role and become university administrators. We find that participation in an experimental role as an administrator can also result in similar value shifts. Lord Acton has taught that power corrupts and we suspect that "simulated power" is just as corrupting as the "real" thing. Special attention should be paid to this in the hope that ways to mitigate damaging effects may be found.

Elements of the Experimental Process

The process of model construction, experimental design, data collection and analysis need not be dwelt upon here since we are an assembly of experimentalists and our methods have little to add to orthodoxy. At Berkeley, we have been concentrating on instrumentation and control over experiments with special attention to precise computer control of the subjects' environment and with data which is logged in real time in machine readable form. We employ a small, real-time computer system to

<u>List of Variables and Processes</u>

$\left.\begin{array}{l}EI\\SI\end{array}\right\} \equiv \left\{\begin{array}{l}\text{experimenter}\\\text{subject}\end{array}\right\}$ state of prior information

$\left.\begin{array}{l}EV\\SV\end{array}\right\} \equiv \left\{\begin{array}{l}\text{experimenter}\\\text{subject}\end{array}\right\}$ state of values

$\left.\begin{array}{l}ES\\SS\end{array}\right\} \equiv \left\{\begin{array}{l}\text{experimenter}\\\text{subject}\end{array}\right\}$ skills

$t \equiv$ discrete clock of the process

$f \equiv$ transform of experimenter variables and states

$g \equiv$ transform of subject variables and states

$h \equiv$ transform of experiment

A time subscript indicates a transform or state which obtains at time t.

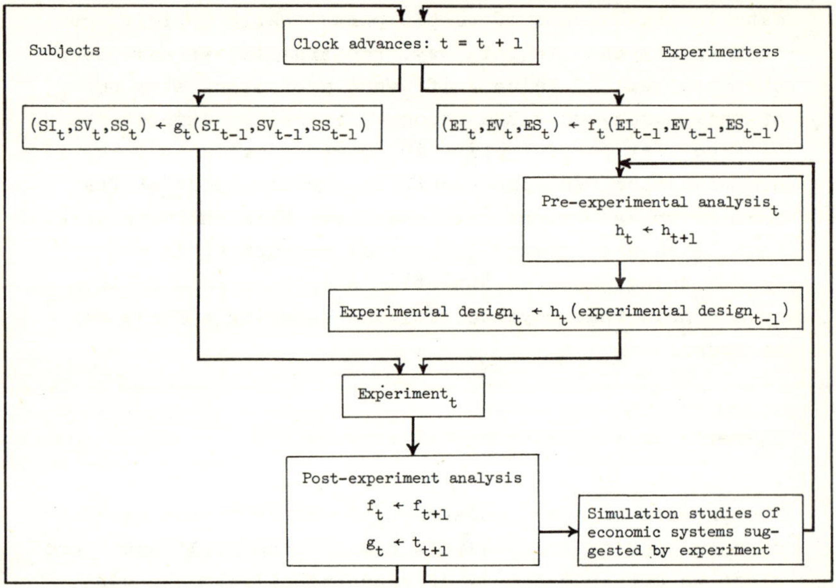

Figure 1 Schematic of the process of experimentation with economic models

control the laboratory and record data, and we employ the large campus computer for data reduction, error detection, and theoretical analysis of the results. We show a schematic of this subsystem in Figure 2. This diagram shows two programming languages: ECL, the environmental control language for the laboratory, and FORTRAN for the campus computer center. A new laboratory system is being developed with a META-4 computer which will be programmed in APL, A Programming Language. With the increasing availability of APL on large machines, this means that we can unify the work of laboratory control, model construction and data analysis within a single language.
As in all automation, we experience a certain rigidity in the system - long lead times of programming and development may be necessary before experiments can begin. However, once it is set up the lab has a vast capacity for collecting carefully controlled data and the feedback to the experimenter can be very rapid.[1] In some respects this places the experimenter in an ideal learning environment. However, Reinhard Selten has raised a fundamental query about this process in that it does remove the experimenter a great distance from the running of his experiment and it interposes a computer between the data and the experimenter. Some experimentalists who have been accustomed to a "hands-on" approach find this objectionable. This is normal when instrumentation is a major factor - we have merely borrowed from our physical science colleagues. Those who are concerned with this should await the calibration of computer controlled experiments against the same si-

---

1 All of the data for the coalition experiments reported in Ofshe, Richard and Lynn Ofshe, Utility and Choice in Social Interaction, Prentice-Hall, 1970, were collected in nine days of activity in the Berkeley Laboratory.

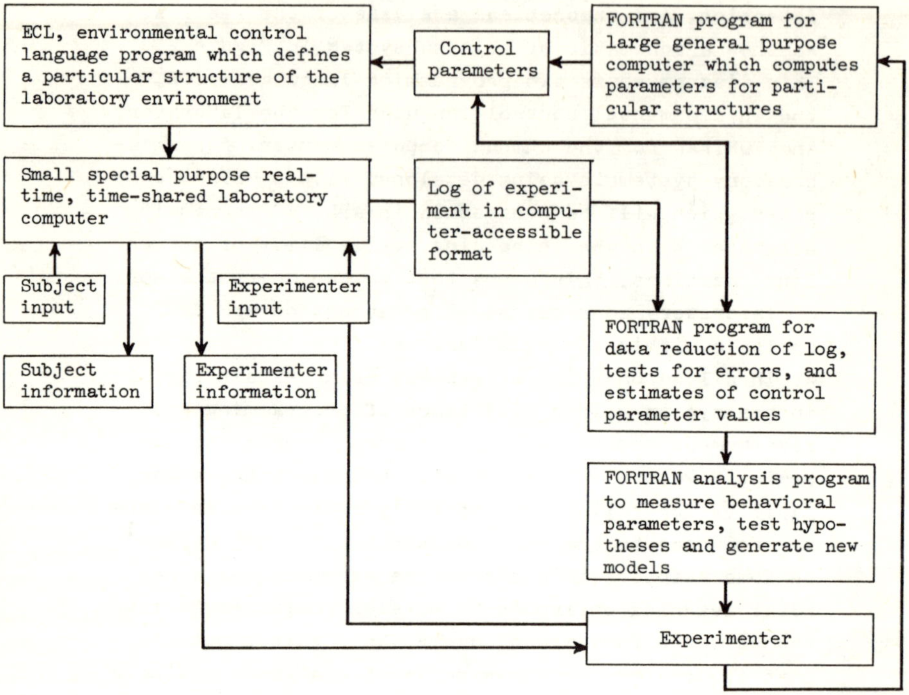

Figure 2. Schematic of computer-controlled experimentation

tuations controlled by hand (see below). It is a question of experiment to determine whether or not these methodological questions are of great importance.

There are several problems which arise in experiments with human decision-makers which do not arise in physical science. Many of these are relevant to the question of subject motivation and the criteria which subjects employ in measuring performance in the laboratory. In the theory of games it is assumed that players derive no utility from the play of the game and are motivated by the utilities of the outcome only. This, of course, is not the case for the actual play. In our work we have tried to motivate subjects by money payoff and instructions which emphasize own money reward. But we still find a large number of subjects who behave as if the payoffs to other subjects were significant determinants to their own decisions. In addition, time foreshortening and boredom are significant factors. This creates problems in modeling which greatly complicate the analysis. In particular, decomposition of events and expected utility calculus of the von Neumann-Morgenstern utility theory cannot be employed. Much experimentation has been done with naive subjects who are not given sufficient training to be familiar with the situations in which they are embedded. It may be an interesting question to study how subjects react to bewildering situations, but values and skills that hold in situations in which subjects at least understand the structure of the environment in which they act are likely to be of more interest as guides to theory construction. Thus in our work we generally try to repeat experimental situations until learning begins to fall off. Then, until boredom dominates, we hope to measure a fairly stable decision-making situation. The effort to identify these "cut-off" points is an important and difficult analytic question.

Values which are employed by subjects in the laboratory are subject to distortion from several sources. First, there is the possibility that subjects will try to determine what the experimenters' values are and then try to match them. Second, they may have a preconceived idea of the values which are employed py persons who play certain roles, and they may adapt their values in the experiment to these ideal types. To this extent experiments can be powerful brainwashing situations and this effect must be measured so that we may compensate for it when theory construction is undertaken.

Having laid out some of the special complexity which faces the experimenter in dealing with human subjects, we see that this cannot be other than a group effort. At least, economists, sociologists and psychologists should have a hand in experimental design and mathematicians and statisticians must surely have a hand in analysis.

3. *Economic Experiments in Economics*

A major weakness which has so far plagued experimental economics is fragmentation. Seldom is an experiment replicated in a given laboratory - never elsewhere. Data from experiments are subject to reduction prior to being published and often are not made available to other experimenters in original form. Thus it is hard for others to check a result or extend an analysis. Because of this, there has been no attempt at calibration of instruments or experimenters (yes, they should be calibrated). The question of calibrating laboratories is premature, but it will come in time. The extent of variation in results from these sources is an unknown at the present time.

Because experimentation in economics requires great physical and intellectual resources, no one experimenter has been in a position to mount a program of experiments to make in-depth studies of a group of subjects which span many areas of theory (for example, oligopoly, bargaining, consumer choice, psychological tests), and to run these in different locales to study cultural differences.[1] A major step forward might be made if such a program could be mounted and sustained. Even to have a group of experimental economists talking about the same data should enhance communication to the point that we could learn from each other. And the large capital costs of facilities could be spread over a wider number of users. These considerations lead to a proposal for co-operative effort among economic experimentalists in order to mount a first series of experiments at a number of different universities to begin a process of integration from which we all may profit.

The experiments ought to be performed in as many locations as possible with data collected in a standard format with situations as standardized as possible and with as much control over variations in conditions as can be accomplished given cultural and other differences. At the present time, this implies that the experiments will be administered by hand. Analysis would proceed with each participating experimenter following his own methods. At the same time, data would be forwarded to a committee

---

1 But see the work of Harnett in this volume in which bargaining experiments with businessmen in several cultures are reported.

which would pursue computerized analysis on the data as collected from the several locations. Thus we would have information about variations in local performance and variation in kind of analysis. Larger samples can be obtained in this way than could be afforded by any one experimenter.

It would be well to calibrate the Berkeley laboratory by running in it some hand-administered and some computer-administered versions of each experiment. We could, in this way, observe the impact that computer control and data logging have on the experimenters and the subjects. Should the effects be crucial we should know this now!

We should be concerned with many aspects of subject response, including:

- skill in benign environment;
- skill in malignant environments;
- value function employed in guiding decisions, including other- and self-directed values, organization- vs. person-directed values;
- risk orientation;
- future discounting.

Obtaining agreement as to how to measure individual responses in each experimental situation would be a major feat of group cooperation. An anthropologist could be employed to study that activity.

We should be concerned with several aspects of overall system performance, including:

- viability (can system function be maintained or is the experiment unstable in the presence of subject interaction?);
- efficiency (how far does the system created in the laboratory depart from nonwasteful use of resources?);

- stability (does the system tend to equilibria or does it hunt?);
- optimality (are there any optimal properties associated with system performance?).

Perhaps it will be possible to get agreement as to how to define and measure these over-all system properties.

In order to have a point of departure for discussing the list of experiments which may be performed in the first round consider the following suggestions:

Individual tests:	decision-making tests[1]
	Papandreou et al., transitivity of choice[2]
Bargaining:	Selten-Hoggatt bargaining experiment[3]
Oligopoly:	Friedman-Hoggatt duopoly[4]

Experience has been obtained with these kinds of situations so we have gone well past initial shakedown and pilot testing; they may all be implemented with no further pilot activity. Further, these selected experiments have all been based on current micro-economic or

---

1 A delightful sequence of tests to measure rational content of a decision-maker's activity has been proposed by Jacob Marschak in "Management Research and Behavioral Science," Western Management Science Institute, Working Paper No. 2, 1961.

2 Hoggatt, A., "Note on the Use of the Data Multiplexor in the Context of a Simple Choice Experiment," CRMS Laboratory Research Report No. 11, April 1969.

3 Selten, R., A. Hoggatt, J. Moore, "Design of a Computer Controlled Bargaining Experiment," CRMS Laboratory Research Report No. 17, October 1971.

4 Friedman, J., A. Hoggatt, D. Crockett, "Programs Employed in a Continuous Oligopoly Experiment," CRMS Laboratory Research Report No. 18, October 1971.

psychological theory, so we will have a good test of the correspondence between theory and behavior. Note that prior to branching out into the analysis of behavior of subjects in novel economic environments we are proposing further experiments in classical situations. This is in keeping with the conservative procedure of separation of difficulties in that the theory of what one ought to do has been worked out and may be brought to bear as a bench mark against which actual behavior may be compared. It is in keeping with arguments which were advanced earlier in this paper.
In order to broaden the subject categories we ought to include:

- students (from both the revolutionary and conservative cultures)
- professors (from both the revolutionary and conservative cultures)
- businessmen (low, middle, and top management).

In order to make a try at comparability of reward it is proposed to pay at an average rate per hour, which approximates the current earning rate of the subject.
We would not specify particular analysis for each set of local experiments. Thus we may later to comparative analysis of the way individual researchers approach the data. We imagine that, whatever else is done at the global level, there would be a large analysis of variance performed across all experiments with regard to both personal performance and over-all system response.
If this effort is successful, it would be possible to seek funds to copy the Berkeley Laboratory Computing System so that computer-based experiments could be conducted in many different locations. Since development

costs could be avoided, a copy of the facility could be obtained at much less cost than was expended to build the first one. Inasmuch as a new system is being designed to be programmed in APL,[1] we will then have the capability to program the experiments, data reduction, analysis, and derivative simulation models, all in the same powerful programming language. We may look to an accumulating file of controlled experiments, an associated centralized, computer-based data bank, and a shared pool of analytic programs all of which are specified in a single language. It is time to unify our efforts - if we have the will, we can do it.

---

1 APL/360: User's Manual, IBM First Edition, September 1969.
Hoggatt, A.C., and Jeffrey Moore, "A Time-Sharing Methodology for Constructing Social Simulations," Working Paper No. 306, Center for Research in Management Science, University of California, Berkeley, August 1970.
Klein, D.A., A.C. Hoggatt, E. Sharon, "Mathematical Programming in APL," Working Paper No. 299, Center for Research in Management Science, University of California, Berkeley, March 1970.

3. ON THE STRUCTURE OF OLIGOPOLY MODELS WITH DIFFERENTIATED PRODUCTS[1]

JAMES W. FRIEDMAN*

1. Introduction

The purpose of this paper is to investigate, in some detail, the structure of a broad class of oligopoly models. It is commonly realized that oligopoly is a game in the sense of von Neumann and Morgenstern [9]; hence a major effort in the present paper will be directed at applying certain results of game theory to models of oligopoly. In the course of doing so, the problem of how to specify the oligopoly model in game theoretic terms will be addressed. Here and there new results may be proven in instances in which the structure of the model will permit.

It is hoped this paper will be of interest both to those interested in oligopoly theory purely for its own sake and to those who perform, or are interested in, experimental research in the area.

Cournot's [4] model of oligopoly has, in various versions, been more widely taught and written about than any other model in the oligopoly literature. Borrowing

---

* Professor of Economics at the University of Rochester

1 I wish to thank the National Science Foundation for providing research support to this work under grant GS-2423.

Chamberlin's [3] insight into differentiated products, it is possible to formulate models in which price is taken to be the decision variable of the firm, and in which small changes in the price of one firm bring about only small changes in the sales of any firm. It is the author's opinion that among all relatively simple oligopoly models, these differentiated products price models are the most realistic and interesting.

It is well known that the famous "Cournot solution" is a special case of the "non-cooperative equilibrium" of Nash. Nash [8] did not prove the existence of the non-cooperative equilibrium for a class of games which included Cournot's model as a subclass; however, this was subsequently done by Debreu [5] and Berge [2]. Indeed, the latter writers deal with games of far greater generality than Cournot.

In addition to (single period) non-cooperative equilibrium, the economist is likely to be interested in characteristics of the profit possibility frontier. It is on this frontier that cooperative solutions will lie and, as the author has shown elsewhere [6], that certain non-cooperative equilibria will lie for games which are played over time.

In section 2 the non-cooperative (Cournot type) equilibrium will be studied. Existence need not be proved, as it has been previously established; however, conditions will be shown under which the equilibrium is unique and under which each firm, at the equilibrium, has strictly positive price and production levels. Section 3 is devoted to studying characteristics of the profit possibility frontier. Sections 4 and 5 deal with multiperiod oligopoly models. In section 4, the "balanced temptation equilibrium", developed in [6], is applied to a multiperiod model lacking "structural time dependence" (i.e., current period payoff depends upon current period prices only). In section 5, non-cooperative equilibrium is studied in a model having structural time dependence (sales in period t depend on prices of both periods t and t-1). Section 6 contains concluding remarks.

2. *The Non-Cooperative Equilibrium*

The equilibrium of Cournot [4] is a non-cooperative equilibrium. In [8] Nash proved the existence of non-cooperative equilibrium in a broad class of n-person, non-constant sum matrix games. Nash's work was simultaneously an extension of Cournot and a generalization of the saddle point equilibrium of von Neumann and Morgenstern [9] for two person zero-sum games.
The present section is devoted to showing how a generalization of the Nash result may be applied to oligopoly models. Additional characteristics of equilibrium, such as uniqueness, will also be shown for some models. Subsection 2.1 deals with demand and cost functions, while 2.2 contains additional assumptions and results concerning the non-cooperative equilibrium.

2.1 The Basic Model

In the present subsection, conditions will be given for demand and cost functions. As some results require stronger assumptions than others, an attempt will be made to use weaker assumptions where possible. Notation follows:

q_i is the amount of output demanded of the ith firm

$q = (q_1,\ldots,q_n)$ is the output (= sales) vector of the industry

p_i is the price charged by the ith firm

$p = (p_1,\ldots,p_n)$ is the price vector of the industry. p may also be denoted $(\bar{p}_i, p_i)$, where $\bar{p}_i$ indicates the n-1 vector of all prices except the ith

Throughout this paper, price will be the decision variable of the firm and sales will always equal demand. Sales of the ith firm depend upon the price vector:

$$q_i = f_i(p) \qquad i = 1,\ldots,n$$

The fundamental rules of this dependence are summarized below.[1]

D1 a. For any $p \in P = \{p | p_i \geq 0,\ i = 1,\ldots,n\}$, $0 \leq f_i(p) < \infty$.

b. For $p \in P$, $f_i(p)$ is continuous.

c. For $p^o \in P$, $p_i^1 > p_i^o$, and $f_i(p^o) > 0$, $f_i(p^o) > f_i(\bar{p}_i^o, p_i^1)$.

d. For $p^o \in P$, $p_j^1 > p_j^o$, $f_i(p^o) > 0$ and $f_j(p^o) > 0$, $f_i(p^o) < f_i(\bar{p}_j^o, p_j^1)$ $(j \neq i)$.

1 The reader requiring definitions of terms from mathematics (eg., continuous, bounded, etc.) should consult a textbook on analysis such as Bartle [1].

e. For $p^o \in P$, $p_j^1 > p_j^o$, and $f_j(p^o) = 0$,

$$f_i(p^o) = f_i(\bar{p}_j^o, p_j^1) \quad (j=1,\ldots,n).$$

f. For $p^o \in P$, $\delta > 0$, $p^1 = (p_1^o + \delta,\ldots,p_n^o + \delta)$,

and $f_i(p^o) > 0$, $f_i(p^1) < f_i(p^o)$.

g. $\overset{o}{A}_i = \{p \mid p \in P, f_i(p) > 0\}$

$\overset{o}{A} = \overset{o}{A}_1 \cap \overset{o}{A}_2 \cap \ldots \cap \overset{o}{A}_n$ is bounded and $0 \in \overset{o}{A}$.

These demand conditions mean a) demand is always non-negative, b) and continuous. c) When a firm raises its price, if it has positive demand its demand will diminish. d) For two firms having positive demand, increasing the price of the first will increase the sales of the second; however, e) if a firm has zero demand, raising its price will have no effect on the sales of any firm. f) If all firms raise prices simultaneously, by equal amounts, then all firms having positive demand will suffer a fall in demand. g) There are positive demands for all firms at zero prices and the set of prices at which all firms (simultaneously) have positive demand is bounded.

Let A be the closure of $\overset{o}{A}$. Forming A means adding to $\overset{o}{A}$ an "upper boundary" of points where one or more of the f_i are zero; however, in any open neighborhood of any such point, there are points for which all f_i are strictly positive. Figure 1 illustrates some of the characteristics of demand for a two firm case. Note that the set A is bounded below and at left by the horizontal and vertical axes, and above and at right by the $f_2 = 0$ and $f_1 = 0$ curves. The $f_2 = q_2^o$ (broken) curve illustrates that when $f_1 = 0$, further increases in p_1(p_2 remaining constant) leave q_2 unaffected.

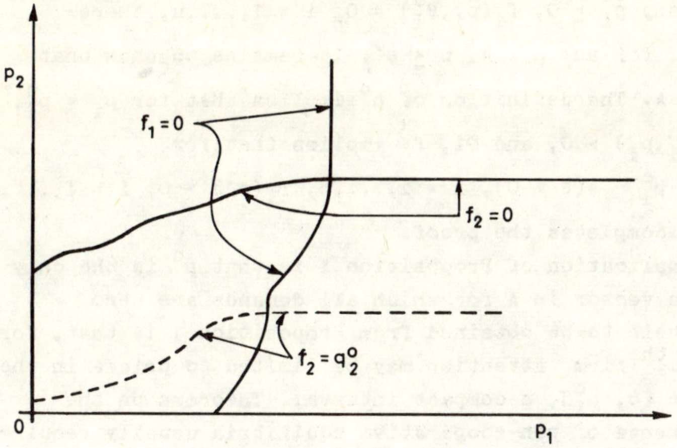

Figure 1

A first result may now be proved:

Proposition 1:[1] D1 implies that the set A has a maximal element. I.e., there is a point $p^o \in A$ such that, for any $p \in A$ $(p \neq p^o)$, $p < p^o$.

Define $p^o = (p_1^o, \ldots, p_n^o)$ as follows: $p_i^o = \sup_{p \in A_i^o} p_i$

---

1 Inequalities among vectors will be denoted as follows:

$x \geq y$ means $x_i \geq y_i$, $i = 1, \ldots, n$

$x > y$ means $x \geq y$ and $x \neq y$

$x \gg y$ means $x_i > y_i$, $i = 1, \ldots, n$.

For any $\bar{p}_i \geq 0$, $f_i(\bar{p}_i, P_i^o) = 0$, $i = 1,\ldots,n$; therefore, for any $p \in A$, $p \leq p^o$. It remains to show that $p^o \in A$. The definition of p^o implies that for $p_i < p_i^o$, $f_i(\bar{p}_i^o, p_i) > 0$, and D1, f. implies that, for $p_i^1 = p_i^o - \delta(\delta > 0)$, $i = 1,\ldots,n$, $f_i(p^1) > 0$, $i = 1,\ldots,n$. This completes the proof.

An implication of Proposition 1 is that p^o is the only price vector in A for which all demands are zero.

The help to be obtained from Proposition 1 is that, for the ith firm, attention may be limited to prices in the range $[o, p_i^o]$, a compact interval. Theorems on the existence of non-cooperative equilibria usually require compact strategy sets; hence, if "strategy" is taken to mean "price", the condition is met.

The basic assumption on total cost functions, C_i, is

C1 $C_i(q_i)$ is continuous, monotone increasing, $C_i(0) \geq 0$ and C_i is finite for finite values of q_i.

Profit for the ith firm is given by:

$$\pi_i(p) = p_i f_i(p) - C_i(f_i(p))$$

It is immediate that $\pi_i(p)$ is bounded on A, as well as continuous.

2.2 Oligopoly as a Game, and the Non-Cooperative Equilibrium

In order to interpret the present oligopoly model as a game in the sense of von Neumann and Morgenstern, it is necessary to identify game theoretic concepts such as "strategy," "strategy set," "payoff function," and "player" with elements of the model. Each firm is a player. As the present section deals with single period oligopoly models, strategy for a firm will be its own price and the payoff function of a firm will be its profit function. In principle a firm could choose a price anywhere in the range $[0,\infty)$; however, consideration may be limited to prices in the range $[0,p_i^o]$ (for the ith firm) because each price greater than p_i^o has identical consequences as p_i^o. At p_i^o or higher, the firm is "out of the market." I.e., it sells zero and any price change which keeps sales at zero leaves all other firms unaffected.

An important concept of equilibrium in game theory is the non-cooperative equilibrium. A vector of strategies, one for each player, comprises a non-cooperative equilibrium if it is impossible for any player to increase his payoff by the choice of any other strategy, given that all other players keep their strategies fixed. Formally, and in terms of the oligopoly model previously described. p^* is a non-cooperative equilibrium if

$$(1) \quad \left.\begin{array}{l} 0 \leq p_i^* \leq p_i^o \\ \pi_i(p^*) \geq \pi_i(\bar{p}_i^*, p_i) \text{ for any } 0 \leq p_i \leq p_i^o \end{array}\right\} i = 1,\ldots,n$$

The equilibrium of Cournot is a non-cooperative equilibrium where a) strategy for the firm is its quantity and b) the payoff function is single period profits. An equilibrium characterized by equations (1) is an equilibrium of the Cournot type. Theorems on existence of non-cooperative equilibrium, such as Proposition 2, below, deal with a much broader class of games than those to be specified in this section.

An important result for non-cooperative games is:

> Proposition 2: If, in an n person game, a) each player's strategy set is a compact, convex subset of a Euclidean space of finite dimension, b) each player's payoff is a continuous function of all player's strategies and c) each player's payoff is a quasi-concave function of his own strategy, then the game has a non-cooperative equilibrium.[1]

Proofs of this proposition may be found in Berge [2] and Debreu [5], among other places. The original theorem on existence of n-person non-cooperative games is due to Nash [8].[2] Note that if n=2 and if $\pi_2(p) = -\pi_1(p)$, the game is two person and zero-sum. Thus restricted, the non-cooperative equilibrium becomes the saddle point, or mini-max. equilibrium of von Neumann and Morgenstern.

---

1 A function, f(x), is said to be "quasi-concave" if $\{x | f(x) \geq a\}$ is convex, for any scalar "a".

The figure at left shows a function which is quasi-concave, but not concave. The argument, x, may be a vector, of course.

2 The Nash theorem deals with matrix games. Each player has a finite number of "pure" strategies he can choose. Also, the player can choose to play a "mixed" strategy--that is, he places a probability distribution over his pure strategies and uses a chance mechanism to actually choose a pure strategy. The player's payoff as a function of mixed strategies is taken to be the expected payoff, given the mixed strategies which have been chosen. The theorems in Debreu and Berge are more general than Proposition 2.

The oligopoly model under consideration satisfies conditions a) and b) of proposition 2, but does not necessarily satisfy c). Listed below are several conditions, any one of which ensures the existence of a non-cooperative equilibrium for two person zero sum games.

$\pi 1$ For fixed $\bar{p}_i, \pi_i(p)$ is a quasi-concave function of p_i for $p_i \in [0, p_i^o]$.

$\pi 2$ Let $p_i = \mu_i(\bar{p}_i)$ be defined by $\pi_i(\bar{p}_i, \mu_i(\bar{p}_i)) = \max \pi_i(\bar{p}_i, p_i), 0 \leq p_i \leq p_i^o$
$\pi_i(p)$ is a quasi-concave function of p_i, for all $\bar{p}_i$ and $p_i \in [\mu_i(\bar{p}_i), p_i^o]$

$\pi 3$ f_i and C_i have continuous second partial derivatives at all points of $\overset{o}{A}$, with $\frac{\partial^2 f_i}{\partial p_i^2} < 0$, $\frac{\partial^2 C_i}{\partial q_i^2} \geq 0$ everywhere in $\overset{o}{A}$. For p_i'' defined by the conditions $f_i(0, p_i'') = 0$ and $(0, p_i'') \in A$, $p_i'' > \frac{\partial C_i(0)}{\partial q_i}$

The condition $\pi 1$ is a direct restatement of condition c). Condition $\pi 2$ modifies $\pi 1$ by requiring quasi-concavity of the payoff function in only a subset of each player's strategy set and then assuring that an equilibrium must necessarily lie within this subset. While these two conditions do make proposition 2 applicable, they have the disadvantage of not revealing what they impose on demand and cost functions. $\pi 3$ is more stringent than $\pi 1$ or $\pi 2$;

however, the conditions it imposes are directly on the demand and cost functions. These conditions are: i) the demand and cost functions be twice differentiable, ii) demand for each firm is a concave function of its own price

$$\frac{\partial^2 f_i}{\partial p_i^2} < 0$$

, iii) the total cost function of each firm is convex ($C'' \geq 0$), and iv) for any given $\bar{p}_i$, the profit maximizing value of p_i corresponds to a strictly positive level of output (at $q_i = 0$, price necessarily exceeds marginal cost). Thus the following result may be stated:

> Proposition 3: In a game satisfying D1 and C1, and which satisfies π1, π2 or π3, there exists a noncooperative equilibrium. If π3 is satisfied, then, for any equilibrium, p^*, demand is strictly positive ($f_i(p^*) > 0$) and price exceeds marginal cost ($p_i^* > C_i'(f_i(p^*))$) for each firm.

It is not necessary to prove the existence of equilibrium; however, it should be shown that D1, C1 and π3 imply that $f_i(p^*) > 0$ and $p_i^* > C_i'(f_i(p^*))$, $i = 1,\ldots,n$. The individual players' strategy sets are the intervals $[0,p_i^o]$, $i = 1,\ldots,n$. Consider the optimal price choice for player i when the other players choose $\bar{p}_i$ (with $p_j \leq p_j^o$, $j \neq i$). $p_i'' > C_i'(0)$ immediately implies that a price which makes $f_i = 0$ is not optimal. Similarly, a price, p_i', at which $p_i' < C_i'(f_i(\bar{p}_i,p_i'))$ also cannot be optimal because marginal revenue is not greater than p_i'. Thus, for every firm, if p^* is a non-cooperative equilibrium,

$$\left.\begin{array}{l} f_i(p^*) > 0 \\ p_i^* \geq C_i'(f_i(p^*)) > 0 \end{array}\right\} i = 1,\ldots,n\,.$$

Thus $p^* \in \overset{o}{A}$; hence p^* must satisfy

$$f_i(p^*) + (p_i^* - C_i'(f_i(p^*)))\,\frac{\partial f_i(p^*)}{\partial p_i} = 0, \quad i = 1,\ldots,n$$

which implies $p_i^* > C_i'(f_i(p^*))$, $i = 1,\ldots,n$. This completes the proof.

If $\pi 3$ were strengthened slightly, the non-cooperative equilibrium would be unique:

$\pi 3'$ In addition to $\pi 3$, $\dfrac{\partial^2 f_i}{\partial p_i^{\,2}} + \sum\limits_{j \neq i} \left|\dfrac{\partial^2 f_i}{\partial p_i \partial p_j}\right| \leq 0.$

Proposition 4: In a game satisfying D1, C1 and $\pi 3'$, the non-cooperative equilibrium is unique.

Any equilibrium p^* must satisfy the conditions

$$\left.\begin{array}{l} \dfrac{\partial \pi_i(p^*)}{\partial p_i} = 0 \\ p_i^* > C_i'(f_i(p^*)) \end{array}\right\} i = 1,\ldots,n$$

Let $B = \{p \mid p_i \geq C_i'(f_i(p)),\ i = 1,\ldots,n;\ p \in \overset{o}{A}\}$. Then $p^* \in B$. Because

$$\frac{\partial^2 \pi_i(p)}{\partial p_i^{\,2}} < 0 \text{ for } p \in B,$$

the condition $\frac{\partial\pi_i}{\partial p_i} = 0$ may be expressed as[1]

$$p_i = \phi_i(\bar{p}_i)$$

and $\phi(p):p \rightarrow p$ is a function mapping points of B into points of B. A fixed point of this function is a non-cooperative equilibrium; however, ϕ is a contraction, which implies the fixed point is unique. This completes the proof.

Summarizing the present section, it was seen that the existence theorem for non-cooperative equilibrium (proposition 2) could be applied to single period oligopoly models when "strategy" for a firm is its own price and the firm's payoff function is its profit function. Conditions were then found under which any non-cooperative equilibrium gives rise to strictly positive prices and production levels for all firms, and under which equilibrium is unique.

3. *Characteristics of the Pareto Frontier*

The Pareto optimal frontier consists of those payoffs which are a) attainable and b) in comparison with which any other attainable point must give less to someone. I.e., $\pi(p')$ is Pareto optimal if $p' \in A$ and there is no other $p \in A$ such that $\pi(p) > \pi(p')$. That such a frontier exists is quite clear: $\pi(p)$ is a continuous function and its domain is both compact and connected; hence, its range is also compact and connected [see Bartle 1].

---

1 The domain of ϕ_i is the projection of B into the n-1 dimensional space containing the p_j $(j \neq i)$.

A part of the Pareto optimal frontier of particular interest is that portion which is "above" the non-cooperative equilibrium. That is, the portion of the frontier where each player gets each player at least as high a payoff as he gets at the non-cooperative equilibrium. For n = 2, several possibilities are shown below:[1]

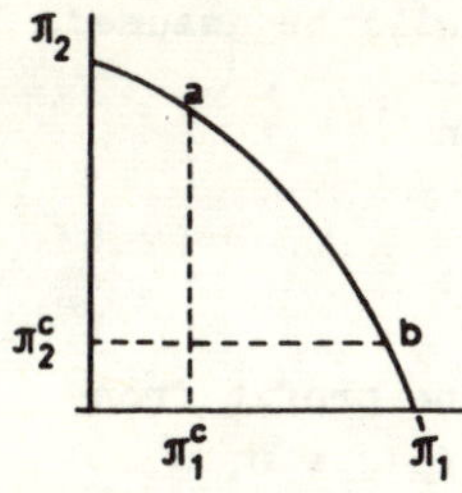

Figure 2

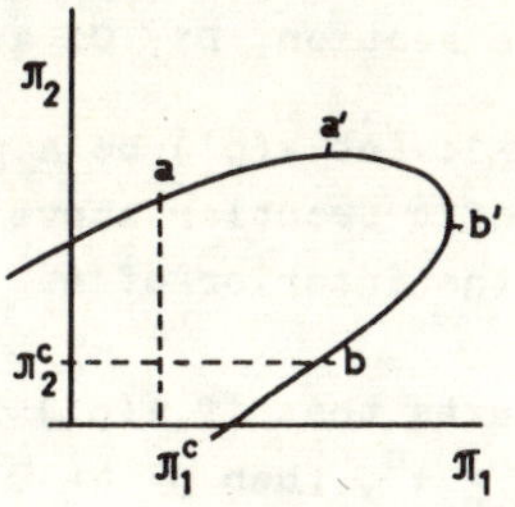

Figure 3

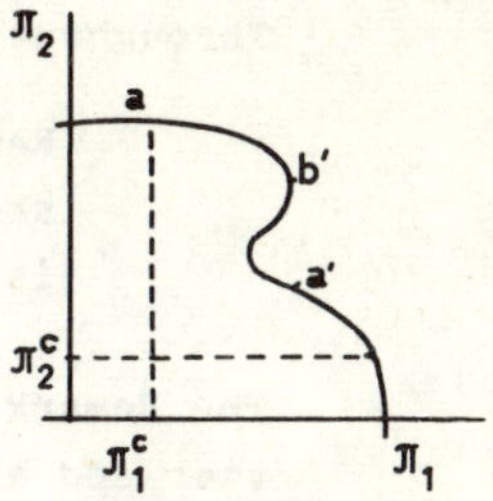

Figure 4

In all three figures, the solid curve from a to b is the boundary of the attainable set of payoffs which is "above" the non-cooperative equilibrium. In figure 2 the Pareto optimal surface above π^c also runs from a to b. In figure 3 it is only from a' to b', while in figure 4 it consists of the segments a to b' and a' to b. In figures 2 and 3 the surface is concave, but in figure 4 it is not.

---

1 The profit levels corresponding to the non-cooperative equilibrium will sometimes be denoted π^c.

Ideally, one would want to know what class of payoff functions give rise to concave profit frontiers and when it is true that the straight line connecting two attainable payoff points consists of attainable payoff points. So far as the present writer is aware, these are unsolved problems. They are not solved below.

In the remainder of this section there will be no systematic results, but some, hopefully useful, pieces of information will be put into the form of "Remarks." Throughout this section, D1, C1 and π3' will be assumed.

> Remark 1: Let $\pi(p')$ be a point on the profit frontier above π^c. p' is in the interior of A.

The Remark asserts that if $\pi(p')$ is on the profit frontier and $\pi(p') \geq \pi^c$, then $p' \gg 0$ and $f_i(p') > 0$, $i = 1,\dots,n$. From Proposition 3 it is known that both price and output are positive at π^c for all firms, and, irrespective of the behavior of other firms, if $p_i = 0$ or $f_i = 0$ then profit is below π_i^c. This implies Remark 1.

> Remark 2: Let $\pi(p')$ be as in Remark 1. The matrix $\left|\left|\frac{\partial\pi_i(p')}{\partial p_j}\right|\right|$ exists and is singular.

The partial derivatives clearly exist because p' is interior to A. If the matrix of first partial derivatives were non-singular, it would have an inverse and the following would hold:

$$\begin{bmatrix} dp_1 \\ \vdots \\ dp_n \end{bmatrix} = \begin{bmatrix} \frac{\partial \pi_1}{\partial p_1} & \cdots & \frac{\partial \pi_1}{\partial p_n} \\ \vdots & & \vdots \\ \frac{\partial \pi_n}{\partial p_1} & \cdots & \frac{\partial \pi_n}{\partial p_n} \end{bmatrix}^{-1} \begin{bmatrix} \delta_1 \\ \vdots \\ \delta_n \end{bmatrix} \varepsilon$$

for any δ_i such that $\sum_{i=1}^{n} |\delta_i| = 1$ and $\varepsilon > 0$. Thus there would be an open neighborhood around $\pi(p')$ all the points of which are generated by elements of A; hence, $\pi(p')$ could be on the profit frontier. I.e., it would be possible to choose $p'' \in A$ such that $\pi(p'')$ lies in any arbitrary direction from $\pi(p')$. Thus $\left\|\frac{\partial \pi_i(p')}{\partial p_j}\right\|$ is singular.

Remark 3: Let $\pi(p')$ be as in Remark 1. There exist constants $\rho_1,\ldots,\rho_n$ such that $\sum_{j=1}^{n} \rho_j \frac{\partial \pi_j(p')}{\partial p_i} = 0$, $i = 1,\ldots,n$;

and $\sum_{i=1}^{n} |\rho_i| > 0$.

If $\left\|\frac{\partial \pi_i(p')}{\partial p_j}\right\|$ has the rank n-1, the vector $\rho = (\rho_1,\ldots,\rho_n)$ is unique up to multiplication by a constant.

This Remark is a direct consequence of the singularity of the matrix of first derivatives and of Remark 1. It is unclear whether a frontier point such as $\pi(p')$ is Pareto optimal; however, insight into this question may be gained by considering frontier points above π^c from another vantage point. Such a point is the solution to the following problem:

$$\max_p \quad \pi_1(p) \text{ subject to}$$

$$\pi_i(p) - \pi_i(p^c) = k_i(\pi_1(p) - \pi_1(p^c))$$

$$k_i \geq 0, \; i = 2,\ldots,n.$$

Or, stated with Lagrange multipliers:

$$\max_p \quad \pi_1(p) + \lambda_2(\pi_2(p) - \pi_2(p^c) - k_2(\pi_1(p) - \pi_1(p^c))) + \ldots + \lambda_n(\pi_n(p) - \pi_n(p^c) - k_n(\pi_1(p) - \pi_1(p^c)))$$

The first order conditions for a maximum are:

$$\frac{\partial \pi_1}{\partial p_1} + \sum_{j=2}^{n} \left[\lambda_j \left(\frac{\partial \pi_j}{\partial p_1} - k_j \frac{\partial \pi_1}{\partial p_1} \right) \right] = 0$$

$$\ldots$$

$$\frac{\partial \pi_1}{\partial p_n} + \sum_{j=2}^{n} \left[\lambda_j \left(\frac{\partial \pi_j}{\partial p_n} - k_j \frac{\partial \pi_1}{\partial p_n} \right) \right] = 0$$

$$\pi_2(p) - \pi_2(p^c) - k_2(\pi_1(p) - \pi_1(p^c)) = 0$$

$$\ldots$$

$$\pi_n(p) - \pi_n(p^c) - k_n(\pi_1(p) - \pi_1(p^c)) = 0$$

Letting $\lambda_1 = 1 - \sum_{j=2}^{n} \lambda_j k_j$, the first n of these conditions may be rewritten:

$$\sum_{j=1}^{n} \lambda_j \frac{\partial \pi_j}{\partial p_i} = 0 \quad i = 1, \ldots, n$$

Solution of these 2n-1 equations, with second order conditions satisfied, leads to a point on the upper boundary of the attainable set.[1] The Lagrange multipliers $\lambda_1, \ldots, \lambda_n$ are the sames as the weights $\rho_1, \ldots, \rho_n$ in Remark 3. This establishes:

> Remark 4: The preceding method for finding points on the payoff frontier above π^c will always work. That is, for given non-negative $k_2, \ldots, k_n$, any frontier point on the ray will correspond to a solution to the first order conditions, and any Pareto optimal point will satisfy the second order conditions as well.

Specifying $k_2, \ldots, k_n$ fixes a ray through π^c, as illustrated in figure 5.

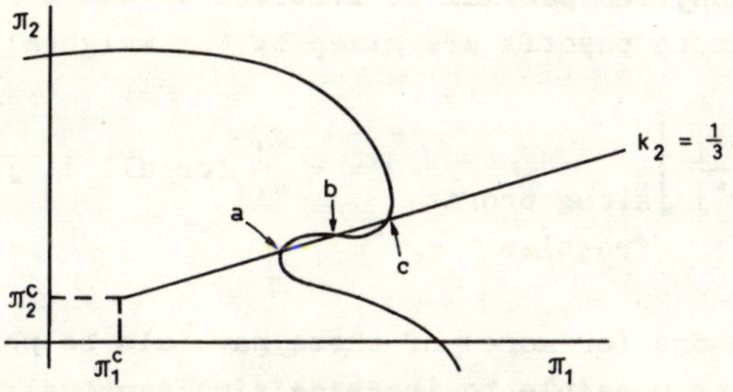

Figure 5

---

1 Of course, if there were several solutions which satisfied the second order conditions, they would have to be examined to determine which were the global maximum.

Note that first order conditions are satisfied at a, b and c, and second order conditions at a and c. Obviously, as between a and c, c is the global maximum; although all three are frontier points and not even one of them is Pareto optimal.

> Remark 5: A necessary condition for a point on the payoff frontier to be Pareto optimal is that all the $\lambda_i (= \rho_i)$ have the same sign.

It has been seen that a frontier point corresponds to a solution of a set of equations which include $\sum_{j=1}^{n} \frac{\partial \pi_j}{\partial p_i} \rho_j, = 0$, $i = 1,\dots,n$. At such a point, the payoff frontier is tangent to a hyperplane given by

$$\sum_{i=1}^{n} \rho_i \pi_i = K$$

for appropriate K. That is, at the frontier point in question, the partial derivatives of the surface with respect to payoffs are given by the weights:

$$\left.\frac{d\pi_i}{d\pi_j}\right|_{\substack{\text{along profit}\\ \text{frontier}}} = -\frac{\rho_j}{\rho_i} \text{ for all } i,\ j,\ \rho_i \neq 0.$$

Should one (or more) of these partials be positive, it would be possible to increase simultaneously the payoffs of all firms.

Remark 6: If, for any non-negatively sloped ray through π^c (given by $k_i \geq 0$, $\sum_{i=1}^{n} k_i = 1$), the associated frontier points have the following characteristics: a) each ray is associated with only one frontier point, b) $\lambda_i > 0$, $i=1,\ldots,n$, c) the matrix of first derivatives $||\partial\pi_i/\partial p_j||$ has rank n-1 and d) the matrix

$$\sum_{i=1}^{n} \lambda_i \left|\left|\frac{\partial^2\pi_i}{\partial p_j \partial p_k}\right|\right|$$

is negative definite; then each frontier point is Pareto optimal, the portion of the Pareto optimal frontier above π^c is concave, and, looking at normalized weights, ($\mu_i = \frac{\lambda_i}{\sum_{j=1}^{n} \lambda_j}$), each frontier point has a unique vector of weights, associated with it.

This remark relies heavily on the continuous differentiability of the payoff frontier and on the information contained in the weights λ_i. A weaker version may be stated:

Remark 7: If all conditions of Remark 6 hold, except condition d) then each frontier point is Pareto optimal.

Figure 2 satisfies the conditions of Remark 6, while Figure 6 satisfies only Remark 7.

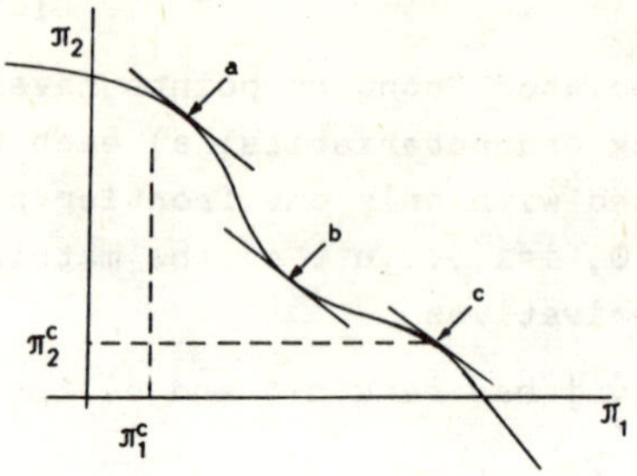

Figure 6

Note that the same (normalized) weights are associated with points a, b and c. This can occur due to the non-concavity of the surface.
Some results rest upon having a concave payoff frontier. The next section provides an example, so it is unfortunate that the conditions which generate such frontiers are not fully understood.

4. The Balanced Temptation Equilibrium[1]

In previous sections, single period models were studied. Economists have recognized that oligopoly is not a single period situation. To deal with it as if it were is to leave out something very important; hence, occasional

---

1 The balanced temptation equilibrium was developed in [6], where existence conditions are also given. The class of models covered in [6] is much broader than in the present paper in such ways as
a) the payoff functions can be different from period to period,
b) payoff functions need not be differentiable, and
c) discount parameters need not be invariant from period to period.

attempts have been made to incorporate time in a realistic manner. All of the "reaction function" literature shares the aim of making a successful analysis of oligopoly with time properly taken into account.

In the model described below time enters in two ways. The firm values prospective profits and may be willing to trade present for future profits, on appropriate terms. Second, the actions a firm takes today may be affected by actions taken in the past by itself or others.

It will be assumed that n firms face, in each time period, the same single period conditions described by D1, C1 and π3'. Price of the ith firm in period t will be denoted p_{it}. Similarly for other variables. Thus

$$\pi_{it} = \pi_i(p_t)$$

$$\text{where } p_t = (p_{1t},\dots,p_{nt}) = (\bar{p}_{it},p_{it})$$

The payoff to which the player is sensitive is

$$\sum_{t=1}^{\infty} \alpha_i^{t-1}\pi_i(p_t)$$

$$\text{where } 0 < \alpha_i < 1$$

Notice that $p_{it} = p_i^c$, $i = 1,\dots,n$, $t = 1,2,\dots$ describes a non-cooperative equilibrium for the model under consideration. Although p^c is the only non-cooperative equilibrium in the single period game, the continual repetition of p^c is not the only non-cooperative equilibrium for the game extended over time. The firms are assumed to possess accurate knowledge about the past. In period t, the firm knows each price vector which was actually chosen in every period through period t-1.

A game of the sort described here, where a group of players are in an "ordinary game" period after period, indefinitely, is called a "supergame." Before proceeding to the balanced temptation equilibrium, an assumption about the Pareto optimal surface will be introduced.

π4 Any point on the payoff frontier, $\pi(p^*)$, which is above $\pi(p^c)$ (i.e., for which $\pi_i(p^*) \geq \pi_i(p^c)$, $i = 1,\ldots,n$) is Pareto optimal. The set of Pareto optimal points above $\pi(p^c)$ forms a concave surface.

In the single period games examined above, a "strategy" for a player can only be a price. The set of possible strategies is the set of possible prices. In a supergame, specifying a strategy for, say, player 1 requires naming a price to be chosen in each time period. Not only may the prices chosen in various periods be different from one another, but the price chosen in period t, p_{it}, may depend upon any or all previous prices of all firms, $p_1,\ldots,p_{t-1}$. Furthermore, p_{it} could depend on $(p_1,\ldots,p_{t-1})$ in a different way than $p_{i,t+1}$ depends upon $(p_1,\ldots,p_t)$. Thus, in full generality, a strategy for the ith firm would be:

$$p_{i1}, \phi_{i2}(p_1), \phi_{i3}(p_2,p_1), \ldots).$$

In this paper, the fullest set of strategies will not be dealt with. It will be seen that interesting results may be found using a more limited class of strategies. Nonetheless, it is worthwhile to be aware of what, in principle, a firm might do.

Now a vector of supergame strategies, one for each firm, will be proposed which may be a non-cooperative equilibrium in which the payoffs are Pareto optimal. Let p^*

denote a price vector yielding a Pareto optimal payoff at which each player is strictly better off than at $\pi(p^c)$. I.e., $\pi_i(p^*) > \pi_i(p^c)$, $i = 1,\ldots,n$. The strategy is given by:

$$p_{i1} = p_i^*$$

$$p_{it} = p_i^* \text{ if } p_{j\tau} = p_j^*,\ j \neq i,\ \tau = 1,\ldots,t-1,\ t > 1, \quad i = 1,\ldots,n$$

$$p_{it} = p_i^c \text{ otherwise}$$

Under this strategy, the ith player will choose his coordinate of p^* (i.e., p_i^*) in the first period and, in each succeeding period he will continue to choose p_i^* if, in all past periods, p^* has been the jointly chosen point. Denote these strategies by σ_i^* $(i = 1,\ldots,n)$. Is σ_i^* optimal for the ith firm when the other firms are playing the σ_j^* $(j \neq i)$? If σ_i^* is played, the discounted payoff stream is

$$\pi_i(p^*) + \alpha_i\pi_i(p^*) + \alpha_i^2\pi_i(p^*) + \ldots$$

$$= \frac{1}{1-\alpha_1}\pi_i(p^*)$$

What if σ_i^* is not played? First, as long as p_i^* is chosen, the others will continue to choose $p_j^*(j\neq i)$; but whenever player i chooses anything other than p_i^*, from the subsequent period onward, the others will choose $p_j^c(j\neq i)$. Say for example that player i chooses p_i^* in each period before t. From period t+1 onward he can do no better than to choose p_i^c. What is best value for p_{it}? The only sensible choice is $p_i^!$ defined by

$$\max_{p_i} \pi_i(\bar{p}_i^*, p_i) = \pi_i(\bar{p}_i^*, p_i^!).$$

Discounted payoff under this strategy is

$$\sum_{\tau=1}^{t-1} \alpha_i^{\tau-1}\pi_i(p^*) + \alpha_i^{t-1}\pi_i(\bar{p}_i^*, p_i') + \sum_{\tau=t+1}^{\infty} \alpha_i^{\tau-1}\pi_i(p^c)$$

The difference between these streams is

$$\sum_{\tau=1}^{\infty} \alpha_i^{\tau-1}\pi_i(p^*) - \sum_{\tau=1}^{t-1} \alpha_i^{\tau-1}\pi_i(p^*) - \alpha_i^{t-1}\pi_i(\bar{p}_i^*, p_i')$$

$$(2) \qquad - \sum_{\tau=t+1}^{\infty} \alpha_i^{\tau-1}\pi_i(p^c)$$

$$= \alpha_i^{t-1} \left[(\pi_i(p^*) - \pi_i(\bar{p}_i^*, p_i')) + \frac{\alpha_i}{1-\alpha_i}(\pi_i(p^*) - \pi_i(p^c))\right]$$

If (2) is negative, indicating the second strategy is superior, then the payoff under this strategy is maximized by choosing t=1. Let $p_{i1} = p_i'$.
If (2) is positive, then σ_i^* is best against the σ_j^*. More generally, if

$$\frac{\pi_i(p_i^*,p_i') - \pi_i(p^*)}{\pi_i(p^*) - \pi_i(p^c)} < \frac{\alpha_i}{1-\alpha_i}, \quad i = 1,\ldots,n$$

then the strategies $\sigma_1^*,\ldots,\sigma_n^*$ form a non-cooperative equilibrium. Obviously, for the chosen point $\pi(p^*)$, if the α_i are sufficiently near 1 the inequalities will be satisfied.
A "balanced temptation equilibrium" is a non-cooperative equilibrium, having the characteristics described above and in addition:

$$\frac{\pi_i(\bar{p}_i^*,p_i') - \pi_i(p^*)}{\pi_i(p^*) - \pi_i(p^c)} = \frac{\pi_j(\bar{p}_j^*,p_j') - \pi_j(p^*)}{\pi_j(p^*) - \pi_j(p^c)} \quad i \neq j, \quad i,j = 1,\ldots,n$$

Notice that $\frac{\pi_i(\bar{p}_i^*, p_i') - \pi_i(p^*)}{\pi_i(p^*) - \pi_i(p^c)}$ is the short run gain associated with choosing p_i' divided by the per period long run loss. This appears to be a suitable normalized measure of the "temptation" faced by a player to short run maximize. In the equal temptation equilibrium, these temptations are equalized across players.

The equal temptation property is illustrated in Figure 7.

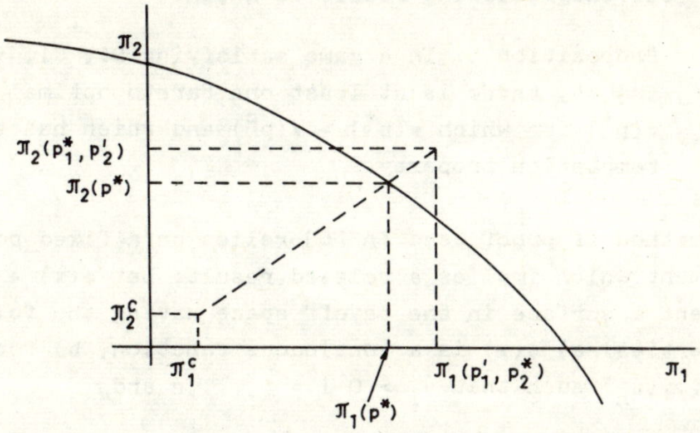

Figure 7

It is possible to distinguish between the "equal temptation property" and the "equal temptation equilibrium." If $\pi(p^o)$ has the equal temptation property, then

$$\pi_i(p^o) \geq \pi_i(p^c), \ i = 1, \ldots, n \text{ and}$$

$$\frac{\pi_i(\bar{p}_i^o, p_i') - \pi_i(p^o)}{\pi_i(p^o) - \pi_i(p^c)} = \frac{\pi_j(\bar{p}_j^o, p_j') - \pi_j(p^o)}{\pi_j(p^o) - \pi_j(p^c)}$$

$$i \neq j, \ i, j = 1, \ldots, n$$

where $\pi_i(\bar{p}_i^o, p_i^!) = \max_{p_i} \pi_i(\bar{p}_i^o, p_i)$, $i = 1,\dots,n$.

If $\pi(p^o)$ is an equal temptation equilibrium, then a) it has the equal temptation property, b) it is Pareto optimal and

$$\text{c)} \qquad \frac{\pi_i(\bar{p}_i^o, p_i^!) - \pi_i(p^o)}{\pi_i(p^o) - \pi_i(p^c)} < \frac{\alpha_i}{1-\alpha_i}, \quad i = 1,\dots,n.$$

From [6], the following result is known:

> Proposition 5: In a game satisfying D1, C1, $\pi3'$ and $\pi4$, there is at least one Pareto optimal point, $\pi(p^*)$ for which $\pi(p^*) > \pi(p^c)$ and which has the equal temptation property.

The method of proof used in [6] relies on a fixed point argument which implies a related result: Let $\phi(\pi) = 0$ represent a surface in the payoff space having the following properties: a) $\phi(\pi)$ is a continuous function, b) for any $(\mu_1,\dots,\mu_n)$ such that $\mu_i \geq 0$ $i = 1,\dots,n$ and

$\sum_{i=1}^{n} \mu_i = 1$, there is exactly one point, $\pi(p(\mu))$, which satisfies $\phi(\pi(p(\mu))) = 0$ and for which $\pi_i(p(\mu)) \geq \pi_i(p^c)$ and

$$\frac{\pi_i p(\mu) - \pi_i(p^c)}{\pi_j p(\mu) - \pi_j(p^c)} = \frac{\mu_i}{\mu_j}$$ for all i and j, $\mu_j \neq 0$. Property b)

merely means that a non-negatively sloped ray through $\pi(p^c)$ intersects the surface $\phi(\pi)$ in exactly one point. This is illustrated in Figure 8.

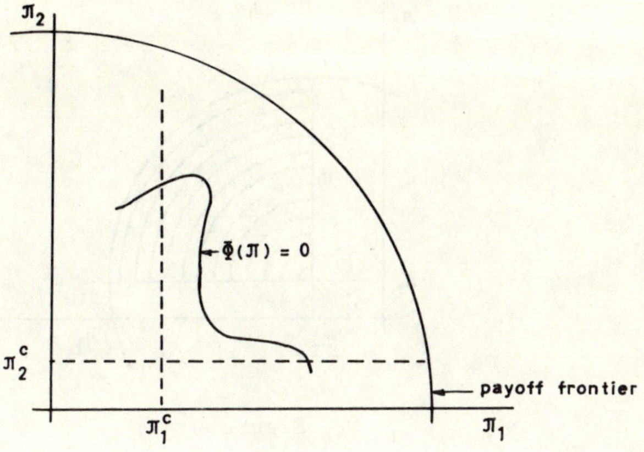

Figure 8

Proposition 6: In a game satisfying D1, C1 and π3', an attainable payoff surface $\phi(\pi)$ has at least one point passessing the equal temptation property.

Note that whether or not a particular point has the equal temptation property depends in no way upon the arbitrary surface passing through that point. Furthermore, the payoff space could have a family of non-intersecting surfaces, dense in the payoff space, each of which has at least one point with the equal temptation property. This is illustrated in figure 9.

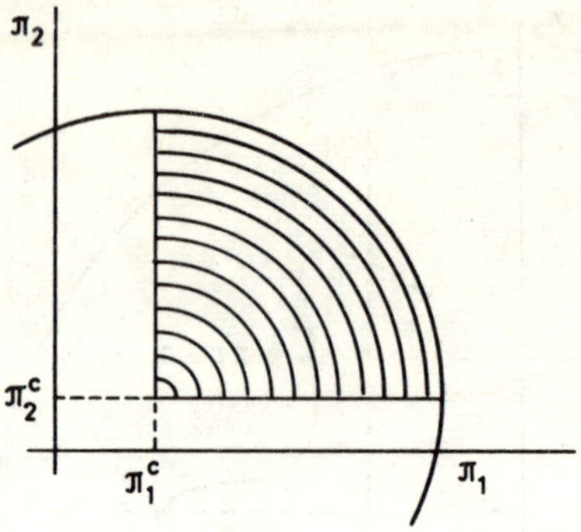

Figure 9

Thus, at any distance from $\pi(p^c)$ no greater than the distance to the nearest frontier point above $\pi(p^c)$ there is a point having the equal temptation property. It would be interesting to know under what circumstances the set of points having the equal temptation property might trace out a continuous curve, as illustrated in figure 10.

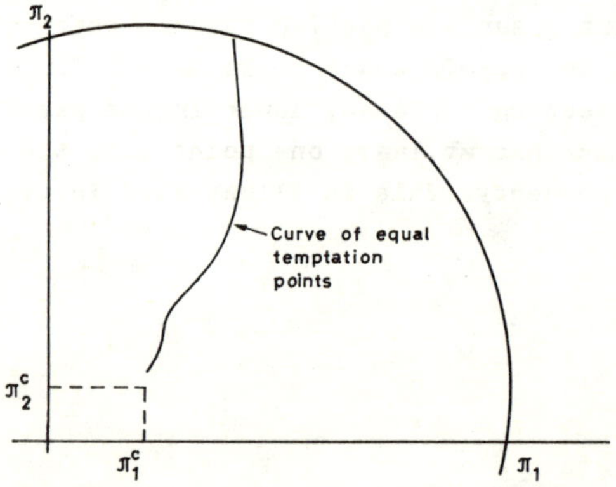

Figure 10

Should such a curve exist, it is possible that firms might move along it from $\pi(p^c)$ to the profit frontier, while groping, in disequilibrium toward an equilibrium state.

That there is such an equilibrium as the balanced temptation equilibrium underscores several important lessons. One is that merely by allowing a game to be temporally repeated, many new non-cooperative equilibria become possible which are unavailable in the single period version of the same basic model. The balanced temptation equilibrium is not only a non-cooperative equilibrium, but it yields Pareto optimal payoffs. Collusion could not simultaneously increase all firms' profits. This insight is in direct contrast to conclusions drawn from the study of single period oligopoly, where the non-cooperative equilibrium is not Pareto optimal, leading to the false conclusion that cooperation is a prerequisite for the attainment of payoffs on the profit frontier.

5. *Steady State Equilibrium in Models with Structural Time Dependence*

In all past sections, the oligopoly model under investigation lacked "structural time dependence." That is, the payoffs received in a given time period depended only on the prices actually chosen in that period. Structural time dependence is present when payoffs in period t are a function of prices in one or more past periods, as well as current period prices. Structural time dependence could stem from demand or cost considerations. For example, sales in period t might be higher, or lower, the greater were sales in the preceding period. On the other hand, total cost in a period might depend upon total production within that period and on the amount by which the production level was changed between periods. Thus structural time dependence is quite separate from "strategic time dependence." The latter was considered in section 4. Strategic time dependence is present when the decisions of one time period may depend upon past choices of oneself or others.

Here structural time dependence will be considered only in a simple form:

$$q_{it} = f_i(p_t, p_{t-1})$$

$$C_{it} = C_i(q_{it})$$

$$\pi_{it} = P_{it} f_i(p_t, p_{t-1}) - C_i(f_i(p_t, p_{t-1})), \quad i = 1, \ldots, n$$

When t=1, π_{i1} depends upon p_o as well as p_1. p_o is taken to be a fixed initial condition. This section will deal only with non-cooperative equilibrium in models with time dependence.

The underlying assumptions used in this section will be a natural modification of those used in earlier sections. Demand now depends upon a pair of price vectors, $(p,r) \in PxP$. The demand assumptions are

D2 a. For any $(p,r) \in PxP$, $0 \leq f_i(p,r) < \infty$

b. For $(p,r) \in PxP$, $f_i(p,r)$ is continuous

c. For $(p^o,r^o) \in PxP$, $p_i^1 > p_i^o$ and $f_i(p^o,r^o) > 0$,

$f_i(p^o,r^o) > f_i(\bar{p}_i^o, p_i^1, r^o)$.

d. For $(p^o,r^o) \in PxP$, $p_j^1 > p_j^o$, $f_i(p^o,r^o) > 0$ and

$f_j(p^o,r^o) > 0$, $f_i(p^o,r^o) < f_i(\bar{p}_j^o, p_j^1, r^o)$, $j \neq i$.

e. For $(p^o,r^o) \in P \times P$, $p_j^1 > p_j^o$ and $f_j(p^o,r^o) = 0$, $f_i(p^o,r^o) = f_i(\bar{p}_j^o,p_j^1,r^o)$.

f. For $(p^o,r^o) \in P \times P$, $\delta > 0$, $p^1 = p_1^o + \delta,\ldots,p_n^o + \delta)$, and $f_i(p^o,r^o) > 0$, $f_i(p^1,r^o) < f_i(p^o,r^o)$.

g. $\overset{o}{A}_i(r) = \{p \mid p \in P,\ f_i(p,r) > 0\}$. For any $r \in P$, $\bigcap_{i=1}^{n} \overset{o}{A}_i(r) = \overset{o}{A}(r)$ is non-empty. $\overset{o}{A} = \bigcup_{r \in P} \overset{o}{A}(r)$ is bounded.

h. For $(p^o,r^o,s^o) \in P \times P \times P$ and $r_j^1 \geq 0$, if $f_j(r^o,s^o) = f_j(\bar{r}_j^o,r_j^1,s^o) = 0$ then $f_i(p^o,r^o) = f_i(p^o,\bar{r}_j^o,r_j^1)$.

D2 a through f state the same conditions for q_{it} as a function of p_t (for given p_{t-1}) as the corresponding conditions of D1. D2 g, in addition to repeating D1 g, states that $f_i(p_t,p_{t-1})$ is zero for p_t outside a bounded set $\overset{o}{A}$, irrespective of the value of p_{t-1}. Finally, D2 h states that changes in $p_{j,t-1}$ cannot affect the value of $f_i(p_t,p_{t-1})$ if, for values of $p_{j,t-1}$ under consideration, $f_j(p_{t-1},p_{t-2})$ is zero. C1 will be retained unchanged.

Additional assumptions are needed.

Let $A^* = \{(p,r) \mid (p,r) \in \overset{o}{A},\ f_i(p,r) > 0,\ i = 1,\ldots,n\}$, and let A be the closure of A^*.

π3" $\pi_i(p_t,p_{t-1})$ has continuous second partial derivatives in the interior of A and is a strictly concave function of $(p_{it},p_{i,t-1})$.

In the class of supergames being considered here, note that the decisions of period t affect structurally the payoffs of periods t and t+1. In the present section attention will be focussed on "simple strategy non-cooperative equilibria." A "simple strategy" is a supergame strategy which displays no strategic time dependence. For example, $p_{i1} = 5.2$, $p_{i2} = 6.84$, $p_{i3} = 5.$, $p_{it} = 6.5$ $(t = 4,5,6,\ldots)$ is such a strategy. The actual price chosen in a given period depends in no way upon any previous choices. I.e., simple strategies are contained in $P \times P \times \ldots$.

Now consider a characteristic of a simple strategy non-cooperative equilibrium for the supergame. If $(p_o^*, p_1^*, p_2^*, \ldots)$ is a non-cooperative equilibrium, then p_t^* is a non-cooperative equilibrium for the game whose payoff functions are

$$\pi_i(p_t, p_{t-1}^*) + \alpha_i \pi_i(p_{t+1}^*, p_t) \qquad i = 1,\ldots,n.$$

More generally, for any fixed (p_{t+1}^o, p_{t-1}^o), the game whose payoff functions are

$$\pi_i(p_t, p_{t-1}^o) + \alpha_i \pi_i(p_{t+1}^o, p_t)$$

has a non-cooperative equilibrium. If there were exactly one such equilibrium corresponding to any given (p_{t+1}, p_{t-1}), the relationship could be denoted

$$p_t = \phi(p_{t+1}, p_{t-1})$$

$\pi 5$ For $p_{t+1} \in \overset{o}{A}(p_t)$ and $p_t \in \overset{o}{A}(p_{t-1})$, ϕ exists and has continuous partial derivatives. In addition

$$\sum_{j=1}^{n} \left| \frac{\partial \phi_i(p_{t+1}, p_{t-1})}{\partial p_{j,t+1}} \right| \leq k_1$$

$$\sum_{j=1}^{n} \left| \frac{\partial \phi_i(p_{t+1}, p_{t-1})}{\partial p_{j,t-1}} \right| \leq k_2$$

$$k_1 + k_2 < 1$$

It would be desirable to find a way of expressing $\pi 5$ by means of direct conditions on the demand and cost functions. At present, the only means of doing this which the author can see are quite cumbersome. In writing the discounted payoff stream,

$\sum_{t=1}^{\infty} \alpha_i^{t-1} \pi_i(p_t, p_{t-1})$, there appears a price vector p_o. This must be taken as an initial condition. In [7] the following results are proved.

> Proposition 7: In a supergame satisfying D2, C1, $\pi 3''$ and $\pi 5$, there is a unique price vector p^c such that, if $p_o = p^c$ then $(p^c, p^c, p^c, \ldots)$ is a non-cooperative equilibrium. I.e., p^c is the only price vector satisfying the condition $p^c = \phi(p^c, p^c)$.
>
> Proposition 8: Let $(p'_o, p'_1, p'_2, \ldots)$ be a simple strategy non-cooperative equilibrium for the supergame satisfying D2, C1, $\pi 3''$ and $\pi 5$. Then $\lim_{t \to \infty} p'_t = p^c$.

These propositions say there is a unique "steady state" non-cooperative equilibrium (using only simple strategies) and, for any simple strategy non-cooperative equilibrium, over time the chosen price vectors will tend to the steady state vector. Reasearch on time-dependent supergames is now only in a very early stage. The results of this section are presented mainly to indicate that such models may be considered in oligopoly.

6. Concluding Comments

When von Neumann and Morgenstern's book was being reviewed in the economics journals over two decades ago, great hopes were often expressed concerning the ways game theory might revolutionize economics. As time went by, some disillusionment set in. It is unrealistic to think a new discipline such as game theory would have a huge, visible impact within very few years. Looking back now it is apparent that it has made considerable contributions in several areas of economics, of which oligopoly theory is an outstanding example.

It is hoped the present paper brings some of these contributions more directly into the main stream of oligopoly theory.

Bibliography

1. Bartle, Robert G., The Elements of Real Analysis, New York: Wiley, 1964.

2. Berge, Claude, "Théorie Générale des Jeux à n Personnes", Mémorial des Sciences Mathematiques, 1957.

3. Chamberlin, Edward H., The Theory of Monopolistic Competition 7th edition, Cambridge: Harvard, 1956.

4. Cournot, Augustin, Researches into the Mathematical Principles of the Theory of Wealth (translated by N.T. Bacon), New York: Kelly, 1960.

5. Debreu, Gerard, "A Social Equilibrium Existence Theorem," Proceedings of the National Academy of Science (1952), pp. 886-893.

6. Friedman, James W., "A Non-cooperative Equilibrium for Supergames," Review of Economic Studies (1971), pp. 1-12.

7. ———, "Non-cooperative Equilibria in Time-Dependent Supergames," University of Rochester, Discussion Paper 72-5, January, 1972.

8. Nash, John F., "Equilibrium Points in n Person Games," Proceedings of the National Academy of Sciences (1950), pp. 48-49.

9. von Neumann, John, and Oskar Morgenstern, The Theory of Games and Economic Behavior, 3rd edition, Princeton: Princeton University Press, 1953.

4. AN ANALYSIS OF LEARNING CHARACTERISTICS IN DUOPOLY EXPERIMENTS

JAMES MURPHY*

I. Introduction

Experimental research in oligopoly has emphasized the degree of cooperation among the bargainers and the theoretical analysis of the solution attained after a series of replicative trials. In many studies, it is well recognized that learning by the bargainers is an important factor in their choice of strategies and in their eventual stable state behavior.

In an early experiment of a duopoly situation, Suppes and Carlsmith [19] concluded that the learning process follows a first order Markov Chain. Siegel and Fouraker [6] expressed the opinion that learning develops as experience progresses and is related to the bargainers aspiration level. Ferguson and Pfouts [5] submit that learning and expectations are clearly related and have a joint effect on the stability of the dynamic bargaining behavior in a duopoly situation. They introduce simple forms of reaction functions which presume that a bargainer learns from past mistakes so that new behavior patterns may emerge during repeated bargaining sessions.

Other studies have suggested learning by various feedback and adaptive processes in various applications of economic or behavioral systems. Particular reaction

---

* University of North Carolina.

functions in duopoly theory have been examined by Friedman [8] to discover the potential set of equilibrium solutions.

While these and other papers have pointed out the need for an analysis of learning, they have also suggested several questions about the learning process, and no study has attempted to set forth a simple, yet general, learning model applicable to duopoly (or oligopoly) bargaining. Clearly, the task of specifying an exhaustive set of learning characteristics evidenced in duopoly bargaining is formidable. Presumably, no model could be comprehensive enough to include all behavioral types. Nevertheless, the purpose of this paper is to make a descriptive and statistical analysis of the bargaining dynamics in simple price-variation duopoly experiments in order to detect the characteristics of learning and to embody them in a simple descriptive dynamic model of a bargainer's learning process.

The particular questions to be considered in the analysis are:

(a) Is there further evidence that the adaptation of bargainers follows a first order Markov process?; and

(b) Do response patterns differ and for what reasons?

II. The Experiments Considered

The selection of the experiments used for analyzing learning in a duopoly situation was based on two criteria, availability of complete bargaining responses and simplicity of experimental design. The former is crucial for the statistical analysis while the latter is important to reduce ambiguity of playing patterns due to confusion or misunderstanding. Furthermore, the amouht of communication and information for the bargainers should be clearly indicated and controlled.[1]

My choices within these criteria are the price variation experiments of Fouraker and Siegel under incomplete and complete information and the author's adaptation of the former.[2] The experiments involve two players bidding on a homogenous good or contract. On each repeated trial, the lower bid is accepted. The players do not know how many trials will be called. The bargainer in each pair making the lowest bid on a given trial receives a profit dependent on the bid price; the other loses a set amount (25¢) representing the cost of making a bid. If both bargainers bid the same price, they each receive an equal profit dependent on the bid price. All the experiments involve 17 pairs of bargainers and follow the same experimental procedure.[3]

Special Differences Between the Experiments

However, several differences must be noted between the Fouraker and Siegel (F-S) experiments and my (M) experiment. The profit table in the (M) experiment is extended to allow a wider range of price bids with negative profits occurring at low rivalistic price bids below the Bertrand solution point. Also, the joint cooperative solution price is distinct from the single

1 This paper is not concerned with the effects on learning of communication. See Harnett and Cummings [10].

2 Fouraker and Siegel, [6], experiments 13 and 16, and J. Murphy [14].

3 J. Murphy, [14], section III describes and compares the methods of these experiments.

profit maximizer price in the (M) experiment while these are indistinguishable in the (F-S) experiments.[1]

A second difference between the experiments is the number of trials. Excluding announced end plays, the (F-S) experiments used 14 trials and the (M) experiment used 24 trials. A final difference is that more information is available to me regarding the bargainers intended strategy and aspiration level in the (M) experiment. This information was acquired from the bargainers after their instruction period but before any practice trials began while they were being seated in their respective cubicles. The two questions which were answered in writing under a condition of silence were:

1. Have you formulated any overall strategy of play? If so, describe your strategy?
2. How much money do you expect to earn by your participation in this experiment?

Bargainers had about 5 minutes to answer these questions. The answers are utilized in making classifications and testing special hypotheses related to learning in the next section.

III. Analysis of the Bargaining Responses

The experiments chosen to examine the response patterns were not originally designed for the purpose of making inferences about learning processes. Consequently, no single test will provide the answer. Instead, many different considerations are presented in an attempt to

---

1 See the respective payoff tables of these experiments, J. Murphy, [14], p. 308.

discover characteristics of the bargaining behavior. Seven basic questions are asked in this section, each followed by one or more hypotheses, tests, and/or tables whose analysis helps to answer the question. Since the motives of the players and the particular bid decisions of their bargaining partner were not controlled in these experiments, most of the analysis is cross-sectional over groups of bargainers. Most of the results are in terms of average behavior characteristics so that individual peculiarities may balance out. Trial outcomes and bid responses are also categorized to maintain relatively large numbers of observations per cell in all transition probability matrices so that chi-square distributed test statistics are applicable.

Question 1. Does bargainer A presume a simple response function for his duopoly rival?

The choice of price bid, $P_{A,t}$ by bargainer A on a given trial t, is dependent on his expectation of his rivals price bid, $E(P_{B,t})$. A simple response function for this rival would be reflected in the expectation rule, $E(P_{B,t}) = P_{B,t-1}$.[1]

To examine if such a simple rule is satisfactory, the bargainer's decision on each trial can be categorized according to whether his price bid is increased (I), unchanged (U) or decreased (D) from his previous one. Also, the outcome for bargainer A at the previous trial ($O_{A,t-1}$) may be classified as won (W) with the lower bid price, tied (T) at the low bid price, or lost (L) by bidding the higher price. A decision ob-

---

1 Although this type response function is often used, each bargainer should recognize that the other has a reaction function and modify his own predictive rule accordingly. See a discussion on this problem by Friedman, [9], p. 413.

servation is defined as the ordered pair relating $(\Delta P)_t$, the price change (I, U, or D) on trial t to O_{t-1}, the outcome (W, T, or L) on trial t-1.

If bargainer A is a profit maximizer (long or short run is indeterminable since the planning horizon, number of trials, was unannounced to the bargainers) and if he uses the rule, $E(P_{B,t}) = P_{B,t-1}$, then certain decision choices would seem irrational. Following a win (W), A would be unwise to decrease his bid price since he would be certain of a greater payoff by keeping it unchanged. He may increase his price bid hoping to win at a higher payoff even though he takes the risk of increasing too much, and hence, tying or even losing. Similarly, A would not rationally ever increase after a tie outcome and would never increase or remain unchanged after a loss. That is, if A envisions $E(P_{B,t})$, = $P_{B,t-1}$, then decision observations (W_{t-1}, D_t), (T_{t-1}, I_t), (L_{t-1}, I_t), or (L_{t-1}, U_t) should seldom occur.

The transition matrices in Figure 1 present the frequency of all decision observations for the (F-S) experiment and for the (M) experiment.[1] The irrational choices discussed obove occur in 18.1% of all transitions in the former and 26.1% in the latter. I do not believe that the bargainers, although students, can be presumed to be irrational this often. Instead, they must be allowing for some adaptation on the part of their rival to their own price bid and to previous results. Such adaptations will be considered further in later questions.

---

1 The source of all such tables are the complete bargaining results excluding observations that would involve practice trials or end plays. The matrices are similar to those used in Friedman, [7].

Figure 1: Total Transition Matrices for (F-S) and (M) Experiments

(F-S)
Trials 2-14

trial t-1 \ trial$_t$	I	U	D	Σ
W	73	46	12	131
T	37	114	29	180
L	9	22	100	131
Σ	119	182	141	442

(M)
Trials 2-24

trial t-1 \ trial$_t$	I	U	D	Σ
W	130	79	26	235
T	88	191	33	312
L	18	72	145	235
Σ	236	342	204	782

Question 2. Do prices stabilize as learning occurs?

It has been suggested that two types of learning occur in such experiments, an "experimental learning" during which the bargainers (as well as the conductors of the experiment) undergo the process and a "within game learning" during which strategy development occurs. When the learning phase is over, a more stable state or equilibrium behavior is presumably attained.[1]

Since an equilibrium behavior suggests that price bids remain unchanged and since learning can occur only if different events are experienced, the detection of the learning phase may be first approximated by examining the average number of price changes within different trial groups throughout the experiment as given in Table 1. The average number of price changes per trial

Table 1: Average Number of Price Changes ($\overline{PC}$)** and Payoffs ($\bar{\pi}$) Per Trial

(F-S) Experiments		
Trial Groups	$\overline{PC}$	$\bar{\pi}$
Incomplete Information		
I 2- 6	22.2	$0.061
II 7-11	20.6	0.051
III* 12-14	15.7	0.032
Complete Information		
I 2- 6	19.4	0.184
II 7-11	18.6	0.148
III* 12-14	17.6	0.149

(M) Experiment		
Trial Groups	$\overline{PC}$	$\bar{\pi}$
I 2- 6	21.2	$0.1134
II 7-11	22.2	0.1002
III 12-16	19.8	0.1728
IV 20-24	13.6	0.1848

* Group III for the (F-S) experiments contains only 3 trials. All other groups contain 5 trials.

** The maximum value for $\overline{PC}$ is 34; each bargainer changes price.

1 See Friedman, [9], pp. 406-7.

by bargainers is consistently higher in the early trials. The t-test for difference between means indicates a significant difference between the average for trials 20-24 and the average for either trial groups 2-6, 7-11, or 12-16. None of the latter groups have averages different from each other.[1] The results give evidence of early experimentation compared to more stability (or loss of interest) in the later trials.

Again, if the bargainers are profit maximizers who are learning from past mistakes by some feedback procedure where $P_{A,t} = f[O_{A,t-1}, E(P_{B,t})]$,[2] then the average payoff per trial should increase due to learning. In the (M) experiment such a relation seems possible as the average payoff in the later trials exceeds that of the learning trials. The difference in average payoffs is significant (0.0005 level) between trial group 2-6 and either groups 12-16 or 20-24. The results for the (F-S) experiments seem to disagree, but these may not include enough trials for the equilibrium to be reasonably approached.

Figure 2 illustrates the average payoff per trial in the (M) experiment. There does seem to be a payoff to the learning in trials 2-10. A higher average level of profit results in trials 12-24 in contrast to the initial decline in profits during the learning phase.[3]

---

1 The calculated t-value of these three tests are 3.18, 3.44, and 3.57 respectively compared to $t_{(.01,\ 8d.f.)} = 2.896$. The difference between standard deviations of average payoffs among any of the groups are not significant at the 0.05 level.

2 Versions of this learning rule are applied by Ferguson and Pfouts, [5], and are shown to result in stability of duopoly bargaining.

3 In both (F-S) experiments, the initial downward trend in average payoffs stopped at trial number 5.

Figure 2: Average Payoff ($\bar{\pi}$) in the (M) Experiment

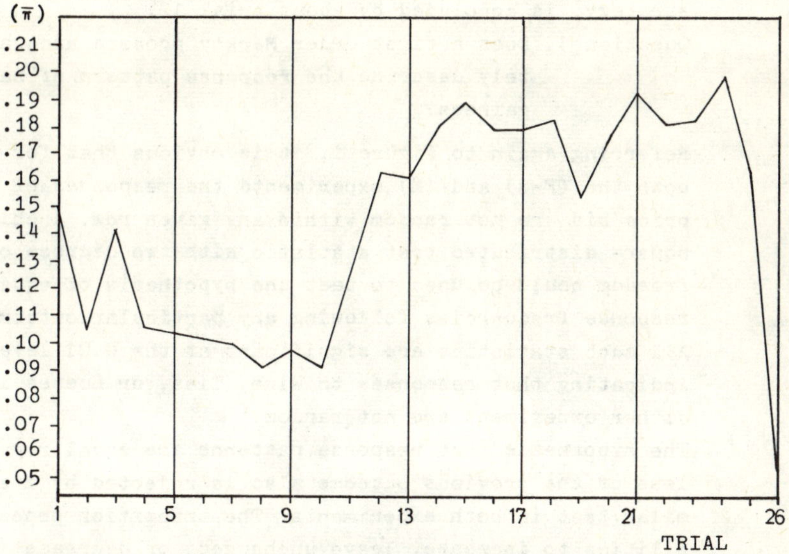

Looking at first differences of the average payoffs, one can posit that a trend of positive changes indicates a payoff to learning while a trend of negative differences indicates a period of learning costs. In the (M) experiment, the first differences in average payoffs (slopes of line regments in Figure 2) are all negative for the five trials 4-8. Then, in the last 15 trials, 9-24, only five differences are negative and never two in succession. The only period in which there occur three or more successive trials without any average payoff decrease of more than \$-0.005 are trials 8-15.[1] For these simple experiments, one might

1 Similar periods occur for the (F-S) incomplete and complete information experiments only during trials (8-12) and (10-13) respectively.

conjecture that the primary learning phase, including both the development of game sense and bargaining strategy, is concluded by about trial 12.

Question 3. Does a first order Markov process adequately describe the response pattern of bargainers?

Referring again to Figure 1, it is obvious that for both the (F-S) and (M) experiments the responses of price bid are not random within any given row. A chi-square distributed test statistic with two degrees of freedom could be used to test the hypothesis of equal response frequencies following any particular outcome.[1] All such statistics are significant at the 0.01 level indicating that responses to Wins, Ties, or Losses in either experiment are not random.

The hypothesis that response patterns are equal regardless of the previous outcome also is rejected by a similar test in both experiments. The transition probabilities to increase, leave unchanged, or decrease price seem to differ depending on whether the previous outcome was a win, tie, or loss.

A first order Markov process may describe the relation. A chi-square test statistic is used to test the null hypothesis that the decision observations are statistically independent against the alternative that they come from a first order Markov process.[2] The null hypothesis is rejected for the (F-S) and (M) experiments at the 0.001 significance levels (χ^2 = 208.7 and 288.9 respectively with 12 degrees of freedom). The decision observations do relate P_t to the previous outcome O_{t-1}.

---

1 For the test statistics, see Richmond, [17], Chapter 11.

2 Anderson and Goodman, [1], pp. 100-103. The tests on Markov processes are generalizations of the previous tests. Ideally, a Markov process of order r should be distinguished from a process of any other order, but there is no available test statistic for such a test.

Second Order Response Patterns

Consideration of higher order processes is limited by the number of observations, but examination of particular bargaining patterns strongly indicate that some bargainers do make use of past information prior to the preceding outcome. Thus, second order transitions are considered by tabling the decision observations according to the 3-tuple, $[O_{t-2}, O_{t-1}, (\Delta P)_t]$ for each bargainer for each trial (practice trials and end plays excluded to give 748 total 3-tuples with the minimum number of decision observations being 5 for $[L_{t-2}, L_{t-1}, I_t]$).[1]

The null hypothesis to be tested is that decision observations come from a first order Markov process as opposed to the alternate that they come from a second order process. The first order process cannot be rejected using the (F-S) experimental results even at a significance level of 0.40 ($\chi^2 = 13.08$ with 12 degrees of freedom). For the (M) experiment this same hypothesis is rejected at the 0.01 significance level, due to the strong second order feedback following ties in trial t-1. (See Table 2, block 1). That is, second order decision observations of the type $[O_{t-2}, W_{t-1}, (\Delta P)_t]$ and $[O_{t-2}, L_{t-1}, (\Delta P)_t]$ are not significantly different from the simple first order transitions $[W_{t-1}, (\Delta P)_t]$ and $[L_{t-1}, (\Delta P)_t]$. However, if O_{t-1} is a tie, then there are significant changes in the response patterns depending on whether O_{t-2} was a win, tie, or loss.

---

1 The ordered 3-tuple involving outcomes rather than the rival's price changes in the previous two periods is used because only the outcomes are known to the bargainer. When the outcome O_{t-1} was a win, for example, he cannot infer how the rival changed price, but only that the rival's price bid was higher than his own.

Table 2: Chi-square Test Results for (M) Experiment Considering Second-order Decisions Observations

Hypotheses:		Outcome in trial t-1 W	T	L	Overall
1. H_o: $\Delta P_t = f(O_{t-1})$	χ^2	3.828	27.06	3.110	33.998
H_a: $\Delta P_t = f(O_{t-1}, O_{t-2})$	DF	4	4	4	12
		Accept	Rej(.01)	Accept	Rej(.01)
2. $(W,O_{t-1},\Delta P_t)=(T,O_{t-1},\Delta P_t)$	χ^2	2.264	17.256	0.075	19.595
	DF	2	2	2	6
		Accept	Rej(.01)	Accept	Rej(.01)
3. $(T,O_{t-1},\Delta P_t)=(L,O_{t-1},\Delta P_t)$	χ^2	3.301	22.330	1.984	27.615
	DF	2	2	2	6
		Accept	Rej(.01)	Accept	Rej(.01)
4. $(W,O_{t-1},\Delta P_t)=(L,O_{t-1},\Delta P_t)$	χ^2	0.062	0.360	5.741	6.163
	DF	2	2	2	6
		Accept	Accept	Rej(.01)	Accept

Another null hypothesis tested using second order transition matrices is that the first order decision observations $[O_{t-1}, (\Delta P)_t]$ are equal following any pair of second order outcomes, O_{t-2}. The results (Table 2, blocks 2-4) show that the overall first order response pattern is similar for second order outcomes of win or lose, but that there is a significant difference between either of these and the responses after second order tie outcomes. The differences are greatest among the second order decision observations $[W_{t-2}, T_{t-1}, (\Delta P_t)]$, $[L_{t-2}, T_{t-1}, (\Delta P)_t]$ and $[T_{t-2}, T_{t-1}, (\Delta P)_t]$. The reaction function may be described, relative to this result, as

$$\Delta P_t = f(O_{t-1}) \quad \text{if } O_{t-1} \text{ is W or L.}$$

$$f(O_{t-1}, O_{t-2}) \text{ if } O_{t-1} \text{ is T.}$$

When bargainers tie, they refer back to the preceding outcome before making their next price decision.

Question 4. Do the response patterns change during the experiment?

Some general conclusions can be drawn about the response patterns during any of these experiments. Early trials are dominated by frequent price changes (See Table 1) and relatively more price decreases. The middle trials reflect developing strategies as the assortment of responses is broader (higher off-diagonal transition probabilities). The later trials show greater stability. Throughout, the most variable response follows a tie outcome; the most consistent response is to lower price following a loss.

Table 3 presents data giving evidence of these statements. The per cent of diagonal decision observations reflect the mechanistic patterns of response, namely (W_{t-1}, I_t), (T_{t-1}, U_t) and (L_{t-1}, D_t). The per cent of "tie-unchanged" responses indicates a stable state situation. The per cent of price decreases indicates competitiveness or attempts to provide experiences of learning for oneself or one's bargaining rival.[1]

---

1 Some separation of these two is attempted in answering question six below. The problem arises since the bargaining results give indication that a bargainer will bid lower in attempts to either locate the bid level of his rival or to punish his rival for not cooperating more.

Table 3: Selected Percentage Responses by Experiment and Trial Groups Over All Bargainers

Trial Groups	Per Cent Diagonal	% Tie-Unchanged	Percent Price Decrease
(M) Exp. 2- 6	60	12	33
7-11	59	13	31
12-16	53	24	21
20-24	66	42	19
(F-S) Exp., incomplete information			
2- 7	64	20	37
6-10	64	18	32
8-14	66	31	28
(F-S) Exp., complete information			
2- 6	66	25	31
10-14	72	38	30

Several ranking tests described by Jonckheere [12] were performed using individual response changes between trial periods rather than these cross-sectional data. No significant trends were found among the number of diagonal choices over the trial periods in either the (F-S) or (M) experiments. The number of "tie-unchanged" responses showed no significant upward trend in the (F-S) experiments using all individuals and trial groups 2-5, 6-9, and 10-13. There is a significant increase in the number of such responses in the (M) experiment using all individuals and trial groups, 2-6, 12-16, and 20-24. In the (F-S) and (M) experiments, a significant decreasing trend occurs in the number of price decreases (using the same trial groups as above).

Results for the (F-S) Experiments

Further tests on possible changes in response patterns are made by comparing the first order transition matrices for subgroups of trials.[1] In the (F-S) experiment, the results indicate that the transition probabilities are not similar (at 0.02 level of significance) between trial groups 2-6 and 10-14. The response pattern is very weakly similar (fail to reject similarity at the 0.15 significance level) between trial groups 2-6 and 7-10. There is indication of a gradual change in the middle trials resulting in a significantly different response pattern in the later trials. The main difference is again in the reaction to tie outcomes.

In the (F-S) experiment under complete information, there is no significant overall difference between response patterns in trials 2-6 and 10-14 even though the response pattern after losses is significantly different by itself at the 0.01 significance level. (Overall $x^2_{6\ df} = 7.605$, and after losses, $x^2_{2\ df} = 5.675$). Apparently, the learning under complete information conditions takes place very early, even in the practice trials, and the beginning overall strategy is not much different from the one developed after some experience. Within the limited scope of choice in this simple experiment, the bargainer acquires so much information early that his anticipations or expectations for the next period are frequently realized within some probability limit.[2] Not much new information is acquired during the trials and not much change occurs in the form or parameters of his response function.

---

1 The chi-square test is again appropriate. Similar uses of this procedure are found in Friedman [7], and Anderson [2].

2 This result is used as a behavioral assumption in Ferguson and Pfouts, [5], p. 225.

Results for the (M) Experiment

The results for tests of changing response patterns in the (M) experiment are given in Table 4. The null hypothesis is that the transition probabilities are the same between the respective pair of trial groups indicated in the first columns. Values of the test statistic with two degrees of freedom are given for difference of responses following each state of outcome as well as the overall values of the chi-square statistic with six degrees of freedom.

Table 4: Chi-square Test Results for (M) Experiment Concerning First-order Response Patterns

Hypothesis: Equal response pattern between trial groups	Outcome in Trial t-1			
	W	T	L	Overall
2-6 and 7-11	0.390 Accept	5.916 Rej(.10)	0.072 Accept	6.378 Accept
2-6 and 12-16	0.254 Accept	11.856 Rej(.01)	0.327 Accept	12.437 Rej(.10)
2-11 and 12-16	0.361 Accept	6.160 Rej(.05)	0.508 Accept	7.029 Accept
2-16 and 20-24	5.527 Rej(.10)	15.040 Rej (.005)	0.111 Accept	20.678 Rej(.01)
12-16 and 20-24	2.529 Accept	13.183 Rej(.01)	0.814 Accept	16.526 Rej(.05)

The response pattern after ties is the most volatile. There seems to be no evidence of changes in the response to losses. The final five trials differ markedly in response patterns from the early trials and somewhat less so from the middle trials.

In addition, the second order transition probabilities were examined for changes during the (M) experiment.

The null hypothesis is that the second order response patterns are similar between trials groups 3-16 and 17-24.[1] The respective chi-square statistics for outcome states W, T, and L in trial t-1 and over all outcome states in trial t-1 are 6.744 (Sig.,.05), 12.35 (Sig.,.01), 6.28 (Sig.,.05) and 25.374 (Sig.,.01) respectively. These significant results imply that the response patterns do indeed change from the early trials to the later trials. Even more significant test results would be obtained by deleting some of the transitory middle trials and comparing more widely separate trial groups. For an individual bargainer, this implies that two successive wins suggest a different price bid response in later trials than in early trials, and similarly, for two successive ties, etc..

For a bargainer to record, update and analyze such second order patterns to determine his rivals expected price bids or his own expected payoffs would require more time for calculation than was available. Indeed, there is no indication that individual bargainers used objective decision theory methods in arriving at these changing response patterns. Thus, it must be concluded that anticipations prior to a trial and evaluation and measurement of the new information after the trial is, to a large extent, subjective. In some way, the bargainer determines a subjective expectation of his payoff and of its uncertainty for each price decision. Although the bid price of his rival is unknown, his de-

---

1 The test is a special case, for order two, of the test from Anderson and Goodman, [1] section 3.4, that several samples are from the same Markov chain of a given order.

cision is still determinate based on his subjective analysis of the previous one, two, or perhaps more outcomes. In making his bid, he has a conviction that his subjective determination is correct. The previous experiences have helped him to subjectively reduce the uncertainty in his decision process.[1]

Question 5. Are the response patterns different among different price ranges?

In the (M) experiment, the potential price bid range is twice as great as in the (F-S) experiments so that much greater variety in behavior is possible. The price bids can be categorized into three separate groups, high level over 6.0, low level below 3.0, and mid-level, 3.0 to 6.0. To a large extent, the high bids indicate cooperative bargaining, low bids indicate competitive or rivalistic bargaining, while the mid-level bids cannot be easily classified. Analysis of the bargaining responses following outcomes in which the bid price is classified into one of these three levels can indicate more specific average behavior patterns and response functions.

For P_{t-1} in the high, cooperative bid level, a definite response pattern is evident which would give nearly perfect prediction (three exceptions in 147 observations) if it were applied to the bargaining trials 2-24. First, there are no wins in this price level.[2] After ties, the expected response is $P_t > P_{t-1}$ if $P_{t-1} < 8.0$, and $P_t = P_{t-1}$ if $P_{t-1} = 8.0$. After losses, the expected response is $P_t = P_{t-1}$ if $t \leq 10$, and $P_t < P_{t-1}$ if $t > 10$.

---

1 Commonly, in adaptive systems, such a reduction in uncertainty is itself defined as learning. See, R. Murphy, [16], Chapter 2.

2 Due to the zeros in the transition matrix, the chi-square tests are not used in analyzing either high or low price level response patterns.

The response pattern for the low price bid reveals no consistent, simple predictive rule. There is a continuing shift in the response pattern following low price bids among trial groups 2-6, 12-16, and 20-24 toward more unchanged responses relative to increases following wins or ties. To the extent that these low price bids come from the same bargainers, this may simply reflect a graduating state of discouragement or disinterest.

For the mid-level prices, changes in response patterns are a true indicator of any learning from experience throughout the trials. For $3 \leq P_{t-1} \leq 6$, bargaining responses (excluding the small number of (W_{t-1}, D_t) and (L_{t-1}, I) transitions) tend to be nearly random in the early trials 2-11. It appears many bargainers attempt to simply outguess their rival with a one-trial profit maximizing motive.

By the middle trials, the transition matrix following all mid-level price bids is not significantly different from the overall transition matrix for all trials and all bargainers. Then, there is a significant (.01 level) change between trials 12-16 and 20-24 in the response pattern following both ties and wins.

This changing reaction is more important when one realizes that the more consistent bargainers who achieve cooperation or who become rivalistic during the course of the experiment have moved out of this mid-level price range. The number of decision observations with $3 \leq P_{t-1} \leq 6$ is 127, 103, and 92 respectively in trial groups 2-6, 12-16, and 20-24. Those bargainers remaining in this mid-level by the end of the experiment are those accounting for a proportionately greater share of price changes and non-diagonal choices. Yet, by using chi-square distributed statistics on the appropriate transition matrices, it is found that their responses on the average change from random to significant first order (.01 level) and significant second order (.02 level) Markov processes in trials 17-24. Such a change implies that the learning which occurs is not simply trial and error, but perhaps more analytical.

Question 6. Are the response patterns different between bargainers with different expressed indices of cooperation?

Each bargainer can be classified by his answer to the question on intended strategy (see section II) resulting in a classification of 15 cooperators, 12 competitors, and 7 others (when the answer does not characterize him as either of the former two). Analysis of the response patterns of these groups of individuals reveals that competitors respond differently from cooperators to tie outcomes ($\chi^2_{2\ df} = 2.81$, significant at 0.001 level) over all trials 2-24 in the (M) experiment. The responses are not significantly different after wins ($\chi^2_{2\ df} = 1.240$) nor after losses ($\chi^2_{2\ df} = 1.502$). The cooperators tend to favor the response (T_{t-1}, I_t) relative to the competitors who favor the response (T_{t-1}, D_t). The relevant transition probabilities are given in Table 5.[1]

Table 5: Transition Probabilities of Cooperators and Competitors following a Tie Outcome

	Bargaining type	Price decision in trial t		
		Increase	Unchanged	Decrease
Tie in	Competitors	.20	.40	.40
trial t-1	Cooperators	.29	.69	.02

1 The grouping throughout this discussion is by bargainers intended strategy, not by actual results of bidding at competitive or cooperative solution levels. Several self-proclaimed competitors ended up at the Pareto solution. Their exclusion would strengthen my remark.

In spite of these tendencies, the results in Table 6 show that the cooperators learn to achieve more wins and ties than do competitors. If both types of bargainers are assumed to be profit maximizers, then it would not seem too inappropriate to use indexes of cooperative behavior as learning parameters.[1] It is also obvious that cooperators seek higher prices and use the diagonal strategies consistently more than competitors.

Table 6: Characteristic Response Percentages of Bargainers by Trial Group and Intended Levels of Cooperativeness

Trial groups	Percent I and U response*			Percent Loss Outcomes			Percent Use of Diagonal Strategies		
	Coop.	Comp.	Other	Coop.	Comp.	Other	Coop.	Comp.	Other
2- 6	71	50	77	43	40	40	71	60	53
7-19	85	63	73	23	37	19	57	50	44
20-24	94	70	73	6	25	30	77	52	70

* I = increase price; U = leave price unchanged

Two interesting features of the results in Table 6 deserve more attention. First, the use of diagonal strategies is lowest in the middle trials for all types of bargainers. Perhaps, these "mechanistic" strategies are the most common sense initial responses but the outcomes resulting from their use lead bargainers to initiate learning experiments to dis-

1 Such indices have been used in Hoggart [11], p. 422. Note that my evidence is based on only 27 subjects whose rivals were not under control.

cover why their expected payoffs are not achieved. After the "analytical" learning phase is completed, bargainers return to the diagonal strategies, perhaps because their anticipations are more often realized and new information is less likely to be valuable now that continual experience has led to a more stable contract price level. (See Table 1 again illustrating a movement to fewer changes and higher payoffs).

Second it is curious, in view of the dominant response among all subgroups analyzed to decrease price after a loss, that for trials, t = 2-6, cooperators suffered a greater percentage of loss outcomes in trial t-1 than did competitors and yet, the cooperators used responses I and U proportionately more often. Even though one might presume that it takes two to cooperate and that a pair with one competitor would tend toward competitiveness, this presumption seems dubious. Even as early as trials 2-6, the evidence suggests that bargainers with a competitive rival attempt (and are successful in several clear instances) to **teach cooperation.** They increase their price bid in spite of losses in order to raise the contract price bid.

This behavior would be consistent with a longer run profit maximation motive. The bargainer would be ascribing a large subjective payoff to learning, due to its future benefits in more profits, which exceeds the expected monetary payoff of any price decision in the current trial.

Question 7. Are response patterns affected by level of success of the bargainer relative to his aspiration level?

Based on the aspiration level expressed by the bargainers (See section II) prior to the experimental trials, an attempt is made to classify the bargainers at the end of trial 5, and again at the end of trial 15, according to their profit achievement relative to this aspiration level. These break points represent the end of one and two hours of the subject's time spent in instruction, practice, and bargaining trials. The total payoff of each subject at these break points were compared to a one and two hour total wage using an hourly wage rate determined from the aspiration level.[1] The decision observations in trials 6-15 of those who were clearly achieving at their aspiration wage rate by trial 5 were combined with those in trials 16-24 who were clearly "achievers" by trial 15. Those who were clearly "not achieving" were similarly grouped as were those that were "not classifiable" in either of the former groups. Thus, some bargainer's responses in trials 6-15 may be in the "achiever" group; yet his responses in trials 16-24 may be in the "non-achiever" or "non-classifiable" group (and vice-versa).

Even though the earlier results on response patterns for low price bidders hinted that non-achievers may have become frustrated, there is no such conclusion possible based on the aspiration level groupings. Using chi-square tests there is no significant (.10 level) difference in response patterns between achievers or non-achievers following any outcome, W, T, or L. Apparently, control for achievement relative to aspiration level (at least by my crude separation method) is

---

1 Many subjects answered the aspiration level question in terms of dollars per hour. Others gave merely a total amount. These latter amounts were divided by three to get an hourly rate for the three hour experiment. Obvious errors are possible since the subjects did not know how long a session to expect. These may be minimal, however, since other preceding experiments in psychology and organizational behavior which recruited subjects from the same student body in the same school year traditionally used three hour sessions. All the derived wage rates are "reasonable," ranging from 66¢ to $5 an hour.

not as important as control for degree of cooperativeness, for amount of learning experience, or for level of price bid.

IV. Summary of Learning Characteristics

Based on the analysis of bargaining patterns in the seven questions of the previous section (referred to in the list below), several important characteristics of learning are evident. These are itemized for reference in the description of a dynamic learning model in the next section.

Learning Characteristics

(1) Adaptation does occur since the expected price bid of a rival bargainer is not assumed to be unchanged from the previous bid and since current price decisions are related to outcomes on at least the previous two trials (especially if O_{t-1} is a tie). (Questions 1,3,4).

(2) Learning seems to occur in the first 10-12 trials and it has a value represented by higher average profits per trial after a decline during the learning-teaching phase. (Questions 2 and 6).

(3) Expectations of payoffs and the uncertainty of the outcome state are not measured objectively by the bargainers, but are necessarily subjective measures. (Question 4).

(4) While some of the changing response patterns may be a result of a mechanistic trial and error learning process, the evidence indicates that a higher order of learning, a more analytical process with feedbacks is also operative. (Questions 3, 4, 5, 6).

(5) Response patterns change most in trial groups when wider experimentation in bargaining occurs, anticipated responses are not realized, and new information is aquired. (Questions 4, 5, 6).

V. A Dynamic, Choice-Learning Model

The learning characteristics, items 1-5 in Section IV., can be embodied in a descriptive model of the bargainer's choice decision at each trial t. As the framework for this particular model, a general model of an analytical choice-learning process is used as developed by Tarascio and Murphy, [15]. This theoretical model emphasizes three characteristics which recommend its use for this particular adaptation.
First, the decision maker is assumed to use a decision rule which considers both maximization of expected utility and minimization of ex ante uncertainty about the decision outcome. Second, it emphasizes the important subjective aspects of the choice-learning process. Third, it is a dynamic model which permits analytical learning to occur after each experience in the form of revised ex ante anticipations relative to the next decision. In these adaptations, the decision-maker may assign a positive utility to learning itself.[1]

Notation for Duopolist Decision Model

In the format of the decision observation for a duopoly bargainer A, one of three actions may be chosen at trial t, $(\Delta P)_{it}$, i = 1, 2, 3, representing an increased,

---

1 Tarascio and Murphy, [15]. See their Figure 4 for a schematic diagram of the dynamic decision process and pages 10-13 for a descriptive outline of each step. My adopted presentation follows similar steps.

unchanged, or decreased price bid. The decision depends on the bargainer's expectation of the price bid of his rival, $E(P_{B,t})$ on that trial. The two price bids result in an outcome state, O_{jt}, j = 1, 2, 3, representing a win, tie, or loss in the current decision experience.

Let the following notation be adopted for an arbitrary bargainer A:

p_{ijt} = subjective probability of outcome state O_j corresponding to his own action choice, $(\Delta P)_i$ denoted by the decision result $[(\Delta P)_{it}, O_{jt}]$;[1]

U_{ijt} = anticipated profit from the payoff table for the decision result $[(\Delta P)_{it}, O_{jt}]$; and $E_L(U_{ijt})$ = subjective evaluation for the decision result $[(\Delta P)_{it}, O_{jt}]$ of the expected future gains in payoffs due to learning based on the value of new experiences and information in reducing uncertainty.

Theoretical Decision Rule

The expected utility of action choice $(\Delta P)_{it}$ is given by $E[U(\Delta P)_{it}] = E_{it} = \sum_j p_{ijt}[U_{ijt} + E_L(U_{ijt})]$.[2] Similarly, a measure of uncertainty or variability in utility corresponding to action $(\Delta P)_{it}$ is given by $V[U(\Delta P)_{it}] = V_{it} = E[U_{ijt}+E_L(U_{ijt})-E_{it}]^2$. The choice of action may then be determinable by finding which action maximizes some appropriate function involving the arguments, E_{it} and V_{it}.

---

1 Note the change in timing and order between the defined, "decision observation," $[O_{t-1}, (\Delta P)_t]$ used in the analysis and the "decision result," $[(\Delta P)_t, O_t]$ used here.

2 The expectation could be generalized to involve explicitly a discounted stream of payoffs over time as suggested by Friedman, [8].

A model requiring the calculation of the values of E_{it} and V_{it} may impose severe constraints on its own applicability since it cannot be assumed that duopoly bargainers making contract bids could or would use such objective decision theory methods.[1] The undergraduate student bargainers participating in the experiments considered in this paper certainly failed to make such objective determinations. (Refer to characteristic 3, section IV). Any decision rule for duopoly bargainers used in a choice-learning model should be much simpler.

The Practical Decision Rule

Suppose the decision maker can subjectively rank E_{it} and V_{it} separately, obtaining the sets of ranks $\{r(E_{it})\}$ and $\{r(V_{it})\}$, each from one to three with unity representing the lowest E_{it}, but the largest V_{it}. The action chosen, $(\Delta P)^*_t$, with expected value E^*_t, is then determined to be $(\Delta P)_{it}$ corresponding to $\max_i \{r(E_{it}) + r(V_{it})\}$. In the case of ties, a single trial profit maximizer may choose the action with the largest $r(E_{it})$ among those tied. A bargainer with a longer horizon may break a tie by choosing the action whose weighted learning component, $\sum_j p_{ijt} E_L(U_{ijt})$, is the highest.

Information Processing

Whatever simple, subjective decision rule is used, a choice is made, $(\Delta P)^*_t$ with a resulting outcome O^*_t. The bargainer then determines subjectively his measure of the utility derived from this outcome including mone-

---

1 See the data requirements for a practical model of choice given by Simon, [18], p. 275.

tary and psychic payoffs, say U_t^*. The beginning of a feedback and adjustment mechanism, implied by characteristic (4) in section IV., involves the processing of this new information from trial t by the bargainer. He must determine the difference, $D_t^* = (U_t^* - E_t^*)$, between his ex post derived utility and his ex ante expected utility for the action chosen.

According to characteristic (5) in section IV., both the sign and size of D_t^* have implications for changes in the response function of the bargainer. If D_t^* is very small, the reinforcement component of learning may be substantial (particularly in the early trials when the amount of previous experience is limited) and some response pattern changes may result. However, such changes are probably larger and more immediate with larger $|D_t^*|$.[1]

Adaptation and Learning

A nonzero value for D_t^* indicates that the bargainer's subjective ex ante measures of $E_L(U_{ijt})$ were inaccurate and/or his subjective estimates of p_{ijt} were wrong. Since both these measures depend on the underlying expectation by bargainer A of the bid price of bargainer B, then their incorrectness implies that $E(P_{B,t}) \neq P_{B,t}^*$, where $P_{B,t}^*$ is the actual price bid of bargainer B in decision period t. Such an error reflects some change in the rivals reaction function that increases the uncertainty in the decision process unless it can be perceived by bargainer A.[2]

---

1 If one applies Boulding's [4, p. 130] behavioral conclusion, then the reaction following a negative D_t^* should be stronger than that following a positive D_t^* of the same absolute size.

2 A change in attitude, motivation, aspiration, experience, etc. may have occurred. For a discussion of the role of these factors in problem solving behavior see Katona, [13], pp. 310-318.

The expected price bid, $E(P_{B,t})$, is a function of a state vector Z_t, $E(P_{B,t}) = f(Z_t)$ where Z_t has historical and background components which form a description of past events as needed for information feeding into the subjective estimation process.[1] From the learning characteristics (1) - (5) in section IV, it is known that some of these components of Z are previous outcomes O_{t-1}, O_{t-2}; the amount of "game experience" represented by the number of previous trials; subjective perception of the rivals motives; the level of the previous bid price; and the bargainers own attitudes and degree of cooperativeness.[2]

Some especially interesting phases of the learning process need to be repeated for emphasis as these are often not considered in analyses of bargaining behavior. When a large difference D_t^* occurs, the bargainer may deviate from his game strategy under a profit maximizing motive to a pattern forming and hypothesis testing strategy under a learning motive. He may design his own sub-experiment lasting several trials to learn more about his rival's motives and isolate the cause of the large difference he experienced between his ex ante anticipated payoff and his ex post realized payoff. During this sub-experiment in which the bargainer is deeply involved in how the game operates and how his rival makes responses, he is implicitly assigning a large subjective value to learning itself so that the terms, $E_L(U_{ijt})$, dominate the expected values E_{it}. A bargainer may conduct more than one of these sub-experiments of varying length within the total bargaining experiment as part of his analytical learning and adaptation behavior.

---

1 R. Murphy, [16], p.30 defines a similar historical state vector useful in formulating adaptive processes.

2 Some indication of interrelations among the factors of attitudes, experience, and cooperativeness is given in Hoggart, [11], p. 422 ff.

When new information is obtained from the experience of decision period t and the measure of D_t^*, the bargainer can make a revision of the expected bid price of his rival for the next contract offer. The feedback characteristic (4) of section IV, is included in the model by the determination of a revised expectation, $\tilde{E}(P_{B,t+1}) = f(Z_{t+1}) = \tilde{g}(Z_t, D_t^*)$.[1] This, in turn, leads to the revisions, $\tilde{E}_L(U_{ij,t+1})$ and $\tilde{p}_{ij,t+1}$; and finally to revised (or reinforced) measures, $E_{i,t+1}$ and $\tilde{V}_{i,t+1}$ to use in the decision rule for decision period t+1.

After many different experiences, expectations may be realized more closely more often. The stable state bargaining process is approached as the sequences over t of $[E(P_{B,t}) - P_{B,t}^*]$, D_t^*, and $\tilde{V}_{it}$ approach zero.[2]

Some Special Cases

The feedback process of this general model permits a wide variety of rational and learning behavior as special cases. Only a few of these potential behavioral patterns are discussed now. The suggested descriptions of different bargaining types are neither unique nor exhaustive.

A non-learning bargainer might be described as one who does not determine E_{it} (or V_{it}) even subjectively, nor need he be concerned with evaluating D_t^*. He may simply use a random mixed strategy, or he may habitually choose diagonal strategies.

1 Bayesian methods might be used in constructing descriptive notation of such a procedure, as in Bakan, [3], p. 361-3. However, since all these measures have subjective aspects in real bargaining, this would be largely an impractical mental exercise.

2 Allowing single period adaptations based on past experiences provides a dynamically stable model. Recall, Ferguson and Pfouts, [5].

A bargainer who does learn, as indicated by characteristic (2) of section IV, may suffer some temporary decline in profits and appear to be choosing irrationally (non profit-maximizing in the short run). However, he may subjectively set a high value on $\tilde{E}_L(U_{ij,t+1})$ for some decision results in a planned, pattern forming personal experiment in order to better perceive why he experienced a large D_t^*.[1] Finally, given the same average experiences, current price bid levels, and perceptions of their rival, two bargainers may both rationally choose opposite price changes following a tie outcome. One may have a competitive motivation and a single trial profit maximizing attitude so that he assigns a very low value to $E_L(U_{ijt})$. He may subjectively determine E_{3t} to be the maximum and choose to lower price one scale unit below $E(P_{Bt})$ in order to win.[2] The other may have a strong cooperative motivation with a "price fix" desire at high mutual payoffs. His own attitude affects his subjective estimations. Thus, he may choose to raise price because he hopefully assigns a large value to p_{12t}, probability of a tie outcome if both he and his rival raise price by one scale unit. Similar examples of seemingly inconsistent or irrational behavior could be itemized by restricting various steps in the choice-learning process or by varying different components of Z and considering the subsequent effect on the revised measures, $E(P_{B,t+1})$

---

1 Such behavior corresponds to the analytical learning block in the model of Tarascio and Murphy, [15].

2 Such motivation is very clear in "end play" trials when $E_L(U_{ijt})$ may be assumed to be zero. Refer to the average payoff for trials 25 and 26 in Figure 2. In the (M) experiment after trial 24 was completed, trial 26 was announced as the final trial.

or $\tilde{p}_{ij,t+1}$. In a dynamic context with learning based largely on subjective evaluation, such behavior may be totally rational.

VI. Suggestions for Further Experimentation

In this paper, analysis of some "second best" data is used to determine learning characteristics from different response transitions of groups of bargainers over groups of trials. These learning characteristics are embodied in a simple, yet general, descriptive model of the dynamic choice-learning process. Some additional well designed experiments could contribute greatly to a more detailed understanding of this process.

Obviously, first and second order transitions and response patterns should be analyzed for oligopoly bargainers. However, even if the duopoly price variation situation is maintained as the basic experiment, important results could be obtained by various extensions and controls.

For the obvious implications of analysis, experiments might be designed so bargainers with different motivation, attitudes, or aspiration levels all participate against the same programmed response function. Also, bargainers grouped by attitudes and levels of cooperativeness might play against several different programmed response patterns. The use of a "computer" as a rival bargainer and as a secretary of all transactions would allow more trials and more combinations to be used in a given experimental session.

In some experiments certain subgroups of bargainers might be provided with some summary statistics concerning their own and/or their rivals response pattern in the previous trials. Various hypotheses of learning and adaptive processes could be specified and tested by examining their accuracy in forecasting bargainers responses.

In conclusion, another experiment of this type might be conducted in which bargainers are allowed to make a partial or complete "no-play" choice at any trial. The partial "no-play" choice would allow a bargainer to make no bid on that trial. He would lose a set amount, say 10¢, as the cost of staying in business and being eligible to make bids again in the future. A complete "no-play" decision drops the player from the game at a fixed cost, say $1.00. For any "no-play" trials by a bargainer, his rival could continue to make bids and receive the winning profit, now as a monopoly power.

Such an experiment would allow greater strategy variation. Thus, both the intentions of the players and the dynamic patterns of the choice-learning process would be more readily discernible. No true rivalistic competitor could afford to drop out. On the other hand, implications about the interest and fatigue of subjects during such experiments, about the subject's utility for money, his aversion to risk, and his aspiration level might be deduced from the timing, frequency, and the distribution of winnings of drop-outs. Finally, after a drop-out, the feedback structure of the learning process could be analyzed by examining the speed of recognition and the convergence of adjustment as implied by the sequence of price bids of the remaining bargainer.

Bibliography

Anderson, T.W., and Leo A. Goodman, "Statistical Inference about Markov Chains," Annals of Mathematical Statistics, (1957).

Anderson, T.W., ed., Mathematical Thinking in the Social Sciences, (Paul Lazarsfeld Press, 1954).

Bakan, David, "Learning and the Principle of Inverse Probability," Psychological Review, (1953), pp. 360-370.

Boulding, Kenneth, "The Verifiability of Economic Images," The Structure of Economic Science, S.R. Krupp, ed., (New Jersey: Prentice-Hall, 1966), pp. 129-141.

Ferguson, C., and R.W. Pfouts, "Learning and Expectations in Dynamic Duopoly Behavior," Behavioral Science, (1962), pp. 223-237.

Fouraker, L.E., and S. Siegel, Bargaining Behavior, (New York: McGraw-Hill, 1963).

Friedman, James W., "An Experimental Study of Cooperative Duopoly," Econometrica, (July-Oct., 1967), pp. 379-398.

Friedman, James W., "Reaction Functions and the Theory of Duopoly," Review of Economic Studies, (July, 1968), pp. 257-272.

Friedman, James W., "On Experimental Research in Oligopoly," Review of Economic Studies, (October, 1969), pp. 397-416.

Harnett, D.L., and L.L. Cummings, "Bargaining Behavior in a Symmetric Bargaining Triad," Review of Economic Studies, (October, 1969), pp. 485-502.

Hoggat, A.C., "Response of Paid Student Subjects to Differential Behavior of Robots in Bifurcated Duopoly Games," Review of Economic Studies, (October, 1969), pp. 417-432.

Jonckheere, A.R., "A Test of Significance for the Relation Between m Rankings and k Ranked Categories," The British Journal of Statistical Psychology, (November 1954), pp. 93-99.

Katona, George, "Rational Behavior and Economic Behavior," Psychological Review, (1953), pp. 360-370.

Murphy, James L., "Effects of the Threat of Losses on Duopoly Bargaining," Quarterly Journal of Economics, (May, 1966), pp. 296-313.

Murphy, James L., and Vincent J. Tarascio, "Uncertainty, Learning, and Dynamic Utility Theory," unpublished paper presented at the Econometric Society Meetings, (Detroit, December, 1971).

Murphy, R.E., Jr., Adaptive Processes in Economic Systems, (New York: Academic Press, 1965).

Richmond, Samuel B., Statistical Analysis, (New York: Ronald Press, 1964).

Simon, Herbert A., "Theories of Decision Making in Economics and Behavioral Science," American Economic Review, (June, 1959), pp. 253-283.

Suppes, P., and J. Carlsmith, "Experimental Analysis of a Duopoly Situation from the Standpoint of Mathematical Learning Theory," International Economic Review, (January, 1962).

5. BILATERAL MONOPOLY BARGAINING: AN INTERNATIONAL STUDY

DONALD L. HARNETT* AND LARRY L. CUMMINGS

The market situation wherein a single seller must transact business with a single buyer is called bilateral monopoly. Although bilateral monopoly models have been the subject of considerable theoretical analysis, it was not until the extensive experimental work by L.E. Fouraker and S. Siegel (7,18) that many assumptions about behavior in these models were tested. The present study is part of a series of experiments designed to expand on the Fouraker-Siegel data, and our own findings (1,8) by investigating various behavioral aspects of bargaining behavior between business executives from both the U.S.A. and Europe.[1]

Our current interest centers on two aspects of bilateral monopoly bargaining under incomplete information (i.e., bargaining where neither party knows the payoffs available to the person bargaining against him). First, we are interested in investigating the

---

* Indiana University

** University of Wisconsin

1 We are grateful to both the Ford Foundation and the Indiana University International Business Research Institute for their support of this research. Support was also provided to D.L. Harnett by the Graduate School of Business, Harvard University.

effect of using parameters in the construction of payoff tables which do not place the buyer and seller in symmetric roles. Generally, we hypothesize that both the process and the results of negotiations between a seller and a buyer will be significantly influenced by giving one of the bargainers a more favorable position from which to begin negotiations. In addition, we hypothesize that the amount of concessions by the two bargainers will be, in part, a function of the relative magnitude of the slopes of their marginal cost and revenue functions. Both these hypotheses are discussed more thoroughly in the section titled "theory."

A second interest reported in this paper involves an effort to determine the effect of nationality differences on bargaining behavior. This type of analysis becomes increasingly important as the world becomes more international in character, and bargaining between individuals and firms of different nations, and their governments, assumes an increasing role in terms of world peace and prosperity. Our hope is to contribute to the small but growing stream of research reporting on cross-cultural aspects of bargaining behavior (e.g., see bibliography 1,5,10,11, 12,15).

The bilateral monopoly experiment reported in this paper involves bargaining between two business executives, representing the roles of seller and buyer, whose task is to agree on a single price and quantity for the exchange of a fictitious product between them. Participants were told the "profit" they would earn for every possible price-quantity agreement, but they were not told the profit their counterpart in the negotiation would earn. In order to provide some measure of realism to the bargaining and to give an incentive for each participant to take the experiment seriously, each person was told he would receive a cash payoff corresponding to the amount of profit he earned in his bargaining agreement. The bargaining process, which was conducted by means of written price-quantity offers, was held in such a manner so that no participant could see, identify, or speak to his bargaining opponent.

It is important to note at the outset that we have no evidence that the executives in our study are representative of the total population of executives in the six countries included in this research. At best, they may be roughly representative of the more "modern and progressive" professional management subset in each country.[1] Even this, of course, is admittedly conjecture.

Theory

Most bargaining literature specifies the solution to the bilateral monopoly problem to be that quantity which maximizes the joint profit of the two bargainers. Joint profits are maximized when the marginal cost to the seller of (buying and then) selling the product equals the marginal revenue derived by the buyer in selling the product (after he has purchased it from the seller). The derivation of the joint maximizing quantity can be demonstrated by considering the following simple model, in which marginal cost and marginal revenue are linear functions.

---

1 This assumption is based on the fact that, at the time of data collection, they were participating in management development programs.

Let A = price axis intercept of the average revenue function,
A' = price axis intercept of the average cost function,
B = the slope of the average revenue function,
B' = the slope of the average cost function,
C = total cost
P = price
Q = quantity
R = revenue
and K, K' = constants

Suppose we assume that the total cost (C) to the seller of selling Q units is a second degree polynomial of the following form:

$$C = A'Q + B'Q^2 + K' .$$

If C assumes the parabolic form shown above, then marginal cost, which is the first derivative of total cost, must be linear:

$$dC/dQ = A' + 2B'Q .$$

If we assume that total revenue (R) to the buyer is also parabolic, where

$$R = AQ - BQ^2 + K ,$$

then marginal revenue (dR/dQ) will have the following linear form:

$$dR/dQ = A - 2BQ .$$

Since maximization occurs when marginal revenue equals marginal cost (assuming the second derivation is negative), then the joint maximizing quantity, Q_M, can be derived by setting the marginal functions equal and solving for Q.

$$dC/dQ = dR/dQ$$

$$A' + 2B'Q = A - 2BQ$$

$$Q_M = (A - A')/(2B + 2B')$$

If quantity is assumed determinate at Q_M, then the division of profits between the seller and the buyer will depend on the price they establish. Although some bilateral models consider price as indeterminate when both parties have equal bargaining power, the price usually accepted as most likely is the one yielding a solution which both participants regard as a draw, or a "fair" division of joint profits. This solution, usually corresponding to a fifty-fifty split of joint payoffs, was suggested by Pigou in 1908 (14) and corresponds to the solution specified by many game theoretic and negotiation models [e.g., Zeuthen (19), Nash (13), Raiffa (16) and Harsanyi (1)]. Schelling (17) also specifies the even split of maximum joint profits as the apparent solution, but stipulates that the "value" of the game must be known to the participants. The experimental studies conducted by Siegel and Fouraker (18) also indicate that assumptions involving the amount of knowledge prossessed by the participants are crucial determinants of the bargaining outcome. Under incomplete information conditions they found their experimental results supported Fellner's analysis (3,4), in which he suggested that the price agreements of randomly paired bargainers would form a symmetrical distribution around the price corresponding to a fifty-fifty split of the maximum joint payoff.

An equal split of maximum joint profit occurs when total profit to the seller equals total profit to the buyer, or when $PQ_M - C = R - PQ_M$. Thus, if we denote P_E as the equal split price, then $P_E = (R + C)/2Q_M$.

In this paper we investigate two aspects of the general conclusions by Siegel and Fouraker concerning the main determinants of differential payoffs and price in bilateral monopoly bargaining under incomplete information. Our first interest involves the extent of the influence of certain characteristics of the payoff structure of the bargainers on their relative earnings. Secondly, we are interested in examining the influence of the nationality of the bargainers on the bargaining process and outcome.

In regard to the first of these interests, we suggest that the lack of any significant difference in average payoff between the buyers and sellers in the Siegel-Fouraker experiments can be attributed, at least in part, to the fact that their payoff matrices were symmetrical to the extent of yielding the same maximum payoff for both bargainers. Our contention is that this symmetry induces a measure of equality between the initial aspiration levels of the buyers and sellers, and it is this equality which leads to the similarity in average profits. In a related study, Chertkoff and Conley (2) found that those bargainers opening with the more extreme offers did better in the negotiations. We thus hypothesize that for bargainers with unequal maximum payoffs, the bargainer with the more favorable position will have a higher aspiration level which, in turn, will result in bargaining behavior generating the larger profit.

Each bargainer's payoff in a negotiation process can be thought of as a function of the total amount of concessions he makes in yielding from his initial aspiration level. Fouraker (6) has suggested that each bargainer will make concessions by quoting price-quantity combinations along his own marginal function (cost or revenue), and equilibrium will occur at the point (on Q_M) where the marginal curves intersect. The price where marginal cost equals marginal revenue can be derived by substituting the quantity Q_m into the formula for either marginal function. Thus, if we denote the price at the intersection of the marginal functions as P_I, then

$$P_I = A - 2B\left(\frac{A-A'}{2B+2B'}\right)$$

Although this solution results in maximum joint payoffs, it yields an equal split of these profits only if the slopes of the two marginal functions are equal (i.e., when $B = B'$). When $B > B'$ the marginal intersection solution will give the buyer the larger profit; when $B' > B$ the seller will earn more than the buyer. These two cases are illustrated in Figure 1.

Although Siegel and Fouraker reject the marginal hypothesis as a result of their 1960 experiments (in favor of the Fellner solution), their results do not preclude the possibility that the concessions the bargainers make will be at least partially influenced by the slope of their marginal functions. This influence, if there is any tendency for the bargainers to conceed in amounts which are related to the slopes of their marginal functions, should favor the bargainer who will earn the larger profit at the marginal intersection solution. Thus, our hypothesis is that when $B \neq B'$, there will be a tendency for the bargainer who has the steeper

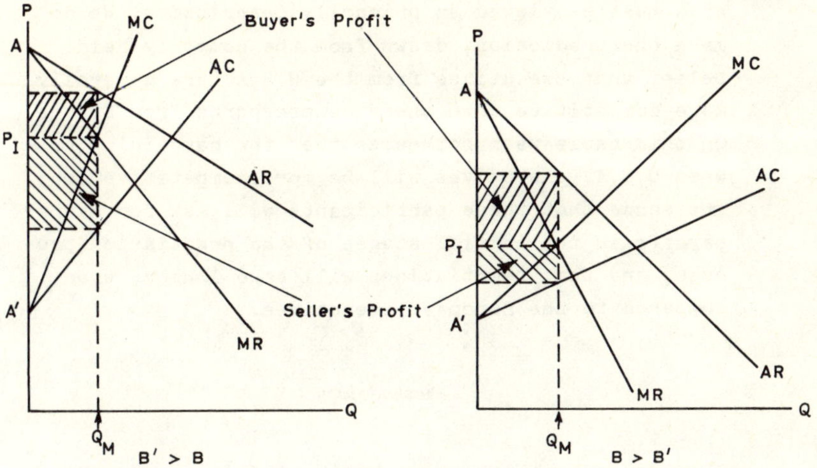

Figure 1: Asymmetrical Marginal Functions

sloping marginal function to make the smaller total concession.[1]

Now to the second interest mentioned previously. Since the culture within which a man is socialized and educated presumably exerts a significant influence on his basic attitudes and dispositions, we might expect to find differences across national boundries in bargaining behaviors (see reference 1). Unfortunately, systematic evidence regarding the nature of such differences is limited, so that our investigation in this

---

1 It might be argued at this point that initial asking level and amount yielded are not independent, and that one would expect a larger concession rate from the bargainer who asks for a higher initial profit. We cannot disprove this argument, but rather point out that since the buyers do not know they are asking for an initially higher amount (i.e., they have incomplete information), there would seem to be little justification for arguing that this fact would influence their yielding pattern.

area must be viewed as primarily descriptive. We do make one prediction, drawn from the commonly held belief that executives from the U.S.A. are generally more competitive than their counterparts from Europe. On this basis we hypothesize that the bargaining between U.S.A. executives will be more competitive in the sense that these participants will ask for higher payoffs in the initial stages of the negotiation process, and that negotiations will take longer, when compared to the European executives.

Methodology

In order to test the hypothesis of this study a bilateral monopoly bargaining experiment under incomplete information was conducted in each of six different countries - Belgium, England, Finland, France, Spain, and the U.S.A. The subjects for these experiments were middle and top-level managers from private business enterprises each of whom was participating in an executive development program in his native country. In all cases the experimental test was arranged with the full cooperation of the administrators of each program, and was an integral part of the normal schedule of the participating executives.[1] All instructions and materials

1 We wish to acknowledge the assistance of and express our gratitude to the following individuals, without whose collaboration this study would have been impossible. Mr. Leo Ahlstedt, Mr. Henri-Claude de Bettignies, Mr. A.J. Eccles, Mr. Salvatore Teresi, Mr. Hugo Van Hassel and Dr. Jose Ma Veciana. We also wish to acknowledge the cooperation of the following organizations: Management Training Center, University of Leuven, Leuven, Belgium, Manchester Business School, The Finnish Institute of Management, The European Institute of Business Administration, and ESADE (School of Administration and Business Management), Barcelona, Spain.

were administered in the native language of the country involved. Selected demographic characteristics of the executives who participated in these experiments are presented in Table 1.

TABLE 1 - DEMOGRAPHIC CHARACTERISTICS OF EXECUTIVES

Region	Number of Participants	Mean Age	Mean No. of Yrs. of Higher Education	Mean No. of Yrs. of Business Experience
Europe*	134	36.0	3.6	14.2
England	44	36.6	3.0	15.5
U.S.A.	26	42.3	4.0	16.8

*Includes Belgium, Finland, France, and Spain

In each country the participating executives were divided, randomly, into an equal number of buyers and sellers. The buyers and sellers were then placed in separate rooms where they were seated by a master plan which (randomly) matched each seller with a specific buyer. As soon as all participants had found their assigned seats, each person was given a set of instructions describing the negotiation process (see Exhibit I) and a payoff table showing the profit he could earn for each possible price-quantity agreement (see Exhibits II and III). For each country the instructions given to the participants had been translated into the language being used at the seminar (i.e., Flemish, French, Finnish, and Spanish), and the payoff tables had been converted to local currency (at the official exchange rate).
After the participants were given sufficient time to read their instructions and ask questions (which were answered by a collaborator who spoke the native language),

the bargaining process was begun. The seller started the negotiations by writing his initial price-quantity offer on a sheet of paper. This sheet was then taken to the buyer, who had the option of either accepting the seller's offer, or of making a counter offer. If he made a counter offer this offer was taken to the seller, who then had the option of accepting it, or of making a new offer. This process of making offers and counter offers continued until an agreement was reached (i.e., one party accepted the other's offer). The negotiations were conducted in silence, with no communication permitted between participants except for the written price-quantity offers and counter offers. The participants were told that if they did not reach an agreement after 90 minutes of bargaining, the negotiations would end and neither person would earn any money.

Operational Definitions

The payoff matrices furnished the buyers and sellers were derived from the following parameters:

$$A = 270,\ B = 5,\ K = 65,\ A' = 0,\ B' = 10,\ \text{and}\ K' = -200.$$

For these values the joint maximizing quantity equals

$$Q_M = \frac{A-A'}{(2B+2B')} = \frac{270}{10+20} = 9\ .$$

For the parameters of this model $R + C = 2700$ when $Q = 9$, so that the equal split price is

$$P_E = (R + C)/2Q_M = \frac{2700}{18} = 150.$$

The payoff (in cents) at $P_E = 150$, $Q_M = 9$ is

$$P_E Q_M - C = R - P_E Q_M = 740 \quad (\text{or } \$7.40) .$$

As shown in Exhibits II and III, the payoff matrix furnished each participant allowed for quantity choices ranging from 1 to 20, and price choices ranging from 105 to 205, in multiples of 5. The maximum payoff to the seller occurs at P = 205, Q = 9, and equals 1250 ($12.50). The buyer's maximum profit occurs at P = 105, Q = 15 or 16, for a profit of 1425 ($14.25).

Notice that the model as outlined above accomplishes our objective of not placing the buyer and seller in symmetric roles in terms of their maximum payoff or in terms of the slopes of their marginal (cost and revenue) functions. At the maximum payoff points this model gives the buyer the advantage as his profit can be as much as $1.75 larger than the seller's ($14.25 - $12.50). Our hypothesis is that this difference will give the buyers a bargaining advantage in terms of the amount of profit earned - i.e., the buyers average payoff will be significantly larger than the average payoff of the sellers.

In our model the slope of the seller's marginal cost function (2B' = 20) is twice the slope of the buyer's marginal revenue function (2B = 10). Thus, since we hypothesized that the bargainer with the steeper sloping function will concede the smaller amount, for the present research we hypothesize that the average concession by the sellers will be significantly less than the average concession by the buyers. To be consistent with our earlier research (8), we have operationally defined the amount a bargainer conceeds to be the difference between his second offer and his final payoff. Each person's second offer was chosen over his first offer as his initial aspiration level because many of the participants made their initial offer at the price-quantity representing their maximum profit, hence it was felt this first offer was more of an exploratory bid rather than a meaningful asking level.

It is important to note that the two hypotheses outlined above lead to opposite predictions in terms of bargaining advantage - i.e., the first predicts an advantage to the buyer because of his more favorable starting position, while the second predicts an advantage to the seller because he has the steeper sloping marginal function. The advantage in the first case is expected to be at most \$1.75, representing the difference in maximum attainable profits. In the second case, the maximum difference is represented by the seller's advantage at the point where marginal cost equals marginal revenue, which is \$5.40 in the present model (\$10.10 vs. \$4.70). Viewed in this manner our experiment becomes a test of the relative influence of differences in maximum payoff versus differences in the slopes of the marginal functions. Based on the Siegel-Fouraker data, however, we have implicitly predicted that the influence of the maximum payoff differential will dominate by hypothesizing an overall bargaining advantage to the buyer.

Results

A total of 204 business executives participated in this research project, 134 from Continental Europe (Belgium, Finland, France, and Spain), 44 from England, and 26 from the U.S.A. Of this total there were four dyads who did not reach an agreement within the allotted 90 minutes. Since we were not able to compute meaningful values on a number of the variables of interest for these participants (i.e., final payoff, amount yielded, number of bids) we decided to exclude these groups from our analysis. Our findings for the remaining 196 participants (98 groups) are reported below.

Our initial hypothesis was that in the present model the buyer will have a bargaining advantage in terms of the amount of profit he earns because he has the higher maximum payoff. To test this hypothesis we calculated the difference between the buyer's payoff and the seller's payoff for each of the 98 bargaining groups. A t-test for matched pairs was then used to test the null hypothesis that the population mean of these difference scores equals zero. The mean buyer-seller difference was $0.97, leading to rejection of the null hypothesis at $p < .0005$ ($t = 3.104$). In order to present a more comprehensive picture of the relationship between the bids of the two participants, we have calculated the average offer by both buyers and sellers (i.e., average profit asked for) for the first twenty transactions. These data, shown in Figure 2, indicate a fairly constant difference between the mean bids of the buyers and the sellers. It thus appears that the buyer's larger maximum obtainable payoff does yield him a bargaining advantage in the present bilateral monopoly model.

As Figure 2 indicates, the average first offer by the buyer ($12.26) was $1.35 higher than the average first offer by the seller ($10.91), a difference which is significant at $p < .0005$ ($t = 3.567$). Thus,

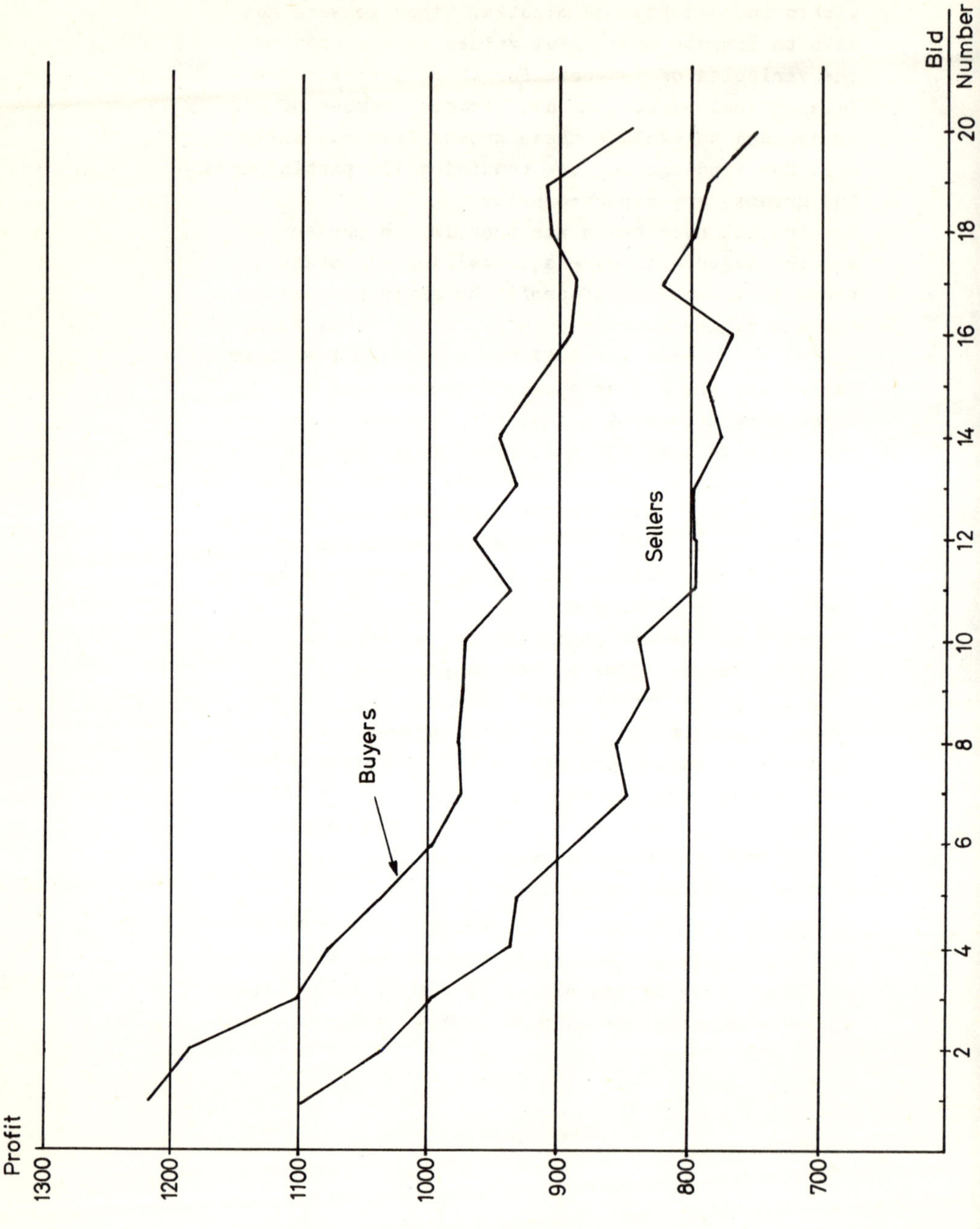

Figure 2: Mean Offers (Profit Asked For)

even on the first bid the buyer-seller difference was less than the maximum of \$1.75, although many of the participants asked for their highest profit on the first offer. This first-offer difference, however, is larger than the buyer's advantage in final payoff (0.97), suggesting that the negotiation process has a moderating influence on the buyer's initial advantage. This moderating influence is the subject of our second hypothesis, concerning the amount conceeded by the bargainers.

Our second hypothesis is that the average buyer-seller difference for the amount yielded (2nd offer minus final payoff) will be significantly greater than zero. That is, we have hypothesized that the seller will yield less than the buyer because $B' > B$. An interesting pattern occured on the second bids in that the buyer-seller difference increased, to \$1.65. This difference, which is significant at $p < .0005$ ($t = 5.008$) resulted from an average asking level of \$11.90 for the buyers as compared to \$10.25 for the sellers. The buyer-seller difference in terms of amount yielded can now be determined by subtracting the final-payoff mean of \$0.97 from the second-offer mean of \$1.65. This difference, of \$0.68, is significant at $p < .05$ ($t = 1.927$), thus supporting our second hypothesis that the seller will yield significantly less than the buyers. These data are shown in Table 2.

From the information in Table 2 and from our discussion thus far it is apparent that this data supports our contention concerning the bargaining advantage of differences in maximum payoff relative to differences in the slopes of these marginal functions. In essence, we found that both of

TABLE 2 - BUYER-SELLER DIFFERENCE SCORES

Variable	Buyer-Seller Mean	t value	Significance
1st offer	\$1.35	3.567	< .0005
2nd offer	1.65	5.008	< .0005
Payoff	0.97	3.104	< .005
2nd-Payoff	0.68	1.927	< .05

these factors influenced the process and results of the bargaining, but that the seller's advantage (due to his steeper sloping marginal function) was significantly less than the buyer's advantage. Hence, in general terms, we found that starting position is the more important factor in terms of relative impact on the bargaining outcome.

To conclude our analysis of the effects of the asymmetrical nature of the payoff tables, we examine the influences of these structural characteristics on the average price and quantity agreement. Recall that the Siegel-Fouraker data supported the Fellner hypothesis that agreements will be randomly distributed about the price and quantity reflecting an equal-split of maximum joint payoffs. For our data the average negotiated price was $\bar{P} = 147.86$, which does not differ from the equal-split price of $P_E = 150$. The average negotiated quantity was $\bar{Q} = 9.66$, which is significantly larger than the joint maximizing quantity of $Q_M = 9$ ($Z = 4.644$, $p < .0001$). Thus, the effect of the changes we introduced, as compared to the Siegel-Fouraker findings, was to move the negotiated quantity away from the joint maximizing quantity (and thus necessarily reduce total joint profits), but not to affect the negotiated price.

Nationality Differences

Our final interest in this study concerns the effect of a person's nationality on the process and results of his negotiations. More specifically, we are interested in comparing the behavior of the U.S.A. executives with the behavior of their Continental European counterparts. Since we were uncertain whether to group the executives from England with their English-speaking counterparts (the U.S.A.), or with their neighbors across the channel, our initial analysis excludes these participants. Later in this paper we will present data which includes the English executives.

We hypothesized that the U.S.A. executives will, because of the assumed competitive nature of their culture, approach the bargaining task more competitively. That is, we would expect them to ask for higher initial profits and to take more time and to use more bids to reach an agreement. To make this comparison we computed a mean score for the buyers from the U.S.A. and Europe, and then used a two-sample t test to test the null hypothesis that the two population mean scores are equal.[1] These data are presented in Table 3.

The first row of Table 3 shows that the average initial profit asked for by the buyers in the U.S.A. study was $1.30 higher than that asked for by the buyers in the European studies, and that this difference is

1 The two-sample t test requires assuming that the variances in the populations being studies are equal. Our data indicates that this assumption is reasonable. Our decision to use the buyer rather than the seller data for this analysis was an arbitrary one. We decided not to aggregate these two sets of data because the seller's score on many of our variables is not independent of the buyer's score.

TABLE 3 - INTERNATIONAL EXECUTIVE COMPARISON: U.S.A. vs Continental Europe

Variable	Mean Scores - Buyers U.S.A.	Europe	t Value	Significance
1st offer	$13.15	$11.85	1.626	< 0.055
2nd offer	12.73	11.43	1.758	< 0.045
Payoff	8.26	7.63	1.229	N.S.*
2nd-Payoff	4.50	3.79	0.921	N.S.*
No. of bids	22.67	15.14	2.603	< 0.055
time (in min.)	71.92	61.75	1.395	< 0.085

*Not Significant (at $p = 0.10$)

significant at $p < .055$. Our competitive hypothesis is also supported by the fact that the mean of the U.S.A. offers was higher on the second bid ($p < .045$), and by the fact that the U.S.A. executives took longer to reach a solution (10.17 more minutes) and a larger number of bids (7.53 more bids) than did the European executives. Note that the difference in mean values for the variables "payoff" and "2nd bid-payoff" is not large enough to be significant. We did not hypothesize a significant difference in these two cases because any additional competitive spirit assumed to exist for the U.S.A. buyers would be expected to be offset by a similar spirit among the sellers. We were thus somewhat surprised that the difference between the U.S.A. buyers and their European counterparts was as large as it was (the difference of $0.63 is significant at $p < .115$).

In view of the above result, and of the fact that maximum joint profit in the present model is limited to $14.80, it is not surprising to find that the U.S.A. sellers earned $0.25 less than the European sellers

($6.48 vs. $6.73). If we sum the buyer and seller profit for each bargaining pair, however, the average U.S.A. total profit is $0.38 higher than the comparable European total ($14.74 vs. $14.36). This difference is significant at approximately $p = 0.10$. Thus, the U.S.A. buyers seemed to be more successful than the European buyers in using their bargaining advantage to earn higher profits, and, in addition, the U.S.A. participants appeared to be more successful in competing against the game and the experiments.

In addition to comparing the bargaining behavior of the U.S.A. executives with the average behavior of all European executives, we have examined the process and results of negotiations on a country-by-country basis. We found, in general, that the same patterns of behavior observed in the aggregate also held for each of the individual countries, although in some cases the sample sizes were too small to indicate significant differences. That is, we found for all five European countries studied that, on the average, the buyers asked for a higher payoff than did the sellers on both the first and second bids, the buyers made more money than did the sellers, and (with the exception of Belgium) the buyers yielded more from their second offer. In comparing the U.S.A. buyers with the European buyers on a country-by-country basis, we found the U.S.A. executives consistently asked for more money on their initial offers, they made more offers during the negotiations, and, with one exception (France), they took longer to reach an agreement.

As we indicated earlier, we were uncertain as to whether the English executives should be grouped with their counterparts from Continental Europe, or with those from the U.S.A. In our country-by-country analysis, however, we found a greater similarity between the behavior of the U.S.A. and the English executives than between the English and the Continental European executives. To indicate the nature and the strength of the differences between the behavior of executives whose native language is English (U.S.A., England) relative to those from Continental Europe, we present (in Table 4) data on the same six variables considered earlier.

TABLE 4 - INTERNATIONAL EXECUTIVE COMPARISON
U.S.A. and England vs. Continental Europe

Variable	Mean Scores - Buyers U.S.A. & England	Mean Scores - Buyers Europe	t value	Significance
1st offer	\$13.08	\$11.85	2.385	< .025
2nd offer	12.85	11.43	2.911	< .003
Payoff	7.82	7.63	0.590	N.S.*
2nd-Payoff	5.03	3.79	2.455	< .008
No.of bids	17.67	15.14	1.326	< .095
Time (in min.)	70.82	61.75	1.867	< .035

*Not significant (at $p = 0.10$)

The effect of adding the English buyers to the U.S.A. buyers can be seen by comparing Tables 3 and 4. Notice that the only difference whose significance level did not decrease was the "no. of bids." For the two variables whose differences were not significant previously, the first (payoff) has remained that way, while the second (2nd offer-Payoff) is now significant at $p < .008$. Thus, if we measure competitiveness in terms of the variables listed in Table 4, the U.S.A. and English executives are seen to be significantly more competitive than the Continental European executives.

Summary

We have examined the effects of two general variables on the process and results of bargaining behavior between business executives in a bilateral monopoly experiment. The first involved certain non-symmetrical properties of the bargaining model, while the second was concerned with the influence of nationality differences among the participants. In the first case our findings indicate that, under incomplete information conditions, the bargainers with the higher maximum obtainable profit tended to ask for higher payoffs in the negotiation process than did their bargaining opponents, and, consequently, they earned a significantly larger profit. We also found that the bargainer with the steeper sloping marginal (cost vs. revenue) function tended to conceed, from an initial asking level, less than his opponent did. In terms of the payoffs earned, the first influence seemed to dominate the second. Our study of differences in behavior attributable to the participants' nationality indicated a significantly more competitive posture in the negotiations among the U.S.A. and English executives than among the Continental European counterparts.

In reviewing our current findings relative to the Siegel-Fouraker data, we find ourselves in general agreement with their conclusion that "personal characteristics of the bargainers seem to be the main determinants of differential payoffs and price in bilateral monopoly bargaining." Our research has extended their results by considering a variable not included in their model (structural asymmetry), and by investigating the influence of a possible source of variability among bargainers (their nationality). The extent to which a person's nationality influences his bargaining behavior may, of course, be a reflection of certain personality traits prevailing in the country in which he was raised (see bibliography 1). The present paper is part of a larger study investigating a number of cross-cultural differences in personality and the influence of these differences on bargaining behavior.

Bibliography

1. Cummings, L.L., Harnett, D.L., and O.J. Stevens, "Conciliation, Risk, Fate, and Trust - An International Study," Academy of Management Journal, 1971, Vol. 14, No. 3, pp. 285-304.

2. Chertkoff, J.S., and M. Conley, "Opening Offer and Frequency of Concession as Bargaining Strategies," Journal of Personality and Social Psychology, 1967, Vol. 7, No. 2, pp. 181-185.

3. Fellner, W., "Prices and Wages Under Bilateral Monopoly," The Quarterly Journal of Economics, 1947, Vol. 61, pp. 503-532.

4. Fellner, W., Competition Among the Few, New York: Knopf, 1949.

5. Foa, U.G., "Cross-Culture Similarity and Differences in Interpersonal Behavior," Journal of Abnormal and Social Psychology, 1964, Vol. 68, No. 5, pp. 517-526.

6. Fouraker, L.E., "Professor Fellner's Bilateral Monopoly Theory," The Southern Economic Journal, 1957, Vol. 24, pp. 182-189.

7. Fouraker, L.E., and S. Siegel, Bargaining Behavior, New York: McGraw-Hill, 1963.

8. Harnett, D.L., Cummings, L.L., and G.D. Hughes, "The Influence of Risk-Taking Propensity on Bargaining Behavior," Behavioral Science, 1968, Vol. 13, No. 2, pp. 91-101.

9. Harsanyi, J.E., "Approaches to the Bargaining Problem Before and After the Theory of Games: A Critical Discussion of Zeuthen's, Hicks' and Nash's Theories," Econometrica, 1956, Vol. 24, pp. 144-157.

10. McClintock, Charles G., and Joseph M. Nuttin, Jr., "Development of Competitive Game Behavior in Children Across Two Cultures," Journal of Experimental Social Psychology, 1969, Vol. 5, pp. 203-218.

11. McClintock, C.G., and S.P. McNell, "Cross-Cultural Comparisons of Interpersonal Motives," Sociometry, 1966, Vol. 29, No. 4, pp. 406-427.

12. Kelley, H.H., G.H. Shure, M. Deutsch, C. Fansheaus, J.T. Lanzetta, S. Moscoviei, J.M. Nuttin, Jr., J.M. Rabbie and J.W. Thibaut, "A Comparative Experimental Study of Negotiation Behavior," Journal of Personality and Social Psychology, 1970, Vol. 16, No. 3, pp. 411-438.

13. Nash, J.F., "The Bargaining Problem," Econometrica, 1950, Vol. 18, pp. 155-162.

14. Pigou, A., "Equilibrium Under Bilateral Monopoly," Economic Journal, 1908, Vol. 18, pp. 205-220.

15. Sawyer, J., and H. Guetzkow, "Bargaining and Negotiation in International Relations," in H.C. Kelman, International Behavior, New York: Holt, 1965.

16. Raiffa, H., "Arbitration Schemes for Generalized Two-Person Games," in H.W. Kuhn and A.W. Tucker (eds.), Contributions to the Theory of Games, Vol. 2. Annals of Mathematical Studies, 28, Princeton: Princeton University Press, 1953.

17. Schelling, T.C., "Bargaining Communication and Limited War," Journal of Conflict Resolution, 1957, Vol. 1, pp. 19-36.

18. Siegel, S., and L.E. Fouraker, Bargaining and Group Decision Making, New York: McGraw-Hill, 1960.

19. Zeuthen, F., Problems of Monopoly and Economic Warfare, London: Routledge, 1930.

Exhibit I

Instructions to the Buyer

Funds have been provided for the conduct of research regarding economic decisions. If you follow instructions carefully and make appropriate decisions, you may earn an appreciable amount of money. You cannot lose your own money, but a poor choice will result in little or no profit to you. You will keep all the money that you earn.
You have been paired, at random, with one other person. You will not be told with whom you have been paried, nor will you be permitted to speak to this person or any person participating in this research, as the decision making process must be carried out in silence. You and your anonymous counterpart will engage in a negotiation process to be carried out by means of written bids. Imagine that you and he must exchange some fictitious commodity. You have been selected (at random) to act as the buyer of this commodity and he has been selected (at random) to act as the seller. The task for the two of you is to negotiate, by means of written price-quantity offers, a single agreement on the price of the commodity to be exchanged between you, and the quantity to be exchanged at this price.

A table labeled Buyer's Payoff Table has been furnished you. The figures in the body of this table represent the profit that we will pay you, depending on the price and quantity you and the seller agree upon. Prices are listed down in the left-hand side, quantities across the top. Thus, if you and the seller agree upon a price of 120 and a quantity of 19, we will pay you $11.10.

At a price of 200 and a quantity of 6, we will pay you $3.05. You will not be told the amount of money we are paying the seller at these prices and quantities. In general, however, price-quantity agreements giving you a high profit will result in a low profit to him, while agreements giving you a low profit will result in a high profit to him.

The negotiation will begin by the seller making a price-quantity offer. He may choose any price along the left-hand margin, and any quantity across the top of his payoff table. He will write his price-quantity offer on a yellow sheet labeled Price-Quantity Offers. This yellow sheet will then be brought to you. You must either accept the seller's offer, in which case you should write "accept" on the yellow sheet, or make a new price-quantity offer of your own in the appropriate columns (Buyer's Price Offer, Buyer's Quantity Offer) on the yellow sheet. Your offer must also be written on the sheet labeled Buyer's Record Sheet. The yellow sheet will then be taken to the seller, who must accept your offer, or make another offer himself.

Each time you make a new offer you must write your offer on the Buyer's Record Sheet as well as on the Price-Quantity Sheet. You may make the same offer as many times as you wish, or vary your offer each time. When you have decided on your next offer raise your hand and the yellow sheet will be taken to the seller. The sheet will be returned to you as soon as he has decided on a new offer, or has accepted your offer. He may accept only your last offer, and you may accept only his latest offer. In other words, neither of you may go back and accept a previous offer. You may not write messages to the seller, or communicate with him in any other way except through the written price-quantity offers.

The proces of exchanging offers thus continues until one of you writes "accept" on the record sheet. Note that only one agreement is to be made between the two of you, and only one payoff will be made. As soon as you two reach agreement on a price and quantity, your part in this research has ended. Normally, you and the seller should reach agreement within one hour's bargaining time, although an additional 30 minutes will be given if necessary. If, at the end of this period of 1 1/2 hours, the two of you have not reached an agreement, the bargaining session will end and both you and the seller will be paid nothing (zero profit) for the session. If you do reach agreement you will be paid an amount equal to the profit shown in your payoff table.

If you have any questions about the negotiation process or the payoff table, please ask them now. Do not, however, inquire about or suggest appropriate bargaining strategies. There is no "correct solution." We are interested in your own approach to this negotiation problem.

Exhibit II

SELLERS PAYOFF TABLE

PRICE	QUANTITY 1	2	3	4	5	6	7	8	9	10	11	12	13	14	15	16	17	18	19	20
205	395	570	725	860	975	1070	1145	1200	1235	1250	1245	1220	1175	1110	1025	920	795	650	485	300
200	390	560	710	840	950	1040	1110	1160	1190	1200	1190	1160	1110	1040	950	840	710	560	390	200
195	385	550	695	820	925	1010	1075	1120	1145	1150	1135	1100	1045	970	875	760	625	470	295	100
190	380	540	680	800	900	980	1040	1080	1100	1100	1080	1040	980	900	800	680	540	380	200	0
185	375	530	665	780	875	950	1005	1040	1055	1050	1025	980	915	830	725	600	455	290	105	0
180	370	520	650	760	850	920	970	1000	1010	1000	970	920	850	760	650	520	370	200	10	0
175	365	510	635	740	825	890	935	960	965	950	915	860	785	690	575	440	285	110	0	0
170	360	500	620	720	800	860	900	920	920	900	860	800	720	620	500	360	200	20	0	0
165	355	490	605	700	775	830	865	880	875	850	805	740	655	550	425	280	115	0	0	0
160	350	480	590	680	750	800	830	840	830	800	750	680	590	480	350	200	30	0	0	0
155	345	470	575	660	725	770	795	800	785	750	695	620	525	410	275	120	0	0	0	0
150	340	460	560	640	700	740	760	760	740	700	640	560	460	340	200	40	0	0	0	0
145	335	450	545	620	675	710	725	720	695	650	585	500	395	270	125	0	0	0	0	0
140	330	440	530	600	650	680	690	680	650	600	530	440	330	200	50	0	0	0	0	0
135	325	430	515	580	625	650	655	640	605	550	475	380	265	130	0	0	0	0	0	0
130	320	420	500	560	600	620	620	600	560	500	420	320	200	60	0	0	0	0	0	0
125	315	410	485	540	575	590	585	560	515	450	365	260	135	0	0	0	0	0	0	0
120	310	400	470	520	550	560	550	520	470	400	310	200	70	0	0	0	0	0	0	0
115	305	390	455	500	525	530	515	480	425	350	255	140	5	0	0	0	0	0	0	0
110	300	380	440	480	500	500	480	440	380	300	200	80	0	0	0	0	0	0	0	0
105	295	370	425	460	475	470	445	400	335	250	145	20	0	0	0	0	0	0	0	0

Exhibit III

BUYERS PAYOFF TABLE

PRICE	QUANTITY 1	2	3	4	5	6	7	8	9	10	11	12	13	14	15	16	17	18	19	20
205	125	175	215	245	265	275	275	265	245	215	175	125	65	0	0	0	0	0	0	0
200	130	185	230	265	290	305	310	305	290	265	230	185	130	65	0	0	0	0	0	0
195	135	195	245	285	315	335	345	345	335	315	285	245	195	135	65	0	0	0	0	0
190	140	205	260	305	340	365	380	385	380	365	340	305	260	205	140	65	0	0	0	0
185	145	215	275	325	365	395	415	425	425	415	395	365	325	275	215	145	65	0	0	0
180	150	225	290	345	390	425	450	465	470	465	450	425	390	345	290	225	150	65	0	0
175	155	235	305	365	415	455	485	505	515	515	505	485	455	415	365	305	235	155	65	0
170	160	245	320	385	440	485	520	545	560	565	560	545	520	485	440	385	320	245	160	65
165	165	255	335	405	465	515	555	585	605	615	615	605	585	555	515	465	405	335	255	165
160	170	265	350	425	490	545	590	625	650	665	670	665	650	625	590	545	490	425	350	265
155	175	275	365	445	515	575	625	665	695	715	725	725	715	695	665	625	575	515	445	365
150	180	285	380	465	540	605	660	705	740	765	780	785	780	765	740	705	660	605	540	465
145	185	295	395	485	565	635	695	745	785	815	835	845	845	835	815	785	745	695	635	565
140	190	305	410	505	590	665	730	785	830	865	890	905	910	905	890	865	830	785	730	665
135	195	315	425	525	615	695	765	825	875	915	945	965	975	975	965	945	915	875	825	765
130	200	325	440	545	640	725	800	865	920	965	1000	1025	1040	1045	1040	1025	1000	965	920	865
125	205	335	455	565	665	755	835	905	965	1015	1055	1085	1105	1115	1115	1105	1085	1055	1015	965
120	210	345	470	585	690	785	870	945	1010	1065	1110	1145	1170	1185	1190	1185	1170	1145	1110	1065
115	215	355	485	605	715	815	905	985	1055	1115	1165	1205	1235	1255	1265	1265	1255	1235	1205	1165
110	220	365	500	625	740	845	940	1025	1100	1165	1220	1265	1300	1325	1340	1345	1340	1325	1300	1265
105	225	375	515	645	765	875	975	1065	1145	1215	1275	1325	1365	1395	1415	1425	1425	1415	1395	1365

6. EQUAL SHARE ANALYSIS OF CHARACTERISTIC FUNCTION EXPERIMENTS

REINHARD SELTEN

There are many ingenious theories applicable to characteristic function games (von Neumann-Morgenstern 1944, Shapley 1953, Luce 1955, Aumann-Maschler 1964, Maschler 1963, Radström 1964, Nering 1964). Some of these have been compared with experimental results (Kalish, Milnor, Nash and Nering 1954, Maschler 1965, Selten-Schuster 1966). The Bargaining Set theory of R.J. Aumann and M. Maschler (Aumann-Maschler 1964) has been most successful from the predictive point of view.

It is the purpose of this paper to develop a new theory called "equal share analysis" and to present experimental evidence. Unlike other theories, the new approach is simplistic rather than sophisticated.

The theory can be expressed in the form of three hypotheses about the outcome of characteristic function games. The first hypothesis says that there will be a strong tendency to form an "exhaustive coalition structure" which means that the final system of coalitions does not allow any profitable merger of several coalitions. This is not new. The condition is a part of the definition of Milnor's class D of reasonable outcomes. (Luce-Raiffa 1954).

---

* Freie Universität Berlin

The second hypothesis introduces a new game theoretic concept: the equal division core. A payoff vector is in the equal division core, if no coalition can divide its value equally among its members and in this way give more to each of the members than they receive in the payoff vector. The second hypothesis asserts that the outcome will have a strong tendency to be in the equal division core.

The third hypothesis says that within a coalition a stronger player will not get less than a weaker player. In most characteristic function games which have been used for experimental purposes it is perfectly clear who is stronger and who is weaker. Nevertheless we shall give a formal definition of the order of strength, which agrees with the intuitive notion in sufficiently simple cases and allows us to prove a theorem about the existence of outcomes which satisfy the three hypotheses.

The intuitive reasoning behind the first and the third hypothesis is easy to understand. But why should the player pay any attention to the equal division core? In the following we shall try to give an answer to this question.

The principle of equal division is a strong distributive norm which influences the behavior of the players. This is true in spite of the fact that in many types of characteristic function games, equal divisions rarely occur as final outcomes. The influence of the norm works indirectly: equal divisions are the most dangerous alternatives, because they are approved by the norm.

It seems to be true that the attention of the players is attracted by coalitions with high equal shares. This means that those players will be perceived as strong whose cooperation is needed for the formation

of coalitions with high equal shares. Our formal definition of the order of strength tries to capture this intuitive idea.
207 cases of experimental games from various sources in the literature and from the author's own experimentation have been compared with the theory. 76% of these cases conform to all three hypotheses.

Theory

Definitions: For the purpose of this paper a characteristic function is a function v which assigns a real number v(C) to all elements of a set P of subsets of N=(1,...,n), where P contains at least all subsets of the form (i) and v satisfies the condition.

$$(1)\qquad v(C) \geq \sum_{i\in C} v(i) \qquad \text{for all } C\in P \text{ with } |C| > 1$$

Here |C| is the number of elements in C and the symbol i stands for set (i). The set N = (1,...,n) is interpreted as the set of all players, the subsets of N are coalitions and the elements of P are called permissible coalitions.
A characteristic function game is played in the following way: The object of the players is to form one or several coalitions C∈P. A player cannot belong to more than one coalition. In order to form a coalition, the players in C must agree upon a division of v(C) among themselves; the numbers v(C) typically represent sums of money.
The result of the play is a configuration

$$(C_1,\ldots,C_m;x_1\ldots,x_n)$$

which consists of a <u>coalition structure</u> $(C_1,\dots,C_m)$ which is a partition of N into permissible coalitions $C_j \varepsilon P$ and a <u>payoff vector</u> $x = (x_1,\dots,x_n)$ which satisfies the conditions

(2) $$\sum_{i \varepsilon C_j} x_i = v(C_j) \quad \text{for } j = 1,\dots,m$$

and

(3) $$x_i \geq v(i) \qquad \text{for } i = 1,\dots,n \quad .$$

<u>Exhaustive structure:</u>

A coalitions structure $(C_1,\dots,C_m)$ with the following property is called <u>exhaustive</u>: If $C \varepsilon P$ is a union of several of the C_j, then we have

(4) $$v(C) \leq \sum_{C_j \subseteq C} v(C_j)$$

This means that nothing can be gained by forming a larger coalition from several coalitions of an exhaustive structure.

<u>Equal division core:</u>

For every $C \varepsilon P$ define

(5) $$e(C) = \frac{v(C)}{|C|}$$

$e(C)$ is called <u>equal share</u> of C.
Let E be the set of all configurations $(C_1,\dots,C_m; x_1,\dots,x_n)$ with the following property: there is no

coalition C with

(6) $x_i < e(C)$ for all $i \in C$.

The set E is called <u>equal division core</u> of v.

<u>Decreased games</u>:

Let $b_1,\ldots,b_R$ with $b_1 < b_2 < \ldots < b_R$ be the values assumed by e(C). The decreased game v_1 of v is the characteristic function which is defined on the same set P of permissible coalitions as v and takes the following values

$$(7) \quad v_1(C) = \begin{cases} v(C) & \text{for } e(C) < b_R \\ |C| b_{R-1} & \text{for } e(C) = b_R \end{cases}$$

For k = 2,..., R-1 let v_k be the decreased game of v_{k-1}. We call v_k the <u>k-th decreased game</u> of v.

<u>Maximal share structure</u>:

Let $(C_1,\ldots,C_m)$ be a coalition structure for v and let P_k be the set of all permissible coalitions which are subsets of $N-C_1-\ldots-C_{k-1}$. The coalition structure $(C_1,\ldots,C_m)$ is called a maximal share structure, iff it has the following property

$$(8) \quad e(C_k) = \max_{C \in P_k} e(C) \quad \text{for } k = 1,\ldots,m$$

A maximal share structure may be interpreted as the result of a coalition forming process, where one coalition forms after the other and the players try to form a coalition C with the highest possible equal share e(C).

Let $(C_1,\ldots,C_m)$ be a coalition structure; the <u>equal share</u> $s_i(C_1,\ldots,C_m)$ of player i in that structure is the equal share $e(C_j)$ of that coalition C_j which contains i.

<u>Order of precedence</u>:

In the following we shall introduce some definitions which prepare our concept of the order of strength. This concept is based on the idea, that those players are strong who tend to have high equal shares in maximal share structures.

Two players i and j are called <u>undistinguished</u> if in at least one maximal share structure player i has a higher share than player j, while in at least one other maximal share structure player j has a higher equal share than player i. Two players i and j are called <u>equal in precedence</u>, if it is possible to find a chain $i_1,\ldots,i_K$ of players, beginning with $i_1 = i$ and ending with $i_K = j$, such that for $k=1,\ldots,K-1$ two neighboring players i_k and i_{k+1} are undistinguished. Obviously the relationship "equal in precedence" is transitive.

We say that player i <u>precedes</u> player j, if i and j are not equal in precedence and there is at least one maximal share structure, where player i has a higher equal share than player j. Obviously, if i precedes j, then there is no maximal share structure where j has a higher equal share than player i. It follows that "precedes" is a transitive relationship. Moreover if i, j and k are three players where i precedes j and j is equal in precedence to k, then i precedes k. This follows from the fact that i cannot be equal in precedence to k, since otherwise i would be equal in precedence to j. In the same way it can be seen that i precedes k if i is equal in precedence to j and j precedes k. Summarizing these results we may say that the relations "equal in precedence" and "precedes" combine to form an incomplete transitive <u>order of precedence</u>.

Two players i and j are called <u>peers</u>, if they are not equal in precedence and

$$(9)\qquad s_i(C_1,\ldots,C_m) = s_j(C_1,\ldots,C_m)$$

holds for every maximal share structure $(C_1,\ldots,C_m)$. Obviously one of two peers cannot precede the other.

<u>Order of strength</u>:

We could complete the order of precedence by regarding two players as equally strong whenever they are peers. Unfortunately this leads to a very coarse order which even in relatively simple cases does not reflect obvious differences of strength. Therefore we construct a more refined order of strength in which one of two peers is regarded as stronger than the other, if he is stronger in the decreased game. Since every maximal share structure of the original game is a fortiori also a maximal share structure of the decreased game, i must either be a peer of j or precede j in the original game, if i precedes j in the decreased game. Therefore it seems to be natural to look at the larger set of maximal share structures of the decreased game in order to distinguish between the strength of two players who are peers in the original game. The order of strength proposed here is characterized by the following five properties:

<u>Property 1</u>: If i precedes j in v then i is stronger than j in v.

<u>Property 2</u>: If i and j are equal with respect to precedence in v, then i and j are equally strong in v.

<u>Property 3</u>: If v is symmetric with respect to i and j (exchanging the numbers of both players does not change the game), then i and j are equally strong in v.

<u>Property 4</u>: If i and j are peers in v and i is stronger than j in the decreased game v_1 of v then i is stronger than j in v.

<u>Property 5</u>: If i and j are peers in v and i and j are equally strong in the decreased game v_1, then i and j are equally strong in v.

<u>Lemma</u>: Properties 1 to 5 uniquely determine a complete transitive order of strength.

<u>Proof</u>: We prove the lemma by describing a recursive procedure of constructing an order of strength with properties 1 to 5. The construction will be such that it is clear that properties 1 to 5 force us to order the players in this way. The procedure begins with the application of properties 1,2 and 3 to v. Two players i and j whose strength relationship remains open after this, must be peers. We then apply properties 1 to 3 to the decreased game v_1 in order to fill in such open relationships with the help of properties 4 and 5. In the same way we can look at the second decreased game in order to fill in those relationships which remain open after the investigation of v_1. If we go on in this way we sooner or later reach a point where no relationship remains open, since sooner or later we meet a decreased game v_k which is symmetric with respect to any given pair of players. The last decreased game v_{R-1} is completely symmetric. The construction also shows that the order of strength has properties 1 to 5. No conflict can occur between properties 1,2 and 3 which obviously define an incomplete and transitive order and the properties 4 and 5 which are applicable only to pairs

of peers. It may happen, that v is symmetric with respect to two peers but in this case also the decreased game is symmetric with respect to them.
If i and j are peers than i and j must have the same precedence relationship to any third player k. If i precedes k, then j precedes k, if k precedes i, then k precedes j. Therefore the application of properties 4 and 5 completes the transitive precedence order for v in a transitive way by the transitive precedence order for v_1. This shows that the final order of strength is transitive.
Example: The practical determination of the order of strength with the help of the recursive procedure described in the lemma generally does not take many steps and leads to intuitively acceptable results. It can be seen easily that it gives the intuitively expected answer for those types of 3- and 4-person games which occur in Maschler's experiments. For the purpose of illustration we may apply the procedure to the game V of Kalish, Milnor, Nash and Nering (table 7). This game has only one maximal share structure which may be described in a somewhat simplified notation as 1234,5 (the first coalition contains players 1,2,3 and 4, the second player 5). This yields 1,2,3, 4 > 5 where the symbol " > " is used for "stronger than". The decreased game has the additional maximal share structure 125,34 and no other. This yields 1,2 > 3,4. The second decreased game again has only one additional maximal share structure, namely 1235,4. It follows that we have 3 > 4. The third decreased game has 2 additional maximal share structures: 1245,3 and 135,24; consequently we have 1 > 2. The order of strength is 1 > 2 > 3 > 4 > 5. We see that strength is connected to membership in coalitions with high equal shares, which agrees with our intuitive notion, that the attention of the players is attracted by high equal shares.

Three Hypotheses

The new theory proposed here asserts that under certain experimental conditions a high percentage of all outcomes will satisfy the following three hypotheses about the final configuration $(C_1,\ldots,C_m;\ x_1,\ldots,x_n)$.

Hypothesis 1 (exhaustive structure):

The coalition structure $(C_1,\ldots,C_m)$ is exhaustive.

Hypothesis 2 (equal division core):

The configuration $(C_1,\ldots,C_m;\ x_1,\ldots,x_n)$ is in the equal division core.

Hypothesis 3 (order of strength):

If in the configuration $(C_1,\ldots,C_m;\ x_1,\ldots,x_n)$ two players i and j belong to the same coalition C_k and i is stronger than j then we have $x_i \geq x_j$.

A configuration which conforms to hypotheses 1, 2 and 3 is called regular; other configurations are called irregular.

Note that neither the equal division core nor the order of strength are invariant with respect to strategic equivalence.

Existence of Regular Configurations

Theorem: The set of all regular configurations is always non-empty.

Proof: We can always construct a maximal share structure $(C_1,\ldots,C_m)$. Let $(C_1,\ldots,C_m;\ x_1,\ldots,x_n)$ be the configuration with

$$(10) \qquad x_i = s_i(C_1,\ldots,C_m)$$

From the fact that $(C_1,\ldots,C_m)$ is a maximal share structure we can conclude that $(C_1,\ldots,C_m;\ x_1,\ldots,x_n)$ is in the equal division core; this can be seen as follows: consider a coalition $C \varepsilon P$ which satisfies (6). Let k be the smallest index with $C_k \cap C \neq \emptyset$. The coalition C is a subset of P_k. This is a contradiction against (8).

The configuration $(C_1,\ldots,C_m;\ x_1,\ldots,x_n)$ trivially satisfies the condition of hypothesis 3, since all members of the same coalition have equal payoffs. If $(C_1,\ldots,C_m)$ is exhaustive, then $(C_1,\ldots,C_m;\ x_1,\ldots,x_n)$ is regular. If $(C_1,\ldots,C_m)$ is not exhaustive, we can always find an exhaustive structure $(C_1',\ldots,C_m')$, which is a coarser partition of N than $(C_1,\ldots,C_m)$. Define

$$(11)\quad y_i = x_i + \frac{1}{|C_j'|}\left(v(C_j') - \sum_{i \varepsilon C_j'} x_i\right) \quad \text{for } i \varepsilon C_j'$$

Obviously the configuration $(C_1',\ldots,C_m';\ y_1,\ldots,y_n)$ is in the equal division core, since $(C_1,\ldots,C_m;\ x_1,\ldots,x_n)$ is in the equal division core.

If two players i and j with $y_i > y_j$ are both in the same coalition C_j' then player i must have a higher equal share in $(C_1,\ldots,C_m)$ than player j. Therefore it follows from properties 1 and 2 of the order of strength that j is not stronger than i. Consequently $(C_1',\ldots,C_m';y_1,\ldots,y_n)$ satisfies hypothesis 3 and is regular.

Remark: Since we did not make use of the properties 3,4 and 5, the theorem remains true if the definition of the order of strength is replaced by another one which satisfies properties 1 and 2.

Favorable Experimental Conditions

The mathematical structure of the characteristic function is not the only factor which influences the outcome of the game. One cannot expect that the same theory fits all kinds of experimental procedures. Equal share analysis seems to be well adapted to a certain set of favorable experimental conditions, which shall be described below. Some characteristic function experiments whose experimental procedures seriously deviate from these conditions were not included into the material presented in tables 1 to 11. Thus, for example, Riker's 3-person games were excluded, since in these games bargaining was structured as a predetermined sequence of nine secret 2-player sessions (Riker 1967); this violates several of the communication conditions stated below.

To a certain extent equal share analysis still works under unfavorable experimental conditions, especially, if the theory is applied in a modified way. In some of the experiments which are included into the material presented in tables 1 to 12, a group of players could make a formal agreement to enter the final coalition as a whole (Kalish, Milnor, Nash and Nering 1954, Frassine, Fürst and Winter 1967); a binding agreement of this kind is called a precoalition. A precoalition may or may not involve conditional agreements on the payoff division for the case that no larger coalition is formed. A precoalition may be viewed as a move which changes the characteristic function. Those coalitions which would break up the precoalition are no longer permissible. A configuration which is irregular for the original characteristic function may

be regular for the new characteristic function. For the purpose of this paper cases of this kind are counted as regular. Among the 57 cases of games where precoalitions are allowed, we find 34 cases which are regular in the stronger sense and 8 cases which are regular in the weaker sense (see table 12).
The following experimental conditions seem to be favorable for the validity of the predictions derived from equal share analysis:

1. Full information: The players are fully informed about the rules of the game.
2. Strong motivation: The players are strongly motivated to succeed in the game.
3. One-shot plays: Each game is played only once by the same set of players.
4. Face to face communication: The players can see each other and can talk to each other.
5. Unrestricted communication: Every player can talk to any other player anytime.
6. Unstructured communication: Bargaining is not formalized; the players are free to choose the content of the communication.
7. Open communication: Secret bargaining is impossible; everything which is said, can be overheard by everybody.
8. Absence of precoalition commitment power: Precoalitions are not allowed. The players can commit themselves to final coalitions only.

Explanation of the Tables

Tables 1 to 11 show the outcomes of 207 cases of characteristic function games coming from various sources in the literature and from the author's own experimentation. The columns named "exhaustive", "eq.div.core" and "strength" refer to the hypotheses 1,2 and 3. The symbol "+" indicates that the case confirms the hypothesis, while "-" indicates lack of confirmation and "/" means that the hypothesis is not applicable to the case in question."(+)" indicates that the hypothesis is satisfied only for the new characteristic function arising after the last precoalition has been formed.

For games where v(i)=0 does not hold for all players, we have added a column named "normed eq.div.core." Here the symbol "+" indicates that after the application of a transformation which transforms the game into a strategically equivalent game, the transformed outcome is in the equal division core of the transformed game (tables 6 and 7).
Where nothing else is said about 1-person coalitions we have v(i)=0 for i=1,...,n. Generally only those coalitions with more than 1 player are permissible, for which values are given in the tables; in table 4 where no values are given, only 1-person and 2-person coalitions are allowed and the value of a 2-person coalition is the sum of the quotas of the two players in the coalition.
In some of the tables the values of coalitions which formed are underlined (tables 1 to 3). In other tables the players with underlined payoffs are in the same coalition, usually the first which formed (tables 4 to 7; it is not always quite clear which coalition formed first). In the rest of the tables, the players with positive payoffs are in the final coalition (tables 8 to 11).

In those cases where the players randomized in order to determine the final outcome, tables 6 and 7 give expected values, while all other tables show the actual payoffs after the randomization: "Expected outcomes are given in the few cases where the players randomized" (Kalish, Milnor, Nash and Nering 1954, p.316). Unfortunately Kalish, Milnor, Nash and Nering do not say which are the few cases. Only run no. 147 is described as the result of a randomization: "all four players randomized in order to see which 3-person coalition would form" (Kalish, Milnor, Nash and Nering 1954, pp. 308-309). Our evaluation is based on the assumption that all other cases did not involve randomizations and that the players in run no. 147 agreed to split evenly among 3 players.
The numbering of the players does not agree with that in the original papers. The players have been numbered according to their strength (the strongest player receives number 1) and as far as this still leaves degrees of freedom according to their payoffs (lower numbers for players with higher payoffs). This system of numbering is convenient for the purpose of comparing the data with hypothesis 3.
The entries in table 12 are numbers of cases. This table summarizes the evaluation of the material presented in tables 1 to 11.

Sources:

Tables 1 to 5:
Maschler 1965.

Tables 6 and 7:
Kalish, Milnor, Nash and Nering, 1955.

Table 8:
Selten and Schuster 1968 - The results of play number 173,174 and 175 became known to the author as a participant of the Jerusalem Workshop on Game Theory in 1965.

Tables 9 and 10:
These experiments were run by the author as part of various courses and lectures for the purpose of classroom demonstration.

Table 11:
Frassine, Fürst and Winter, 1967.

Subjects

Tables 1 to 5:
Maschler's subjects were 39 11-th grade class students of the Hebrew University Secondary School (29 boys and 9 girls). Each subject participated in many plays.

Tables 6 and 7:
The subjects of Kalish, Milnor, Nash and Nering were 4 men and 4 women, including 5 college students, 2 housewives and one teacher. Each subject participated in many plays.

Table 8:
The subjects of the SELTEN-SCHUSTER experiment were 60 male undergraduates of Frankfurt University (Germany), 59 majoring in economics and 1 in psychology. Runs number 173,174,175 were played by game theorists. Each subject participated only once. The big player in run 175 (the author) had the benefit of having observed runs 161-172.

Tables 9 and 10:
University students (runs 176,178,179,180,181,185) students of the Vienna diplomatic academy (run 186) managers (runs 183 and 184) operations research analysts and military men (runs 177,182 and 187). Each subject participated only once.

Table 11:
The subjects were 59 high school students in the age group between 16 and 18 years and one university graduate (age 25). Each subject participated only once.

Experimental Procedures

The experiments which are collected in our tables are the result of several similar experimental procedures. In the following we give a short description of the procedures which concentrates on the differences. Where nothing else is said, the procedures satisfy the experimental conditions, which we have described as favorable to our theory.

Tables 1 to 5:
Maschler's experiments were not run in the laboratory. The participants could choose when and where the bargaining would take place. The rules prescribed open bargaining, but because of lack of control one cannot exclude the possibility that secret negotiations took place in some cases. For each game the players received a card with a description of the game and the names of the participants. The final agreement was written on the card which then was turned in to the experimenter. The payoffs were in points. The experiment was run as a contest with book coupon prizes for the 3 most successful subjects. The prizes had the values of 10, 5 and 3 Israeli Pounds.

Tables 6 and 7:
The games were played in the laboratory. A time limit of 10 minutes was imposed on the negotiations of each game. Formal commitments to precoalitions were possible. The subjects played for modest monetary rewards.

Table 8, no. 161-172:
The games were played in the laboratory. An agreement had to survive a registration time of 10 minutes in order to become final, but no time limit was imposed on the negotiations. The subjects played for substantial monetary rewards.

Table 8, no. 173-175:

Maschler's Jerusalem conference games were run in a similar way as Maschler's experiments in tables 1 to 5, but secret negotiations were not explicitly forbidden and did take place. Three days after the beginning of the plays the agreements had to be turned in at a specified time. The money rewards were not negligible.

Tables 9 and 10:

The games were played as classroom demonstrations, but apart from the fact that this involves a lower degree of experimental control, the procedure was that of table 8, no. 161-172. The monetary rewards were substantial or at least not negligible.

Table 11:

Players 2 and 3 were allowed to form a precoalition, but otherwise the procedure is that of table 8, no. 161-172. The registration time rule applied to precoalition agreements too. The subjects played for substantial money rewards.

No.	values of the coalitions 12	13	23	123	payoffs 1	2	3	exhaustive	eq.div.core	strength
1	100	100	50	0	74	26	0	+	+	+
2	100	100	50	100	60	40	0	+	+	+
3	100	100	50	110	50	30	30	+	+	+
4	100	100	50	125	55	35	35	+	+	+
5	100	100	50	150	50	50	50	+	+	+
6	80	80	40	0	0	20	20	+	−	+
7	80	80	40	80	50	30	0	+	+	+
8	80	80	40	90	60	20	0	−	+	+
9	80	80	40	100	36	32	32	+	−	+
10	80	80	40	110	50	30	30	+	+	+
11	90	70	60	0	55	35	0	+	+	+
12	90	70	60	90	45	45	0	+	+	+
13	90	70	60	110	40	40	30	+	−	+
14	90	70	60	150	50	50	50	+	+	+
15	100	80	60	0	55	0	25	+	−	+
16	100	80	60	100	57	43	0	+	+	+
17	100	80	60	110	50	50	10	+	+	+
18	100	80	60	120	50	35	35	+	+	+
19	100	80	60	150	54	50	46	+	+	+
20	60	30	20	0	32	28	0	+	+	+
21	60	30	20	40	35	25	0	+	+	+
22	60	30	20	55	37	23	0	+	+	+
23	60	30	20	60	0	15	5	−	−	+
24	60	30	20	100	50	30	20	+	+	+
25	80	30	30	0	40	40	0	+	+	+
26	80	30	30	20	40	40	0	+	+	+
27	80	30	30	70	40	40	0	+	+	+
28	80	30	30	80	40	40	0	+	+	+
29	80	30	30	100	45	45	10	+	+	+
30	120	90	70	0	70	0	20	+	−	+
31	120	90	70	0	0	35	35	+	−	+
32	60	30	20	60	20	0	10	−	−	+
33	50	50	0	50	30	20	0	+	+	+
34	50	50	0	60	30	15	15	+	+	+
35	50	50	0	100	50	25	25	+	+	+
36	50	50	0	120	48	36	36	+	+	+
37	70	50	0	0	58	12	0	+	+	+
38	70	50	0	60	55	15	0	+	+	+
39	70	50	0	70	50	18	2	+	+	+
40	70	50	0	80	50	25	5	+	+	+
41	70	50	0	100	41	39	20	+	+	+

TABLE 1: MASCHLER'S 3-PERSON GAMES

No.	values of the coalitions 12	13	23	payoffs 1	2	3	exhaustive	eq.div.core	strength
42	50	50	0	49	1	0	+	+	+
43	50	50	0	0	0	0	-	-	/
44	50	50	0	30	20	0	+	+	+
45	50	50	0	40	10	0	+	+	+
46	50	50	0	49	1	0	+	+	+
47	50	50	0	40	10	0	+	+	+
48	50	50	0	35	15	0	+	+	+
49	50	50	0	49	1	0	+	+	+
50	50	50	0	25	25	0	+	+	+
51	50	50	0	0	0	0	-	-	/
52	50	50	0	49	1	0	+	+	+
53	50	50	0	25	25	0	+	+	+
54	50	50	0	25	25	0	+	+	+
55	60	60	10	40	20	0	+	+	+
56	60	60	10	40	20	0	+	+	+
57	60	60	10	45	15	0	+	+	+
58	60	60	10	48	12	0	+	+	+
59	60	60	10	45	15	0	+	+	+
60	60	60	10	40	20	0	+	+	+
61	60	60	10	35	25	0	+	+	+
62	60	60	10	0	5	5	+	-	+
63	60	60	10	40	20	0	+	+	+
64	60	60	10	20	40	0	+	+	-
65	60	60	10	30	30	0	+	+	+
66	60	60	10	45	15	0	+	+	+
67	60	60	10	38	22	0	+	+	+
68	60	60	10	0	5	5	+	-	+
69	60	60	10	0	5	5	+	-	+
70	60	60	10	40	20	0	+	+	+
71	60	60	10	45	15	0	+	+	+
72	60	60	10	35	25	0	+	+	+
73	60	60	10	29	31	0	+	+	-
74	60	60	10	31	29	0	+	+	+
75	60	60	10	55	5	0	+	+	+
76	60	60	10	35	25	0	+	+	+
77	60	60	10	45	15	0	+	+	+
78	60	60	10	0	5	5	+	-	+

TABLE 2: MASCHLER'S EXTREME 3-PERSON GAMES

No.	values of the coalitions 123	124	134	234	1234	payoffs 1	2	3	4	exhaustive	eq.div.core	strength
79	<u>100</u>	90	70	50	0	45	40	15	0	+	+	+
80	<u>100</u>	90	70	50	110	33	34	33	0	-	+	+
81	100	90	70	50	<u>100</u>	39	36	15	10	+	+	+
82	<u>90</u>	80	70	60	0	30	30	30	0	+	+	+
83	90	80	70	60	<u>100</u>	30	30	20	20	+	+	+
84	90	80	<u>70</u>	60	95	30	30	0	10	-	+	+
85	120	<u>110</u>	100	90	0	45	42	0	23	+	+	+
86	120	110	100	90	<u>140</u>	29	47	42	22	+	+	-
87	120	110	100	90	<u>130</u>	41	41	41	7	+	+	+
88	<u>120</u>	100	80	60	0	50	35	35	0	+	+	+
89	120	100	80	60	<u>130</u>	46	40	40	4	+	+	+
90	120	100	80	60	<u>150</u>	69	38	27	16	+	+	+
91	<u>120</u>	100	80	60	0	55	40	25	0	+	+	+
92	<u>120</u>	100	80	60	0	40	40	40	0	+	+	+
93	120	100	80	60	0	0	0	0	0	-	-	/
94	120	<u>100</u>	80	60	0	45	45	0	10	+	+	+
95	<u>120</u>	100	80	60	0	40	40	40	0	+	+	+

TABLE 3: MASCHLER'S 4-PERSON GAMES WITH FLAT 2-PERSON COALITIONS

No.	quotas				payoffs				exhaustive	eq.div.core	strength
	1	2	3	4	1	2	3	4			
96	70	50	30	10	75	36	25	24	+	-	+
97	60	60	20	20	60	60	20	20	+	+	+
98	30	10	10	10	20	20	10	10	+	+	+
99	60	30	10	10	55	35	10	10	+	+	+
100	80	70	20	10	75	75	15	15	+	+	+
101	60	50	40	30	50	48	42	40	+	-	+
102	80	70	20	10	80	70	15	15	+	+	+
103	80	80	60	40	80	80	60	40	+	+	+
104	60	40	20	10	60	35	20	15	+	+	+
105	80	70	50	0	80	70	30	20	+	+	+
106	60	40	0	0	60	40	0	0	+	+	+
107	80	0	0	0	75	5	0	0	+	+	+
108	80	60	10	10	65	45	25	25	+	-	+
109	80	10	10	10	55	35	10	10	+	+	+
110	90	70	10	10	89	40	40	11	+	+	+
111	80	10	10	10	70	20	10	10	+	+	+
112	90	70	0	0	90	70	0	0	+	+	+
113	70	70	30	0	75	0	25	0	-	-	+

TABLE 4: MASCHLER'S 4-PERSON QUOTA GAMES

No.	value of 2-person coalitions	value of coalition 123	payoffs 1	2	3	4	exhaustive	eq.div.core	strength
114	50	120	45	25	25	5	+	+	+
115	50	111	40	25	25	10	+	+	+
116	50	111	38	0	0	12	-	-	+
117	50	120	45	25	25	5	+	+	+
118	50	111	45	25	25	5	+	+	+
119	50	120	41	25	25	9	+	+	+
120	50	111	40	25	25	10	+	+	+
121	50	120	40	40	40	0	+	+	+
122	50	111	40	25	25	10	+	+	+
123	50	120	41	25	25	9	+	+	+

TABLE 5: MASCHLER'S SPECIAL 4-PERSON GAMES

Characteristic Functions				
coalition	game I	game II	game III	game IV
1	0	10	-20	-20
2	0	0	-20	-40
3	0	-40	-20	-20
4	0	-50	-20	-40
12	60	50	0	30
13	60	10	0	-10
14	40	0	0	0
23	40	0	0	0
24	20	-10	0	10
34	20	-50	0	-30
123	80	50	20	40
124	80	40	20	20
134	80	0	20	40
234	80	-10	20	20

No.	game	payoffs 1	2	3	4	precoalition	exhaustive	eq.div.core	strength normed	eq.div.core
124	I	32	24	0	24	24	+	-	+	
125	I	34	34	0	12	12	+	+	+	
126	I	30	30	10	10	12	+	+	+	
127	I	35	35	10	0	12	+	+	+	
128	I	40	20	10	10	12	+	(+)	+	
129	I	34	34	0	12		+	+	+	
130	I	35	30	15	0	12	+	+	+	
131	I	35,5	35,5	0	9	12	+	-	+	
132	II	20	30	- 4	-46	34	+	+	-	-
133	II	26	26	- 2	-50	12	+	+	+	-
134	II	25	25	-25	-25	34	+	+	+	-
135	II	35	35	-20	-50		+	+	+	-
136	II	25	25	-23	-27	12	+	+	+	-
137	II	25	25	-18	-32	12	+	+	+	-
138	II	42	41	-40	-43		+	-	+	-
139	II	34	34	-40	-28	12	+	+	+	+
140	III	0	0	0	0	12	+	-	/	
141	III	10	9	1	-20	12	+	+	/	
142	III	7	7	6	-20		+	+	/	
143	III	10	9	1	-20	12	+	+	/	
144	III	0	0	0	0	12	+	-	/	
145	III	9	9	2	-20	12	+	+	/	
146	III	0	0	0	0	12	+	-	/	
147	III	0	0	0	0	*)	+	+	/	
148	IV	25	-40	25	-10		+	-	+	-
149	IV	-20	10	0	10	24	+	(+)	(+)	+
150	IV	15	-40	10	15	14	+	+	-	-
151	IV	25	25	-10	-40	12	+	+	+	-
152	IV	24	24	- 8	-40	12	+	+	+	-
153	IV	- 5	5	- 5	5	24	+	-	+	+
154	IV	25	25	-10	-40	12	+	+	+	-
155	IV	15	-40	15	10		+	+	+	-

*) randomization, see Explanation of the Tables

TABLE 6: THE 4-PERSON GAMES OF
KALISH, MILNOR, NASH AND NERING

game V

coalition	value	coalition	value
1	-20	123	10
2	-30	124	0
3	-40	125	40
4	-50	134	-10
5	-60	135	30
12	0	145	20
13	-10	234	-20
14	-20	235	20
15	20	245	10
23	-20	345	0
24	-30	1234	60
25	10	1235	50
34	-40	1245	40
35	0	1345	30
45	-10	2345	20

game VI

coalition	value
1 player	-40
2 players	0
3 players	-20
4 players	20
5 players	0
6 players	40

Characteristic Functions of Games V and VI

	No.	payoffs 1	2	3	4	5	precoalitions	exhaustive	eq.div.core	strength normed	eq.div.core
	156	10	10	-40	10	10	12,45	+	(+)	+	+
game V	157	23	23	-19	-50	23	125	+	+	-	-
	158	20	20	10	10	-60	12,124	+	+	+	-

	No.	payoffs 1	2	3	4	5	6	7	precoalitions and final structure	exhaustive	eq.div.core	strength
game VI	159	7	7	7	7	6	6	-40	56,12,34,1234 (123456,7)	+	+	/
	160	3	5	5	5	5	3	-26	23,45,16,2345 (2345,167)	+	(+)	/

TABLE 7: THE 5- AND 6-PERSON GAMES OF KALISH, MILNOR, NASH AND NERING

AUNT-AND-I GAME
Number of "big" and "small" players in the 2 types of minimal winning coalitions
1) 1 big and 1 small
2) 4 small

1 of the 5 players is "big" and 4 are "small"

Non-Minimal winning coalitions are coalitions which contain a minimal winning coalition. In the SELTEN-SCHUSTER EXPERIMENTS non-minimal winning coalitions were permissible, but as far as I remember, only minimal winning coalitions were allowed in MASCHLER'S JERUSALEM CONFERENCE GAMES.

SELTEN-SCHUSTER EXPERIMENTS

Value of a winning coalition: 40,00 German Marks

No.	payoffs big	small	small	small	small	exhaustive	eq.div.core	strength
161	25,00	15,00	-	-	-	+	+	+
162	25,00	15,00	-	-	-	+	+	+
163	25,00	15,00	-	-	-	+	+	+
164	25,00	15,00	-	-	-	+	+	+
165	-	14,00	8,66	8,66	8,66	+	-	+
166	-	19,00	7,00	7,00	7,00	+	-	+
167	18,00	22,00	-	-	-	+	-	-
168	25,00	5,00	5,00	5,00	-	+	-	+
169	28,00	12,00	-	-	-	+	+	+
170	20,00	6,66	6,66	6,66	-	+	-	+
171	25,00	15,00	-	-	-	+	+	+
172	8,00	8,00	8,00	8,00	8,00	+	-	+

MASCHLER'S JERUSALEM CONFERENCE GAMES

Value of a winning coalition: 100,00 Israeli Pounds

No.	payoffs big	small	small	small	small	exhaustive	eq.div,core	strength
173	65,00	35,00	-	-	-	+	+	+
174	65,00	35,00	-	-	-	+	+	+
175	62,50	37,50	-	-	-	+	+	+

TABLE 8: SELTEN-SCHUSTER EXPERIMENTS AND MASCHLER'S JERUSALEM CONFERENCE GAMES (AUNT-AND-I GAME)

DEMONSTRATION GAME
Number of "big" and "small" players in the 3 types of minimal winning coalitions
1) 2 big and 1 small
2) 1 big and 3 small
3) 5 small

Non-minimal coalitions were permissible.

Abbreviation:

A: Austrian Shillings

$: American Dollars

M: German Marks

2 of the 7 players are "big" and 5 are "small".									exhaustive	eq.div.core	strength
No.	value of winning coalition	payoffs big	big	small	small	small	small	small			
176	200A	70,00	70,00	60,00	-	-	-	-	+	+	+
177	40M	-	-	8,00	8,00	8,00	8,00	8,00	+	-	+
178	40M	18,00	-	7,33	7,33	7,33	-	-	+	-	+
179	20$	6,66	6,66	6,67	-	-	-	-	+	+	+
180	18$	7,00	7,00	4,00	-	-	-	-	+	+	+
181	19$	7,00	7,00	5,00	-	-	-	-	+	+	+
182	27$	9,00	9,00	9,00	-	-	-	-	+	+	+
183	100M	35,00	35,00	30,00	-	-	-	-	+	+	+
184	100M	40,00	-	20,00	20,00	20,00	-	-	+	-	+
185	40M	14,00	14,00	12,00	-	-	-	-	+	+	+

TABLE 9: DEMONSTRATION GAME (SELTEN)

COMMON MARKET GAME
Number of "big", "small" and "medium" players in the 3 types of minimal winning coalitions
1) 3 big and 1 small 2) 3 big and 1 medium 3) 2 big and 2 medium

Non-minimal winning coalitions were permissible.

Abbreviations:

A: Austrian Shillings

M: German Marks

3 of the 6 players are "big" 2 are "medium" and 1 is "small".								exhaustive	eq.div.core	strength
No.	value of winning coalition	payoffs big	big	big	medium	medium	small			
186	120A	39,00	39,00	39,00	-	-	3,00	+	+	+
187	60M	24,00	24,00	-	6,00	6,00	-	+	+	+

TABLE 10: COMMON MARKET GAME (SELTEN)

VIENNA GAME

coalition	value
12	120
13	120
23	60
123	120

one-person coalitions have value 0.
payoffs in Austrian Shillings.

Players 2 and 3 had the possibility to commit themselves to a division of $v(2,3) = 60$ and to bargain with player 1 about the division of $v(1,2,3) - v(2,3) = 60$.

No.	payoffs			commitment		exhaustive	eq.div.core	strength
	1	2	3	2	3			
188	65,00	55,00	-			+	+	+
189	50,00	70,00	-			+	-	-
190	75,00	45,00	-			+	+	+
191	70,00	50,00	-			+	+	+
192	70,00	50,00	-			+	+	+
193	60,00	60,00	-			+	+	+
194	70,00	50,00	-			+	+	+
195	60,00	60,00	-			+	+	+
196	60,00	60,00	-			+	+	+
197	30,00	50,00	40,00	40,00	20,00	+	(+)	(+)
198	65,00	55,00	-			+	+	+
199	50,00	70,00	-			+	-	-
200	60,00	60,00	-			+	+	+
201	40,00	40,00	40,00			+	-	+
202	10,00	55,00	55,00	30,00	30,00	+	(+)	(+)
203	20,00	50,00	50,00	30,00	30,00	+	(+)	(+)
204	65,00	55,00	-			+	+	+
205	35,00	60,00	25,00	50,00	10,00	+	+	(+)
206	20,00	50,00	50,00			+	-	-
207	70,00	50,00	-			+	+	+

TABLE 11: VIENNA GAME (FRASSINE-FÜRST-WINTER)

TABLE 1: MASCHLER'S 3-PERSON GAMES
TABLE 2: MASCHLER'S EXTREME 3-PERSON GAMES
TABLE 3: MASCHLER'S 4-PERSON GAMES WITH FLAT 2-PERSON COALITION
TABLE 4: MASCHLER'S 4-PERSON QUOTA GAMES
TABLE 5: MASCHLER'S SPECIAL 4-PERSON GAMES
TABLE 6: 4-PERSON GAMES OF KALISH, MILNOR, NASH AND NERING
TABLE 7: 5-AND 6-PERSON GAMES OF KALISH, MILNOR, NASH AND NERING
TABLE 8: AUNT-AND-I-GAME
TABLE 9: DEMONSTRATION GAME
TABLE 10: COMMON MARKET GAME
TABLE 11: VIENNA GAME

exhaus-tive	eq.div. core	strength	TABLES 1	2	3	4	5	6	7	8	9	10	11	All tables
+	+	+	32	29	13	14	9	16	1	9	7	2	12	144
+	+	/						4	1					5
+	(+)	+						1						1
+	+	(+)											1	1
+	(+)	/							1					1
+	(+)	(+)						1	1				3	5
regular			32	29	13	14	9	22	4	9	7	2	16	157
+	+	-		2	1			2	1					6
+	-	+	6	4		3		4		5	3		1	26
+	-	/						4						4
+	-	-								1			3	4
-	+	+	1		2									3
-	+	/												
-	-	+	2			1	1							4
-	-	/		2	1									3
-	-	-												
irregular			9	8	4	4	1	10	1	6	3	0	4	50
			41	37	17	18	10	32	5	15	10	2	20	207

non exhaustive structure: 10
not in the equal division core: 41
not conforming to order of strength: 11

TABLE 12: EVALUATION OF TABLES 1 TO 11

Discussion

As we can see from table 12, equal share analysis fits the data quite well. In this paper no attempt will be made to compare the goodness of fit with that of other theories, but on the basis of our results one may conjecture that our approach does at least as well as other solution concepts for characteristic function games.

One of the most important results of Kalish, Milnor, Nash and Nering was the fact that strategically equivalent games did not show strategically equivalent behavior. Our theory contributes to the explanation of this phenomenon. The outcomes of 14 of the 19 cases of games with $v(i) \neq 0$ for some players are in the equal division core, but only 4 of these 19 cases are in the normed equal division core (tables 6 and 7).

It would be desirable to arrive at a narrower definition of "regular" outcomes by adding some further hypotheses to the theory. In order to do this in a meaningful way many more experiments must be made. As an example of a possible fourth hypothesis we may look at the assumption that a player i, who is a dummy receives $v(i)$ in the final outcome. Unfortunately up to now none of the experimental games known to me contains a dummy.

Another hypothesis which was not included into our theory in spite of the fact that it is satisfied for many cases is a strengthening of hypothesis 3: Two players in the same coalition who are equally strong receive equal payoffs. - The reason for not making this assumption is non-empirical; for some characteristic functions it is impossible to find a regular outcome with this property. An example is the 3-person game v with

$$v(1) = v(2) = v(3) = 0,$$
$$v(1,2) = v(1,3) = v(2,3) = 100,$$
$$v(1,2,3) = 120.$$

The 3-person coalition constitutes the only exhaustive coalition structure. All players are equally strong. According to the new assumption each of the players receives 40. But this is not in the equal division core. It would be interesting to run a series of experiments on this game in order to see whether our theory is confirmed by payoff distributions such as (55, 55, 10), which are in the equal division core. It is quite possible that such experiments could refute either hypothesis 1 or hypothesis 2.
The author of this paper would not be surprised, if equal share analysis in its present form does not survive the next 200 cases of experimental games but he feels confident that the spirit of the new approach will continue to be useful in the construction of empirical theories for characteristic function games. In this respect two features of our theory are of special interest: 1. Emphasis on easy computability. 2. Emphasis on distributive norms.

1. Emphasis on easy computability:
Since the players do not perform complicated computation, the stability requirements should be easy to check. Equal share analysis meets this requirement to a higher degree than other theories.

2. Emphasis on distributive norms:
The intuitive reasoning behind our hypotheses connects individual rationality with distributive norms. A distributive norm may be described as a mode of distributive

behavior which is socially approved. Hypothesis 1 may be interpreted as a norm, which says that the players should exhaust the game, since it is wasteful not do so. Hypothesis 2 can be explained by the idea that the equal divisions are the most dangerous alternatives to any possible outcome, since they are approved by a distributive norm. Hypothesis 3 can be regarded as a modification of the equal division principle. If an unequal division is accepted, then a weaker player should not receive more than a stronger player.

Distributive norms combine with individual rationality. Since social approval enhances the stability of a proposed agreement, it is individually rational to obey them. Since it is individually rational to obey them, distributive norms can survive.

The importance of distributive norms has the consequence that the influence of individual utility functions on the behavior of the players is overshadowed by the prescriptions of norms, which do not refer to utilities, but to directly observable variables such as money payoffs.

Bibliography

Aumann, R.J., and Maschler, M., The Bargaining Set for Cooperative Games, in: Dresher, M., Shapley, L.S., and Tucker, A.W. (eds.), Advances in Game Theory, Ann. Math. Stud. 52, Princeton, N.J. 1964, pp. 443-476.

Frassine, I., Fürst, E., and Winter, H., Verhandlungsspiele, ein experimenteller Beitrag. Forschungsbericht Nr. 7 des Instituts für Höhere Studien und Wissenschaftliche Forschung Wien, Wien 1967.

Kalish, G.K., Milnor, S.W., Nash, J.F., and Nering, E.D., Some Experimental n-Person Games, in: Thrall, R.M., Coambs, C.H., and Davis, R.L. (eds.), Decision Processes, New York-London 1954, pp. 301-327.

Luce, R.D., ψ-Stability, a New Equilibrium Concept for n-Person Game Theory, in: Mathematical Models of Human Behavior, Proceedings of a Symposium Dunlap and Associates, 1955, pp. 32-44.

Luce, R.D., and Raiffa, H., Games and Decisions, John Wiley and Sons, New York 1957.

Maschler, M., The Power of a Coalition, in: Management Science, Vol. 10, 1963, pp. 8-29.

Maschler, M., Playing an n-Person Game, in: Econometric Research Program, Research Memorandum No. 73, Princeton 1965.

Nering, E.D., Coalition Bargaining in n-Person Games, in: Dresher, M., Shapley, L.S., and Tucker, A.W. (eds.), Advances in Game Theory, Ann. Math. Stud. 52, Princeton, N.J. 1964, pp. 443-476.

von Neumann, J., and Morgenstern, O., Theory of Games and Economic Behavior, Princeton N.J. 1944.

Radström, H., A Property of Stability Possessed by Certain Imputations, in: Dresher, M., Shapley, L.S., and Tucker, A.W. (eds.), Advances in Game Theory, Ann. Math. Stud. 52, Princeton, N.J. 1964, pp. 513-530.

Riker, W.H., Bargaining in a Three-Person Game, in: The American Political Science Review LXI, 3, 1967, pp. 642-656.

Selten, R., and Schuster, K.G., Psychological Variables and Coalition Forming Behavior, in: Borch, K., and Mossin, J. (eds.), Risk and Uncertainty, New York 1968, pp. 221-240.

Shapley, L.S., A Value for n-Person Games, in: Kuhn, H., and Tucker, A.W. (eds.), Contributions to the Theory of Games II, Ann. Math. Stud. 28, Princeton, N.J. 1953, pp. 307-317.

7. IS TOUGHNESS PROFITABLE?*

OTOMAR J. BARTOS**

One of the most controversial aspects of negotiation is the desirability of toughness. Should one be "soft" and make low demands because such a strategy induces the opponent to be soft as well and leads to an early and fair agreement? Or should one be "tough" and make high demands because then the opponent has to make low demands and hence such strategy leads to a high final payoff for the tough negotiator?

We shall present some experimental data bearing on this question. We shall also formulate a rather simple theory that permits us to generalize these results beyond the confines of our experimental situation. And we shall provide a qualified answer to the question whether toughness is a profitable strategy.

Procedures

The basic result concerning the profitableness of toughness can be presented with ease in a graphic form. However, in order to understand this result it is desirable to discuss first the design of the experiments from which

* The experimental data was obtained from the research conducted under the Air Force Office of Scientific Research Grant AF-AFOSR-62-314. I am also indebted to the Bureau of Sociological Research at the University of Colorado for help in preparing the paper.

** University of Colorado.

the data came, and the general procedure used to analyze them.

The Experiments

The design of the experiments has been reported with considerable detail elsewhere,[1] so it may suffice to present only their most essential features. Although the basic design of the experiments differed - some involving teams, others individuals; some comprising only two opponents, others as many as five; some allowing for free communications, others restricting it rather severely; and so on - the main ideas common to all designs can be best explained by considering a two-team experiments with unlimited communication.

The subjects were college students (mostly undergraduates from various social science departments) who volunteered to participate. Prior to coming to an experiment, each subject was assigned a role to play (e.g., the role of Mao Tse-tung at a Summitt meeting with Kennedy) and was given a dossier describing the agenda which was to serve as the basis of the experiments. Included in the dossier were some realistic arguments supporting the position the subject was supposed to uphold, thus giving the subject some notion of what to say.

The agenda was so constructed that it included a number (usually five) of realistic issues, two heads of state (such as Mao Tse-tung and Kennedy), or members of a congressional committee (composed of Democrats and Republicans) might wish to debate. For example, the agenda for a meeting between Mao Tse-tung and Kennedy might look as follows:

---

1 See Bartos (1966, 1967 and 1972).

1. Disarmament (reduction of conventional weapons).
2. Ban on nuclear testing.
3. Creation of a strong UN police force.
4. World-wide network of inspection stations. (to monitor military preparations).
5. Destruction of existing nuclear weapons.

In order to create a conflict of interests without which negotiation is unnecessary, each proposal had associated with it a pair of payoffs such as shown in Table 1. Observe that the numerical values were so chosen that they roughly corresponded to the interests of the two nations. In order to motivate the subjects to represent the interests of the two nations faithfully, these payoffs were actually amounts of money that each team would receive. Specifically, the two payoffs in row i of the table, v_i and $\not{v}_i$, represented the payoff the two teams would receive if they both agreed on proposal i.

TABLE 1

One of the Payoff Matrices Used in the Team Experiments

	Outcome	Resulting Payoff to China	Resulting Payoff to USA
	0 Disagreement	\$ 0	\$ 0
Agreement On	1 Disarmament	\$12	-\$ 9
	2 Nuclear test ban	-\$ 1	\$ 4
	3 UN Police	-\$ 2	\$ 5
	4 Inspection stations	-\$10	\$13
	5 Destruction of nuclear stockpiles	\$20	-\$17

Since it is our belief that in real life a negotiator never knows exactly the interests of his opponent, each subject knew only his own payoffs. Moreover, he was not allowed to reveal the exact size of his payoffs to his opponent, before, during or after the experimental negotiation. However, each subject knew that if a unanimous agreement was not reached, both he and his opponent's team would receive zero payoff.

In the actual experimental negotiation the subjects were allowed to agree not only on one of the several proposals on the agenda, but also on a "package deal" involving two or more proposals. The payoff from such a package deal was equal to the sum of the payoffs from the proposals included in the package. Table 2 shows the 32 possible outcomes that the game of Table 1 can have, as well as the payoff associated with each such outcome.

Before the subjects were allowed to engage in actual experimental behavior, they went through a "dry run" to gain experience. Both the training dry runs and the actual experiments had the following aspect in common:

1. Each side was represented by two subjects. (For our example, a team of two subjects represented China, another team of two subjects represented USA).
2. The subjects knew that:
   a. Each side will be allowed to make a maximum of 12 speeches.
   b. Each speech must indicate clearly what proposal or package deal the speaker advocates "at this time." Otherwise, there were no limitations of what was said (other than the prohibition on revealing own payoffs).

TABLE 2

The Possible Outcomes and Payoffs Associated with the Game Shown in Table 1

Outcome[a]	Resulting Payoff[b] to China	Resulting Payoff[b] to USA
0	0	0
1	12	- 9
2	- 1	4
3	- 2	5
4	-10	13
5	20	-17
1&2	11	- 5
1&3	10	- 4
1&4	2	4
1&5	32	-26
2&3	- 3	9
2&4	-11	17
2&5	19	-13
3&4	-12	18
3&5	18	-12
4&5	10	- 4
1&2&3	9	0
1&3&4	0	9
1&4&5	22	-13
1&2&4	1	8
1&2&5	31	-22
1&3&5	30	-21
2&3&4	-13	22
2&3&5	17	- 8
2&4&5	9	0
3&4&5	8	1
1&2&3&4	- 1	13
1&2&4&5	21	- 9
1&3&4&5	20	- 8
2&3&4&5	7	5
1&2&3&5	29	-17
1&2&3&4&5	19	- 4

[a]The possible outcomes include not only "disagreement" (outcome 0) and agreement on a single proposal (outcomes 1 to 5) but also "package deals" such as 1&2&4 (i.e., agreement on proposals 1 and 2 and 4).

[b]Payoff is in US dollars.

c. Following a sequence of 6 speeches (3 from each side), the negotiation will be interrupted and each side will be allowed to confer in privacy.
d. If no agreement is reached at the end of the twelfth round of speeches, the subjects will be permitted exactly 10 minutes in which they could reach an agreement.
e. An agreement is reached as soon as one team agrees to the proposal or package deal suggested by the opposite team.

3. The order in which the teams spoke was experimentally fixed. However, it was up to the members of each team to decide which one of the two members will represent the team during a given set of three rounds of speeches.

It is perhaps clear that in these so-called "team" experiments we tried to simulate real life negotiations as much as possible: each side was represented by a team, the teams adjourned regularily to plan their strategy, their speeches were free to communicate anything they wished, and there was some uncertainity not only about their opponent's true interests but, since they were given explicitly only the payoffs for single proposals but not for the package deals (and hence had often to estimate the value of a package deal during the actual negotiation, when to compute them exactly would have been too time-consumming), about their own interests as well.

It is obvious that we thus allowed our design to be "polluted" by numerous influences which we could not take into account by any simple theory. We did this purposely, on the grounds that a good theory should fit the data well even under such adverse conditions. However, we wished to compare the results obtained under these conditions with those that were "pure" from the experimental point of view. For this reason, we utilized two additional types of experimental design, "abstract" and "spoken."

The purer of the two was the so-called "abstract" design. In this design there were no teams (each subject represented himself only), the proposals had no real life meaning (became simply "proposal 1" or "proposal 2" and so on), and there were no package deals possible (e.g., the game might consist of 32 possible outcomes, 31 of them being distinct proposals). The name "abstract" came from the fact that the "speeches" were limited to naming the number of proposals the subject was proposing "now."

The "spoken" experiments were identical with the team experiments except that they involved individuals acting on their own rather than teams. Consequently there were no caucuses and the deadline was defined in real time (say, 10:00 p.m.) rather than as something that follows 10 minutes after the twelfth round of speeches. Both the spoken and the abstract experiments often involved more than two sides, the maximum being five.

Measures of Toughness

It is perhaps obvious from the discussion of the design that it is possible to conceptualize our negotiations as involving discrete time periods $t=1,2,3,\ldots,k$ and associate with each t a demand D_t and offer O_t. To accomplish this, we merely stipulate that each time period coincide with a negotiator's speech and decide to refer to the first-speaking negotiator as negotiator 1. It is true that negotiator 1 does not make explicit demands and offers, that he merely states which proposal he wishes to endorse. But, as is obvious from Table 2, to endorse a proposal (or a package deal) also means

to select a pair of payoffs, one for the negotiator and one for his opponent. And it is obvious that the payoff associated with the endorsed proposal(s) for the speaker is his implicit demand; the payoff associated with that very same proposal(s) for opponent j is the speaker's implicit offer to opponent j. For example, should negotiator 1 endorse at time t proposal 1 of Table 2, he is demanding 12 dollars ($D_t = 12$) and offering his opponent -9 dollars ($O_t = -9$).
To simplify our discussion, we shall limit ourselves to the case of two negotiators. It is perhaps obvious from the preceeding discussion that in that case we can distinguish the following sequence of demands and offers:

Time t	Negotiator 1		Negotiator 2	
	His demands D_t	His offers O_t	His demands $Ð_t$	His offers $Ø_t$
1	D_1	O_1	--	--
2	--	--	$Ð_2$	$Ø_2$
3	D_3	O_3	--	--
4	--	--	$Ð_4$	$Ø_4$
:	:	:	:	:
k	D_k	O_k	--	--
k+1	--	--	$Ð_{k+1}$	$Ø_{k+1}$

Observe that negotiator 1 speaks at odd-numbered times and that O_t refers to the offer made by him to his opponent. It should be added that while negotiator 1 is always - by definition - the first speaker, negotiator 2 may but need not be the last: there is nothing in the rules to say that he must be the one who agrees to the previous offer.

Now suppose it were an empirical fact that the time-paths of various demands followed a rather simple set of rules: each demand path looks more or less like another, so that the paths of different negotiators are parallel with each other, as shown in Figure 1. Then one could characterize a negotiator's toughness fully by reference to his very first demand: the higher is his first demand, the higher will be the entire path of his demands, and hence the tougher he may be said to be since he converges to a high final demand.

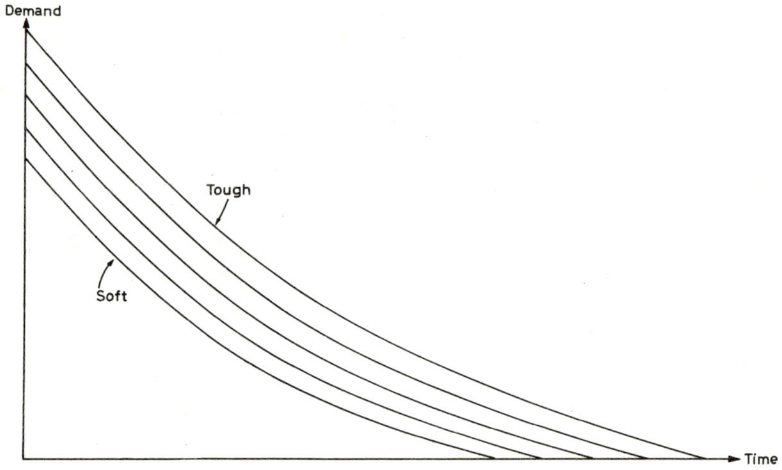

FIGURE 1. Demand Paths of Negotiators With Varying Degree of Toughness

Moreover, if the demand paths were of the kind represented in Figure 1, one could also characterize a negotiator's toughness by the mean of his demands: the higher his mean demand, the tougher he is. For example, for the first negotiator the mean demand is given by

$$(1) \quad \bar{D} = \frac{2}{k} \sum_{t=1}^{k} D_t \quad \text{for } t = 1,3,5,\ldots,k$$

To be sure, when the demand paths are parallel there is no reason to compute this measure since it gives the same results as the simple measure taking into account only the first demand. Nevertheless, we shall use $\bar{D}$ as our measure of toughness because our data only approximate the conditions outlined in Figure 1. Thus, in general, this measure implies merely that a tough negotiator tended to have high demands. Only when the demand paths are in fact parallel can we make an additional inference about the concession making: although under those conditions concessions may vary with time, for a given time they do not vary with toughness. Thus under "ideal" conditions our measure of toughness does not have the property deemed desirable by some: it does not reflect different rates of concession.

Measures of Profitableness

Although the reader may feel that the profit derived from a negotiation strategy should be conceived rather broadly to include such intangible assets as creation of good will, we shall limit ourselves to a more narrow definition. We shall assume that the subjects were motivated to maximize their payoff; hence we shall use the payoff the subjects actually received (their "final payoff") as a measure of their success: the higher the final payoff associated with a strategy, the more profitable it will be said to be.

There is a sense in which the relationship between a strategy and toughness is a foregone conclusion, particularily under the idealized conditions of Figure 1. When the demand paths are parallel, it follows in a completely tautological sense that for a given t the tough negotiator's demand is always higher than that of a soft negotiator. Hence if an agreement occurs at time t, then the tough negotiator must receive higher payoff than a soft negotiator would have. And it follows that toughness is a profitable strategy.

What prevents us from accepting that obvious conclusion is the fact that (1) there may be a relationship between toughness and the time of agreement (it may take a tough negotiator longer to reach an agreement and hence his payoff may be the same as that of a soft negotiator who reached an agreement earlier), and that (2) there may be a relationship between toughness and the fact of reaching an agreement at all (tough negotiators may deadlock the negotiation, particularily when there is a deadline). Hence we need a theory that takes these additional possibilities into account.

A Theory

The theory we shall present arose from a specific problem: we had certain findings and we wished to determine whether these results can be generalized. Let us start by considering these specific results.

Some Findings

In order to determine whether toughness was a good strategy in our experiments, we adopted a simple procedure. We divided all our subjects into five categories, depending on whether their mean demand was high or low. Technically, we accomplished this by considering separately each set of subjects who played the same role (e.g., the role of Kennedy in the experiments using the payoff matrix of Table 1). We standardized the mean demands of all subjects falling into the same set so that the mean of these standardized mean demands was zero and their standard deviation was 1. Subjects playing different roles and having different payoff thus became comparable because those with the same standardized mean demand could be said to have displayed the same degree of toughness.

Once we had the standardized mean demands, we put each subject into one of five categories:

i=1 (extreme softness): Included were the subjects whose standardized mean demands were -1.00 or less.[1]

i=2 (moderate softness): Included were the subjects whose standardized demands were between -.999... and -.3.

i=3 (average toughness): Included were the subjects with standardized means falling between -.2999... and +.2999... .

i=4 (moderate toughness): Included were the subjects whose standardized mean demands were between +.3 and +.999... .

i=5 (extreme toughness): Included were the subjects whose standardized means were +1.00 or more.

The next step was to divide the payoffs actually received by the subjects into "high" and "low." We did this by standardizing the final payoffs in the same manner as the mean demands, and called the positive (above the average) standardized payoffs "high," the rest "low." We were then able to construct the following table showing the relationship between toughness and final payoff:

---

1 In other words, a subject was put into category i=1 if his (raw) mean demand was at least one standard deviation below the (raw) grand mean demand.

		Final Payoff High	Final Payoff Low	Total Proportion	Total Number of Cases
i=1	Extremely soft	.23	.77	1.00	183
i=2	Moderately soft	.32	.68	1.00	243
i=3	Average soft	.45	.55	1.00	256
i=4	Moderately tough	.53	.47	1.00	281
i=5	Extremely tough	.54	.46	1.00	158

Figure 2 represents this relationship between toughness and proportion receiving high payoff graphically.

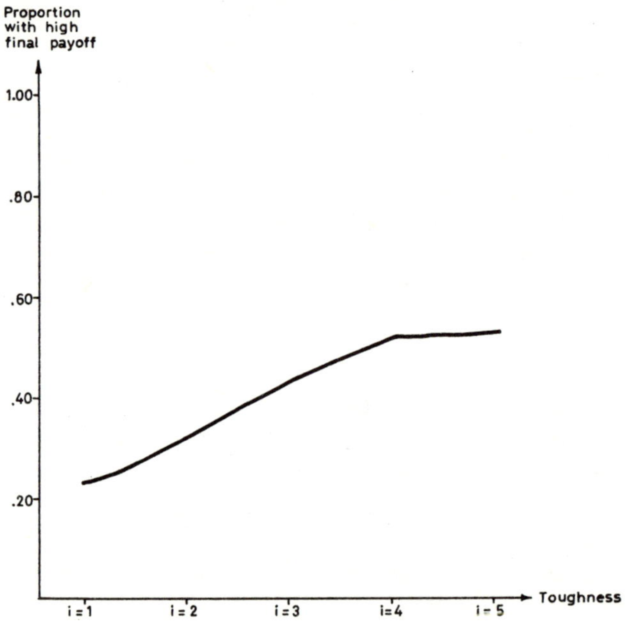

FIGURE 2. Empirical Relationship Between Toughness and Final Payoff

Inspection of Figure 2 suggests that the high final payoff was received most often by the subjects who were extremely tough. Moreover, we see that the relationship between toughness and the probability of high final payoff is monotone increasing: the tougher the subject was, the more likely he was to receive a high final payoff. Thus, **ex** post facto at least, toughness is shown by our data to be a good strategy. Although these findings are interesting, they are by themselves of little practical or theoretical interest: we must be most hesitant to generalize from our findings and recommend to any and all negotiators that they be as tough as possible. The reason for our hesitation is not so much that real life negotiations are different than those created in our experiments - although we no doubt should take this difference seriously - but rather that we understand nothing about the forces that are responsible for the result. We shall now outline a simple theory that attempts to pinpoint the most important of such forces.

Assumptions

As already indicated, two factors may work against the rather obvious conclusion that toughness is a good strategy: first, toughness may have an effect upon the opponent's toughness, either making him less or more tough; second, a present deadline may render extreme toughness likely to lead to a deadlock. We shall make use of our general finding (reported elsewhere[1]) that opponent's toughness is negatively correlated (the tougher is one, the softer is the other) to take care of the first consideration. The second consideration - the effect of a deadline - will be treated theoretically rather than empirically.

---

1 See Bartos (1973).

In order to be able to derive the results we desire, we shall simplify our problem along the lines shown in Figure 1. Actually, our assumptions will not be as strong as shown there, since we need be concerned only with the end of the negotiations. Thus we shall assume that the end-part of the negotiation (the part during which agreements occur) is characterized by parallel demand paths. In order to make our problem simple - and because of some findings permitting us to do so[1] - we shall assume that the rate of concession in the end-part is fixed so that the demand paths there are straight. Furthermore, since we chose the five categories of toughness so that their means are equally distant (the distance being one-half of a standard deviation), it seems plausible to assume that the demand paths are equally distant as well.
The final assumption to be made about the shape of the demand paths is quite natural: if there is an agreement to be reached, the demands in the end-part must be decreasing with time. We state all these assumptions formally as follows:

Assumption 1 (Demand Paths):

The demand paths of the negotiators who play the same role are, in their end-part,

a. straight,
b. parallel with each other,
c. equally distant from each other, and
d. decreasing with time.

The next assumption further simplifies our problem by implying that the demands a negotiator makes for himself and the offers that are made to him are symmetric in the sense that the change in his demand at time t is of exactly the same size as the change in the offer made to

---

1 See ibid.

him at time t+1.

Assumption 2 (Demands and Offers):

The concession made by a negotiator at time t is of the same size as the increase in offer made by his opponent at time t+1, i.e.,

$$(2) \qquad \Delta D_t = -\Delta \emptyset_{t+1}$$

There is not much one can say in support of this assumption other than it either is or is not empirically true, and that it is possible to relax it under certain conditions without altering our substantial results. Observe, however, that the above assumption does not necessarily imply that negotiators playing different roles (i.e., those who are opponents) make the same concession at time t and t+1. To see this, let us assume that the payoff function of the two opponents are negatively linear with each other, i.e.,

$$(3) \qquad v = -A\not{v}+B$$

where v is the payoff of negotiator 1, $\not{v}$ the payoff of negotiator 2. Suppose that negotiator 1 demands D_{t-2} and D_t while his opponent demands $\not{D}_{t-1}$ and $\not{D}_{t+1}$. Then we know from eq. 3 that the offers made to negotiator 1 are $\emptyset_{t-1} = -A\not{D}_{t-1}+B$ and $\emptyset_{t+1} = -A\not{D}_{t+1}+B$. Hence the change (increase) in offers made to negotiator 1 is

$$\Delta\emptyset_{t+1} = \emptyset_{t-1}-\emptyset_{t+1} = -A(\not{D}_{t-1}-\not{D}_{t+1}) = -A\Delta\not{D}_{t+1}$$

The change in negotiator 1's demand (his concession) is

$$\Delta D_t = D_{t-2}-D_t$$

Substituting into eq. 2 we get

$$\Delta D_t = -\Delta\emptyset_{t+1} = A\Delta\emptyset_{t+1}$$

Hence, unless A=1, the above assumption 2 does not imply that the opponents must be making equal concessions. It does imply, in the case of payoffs that are negatively linear, that the ratio of the concessions be the same as the slope of the linear relationship between the payoffs:

$$(4) \qquad \frac{\Delta D_t}{\Delta\emptyset_{t+1}} = A$$

The next assumption is based on the already mentioned finding that opponent's toughness is negatively correlated. We shall give this assumption specific meaning shortly, but right now we state the assumption only in general terms:

Assumption 3 (Opponent's Toughness

The higher (tougher) is the demand path chosen by the negotiator, the lower (softer) does the path chosen by his opponent tend to be.

The final assumption simply refers to the fact that all experiments we conducted - and most negotiations in real life - have a deadline by which an agreement must be reached.

Assumption 4 (Deadline):

Each negotiation has a deadline, i.e., an agreement must be reached at or before a fixed time t^*.

Reaction Matrix P

Assumption 3 specifies the main empirical basis of the theory and hence will prove crucial in deriving implications from the theory. Our discussion will be considerably simplified if we specify what it means for our experiments. We shall therefore not only spell out what assumption 3 means in general, but also what it meant specifically for the data gathered in our experiments.

To start with, observe that assumption 3 really speaks about probability $P(\bar{D}_j|D_i)$, i.e., the probability that the opponent will choose the demand path j if the negotiator chose the demand path i. In order to obtain empirical estimates of these probabilities we need only to crosstabulate the opponents with respect to the five toughness categories and compute the proportion of cases in which the opponent fell into toughness category j when the negotiator fell into category i. Although we spoke only about negotiations involving two participants, we can generalize this procedure to n participants. All we need to do is to lump all opponents of a given negotiator into one set, compute the mean of their mean demands, and determine the toughness category of this average toughness of the opponents.[1] Applying this procedure to both 2-person and n-person experiments, we get the following matrix $\hat{T}$:

$\hat{T}$ =

	$\bar{M}_1$	$\bar{M}_2$	$\bar{M}_3$	$\bar{M}_4$	$\bar{M}_5$	Number of subjects
M_1	.12	.13	.21	.31	.23	183
M_2	.11	.16	.26	.35	.12	243
M_3	.11	.21	.24	.33	.10	256
M_4	.17	.24	.31	.17	.11	281
M_5	.27	.24	.14	.19	.16	158

1 Our justification for this procedure is that the probability estimates obtained for n-person negotiations are remarkably similar to those obtained for the 2-person negotiations.

Observe that we marked T by a hat ^ to indicate its empirical base. Furthermore, note that the components of $\hat{T}$ are $P(M_j|M_i)$, i.e., the probabilities that the opponent is in toughness category M_j if the negotiator is in toughness category M_i. Finally, observe that the relationship is indeed negative: the fact that the largest entries cluster near the minor diagonal suggest that the tougher the negotiator was, the softer did his opponent tend to be.

Matrix $\hat{T}$ becomes directly useful for our theory if we make two assumptions that appear to be quite plausible:[1]

Assumption 5:

The negotiator whose mean demand fell into category M_i chose demand path D_i.

Assumption 6:

The opponent whose mean demand fell into category M_j chose offer path $\emptyset_j$.

It is perhaps obvious that whenever assumption 5 is met and eq. 3 holds, then assumption 6 follows logically and hence need not be stated as a separate assumption. In any case, given these two assumptions, we can write a reaction matrix $\hat{P}$ the labels of which are the demand and offer paths and the components of which specify the desired probabilities $P(\emptyset_j|D_i)$:

$$(5) \qquad \hat{P} = \begin{array}{c} \\ D_1 \\ D_2 \\ D_3 \\ D_4 \\ D_5 \end{array} \begin{array}{c} \begin{array}{ccccc} \emptyset_1 & \emptyset_2 & \emptyset_3 & \emptyset_4 & \emptyset_5 \end{array} \\ \begin{bmatrix} .12 & .13 & .21 & .31 & .23 \\ .11 & .16 & .26 & .35 & .12 \\ .11 & .21 & .24 & .33 & .10 \\ .17 & .24 & .31 & .17 & .11 \\ .27 & .24 & .14 & .19 & .16 \end{bmatrix} \end{array}$$

1 However, we shall have to modify them later.

Observe that $\hat{p}_{ij}$ - which we shall use instead of the cumbersome $\hat{P}(\emptyset_j|D_i)$ - refers to the probability that the opponent will choose offer path j if the negotiator choose demand path D_i. Since p_{ij} represents opponent's reaction to our negotiator's choice, we shall term P of eq. 5 the "reaction matrix" of the game.

Essence of the Theory

Our conclusion that under certain fairly restricted conditions toughness is a good strategy was said to be subject to two main qualifications: the effects of opponent's reaction and the effect of the deadline. Since matrix $\hat{P}$ describes opponent's reactions, it remains to assess the effect of the deadline.

It is quite easy to see that the interference of the deadline with the generally profitable nature of toughness comes from the fact that if the negotiators do not reach an agreement they generally receive a low payoff. It is therefore useful to partition negotiations into two sets, those that reached an agreement and those that did not. It is then easy to see that the profitableness of toughness of degree i is given by the expected payoff u_i

$$u_i = P_{Ai}v_i + (1-P_{Ai})w_i \tag{6}$$

where P_{Ai} is the probability that an agreement will be reached if our negotiator uses strategy of chosing demand path D_i, v_i is his payoff when he chooses D_i and an agreement is reached, w_i is his payoff when he chooses D_i and an agreement is not reached.

We shall use eq. 6 for determining the profitableness of toughness for certain purposes. However, we cannot use it to test the theory against our data because the results of Table 2 relate toughness to the probability of high payoff rather than to expected high payoff itself. In that case the relevant expression is:

$$(7) \quad P(u_{Hi}) = P_{Ai}P(v_{Hi}) + (1-P_{Ai})P(w_{Hi})$$

where $P(v_{Hi})$ is the probability that our negotiator's payoff will be high if he chooses path D_i and an agreement is reached, $P(w_{Hi})$ is the probability that our negotiator's payoff will be high if he chooses D_i and an agreement is not reached.

Observe that our theory deals with the following three variables:

$P_A, 1-P_A$ ... probability of agreement and disagreement;

v_i, w_i ... "conditional" payoff (payoff from agreement and disagreement)

u_i ... total (expected) payoff

We shall now turn to each of these three variables, inquiring into the implications our assumptions have for them.

Probability of Agreement

The very first implication of our assumptions is that the end part of the negotiation session looks like the grid shown in Figure 3. The reader should satisfy himself that assumptions 1 and 2 guarantee that the grid will consist of lines that are

a. straight,
b. parallel,
c. equally distant, that
d. intersect, and are
e. symmetric with respect to a horizontal axis.

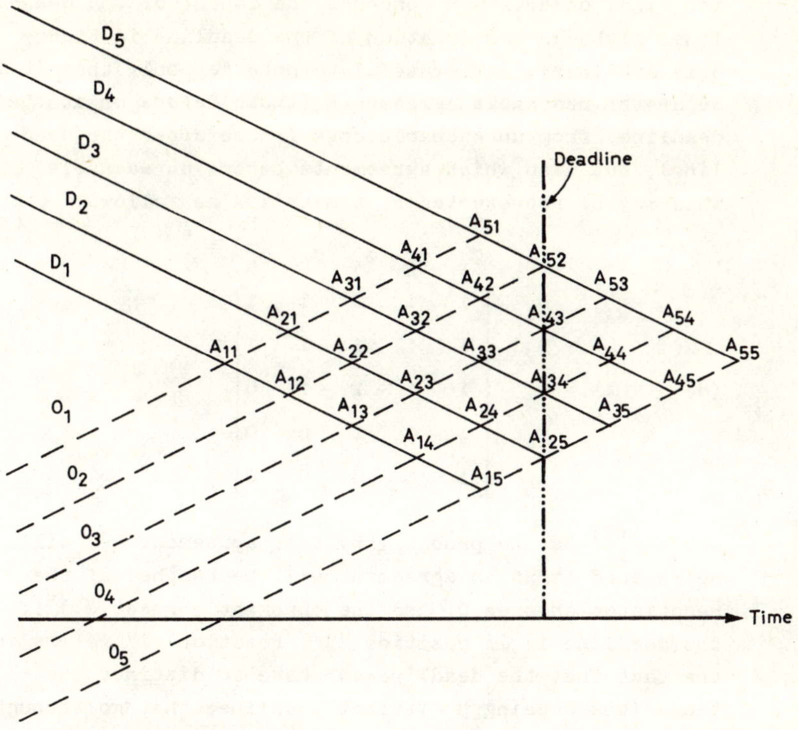

FIGURE 3. Demands and Offers in the Tail End of the Negotiation Session

The next thing to observe is that each intersect of the grid of Figure 3 corresponds to a possible agreement A_{ij}: it is the agreement reached when the negotiator chooses D_i and his opponent chooses $\emptyset_j$. That the intersects indeed correspond to an agreement is obvious when we realize that an intersect denotes the point in time when demand equals offer, which of course is a definition of an agreement.

The final observation concerns the impact of the deadline. Although the location of the deadline in Figure 3 is arbitrary, it is useful to note not only that it separates reachable agreements (those before or at the deadline) from unreachable ones (those after the deadline), but also which agreements become unreachable. This may be represented by a matrix X as follows:

$$(8) \qquad X^{(7)} \quad \begin{array}{c} \\ D_1 \\ D_2 \\ D_3 \\ D_4 \\ D_5 \end{array} \begin{array}{c} \begin{array}{ccccc} \emptyset_1 & \emptyset_2 & \emptyset_3 & \emptyset_4 & \emptyset_5 \end{array} \\ \begin{bmatrix} 1 & 1 & 1 & 1 & 1 \\ 1 & 1 & 1 & 1 & 1 \\ 1 & 1 & 1 & 1 & 0 \\ 1 & 1 & 1 & 0 & 0 \\ 1 & 1 & 0 & 0 & 0 \end{bmatrix} \end{array}.$$

where $x_{ij}^{(7)}$ is the probability that agreement A_{ij} will be reached (that an agreement will be reached if the negotiator chooses D_i and the opponent chooses $\emptyset_j$) if the deadline is in position "7". Position "7" refers to the fact that the deadline can have 10 distinct locations (there being 9 distinct deadlines that go through some points A_{ij} and one that lies to the right of A_{55}), and that Figure 3 places the deadline to the seventh position from the extreme right. The reader should satisfy himself that $X^{(d)}$ will always have zeroes below a line parallel with the minor diagonal: the outcomes that correspond to joint toughness are thus removed from the reachable set.

Of course, $x_{ij}^{(d)}$ does not specify the probability of agreement we are looking for, since it represents triple-contingent probabilities $P(A|D_i,\emptyset_j,d)$ - that is the probability of agreement when D_j, $\emptyset_j$ and location of the deadline d are all given - while we are looking for double-contingent probabilities $P(A|D_i,d)$. It is perhaps obvious that these probabilities are obtained directly from $\hat{P}$ when we substitute zeroes in exactly the same locations as in $X^{(d)}$. For d = 7 as given in Figure 3 we therefore transform P into a matrix we shall call $S^{(7)}$.

$$S^{(7)} = \begin{bmatrix} .12 & .13 & .21 & .31 & .23 \\ .11 & .16 & .26 & .35 & .12 \\ .11 & .21 & .24 & .33 & .0 \\ .17 & .24 & .31 & .0 & 0 \\ .27 & .24 & .0 & .0 & .0 \end{bmatrix}$$

and then we obtain the probabilities of agreement (when the deadline is in location d = 4) by summing each row of the above matrix:

$$P_A^{(7)} = \begin{bmatrix} 1.00 \\ 1.00 \\ .89 \\ .72 \\ .51 \end{bmatrix}$$

It is perhaps clear that the i-th component of $P_A^{(7)}$ corresponds to the probability that an agreement (any agreement) will be reached if our negotiator chooses D_i and the deadline is in location d = 7 (and, of course, when P is given by eq. 5).

To express our result in general terms we shall introduce symbol ⓧ to correspond to element-by-element multiplication. Thus, for example, A ⓧ B for two 2x2 matrices means

$$\begin{bmatrix} a_{11} & a_{12} \\ a_{21} & a_{22} \end{bmatrix} \otimes \begin{bmatrix} b_{11} & b_{12} \\ b_{21} & b_{22} \end{bmatrix} = \begin{bmatrix} a_{11}b_{11} & a_{12}b_{12} \\ a_{21}b_{21} & a_{22}b_{22} \end{bmatrix}$$

This multiplication should not be confused with the customary matrix (inner product) multiplication which will be designated by AB and will mean

$$AB = \begin{bmatrix} a_{11} & a_{12} \\ a_{21} & a_{22} \end{bmatrix} \begin{bmatrix} b_{11} & b_{12} \\ b_{21} & b_{22} \end{bmatrix}$$

$$= \begin{bmatrix} a_{11}b_{11}+a_{12}b_{21} & a_{11}b_{12}+a_{12}b_{22} \\ a_{21}b_{11}+a_{22}b_{21} & a_{21}b_{12}+a_{22}b_{22} \end{bmatrix}$$

Given this notation, we can write that

$$(9) \qquad P_A^{(d)} = (P \otimes X^{(d)})\ \underline{1'}$$

where P is the reaction matrix, $X^{(d)}$ is a matrix as illustrated in eq. 8 and 1' is a column of ones. Observe that $P \otimes X^{(d)}$ supplies zeroes for the upper right corner of P, postumultiplying by 1' provides the sums of the resulting rows.

Agreement Payoff

The second variable that appears in eqs. 6 and 7 is "conditional" payoff, i.e., the payoff the negotiator receives when there is an agreement (v) as well as the payoff he receives when an agreement is not reached (w). For reasons mentioned earlier, we shall be now interested in the probability that the conditional payoff is high $P(v_{Hi})$ and $P(w_{Hi})$ rather than in the values of the payoff itself. For reasons to become obvious later, we shall limit our attention to the "agreement payoff" v_{Hi}.

As a first step we note that our assumptions imply that the possible agreements have closely related payoff. Suppose that we denote the lowest possible payoff our negotiator can receive from an agreement by m, and the distance between any payoff and the next higher payoff by z; then we can write the matrix of the possible agreement payoffs as

$$(10) \qquad V^{(1)} = \begin{array}{c} \\ D_1 \\ D_2 \\ D_3 \\ D_4 \\ D_5 \end{array} \begin{array}{c} \begin{array}{ccccc} \emptyset_1 & \emptyset_2 & \emptyset_3 & \emptyset_4 & \emptyset_5 \end{array} \\ \begin{bmatrix} m+4z & m+3z & m+2z & m+1z & m+0z \\ m+5z & m+4z & m+3z & m+2z & m+1z \\ m+6z & m+5z & m+4z & m+3z & m+2z \\ m+7z & m+6z & m+5z & m+4z & m+3z \\ m+8z & m+7z & m+6z & m+5z & m+4z \end{bmatrix} \end{array}$$

Observe that we denoted the above matrix as $V^{(1)}$, i.e., that it represents the conditional payoffs when the deadline is in position d=1 and hence all agreements are reachable. We used that position since it permits us to display all of the possible payoffs. Inspect Figure 3 and note that m, the minimum payoff, corresponds to the payoff from agreement A_{15}, and that 2z represents the distance between any two agreements directly above each other.

We now define what "high" payoff is. This definition is in a sense arbitrary, but since we wish our results to apply to our data, we should choose a definition that is similar to that used in our empirical analysis. Recall that we termed a payoff to be high if it was above average for a given role. Now observe that the mean of the 25 components of matrix $V^{(1)}$ of eq. 10 is m+4z. Therefore, it is consistent with our empirical analysis to define the theoretical payoff in $V^{(1)}$ as being high if it is higher than m+4z. Given this definition, it is clear that the following matrix

$$
(11) \qquad Y = \begin{array}{c} \\ D_1 \\ D_2 \\ D_3 \\ D_4 \\ D_5 \end{array} \begin{array}{c} \begin{array}{ccccc} \emptyset_1 & \emptyset_2 & \emptyset_3 & \emptyset_4 & \emptyset_5 \end{array} \\ \begin{bmatrix} 0 & 0 & 0 & 0 & 0 \\ 1 & 0 & 0 & 0 & 0 \\ 1 & 1 & 0 & 0 & 0 \\ 1 & 1 & 1 & 0 & 0 \\ 1 & 1 & 1 & 1 & 0 \end{bmatrix} \end{array}
$$

tells us which agreements A_{ij} have high payoff for our negotiator if we interpret $y_{ij} = 1$ as meaning that payoff from A_{ij} is high, $y_{ij} = 0$ as meaning that payoff from A_{ij} is low.

We now recall that our problem concerns the agreement payoff associated with the choice of D_i. More precisely, we wish to determine the probability $P(v_{Hi})$ that the payoff of our negotiator will be high if he chooses demand path D_i and an agreement is reached. We start by observing in Figure 3 that if we know both the choice of D_i and of $\emptyset_j$, then the probability of agreement is either 1 or 0. For example, since A_{11} lies before the deadline, when D_1 and $\emptyset_1$ are chosen, an agreement (the agreement A_{11}) is certain to be reached; since A_{14} lies behind the deadline, a choice of D_1 and $\emptyset_4$ is certain to lead, to a disagreement; and so on. However, our problem now is different. After some thought, we conclude that we wish to know the probability that $\emptyset_j$ was chosen given that (i) D_i was chosen and (ii) that an agreement was reached. It is perhaps obvious that this probability $P(\emptyset_j | D_i, y_{ij}=1)$

can be obtained by transforming matrix $\hat{P}$ in two ways: first, we make the influence of the deadline felt by substituting zeroes in the appropriate lower-right cells; second, we transform each row of the matrix so that it sums up to one. We already performed the first step earlier for our matrix $\hat{P}$ and location of deadline d=7 and called the resulting matrix $S^{(7)}$:

$$S^{(7)} = \begin{bmatrix} .12 & .13 & .21 & .31 & .23 \\ .11 & .16 & .26 & .35 & .12 \\ .11 & .21 & .24 & .33 & .0 \\ .17 & .24 & .31 & .0 & .0 \\ .27 & .24 & .0 & .0 & .0 \end{bmatrix}$$

The second step involves "standardizing" each row of $S^{(7)}$ so that each row sums up to 1. This is accomplished by dividing each component of $S^{(7)}$ by the sum of the appropriate row of $S^{(7)}$. Performing that operation and calling the resulting matrix Q, we obtain

$$Q^{(7)} = \begin{bmatrix} .12 & .13 & .21 & .31 & .23 \\ .11 & .16 & .26 & .35 & .12 \\ .12 & .24 & .27 & .37 & .0 \\ .24 & .33 & .43 & .0 & .0 \\ .53 & .47 & .0 & .0 & .0 \end{bmatrix}$$

It is perhaps obvious that the component $q_{ij}^{(7)}$ is the probability we want: the probability that the opponent chose $\emptyset_j$ if the negotiator chose D_i and an agreement was reached.

We are now ready to compute the probability we ultimately wish to know, the probability that the final payoff will be high if D_i was chosen and an agreement was reached. Clearly, what we must do is distinguish in matrix Q agreement that give our negotiators a high payoff from those that give him low payoff. Recalling the definition of eq. 11, we obtain these probabilities by substituting zeroes in Q in the very same locations that there are zeroes in Y:

$$\begin{bmatrix} 0 & 0 & 0 & 0 & 0 \\ .11 & 0 & 0 & 0 & 0 \\ .12 & .24 & 0 & 0 & 0 \\ .24 & .33 & .43 & 0 & 0 \\ .53 & .47 & 0 & 0 & 0 \end{bmatrix}$$

Clearly, the component in the i-th row and j-th column of the above matrix denotes the probability that our negotiator's payoff will be high if he chose D_i, his opponent chose $Ø_j$ and an agreement was reached. And the sum of the i-th row of the above matrix denotes the desired probability $P(v_{Hi})$:

$$P(v_H) = \begin{bmatrix} 0 \\ .11 \\ .36 \\ 1 \\ 1 \end{bmatrix}$$

where the i-th row of the vector $P(v_H)$ corresponds to the probability that our negotiator's final payoff will be high if he chooses D_i and an agreement is reached. In short, it gives us the probabilities of high agreement payoff.

Let us now generalize our procedures. In order to obtain the vector $P(v_H)$, we first transform matrix P into S so as to indicate the influence of the deadline, i.e.,

(12) $$S^{(d)} = P \otimes X^{(d)}$$

As a next step, we convert $S^{(d)}$ into $Q^{(d)}$. We do this by standardizing each row of $S^{(d)}$, i.e., by dividing each $s_{ij}^{(d)}$ by the sum $\Sigma s_{ij}^{(d)}$ for a given i. But, as we saw, the sum of the i-th row of $S^{(d)}$ gave us the probability that an agreement will be reached if D_i is chosen, $P_{Ai}^{(d)}$; hence we may write that

(13) $$q_{ij}^{(d)} = \frac{s_{ij}^{(d)}}{P_{Ai}^{(d)}}$$

Finally, we obtain the desired probabilities $P(v_{Hi})$ by applying our definition of high payoff to Q and summing up each row, i.e.,

(14) $$P_d(v_H) = (Q^{(d)} \otimes Y)1'$$

where Q is defined by eq. 13, Y by eq. 11, and 1' is a column vector of 1's.

A word of explanation concerning the use of matrix Y is in order. It is perhaps clear that Y of eq. 11 designates high payoff only in the case when the deadline is in position d=10, i.e., when all agreements lie before the deadline. When the deadline is, say, in position d=7 (as in our example of Figure 3), then Y becomes

$$Y^{(7)} = \begin{bmatrix} 0 & 0 & 0 & 0 & 0 \\ 1 & 0 & 0 & 0 & 0 \\ 1 & 1 & 0 & 0 & 0 \\ 1 & 1 & 1 & 0 & 0 \\ 1 & 1 & 0 & 0 & 0 \end{bmatrix}$$

because in our experiments the payoff from disagreement is zero and that certainly is not a "high" payoff. How then can we use the same Y for all locations of the deadline, as we do in eq. 14? The answer is, of course, that introducing the effect of the deadline in eq. 12 makes distinguish between different Y superfluous, and hence we can use the same Y of eq. 11. To put it differently, eq. 12 guarantees that the right-upper corner of matrix $Q^{(d)} \otimes Y$ will have zeroes in the same way $Y^{(7)}$ does, and hence use of a distinct $Y^{(7)}$ is unnecessary.

Total Payoff

We are now ready to consider the payoff that is the appropriate evaluation of our negotiator's strategy, the total (expected) payoff u. We saw in eq. 7 that the probability that the total payoff will be high is given by

$$P_d(u_{Hi}) = P_{Ai}^{(d)} P_d(v_{Hi}) + (1-P_{Ai}^{(d)}) P_d(w_{Hi})$$

where P_{Ai} and $P(v_{Hi})$ are the just considered probabilities of agreement and of high agreement payoff respectively, given the choice of D_i, and $P(w_{Hi})$ is the probability of high disagreement payoff. But we just argued that in our experiments (and in real life as well) the payoff from disagreement is low, and hence $P(w_{Hi}) = 0$. Thus we can write simply that

(15) $$P_d(u_{Hi}) = P_{Ai}^{(d)} P_d(v_{Hi})$$

Since P_{Ai} can be computed from eq. 9 and $P(v_{Hi})$ from eq. 14, eq. 15 is immediately given as well. And we can turn our attention to testing our theory against the empirical data.

Empirical Plausibility of the Theory

It should be recognized that, although all of our experiments had a deadline and although this deadline was fixed in real time, the "conceptual location" of the deadline - i.e., the location referred to by our theory - could not be derived from the real-time location in a unique fashion. The reason for this is that we must view the grid of Figure 3 as being a result of the strategic adjustments occurring prior to the end segment of the negotiation. In particular, it is quite consistent with our theory to assume that the slope of the demand paths will be steeper when the deadline is early than when it is late. Hence knowing the real-time location of the deadline gives us no a priori information about the location of the deadline with respect to the grid illustrated in Figure 3, i.e., its conceptual location. Consequently, we can test our theory only by considering all ten possible locations of the deadline, attempting to determine whether any one of them generates a theoretical relationship that is similar to the empirical one given in Figure 2.

Test of the Theory

One of the advantages of having our explicit theory is that we can test not only its predictions concerning the total (expected) payoff, but also its predictions concerning the "partial" consequences of toughness, the probability of agreement and the agreement payoff. In order to determine whether our theory predicts correctly the probability of agreement P_A, we shall rely primarily on graphic methods. Using eq. 9 for every one of the ten possible $X^{(d)}$, we obtain ten different relationships between toughness i and probability of agreement P_{Ai}. Figure 4 displays these theoretical relationships through broken lines. Observe that for d=1 (when all agreements fall before the deadline), the agreement is certain to occur, and the relationship between i and P_{Ai} is a horizontal line at $P_{Ai}=1$. Similarily, when d=10 (when none of the agreements fall before the deadline), an agreement cannot occur and the relationship is a line horizontal and located at $P_{Ai}=0$.

The solid line in Figure 4 represents the empirical relationship between toughness and probability of agreement. Observe that the tough segment of the relationship (for i=3,4,5) fits the predicted relationship in that it falls between the relationships predicted for d=3 and d=4, and is roughly parallel with them. This suggests that if we assumed that the deadline was located at location d=3 with probability p and at location d=4 with probability 1-p, we would obtain a fairly good fit for that part of toughness.

For the soft part of the relationship, however (for i=1,2,3), the actual relationship appears quite different from the predicted one. Observe that all predicted relationships have nonpositive slope for all i, while the actual relationship has positive slope for i=1,2,3. In order to determine whether this tendency for the actual relationship to have positive slope for i=1,2,3 is significantly different from the nonpositive relationship predicted by our theory, consider the following table:

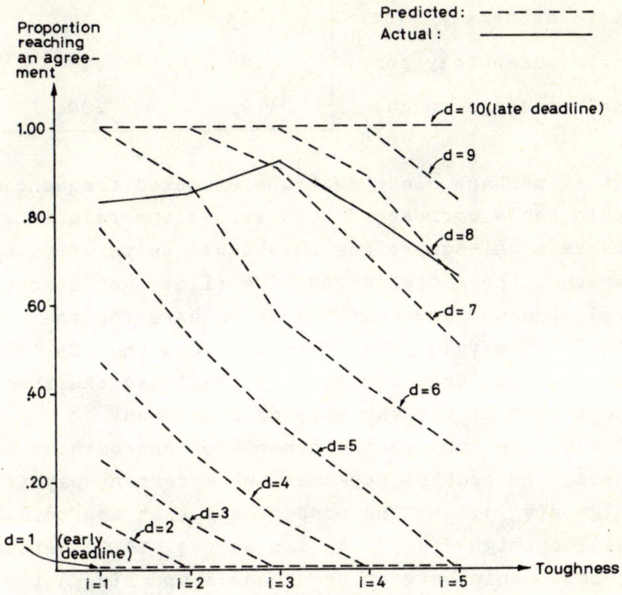

FIGURE 4. Relationship Between Toughness and Probability of Agreement

	Proportion of Experiments Reaching an Agreement	Failing to reach an Agreement	Total
i=1 (extremely soft)	.83	.17	1.00 (183)
i=2 (moderately soft)	.85	.15	1.00 (243)
i=3 (average tough)	.91	.09	1.00 (256)

It is perhaps clear that the expected frequencies for this table correspond to a zero-slope relationship, and hence a chi-square for this table helps us to determine whether the slope is positive (i.e., not zero or negative). And we find that the chi-square for the above table is 7.59, a value significant beyond the .05 level. Hence we conclude that our data contradicted the theory for the soft part of the variable of toughness.

Let us now turn to the other two consequences of toughness, the probability that the agreement payoff will be high $P(v_{Hi})$, and the probability that the total payoff will be high $P(u_{Hi})$. We can use eq. 14 to determine the relationship between toughness i and $P(v_{Hi})$ for every one of the ten possible locations of the deadline. Figure 5 again depicts these predicted relations through broken lines, the actually observed relationship through a solid line. It should be observed that for the early locations of the deadline the relationship is not defined for all values of i, because then high toughness always leads to an agreement that lies behind the deadline and hence there are no agreements possible. But the most important fact for our purposes is that the slope of the actual relationship is lower than the slope of any one of the predicted relationships. Thus we again find here a discrepancy between the predictions generated by our theory and the findings.

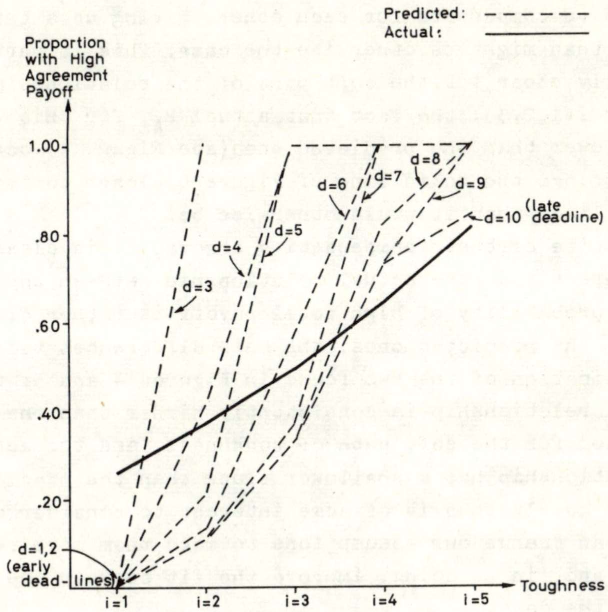

FIGURE 5. Relationship Between Toughness and Probability of High Agreement Payoff

Given the fact that eq. 15 shows $P(u_{Hi})$ to be a simple product of P_{Ai} and $P(v_{Hi})$, and that we found both partial predictions defective, it is hardly surprising to find our predictions of $P(u_{Hi})$ defective as well. Figure 6 shows both the predicted relationships based on eq. 15 (broken lines) and the actual relationship obtained from our experiments (solid line). Observe, however, that the defects of the two partial predictions tend to compensate for each other, giving us a better fit than might be otherwise the case. This is particularily clear for the soft part of the relationship (for i=1,2,3): the fact that actual P_{Ai} for this range is lower than the predicted one (see Figure 4) actually brings the solid line of Figure 6 closer to the broken lines than it would otherwise be.

In spite of these compensating errors, it is clear from Figure 6 that the actual relationship between toughness and probability of high total payoff is rather different from the predicted ones, the main differences being a combination of the two found in Figures 4 and 5: the actual relationship is consistently higher than the predicted for the soft path of toughness, and the actual relationship has a shallower slope than the predicted ones do. It thus is of some interest to consider whether we can change our assumptions to make them more realistic and, in so doing, improve the fit between the theory and the data.

Theory Reconsidered

The two assumptions we had to make to estimate matrix P were assumptions 5 and 6 stating that a subject whose mean demand fell into category M_i also chose a demand path D_1 and also chose offer path O_j such that j=i. But these assumptions - which concern more the interpretation of our data than the theory itself - could be false:

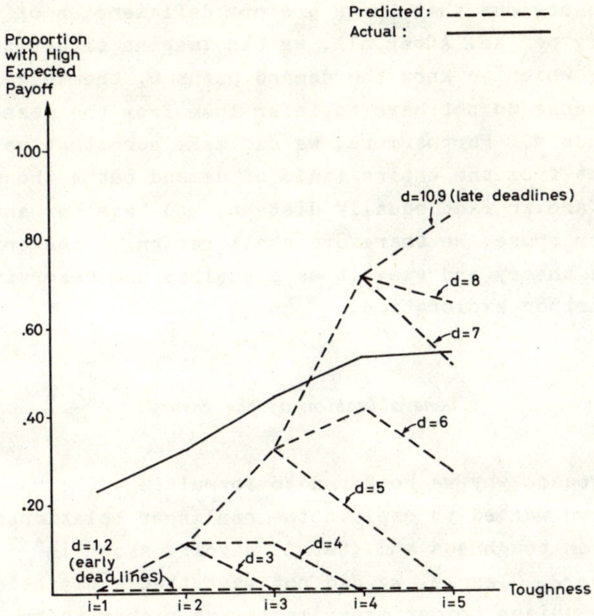

FIGURE 6. Relationship Between Toughness and Probability of High Expected (Total) Payoff

it could be that knowing the mean demand gives us only an approximate knowledge of which demand and offer path was chosen. It turns out that when we relax assumptions

5 and 6 so that knowing demand category k gives us only a stochastic knowledge of the categories i and j, much of the discrepancy between our data and prediction disappears. Further improvement is obtained if we assume that the demand paths are not equally distant.[1]

It is obvious that these are not deficiencies of the theory per se. After all, we can imagine situations under which we know the demand paths D_i themselves and hence do not have to infer them from the mean demands M_i. Furthermore, we can make sure that we select from the entire field of demand paths those that are in fact equally distant, and base our analysis on those. We therefore shall return to the original theory and view it as plausible and deserving of further exploration.

Generalization of the Theory

The reason why we bothered to formulate a theory was that we wanted to explain the nonlinear relationship between toughness and (total) payoff, shown in Figure 2. Clearly, we did not want that explanation to be unique to our experiments but rather to be general, one which holds for most negotiations. Have we reached our objective?

Partial Consequences

Let us start by considering a specific location of the deadline, say at d=4. We know from eq. 9 that the probability of agreement is - when there are five demand paths to chose from -

---

1 For the relevant data, see Bartos (1973), Appendix H.

$$P_{Ai}^{(4)}=(P \otimes X^{(4)})1'=\begin{bmatrix} p_{11} & p_{12} & p_{13} & p_{14} & p_{15} \\ p_{21} & p_{22} & p_{23} & p_{24} & p_{25} \\ p_{31} & p_{32} & p_{33} & p_{34} & 0 \\ p_{41} & p_{42} & p_{43} & 0 & 0 \\ p_{51} & p_{52} & 0 & 0 & 0 \end{bmatrix}\begin{bmatrix} 1 \\ 1 \\ 1 \\ 1 \\ 1 \end{bmatrix}=\begin{bmatrix} 1 \\ 1 \\ p_{31}+p_{32}+p_{33}+p_{34} \\ p_{41}+p_{42}+p_{43} \\ p_{51}+p_{52} \end{bmatrix}$$

Since P_{A1} stands for probability of agreement when the negotiator is as tough as possible, the above results suggest that soft strategies lead to a higher probability of agreement ($P_{A1}=P_{A2}=1$) than tough strategies ($P_{A3}, P_{A4}, P_{A5} \leq 1$). The question we must ask is this: is it reasonable to assume that P will generally be of such kind that the probability of agreement P_{Ai} decreases as toughness i is increased?

It is perhaps not too difficult to see that, given our theory, this negative relationship between toughness and probability of agreement will hold true whenever the sums of the rows in $P \otimes X^{(d)}$ decrease as we move down the rows (as we increase i). Thus we are asking whether it is reasonable to assume that

$$(16) \qquad \sum_{j=1}^{s+1} p_{ij}^{(d)} \geq \sum_{j=1}^{s} p_{i+1,j}^{(d)} \qquad \text{for all } i,d,s$$

where s is a number between 0 and 4 and d=1,2,...,10.

Observe that - as we mentioned earlier - the matrix $P \otimes X^{(d)}$ will have always zeroes below the boundary that is parallel with the minor diagonal, so that as we compute the sums of row i we are progressively adding fewer and fewer nonzero components p_{ij} (as we go down the rows, i.e., as i increases). It is customary to assume that the relationship between any two variables is bivariate normal; it seems therefore reasonable to assume that the more p_{ij}'s are involved in the summing operation, the larger will be the resulting sum. Hence it seems quite plausible to expect that reaction matrices P will have the property required in eq. 18. And hence it seems safe to generalize that in most negotiations toughness is "partially counter-productive" in that tougher negotiators reach an agreement less frequently than softer negotiators.

Let us now turn to the second "partial" consequence of toughness, the probability that high payoff is received in the case an agreement is reached $P(v_{Hi})$. Let us start by considering the case when all agreements can be reached, i.e., when the deadline is in position d=1. In that case eq. 14 becomes

$$P_1(v_H) = (Q^{(1)} \otimes Y)1' = \begin{bmatrix} 0 & 0 & 0 & 0 & 0 \\ q_{21} & 0 & 0 & 0 & 0 \\ q_{31} & q_{32} & 0 & 0 & 0 \\ q_{41} & q_{42} & q_{43} & 0 & 0 \\ q_{51} & q_{52} & q_{53} & q_{54} & 0 \end{bmatrix} \begin{bmatrix} 1 \\ 1 \\ 1 \\ 1 \\ 1 \end{bmatrix}$$

But, since we consider the case when all agreements are possible, Q=P and we may write that

$$P_1(v_H) = \begin{bmatrix} 0 & 0 & 0 & 0 & 0 \\ p_{21} & 0 & 0 & 0 & 0 \\ p_{31} & p_{32} & 0 & 0 & 0 \\ p_{41} & p_{42} & p_{43} & 0 & 0 \\ p_{51} & p_{52} & p_{53} & p_{54} & 0 \end{bmatrix} \begin{bmatrix} 1 \\ 1 \\ 1 \\ 1 \\ 1 \end{bmatrix}$$

And we see that the probability that the agreement payoff will be high increases as toughness increases (that is, that the sum of the i-th row in the above matrix increases as i increases) if it holds that

$$(17) \qquad \sum_{j=1}^{s} p_{ij} \leq \sum_{j=1}^{s+1} p_{i+1,j} \qquad \text{for all } i,d,s$$

where s again is integer between 0 and 4.
We can use exactly the same argument as we used in connection with condition of eq. 16, except now it applies in a reverse way. What is happening now is that we are adding progressively more p_{ij}'s as we move down the rows to compute the sums. And, given the type of data one has come to expect in the behavioral sciences - data sets in which variables are paired in bivariate normal fashion -, one can expect the condition of eq. 17 to hold in most cases.
But we have not shown as yet that toughness and agreement payoff are positively related. To do so, we must consider all the ten possible locations of the deadline. But it is not difficult to see that the effect of shifting the deadline to an earlier position is to make certain that extreme toughness leads to high payoff! To illustrate, consider, say the location d=4. Then

$$P_4(v_H) = \begin{bmatrix} 0 & 0 & 0 & 0 & 0 \\ q_{21} & 0 & 0 & 0 & 0 \\ q_{31} & q_{32} & 0 & 0 & 0 \\ q_{41} & q_{42} & q_{43} & 0 & 0 \\ q_{51} & q_{52} & 0 & 0 & 0 \end{bmatrix} \begin{bmatrix} 1 \\ 1 \\ 1 \\ 1 \\ 1 \end{bmatrix}$$

We know that, by definition, the sum of q_{ij} up to the "deadline boundary" (i.e., the boundary that is parallel to the minor diagonal) always sum up to unity. Hence we see immediately that $q_{51}+q_{52}=q_{41}+q_{42}+q_{43}=1$, that is, extreme toughness is now certain to lead to high agreement payoff.

It is perhaps not difficult to see what the conclusion is: if both eq. 16 and 17 are satified, then toughness makes high agreement payoff likely. Since we have argued that both assumptions are usually met, it follows that in most negotiations toughness is "partially productive" in the sense that the tougher negotiators are more likely to receive high agreement payoff than soft negotiators.

Thus we reach a conclusion that seems to be quite in agreement with our intuition: toughness has both "good" and "bad" consequences. Its good consequence is that it tends to lead to high payoff when an agreement is reached; its bad consequence that it tends to decrease the probability that an agreement will be reached. Since the total consequence of toughness has been shown to be a simple function of these two partial consequences - the two partial consequences being linked by simple multiplicative relationship shown in eq. 15 - it follows that we must expect the total profit derived from toughness to be of curvilinear in nature, forming an upwardly concave function: at the extreme softness side of the variable, are increase in profit resulting from the increase in toughness is largest, but this increment decreases as we consider tougher and tougher choices. Thus we have come to identify a version of diminishing returns from toughness.

Profit Derived from Toughness

We now come to consider what generalizations can be stated about the "total" consequence of toughness, that is, the overall profit that is derived from it. We have shown that the probability that the total payoff will be high is

$$P_d(u_{Hi}) = P_{Ai}^{(d)} P_d(v_{Hi})$$

For, say, d=4, this becomes

$$P_4(u_{Hi}) = \left\{ \begin{bmatrix} p_{11} & p_{12} & p_{13} & p_{14} & p_{15} \\ p_{21} & p_{22} & p_{23} & p_{24} & p_{25} \\ p_{31} & p_{32} & p_{33} & p_{34} & 0 \\ p_{41} & p_{42} & p_{43} & 0 & 0 \\ p_{51} & p_{52} & 0 & 0 & 0 \end{bmatrix} \begin{bmatrix} 1 \\ 1 \\ 1 \\ 1 \\ 1 \end{bmatrix} \right\} \otimes \left\{ \begin{bmatrix} 0 & 0 & 0 & 0 & 0 \\ q_{21} & 0 & 0 & 0 & 0 \\ q_{31} & q_{32} & 0 & 0 & 0 \\ q_{41} & q_{42} & q_{43} & 0 & 0 \\ q_{51} & q_{52} & 0 & 0 & 0 \end{bmatrix} \begin{bmatrix} 1 \\ 1 \\ 1 \\ 1 \\ 1 \end{bmatrix} \right\}$$

But we recall how matrix $Q^{(d)}$ was constructed: it is matrix $P^{(d)}$ transformed so that each of its rows sums up to 1. Hence, for example, the sum of the last row of $Q^{(4)}$ is $q_{51}+q_{52}=(p_{51}+p_{52})/(p_{51}+p_{52})$. And it is obvious that we may compute $P_4(u_{Hi})$ directly from matrix P, by converting it into a new matrix in which both the deadline boundary and the high payoff boundary are effective:

$$P_4(u_{Hi}) = (P^{(4)} \otimes X^{(4)} \otimes Y)1' = \begin{bmatrix} 0 & 0 & 0 & 0 & 0 \\ p_{21} & 0 & 0 & 0 & 0 \\ p_{31} & p_{32} & 0 & 0 & 0 \\ p_{41} & p_{42} & p_{43} & 0 & 0 \\ p_{51} & p_{52} & 0 & 0 & 0 \end{bmatrix} \begin{bmatrix} 1 \\ 1 \\ 1 \\ 1 \\ 1 \end{bmatrix}$$

In general, we may define the probability that the total payoff will be high simply as

$$P_d(u_{Hi}) = (P^{(d)} \otimes X^{(d)} \otimes Y)1' \tag{18}$$

If conditions of eqs. 16 and 17 hold - and we argued that they will in most cases -, then it follows that the relationship between toughness and the probability of high payoff will in most cases be curvilinear: increasing at first (as we move down the rows of $P \otimes X \otimes Y$, the influence of Y is felt at first), then decreasing (as we continue to move down the rows, influence of X becomes dominant). Since matrix Y is constant in all cases, the slope of the function will always be positive at first (for the soft part of the toughness variable); since $X^{(d)}$ varies with the deadline, it follows that the point at which the slope of the function becomes negative depends on the location of the deadline: the earlier the deadline, the less likely it is that extreme toughness will be profitable.

So far, we have viewed total payoff as a dichotomized variable, high and low. We did this because our data by necessity were of this kind, and we needed to test our theory against those data. At this point, however, we may abandon this restriction and inquire about the relationship between toughness and total payoff itself. It is obvious from our discussion that the total payoff we are referring to is really expected payoff, i.e., that

$$u_i^{(d)} = \sum_{j=1}^{5} p_{ij} w_{ij}^{(d)}$$

where p_{ij} is the component of matrix P, and $w_{ij}^{(d)}$ is the matrix of payoffs our negotiator will receive if he uses D_i, his opponent uses $\emptyset_j$, and the deadline is in position d. Thus, for example, for d=4 we get that

$$W^{(d)} = \begin{bmatrix} m+4z & m+3z & m+2z & m+z & m \\ m+5z & m+4z & m+3z & m+2z & m+2 \\ m+6z & m+5z & m\_4z & m+3z & 0 \\ m+7z & m+6z & m+5z & 0 & 0 \\ m+8z & m+7z & 0 & 0 & 0 \end{bmatrix}$$

It is perhaps obvious that $W^{(d)}$ is related to $V^{(1)}$ in eq. 10 so that $W^{(d)}=V^{(1)} \otimes X^{(d)}$. Hence we can write total (expected) payoff as

$$(19) \qquad u_i^{(d)} = (V^{(1)} \otimes X^{(d)} \otimes P)1'$$

For d=4 we may therefore write

$$u^{(4)} = \begin{bmatrix} p_{11}(m+4z) & p_{12}(m+3z) & p_{13}(m+2z) & p_{14}(m+2) & p_{15}m \\ p_{21}(m+5z) & p_{22}(m+4z) & p_{23}(m+3z) & p_{24}(m+2z) & p_{25}(m+z) \\ p_{31}(m+6z) & p_{32}(m+5z) & p_{33}(m+4z) & p_{34}(m+3z) & 0 \\ p_{41}(m+7z) & p_{42}(m+6z) & p_{43}(m+5z) & 0 & 0 \\ p_{51}(m+8z) & p_{52}(m+7z) & 0 & 0 & 0 \end{bmatrix} \begin{bmatrix} 1 \\ 1 \\ 1 \\ 1 \\ 1 \end{bmatrix}$$

Observe that the sums of the rows will be

$$u_1^{(4)}=m(p_{11}+p_{12}+\ldots+p_{15}) + z(4p_{11}+3p_{12}+\ldots+p_{14}+0)$$

$$u_2^{(4)}=m(p_{21}+p_{22}+\ldots+p_{25}) + z(5p_{21}+p_{22}+\ldots 2p_{25})$$

But the first term always equals mP_{Ai}; hence we may write that,in general, $u_i^{(d)}$ will be of the form

$$(20) \qquad u_i^{(d)} = mP_{Ai}^{(d)} + z \sum_{j=1}^{5} c_{ij}p_{ij}x_{ij}^{(d)}$$

where c_{ij} are the integers appearing in eq. 10, i.e.,

$$C = \begin{bmatrix} 4 & 3 & 2 & 1 & 0 \\ 5 & 4 & 3 & 2 & 1 \\ 6 & 5 & 4 & 3 & 2 \\ 7 & 6 & 5 & 4 & 2 \\ 8 & 7 & 6 & 5 & 4 \end{bmatrix}$$

and $x_{ij}^{(d)}$ is the component of $X^{(d)}$ illustrated in eq. 8. What does eq. 20 imply about the relationship between toughness and total payoff? Observe that the first term $mP_{Ai}^{(d)}$ will decrease as toughness i increases, since we have shown that $P_{Ai}^{(d)}$ under normal conditions will decrease as toughness increases. The second term $\Sigma c_{ij}p_{ij}x_{ij}^{(d)}$ is harder to characterize in general. However, observe that when we omit p_{ij} from that term, we obtain a curvilinear relationship between toughness and the remaining expression $\Sigma c_{ij}x_{ij}^{(d)}$. For example, for d=4 we may write this remainder as

$$(C \otimes X^{(4)})1' = \begin{bmatrix} 4 & 3 & 2 & 1 & 0 \\ 5 & 4 & 3 & 2 & 1 \\ 6 & 5 & 4 & 3 & 0 \\ 7 & 6 & 5 & 0 & 0 \\ 8 & 4 & 0 & 0 & 0 \end{bmatrix} \begin{bmatrix} 1 \\ 1 \\ 1 \\ 1 \\ 1 \end{bmatrix} = \begin{bmatrix} 10 \\ 15 \\ 18 \\ 18 \\ 15 \end{bmatrix}$$

Of interest is the fact that the sum increases for the soft part of the toughness variable (up to the point where the deadline is felt, for i=1,2,3 when d=4). But observe that when the reaction matrix P displays a negative relationship between opponents' toughness (as it does for our data), the bivariate normal assumption means that the largest p_{ij} will be on the minor diagonal of P, decreasing gradually in both directions. This in turn means that, up to the point where the deadline is felt, the value of the second term in eq. 22 must increase as we move from extreme softness i=1 to tougher stance i=2,3. Thus we see that for the soft part of the toughness variable eq. 22 captures two contradictory tendencies: as we consider progressively tougher negotiators, the value of the first term decreases while the value of the second term increases.

This being the case, let us observe that the resolution of these two opposite tendencies depends on the two constants characterizing $V^{(1)}$ of eq. 8, that is, constants m and z: the larger is m relative to z, the more influential the first term of eq. 20 becomes and the more likely it is that toughness is a "bad" strategy. But what are m and z? We recall that m is the minimum payoff that our negotiator can receive (the distance of A_{15} from the horizontal axis in Figure 3), while z is the (vertical) distance between the demand paths. Thus our conclusion is that toughness is most likely to be a thoroughly unprofitable strategy (that is, the slope of the relationship between u_i and toughness is likely to be negative for all i) if:

1. the minimum payoff is large (m is large)
2. the demand paths are closely spaced (z is small).

If, on the other hand the minimum payoff is close to zero and the demand paths are widely spaced, then toughness is profitable up to the point where the effect of the deadline is felt.

One more observation is in order. Up to this point we assumed that all agreements A_{ij} lie above the horizontal axis, i.e., that the feasible payoffs are not negative. What happens if some of these payoffs are in fact negative? Consider the case when d=4 and A_{15},A_{24} and A_{25} lie below the horizontal axis. Then it follows that

$$(C \otimes X^{(4)})1' = \begin{bmatrix} 4 & 3 & 2 & 0 & 0 \\ 5 & 4 & 3 & 2 & 0 \\ 6 & 5 & 4 & 3 & 0 \\ 7 & 6 & 5 & 0 & 0 \\ 8 & 7 & 0 & 0 & 0 \end{bmatrix} \begin{bmatrix} 1 \\ 1 \\ 1 \\ 1 \\ 1 \end{bmatrix} = \begin{bmatrix} 9 \\ 14 \\ 18 \\ 18 \\ 15 \end{bmatrix}$$

This is to say, the increase in total payoff associated with increase in toughness (for i=1,2,3) is even sharper than it was when all payoffs were nonnegative.

Accomplishments and Problems

It is worthwhile to pause for a moment to take a fresh look at the results of this paper. What contribution does it make to our understanding of negotiation? What are some ambiguities that need further exploration?

Choice of an Optimal Strategy

We set up our problem in such a way that the choice of the demand path D_i may be viewed as a strategic choice. It is therefore natural to inquire what prescription, if any, do our results offer to a negotiator about what to do at the negotiating table. What demand path should he choose? Should he be very tough, very soft, or should he choose a stance that falls somewhere between these two extremes?

It is perhaps clear that our theory is only quasi-normative, because it permits us to prescribe the optimal strategy only if we view the game as being assymetric, as a "game against Nature",[1] in which "our" negotiator is free to make a choice of the optimal strategy, but his opponent is not, since his reactions are governed by the reaction matrix P. To put it differently, if we can imagine that the results of this paper are a well-kept secret, one which is revealed to only one side in every negotiation session, then for the informed party we can give a prescription. And the prescription is of the following kind: using the procedure we outlined in this paper, compute $u_i^{(d)}$ for all possible i, and use D_i for which $u_i^{(d)}$ is largest.

In addition to being quasi-normative, our theory is descriptive. It tells us that, given a reaction matrix P and deadline in location d, the negotiator who "happened" to choose demand path D_i can expect to receive total payoff u_i. But obviously, our theory is not what many would like it to be, it is not (purely) normative, since it does not tell us what both negotiators should do. That our theory is not normative in the symmetric sense becomes obvious when we note that it permits us to select one demand path as being quasi-optimal. If we made this advice symmetric and applicable to both opponents, then obviously the rational choice would be for both to choose that demand path D_i. Which means that the opponent would be choosing certain offer path $\emptyset_j$ with probability 1, all the rest with probability 0. Which, in turn would mean that our reaction matrix P is no longer applicable and that fact would destroy the optimal status of the choices we recommended.

We have argued elsewhere that this, in our opinion, is the dilemma that confronts any researcher who wishes to apply empirical data to game-theoretical models: such an application prevents him from viewing his model as

---

1 For a discussion of such games see Luce and Raiffa (1950).

normative in the game-theoretical sense.[1] It is not so much that this dilemma is unresolveable, but rather that any resolution is far from being fully satisfactory. Our suggestion that we view negotiation as an assymetric game against Nature is faulty because to assume such assymetry is usually empirically wrong (since both sides usually have access to papers such as ours) as well as theoretically suspect. The other possible answer is to search for a symmetric game for which the reaction matrix P is a solution so that the recommended behavior is one which in effect reproduces the reaction matrix P.[2] The shortcoming of this approach is that it equates what "is" with what "should be." It presupposes that the subjects in fact are rational and it serves to provide a theoretical underpinning for this presumed rationality. In so doing, it abandons one of the most important roles a normative model can play: that of a corrective device, through which current practice is changed to a better one.

Future Work

Depending on one's preferences, one can use the work presented here as a point of departure in several ways. On one hand, one can view the assymetry inherent in our approach as by far the most disturbing aspect of the theory, and follow the alternative of showing that the actual behavior is in fact optimal. On the other hand, one may wish to preserve the corrective potential of the theory without abandoning its empirical basis, and pursue our formulations further. To those willing to pursue in the latter approach, several points are of interest.

---

1 See Bartos (1967), pp. 301-303.

2 I am indebted to Professor Selten for suggesting that it might be possible to define a game with incomplete information, the optimal strategies of which would reproduce matrix P.

In the first place, it remains to establish more clearly than was possible in this paper the meaning of the "location of the deadline." It is perhaps obvious from our discussion that the real-time location of the deadline bears only remote connection with the conceptual location our theory refers to. In fact, it is quite possible that the conceptual location is fixed for all negotiations, somewhere where it seems to occur in our experiments, near position d=4. If this were found to be true, than we might be able to derive much stronger conclusions about the consequences of toughness, since the shape of the relationship between toughness and total payoff would be more determined: the location of the deadline determines the turning point at which toughness stops being profitable.

The possibility that the conceptual location of the deadline may be viewed as fixed although the real-time deadline changes arises from the fact that our theory allows us to assume that the early part of the negotiation session involves a struggle whereby both negotiators adjust their concession rates not only to each other, but also to the deadline. Thus the grid of Figure 3 which presumably characterizes the end of the session may represent an equilibrium situation in which all these conflicting pressures have been resolved. Specifically, it may represent demand paths the slope of which are so chosen that the deadline falls in a "reasonable" position, say near location d=4.

Given the possibility that the grid may represent a standard resolution of highly diversified conflicts of interests, it is of some interest to inquire (1) empirically whether our theory possesses elements of stability that would enable it to indicate what the standard resolution is and (2) theoretically what changes in the assumptions are irrelevant because they do not alter our main conclusions.

With respect to the first question, it is of some interest to report that the reaction matrix $\hat{P}$ (or, more exactly, the matrix $\hat{T}$ relating toughness of the two opponents) is remarkably similar whether we compute it from the team experiments (which were short and involved two teams pitted against each other) or from abstract and spoken experiments (which tended to be much longer and usually involved several individual opponents). With respect to the second question, it can be shown that neither the slope of the demand paths nor their shape matters (they need not be straight), as long as their vertical distance remains constant for all t in the final segment and for all paths, and as long as the demand paths and the offer paths are symmetrical with respect to a horizontal axis: our conclusions about the relationship between toughness and probability of agreement, of high agreement payoff and of high total payoff remain the same. Thus there are indications that the conclusions based on our theory are of considerable generality. However, more extensive theoretical and empirical work is required before this claim is validated.

Bibliography

Bartos, O.J., "Concession-Making in Experimental Negotiations," in Berger et al. (eds), Sociological Theories in Progress, Vol. 1, Boston: Houghton Mifflin, 1966.

---, Simple Models of Group Behavior, New York: Columbia University Press, 1967.

---, Process and Outcome of Negotiations, New York: Columbia University Press, 1973 (in press).

Raiffa, H., and R.D. Luce, Games and Decisions, New York: Wiley, 1958.

8. A UTILITY-BASED THEORY OF DECISION MAKING

RICHARD OFSHE AND LYNNE ROBERTS*

This paper reviews the progress of a research program directed towards the goal of development of a general theory of decision making. The theory is based on axioms of maximization of expected utility and proposes a formal model which permits the prediction of choice behavior in situations in which individuals assign utilities to both monetary and non-monetary commodities. The model yields predictions for the precise choice distribution individuals should adopt if it is true that they are acting to maximize expected utility. The model is also generalized to permit predictions for the behavior of n-person interaction systems through combination of predictions for the behaviors of the participants in the interaction. The theory is tested in the context of the Humphreys' light-guessing experiment, the coalition game, and the prisoner's dilemma game.

---

* University of California at Berkeley.

1. Introduction

The generality of a theory is typically calculated in terms of the number and importance of the phenomena that can be explained when its axioms are coordinated to variables operating in concrete situations, and by the number of "middle-range" theories that can be treated as its special cases. Given these criteria, it is obvious that a viable theory of decision making would rank as a highly general formulation and would therefore provide a powerful explanatory device for the analysis of human behavior. Recognition of the importance of the phenomenon as a problem for investigation is reflected by the fact that a substantial proportion of the energy expended by social and behavioral scientists can be considered to be either clearly directed at, or can be organized in terms of, attempts to create an explanation of decision making. The amount of attention the problem receives is clearly commensurate with its scientific status.

That a theory of human decision making is essential to the development of a powerful social science is illustrated by consideration of the work of Von Neumann and Morgenstern in their Theory of Games and Economic Behavior (1944). Their work addressed the problem of finding "an exact description of the endeavor of the individual to obtain a maximum of utility, or, in the case of the entrepreneur, a maximum of profit from his alternative choices" (p.1). Their theory united previously unrelated aspects of mathematics and economics and proposed an elegant theory for a major facet of human behavior. There is no question that Von Neumann and Morgenstern's contribution to the theoretical literature was of considerable importance. As Luce and Raiffa have summarized,

> The achievement of Von Neumann and Morgenstern is remarkable: In the first major publication on the subject, they formulated a clear abstraction from the relatively vague social sciences, having both considerable breadth and mathematical depth, and they developed an elaborate and subtle superstructure with masterful scope. (Luce and Raiffa, 1965, p.11)

Luce and Raiffa also note that:

> ...we have the historical fact that many scientists have become disillusioned with game theory. Initially there was a naive bandwagon feeling that game theory solved innumerable problems of sociology and economics, or that it made their solution a practical matter of a few years' work (p.10).

The disenchantment with game theory is not accounted for by the fact that its mathematical structure has proven inconsistent. The problem is that it simply does not predict the behavior of individuals in situations in which their decision making should be explained by the theory. There are at least three ways in which to account for the failure of the theory to predict behavior. The theory's axioms may lead to incorrect predictions, it may be an insufficient explanation and hence yield incorrect predictions, or the tests to which it was subjected may not have been conducted under appropriate conditions for evaluation of the theory. The failure of game theory to predict decision making (and therefore to predict behavior) is held to be accounted for by a combination of the latter two alternatives.

Von Neumann and Morgenstern constructed their theory to predict decision making in situations in which it is assumed "that the aim of all participants in the economic system, consumers as well as entrepreneurs, is money, or equivalently a single monetary commodity" (p.8). Given their problem, constructing a mathematical theory that yields strategies which maximize an individual's gain, the assumption that actors could be treated as being motivated solely by money was of minor importance and probably made for convenience. The great disappointment with game theory has come about primarily as a result of the fact that researchers have applied the theory without due regard to the limitations of the heuristic assumption made by the theorists. It is naive for behavioral scientists to believe that individuals are motivated solely by monetary gain. This assumption is inappropriate when "real life" decisions are being considered, and it is equally inappropriate for consideration of decision making in even highly rarified and controlled experimental situations. The mathematics of game theory can be applied once the inputs to the equations are correctly identified. Without such identification, game theory, or any other theory which incorporates a model of human decision making in its foundations, will certainly yield predictions for behavior which do not match the manner in which individuals act.

The purpose of this paper is to review an on-going program of research which attempts to demonstrate that it is possible to combine the basic idea of rationality in human decision making with a social-psychologically sophisticated analysis of human goals and to produce a mathematical model of decision making which yields precise and testable predictions for human behavior. The model of decision making which provides the vehicle for this research has been tested in three quite different situations: (1) the Humphreys' light-guessing experiment; (2) the coalition game; and (3) the prisoner's dilemma game.

2. *A Model for Non-Social Decision Making*

In this section, the work of Siegel and his associates (1964) in the area of non-social decision-making will be reviewed. Siegel proposed a general, utility-based model for decision making and tested it in a repetitive, non-interactive, non-social situation. That is, in a setting in which individuals were required to make a series of decisions under basically similar circumstances, in which the behavior of an individual on trial N in no way affected the decision structure he would face on trial N + K, and in which there were no other actors involved; hence there was neither interaction nor any "social" aspect to the decision problem.

The particular context in which the research was carried out was that of the Humphreys' light-guessing experiment (Humphreys, 1939). This situation can be described as follows: A subject is seated before two light bulbs and is instructed to predict which bulb will illuminate on each of a series of trials. Usually, one and only one bulb illuminates on any trial, and the probabilities with which the two events occur sum to one. After he makes his prediction, the subject is able to see whether or not he is correct by

simply observing which light subsequently illuminates. If the subject is correct he receives some sort of reward. The probability that a given bulb illuminates is fixed in advance and is typically figured for a block of trials. If, for example, the probabilities were .80 and .20 and figured over blocks of twenty trials, one light would come on sixteen times and the other four times in each block.[1]
At the start of the experiment subjects typically distribute their choices equally between the two lights. As the experiment continues, they tend to increase their choices of the more frequently reinforced light. After one to two hundred trials, the behavior of subjects generally stabilizes, and they choose each light with about the same probability with which it illuminates; this is generally called a "matching strategy."[2] For example, in the case in which the right-hand light illuminates on eighty percent of the trials and the left light on twenty percent, the subject will, when he reaches stable-state, distribute his choices with a probability of approximately .80 for the right light and .20 for the left-hand light.

---

1 Blocking the probabilities permits the analysis of process effects (that is, experience-dependent changes in behavior) through inspection of the change in a subject's distribution of choices over blocks of trials, all of which have the same probability structure.

2 The game-theoretic term, strategy, refers to the distribution of choices for the possible alternatives. The term implies that a plan has been adopted and that subjects can be treated as having selected a probability distribution for their behaviors which will be adhered to for a substantial period of time.

The experiment has created considerable interest for two reasons. First, it provides a setting in which subjects gradually change their behavior over a lengthy series of trials and hence can be used as a situation in which to test alternative theories of the learning process. Two learning models which have been extensively tested in this situation are the Bush-Mosteller linear-operator model (Bush and Mosteller, 1955) and Estes' stimulus-sampling formulation (Estes, 1950, 1954). In addition, interest in the experiment has been provoked because of its apparent aspects of economic irrationality. Since subjects are only rewarded when they correctly predict which of the two lights will illuminate, their optimal strategy for maximization of gain (winning the greatest number of rewards) is to select the more frequent event with a probability of 1. If this strategy is adopted, the expected number of rewards obtained over a series of 100 trials would be 80 [(.80)(100)]. With a matching strategy, the expected number of rewards a subject would win is 68 [(.80)(80) + (.20)(20)]. If the payoff in an experiment were ten cents for each correct prediction, the average winnings for a subject following the matching strategy would be $6.80. For subjects playing the optimal strategy, the total payoff would be $8.00.

Although on the surface it appears that subjects behave in an economically irrational fashion, this follows only if it is assumed that individuals are solely concerned with maximizing their monetary gain. The strategy of always selecting the event with the higher probability of occurrence is optimal only for producing the greatest number of sure wins. It cannot be concluded that subjects are behaving irrationally if it is the case that they are not solely concerned with maximizing their monetary rewards. It could be argued that individuals are concerned with maximizing expected utility in their decision making, that is, with maximizing subjective value in their selection of an alternative, and that there are sources of value in the situation other than the monetary payoff associated with a correct prediction. Given this conception of the subject's aim, it is not clear that he is behaving irrationally with respect to his goals.

Siegel developed a theory based on the idea that individuals act so as to maximize expected utility in their decision making. He proposed that in the context of the light-guessing experiment there were two sources of utility. The first was the utility of a correct choice. The utility of a correct choice referred to the monetary payoff associated with an alternative, as well as to any other considerations which served to increase a subject's subjective value for that choice. Since the reward associated with an alternative was realized only if the prediction was correct for that trial, it was necessary to consider the expected utility of a correct choice. Expected utility was defined as a product of the utility of a choice and the probability with which it is correct.

The second source of utility was for choice variability due to the intrinsic boredom of the pure strategy (choosing one light consistently), as well as from the greater satisfaction connected with being able to correctly predict the less frequent event. In post-experiment interviews with subjects, Siegel and Goldstein (1959) found that many subjects periodically predicted the less frequent event for one or the other of the reasons mentioned above. Subjects behaved in this fashion even though they reported that they were aware that the "best" strategy was to choose the more frequent event with certainty. Goodnow (1955) has also reported that subjects were able to follow a pure strategy only by inventing games which served to decrease the monotony inherent in repeatedly choosing the same alternative. Subjects in Goodnow's experiments devised games such as varying the hand used to operate the response key or varying the pressure applied to the key.[1]

Siegel constructed a formal model which was intended to predict stable-state choice strategies.[2] In deriving the model the following notation was used:[3]

π_i = the probability that the ith light comes on, i = 1,2

a_i = the marginal utility of a correct choice of the ith alternative, i = 1,2

b = the marginal utility of response variability

P_i = the stable-state probability that the subject chooses the ith alternative, i = 1,2.

---

1 The results of an experiment conducted by Siegel which clearly demonstrated the existence of this source of utility can be found in Siegel's monograph, Choice, Strategy and Utility (Siegel et al.,1964, pp. 64-81).

2 Stable-state choice strategy refers to an individual's decision strategy after he has "adjusted" to the situation. In choice experiments of the type discussed in this paper, it is typically observed that subjects adopt a stable choice strategy after a learning period of variable length. The model was designed to predict only the subjects' stable-state strategies. It was not intended to account for the learning process prior to stabilization.

3 For a more complete presentation of the model and derivation of the n alternative case, see Siegel, et al., 1964.

The goal of this model was to predict the subject's stable-state strategy, P_1 and P_2, from the values of the other variables. Employing the concept of mathematical expectation and the above definitions, the expectation that the subject's choice will be correct is obviously the sum of the probabilities that he gets each light correct, or $P_1\pi_1 + P_2\pi_2$, and the expected utility of a correct choice is the sum of the expected utilities for all alternatives, or $a_1P_1\pi_1 + a_2P_2\pi_2$. Assuming that the utility of choice variability is proportional to the variance of the subject's choice, it is clear that in the case of two alternatives the interpretation of the utility of choice variability function is simple. Assuming that with probability P_1 the subject chooses the first alternative and with probability $P_2 = 1-P_1$ he chooses the second alternative, it is the case that the model of his choices is that of a sequence of Bernoulli trials with parameter P_1. Thus the variance of each choice is $P_1(1-P_1)$, and it is assumed in the model that an individual's utility of choice variability is proportional to the variance of his (random) choice, that is $2bP_1(1-P_1)$.
The expected utility, U, of the choice strategy, P_1, is assumed to be the sum of these two utility functions:

$$U=a_1P_1\pi_1+a_2P_2\pi_2+2bP_1(1-P_1)=-2bP_1^2+(a_1\pi_1-a_2\pi_2+2b)P_1+a_2\pi_2$$

It is further assumed that the individual is maximizing his expected utility U, by his choice of a strategy, that is, by his choice of P_1. The problem is to find the value of P_1 which will maximize U in the above equation. Since U is a concave function of P_1, the maximum of U with respect to P_1 occurs when $\frac{\partial U}{\partial P_1} = 0$:

$$0 = \frac{\partial U}{\partial P_1} = -4bP_1 + a_1\pi_1 - a_2\pi_2 + 2b$$

This equation can be solved for P_1; therefore, the maximum of U occurs when

$$P_1 = \frac{(a_1\pi_1 - a_2\pi_2 + 2b)}{4b} = (1/4)(\frac{a_1}{b}\pi_1 - \frac{a_2}{b}\pi_2) + \frac{1}{2}$$

and substituting α_i for $\frac{a_i}{b}$;

(1) $P_1 = (1/4)(\alpha_1\pi_1 - \alpha_2\pi_2) + 1/2 \qquad P_2 = 1 - P_1$

This can be simplified in the case in which the utilities of the two alternatives are equal, that is, $a_1=a_2$ ($\alpha_1 = \alpha_2 = \alpha$):

(2) $P_1 = (1/4)\alpha(\pi_1 - \pi_2) + 1/2 \qquad P_2 = 1 - P_1$

These two sets of equations will predict the stable-state behavior of an individual given the probabilities of feedback and the values of the utilities. It should be noted that in deriving the model, several additional assumptions about the variables have been made; for example, the expected utility of a choice strategy is the sum of the utilities of correct choices and of choice variability. While certain assumptions could be made differently, the set chosen by Siegel has resulted in quite accurate predictions.

The choice theory was tested in a two-stage experimental program. The first series of experiments was designed to test a number of ordinal predictions from the theory, predictions of the form: the greater the marginal utility of a reward for correct prediction of events, the more nearly will subjects adopt a pure strategy. The second set of tests was designed to evaluate the predictive power of the formal choice model developed from the theory. Since the formal model is a precise statement of the general axioms from which the ordinal tests were derived, it is unnecessary, at this time, to report the results of the ordinal tests. In order for the model to predict accurately it must be true that the ordinal predictions are correct.

Siegel conducted a number of tests of the formal model. The first set of investigations consisted of three tests of the model under equal alpha conditions. Since in the notation used in the model, α refers to the ratio of the marginal utility of a correct decision to the marginal utility of response variation, situations in which the utility of a correct decision is equal for all alternatives and the utility of response variation is fixed are referred to as equal alpha conditions. In this first set of experiments, the utility of a correct choice was equated for both alternatives by simply assigning the same payoffs to a correct or incorrect prediction of either event. Subjects were paid five cents for every correct prediction and lost five cents every time they made a prediction that failed. This condition was held constant over all experimental treatments. The only differences between treatment conditions were in the probabilities with which the two events occurred. Table 1 summarizes the formal characteristics of the three treatment conditions; π_1 and π_2 refer to the probabilities with which the two events occur, and a_1 and a_2 denote the payoffs associated with each event.

Table 1: Formal Characteristics of Decision-Making Experiments in a Non-Social Situation (Equal Alpha Model)

Condition	Probabilities of Events 1 and 2		Payoffs for Predictions of Events 1 and 2		Number of Subjects
	π_1	π_2	a_1	a_2	
A	.75	.25	±5¢	±5¢	17
B	.65	.35	±5¢	±5¢	16
C	.70	.30	±5¢	±5¢	20

The structure of the formal model is such that there are three unknowns in the equations used to predict stable-state choice strategies. The unknowns are (1) the probabilities with which the events occur, (2) the subjects' utility for the payoff for prediction of each event, and (3) the subjects' utility for choice variability. Given the values of these three unknowns, the model yields a stable-state choice strategy which maximizes expected utility.

Since the model treats the utilities for choice variability and for the payoff for predicting an event rather than the monetary value of the payoff or the objective characteristics of the experiment, it is necessary to measure the utilities of these factors in order to test the model's predictive power. The procedure for testing the model under equal alpha conditions requires a pair of observations, one for measurement and one for testing predictions.
The purpose of the first observation (experiment) is to provide an estimate of the ratio of the utility of the monetary payoff associated with a correct

prediction to the utility of response variation induced by a specified set of experimental procedures. Given all the information from one experiment it is possible to solve the choice equations for the ratio of these utilities. That is, the choice equations are structured such that given knowledge of (1) the probabilities with which each of the events occurs, and (2) the subject's observed stable-state choice strategy, it is possible to solve for the ratio of a subject's utility for the payoff for prediction of an event to his utility for response variation. In arriving at this estimate of the subject's utilities, the operating assumption is that he acts so as to maximize expected utility in his decision making.

In the second, prediction experiment, only one aspect of the treatment is changed. Both the boredom-inducing aspects of the situation and the monetary payoffs for predicting events remain the same as in the measurement experiment, while the probabilities with which the events occur are altered. Theoretically, changing these probabilities has the effect of changing the stable-state strategy which maximizes a subject's expected utility. The test of the formal model is its ability to predict the precise numeric value of the stable-state strategy adopted by subjects in the second experiment. It should be clearly understood that the procedure for testing the model leads to non-tautological predictions. Note that no information from the test condition is used to generate predictions; although it is not strictly necessary, different subjects are used in the measurement and prediction conditions, and changes in the π values lead to substantially different maximizing strategies in the measurement and prediction experiments.

The test procedure can be summarized as follows: An estimate of the α value is obtained from a measurement experiment. This is accomplished by using all the data from one experimental treatment and solving an equation constructed on the assumption that individuals act so as to maximize expected utility in their decision making. The alpha estimate is then employed in a set of equations designed to predict the behavior of a second sample of subjects in an experiment in which the α-determining factors are unchanged and the event parameters ($\pi_1 \ldots \pi_N$) are varied. Changing these parameters changes the strategy that subjects should adopt if they wish to maximize their expected utility and the formal theory is correct. The accuracy with which the model's predictions match observed behavior in the test experiment is an index of the power of the model.

The following is an example of the application of the measurement and prediction procedure to the data from Conditions A and B of the experiments. In this application, Condition A serves as the measurement experiment and B as the prediction condition. With Condition A as the measurement experiment the following estimate of alpha is obtained:

$$\alpha = (P_1 - .5)\left(\frac{4}{\pi_1 - \pi_2}\right)$$

$$= (.929412 - .5)\left(\frac{4}{.75 - .25}\right)$$

$$= 3.435$$

Entering this alpha value and the new values of π_1 and π_2 into the choice equation, the following are the predictions for stable-state choice behavior for subjects in Condition B.[1]

$$P_1 = \frac{\alpha}{4}(\pi_1 - \pi_2) + .5$$

$$= \frac{3.435}{4}(.65 - .35) + .5$$

$$= .758 \qquad\qquad P_2 = 1 - P_1 = .242$$

The observed values for P_1 and P_2 in Condition B were $P_1 = .753$ and $P_2 = .247$. The absolute values of the discrepancies between the observed and predicted values was .005.

Table 2 summarizes the results of the three applications of the model carried out by Siegel. In the second application of the model, Condition B was used as the measurement experiment and the behavior of subjects in Condition A was predicted. In this case the model yielded a prediction which was discrepant from the observed choice behavior by only .007. In the third application, both Conditions A and B were used in order to generate an alpha estimate, and predictions were tested in Condition C. For this application, the model predicted to within .020 of the observed stable-state choice strategy adopted by subjects.

---

1 The values of the stable-state choice strategies in the equal alpha experiments were calculated using the last twenty trials in each experimental condition. Due to the increased complexity of the unequal alpha experiments (reported below), the last eighty trials of the experiments were used in the calculation of subjects' stable-state choice strategies for applications of the model.

Table 2: Results of Applications of the Equal Alpha Model to Non-Social Decision Making

Measurement Condition(s)	Prediction Condition	π_1 π_2	Observed P_1 and P_2*	Predicted P_1 and P_2	|Discrepancy|
A	B	.65	.753	.758	.005
		.35	.247	.242	
B	A	.75	.929	.922	.007
		.25	.071	.078	
A and B	C	.70	.862	.842	.020
		.30	.138	.158	

*The calculation of the subjects' observed stable-state choice strategy was based on the last twenty trials of the experiments.

Note that there are considerable differences between the choice strategies adopted by subjects in the three conditions. For example, in Condition A the stable-state probability of a prediction of event 1 was .929, and in Condition B it was .753. The change in the values of π_1 and π_2 from Condition A to Condition B was only .10 (in Condition A, π_1 was .75, and in Condition B it was .65; π_2 was changed from .25 to .35). These minimal changes in the structure of the experiment produced a substantial change in the behavior of subjects. The observed difference in the mean values of the probability of a prediction of both events 1 and 2 was .176. For Condition B the model's prediction of the probability with which subjects would select alternative 1 if they were maximizing expected utility was .758, and the probability with which they chose this alternative was .753.

In a second set of tests, the model was applied to a more complex situation in which there were three different events to be predicted and the ratio of the expected utility of a choice to the utility of response variability was not equal for all events. In these experiments, the payoff for prediction of event 1 was ± five cents for correct and incorrect predictions, and the payoff for correct or incorrect predictions of events 2 and 3 was ± one cent. Table 3 summarizes the values of the event parameters and the payoffs for predictions in each of the four experiments.

Table 3: Formal Characteristics of Decision-Making Experiments in a Non-Social Situation (Unequal Alpha Model)

Condition	Probabilities of Events 1, 2, and 3			Payoffs for Predictions of 1, 2, and 3			Number of Subjects
	π_1	π_2	π_3	a_1	a_2	a_3	
D	.65	.25	.10	±5¢	±1¢	±1¢	18
E	.75	.20	.05	±5¢	±1¢	±1¢	18
F	.70	.15	.15	±5¢	±1¢	±1¢	18
G	.70	.50	.40	±5¢	±1¢	±1¢	18

In testing the model, any three of the treatment conditions can be used to perform the measurements necessary to make predictions for subject behavior in the fourth experiment. Table 4 presents a summary of the results of the four possible applications of the model. It is clear that the model again proves to be an extraordinarily powerful predictor of behavior. For example, when Conditions D, E and F are used to estimate the alphas, the absolute discrepancies between the predicted and observed choice strategies adopted by subjects in Condition G are P_1 = .034, P_2 = .009, and P_3 = .029. When the results of all the tests of the unequal alpha version of the model are considered, the average absolute discrepancy between observed and predicted choice strategies is only .016.

Table 4: Results of Applications of the Unequal Alpha Model to Non-Social Decision Making

Measurement Conditions	Prediction Conditions	π_1 π_2 π_3	Observed P_1, P_2 and P_3*	Predicted P_1, P_2 and P_3	|Discrepancy|
E, F and G	D	.65 .25 .10	.785 .119 .096	.819 .110 .170	.034 .009 .029
D, G and F	E	.75 .20 .05	.891 .076 .033	.895 .068 .037	.004 .008 .004
D, E and G	F	.70 .15 .15	.876 .058 .066	.842 .079 .079	.034 .021 .013
D, E and F	G	.70 .50 .40	.891 .076 .033	.895 .068 .037	.004 .008 .004

* The calculation of the subjects' stable-state choice strategy was based on data from the last eighty trials of the experiments. The selection of the stabilization point was based on inspection of the process data from the experiments (see Siegel, et. al., 1964, pp. 125-131).

The choice model developed by Siegel and his associates was based on a theory which incorporated the assumptions that individuals act so as to maximize expected utility in their decision making and that the utilities from different sources were additive. The formal model of the theory was subjected to intensive testing and was proven to be a powerful predictor of human decision making. The model was, however, only tested on a single research setting and under a set of rather restrictive conditions. For example, subjects were instructed that the future behavior of the light bulbs would not be affected by their decisions. That is, subjects believed that they were playing a game against an environment in which their behavior would not determine future states of nature. Also, the considerations entering into their assignment of utility to an alternative presumably involved only consideration of their utility for the monetary payoff. In order to begin assessing the generality of the choice theory it is necessary to test the model in experimental settings which eliminate some of the restrictive conditions required for its application.

3. A Model for Social Decision Making in the Coalition Game

This section will review the work of Ofshe and Roberts (1968a,b,c,d;1970) the application of the choice theory to a situation which required decision making in a social setting. The choice model was applied to a repetitive, perceived interactive, perceived social situation. The research setting was one in which subjects were required to make a series of decisions in a situation in which they believed that their decision on trial N would affect future states of nature, in which they believed that they were interacting with two other individuals, and in which they were induced to be either greatly or minimally concerned about the welfare of the other participants in the game.

The context of the research was an n-person mixed motive game generally referred to as the coalition game. The game is considered to be one of mixed motives, since there are elements of competition in that no outcome satisfies everyone, and there are elements of cooperation in that two players must ally in order to win. A typical game employs three players, each of whom is assigned a certain weight or resource on each trial. The players are instructed that on each trial a payoff, usually monetary, will be given to the individual, or coalition, controlling the majority of resources. The assignment of resources is usually designed to structure the situation such that if any two players combine, they control a majority of the resources. Variations on the game include increasing the number of players and adding some additional situational factors which increase player interest but do not change the game's basic structure.

Much of the current focus in coalition studies is on the effect of the distribution of resources on the selection of partners and the subsequent division of rewards.[1] It has, however, been argued (Ofshe and Roberts, 1968a) that the notable lack of progress in explaining behavior in the game is due to the attempt to treat both the choice process (selection of a potential coalition partner) and the bargaining aspects

---

1 For an excellent review and critique of the traditional approach to coalition game research, see Gamson (1964).

of the game (division of payoffs between coalition partners) at the same time and without the aid of powerful theories of either of the separate processes. In any concrete situation there is obviously an interaction effect between the two processes. In fact, lacking a conceptual analysis of these processes and a theory of their interaction, aggregated data from coalition experiments may not appear to have any patterning. If, for example, person "a" in a coalition game finds person "b" to "drive a hard bargain," he may choose person "c" regardless of the resource and reward distribution. Since most explanations consider only factors of resources and rewards, while the data reflect many additional variables, the relationship between the variables of primary interest is frequently obscured.

It is possible to consider the two processes separately, that is, to decompose the complex game and attempt to develop theories of its constituent general processes prior to attempting to predict their interaction. The empirical counterpart of the decomposition can readily be accomplished by fixing the payoffs for forming alternative coalitions. This permits the separate study of the choice process. Given this decomposition, the game may be viewed as an individual decision-making problem, in which each of the players is faced with a series of binary choices; that is, he can choose either of the other two players on each trial. This approach permits an analysis of the bulk of the coalition game literature in terms of three variables: the probability that a player's choice will be reciprocated; the payoff for forming alternative coalitions; and the player's desire to maintain an equitable distribution of the total available rewards among the three players in the game.[1]

Choice behavior in the coalition game is assumed to be affected by three factors: the probability of reciprocation, the rewards associated with each alternative, and the equity considerations. These factors are believed to operate in the same manner as the three factors affecting behavior in the light-guessing experiment: the probability of a correct choice; the payoffs associated with each alternative; and the basic monotony of the situation.

In a coalition game, an individual can win a reward only if his choice is reciprocated. This directly corresponds to a correct choice in the light-guessing experiment: an individual receives a payoff only if the light which he has chosen subsequently illuminates. Thus, it is obvious that a reciprocated choice in the coalition game is strictly analogous to a correct choice in the light-guessing experiment. Letting

a_i = the marginal utility of a reciprocated choice with participant i, i = 1,2

P_i = the stable-state probability that the player chooses participant i, i = 1,2, and

π_i = the probability that the player is chosen by participant i, i = 1,2,

the expected utility of a reciprocated choice is $\pi_1 P_1 a_1 + \pi_2 P_2 a_2$. This function employs the same implicit assumptions which were used in developing the model of decision making in the light-guessing experiment.

---

1 For a detailed analysis that organizes the literature on coalition gaming in terms of these three factors, see Ofshe and Roberts (1968a).

The second utility considered in the light-guessing situation, the utility of choice variability, may not seem to apply in this situation, for it can be argued that the game itself destroys boredom as well as any desire to choose the less frequently reinforced choice. However, there is a factor in this situation which is not operating in the light-guessing experiment. Each time an individual forms a coalition, the other person is rewarded as well as himself. This means that if two players constantly form a coalition, the third player wins nothing. There is evidence that an equity norm causes a utility of choice variability. Lieberman (1962) points out that the results of one of his experiments "describe the behavior of three individuals in a situation where two have a clear incentive to unite forces to the detriment of the third. In a majority of choices [70%] the two did just that. However, in a sizeable minority of choices [30%] this prescribed behavior did not occur.... Some subjects felt it was not fair to do this." Since the equity norm results in a subjective utility for varying choices, it is directly comparable to the utility of choice variability in the light-guessing experiment. Thus, letting

$$b = \text{marginal utility of choice variability,}$$

the equations for the player's behavior can be derived in exactly the same manner as for choice behavior in the non-social situation. Therefore, the following equations should describe choice behavior in the coalition game. (The symbol α_i in the equations is defined as follows: $\alpha_i = \frac{a_i}{b}$.)

$$P_1 = (1/4)(\alpha_1\pi_1 - \alpha_2\pi_2) + 1/2$$

(unequal payoffs)

$$P_2 = 1 - P_1$$

$$P_1 = \frac{\alpha}{4}(\pi_1 - \pi_2) + 1/2$$

(equal payoffs)

$$P_2 = 1 - P_1$$

Note that the general choice model being used here is identical to the one employed for the non-social situation; the only changes are in the substantive interpretations of certain variables.

The program of experiments designed to test the applicability of the choice model to social decision making paralleled the series of researches carried out in the non-social setting. The results of the series of ordinal tests of the theory will not be reported at this time.[1] The formal model was first applied to a situation in which the ratio of the utility for forming a coalition to the utility for equity was the same for all alternatives. In the second set of tests, the experiments were structured such that these ratios were unequal for alternative coalitions.

The research was conducted at a computer-controlled laboratory facility operated by the Center for Research in Management Science at the University of California at Berkeley. The major hardware of the laboratory was a PDP 5/8 computer with a time-sharing system that operated up to ten teletype stations around the laboratory. Utilization of the laboratory facility permitted nine games (nine subjects) to be

---

1 Tests of the ordinal predictions are reported in Ofshe and Roberts (1968b).

run simultaneously with computer control of the experiment and automatic data recording.

The experiment was described to subjects as a study of behavior in a coalition game, a game in which three persons participate and on each of a series of trials all players select one, and only one, of the other players as a coalition partner. After all three players make their choices, they are each informed of the selections of the other individuals in the game. If two players select each other, they form a coalition for that trial and win a monetary payoff. The experiments in the series used to test the model were all run under a "low equity" manipulation.[1] This consisted of a set of statements in the instructions which defined it as proper for subjects to be concerned solely with winning as much money as they could.

In order to attain the degree of control necessary to apply the model it was required that the probabilities with which each of the other players chose the subject be predetermined and blocked over sets of trials. This precluded letting subjects actually interact. Therefore, each subject in the experiment participated in a game in which the behavior of the other two players was simulated and could be precisely determined. Subjects were led to believe that they were playing against two human decision makers. Post-experiment questionnaires and interviews revealed no instance in which a subject became suspicious of the situation. On the contrary, subjects reported that they believed that their decisions affected the behavior of the two

---

1 One of the experiments reported in Ofshe and Roberts (1968b) demonstrates that the effect of increasing subjects' marginal utility for equity is to produce a choice-strategy in which, as the theory predicts, subjects more equally divide their choices between the other players in the game.

robots. They occasionally became angry at another player if he defected from a coalition which they believed would hold up for a few more trials, and occasionally attempted to punish defection by refusing to choose the disloyal player for a number of trials. Although the situation was structurally analogous to the light-guessing situation, and from the point of view of the choice theory it was isomorphic to the non-social decision situation, from the point of view of subjects it was a vastly different situation. From a subject's perspective perhaps the two most important differences between the settings were the facts that (1) in the coalition game the probabilistically-determined events were believed to be the behaviors of other humans, while in the light-guessing situation they were simply states of nature, and (2) in the coalition game it was believed that the future behavior of the other players could be affected by the subject's current decision, while in the light-guessing experiment it was impressed upon subjects that the behavior of the lights was determined prior to the start of the experiment.

For the tests of the equal alpha version of the model a pair of experiments were conducted with male subjects and then replicated with small samples of female subjects. In these experiments, the payoffs for forming coalitions were held constant for all treatment conditions; subjects were paid five cents each time they were able to enter either possible coalition. The only aspects of the experiments that were varied between conditions were the probabilities with which the subject was chosen by the other players. Table 5 summarizes the formal characteristics of the experiments and replications.

Table 5: Formal Characteristics of Decision-Making Experiments in the Coalition Game (Equal Alpha Model)

Condition	Sex of Subjects	Probabilities of Selection by Players 1 and 2		Payoffs for Formation of Coalitions with Players 1 and 2		Number of Subjects
		π_1	π_2	a_1	a_2	
H	Male	.70*	.30	5¢	5¢	22
I	Male	.60	.40	5¢	5¢	21
H'	Female	.70	.30	5¢	5¢	6
I'	Female	.60	.40	5¢	5¢	9

*In the experiments, all subjects thought themselves player number three. Half the subjects found that player number one chose them more frequently, and half discovered that it was player two who was choosing them more frequently. For reasons of clarity in presentation of data, the player who chose the subject more frequently will be identified as player one in all tables.

The experiments and replications permit two completely independent tests of the model and four different applications. Although using one condition as the measurement experiment and the other as the prediction condition and then reversing the order permits two applications of the model, each pair of applications can be considered to constitute only one independent test (carried out in two different directions as a consistency check).

Table 6 summarizes the results of the four applications of the choice model. When Condition H is used as the measurement experiment and predictions are made for the stable-state choice strategies of subjects in Condition I, the model yields a prediction which is discrepant from the observed behavior by only .0008. When the direction of the prediction is reversed, I used for measurement and H for prediction, the model's predictions are discrepant from the observed behavior by .0017. Note that the difference in the strategy adopted by subjects in the two conditions is substantial; for example, in Condition H the mean stable-state probability of a player one choice is .8636, and in Condition I the probability of a choice of player one is .6810. The difference between the two conditions is on the order of eighteen points.

Table 6: Results of Applications of the Equal Alpha Model to Decision Making in the Coalition Game

Measurement Condition	Prediction Condition	π_1 π_2	Observed P_1 and P_2*	Predicted P_1 and P_2	Discrepancy
H	I	.60	.6810	.6818	.0008
		.40	.3190	.3182	
I	H	.70	.8636	.8619	.0017
		.30	.1364	.1381	
H'	I'	.60	.7056	.7167	.0111
		.40	.2944	.2833	
I'	H'	.70	.9333	.9111	.0222
		.30	.0667	.0889	

* The calculation of the subjects' stable-state choice strategy was based on the data from the last twenty trials of the experiments.

The data generated by female subjects in the replication permit a second independent test of the model. The number of subjects in these two experiments (H' = 6, I' = 9) is exceedingly small for the type of prediction attempted by the model. The data reported in Table 6 indicate, however, that the model proves to be a reasonably accurate predictor of behavior. When H' is the measurement experiment, the choice strategy adopted by subjects in I' is different from the predictions by only .0111. In the reverse application of the model the discrepancy is .0222.

A second set of experiments was designed to test the unequal alpha form of the model. In these experiments, the ratio of the marginal utility for formation of a coalition to the marginal utility for maintenance of equity was different for each of the alternative coalitions. In this set of experiments, the payoff for forming a coalition with player one was five cents, while the payoff for a coalition with player two was ten cents. In all of the experiments the robot who chose the subject more frequently is identified as player one. A subject was therefore faced with a decision situation in which he could obtain a small payoff for forming a coalition with a player who was "anxious" to unite with him, or a relatively large payoff for forming a coalition with the player who chose him less frequently. Table 7 summarizes the formal characteristics of the three experimental conditions.

In order to apply the model it is necessary to use the data from two measurement conditions in order to estimate the values of α_1 and α_2. Since there are three treatment conditions and any two can be used for measurement, with the third serving as the test condition, it is possible to make three different ap-

Table 7: Formal Characteristics of Decision-Making Experiments in the Coalition Game (Unequal Alpha Model)

Condition	Sex of Subjects	Probabilities of Selection by Players 1 and 2		Payoffs for Formation of Coalitions with Players 1 and 2		Number of Subjects
		π_1	π_2	a_1	a_2	
J	Male	.80	.20	5¢	10¢	9
K	Male	.70	.30	5¢	10¢	14
L	Male	.60	.40	5¢	10¢	13

plications of the model. In the first application, the data from Conditions J and K were used to estimate the α's, and Condition L was employed as the test condition. In this case, the model predicted that in stable-state the probability of a player one choice would be .4070 and the probability of a player two choice would be .5930. The observed, stable-state choice strategy of subjects in Condition L was to select player one with a probability of .4397 and player two with a probability of .5603. The absolute discrepancy between the predicted and observed behaviors of subjects in Condition L was .0327. When Conditions J and L were used to predict the choice strategies of subjects in Condition K, the discrepancy between predicted and observed strategies was .0164. Finally, when Conditions K and L served as the measurement experiments and J was the prediction condition, the discrepancy was .0328. The results of the three applications of the model are summarized in Table 8.

Table 8: Results of Applications of the Unequal Alpha Model to Decision Making in the Coalition Game

Measurement Conditions	Prediction Condition	π_1 π_2	Observed P_1 and P_2*	Predicted P_1 and P_2	Discrepancy
J and K	L	.60	.4397	.4070	.0327
		.40	.5603	.5930	
J and L	K	.70	.5393	.5557	.0164
		.30	.4607	.4443	
L and K	J	.80	.6716	.6388	.0328
		.20	.3284	.3612	

* Calculations of subjects' stable-state choice strategies were based on the last ninety trials of Condition J and on the last sixty trials of Conditions K and L.

The general decision-making theory was applied to a social situation, and the formal model of the theory was subjected to three independent tests. In each case the model proved to be as powerful a predictor of choice behavior in the coalition game as it was in the light-guessing experiment. The coalition game setting provided a research situation which was considerably "richer" than the light-guessing experiment. Subjects in the coalition game considered the effects of their behaviors on future relations with the other players in the game, considered the welfare of the other players, and believed that the behavior of the other players would be affected by their actions. The greater "noise" in the coalition game did not reduce the predictive power of the model.

With regard to certain gross aspects of behavior in the two situations, subjects in the light-guessing experiment and the coalition game behave in quite dissimilar fashions. The most important difference is the length of time it takes to adapt to the probability structure of the experiments. The difference is most apparent in cases in which the probabilities of the two events are greatly divergent from .50 for each event. In the light-guessing experiment, Siegel observed that choice behavior stabilized after about 200 trials. For example, in one of Siegel's experiments the probabilities with which the events occurred were $\pi_1 = .75$ and $\pi_2 = .25$, and the payoffs, a_1 and a_2, were both five cents. In this experiment, subjects moved from a probability of prediction of event one of approximately .47 in the first twenty-trial block to a probability of making this prediction of .85 (approximate) in the tenth twenty-trial block. Over the course of 200 trials the shift in the probability of predicting event one was approximately 38 points. The most similar coalition game experiment was one in which $\pi_1 = .70$, $\pi_2 = .30$, and a_1 and a_2 were both five cents. In this experiment, subjects moved from a probability of selecting player one in the first five-trial block of .391 to a probability of making this decision of .791 in the third five-trial block. In a situation in which the probabilistic events were believed to be the behaviors of other individuals, subjects evidenced a probability shift in their behavior of .400 over fifteen trials. Apart from the negligible difference in the parameters under which the experiments were run, the only possible source for an explanation of the marked differences in behavior in the two situations rests with the effects of believing that one is in interaction with other individuals rather than trying to predict a series of probabilistically determined events.

It is important to note that despite the major differences in the subjects' cognitions about the decision situation and the substantial differences in the rate at which subjects adapt to the probability structure of the experiments, the same general decision-making model is able to predict behavior in both non-social and social situations.

4. An Application of the Model to the Prisoner's Dilemma Game

Perhaps the classic two-person game situation is that of the prisoner's dilemma. The structure of the decision problem is built on the lines of the following situation:

> Two suspects are taken into custody and separated. The district attorney is certain that they are guilty of a specific crime, but he does not have adequate evidence to convict them at a trial. He points out to each prisoner that each has two alternatives: to confess to the crime the police are sure they have done, or not to confess. If they both do not confess, then the district attorney states that he will book them on some very minor trumped-up charge, such as petty larceny and illegal possession of a weapon, and they both will receive minor punishment; if they both confess, they will be prosecuted, but he will recommend less than the most severe sentence; but if one confesses and the other does not, then the confessor will receive lenient treatment for turning state's evidence, whereas the latter will get "the book" slapped at him. (Luce and Raiffa, 1957).

The basic elements of the situation are that each individual is confronted with making a decision which is conditioned by his beliefs about how the other actor will choose, and by the fact that the best outcome for the pair (each not confessing) results in a less favorable outcome than does turning state's evidence (providing that the other individual is foolish enough to trust his partner). The payoff matrix for the situation described above can be represented as follows:

		Prisoner X	
		Not confess	Confess
Prisoner Y	Not Confess	1 year each	Y gets 10 years X gets 3 months
	Confess	Y gets 3 months X gets 10 years	8 years each

In research on interpersonal conflict, the basic elements of the situation are preserved, although the prison sentences are replaced with monetary payoffs and the criminals with college students. The dilemma faced by the two decision-makers is analogous to the problem faced by the prisoners since the payoffs are arranged such that a cooperative choice (no confession) carries a smaller payoff than a competitive choice (confession) if the other individual trusts his partner. A typical payoff matrix is the following:

		Player Y	
		1	2
Player X	1	(5,5)	(-5,+10)
	2	(+10,-5)	(1,1)

The matrix is set up such that the first entry in each cell is the payoff for player X. If players X and Y both choose alternative 1, they each receive five dollars. If player X chooses 1 and Y chooses 2, X loses five dollars and Y is paid ten dollars.

The game situation has become a focus of research for two reasons. The first is related to the issue of "rationality" in choice behavior, and the second is accounted for by the fact that the situation is a convenient one in which to study factors affecting cooperative and competitive behavior.

The "rationality" aspect of the interest centers around consideration of the fact that a player's safest strategy is to choose alternative two under all circumstances, while the best strategy to maximize gain for both players in the game is to always choose alternative one. Luce and Raiffa have argued that for games with only a single play, there is nothing "irrational or perverse about the choice of α_2 and β_2 [each player's alternative 2], and we must admit that if we were actually in this position we would make these choices" (Luce and Raiffa, 1957, p. 96). When there are several iterations of the game, the situation is somewhat altered. Under this condition, it is proposed that "an unarticulated collusion between players will develop" (p.101). The difference between expected behavior in single-play games and games with multiple iterations is accounted for by the fact that with repeated plays, it is possible for the two opponents to establish a pattern of behavior that results in greater benefit for each than would be achieved if both chose the uncooperative alternative (alternative 2).

It is the case, however, that even given the possibility of establishing a form of communication by signaling intent through consistent action, players do not "lock into" the cooperative, jointly and usually individually maximizing strategy. Nor do they establish any type of complex alternation pattern which, with perfect coordination and under certain combinations of payoffs, would result in a greater joint gain than could be obtained through simple cooperation. The problem which confronts researchers is to account for the display of a choice-strategy which does not maximize the monetary payoffs available to players in the game.

In addition to providing a setting in which to test theories of decision making, the game situation provides a convenient setting in which to test the effects of changes in variables which are hypothesized to be related to cooperation and competition, and trust and mistrust. The ease with which factors such as temptation and power can be manipulated makes the game a desirable setting in which to conduct such research. Consider, for example, the hypothesis that the greater the gain for defection, the greater the probability of defection. It is a simple task to design an experiment suitable for testing this hypothesis within the structure of the prisoner's dilemma game. All that is necessary is to increase the payoff for defection (an alternative 2 choice) from control to experimental treatment and observe the effects on the dependent variable. The convenience with which research on extremely provocative topics can be conducted has resulted in a deluge of frequently quite interesting but theoretically disconnected studies.

Even the most extensive and detailed treatment of behavior in the game situation, Rapoport and Chammah's Prisoner's Dilemma (1965) has not resulted in a powerful explanatory theory.

Given the structure of the decision theory considered in this paper, it is obvious that the formulation should be applicable to decision making in the prisoner's dilemma game. An analysis of the game situation in terms of the concepts of the theory is as follows.

A player in a prisoner's dilemma type game is faced with a series of binary decisions; he can choose either the cooperative alternative (choice 1) or the competitive alternative (choice 2). It is assumed that in his decision making an individual will act so as to maximize expected utility and that there are two sources of utility in the situation. The first is the marginal utility of the payoffs for each of the possible outcomes, and the second is the individual's marginal utility for "relative gain."

The utility of a payoff denotes not only the utility of the monetary reward associated with an outcome but also any additional factors which increase an individual's subjective value for that outcome. For example, for a male playing against an attractive female, the marginal utility for a cooperative choice might be increased (over the assignment following from just the monetary payoff) due to recognition of cooperation's potential effects on establishment of an extra-game relationship with the opponent. For a male playing against another male, the marginal utility of a cooperative choice is not likely to be increased for this reason.

It is proposed that the second source of utility in the situation stems from the individual's desire to demonstrate superior ability at the strategic aspects of the game situation. This is denoted as the individual's marginal utility for "relative gain." With regard to the issue of rationality, the problematic aspect of behavior in multiple iteration games is that individuals fail to achieve a stable, permanent alternative 1 response pattern. Although an individual's maximum long-run gain is realized through establishment of an alliance with the other player, subjects usually display some propensity to attempt to "one-up" their opponents. It is suggested that this result comes about because subjects recognize the competitive nature of the game and desire to out-perform the other players. The work of Orne (1959, 1962) and Rosenthal (1966) clearly demonstrates that subjects in social-psychological experiments are in part motivated to perform well because they desire to adequately fulfill the role of experimental subject and are concerned about evaluating their abilities in new areas. The degree to which subjects are induced to value "beating" their opponents will, of course, vary with the particular set of instructions employed in an experiment.

Participants in a prisoner's dilemma game are confronted with a choice situation in which they are conceived of as attempting to maximize the combination of utilities stemming from payoffs associated with outcomes of choices and utilities stemming from desires to out-perform their opponents. The formal model for decision making in the game is as follows. Letting

π_i = the probability that the opponent chooses alternative i, i = 1,2

a_i = the marginal utility of the payoff for choice i, i = 1,2

b = the marginal utility of relative gain

α_i = the ratio a_i/b_i, i = 1,2

P_i = the stable-state probability that the player chooses alternative i, i = 1,2.

Following the derivation presented earlier, the final equations of the model are:

$$P_1 = (1/4)(\alpha_1\pi_1 - \alpha_2\pi_2) + 1/2$$

$$P_2 = 1 - P_1.$$

The model has not yet been empirically tested in a research program specifically designed for the evaluation of this formulation. There does, however, exist in the literature a set of three experiments in which the same payoff matrix was used, the behavior of one of the players was simulated, and the π parameters were varied in a manner which permits application of the model.

Application of the model to this data is not strictly appropriate since certain necessary experimental conditions for its application are not achieved in the researches. For example, the published data report only the mean probabilities of alternative 1 and 2 choices for thirty trials in two experiments and for fifty trials in the third experiment. It is impossible, from this data, to judge the point at which a stable-state choice strategy is attained. Therefore, it is necessary to apply the model to the entire length of the experiments.

A second consideration is that the data were gathered by two different teams of researchers, and the procedures under which the experiments were run differed between experiments. In light of the assumption that the magnitude of utility assigned to relative gain varies with the set of instructions employed by the researcher, this is an important problem.

The third point to note is that the researches were carried out at two different universities, and therefore subjects for the three treatment conditions did not come from the same population. Since the testing procedure for the model employs estimation of α

ratios from the data generated by one set of subjects and comparison of predictions against the behavior of a second set, it is necessary to make the assumption that the distribution of α ratios will be the same in both populations. Students at different institutions could differ substantially in their assignments of utility to the monetary payoffs and to relative gain. For example, Lave (1962) conducted three separate but identical prisoner's dilemma experiments with students at Harvard, M.I.T. and Northeastern. The choice strategies adopted by Harvard and M.I.T. students were identical, while the strategies displayed by Northeastern students were substantially different. In the applications of the model to the light-guessing experiment and the coalition game, subjects were sampled from a single population and randomly assigned to treatment conditions. This procedure was employed in order to control for individual variations in assignment of utilities. In the published researches on the prisoner's dilemma game, this procedure was not employed. The two teams of researchers were, of course, conducting the experiments for their own purposes, and there was no reason to employ procedures which would permit an unambiguous test of the model being considered here. Application of the model to this data should be regarded as constituting a preliminary test, since many of the necessary conditions for its application have clearly been violated.

The data to which the model will be applied are reported in Minas, et al. (1960) and Bixenstine, et al. (1963). The research reported in the first paper was conducted at Ohio State University, while the data reported in the second paper were obtained at Kent State University. The results reported below are for male subjects.

Subjects in three different treatment conditions participated in a prisoner's dilemma game against a simulated opponent. The probabilities with which the robot chose the two alternatives were varied across conditions. The payoff matrix was fixed for all treatment conditions, with the values of the payoffs (in cents) as shown below.

		Robot 1	Robot 2
Subject	1	(3,3)	(0,5)
	2	(5,0)	(1,1)

The formal characteristics of the treatment conditions are presented in Table 9. Conditions M and N were run by Bixenstine, et al., and Condition O by Minas, et al.

Table 9: Formal Characteristics of Decision-Making Experiments in the Prisoner's Dilemma Game

Condition	Probabilities of Robot Selections of Alternatives 1 and 2		Payoffs for Alternatives 1 and 2		Number of Subjects	Number of Trials
	π_1	π_2	a_1	a_2		
M	.17	.83	(3,0)	(5,1)	12	30
N	.83	.17	(3,0)	(5,1)	12	30
O	1.0	0	(3,0)	(5,1)	26	50

Since the payoffs for alternatives 1 and 2 are unequal, two measurement conditions are required to predict behavior in the test condition. The three treatment conditions therefore permit three applications of the model. The results of these applications are summarized in Table 10.

Table 10: Results of Application of the Unequal Alpha Model to the Prisoner's Dilemma Game

Measurement Conditions	Prediction Condition	π_1 π_2	Observed P_1 and P_2	Predicted P_1 and P_2	|Discrepancy|
M and N	O	1.	.38	.36	.02
		0	.62	.64	
M and O	N	.83	.33	.36	.03
		.17	.67	.64	
N and O	M	.17	.30	.14	.16
		.83	.70	.86	

When Conditions M and N are used in order to estimate the alphas, the model predicts that under the π parameters used in Condition O, the probability of a cooperative choice (alternative 1) will be .36. The observed probability of a cooperative choice in this condition is .38. The absolute value of the discrepancy between the observed and predicted probabilities is .02. When Conditions M and O are used to predict behavior in Condition N, the absolute value of the discrepancy between observed and predicted choice strategies is .03. In the final application of the model, Conditions N and O are used in order to measure the alphas, and predictions are tested against observations made in Condition M. In this case, the absolute value of the discrepancy between the predicted and observed choice strategy is .16. If the discrepancies between predicted and observed choice strategies are averaged for the three applications of the model, the result is a mean absolute discrepancy of .07.

Given the experimental conditions under which the model was applied, its predictive power is quite impressive. The results indicate that, at minimum, the general decision-making formulation gives reasonably accurate predictions for choice behavior in a two-person competitive social situation. Despite rather gross violations of crucial experimental conditions, the model's predictions reflect the effects of changes in the values of the π parameter and in two of the three conditions are as accurate as predictions tested under better controlled conditions.

Bibliography

Bixenstine, V.E., and K.V. Wilson, Effects of Level of Cooperative Choice by the Other Player on Choices in a Prisoner's Dilemma Game, Part I, Journal of Abnormal and Social Psychology, 66, 1963, pp. 308-313.

Bixenstine, V.E., and K.V. Wilson, Effects of Level of Cooperative Choice by the Other Player on Choices in a Prisoner's Dilemma Game, Part II, Journal of Abnormal and Social Psychology, 67, 1963, pp. 139-147.

Bush, R.R., and F. Mosteller, Stochastic Models for Learning, New York: John Wiley & Sons, Inc., 1955.

Estes, W.K., Toward a Statistical Theory of Learning, Psychological Review, 57, pp. 94-107.

Estes, W.K., Individual Behavior in Certain Outcome Situations; An Interpretation in Terms of Statistical Association Theory, in R.M. Thrall, C.H. Coombs, and R.L. Davis (eds.), Decision Processes, New York: John Wiley & Sons, Inc., 1954, pp. 127-137.

Gamson, W.A., Experimental Studies of Coalition Formation, in L. Berkowitz (ed.), Advances in Experimental Social Psychology, Vol. I, New York: Academic Press, 1964.

Goodnow, J.J., Determinants of Choice-distribution in Two-choice Situations, American Journal of Psychology, 68, 1955, pp. 106-116.

Humphreys, L.G., Acquisition and Extinction of Verbal Expectations in a Situation Analogous to Conditioning, Journal of Experimental Psychology, 25, 1939, pp. 294-301.

Lave, Lester B., Factors Affecting Cooperation in the Prisoner's Dilemma, Behavioral Science, 10, 1965, pp. 26-38.

Lieberman, B., Experimental Studies of Conflict in Some Two-person Games, in J. Criswell, H. Solomon, and P. Suppes (eds.), Mathematical Methods in Small Group Processes, Stanford: Stanford University Press, 1963.

Luce, R.D., and Howard Raiffa, Games and Decisions, New York: John Wiley & Sons, Inc., 1957.

Minas, J.S., Scodel, A., Marlowe, D., and H. Rawson, Some Descriptive Aspects of Two-person, Non-zero Sum Games, Part II, Journal of Conflict Resolution, 4, 1960, pp. 193-197.

Ofshe, Richard, and Lynne Roberts, Utility and Choice in Social Interaction, I. Theory, in Research Report in Computer-Controlled Behavioral Experimentation, No. 2, Center for Research in Management Science, University of California (Berkeley), 1968(a).

Ofshe, Richard, and Lynne Roberts, Utility and Choice in Social Interaction, II. Basic Experimental Tests, in Research Report in Computer-Controlled Behavioral Experimentation, No. 3, Center for Research in Management Science, University of California (Berkeley), 1968(b).

Ofshe, Richard, and Lynne Roberts, Utility and Choice in Social Interaction, III. A Model for Equal Alpha Conditions, in Research Report in Computer-Controlled Behavioral Experimentation, No. 4, Center for Research in Management Science, University of California (Berkeley), 1968(c).

Ofshe, Richard, and Lynne Roberts, Utility and Choice in Social Interaction, IV. A Model for Unequal Alpha Conditions, in Research Report in Computer-Controlled Behavioral Experimentation, No. 5, Center for Research in Management Science, University of California (Berkeley), 1968(d).

Ofshe, Richard, and Lynne Roberts, Utility and Choice in Social Interaction, New York: Prentice-Hall, 1970.

Orne, M.T., The Nature of Hypnosis: Artifact and Essence, Journal of Abnormal and Social Psychology, 58, 1959, pp. 277-299.

Orne, M.T., On the Social Psychology of the Psychological Experiment: With Particular Reference to Demand Characteristics and their Implications, American Psychologist, 17, 1962, pp. 776-783.

Rapoport, A., and A.M. Chammah, Prisoner's Dilemma: A Study of Conflict and Cooperation, Ann Arbor: The University of Michigan Press, 1965.

Rosenthal, Robert, Experimenter Effects in Behavioral Research, New York: Appleton-Century-Crofts, 1966.

Siegel, S., Siegel, A.E., and J.M. Andrews, Choice, Strategy, and Utility, New York: McGraw Hill, 1964.

Siegel, S., and D.A. Goldstein, Decision-making Behavior in a Two-choice Uncertain Outcome Situation, Journal of Experimental Psychology, 57, 1959, pp. 37-42.

Von Neumann, John, and Oskar Morgenstern, Theory of Games and Economic Behavior, New York: John Wiley & Sons, Inc., 1944.

9. THE MACROECONOMIC EXPERIMENTAL GAME KRESKO

— Experimental Design and the Influence of Economic Knowledge on Decision Behavior[1] —

REINHARD TIETZ*

The experiences made in microeconomic experiments induce us to extend experimental investigations to macroeconomic problems. It is rather difficult to create an experimental situation in which many persons have to make decisions. That makes it necessary to select such problems, where individuals or small teams have to make decisions with relevant influences on the macroeconomic development. Such problems are, for instance, collective bargaining or central bank decision making.

---

* Universität Frankfurt/Main

1 This and the three following papers report on the first results obtained from the experimental game KRESKO. We intend to make further investigations.
We are indebted to Deutsche Forschungsgemeinschaft, Bad Godesberg, and to Deutsches Rechenzentrum, Darmstadt, who enabled us to compute and to perform the experiment, and to all colleagues engaged in the experiment. For the evaluation we used the UNIVAC 1108 computer of the Zentrales Recheninstitut der Johann Wolfgang Goethe-Universität, Frankfurt am Main.

The Model[1]

First we will give a short introduction to the model which, by means of an ALGOL-program, generates the information about the economy KRESKO. The model represents a closed economic system with 5 sectors: industry, households, credit banks, the central bank, and the government, whose activity is restricted to unemployment insurance and to buying capital goods for improvement of infrastructure.

The sectors are handled as representative decision units. They are interconnected by means of five markets. The labor market determines the effective number of workers under contract and the effective wage rate which generally differs from the standard of wage rate. Two markets coordinate supply and demand of consumer and capital goods. The volumes of short-term and long-term credits given by banks to industry and the respective interest rates are also market results. The market relationships are completed by the concept of "information bridges." This concept takes into consideration that on some markets the demanders get more or less accurate information on the quantities planned by the suppliers. This information can influence the planning of demanders, before both parties actually meet on the market.

Figure 1 shows a simple schematic representation of the money circulation between the five sectors (rectangles) connected by the five markets (circles)

---

1 A detailed description of the model will be published later in Volume IV. of these Contributions.

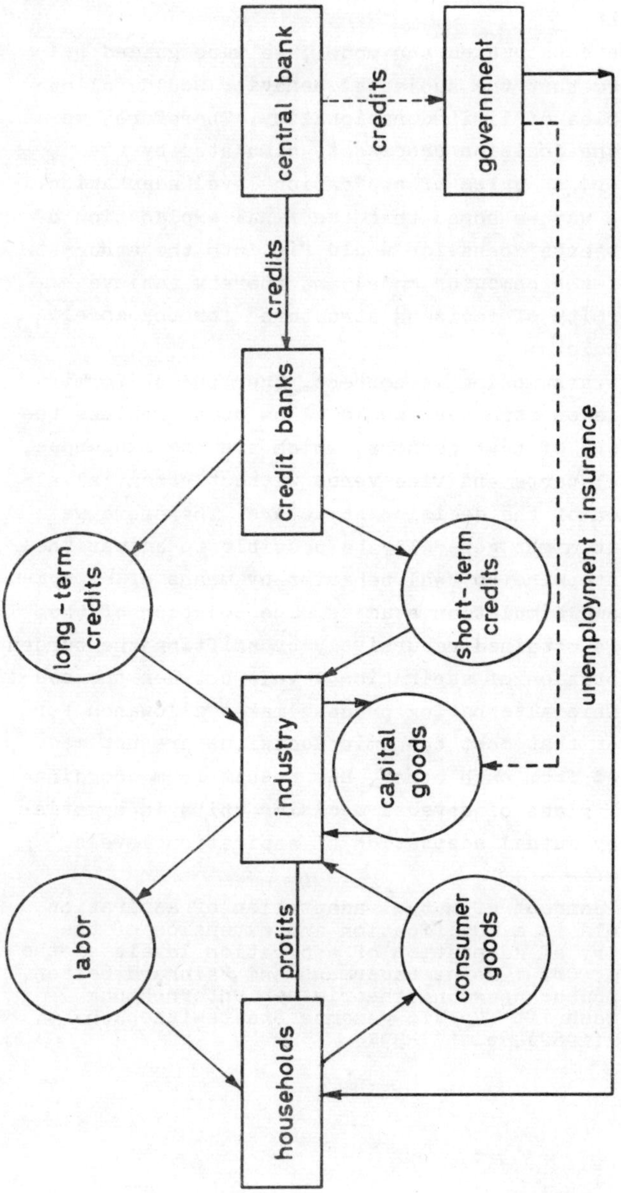

Figure 1: The monetary circulation of the KRESKO economy

and some other important flows (profits, credits given by the central bank, and unemployment insurance).
When we constructed the model, we were guided by the idea that the subjects' behavior would follow principles of limited rationality. Therefore, we based the decision processes, simulated by the computer, on rules of aspiration level adaptation. In this way we hoped that the final explanation of the subjects' behavior would fit into the structure of the computer model and thereby achieve "uniformity of decision structure" for the model as a whole.
If this assumption is correct, then the uniformity of decision structure would allow us to replace the decisions of test persons, which are now exogenous, by model parts and vice versa without essential alteration of the decision structure. Therefore we think it might generally be possible to adjust the model stepwise to real behavior by means of experiments and simulation studies. The solution of the model is obtained recursively by shifting the burden of adaptation of aspiration levels between the sectors. This alternating process makes allowance for the fact that most economic decisions are not made isolated from each other, but result from coordination of plans of several decision units in negotiations by mutual adaptation of aspiration levels.[1]

---

1 The concept of mutual adaptation of aspiration levels is a modification and extension of the theory of adaptation of aspiration levels of the firm. Cf. : Heinz Sauermann and Reinhard Selten, Anspruchsanpassungstheorie der Unternehmung, Zeitschrift für die gesamte Staatswissenschaft, 118 (1962),pp. 577-597.

The model is constructed in such a way that equilibrium growth is possible. As a consequence of endogenous technical progress three paths of equilibrium growth exist. The model also allows for business cycles.

Three typical experimental game developments in terms of the growth rates of real net national product ($Y^{nr.\gamma}$) are shown in Figure 2. The games differ in respect to fluctuations (uniform growth, early or late depression). The different developments of the three games result from the different exogenous decisions of the experimental subjects only.

The Experimental Design

With the experiences of six pilot studies in 1969 we ran our experiment with 37 students of economic sciences in 1970 in four "first" and twelve "second games."

Before beginning the experiment a surprise examination was given to the students in order to determine the extent of their knowledge of macroeconomic theory. The students were graded according to their performance in this examination. The assignment of the players to games was done in such a way that the macroeconomic knowledge of all subjects playing the same game was as equal as possible. This gives us the possibility to investigate the influence of the level of macroeconomic knowledge on the collective performance of the game group.

In the experimental game KRESKO there are three parties playing the roles: the employers' association (A), the labor union (G), and the central bank (Z).

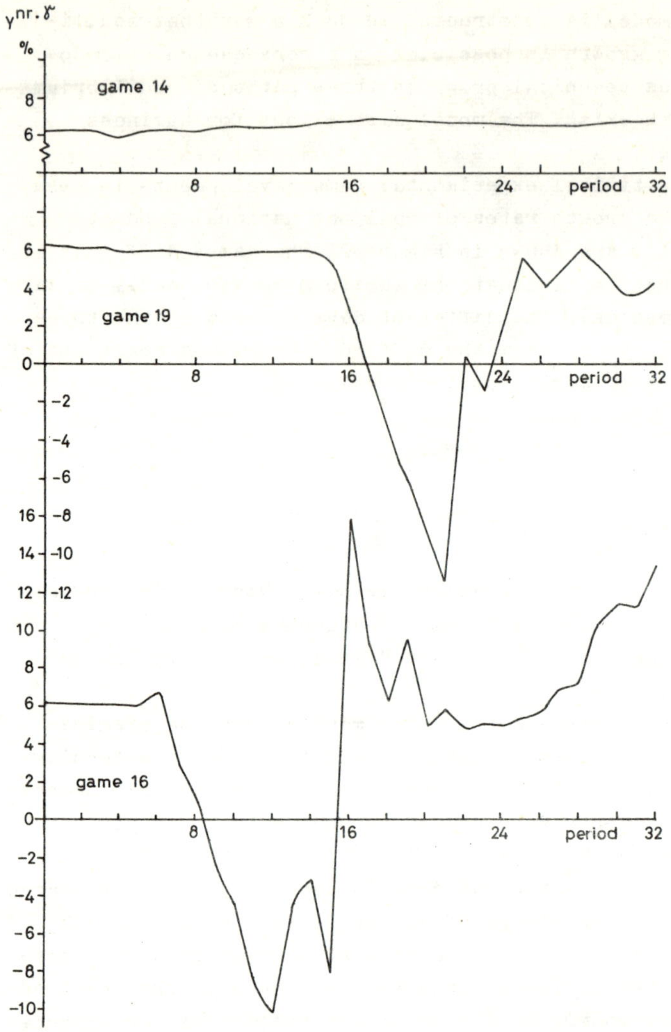

Figure 2: Three typical experimental game developments

The first two parties bargain on the standard wage rate (w_T), the standard of working hours weekly (h_T), and the periods of notice for the employment contracts (Küf). The central bank decides on 10 variables in the field of monetary policy. The central bank player was allowed to make suggestions on the bargaining variables during the bargaining session.

For each period the players get information on approximately 200 variables which were computed by the ALGOL-Program by means of an IBM 7094. The information is presented by a national accounting separated in three sections: the accounting of assets, the income accounting, and an accounting of the changes of financial relations. In addition, some other important variables are given in tables and sometimes graphically.

To get more insight into the planning behavior of the subjects and to have the possibility of testing our behavioral hypothesis of mutual adaptation of aspiration levels used in constructing the model, each player has to fill in a planning form for each period.

The most important variables asked for A and G are shown in Table 1. The symbols of the variables are composed in the following way:

(1) There are three decision parameters:
- h standard of working hours weekly,
- w growth rate of standard wage rate,
- k periods of notice for the employment contracts.

(2) Both A and G have the following set of seven planning variables:

(2a) Upper indices:

KG planned conflict limit,

KD planned conflict threat,

DU bargaining result regarded as attainable,[1]

G planned bargaining result,[2]

W1 first demand.

(2b) The additional symbol (^) stands for the expectation for two planning variables of the other party (KG and W1).

(3) The lower indices A and G mean the two parties.

The planning variables of the central bank player are shown in Table 2. They are composed in a similar manner.

---

1 The question was in German: "Welches Verhandlungsergebnis halten Sie mindestens für durchsetzbar?".

2 The question was in German: "Welches Verhandlungsergebnis streben Sie an?".

Table 1: Planning and bargaining variables of the employers' association (A) and the labor union (G)

groups of variables	standard of working hours weekly		growth rate of standard wage rate		periods of notice for the employment contracts		conflict variables	
							lock-out	strike
roles	A	G	A	G	A	G	A	G
1) <u>The variables in the planning form (P)</u>								
planned conflict limit	h_A^{KG}	h_G^{KG}	w_A^{KG}	w_G^{KG}	k_A^{KG}	k_G^{KG}		
planned conflict threat	h_A^{KD}	h_G^{KD}	w_A^{KD}	w_G^{KD}	k_A^{KD}	k_G^{KD}		
expected first demand of the opposite party	$\hat{h}_A^{W1}$	$\hat{h}_G^{W1}$	$\hat{w}_A^{W1}$	$\hat{w}_G^{W1}$	$\hat{k}_A^{W1}$	$\hat{k}_G^{W1}$		
bargaining result regarded as attainable	h_A^{DU}	h_G^{DU}	w_A^{DU}	w_G^{DU}	k_A^{DU}	k_G^{DU}		
planned bargaining result	h_A^{G}	h_G^{G}	w_A^{G}	w_G^{G}	k_A^{G}	k_G^{G}		
first demand	h_A^{W1}	h_G^{W1}	w_A^{W1}	w_G^{W1}	k_A^{W1}	k_G^{W1}		
expected conflict limit of the opposite party	$\hat{h}_A^{KG}$	$\hat{h}_G^{KG}$	$\hat{w}_A^{KG}$	$\hat{w}_G^{KG}$	$\hat{k}_A^{KG}$	$\hat{k}_G^{KG}$		
priority	Pr_A^h	Pr_G^h	Pr_A^w	Pr_G^w	Pr_A^k	Pr_G^k		
planned number of persons for whom strike or lock-out may be declared							AUS_A^G	STR_G^G
2) <u>The variables in the bid form (Wi = W1,W2,...)</u>								
demand	h_A^{Wi}	h_G^{Wi}	w_A^{Wi}	w_G^{Wi}	k_A^{Wi}	k_G^{Wi}		
corrected planned bargaining result	$h_A^{G.Wi}$	$h_G^{G.Wi}$	$w_A^{G.Wi}$	$w_G^{G.Wi}$	$k_A^{G.Wi}$	$k_G^{G.Wi}$		
corrected conflict limit	$h_A^{KG.Wi}$	$h_G^{KG.Wi}$	$w_A^{KG.Wi}$	$w_G^{KG.Wi}$	$k_A^{KG.Wi}$	$k_G^{KG.Wi}$		
3) <u>The variables in the decision form (E)</u>	h_T^W		w_T^Y		Küf		AUSSPG	STREIK

Table 2: Planning and decision variables of the central bank (Z)

1) <u>Bargaining expectations in the planning form (P)</u>	standard of working hours weekly	growth rate of standard wage rate	periods of notice for the employment contracts
expected bargaining result	$\hat{h}_Z$	$\hat{w}_Z$	$\hat{k}_Z$
expected first demand of A	$\hat{h}_Z^{W1.A}$	$\hat{w}_Z^{W1.A}$	$\hat{k}_Z^{W1.A}$
expected first demand of G	$\hat{h}_Z^{W1.G}$	$\hat{w}_Z^{W1.G}$	$\hat{k}_Z^{W1.G}$

2) <u>planning and decisions of Z</u>	planning form (P)		bid form (W)	decision form (E)
	in the case that the expected bargaining result occurs (a)	alternative planning (b)	correction on bid form (Wi=W1, W2,...)	final decision
rediscount rate	$z_D^{G.a}$	$z_D^{G.b}$	$z_D^{G.Wi}$	z_D
interest rate for open market papers	$z_O^{G.a}$	$z_O^{G.b}$	$z_O^{G.Wi}$	z_O
contingent of rediscount	$Q_{Red}^{G.a}$	$Q_{Red}^{G.b}$	$Q_{Red}^{G.Wi}$	Q_{Red}
rate of minimum reserve on sight deposits	$r_G^{G.a}$	$r_G^{G.b}$	$r_G^{G.Wi}$	r_G
rate of minimum reserve on time deposits	$r_T^{G.a}$	$r_T^{G.b}$	$r_T^{G.Wi}$	r_T
rate of minimum reserve on saving deposits	$r_S^{G.a}$	$r_S^{G.b}$	$r_S^{G.Wi}$	r_S
interest rate on minimum reserve deficit	$z_{MrD}^{G.a}$	$z_{MrD}^{G.b}$	$z_{MrD}^{G.Wi}$	z_{MrD}
supply/demand of long-term credits	$Q_{Vl}^{G.a}$	$Q_{Vl}^{G.b}$	$Q_{Vl}^{G.Wi}$	$Q_{V_Z^l}$
maximum volume of open market papers	$Q_{EO}^{G.a}$	$Q_{EO}^{G.b}$	$Q_{EO}^{G.Wi}$	$Q_E{}^O$
granted credit for government activities in infrastructure	$Q_{VI}^{G.a}$	$Q_{VI}^{G.b}$	$Q_{VI}^{G.Wi}$	$Q_{VI_S^m}$

The Bargaining Procedure

The players are placed around a table in the following arrangement:

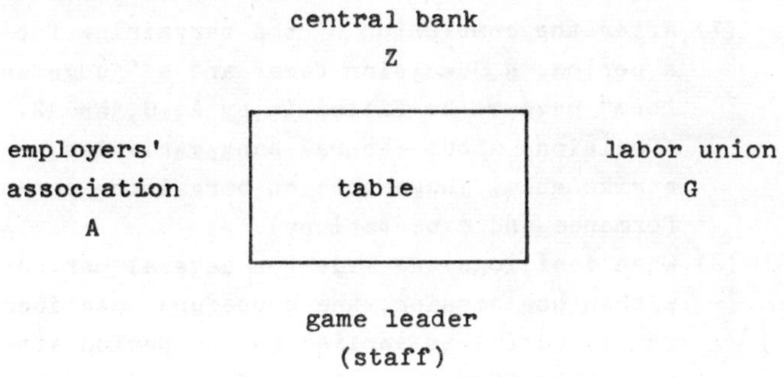

The bargaining procedure may be described by the following steps:

(1) Game leader receives planning forms from A, G, and Z.
(2) Game leader announces "first demands" of A's and G's planning form.
(3) Game leader performs a random experiment which decides the order in which A, G, and Z present their opening remarks (reasons for or against first demands by A and G).
(4) Opening remarks by A, G, and Z (argueing).
(5) If a new bid form is presented by A, G, or Z, the game leader gives the floor to the particular party. (The bid form may be empty if the party wants to confirm its earlier demands).

(6) Bargaining stops after agreement has been reached or time is up. (The fixed bargaining time is given in Table 3. The game leader could grant a small extension of the bargaining time, if reaching an agreement soon seemed to be highly probable).

(7) After the completion of the bargaining for a period, a "decision form" and a "judgement form" have to be filled in by A, G, and Z. (Decisions about central bank variables, strike etc., judgements on bargaining performance and expectations).

(8) When decisions are made for several periods within one session, the procedure described in (1) to (7) is applied to one period after the other (for the number of periods within one session, see Table 3).

The players met for 12 sessions, one per week. They had to make decisions for the total of 31 periods corresponding to Table 3.

Table 3: The decision periods of the sessions and the fixed bargaining time.

session	period number	fixed bargaining time in min.
1	2	50
2	3, 4	20
3	5, 6	20
4	7, 8	20
5	9, 10	20
6	11, 12	20
7	13, 14	20
8	15, 16	20
9	17, 18	20
10	19-22	15
11	23-26	15
12	27,	15
	28-32	10

Interesting Investigation Problems

From this experiment we obtained about 200000 numbers. The large data base gives us the possibility to begin an extensive research. A schematic representation of the data generation by the experiment is given in Figure 3. The rectangles contain the different occasions from which we obtained experimental data. The arrows show the chronological order of the different occasions in the whole decision process. The triangles point to the data which have been partly analyzed until now. The methods used for this are:

SC = selection and classification,
F = factor analysis,
R = regression analysis.

Our method for selection (S) and classification (C) is described in the following section of this paper. We will also discuss the influence of macroeconomic knowledge on the experimental behavior.
The second paper[1] is concerned with the problem of data handling. Factor analysis (F) leads, among other conclusions, to data reduction and data transformation in order to prevent us from misinterpreting correlations. This instrument was applied to information, planning, and sociometric data.

---

1 Reinhard Tietz, Karl-Heinz Fischer and Klaus G. Schuster, On Handling Experimental Data of the KRESKO-Game with Factor Analysis and some Remarks on Interpersonal Relations, in this volume, pp.289-299.

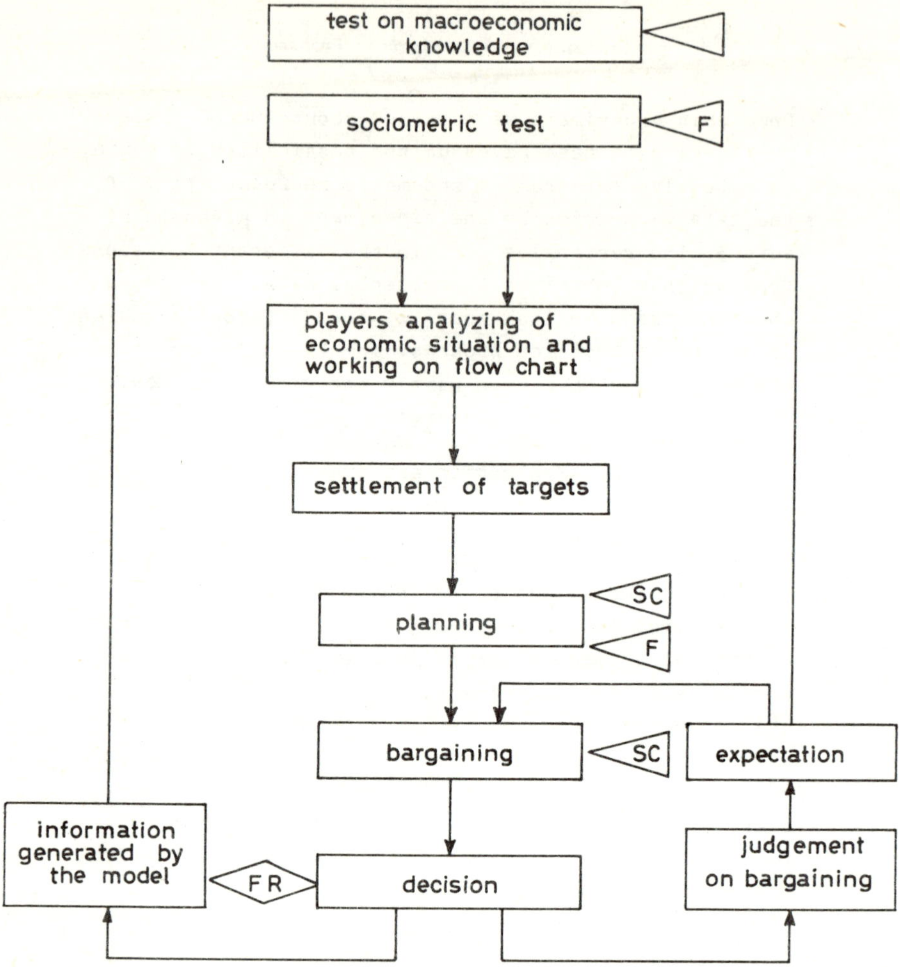

Figure 3: Data generation in the KRESKO experiment

Based on factoranalytical results the third paper[1] reports on some experiences with regression analysis (R) of the wage decisions in relation to information data. It may be fruitful to apply further regression analyses to planning and information data.

In the fourth paper[2] we present the first results on bargaining behavior obtained by regarding pure wage bargaining periods only. The explanation of the bargaining behavior is given by an spproach for a theory of mutual adaptation of aspiration levels, similar to the behavior theory of the abstract computer model. Regarding the planning forms, this approach will answer the following questions:

1.) Who makes the first concession?
2.) Which level of aspiration is reached by the first concession maker with the first concession?
3.) Which level of aspiration is reached by the first concession maker in the final bargaining result?

Criteria for the Description of Bargaining Variables Constellations

We examined for each of the three decision parameters the first seven planning variables of Table 1 (section 1) for both parties A and G, and two reali-

---

1 Reinhard Tietz and Volker Assmus, Some Experiences with Regression Analysis of the Wage Determination in the KRESKO-Game, in this volume, pp.300-304.

2 Reinhard Tietz and Hans-Jürgen Weber, On the Nature of the Bargaining Process in the KRESKO-Game, in this volume, pp.305-334.

zation variables, the variables of the decision form of the current and previous period (Table 1, section 3).

The 120 differences between the 16 planning and realization variables were transformed into 120 variables called "criteria", which can assume three values. If x and y are compared, the value is 1 for $x-y < 0$, 2 for $x-y = 0$, and 3 for $x-y > 0$. The three decision parameters yield altogether 360 criteria.

The mapping of the continuous variables into the discrete criteria allows easy selection by the computer of those of the 372 game periods which fulfill a given special planning structure determining the character of the period in respect to the start of the bargaining process. The criteria can be used to classify the periods. We can build up samples which are homogeneous in respect to a combination of criteria. This eliminates specific influences of the planning structure on the bargaining process and allows the investigation of specific hypotheses.

The criteria are also used to determine the similarity of two periods in respect to the planning structure by the following measures:

(1) Measure of similarity: The number of criteria taking the same value in two different periods (360 criteria).

(2) Restricted similarity measure: The number of criteria taking the same value in two different periods regarding the planning variables for the wage rate only (91 criteria).

We find the following result: Periods are very similar within sessions and dissimilar between sessions. In 122 out of 132 cases "the first decision period of a session" (FDP) is more similar to the second period of the same session than to the last period of the previous session.[1] This is true for the full similarity measure (binomial test: $\alpha < .0001$).

The high similarity between the FDP and the second period of a session, which amounts on the average to 302 of the maximum of 360 (84%), may follow from the fact that the plannings for both periods were done at the same time, based on the same information data. For this reason the FDP may be regarded as representative in a certain sense for the following decision periods of a session.

On the other hand there are differences in the information and decision situation in both bargaining periods. In the FDP the players have the information about the economic past. For the following periods of a session the players make decisions regarding their expectations on the economic development influenced by their last decisions in the FDP as well. Since we have not investigated the formation of expectations until now, we reduce, for certain purposes, the sample size from 372 periods to the 144 FDP only. Considering the similarity mentioned above, we hope to find the most important interdependence of the experiment in this reduced sample.

---

1 As Table 3 shows there are 11 sessions in which the decisions were made for more than one period.

The Influence of Time on the Bargaining Behavior

It is of some importance for the whole investigation to know the influence of time on the experimental behavior. For finding general tendencies we correlate - by means of the Spearman rank correlation r_S[1] - the time in terms of the session numbers (according to Table 3) with the average ranks of some characteristic variables through the FDP of the twelve games. The concordance between the games is tested by the Kendall coefficient of concordance W.

Table 4 shows that the number of bids and the relative bargaining time are significantly negatively correlated with the session numbers. This means that the activity in bargaining tends to become lower with the proceeding of time.
The range of bargaining (3) and tactical reserves (4 and 5) also decrease during the game. This seems to indicate that tactical aspects lose importance with increasing bargaining experience. The tendency seems to be greater for A than for G.
In contrast to that, the goodness of expectations on the behavior of the opposite party (6) is not significantly influenced by the passing of time.
These influences of time in the course of the whole experiment show that there is a learning process in bargaining behavior. The subjects become able to reach an agreement in a shorter time by means of fewer bids. The decrease of the range of bargaining and of

---

1 We use in the following the Spearman rank correlation coefficient r_S. The computations were done by means of the program RANG, written by F. Gebhardt, Deutsches Rechenzentrum, Darmstadt.

Table 4: Correlations between the time (session numbers) and some characteristic variables throughout 12 games in the FDP[1]

variable	correlation		concordance		
	r_S	$\alpha <$	W	χ^2	$\alpha <$
1) number of bids	-.87	.001	.32	42.3	.001
2) total bargaining time in percent of fixed bargaining time					
a) session 1 - 12	-.45	.10	.16	20.8	.05
b) session 2 - 12	-.89	.001			
3) range of bargaining $\Delta w_{AG}^{W1} = w_G^{W1} - w_A^{W1}$	-.86	.001	.18	24.8	.01
4) tactical reserve in respect to the bargaining result regarded as attainable (DU)					
a) of A: $w_A^{TRD} = w_A^{DU} - w_A^{W1}$	-.80	.005	.18	24.3	.02
b) of G: $w_G^{TRD} = w_G^{W1} - w_G^{DU}$	-.70	.01	.10	13.0	.30
5) tactical reserve in respect to planning (G)					
a) of A: $w_A^{TRG} = w_A^{G} - w_A^{W1}$	-.97	.001	.16	21.0	.05
b) of G: $w_G^{TRG} = w_G^{W1} - w_G^{G}$	-.79	.005	.12	16.4	.20
6) goodness of expectation for the first demand of the opposite party					
a) of A: $\lvert \hat{w}_A^{W1} - w_G^{W1} \rvert$	+.17	.30	.09	11.6	.50
b) of G: $\lvert w_A^{W1} - \hat{w}_G^{W1} \rvert$	-.27	.20	.09	12.1	.50

1 Only the growth rate of standard wage rate is used for the variables 3 to 6.

tactical reserves shows that the subjects start the bargaining process on a bargaining position which comes closer to final agreement. They learn to estimate the realization possibilities.

The Influence of Macroeconomic Knowledge

The experimental design allows to make some observations on the influence of macroeconomic knowledge and factors behind it. Such factors may be, for instance, discriminating power, open-mindedness, general interest or assiduity.

(1) Collective success is higher for games with a high level of macroeconomic knowledge ($r_S = .46$, $\alpha < .10$).

As a measure of the collective success of each game, we used the average of the growth rates of real net national product throughout all periods.
It should be mentioned that one student was not willing to take the test on macroeconomic knowledge earnestly. He finished the test after half the time. If we disregard this game, the correlation is $r_S = .65$ ($\alpha < .02$).
This tendency, that a better economic knowledge leads to a better game success, implies that better qualified students have more understanding for the economic relations underlying the experiment and are able to make better decisions. Their planning and decisions are more flexible and differentiated. This can, for instance, be shown by the similarity measure.

(2) The similarity of adjacent periods in consecutive sessions is greater for games with a lower level of macroeconomic knowledge ($r_S = .73$, $\alpha < .01$). (This is true for the restricted similarity measure).

Students with a higher level in macroeconomic knowledge react more sensitively on alteration of the economic situation.
In contrast to macroeconomic knowledge, there is no significant correlation between the collective success and the similarity measures.
If we examine the structure of planning variables we may state a normal structure:

	↑
W1	Direction of
G	favourability
DU	in the normal
KD	structure
KG	

The weak inequalities " $\leq$ " are fulfilled for A or G in at least 318 of 372 periods (86%).

(3) The normal structure in which planning variables show strict inequalities in the expected direction is more frequent in games with lower macroeconomic knowledge ($r_S = .52$, $\alpha < .05$).[1]

Since the number of periods in which the weak inequalities hold for A or G is not significantly influenced by the level of macroeconomic knowledge in a game

---

1 If we regard the structure of planning for A and G separately, we get the following correlation coefficients for A: $r_S = .86$ ($\alpha < .001$) and for G: $r_S = .56$ ($\alpha < .05$). This means that the influence of macroeconomic knowledge on the planning structure seems to be lower for the labor union players.

($r_S < .19$, $\alpha > .36$), this correlation shows that knowledgeable students more frequently set at least two of their planning variables at the same value. This means that on the other hand students with a lower level in macroeconomic knowledge tend to set each of their planning variables at a different value in the direction of favourability.[1] The differences in the planning structure might result from different abilities to understand the right meaning of planning variables, from different degrees of subjective uncertainty about the economic and bargaining situation, from different risk aversion, or from different uniformity of the game development.

We have stressed the macroeconomic knowledge in this context since we consider economic knowledge to have an important influence on the reliability of the results obtained by experimental economics, especially, if more complex decision situations are analyzed. As will be demonstrated in the fourth paper, there is a tendency to explain the experimental behavior by means of theoretical approaches more correctly, if the players' macroeconomic knowledge is high.

---

1 This can also be seen, if we regard the two variables w^G and w^{DU} only. The correlation coefficients between the macroeconomic knowledge of a game and the frequency of periods in which the strict inequality between w^G and w^{DU} holds in the direction of favourability are for A: $r_S = -.67$ ($\alpha < .02$), and for G: $r_S = -.46$ ($\alpha < .10$), whereas the corresponding correlations for the weak inequalities are only, for A: $r_S = -.37$ ($\alpha > .10$), and for G: $r_S = -.27$ ($\alpha > .15$).

10. ON HANDLING EXPERIMENTAL DATA OF THE KRESKO-GAME WITH FACTOR ANALYSIS AND SOME REMARKS ON INTERPERSONAL RELATIONS[1]

REINHARD TIETZ, KARL-HEINZ FISCHER AND KLAUS G. SCHUSTER*

One of the central problems of our investigation is the large number of about 200.000 pieces of data we obtained from the experiment KRESKO. Among them are the participants' decisions and the information data on the KRESKO economy computed by the model. Other groups of data are the expectation, planning, and bargaining data of the participants.[2] Additionally, we obtained data from sociometric tests.

We used factor analysis to get information on the correlation structure of data, and thus hints for further detailed evaluation. Our factor analysis is based on the principal component method. As input data we used a matrix of Pearson correlation coefficients. The estimation of communalities was done by means of squared multiple correlations or in some cases by the highest bivariate correlation coefficient. The correction of the estimates was done iteratively by refactoring. The original factor ma-

---

* Universität Frankfurt/Main

1 This paper should be read in connection with the preceding paper : Reinhard Tietz, The Macroeconomic Experimental Game KRESKO, in this volume, pp. 267-288.

2 Cf. Table 1 and 2 in: R. Tietz, op. cit., pp. 275-276.

trix was transformed by varimax rotation.[1/2] As a rule we consider only factor loadings not less than .5 .

Some Factoranalytical Results on Decision and Information Data

There are 193 decision and information variables for 32 periods in 12 second games. To eliminate linear dependencies and similarities between variables by definition we reduce the number of variables to 66.

To emphasize the causal influences of information on decisions, we consider the decision data together with the information data of the previous period.
The factor analysis throughout all 12 games extracted 13 factors. The total communality was 87.0% of the total variance. The factors represent 93.2% of the total original communality. There are 6 factors which were loaded only by information data and which show interdependences in the model.

---

1 The computations were done by means of the program PAFA, written by P. Schnell and F. Gebhardt, Deutsches Rechenzentrum, Darmstadt. We modified this program for our purposes.

2 On factor analysis see e.g. Harry H. Harman, Modern Factor Analysis, Second Edition, Revised, Chicago and London 1967;
Kurt Pawlik, Dimensionen des Verhaltens, Bern und Stuttgart 1968;
Karl Überla, Faktorenanalyse, Berlin-Heidelberg-New York 1968.

The three decision variables resulting from bargaining between the two parties - labor union (A) and employers' association (G) - loaded only 2 factors. The type of information variables loading the same factor as the growth rate of standard wage rate (w_T^Y) suggests that, on the average, bargaining parties tend to orientate their wage policy on the development of capital intensity and of labor productivity. The standard of working hours weekly (h_T^W) and the periods of notice for the employment contracts (Küf) are connected with employment of capacity and variables of the labor market, which also shows a reasonable orientation of bargaining.
The decision variables of the central bank players load five other factors. One of them is a factor representing the liquidity situation of the economy. The rediscount rate (z_D and also z_O) is connected with market interest rates. The remaining three factors are loaded by the central bank decisions only.
Additionally, we factoranalysed the same data for the 12 individual games separately. As a consequence of the small sample size, the results are not as reliable as in the aggregate case. Nevertheless, we will try to discuss some relations:

1. In games with a higher level of macroeconomic knowledge[1] the bargaining decision variables load more factors ($r_S = .75$; $\alpha < .01$).[2] More knowledgeable players base their decisions on more aspects

---

1 For the measurement of macroeconomic knowledge, cf. R. Tietz, op. cit., pp. 271 and 286-288

2 We use here and in the following the Spearman rank correlation coefficient signed with r_S. If the computation of rank correlations was done by computer, we used the program RANG, written by F. Gebhardt, Deutsches Rechenzentrum, Darmstadt.

of the situation.

2. The contribution of the first factor to total variance is higher in games with a greater collective success ($r_S = .46$, $\alpha < .10$).[1] Successful games typically have a smooth path of economic growth with high intercorrelations of economic variables. The contribution of the first factor is a measure of coherence.

The second result is not in contradiction to the first, because a low differentiation on a high number of information variables must not mean that the three bargaining variables are weakly differentiated at the same time.[2]

On the Handling of Planning Data

For testing hypotheses on the bargaining process, expectation and planning data are of main interest to us. For this reason a factor analysis was run on 108 variables, which include 79 variables of planning and bid forms, and 14 important information and decision data of the current and the previous periods. As noted earlier, we investigated only the 12 first decision

---

1 The collective success is measured in terms of the average of the growth rates of real net national product.

2 There are non-significant correlation coefficients between the contribution of the first factor and macroeconomic knowledge ($r_S = .13$, $\alpha = .33$), and between the contribution of the first factor and the number of factors loaded by the three bargaining variables ($r_S = -\ .27$, $\alpha = .20$). The correlation between the macroeconomic knowledge and collective success is $r_S = .46$ ($\alpha < .10$).

periods of a session (FDP).[1]
Throughout the 12 games we extracted 27 factors, which represent 95.5 % of the total original communality. The total communality was 94.9 % of the total variance. The first factor was loaded by the planning and bidding data for notice, the second by the corresponding data for working hours, and the third by the data for the wage rate. The planning data of the central bank were represented by 9 different factors,which may be partly interpreted as unique factors. Other factors were loaded by the planned strike and lock-out, by the priorities of the bargaining variables or by the limits for conflict.
The fact that the three first factors represent 51.9% of the total variance shows that the correlation within these three groups tends to be higher than to other variables, such as information data. These high correlations make it very difficult to disentangle separate influences within the three groups.
Consequently we transform each of these groups of variables by subtracting the bargaining result. The correlations now reveal more of the inner structure of the three groups. A new factor analysis on this data also results in 27 factors which represent 92.3% of the total communality. The total communality is 91.6% of the total variance. The first three factors represent now only 38.0% of the total variance which indicates a greater differentiation of the transformed data.

---

1 Cf. R. Tietz, op. cit., pp. 278 and 281-283

The distribution effect of the transformation becomes most clear in the case of notice variables, which load now 5 factors, in contrast to the non-transformed case, where all 19 notice variables load one factor. For the two other groups of transformed variables the situation is similar. The factor structure of the variables not transformed remains essentially unchanged by transformation. Thus, for further investigations of the bargaining process,we may use the correlations between the transformed variables with more confidence.

Factor Analysis of Sociometric Data

In the sociometric tests the players rated each other on a non-semantic rating scale ranging from 0 to 9. Attributes rated were:

- sympathy
- complaisance
- understanding of economic relations
- persuasive power
- fairness
- credibility
- courtesy

These ratings were run to determine whether interpersonal relations (social perception) had any influence on bargaining behavior. Ratings were carried out three time during the experiment: before starting the first games, i.e. before players knew tneir roles in the game; at the end of the first games, and finally at the end of the second games.

A first run of factor analyses showed high loadings of too many sociometric variables in the first factor. We assume that this was due to the following fact: Some of the participants were not able or not willing to do the ratings and rather gave the same points to all other players on one or more of the scales. This leads to rather high correlations between the individual scales, producing the clustering of variables in the first factor.
In this context it may be of some interest that the number of cases in which a subject gives identical ratings to all fellow subjects in a sociometric test is higher for subjects with a lower level of macroeconomic knowledge[1] ($r_S = .60$, $\alpha < .001$). Various interpretations are possible. Scales especially susceptible to low discrimination were those on fairness, credibility and courtesy. Additionally, it may be mentioned that players with a higher level in macroeconomic knowledge are, at the same time, more stable in their rating behavior.
To eliminate the effect of little-discriminating judges, the rating scores of all individual judges were transformed as follows: For each judge and each of the 3 tests the mean of scores given to other players was computed and subtracted from the original scores. The transformed scores were used to run a new factor analysis to check whether the sociometric scales did measure the same on different occasions, i.e. whether the factor pattern remained stable during the experiment or showed some systematic change:

---

1 Cf. R. Tietz, op. cit. pp. 271 and 286-288

1. Patterns of 3 factors were computed for each of the three occasions of rating. Results show that the factor patterns are nearly stable for the 3 occasions, if factor analysis is done throughout all games. This suggests that the sociometric scales measure the same on all three occasions.
2. The factor pattern looks as follows: One factor is loaded by the variables understanding of economic relations, persuasive power and sympathy; the variables fairness, credibility and courtesy load on other factors. The variable sympathy loads also a third factor together with complaisance and courtesy, showing that sympathy is in relation to two types of other variables. Type one relates to understanding of economic relations and persuasive power, which are more ready to objective assessment, whereas type two relates to complaisance and courtesy, which are more susceptible to subjective interpretation.
3. The contributions of the three factors to reproduced communality tend to become more equally distributed from occasion 1 to occasion 3. This finding may suggest that with growing familiarity of players with each other there is a tendency to more specific interpersonal perception.

Interpersonal Relations and Bargaining Behavior

We incorporate social-perception-items in our experimental design to receive a better understanding of the bargaining behavior

as affected by interpersonal relations and
as affecting interpersonal relations.

As far as the large body of data could be analyzed until now, there seems to be some evidence that both cases may apply, depending on which variables of the game are considered.
Regarding the influence of bargaining on interpersonal relations, some samples may be quoted: There is a significant positive correlation between collective success and average sympathy level at the end of second games ($r_S = .76$, $\alpha < .01$). At the same time there is a high significant positive correlation between rising sympathy level during the games and collective success, which indicates that players in successful games tend to increase their sympathy relations. At the beginning of second games, there was a negative correlation.
This negative correlation derives from the fact that players with a high level of macroeconomic knowledge tend to rate each other low in sympathy at the beginning of second games ($r_S = -.55$, $\alpha < .05$) and, at the same time, tend to achieve a higher collective success.[1] Very similar relations hold for ratings on complaisance and understanding of economic relations, thus showing some positive influence of successful interaction on interpersonal perception.

Another general finding has some bearing on the mutual relation of complaisance level and number of bids during the games: the lower the level of complaisance at the beginning of the second games, the higher is the number of bids in the FDP; and the higher the number of bids in a game, the stronger is the decrease of complaisance level during the

---

1 $r_S = .46$, cf. R. Tietz, op. cit. p. 286

games. Thus, a low complaisance level involves a stronger bargaining activity in terms of bids to reach an agreement. (The corresponding correlations are significant at the .10 level).
On the other hand, some conclusions may be drawn tentatively regarding the influence of interpersonal perception in particular on the "bargaining success" of labor union and employers' association.
There are some significant correlations between bargaining success of labor unions - as measured in terms of the (increasing) final agreement coefficient[1] - and sociometric ratings by the end of the first games. Ratings on this occasion may be assumed to show the base-line of interpersonal relations at the beginning of the second games.
Quoted individually, correlations indicate that a labor union is more successful in the game, if higher ratings on sympathy ($r_S = .40$, $\alpha < .10$), complaisance ($r_S = .55$, $\alpha < .05$), understanding of economic relations ($r_S = .51$, $\alpha < .05$) and persuasive power ($r_S = .61$, $\alpha < .05$) are given to the central bank by the employers' association as compared with ratings given by the labor union. It should be mentioned that the success of the labor union is not at all related to any preference of the central bank with regard to the labor union (or employers' association). The same is true for mutual ratings of the employers' association and the labor union on sympathy, complaisance and understanding of economic relations. At the same

---

1 The final agreement coefficient for w_T^{γ} is defined as:

$$\frac{w_T^{\gamma} - w_A^{W1}}{w_G^{W1} - w_A^{W1}}$$

It is a measure of relative concession.

time it is true that the success of the labor union is the greater, the higher it is rated on persuasive power by the employers' association and the lower the employers' association is rated by the labor union on this scale ($r_S = .45$, $\alpha < .10$).

Thus, it seems that the employers' association has to make larger concessions if it relies heavily on a positive but unrewarded and unresponded attitude towards the central bank, especially if mutual rating on persuasive power is unequal in favour of the labor union.

Correlations connecting the same ratings at the end of the second games and labor unions' success failed to be significant, thus showing an influence of initial sociometric status of parties on their bargaining success.

Thus it should be evident that influence of social interaction (as affected by bargaining) on interpersonal 'climate' within the group as a whole and influence of initial sociometric status of individual parties on their bargaining success are two matters of different concern.

Further investigations of our data should enable us to set up more specific hypotheses which could be subject to controlled experimentation.

11. SOME EXPERIENCES WITH REGRESSION ANALYSIS OF THE WAGE DETERMINATION IN THE KRESKO-GAME[1]

REINHARD TIETZ AND VOLKER ASSMUS*

In order to find some of the main influences on the experimental decisions in the KRESKO-game it seems reasonable to use regression analysis as part of the investigation program. Since the growth rate of the standard wage (w_T^Y) is of main interest, we restrict our investigation to this variable. This paper reports on first experiences with regression analysis of the available experimental data.

Our regression analysis is based on the method of single stage least squares estimation.[2] The computer program generates also the most important statistical measures for econometric tests.[3]

In the regressions we used the information data of the players. In order to analyze influences from information data on wage decisions, we lagged the explanatory variables by one period. As motivated earlier, we res-

---

* Universität Frankfurt/Main

1 This paper should be read in connection with the preceding paper: Reinhard Tietz, The Macroeconomic Experimental Game KRESKO, in this volume, pp.267-288.

2 Cf. e.g. Arthur S. Goldberger, Econometric Theory, New York-London-Sydney 1964.

3 We are indebted to Professor Gerhard Gehrig, who made his program MKQ1 available to us and gave valuable suggestions.

tricted the data base to the twelve first decision periods of a session (FDP).[1]
For the selection of hypotheses we regard the results obtained by factor analysis on decision and information data.[2] It seems useful to select as the first regressor a variable which loads the same factor as the regressand. To avoid hypotheses which have, a priori, a large probability to be burdened with high multicollinearity, it seems reasonable to combine the first regressor only with such variables which load other factors.[3]
The attempt to find regressions on w_T^Y for each of the twelve second games which fulfill statistical requirements in a strict manner was not successful. For the games with a high and uniform economic growth the problem of multicollinearity arises. In the other games the problem exists that the decision variables have - as a consequence of the different economic situations in the course of the game - high variances, and residuals not uniformly distributed.
As will be demonstrated in the fourth paper[4], it is useful to concentrate the investigations on 29 periods in which the bargaining is concerned with the standard wage rate only. From 14 hypotheses we select the fol-

---

1 Cf. R. Tietz, op. cit., pp. 278 and 281-283

2 Cf. the preceding paper: Reinhard Tietz, Karl-Heinz Fischer and Klaus G. Schuster, On Handling Experimental Data of the KRESKO-Game with Factor Analysis and some Remarks on Interpersonal Relations, in this volume, pp.289-299.

3 Cf., e.g., Karl Otwin Becker, Ökonometrische Prognosemethoden, Habilitationsschrift, Frankfurt 1969, pp. 178-184, (unpublished).

4 Reinhard Tietz and Hans-Jürgen Weber, On the Nature of the Bargaining Process in the KRESKO-Game, in this volume, pp.305-334.

lowing one which has with .02 the highest significance for the coefficients:

$$w_T^Y = .029\, G_U^Y + .757\, \pi_B^Y - .074\, q_{L_B a} \quad (1)$$

$$(.011) \quad (.050) \quad (.018)$$

The coefficient of determination R^2 amounts only to .60 which does not allow acceptance of this function without objections. The highest correlation coefficient between the regressors is .57.
Nevertheless, we will try to interpret this regression. It shows that w_T^Y is positively influenced by the growth rate of industry profits (G_U^Y) and by the growth rate of labour productivity (π_B^Y). The ratio of unemployment ($q_{L_B a}$) indicates a negative influence on w_T^Y.
This means that an increase in the growth rate of labour productivity of 1 per cent is followed by an increase of .76 per cent in the growth rate of the standard wage. The profit variable G_U^Y may represent, as a demand factor, the willingness of the employers' association to concede higher wages. The unemployment variable $q_{L_B a}$ may be regarded as a supply factor which influences the readiness of the labour union to be satisfied with lower wages.
As will be discussed in the fourth paper[1], it is useful to classify the selected 29 periods in three cases according to the difference between the planned bargaining results of the employers' association A (w_A^G) and the labour union G (w_G^G). This difference may represent the toughness of the bargaining situation.
The three cases are:

---

1 R. Tietz and H.-J. Weber, op. cit., pp. 306-310

1) Normal planning (N_w^P), with

$$w_A^G < w_G^G \qquad \text{(11 periods).}$$

2) Agreement of planning (A_w^P), with

$$w_A^G = w_G^G \qquad \text{(12 periods).}$$

3) Inverse planning (I_w^P), with

$$w_A^G > w_G^G \qquad \text{(6 periods).}$$

We ran a regression analysis for the hypothesis (1) for each of the three cases separately. The result for the N_w^P-case is nearly the same as for the total sample. But the regression for the A_w^P-case is different:

$$w_T^\gamma = .162\, G_U^\gamma + .610\, \pi_B^\gamma - .141\, q_{L_B a} \qquad (2)$$
$$(.056) \qquad (.089) \qquad (.037)$$

The regression coefficients are significant on the .01 level. The coefficient of determination R^2 increases to .82.[1]

The absolutely increased coefficients of G_U^γ and $q_{L_B a}$, in comparison with the total sample, indicate that in the A_w^P-case the final bargaining result w_T^γ is influenced to a larger extent by the specific orientation data of each role. In the A_w^P-case, in which the plan-

---

1 The I_w^P-case contains only six periods; therefore we also ran a regression for a sample containing the A_w^P- and I_w^P-case which shows nearly the same result as in the A_w^P-case.

nings of both parties coincide per definition, the bargaining process leads to a result which coincides with the planning, too. Since the coefficient of determination is with .82 in the A_w^P-case .30 higher than in the N_w^P-case we can explain the A_w^P-case better than the N_w^P-case by regression. For this reason we can assume that the planning is influenced by information on the economic development to a higher degree than the bargaining result itself. Therefore, it seems to be promising to use regression methods for that complex of the investigation in which the influence of information on planning will be analyzed.

12. ON THE NATURE OF THE BARGAINING PROCESS IN THE KRESKO-GAME[1]

REINHARD TIETZ AND HANS-JÜRGEN WEBER*

In this paper we will discuss the bargaining behavior of players in the KRESKO experiment. A theory which describes the behavior of the players during the bargaining process should virtually answer the following three questions:

(1) Which of the two bargaining parties - the employers' association (A) or the labour union (G) - makes the first concession after the game leader has announced, and the three players have argued for, the first demands?

(2) Is the amount of the first concession explainable?

(3) Which factors determine the bargaining result?

---

* Universität Frankfurt/Main.

1 This paper should be read in connection with the preceding paper: Reinhard Tietz, The Macroeconomic Experimental Game KRESKO, in this volume, pp. 267-288.

The Selection of the Sample

This investigation is based on a small sample of bargaining periods. Complex cases, especially those involving problems of compensation, are reserved for further studies.

From the 144 "first decision periods of a session" (FDP) we separate by means of special criteria[1] 31 periods in which the two parties bargain only about the standard of wage rate. In these periods the first demand of A is lower than that of G ($w_A^{W1} < w_G^{W1}$).

The Planning Structure

In 29 periods the structure of the planning variables[2] fulfills the following relations:

$$(1)\quad \begin{aligned} w_A^{W1} &\leq w_A^{G} \leq w_A^{DU} \leq w_A^{KD} \leq w_A^{KG} \\ w_G^{W1} &\geq w_G^{G} \geq w_G^{DU} \geq w_G^{KD} \geq w_G^{KG} . \end{aligned}$$

This means for the labour unions that the planning (w_G^G) is not greater than the first demand (w_G^{W1}) and not less than the "bargaining result regarded as attainable" (w_G^{DU}), and that the planned conflict threat (w_G^{KD}) is not greater than the bargaining result regarded as attainable and not less than the planned

1 Cf. R. Tietz, op. cit., pp. 281-283

2 Cf. List of Variables, Appendix A, and Values of Variables, Appendix B, pp.331-332.

conflict limit (w_G^{KG}), and vice versa for A. Only in two periods of game No. 16 does this relation not hold.

It is fruitful to examine three cases which differ in the constellation of the two planned bargaining results:

(1) Normal planning (N_w^P), where the planned standard of wage rate of A is lower than that of G ($w_A^G < w_G^G$).

(2) Agreement of planning (A_w^P), where the planning coincides ($w_A^G = w_G^G$).

(3) Inverse planning (I_w^P), where the planning of A is higher than that of G ($w_A^G > w_G^G$).

Table 1 presents some characteristics of the three cases. Column 2 shows that each of the 12 second games is represented in this sample at least once. The three cases do not differ in respect to the average of the session numbers (column 3).[1] This means that the three cases have nearly the same probability to occur in the course of the whole experiment.

Column 4 contains the planning difference $\Delta G = w_G^G - w_A^G$, the selecting criterion of the three cases. The averages of the other characteristics (column 5-9) have the same falling tendency as ΔG.

The greater the planning difference ΔG (column 4), the larger is also the range of bargaining, which is defined as the difference between the first demands

---

1 The test value H of the Kruskal-Wallis one-way analysis of variance by ranks is .27 which corresponds to a probability under the null hypothesis greater than 80 %.

Table 1: Some characteristics of the three planning constellations

case	game	period	$\Delta G = w_G^G - w_A^G$	$\Delta w_{AG}^{W1} = w_G^{W1} - w_A^{W1}$	number of bids of the two parties after the first bids: without concession	with concession	total	total bargaining time in % of fixed bargaining time
(1)	(2)	(3)	(4)	(5)	(6)	(7)	(8)	(9)
N_w^P	11	17	7	7	1	2	3	120
	12	5	.48	1.5	0	3	3	130
	13	11	1.5	4	2	2	4	110
		15	4	5.5	3	0	3	95
		19	1	1.5	0	2	2	53
	14	3	1	1	5	2	7	120
	16	17	1	6	0	3	3	85
	17	2	5.78	5.78	5	6	11	98
		19	23	30	0	3	3	113
	20	13	.5	.5	4	2	6	75
	21	2	3	4.5	3	3	6	58
		15	.2	.2	0	1	1	40
		23	.1	.1	0	2	2	60
average:			3.74	5.20	1.77	2.39	4.17	89
A_w^P	16	5	0	2	0	2	2	85
		15	0	8	0	3	3	80
	17	5	0	1.75	0	4	4	75
	18	13	0	1	0	2	2	35
		23	0	.5	0	1	1	53
	19	7	0	1.32	3	2	5	105
	20	2	0	4	0	3	3	24
		7	0	1	1	2	3	70
		9	0	.5	3	2	5	60
		11	0	.5	1	2	3	60
		23	0	.5	0	2	2	40
	22	19	0	.4	0	2	2	73
average:			0	1.79	.67	2.25	2.92	63
I_w^P	12	9	-.03	.97	0	4	4	95
	15	2	-1.5	3	0	2	2	18
	18	9	-.22	1	0	3	3	60
	20	5	-.26	1	1	2	3	65
	21	27	-.05	.05	0	1	1	20
	22	23	-.1	.1	0	1	1	40
average:			-.36	1.02	.17	2.17	2.33	50

(Δw_{AG}^{W1}, column 5). The Spearman rank correlation coefficient[1] r_S = .51 is significant on the .005 level, which supports our above statements on the planning structure.

We suppose that the three cases differ in the toughness of the bargaining. For instance, it is more difficult in the N_w^P-case to come to an agreement satisfying both parties than in the A_w^P-case. The same tendency can be seen by comparing the A_w^P- and I_w^P-cases.

The toughness of bargaining may be measured by the number of bids without a concession (column 6), and also by the length of the bargaining time (column 9).

The rank correlation between column 4 and column 6 is with r_S = .41 on the .05 level significant. The correlation between the planning difference and the bargaining time is even more significant (r_S = .55, α < .001).

The planning difference ΔG, the selection criterion of the three cases, is an important determinant of the toughness of the bargaining.

Table 2: Correlations between the planning constellation and the number of bids (r_S)

	number of bids	
	without concession	with concession
planning difference ΔG	.412	.132
range of bargaining $\Delta W1$	.161	.529

1 We use here and in the following the Spearman rank correlation coefficient r_S, which was computed by the program RANG, written by F. Gebhardt, Deutsches Rechenzentrum, Darmstadt.

It is interesting to see from Table 2 that the number of concessions is not significantly influenced by the planning difference. Substituting the range of bargaining Δw_{AG}^{W1} for the planning difference ΔG we find the opposite result. This suggests that the toughness of the bargaining does not influence the number of concessions. Only the range of bargaining is highly significantly correlated ($\alpha < .005$) with the number of concessions.[1]

Further Reduction of the Sample

Before we turn to our three main problems mentioned above, we have to reduce our sample to 29 bargaining periods, because two of the 31 periods can only be explained by the intervention of the central bank player. In game 13, period 15, the central bank player suggested no increase of the wage rate. Therefore, the bargaining parties saved their face and broke down the negotiation, which they considered to be equivalent to a concession to 0 %.

In the same game in period 19 the central bank player declared a wage increase of 4 % to be useful for the development of the economy. He insisted on a result, which is outside the bargaining range Δw_{AG}^{W1}. As a result the union player increased his demand from 1.5% to 4% and the other party conceded from 0% to 4%. Such behavior can never be explained by a theory of concession.

---

1 From table 1 it may also be seen that the total number of bids decreases in the course of the experiment ($r_S = -.62$, $\alpha < .001$). The same tendency shows the range of bargaining but not the planning difference.

The Theory of Zeuthen

Point 1: Who Makes the First Concession?

From the numerous bargaining theories the theory of Zeuthen[1] seems to be most applicable to the experimental set-up.
In this model the possibility of conflict is taken as a motivation for concession. He assumes that the parties know their utility values at the conflict points which remain unchanged throughout the bargaining process. We assume that the growth rates of wages can be linearly transformed into utilities (Fig.1). Therefore we may use the growth rate of the standard wage instead of utilities.

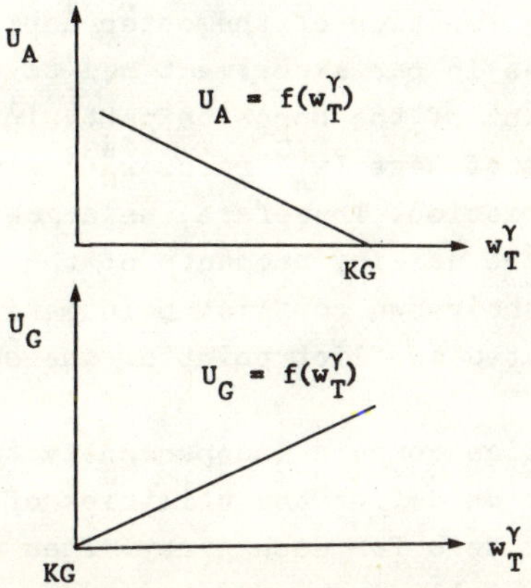

w_T^{γ} = Growth rate of standard wages

KG = Conflict point

U_A = Utilities for the employers' association

U_G = Utilities for the labour union

Figure 1: Utilities and growth rates of standard wages for the employers' association and the labor union.

---

1 Frederik Zeuthen, Problems of Monopoly and Warfare, London 1930, Chap. IV, pp. 104-150.

Zeuthen now argues (in the interpretation of Harsanyi[1]) that player A will concede if the utility product ($U_A^\alpha \cdot U_G^\alpha$) resulting from his demand α is lower than the utility product ($U_A^\beta \cdot U_G^\beta$) which results from the demand β of player G.
I.e., if

$$U_A^\alpha \cdot U_G^\alpha < U_A^\beta \cdot U_G^\beta, \tag{2}$$

player A will concede.

The Theory of Zeuthen Under Incomplete Information

Zeuthen makes the assumption of perfect knowledge, that means: each party knows correctly the conflict point and the utility function of the other party. The bargaining parties in our experiment had to estimate the conflict point of the opposite party in terms of growth rates of wage ($\hat{w}_A^{KG}$ resp. $\hat{w}_G^{KG}$) without having complete information. Therefore, we argue that each party compares the utility products of the first offers according to their own conflict point and according to the estimated conflict point of the opposite party.
In this way both parties compare independently two utility products. Let us define the utilities of the conflict points to be zero for each party. Then the party A considers the following products:

---

1 John C. Harsanyi, Approaches to the Bargaining Problem Before and After the Theory of Games: A Critical Discussion of Zeuthen's, Hick's, and Nash's Theories, Econometrica 24, 1956, pp. 144-157.

$$(w_A^{KG} - w_A^{W1}) \cdot (w_A^{W1} - \hat{w}_A^{KG}) \quad \text{and}$$
$$(w_A^{KG} - w_G^{W1}) \cdot (w_G^{W1} - \hat{w}_A^{KG}) \; .$$

The corresponding products for G are:

$$(w_G^{W1} - w_G^{KG}) \cdot (\hat{w}_G^{KG} - w_G^{W1}) \quad \text{and}$$
$$(w_A^{W1} - w_G^{KG}) \cdot (\hat{w}_G^{KG} - w_A^{W1}) \; .$$

In this way both parties make up their minds, which of them has to concede. Table 3 illustrates the possible outcomes.

Table 3: The first concession according to the theory of Zeuthen under the assumption of imperfect knowledge

case	must concede in the opinion of A	must concede in the opinion of G	prediction according to Zeuthen; who makes a concession?
1	A	A	A
2	A	G	indeterminate
3	G	A	no one
4	G	G	G

If, for instance, the employer's association A thinks that he has to concede, and the labour union G also thinks that A has to concede, then we suppose that the theory of Zeuthen predicts that A makes the first concession (Table 3, case 1).

In case 2 each party is of the opinion that he himself has to concede. Therefore, the theory cannot make a prediction.
In case 3 each party thinks that the opponent must concede. Then no party should concede according to the theory.
Case 4 must be regarded in the same way as case 1.

The outcomes of 25 of the 29 investigated periods are distributed among the four cases of Table 3 according to the following Table 4. For instance, case 4 occurred 6 times. The hypothesis is that G has to concede. This prediction was proved 3 times right and 3 times wrong.

Table 4: The prediction of the first concession according to Zeuthen under the assumption of imperfect knowledge

case	occurs	the prediction is		
		right	indeterminate	wrong
1	7	6	-	1
2	7	-	7	-
3	5	-	-	5
4	6	3	-	3
1-4	25	9	7	9
5	4	-	2	2
total	29	9	9	11

In four periods one party is indifferent as a consequence of equal utility products. We assume in accordance with Zeuthen[1] that this party has to concede. Then we may regard a fifth case which is transformable into cases 1-4. In this way two of the four periods of case 5 can be classified into case 1 and the other two into case 2.
Our hypothesis is that the theory of Zeuthen predicts, which of the bargaining parties will make the first concession. This hypothesis must be rejected in favour of the null hypothesis that the prediction is randomly distributed with $\chi^2 = .67$, which corresponds to a probability greater than .70. The corresponding value of χ^2 for the 25 periods without case 5 amounts to .12 associated with a probability of more than .90.

Cases 2 and 3 can only occur under the assumption of imperfect knowledge. This assumption was not made by Zeuthen. Therefore one may take the view that his theory can predict the first concession maker only, if definite constellations occur, as in cases 1 and 4. Under this assumption nine predictions are right and four are wrong. For this result the binomial test gives a probability under the null hypothesis of .13.

The Influence of Argueing for the First Demands on the Level of Information

The unpredictability of the first concession maker might result from the argueing for the first demands. Due to that reasoning the bargaining parties got quite a good idea of the actual bargaining situation. If we assume that the level of information is raised

---

1 Cf. J.C. Harsanyi, op. cit., p. 148.

so high that the players gain nearly perfect knowledge, we may expect that the original theory of Zeuthen will give better results than our modification above.
To test this hypothesis we substitute the expected conflict limits ($\hat{w}_A^{KG}$ resp. $\hat{w}_G^{KG}$) for the planned conflict limits (w_G^{KG} resp. w_A^{KG}). The first concession maker is then determined by comparing the following products:

$$(5)\quad \begin{array}{l} (w_A^{KG} - w_A^{W1}) \cdot (w_A^{W1} - w_G^{KG}) \quad \text{and} \\ (w_A^{KG} - w_G^{W1}) \cdot (w_G^{W1} - w_G^{KG}) \quad . \end{array}$$

The result may be seen in Table 5.

Table 5: The prediction of the first concession according to the theory of Zeuthen under the assumption of perfect knowledge

the prediction is		
right	indeterminate	wrong
20	1	8

Obviously 20 right predictions differ positively from the results of Table 4. The hypothesis that Zeuthen's theory cannot predict which party will concede first, can be rejected under the assumption of perfect knowledge by means of the binomial test with $\alpha < .05$.
So we might say that the players are able to correct their estimations of the conflict limits by comparing

the reasoning of the opposite party with their own expectations. Since the planned conflict limits are not announced it is not surprising that for 8 periods the predictions are wrong.
By this highly interesting result the idea suggests itself that in real bargaining situations, as they occur in KRESKO, in which two parties try to get better results by motivating their own points of view, the level of information rapidly becomes sufficiently high so that we can explain the bargaining behavior by a theory developed for games with complete information.

Point 2: The Amount of the First Concession

According to Zeuthen (in the interpretation of Harsanyi) the first concession has to change the sign of inequality of equation (2) resp. (5), if the first concession maker wants the opposite party to concede next. This is not true in 23 of 29 periods. It makes clear that the theory of Zeuthen cannot explain the amount of the first concession in the KRESKO experiment.

Point 3: The Final Bargaining Result

The final bargaining result γ should maximize the utility product:

$$U_A^\gamma \cdot U_G^\gamma \rightarrow \max !$$

In comparing the hypothetical result according to Zeuthen with the empirical KRESKO data we found that only in two periods was this maximum reached exactly. In seven other periods the empirical and hypothetical results were close together. In the other 20 periods the hypothetical and empirical results differed not less than $|.50|$ of w_T^{γ}.

These results show that the theory of Zeuthen cannot explain the amount of the first concession nor the final bargaining result.

A Concession Approach for a Theory of Mutual Adaptation of Aspiration Levels

Point 1: Who Makes the First Concession?

Instead of regarding the conflict limits as the main determinants, we should now consider other planning and expectation variables which possibly determine which party will concede first.

The willingness to make concessions during the negotiation is embodied in the difference between the "bargaining result regarded as attainable" (w_A^{DU} resp. w_G^{DU}) and the first demand (w_A^{W1} resp. w_G^{W1}). We call the differences,

$$(w_A^{DU} - w_A^{W1}) \text{ and}$$

$$(w_G^{W1} - w_G^{DU}) \quad ,$$

"tactical reserves." By comparing both tactical reserves the party with the higher willingness to make concessions can be determined. That means, if

$$(6) \qquad (w_A^{DU} - w_A^{W1}) > (w_G^{W1} - w_G^{DU}) \ ,$$

the employers' association has to concede first, and vice versa.
The hypothesis that (6) predicts the party which concedes first is right in 20 periods (Table 6, column 4). The better predictability in the N_w^P-case hints that the variables w_A^{DU} and w_G^{DU} have more importance in the case of normal planning than in the other cases. Substituting in (6) w_A^{DU} resp. w_G^{DU} by the "planned bargaining results" (w_A^G resp. w_G^G) the corresponding hypothesis cannot be verified.
Another possibility of predicting the party which concedes first follows from the fact that the first demands are announced simultaneously by the game leader before the players argue for their demands.[1] With the announcement of w_A^{W1} resp. w_G^{W1} the players get an accurate correction of their estimations ($\hat{w}_A^{W1}$ resp. $\hat{w}_G^{W1}$).

We found a significant correlation between A's own tactical reserve ($w_A^{DU} - w_A^{W1}$) and the difference ($\hat{w}_A^{W1} - w_A^{DU}$), with $r_S = .79$ ($\alpha < .001$). The corresponding correlation for G shows $r_S = .64$ ($\alpha < .001$). The difference ($\hat{w}_A^{W1} - w_A^{DU}$) might be interpreted as A's estimation of G's tactical reserve. The high correlations indicate a rather stable splitting of the expected bargaining range ($\hat{w}_A^{W1} - w_A^{W1}$) resp. ($w_G^{W1} - \hat{w}_G^{W1}$) by the own bargaining result regarded as attainable (w_A^{DU} resp. w_G^{DU}).
Supposing that the players would have known the correct first demands of their opponents before their own planning, one may assume that the own tactical reserve might have been influenced. With the knowledge of the first opposite demand the players argue more or less vigorously and attack more or less keenly the opposite demand. In this way both players get an idea

1 Cf. R. Tietz, op. cit., p. 277

Table 6: The first concession maker explained by the comparison of tactical reserves or tacit concessions

case	game	period	prediction by the comparison of tactical reserves			prediction by the comparison of tacit concessions			prediction by the theory of Zeuthen		
(1)	(2)	(3)	(4)			(5)			(6)		
N_w^P	11	17	+			+			+		
	12	5	+					–	+		
	13	11	+			+			+		
	14	3	+				0				–
	16	17	+			+			+		
	17	2			–			–			–
		19	+			+			+		
	20	13	+				0				–
	21	2	+			+			+		
		15	+			+			+		
		23	+			+			+		
frequencies :			10	–	1	7	2	2	8	–	3
A_w^P	16	5	+			+			+		
		15			–			–			–
	17	5	+			+				0	
	18	13	+			+			+		
		23	+			+			+		
	19	7	+			+			+		
	20	2		0		+			+		
		7			–			–			–
		9		0		+			+		
		11	+			+			+		
		23	+			+			+		
	22	19	+			+					–
frequencies :			8	2	2	10	–	2	8	1	3
I_w^P	12	9			–	+			+		
	15	2		0		+			+		
	18	9			–		0				–
	20	5	+			+			+		
	21	27	+			+			+		
	22	23		0				–			–
frequencies :			2	2	2	4	1	1	4	–	2
total frequencies:			20	4	5	21	3	5	20	1	8

legend: + = the prediction is right

0 = the prediction is indeterminate

– = the prediction is wrong

of the strength of both bargaining positions. The strength of the bargaining position may be expressed by the correction of the estimation of the opposite tactical reserve.
For a bargaining party such a correction of his estimation has an effect similar to an opponent's concession in the case where he would have estimated the opponent's first demand correctly. For this reason we define the corrections of the estimation of the opposite first demand as "tacit concessions."
By comparing both tacit concessions we may find that the party which made the smaller tacit concession concedes first. If, for instance,

$$(7) \qquad (\hat{w}_A^{W1} - w_G^{W1}) > (w_A^{W1} - \hat{w}_G^{W1})$$

player A makes the first concession. Table 6, column 5, shows 21 right predictions obtained from (7). It is of interest that in the A_w^P-case the best results are obtained by the comparison of tacit concessions.
Obviously, all three approaches result in nearly the same total number of right predictions. It is possible to increase the number of right predictions to 24 by combining column 4 (N_w^P-case) and column 5 (A_w^P- and I_w^P-case). Only in five periods all of the three approaches fail.
It is interesting to note that the prediction of the first concession maker tends to be easier in games with better macroeconomic knowledge. Considering the 24 explainable periods the null hypothesis may be rejected with an error probability of $\alpha < .10$ according to the Mann-Whitney U Test.[1]

---

1 For the theory of Zeuthen the same hypothesis gives an error probability of $\alpha < .17$.

Point 2: The Amount of the First Concession

Having discussed the problem concerning the first concession maker, we will now investigate the amount of the first concession.

Since the amount of the first concession ($w_{C1}^{\Delta W}$)[1] is highly correlated with the range of bargaining (Δw_{AG}^{W1}) ($r_S = .93$), we eliminate the influence of the bargaining range by regarding the coefficient of the first concession:

$$\frac{w_{C1}^{\Delta W}}{\Delta w_{AG}^{W1}} .$$

This coefficient correlates positively with the corresponding coefficient of netto tacit concession[2]:

$$\frac{w_{NC1}^{TC} - w_{C1}^{TC}}{\Delta w_{AG}^{W1}}$$

($r_S = .35$, $\alpha < .05$).

---

1 $$w_{C1}^{\Delta W} = \begin{cases} w_A^{Wi} - w_A^{W1}, & \text{if A makes the first concession in his bid form i, and} \\ w_G^{W1} - w_G^{Wi}, & \text{if G makes the first concession in his bid form i.} \end{cases}$$

2 The tacit concession of the first concession maker (C1) is defined:

$$w_{C1}^{TC} = \begin{cases} w_A^{W1} - \hat{w}_G^{W1}, & \text{if A is C1, and} \\ \hat{w}_A^{W1} - w_G^{W1}, & \text{if G is C1.} \end{cases}$$

The tacit concession of the party which is not the first concession maker (NC1) is defined:

$$w_{NC1}^{TC} = \begin{cases} \hat{w}_A^{W1} - w_G^{W1}, & \text{if G is NC1, and} \\ w_A^{W1} - \hat{w}_G^{W1}, & \text{if A is NC1.} \end{cases}$$

This tendency supports our "tacit concession approach." It shows that the amount of the first concession does not only depend on the range of bargaining, but is additionally influenced by the netto tacit concession.

If we regard the values to which the first concessions have led, we find four prominent levels, which can be derived from the planning variables of the first concession maker. The four levels are:

(1) the mean between the first demand of the first concession maker w_{C1}^{W1} and his planned bargaining result w_{C1}^{G},

(2) the planned bargaining result w_{C1}^{G},

(3) the mean between w_{C1}^{G} and the bargaining result regarded as attainable w_{C1}^{DU}, and

(4) the bargaining result regarded as attainable w_{C1}^{DU}.

Evidently 26 first concessions lead exactly to one of the four levels, as can be seen in Table 7. This shows that the players regard these prominent points as levels of aspiration. In 13 periods the concession leads to the nearest aspiration level. In 15 periods the second nearest level is reached. In 6 periods of the N_{w}^{P}-case the first demand coincides exactly with the planned bargaining result, and therefore the concessions lead to the levels 3 and 4.
The hypothesis that the first concession maker will make further concessions if his first concession leads to the next level, and that he will make no further concessions if his first concession leads to the second nearest aspiration level, is significant with $\alpha < .01$ by means of the binomial test.

Table 7: Levels of aspiration reached by the first concession[1]

aspiration level / case	$\frac{w_{C1}^{W1} + w_{C1}^{G}}{2}$ (1)	w_{C1}^{G} (2)	$\frac{w_{C1}^{G} + w_{C1}^{DU}}{2}$ (3)	w_{C1}^{DU} (4)
N_w^P	1	3	3	3+(1)*
A_w^P	5	7	-	-
I_w^P	4†	2	-	-
total	10	12	3	3+(1)*

1 The four periods in which the level reached equals $w_{C1}^{G} = w_{C1}^{DU}$ are classified in column 2.

* One concession did not lead to one of the four aspiration levels. This concession must be explained by the suggestion of the central bank player after exceeding the fixed bargaining time. The concession led then to a value lower than w_{C1}^{DU}.

† Two concessions did not lead exactly but close to this aspiration level.

As a similar result we found: The coefficient of the first concession is lower if further concessions follow, and is higher if no further concessions are made. This hypothesis is supported by the Mann-Whitney U Test, with $\alpha < .001$.
These results show that the amount of the first concession is highly influenced by aspiration levels. The player decides by tactical considerations, which of his two nearest levels the first concession will reach. The factors determining the tactical behavior will be investigated in the future.

Point 3: The Final Bargaining Result

The final bargaining results of the investigated 29 periods are within the range of bargaining. Therefore we are allowed to discuss the final result only from the viewpoint of the first concession maker. Furthermore, we eliminate the influence of the bargaining range as we did before.
The total number of concessions of the party which concedes first had no significant influence on the "agreement coefficient of the first concession maker."[1]
The hypothesis that the first concession maker concedes not less than the opposite party is significant on the .0005 level according to the binomial test. This means that the agreement coefficient

---

1 The agreement coefficient of the first concession maker is defined as:

$$\frac{w_{C1}^{\Delta WT}}{\Delta w_{AG}^{W1}} = \frac{\text{total concession of the first concession maker}}{\text{range of bargaining}}$$

$$\frac{w_{C1}^{\Delta WT}}{\Delta w_{AG}^{W1}} \geq .5.$$

It fits with this hypothesis that the first concession maker will finally concede rather more than less than the opposite party. The corresponding null hypothesis may be rejected on the .02 level.[1]
These results show that the player, who has the weaker bargaining position, must not only make the first concession but finally has to concede relatively more than the opposite party.
We found even better results by considering the aspiration levels. The three cases differ definitely in their final bargaining results,if we consider the aspiration levels of the first concession maker. Figure 2 presents the final bargaining result in aspiration levels. The ordinate shows the aspiration levels of both parties. For every period the final bargaining result is mapped for both parties ("x" for C1 and "o" for NC1). If the final bargaining result does not reach exactly one of the aspiration levels, we have mapped it in relation to the difference of the two neighbouring aspiration levels of the considered party.
In the N_w^P-case the first concession maker agrees with the opposite party at his "bargaining result regarded as attainable" (w_{C1}^{DU}). Only if the "bargaining result regarded as attainable of the opposite party" (w_{NC1}^{DU}) is better for him, the first concession maker agrees

---

1 There are 16 periods in which $\frac{w_{C1}^{\Delta WT}}{\Delta w_{AG}^{W1}} > .5$ and 5 periods in which $\frac{w_{C1}^{\Delta WT}}{\Delta w_{AG}^{W1}} < .5$.

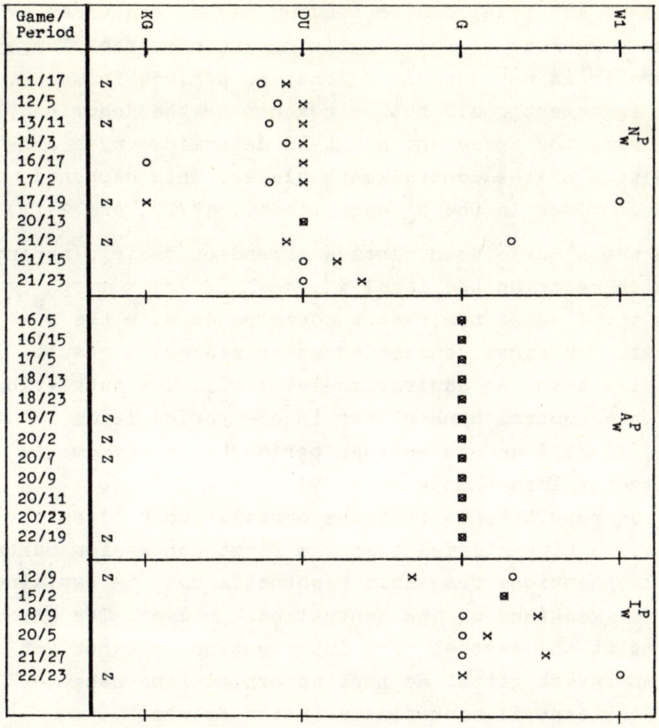

Figure 2: The final bargaining result in aspiration levels.

x = final bargaining result in aspiration levels of the first concession maker
o = final bargaining result in aspiration levels of the party which did not concede first
Z = central bank player suggests a bargaining result

W1 = first demand
G = planned bargaining result
DU = bargaining result regarded as attainable
KG = planned conflict limit

(Example: game 17, period 19 : $w_{C1}^{KG} = w_{T}^{\gamma} = w_{NC1}^{W1}$)

to w_{NC1}^{DU} (period 21/15, 21/23). The fact that only such a low level can be reached may be explained by the toughness of the bargaining in this case. Therefore it is not surprising that in periods in which an agreement could not be reached in the described manner, the agreement point is determined by a suggestion of the central bank player. This happened three times in the N_w^P-case (11/17, 17/19, and 21/2).

In the A_w^P-case both parties agreed on their planning, which means on the level $w_{C1}^G = w_{NC1}^G$.

In the I_w^P-case the result corresponds with the N_w^P-case. The first concession maker reaches a result better than the aspiration level w_{C1}^G. The suggestion of the central bank player in one period leads to w_{C1}^G (22/23) and in another period to an agreement slightly less than w_{C1}^G (12/9).

These results show that the opposite party does not reach a higher level than the first concession maker. All exceptions from this hypothesis must be explained by suggestions of the central bank player. The problems of the central bank intervention have not yet been investigated. We hope to explain the behavior of the central bank player in the future.

The first concession maker has to make greater concessions, but achieves a better aspiration level than the opposite party. This seemingly inconsistent result can be explained as follows: the greater tactical reserve enables the first concession maker to concede in terms of growth rates of standard wages more than the opposite party without violating his corresponding aspiration level. This means that a great tactical reserve gives the player a weak bargaining position in the beginning of the negotiation, but enables him to reach a stronger position to defend his aspiration levels. In this way the opposite party is given the impression that it achieves a better result in terms of the bargaining variable than the first concession maker. Therefore the result obtained might satisfy both parties.

Conclusion

In the KRESKO experiment the students started the second games with the experience of 24 periods of the first games. The experiment required an intensive engagement of the students during three months. Our main results from the wage bargaining in the second games are as follows:

1) The argueing for demands raises the level of information rapidly. Therefore, theories which suppose perfect knowledge are sufficient to explain bargaining behavior.
2) The concession approach offers a possibility of explaining bargaining behavior without regarding threat points.
3) Concession making heavily depend upon levels of aspiration.
4) In tough bargaining situations the realisation of the lowest satisfactory aspiration level is not secured and must be defended. A reasonably high "tactical reserve" gives the players the possibility of having success in defending this level.
5) In bargaining situations with lower tension, where both parties can reach a higher level of aspiration, the lowest satisfactory aspiration level is not jeopardized. It must not be defen-

ded and loses its importance as a point of orientation. Therefore, the reasoning gives no clue with respect to this level, and other points of orientation gain importance. Then "tacit concessions" measure the relative weakness of the bargaining positions.

6) Each demand is connected with a claim upon the other party to accept an obligation to respond. This obligation is accepted if the opposite party's concession is large enough.

7) Not only "tacit concessions" and concessions in the sense of our paper are regarded as concessions to create an obligation to respond, but also "tactical reserves," because the difference of both tactical reserves can be considered as an implicit concession of one party.

8) The final bargaining result is determined by the toughness of the bargaining and by the aspiration levels of the first concession maker.

9) The importance of a bargaining theory of mutual adaptation of aspiration levels is demonstrated in the experiment.

Appendix

Appendix A : List of Variables

names of variables	for player			
	A	G	C1	NC1
planned conflict limit	w_A^{KG}	w_G^{KG}	w_{C1}^{KG}	w_{NC1}^{KG}
planned conflict threat	w_A^{KD}	w_G^{KD}	w_{C1}^{KD}	w_{NC1}^{KD}
expected first demand of the opposite party	$w_A^{\hat{}W1}$	$w_G^{\hat{}W1}$	$w_{C1}^{\hat{}W1}$	$w_{NC1}^{\hat{}W1}$
bargaining result regarded as attainable	w_A^{DU}	w_G^{DU}	w_{C1}^{DU}	w_{NC1}^{DU}
planned bargaining result	w_A^{G}	w_G^{G}	w_{C1}^{G}	w_{NC1}^{G}
first demand	w_A^{W1}	w_G^{W1}	w_{C1}^{W1}	w_{NC1}^{W1}
expected conflict limit of the opposite party	$w_A^{\hat{}KG}$	$w_G^{\hat{}KG}$	$w_{C1}^{\hat{}KG}$	$w_{NC1}^{\hat{}KG}$
tacit concession	w_A^{TC}	w_G^{TC}	w_{C1}^{TC}	w_{NC1}^{TC}
total concession	$w_A^{\Delta WT}$	$w_G^{\Delta WT}$	$w_{C1}^{\Delta WT}$	$w_{NC1}^{\Delta WT}$
amount of the first concession			$w_{C1}^{\Delta W}$	

w_T^Y final bargaining result (growth rate of standard wages)

Δw_{AG}^{W1} range of bargaining

A b b r e v i a t i o n s

A employer's association

G labour union

Z central bank

C1 first concession maker

NC1 party which is not the first concession maker

FDP first decision periods of a session

N_w^P case of normal planning

A_w^P case of equal planning (agreement of planning)

I_w^P case of inverse planning

Appendix B1: Values of the Variables in the N_W^P-case (in per cent)

	Variables		Game / Period										
			11/17	12/5	13/11	14/3	16/17	17/2	17/19	20/13	21/2	21/15	21/23
labour union	expected first demand of A	$\hat{w}_G^{W1}$	0.00	4.50	2.00	3.00	4.00	.00	-5.00	4.50	.00	5.50	5.90
	expected conflict limit	$\hat{w}_G^{KG}$	9.00	6.25	5.00	12.00	25.00	6.00	5.00	6.00	7.00	6.00	6.20
	planned conflict limit	w_G^{KG}	-15.00	4.00	.00	.00	-5.00	-2.00	-10.00	4.00	.00	5.48	5.75
	planned conflict threat	w_G^{KD}	-10.50	4.50	2.00	2.00	-5.00	.00	-5.00	4.50	1.00	5.49	5.80
	bargaining result regarded as attainable	w_G^{DU}	5.00	5.73	2.50	5.00	6.00	3.00	-3.00	5.00	2.00	5.50	5.90
	planned bargaining result	w_G^{G}	7.00	5.73	3.50	5.00	7.50	5.78	-2.00	5.50	3.00	5.75	6.00
	first demand of G	w_G^{W1}	7.00	6.25	4.00	5.00	10.00	5.78	.00	5.50	4.50	5.75	6.00
	first concession leads to	w_G^{C1}	3.00	-	-	-	7.50	-	-	5.25	-	5.55	5.95
	realisation	w_T^{Y}	3.00	5.50	2.00	4.50	6.00	2.00	.00	5.00	3.50	5.55	5.95
employer's association	first concession leads to	w_A^{C1}	-	5.00	2.00	4.50	-	1.00	-25.00	-	3.00	-	-
	first demand of A	w_A^{W1}	.00	4.75	.00	4.00	4.00	.00	-30.00	5.00	.00	5.55	5.90
	planned bargaining result	w_A^{G}	.00	5.25	2.00	4.00	6.50	.00	-25.00	5.00	.00	5.55	5.90
	bargaining result regarded as attainable	w_A^{DU}	.00	5.50	2.00	4.50	7.00	2.00	-12.50	5.00	3.00	5.55	5.95
	planned conflict threat	w_A^{KD}	9.00	7.50	5.00	5.74	5.00	6.00	.00	7.00	7.00	5.60	6.10
	planned conflict limit	w_A^{KG}	10.00	9.00	5.50	6.00	6.00	6.00	.00	8.00	8.00	5.60	6.10
	expected conflict limit	$\hat{w}_A^{KG}$	-5.00	3.50	-.05	2.00	.00	-2.00	-15.00	4.00	-3.00	5.40	5.70
	expected first demand of G	$\hat{w}_A^{W1}$	.00	6.00	2.50	6.00	9.00	3.00	.00	6.00	6.00	5.55	5.95

Appendix B2: Values of the Variables in the A_W^P-case (in per cent)

	Variables		16/5	16/15	17/5	18/13	18/23	19/7	20/2	20/7	20/9	20/11	20/23	22/19
labour union	expected first demand of A	$\hat{w}_G^{WI}$	4.00	5.00	3.00	.00	1.00	4.00	.00	4.00	4.50	4.50	3.00	5.50
	expected conflict limit	$\hat{w}_G^{KG}$	10.00	20.00	5.50	6.00	5.00	6.00	7.00	6.00	6.00	6.50	6.00	6.00
	planned conflict limit	w_G^{KG}	1.00	-10.00	4.25	-.01	-.01	4.50	.00	4.00	4.00	4.00	3.00	5.30
	planned conflict threat	w_G^{KD}	2.00	.00	4.25	.00	.00	5.00	.00	4.00	4.50	4.50	4.00	5.40
	bargaining result regarded as attainable	w_G^{DU}	5.80	10.00	4.50	.50	1.50	5.00	3.00	4.50	5.00	5.00	5.00	5.50
	planned bargaining result	w_G^{C}	6.50	10.00	5.00	.50	2.00	5.50	4.00	4.50	5.50	5.50	5.50	5.60
	first demand of G	w_G^{WI}	7.50	15.00	6.00	1.00	2.50	5.82	6.00	5.00	5.50	5.50	5.70	5.90
	first concession leads to	w_G^{CI}	6.50	-	5.50	-	2.00	-	-	4.50	-	-	5.50	5.60
	realisation	w_T^{Y}	6.50	10.00	5.00	.50	2.00	5.50	4.00	4.50	5.50	5.50	5.50	5.60
employer's association	first concession leads to	w_A^{CI}	-	8.50	-	.50	-	5.50	3.00	-	5.25	5.25	-	-
	first demand of A	w_A^{WI}	5.50	7.00	4.25	.00	2.00	4.50	2.00	4.00	5.00	5.00	5.20	5.50
	planned bargaining result	w_A^{C}	6.50	10.00	5.00	.50	2.00	5.50	4.00	4.50	5.50	5.50	5.50	5.60
	bargaining result regarded as attainable	w_A^{DU}	6.50	10.00	5.50	1.00	2.25	5.50	5.00	5.00	5.50	6.00	5.50	5.60
	planned conflict threat	w_A^{KD}	8.00	8.00	6.00	3.00	4.00	6.50	10.00	10.00	8.00	7.00	6.00	7.00
	planned conflict limit	w_A^{KG}	10.00	8.00	6.00	4.00	4.50	7.00	10.00	10.00	10.00	8.00	7.00	7.50
	expected conflict limit	$\hat{w}_A^{KG}$	2.00	3.00	4.25	-1.00	.00	4.50	1.00	.00	.00	4.00	4.50	.00
	expected first demand of G	$\hat{w}_A^{WI}$	8.00	14.00	7.00	1.50	2.50	6.50	10.00	7.00	6.50	6.50	6.00	5.80

Columns 16/5 to 22/19: Game / Period

Appendix B3: Values of the Variables in the I_W^P-case (in per cent)

Variables			Game / Period					
			12/9	15/2	18/9	20/5	21/27	22/23
labour union	expected first demand of A	$\hat{w}_G^{W1}$	3.50	.00	4.00	4.00	6.00	5.60
	expected conflict limit	$\hat{w}_G^{KG}$	6.00	3.00	10.00	7.00	6.20	6.50
	planned conflict limit	w_G^{KG}	3.00	-1.00	1.00	4.50	5.90	5.40
	planned conflict threat	w_G^{KD}	3.25	.00	3.00	5.00	6.00	5.50
	bargaining result regarded as attainable	w_G^{DU}	4.75	.00	4.25	5.00	6.00	5.60
	planned bargaining result	w_G^{G}	5.47	1.50	4.50	5.50	6.00	5.60
	first demand of G	w_G^{W1}	5.72	3.00	5.00	5.50	6.10	5.70
	first concession leads to	w_G^{C1}	5.47	-	4.75	-	6.05	5.60
	realisation	w_T^{Y}	5.25	2.00	4.72	5.50	6.05	5.60
employer's association	first concession leads to	w_A^{C1}	-	2.00	-	5.00	-	-
	first demand of A	w_A^{W1}	4.75	.00	4.00	4.50	6.05	5.60
	planned bargaining result	w_A^{G}	5.50	3.00	4.72	5.76	6.05	5.70
	bargaining result regarded as attainable	w_A^{DU}	5.75	3.00	5.00	5.76	6.05	5.70
	planned conflict threat	w_A^{KD}	6.50	6.00	8.00	15.00	6.20	7.00
	planned conflict limit	w_A^{KG}	7.25	7.00	9.00	20.00	6.20	7.50
	expected conflict limit	$\hat{w}_A^{KG}$	4.00	-1.00	.00	.00	6.00	.00
	expected first demand of G	$\hat{w}_A^{W1}$	6.25	6.00	5.00	7.00	6.05	5.80

13. EXPERIMENTAL FORMATION OF CONTINGENT UTILITY FUNCTIONS: SOME IMPLICATIONS FOR PORTFOLIO CHOICE

GEORGE C. PHILIPPATOS* AND DONALD R. MOSCATO**

Some Perspectives

Recent research in security valuation and portfolio choice has been highlighted by serious controversy regarding the effects of uncertainty upon market values and the relevant ex ante risk surrogates. Primary concern has centered about the nature of securities, that are viewed as bundles of contingent payments whose contractual outcomes depend on the states of nature.[1] This contingency of future payments realizable from securities results in their riskiness, which is, in turn, characterized by four dimensions:[2] (a) The form and characteristics of the probability distribution of returns. (b) The covariance of returns between ordered pairs of securities in the same portfolio. (c) The potential effects of

---

* The Pennsylvania State University

** Iona College

1 Such securities are also referred to as "primitive" or "pure securities," and are defined as contracts to pay one dollar if a specific state occurs, and pay nothing if any other state occurs. The states in this case are mutually exclusive and exhaustive. See Arrow [1], and Hirshleifer [14] [15].

2 The four dimensions of risk in the market valuation of assets are discussed in detail in Robichek and Myers [25].

the various states of nature, i.e., economy, on the utility of returns function. (d) The resolution of uncertainty in multiperiod-multiproject decisions.

The first dimension is largely empirical and revolves about the family of limiting distributions that best describe the temporal returns.[1] The second refers to the technical separation of portfolio efficiency and the risk-attitudes of investors.[2] The third dimension suggests that the relative value of future returns, associated with each state of nature, can be best expressed by separate utility functions contingent upon the various states of the economy. Finally, the fourth dimension refers to the maximization of lifetime utility functions.[3] Financial literature has been primarily concerned with the first two dimensions, although recent advances in time-state-preference theory point to promising directions for the resolution of uncertainty over time.
However, dimension (c), concerned with the effect of the various states of the economy upon the utility functions of the decision-makers, has been virtually ignored in the security valuation and portfolio selection literature. To wit, there are three important issues involved in this dimension: (1) Are investors maximizing the expected value of future returns, thus exhibiting linear utility functions within the relevant range of monetary rewards? (2) Are investors ma-

---

1 See, for example, Fama and Roll [11] for what seems to be the prevailing view on this issue.

2 Known as the "Separation Theorem," it is attributed to Tobin [30].

3 It has been shown by Mossin [20], and others that, in the absence of transactions costs, the maximization of a lifetime utility function will lead to the selection of efficient portfolios for a series of single-period decisions.

ximizing some expected utility of future returns, approximated by a quadratic function? (3) Are the utility functions of investors affected by anticipated extreme states of the economy?

Answers to the above questions are by no means clear. For example, research by Swalm [29], on the experimental formation of utility functions for corporate executives, has shown that the popular form of the quadratic utility function did not provide a good approximation for one out of three experimental groups.[1] Indeed the utility functions of a group of executives were nearly linear in the range of high positive gains, implying that some form of a hybrid utility function would better approximate their behavior.[2] On the other hand, in their classic experimental study, Mosteller and Nogee [19], provided evidence of the empirical validity of the expected utility maxim and the existence of approximately quadratic utility functions.[3] And, in a more recent study of actual pari-mutuel bettor data, Weitzman [32] found evidence of utility functions strikingly similar to the one pro-

---

1 It should be noted here that we chose to bypass the larger issue of specific cases in which experimental subjects, after due deliberation, select alternatives inconsistent with the expected utility maxim. For a defense of the expected utility maxim, including a review of two classic experiments by M. Allais, see Markowitz [18].

2 Such hybrid utility functions implying diminishing marginal utility for returns, R, below a critical value, K, i.e., $0 \leq R \leq K$, and constant marginal utility for $R \geq K \geq 0$, also admit to the usefulness of the semi-variance as an ex ante portfolio risk surrogate.

3 Interestingly enough the authors found no contradiction for the inflexion-point type of function postulated by Friedman and Savage, and even some meager support. See Mosteller and Nogee [19].

posed by Markowitz [18].[1]
However, to the best of the authors' knowledge, the important issue of contingent utility functions has not been studied empirically, although a number of suggestions have been offered in the past. To wit, it has been originally suggested by Markowitz [18], that the problems of valuation and portfolio selection might be more appropriately analyzed within the methodology of decision theory. In subsequent research, Baumol [2], elaborated on the effects of investor's risk aversion coefficient upon the choice of the optimal portfolio, by positing the lower confidence interval as a surrogate for portfolio risk.[2]
In the same vein, employing a Bayesian framework, Mao and Särndal [17], delineated some of the effects of contingent returns upon the investor's risk aversion coefficient; which, in turn, leads to adjustments on the efficient frontier.
Since expected returns from a portfolio are expressed in monetary terms, the value of these returns for the various states of the economy will differ, and, subsequently, their associated utilities will also differ. For example, if we assume that economic expansion, S_1, is inflationary and economic contraction,

---

1 Markowitz proposed to correct some irregularities in the Friedman-Savage hypothesis by postulating a utility function that possesses no absolute domain, and is defined by the investor's present wealth. See [18] and [26].

2 In the words of Baumol, the choice of the risk aversion coefficient, [A] "depends upon the investor's attitude toward risk, and that this psychological element determines the region within which one can expect to find points of tangency of the investor's indifference curves and the (E,σ) efficient locus. The smaller the value of [A] the greater, ceteris paribus, will be the slopes of the indifference curves and, therefore, the further to the right on [the efficient frontier] must the possible tangency points lie." Cf. Baumol [2], fn. 14.

S_3, is deflationary, we can hypothesize that, in the absence of money illusion (real balance effects), the returns contingent on S_1, and their associated utilities, will be valued less than those contingent on S_3. In the same vein, purchasing power notwithstanding, it is conceivable that other contingent risks, like the possibility of unemployment, might induce the investor to value the returns and utilities associated with S_1 more highly than those contingent on S_3. Indeed, as has been shown by Hirshleifer [14][15], portfolios that are feasible but not efficient, might become efficient when contingency of returns is also introduced into their risk profiles.

Once we admit to possible effects of contingent returns upon the investor's utility function, we might also be interested on the symmetry of investor reactions to extreme states of the economy. Furthermore, we might wish to investigate the symmetry of reaction within each state to large and small stakes, as well as other behavioral attitudes toward risk. In line with the earlier discussion, the authors report on two separate experiments with two distinct groups of student subjects - hereafter Ss - to ascertain whether,

(a) various expected states of the economy, in graduated intensities, affected the utility of returns functions of individual players;
(b) the utility functions of the Ss in the two groups shifted in the same manner, and with the same degree of symmetry, when extreme states of the economy were admitted into the experiment;
(c) the Ss exhibited symmetric reactions in the entire range of monetary rewards.

Method of Experimentation

Reference Contracts

The gambling experiments utilized in our study were simple single-stage reference contracts designed to elicit information from the Ss about their indifference probabilities for various amounts of money, under three equiprobable states of nature. Specifically, the Ss were asked to state the probabilities that would leave them indifferent between certain amounts ranging from \$0 to \$9,000, in \$1,000-multiples, and a risky alternative payoff of \$10,000 under the following expected states of the economy:[1]

S_1: Signifying economic expansion, associated with a 5% (10%) increase in the Consumer Price Index, CPI, and improved employment opportunities.

S_2: Signifying economic conditions exactly similar to the current state of affairs.

S_3: Signifying economic contraction, associated with a 5% (10%) decrease in the CPI and reduced employment opportunities.

The values obtained from the experimental subjects were compared with those of four hypothetical investors - hereafter H.1, H.2, H.3, and H.4 - designed before the experiment to portray preference, neutrality and aversion to risk. In the same vein, randomly selecting from the values originally presented to the Ss, we constructed four portfolios - hereafter P_1, P_2, P_3, and P_4 - whose end-of-period payoffs were contingent upon the equiprobable states of the economy, S_1, S_2,

---

1 Probabilities for \$0 and \$10,000 were arbitrarily set at 0 and 1.00, respectively.

S_3.[1] In effect, the Ss were asked to supply the probabilities that would leave them indifferent between the certain and risky alternatives in each state, such that the expected utilities of the four ex post portfolios were equivalent, i.e., $EU(P_1)=EU(P_2)=EU(P_3)=EU(P_4)$.[2]

---

1 Note that the valuation of wagers with a constant probability is sufficient for the construction of cardinal utility scales that allow for a divergence between subjective and objective probabilities. See Pfanzag [22]. The authors are only too painfully aware of the possible nonadditivity (distortion) of subjective probabilities when applied to non-standard processes, as analyzed by Fellner [13], Ellsberg [5], and others. However, we have attempted to overcome this problem in terms of the following specific steps: (1) The Ss were confronted with equiprobable choices. (2) The Ss were presented with a standard lottery process. (3) The experimental goal was to derive specific indifference points rather than operational utility functions of the von Neumann-Morgenstern type, searched for by Mosteller and Nogee [19]. In this spirit, we believe that the use of uncorrected (impure) probabilities, under the above circumstances, is appropriate, particularly if we postulate that Ss do not necessarily maximize the mathematical expectation of the utility of wealth but rather some analogous function.

2 Once the weights assigned by the Ss are formalized into subjective indifference probabilities, we can construct the cash-equivalence function for each individual. Then, utilizing the arbitrary assignment of EU($0)=0.0 and EU($10,000)=1.0, we can easily convert the cash-equivalence function to its respective expected utility function. See Horowitz [16]. An alternative method of formalizing the evidence into a prospect - known as "introspection" - admits two methods of reduction - namely, the "Jevonsian operation" and the "marking operation." For the former, see Ellsberg [6] and Ozga [21]. For the latter, attributed to Professor Popper, see Watkins [31].

Subjects and Treatments

Eighty-five Ss from two different schools participated in the experiment under two treatments. In both treatments the certain and risky alternatives were the same but the magnitude of index changes differed. Thus, in Treatment I contingent states S_1 and S_3 allowed changes in the indices of economic activity equal to ±5%, while in Treatment II, the changes were set at ±10%. As it often happens in such experiments, some of the Ss who participated in our experiment under Treatment I did not complete Treatment II, and conversely. For this reason we performed separate analyses on the matched observations and the mixed population.[1] Details on the number of Ss participating in each Treatment are presented in Table 1.

Table 1: Student Subjects in Two Treatments

	Matched Treatments		Unmatched Treatments	
	LAB.1	LAB.2	LAB.1	LAB.2
Treatment I	42	16	16	8
Treatment II	42	16	19	3

The two treatments were administered to two groups of Ss referred to as LAB.1 and LAB.2. In LAB.1 the Ss were undergraduates ranging in age from 19 to 21 years, single, with no-known work experience, personal income or personal wealth. In short, they were typical undergraduate business students in a large state university.

1 This is indicated in the various tables and figures under the headings "Matched Treatments" and "All Observations."

In LAB.2 the Ss were enrolled in an evening MBA program, ranging in age from 22 to 35 years. The large majority of these students (70%) have had considerable managerial experience - at the middle and upper-middle management levels of large corporations. They were, at the time of the experiment, fully-employed and part-time students, mostly married, with an estimated income in excess of $10,000, and typically homeowners. The remaining (30%) were full-time students with attributes similar to those in LAB.1, but slightly older.

Method of Validation

The validation procedure for the experimental results proceeded in two steps. We first selected a random sample of 25%, i.e., 14 Ss, for preliminary screening of individual behavior and general directions. To perform the preliminary tests we proposed as the null hypothesis that there is no statistically significant difference between the mean-indifference probabilities assigned by the Ss at the three states of nature in either treatment. This was proposed to be the case for both LABS as well as the combined data, and, on the basis of analyses of variance, it was concluded that in all cases the null hypothesis was rejected. Moreover, it was found that the probabilities assigned to S_3 were consistently higher than those for S_1 and S_2, thus indicating lower utility of returns. In this vein, the effects were more pronounced in Treatment II.
In order to approximate the Ss utility functions we fit their indifference probabilities into first and second degree polynomials - the latter providing the best approximation of the data in most cases. The regression

coefficients possessed the right sign, although they were very small, indicating a very slight risk aversion within the relevant range of monetary rewards. Some additional observations are also in order. Five out of fourteen Ss assigned probabilities less than .90 at the \$9,000 stake for S_1, although their behavior for all other values was consistently risk-averse. It is possible that the combined prospects of economic expansion and \$9,000 made them more aggressive. However, the range of values in our experiment did not permit any further investigation to verify the hybrid-utility results of Swalm [29], or the inflexion-point hypothesis of Friedman and Savage [26]. Finally, more Ss assigned the indifference probability of 1.00 in Treatment II than in Treatment I, perhaps indicating very high risk aversion at high stakes combined with large fluctuations in the indices of economic activity.

On the other hand, when all observations were analyzed some interesting patterns became evident. To wit, Ss in LAB.2 were consistently more risk averse than Ss in LAB.1, over the entire range of risky alternatives, in both treatments and for all three states of the economy. This behavior persists through both the matched treatments and the entire population, and is shown in Figure 1. Such behavior was expected on a priori grounds from the student composition in LAB.2, and it becomes more pronounced when the group is separated into full and part-time students. Reference to Figure 1 also indicates that the utility functions of the hypothetical investor H.2 are strongly concave to the origin, while the experimental mean-value functions are slightly concave for all three states and in both treatments. Moreover, when the two LABS are combined, the concavity of the experimental function is further decreased, as shown in Figure 2.

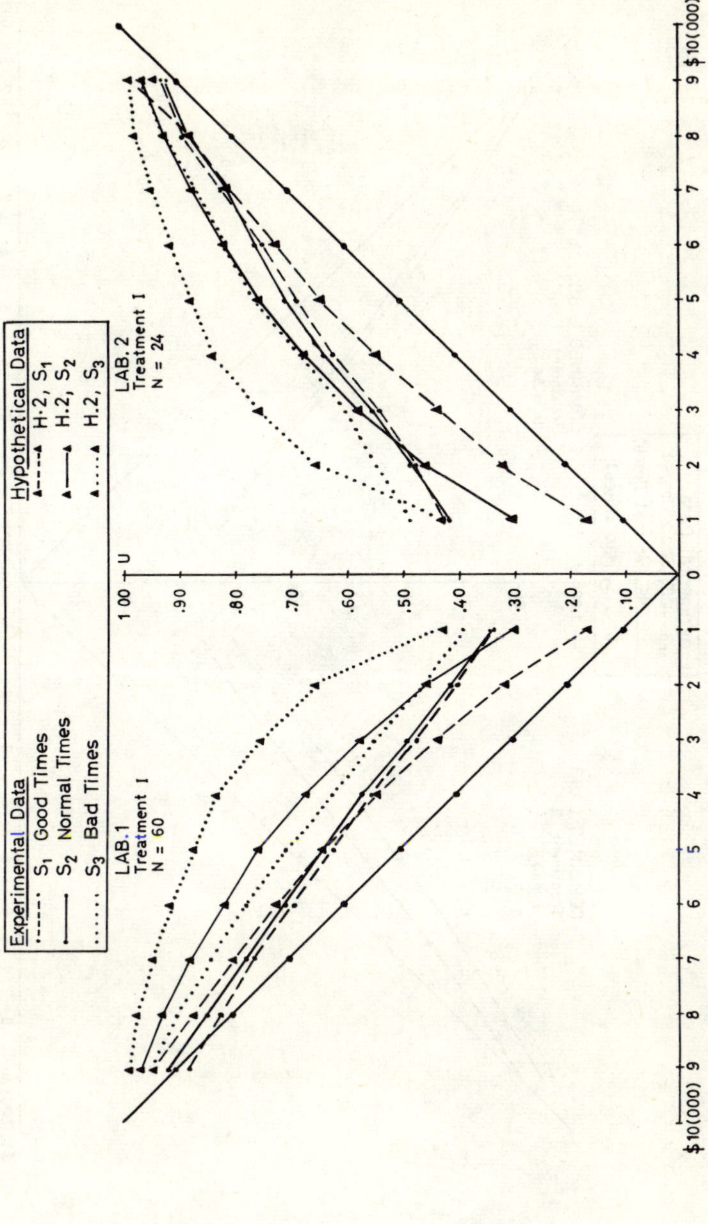
Experimental Data
S1 Good Times
S2 Normal Times
S3 Bad Times
Hypothetical Data
H.2, S1
H.2, S2
H.2, S3
LAB.1
Treatment I
N = 60
LAB.2
Treatment I
N = 24
U
1 00
.90
.80
.70
.60
.50
.40
.30
.20
.10
0
1
2
3
4
5
6
7
8
9
$10(000)
$10(000)

FIGURE 1

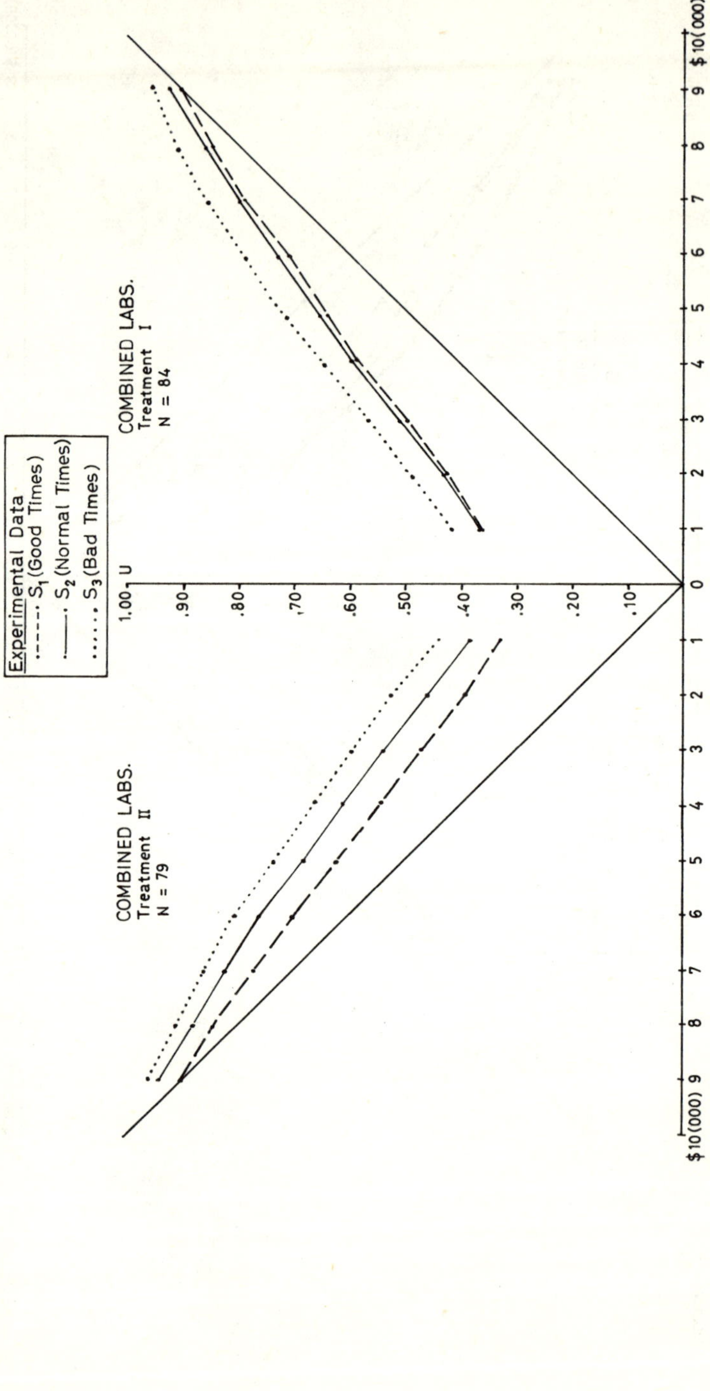

Experimental Data
S_1 (Good Times)
S_2 (Normal Times)
S_3 (Bad Times)
COMBINED LABS.
Treatment I
N = 84
COMBINED LABS.
Treatment II
N = 79
U
1.00
.90
.80
.70
.60
.50
.40
.30
.20
.10
0
1
2
3
4
5
6
7
8
9
$10(000)

FIGURE 2

When the values of the cash-equivalence function were utilized to construct randomly selected portfolios and compute their contingent expected utilities, it became apparent that the choices of portfolios were consistent. The consistency, as shown in Table 2, persists through both treatments, although they were administered nearly 20 days apart. Reference to Table 2 indicates that Ss in LAB.1 selected portfolio 3, while Ss in LAB.2 selected portfolio 4. It is interesting to note that LAB.2 portfolio choice was identical to that of hypothetical investor H.2. On the other hand, LAB.1 choices did not match any of the hypothetical investors, although the Ss risk aversion was higher than H.2 and lower than H.3. A detailed breakdown of Ss portfolio rankings and optimal choices is given in Table 3 and Table 4.

Table 2: Choices of Portfolios by Ss and Hypothetical Investors

	LAB.1	LAB.2	H.1*	H.2*	H.3*	H.4*
Treatment I	P_3	P_4	P_1	P_4	P_2	P_1
Treatment II	P_3	P_4	P_1	P_4	P_2	P_1

Note: *Refers to hypothetical investors designed before the experiment.

Table 3

Ss Agreement on Optimal Portfolios

		LAB.1				LAB.2			
		Treatment I		Treatment II		Treatment I		Treatment II	
		Type of Agreement		Type of Agreement		Type of Agreement		Type of Agreement	
	Portfolios	Strict	Weak	Strict	Weak	Strict	Weak	Strict	Weak
Matched Treatments	1	11	1	8	5	2	1	3	0
	2	3	4	3	2	2	0	2	0
	3	15	4	14	6	4	2	4	0
	4	7	4	9	5	6	2	5	2
All Observations	1	16	2	12	6	2	1	3	0
	2	5	4	5	2	4	2	3	2
	3	22	5	18	7	5	3	4	0
	4	10	4	17	5	9	4	6	2

Note: The numbers 1,2,3,4 refer to portfolios P_1, P_2, P_3, P_4, respectively.

Table 4

Ss and Hypothetical Investors Rankings of Portfolios

	Matched Treatments		All Observations		Hypothetical Investors	
	LAB.1		LAB.1			
	Treatment I	Treatment II	Treatment I	Treatment II	H.1	H.2
Total	3>1>4>2	3>4>1>2	3>1>4>2	3>4>1>2	1>3>4>2	4>2>3>1
Strict Agreement	3>1>4>2	3>4>1>2	3>1>4>2	3>4>1>2	1>3>4>2	4>2>3>1
	LAB.2		LAB.2		H.3	H.4
Total	4>3>1>2	4>3=2>1	4>3>2>1	4>2>3>1	2>4>3>1	1>3>4>2
Strict Agreement	4>3>1=2	4>3>1>2	4>3>2>1	4>3>2=1	2>4>3>1	1>3>4>2

Note: The numbers 1,2,3,4 refer to portfolios P_1, P_2, P_3, P_4, respectively. The symbol (>) indicates preference and (=) indicates indifference.

Results and Discussion

Analysis of the complete set of data led to a number of interesting avenues of investigation. As a first approximation we searched for consistency in the Ss responses, between the two treatments in each LAB. As we recall, Ss in LAB.1 selected portfolio P_3 in both treatments, and, on the basis of t-tests, it was determined that there was no significant difference in the mean values at the 5% and 10% levels of economic fluctuations. Similarly, for the Ss in LAB.2, who chose portfolio P_4 in both treatments, the null hypothesis was also accepted. Hence, the Ss in LAB.1 and LAB.2 behaved consistently in the two separate treatments, and their consistency cannot be attributed to chance.

In a related test we searched for the possible significance in the differences between the mean values of the two LABS at each treatment level. Again, on the basis of t-tests, it was determined that in Treatment I (5%) the null hypothesis was rejected, implying a statistically significant difference in the mean values of LAB.1 and LAB.2. However, in Treatment II (10%) the null hypothesis was accepted, implying no significant differences between the mean values of the two LABS. Two possible explanations are in order:

(1) The heterogeneity of Ss in LAB.2 resulted in this effect, since the young full-time Ss in this LAB exhibited risk-attitudes similar to the Ss in LAB.1. This was also evident from the greater variability of Ss responses in LAB.2, as shown in Table 5, where both the means and variances of LAB.2 are higher than the respective values of LAB.1

Table 5: Means and Standard Deviations for Selected Portfolios

	Treatment I			Treatment II		
	P	μ	σ	P	μ	σ
LAB.1	P_3	.67	.126	P_3	.68	.124
LAB.2	P_4	.72	.153	P_4	.70	.131

(2) In Treatment II, the expected extremity of the states of the economy, i.e., ±10% change, forced similarity of risk-aversion in both LABS.

Although the rationale of the second explanation is appealing, in introducing the influence of shock-effects on Ss convergence toward approximately equivalent values, the authors are more inclined to attribute the results to the heterogeneity of Ss in LAB.2.

Before we proceed further with the data analysis, we must consider two interesting asides. First, inspection of the raw data indicates a strong preference of the Ss for some specific probabilities, which confirms the results of several other experiments conducted by Edwards.[1] In our experiment, the Ss demonstrated a definite preference for probability values ending in 0 or 5. Second, portfolio P_1, ordinarily preferred by the risk-neutral individual, in all cases possessed the smallest mean-variance values. It seems that the threshold (lowest) point on the portfolio frontier always coincided with P_1, while the saturation (highest) point occurred at different portfolios, as shown in Figure 3. Reference to this figure also indicates that

1 Edwards suggests that subjects, when they bet, prefer some probabilities to others and these preferences cannot be accounted by utility considerations. See Edwards [7][8][9][10].

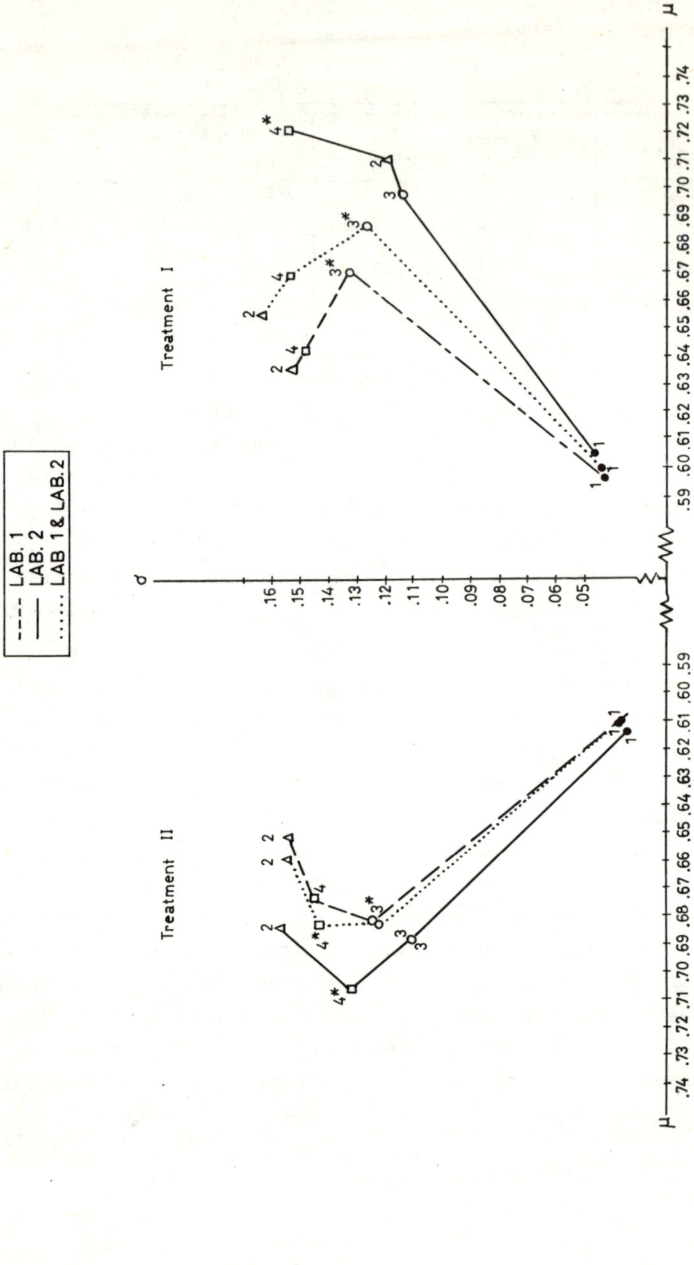

FIGURE 3

the more risk averse LAB.2 frontier consistently dominated the LAB.1 frontier.

Finally, the entire set of mean-indifference probabilities for each of the three states was subjected to a battery of t-tests within each LAB and treatment as well as for the combined population. The tests were performed only on the extreme values, i.e., $1,000 and $9,000, for the following reasons. (1) The $1,000 values had the greatest variance in the Ss responses. (2) The $9,000 values had the smallest variance in the Ss responses. The results are shown in Table 7. The t-tests in this last series are based on normal times, S_2, compared with economic expansion, S_1, and then with economic contraction, S_3. Reference to Table 7 indicates that at the $1,000 stakes we must generally accept the null hypothesis. That is, the average indifference probabilities at each state are not in fact different from shifts above or below the S_2 function, despite their distinctive appearance in Figures 1 and 2. This might also explain the coincidence of the threshold point in the portfolio frontier with portfolio P_1, in all cases, as seen in Figure 3. However, at the $9,000 stakes we do experience a result which indicates that there is a statistically significant difference between the means. The authors attribute this result to the inability of some Ss to achieve a consensus about the value of the risky alternative at the low end of the lottery amounts, i.e., $1,000 to $5,000. Indeed, observation of the raw data makes this explanation defensible.

Two interesting results become apparent at this juncture:

(1) When the t-tests were performed for the extreme states, S_1 and S_3, as shown in Table 7, it became clear that the means for LAB.1 and LAB.2

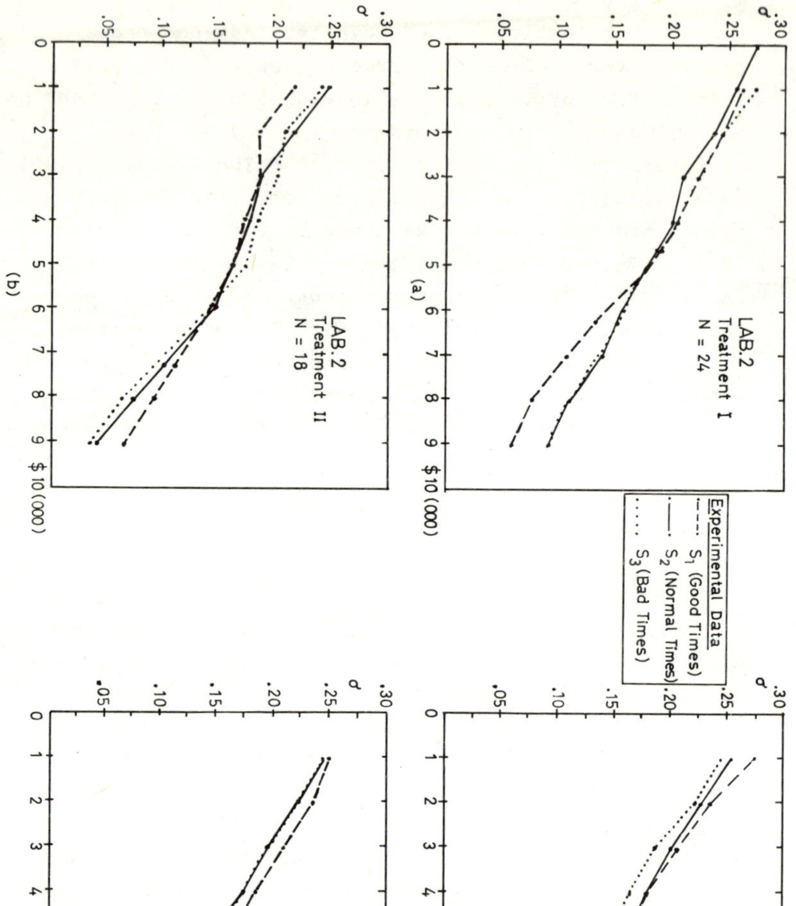
LAB. 2
Treatment I
N = 24
(a)
Experimental Data
S1 (Good Times)
S2 (Normal Times)
S3 (Bad Times)
LAB. 1
Treatment I
N = 60
(c)
LAB. 2
Treatment II
N = 18
(b)
LAB. 1
Treatment II
N = 61
(d)
σ
$10 (000)

FIGURE 4

Table 6: Mean Values and Standard Deviations of Portfolios Selected by Ss (All Observations)

Lab. No.	Sample Size	Treatment	Portfolio No.	Mean	Standard Deviation
LAB.1	60	I	1	.59644	.041
			2	.63555	.152
			3*	.67227	.126
			4	.64822	.146
LAB.2	24	I	1	.60472	.046
			2	.68805	.117
			3	.71972	.119
			4*	.72041	.153
COMBINED LABS	84	I	1	.59880	.043
			2	.65341	.162
			3*	.68583	.126
			4	.66884	.152
LAB.1	61	II	1	.60486	.035
			2	.65196	.153
			3*	.68262	.124
			4	.67633	.145
LAB.2	18	II	1	.61611	.034
			2	.68444	.157
			3	.68574	.110
			4*	.70870	.131
COMBINED LABS	79	II	1	.60742	.035
			2	.65936	.154
			3	.68333	.121
			4*	.68371	.143

Note: *Indicates optimal portfolio.

Table 7

Test for Equality of Means[α]

Null Hypothesis	Treat-ment	Dollar Values	Computed t-values			Degrees of Freedom			Accept H_o at $t_{.90}$			Reject H_o at $t_{.90}$		
			LAB.1	LAB.2	LABS.1&2	LAB.1	LAB.2	LABS.1&2	LAB.1	LAB.2	LABS.1&2	LAB.1	LAB.2	LABS.1&2
$H_o:\mu_1=\mu_3=\mu$, $\Delta H=0$	I	1,000	1.18	.73		118	46		Accept	Accept				
	I	9,000	5.70	2.30		118	46					Reject	Reject	
	II	1,000	2.30	1.70		120	34					Reject	Reject	
	II	9,000	4.30	3.00		120	34					Reject	Reject	
$H_o:\mu_3=\mu_2=\mu$, $\Delta H=0$	I	1,000	1.09	.78	1.30	118	46	166	Accept	Accept				Reject*
	I	9,000	4.30	1.90	4.60	118	46	166				Reject	Reject	Reject
	II	1,000	1.14	.86	1.48	120	34	156	Accept	Accept				Reject*
	II	9,000	2.40	1.80	2.60	120	34	156				Reject	Reject	Reject
$H_o:\mu_1=\mu_2=\mu$, $\Delta H=0$	I	1,000	.09	.05	.06	118	46	166	Accept	Accept	Accept			
	I	9,000	2.70	.40	2.08	118	46	166		Accept		Reject		Reject
	II	1,000	1.23	.86	1.55	120	34	156	Accept	Accept				Reject*
	II	9,000	3.30	1.69	4.04	120	34	156				Reject	Reject*	Reject

Note: *Indicates that H_o is accepted at $t_{.95}$ and rejected at $t_{.90}$.

[α]It should also be noted that, when the raw data were properly adjusted for the 5% and 10% shifts, the results were similar. That is, the differences in responses at the low and high-stakes followed the same pattern as with the unadjusted data. In the former case, the responses appear more in the nature of percentage adjustments. In the latter, the results attain statistical significance. The pattern, as in earlier cases, is more manifestly pronounced in Treatment II than in Treatment I - perhaps signaling a "threshold adjustment level" - while the effects of the Treatments appear again more significant in LAB.2 than in LAB.1.

were significantly different, in each treatment. We also note that there is more distortion in Treatment I, LAB.2, at the $1,000 stakes than elsewhere.

(2) The disparity in the variations at the high and low stakes suggested a separate analysis of the standard deviations in the mean-indifference probabilities.

The standard deviations are shown in Figure 4, where it is apparent that the states of the economy affect the standard deviations differently than the mean-values. This appears to be the cause of the poor t-tests, even though the means at S_1 and S_3 appear different from those in S_2. It is obvious that the learning rate increased, as the Ss approached high stakes; this is evidenced by the reduced variability. Also note that the σ-values for S_3 had the least variability at the highest stakes, i.e., $9,000, for both LABS and treatments. We can perhaps infer from this behavior that under the pressure of economic contraction, when the stakes became very high, the Ss achieved consensus.
Moreover, S_1 had the highest variability for Ss in LAB.1, whereas S_3 had its greatest variability for Ss in LAB.2, particularly at the low stakes. We believe that this is due to the different risk attitudes of the Ss in the two groups. For example, Ss in LAB.1 had more difficulty deciding on what to accept under S_1, while Ss in LAB.2 experienced the same lack of consensus under S_3.[1] Note that the members of LAB.2 had made significant real-life investments in the past. The authors find the implications of the

1 This is reflected in the high variability of the responses.

inverse relationship between σ-values and the stakes more appealing than the direct relationship between the μ-values and the stakes. Indeed, the consistency of the results is very interesting.

In perspective, we can conclude that the Ss varied substantially in their preferences for the certain amounts at the low stakes, while their variability decreased considerably at the high stakes. This appears to be clear evidence of different Ss risk attitudes in "less costly" lotteries and invites further study into the usefulness of the semivariance as an ex ante portfolio risk surrogate.[1] Moreover, since the linearities in the utility curves became more pronounced when the responses are aggregated, it will be tempting to conduct some experiments in order to delineate the "organizational" and "clientele" effects upon the final utility functions of corporate executives and fund-managers. It is clear that contingent returns require adjustments both on the efficient frontier, as shown by Mao and Särndal [17] and on the investor's utility functions as evidenced by our results.

Conclusions

On the basis of the experimental results above, the authors derive the following tentative conclusions:

(1) The various states of nature affected the utility of returns functions of the players.

---

1 Some Ss diverge from their conservative positions at the low-end of the payoffs, but achieve consensus at the high-end, where they are still risk averse, but more in agreement on the value of the bet.

(2) The effect of the states of nature was asymmetric; for the most part higher probability values were assigned to the state of economic contraction and lower values to the state of economic expansion.

(3) The utility of returns functions shifted in the same manner for most investors.

(4) The individual utility functions were generally concave to the origin (quadratic). However, when aggregated, the resultant vector was a linear utility function, whose intercept was higher than that derived from the strategy of maximizing expected monetary value.

Conclusions (1), (2), and (3), above, lend laboratory-type empirical support to what Robichek and Myers call "Dimension C" in investment decisions. Conclusion (4) is largely congruent with recent attempts in the literature by Sharpe [28], and others, to simplify the portfolio selection problem by the use of a simple linear relationship between the individual asset returns and the level of some economic index.

Bibliography

[1] Arrow, K.J., "The Role of Securities in the Optimal Allocation of Risk-Bearing," Review of Economic Studies, April, 1964, pp. 91-96.

[2] Baumol, Wm.,J., "An Expected Gain-Confidence Limit Criterion for Portfolio Selection," Management Science, October, 1965, pp. 174-182.

[3] Baumol, Wm., "The Neumann-Morgenstern Utility Index," Journal of Political Economy, 59, 1951, pp. 61-66.

[4] Carter, C.F., Meredith, J.P., and G.L.S. Shackle (Eds.), Uncertainty and Business Decisions, Liverpool University Press, 1957.

[5] Ellsberg, D., "Risk, Ambiguity, and the Savage Axioms," Quarterly Journal of Economics, November, 1961, pp. 643-669.

[6] Ellsberg, D., "Classic and Current Notions of Measurable Utility," Economic Journal, September, 1954.

[7] Edwards, W., "Utility, Subjective Probability, Their Interaction, and Variance Preferences," Journal of Conflict Resolution, 16, 1962, pp. 42-51.

[8] Edwards, W., "The Reliability of Probability Preferences," American Journal of Psychology, 67, 1954, pp. 68-95.

[9] Edwards, W., "Probability Preferences Among Bets with Differing Expected Values," American Journal of Psychology, 67, 1954, pp. 56-67.

[10] Edwards, W., "Probability-Preferences in Gambling," American Journal of Psychology, 66, 1953, pp. 349-364.

[11] Fama, E.F., and R. Roll, "Some Properties of Symmetric Stable Distributions," Journal of the American Statistical Association, September, 1968, pp. 817-836.

[12] Farrar, D.E., The Investment Decision Under Uncertainty, Prentice-Hall, Englewood-Cliffs, N.J., 1962.

[13] Fellner, Wm., "Distortion of Subjective Probabilities as a Reaction to Uncertainty," Quarterly Journal of Economics, November, 1961, pp. 670-689.

[14] Hirshleifer, J., "Investment Decision Under Uncertainty: Applications of the State Preference Approach," Quarterly Journal of Economics, May, 1966, pp. 252-277.

[15] Hirshleifer, J., "Investment Decisions Under Uncertainty: Choice Theoretic Approaches," Quarterly Journal of Economics, November, 1965, pp. 509-536.

[16] Horowitz, I., Quantitative Business Analysis, McGraw-Hill, New York, 1965.

[17] Mao, J.C.T., and E. Särndal, "A Decision Theory Approach to Portfolio Selection," Management Science, April, 1966, pp. 323-333.

[18] Markowitz, H.M., Portfolio Selection: Efficient Diversification of Investments, Yale University Press, 1970.

[19] Mosteller, F., and P. Nogee, "An Experimental Measurement of Utility," The Journal of Political Economy, October, 1951, pp. 371-404.

[20] Mossin, J., "Optimal Multiperiod Portfolio Policies," Journal of Business, April, 1968, pp. 215-229.

[21] Ozga, S.A., "Utility and Probability: A Simplified Rendering," Economic Journal, September, 1956.

[22] Pfanzag, J., "A General Theory of Measurement: Applications to Utility," Naval Research Logistics Quarterly, 6, 1959, pp. 283-294.

[23] Pratt, J.W., "Risk Aversion in the Small and in the Large," Econometrica, 32, 1964, pp. 122-136.

[24] Raiffa, H., "Risk, Ambiguity, and the Savage Axioms: Comment," Quarterly Journal of Economics, November, 1961, pp. 690-694.

[25] Robichek, A.A., and S.C. Myers, "Valuation of the Firm: Effects of Uncertainty in a Market Context," Journal of Finance, May, 1966.

[26] Savage, L.J., The Foundations of Statistics, John Wiley & Sons, New York, 1954.

[27] Shackle, G.L.S., Expectations in Economics, 2nd Edition, Cambridge University Press, 1952.

[28] Sharpe, Wm.F., "A Simplified Model for Portfolio Analysis," Management Science, January, 1963, pp. 277-293.

[29] Swalm, R.O., "Utility Theory-Insights into Risk-Taking," Harvard Business Review, 44, 1966, pp. 123-136.

[30] Tobin, J., "Liquidity Preference as Behavior Towards Risk," Review of Economic Studies, February, 1958, pp. 65-86.

[31] Watkins, J.W.N., "Decisions and Uncertainty," in [4].

[32] Weitzman, M., "Utility Analysis and Group Behavior: An Empirical Study," Journal of Political Economy, February, 1965, pp. 18-26.

14. A STOCHASTIC MODEL OF PREFERENCE IN DECOMPOSED GAMES[1]

DAVID M. MESSICK*

In discussions of experimental economics, one occasionally comes across two erroneous notions. The first of these is the idea that the "utility" of a commodity is some enduring attribute of the commodity. The second is the assumption that the "utility" of a valued commodity (e.g., money) should be a non-decreasing function of the amount of the commodity and that it is "irrational" for one to prefer less money, for example, to more. The first of these fallacious ideas stems from the tendency to consider the measured utility of a stimulus as a characteristic of the stimulus, rather than a characteristic of the organism from whose preferences the utility function is constructed. The second fallacy probably arises from the economic facts of life which would make a businessman's prospects for economic survival gloomy if his utility for money decreased

---

* University of California, Santa Barbara

1 The research discussed in this paper has been supported by Grants GS-1032 and GS-3061 from the National Science Foundation and by Grant HDO 3258 from the National Institutes of Health. I would also like to cordially acknowledge the aid of Charles G. McClintock, Francis T. Campos, David M. Kuhlman, Daniel Williams, and Joy Stapp for their contributions to this research.

with increasing amounts of money. The "rationality" of a non-decreasing utility function derives from its consistency with the super-ordinate goal of economic success and not because such a utility assignment is the only one consistent with the Von Neumann-Morgenstern axioms. One could be consistent with these axioms and consistently prefer less money to more.

One context in which such "aberrant" preferences occasionally arise is that in which an individual's choice determines an outcome for another person as well as an outcome for himself. To illustrate this phenomenon, consider a simple experiment I performed several years ago with my two sons, in which I offered each of them one of two dishes of peanuts. Each of them chose a dish containing three peanuts in preference to one containing only two. The next step in this experiment was to place four peanuts next to the dish containing three, and to place one peanut next to the dish containing two. The boys were told that they could again select either of the dishes and take the peanuts it contained. In this case, however, the peanuts beside the dish selected would be given to the other boy. Thus their choice in this situation not only determined how many peanuts they would receive, it also determined how many peanuts their brother would receive.

The older boy still preferred the dish containing three peanuts. The younger boy reversed his previous choice and opted for the dish containing two. When asked why they had chosen as they did, the older boy explained that he didn't mind giving his brother more peanuts than he himself got since he felt sure he could get some back later. The younger boy, less confident of his persuasive or coercive abilities, simply said that he chose the dish containing two because he didn't want his brother to get more than he got.

The types of social influences manifested by my sons in this little experiment are not unique to young children. More systematic experimentation with college students has found similar results (Messick & Thorngate, 1967). My goal in this paper will be to describe the results of three experiments we have conducted to analyze these social influences and to relate these results to a simple probabilistic preference model in an effort to clarify the nature of the choice or preference process in such situations.

Decomposed Games

Decomposed games were devised independently by Pruitt (1967) and Messick and McClintock (1968). Prior to this development, practically all experimental work with two person games had employed payoff matrices which displayed the payoffs to the two players for every possible pair of joint choices. While a matrix format is useful for some research purposes, it is cumbersome if one's goal is the determination of preference structures for pairs of payoffs in which one payoff is that of S and the other a payoff to another person (e.g., Wyer, 1967, 1971).

In a two-choice decomposed game, each S is given a choice of two options, A and B, each of which specifies a payoff to S, a_1 and b_1 respectively, and a payoff to the other person, a_2 and b_2, respectively. One can easily compute the matrix game corresponding to any decomposed game by computing, for each pair of choices of the two Ss, the sum of the payoff S's choice affords him and the payoff afforded S by the other's choice. While any decomposed game implies a unique matrix game, the converse is not true. Some matrix games are "non-decomposable," and any matrix game which is decomposable may be decomposed into an infinite number of games. Since these issues are discussed by Messick and McClintock (1968) they need not be pursued further here.

Social Motives and Motivational Dominance Structures

The theory which we describe in the next section assumes that at a given instance, S will select one of the two (for two-choice games) options on the basis of one of several criteria. It has been traditionally assumed in much experimental game research that S's goal is to maximize the number of points (or the amount of money) he receives. Such an orientation, which we have called individualism since it implies that S ignores the payoffs his choices afford the other person, implies that in a decomposed game, S will choose A if $a_1 > b_1$ and B otherwise (excluding the possibility of equality). Other factors are also involved, however. Messick and Thorngate (1967) clearly showed that S's may also attempt to maximize their relative gain or the difference between their payoff and that of the other. We have labelled this motivational orientation competition since it involves an attempt to obtain more than the other. An S choosing on the basis of competitive motives will choose A if $a_1-a_2 > b_1-b_2$ and B otherwise (excluding, for the moment, the case in which $a_1-a_2 = b_1-b_2$). Finally, Deutsch (1960) and others have shown that Ss may be cooperative and attempt to maximize the sum of the payoffs to the two players. With such a motivational disposition, S will choose A if $a_1+a_2 > b_1+b_2$, and B otherwise (again briefly ignoring the possibility of the sums being equal).

That only three of a multitude of possible social motives have been considered does not imply that we regard them to be the only important ones. We consider the motives of individualism, competition, and cooperation to be the minimal set, but not necessarily an exclusive set as we shall see in a later section. A more extended discussion of the question of motives has been given by Messick (1970).

The next step in our endeavor to develop a meaningful method to investigate preferences in decomposed games requires that we examine the extent to which it is possible to isolate the three choice criteria just discussed. Is it possible, for example, to construct a decomposed game in which one of the choices (either A or B) will be made only if S is choosing on the basis of individualistic motives and in which the other choice will be made if S is choosing either competitively or cooperatively? Table 1 lists the six possible types of two-choice decomposed games with an example of each type. The game referred to above is impossible to construct.

Table 1: Six Motivational Dominance Structures for 2-choice Decomposed Games

	j·r(o)		oj·r		or·j		orj		or(j)		oj(r)	
	A	B	A	B	A	B	A	B	A	B	A	B
Own outcome	8	8	8	7	6	5	4	9	6	8	9	6
Other's outcome	3	2	5	3	1	4	3	2	6	4	4	1

Each of the six motivational dominance structures listed in Table 1 denotes a unique configuration of the choices dictated by the three motives discussed earlier in this section. The code used to summarize these patterns can be described as follows. The letters o, r, and j designate own gain, relative gain, and joint gain, respectively. If one of these letters is in parentheses, then the two alternatives are equal with respect to that criterion for all the games of that type. If a period is between two letters (ignoring, of course, letters in parentheses) this indicates that the criteria on one side of the period dictate one of the choices (either A or B) while the criterion on the other side of the period leads to a choice of the other alternative.

To illustrate this seemingly awkward notation, look at the first class of games with the j·r(o) structure. In this class of games, own gain is always equal for the two options. The own payoff in the example is equal to 8 units for both A and B. The period between j and r indicates that one alternative will be dictated by relative gain (option B in the example) and the other, option A, will be chosen if S is choosing on the basis of joint gain maximization. In the fourth game, orj, all three criteria lead to the same choice. In the example, this choice is the B choice.

In conclusion, it is important to realize that the motivational dominance structures for two-choice or three-choice games (as we will see in a later section) depend on the set of motives one selects for investigation. Clearly, had we used different motives, the motivational dominance structures we would have obtained would have been different.

Preference Models in Decomposed Games

Messick and Thorngate (1967), after describing a series of experiments demonstrating the importance of relative gain maximization in experimental games, concluded by suggesting that it might be possible to construct a utility model for pairs of outcomes in which the utility of a pair (x_1, x_2) could be described as

$$u(x_1, x_2) = f(x_1) + g(x_1 - x_2). \tag{1}$$

In this expression, x_1 is S's payoff and x_2 is the payoff to the other. Messick and McClintock (1968) subjected this model to an admittedly strict empirical test. Assuming f to be monotonic increasing on x_1, the model was violated at least once by 166 of 180 Ss. (A different algebraic formulation which has met with considerable success has been developed by Livingston (1971), but a discussion of this work is beyond the scope of this paper).

Our lack of success with the algebraic formulation led us to seek a probabilistic choice model. The simple model to be described is the result of that effort.

We assume that at any given instant, S can be in any one of four hypothetical states listed in Table 2. If he is in one of the first three states, he will make his choice on the basis of own gain, relative gain, or joint gain maximization respectively. If he is in the fourth state, he makes his choice randomly, selecting A and B with equal probability. It is further assumed that probabilities of S being in any of these four states at a given time, w, x, y, and z, respectively, are constant across individuals, games, and trials, and that the choices are independent of S's previous choices and the choices of the other.

Table 2: Assumed Motivational States

S_1 - Individualistic	$P(S_1) = w$
S_2 - Competitive	$P(S_2) = x$
S_3 - Cooperative	$P(S_3) - y$
S_4 - Indifferent	$P(S_4) = z$

With these assumptions it is possible to write the expected choice probabilities for each of the six types of dominance structures as a function of the parameters of the model. As a convention, we will write the expected probability for the choice dictated by own gain. Since no such choice exists in the j·r(o) game, we will write the choice probability for the alternative leading to relative gain maximization. These probabilities are presented in Table 3.

Table 3: Expected Choice Probabilities

1. $P[orj] = w+x+y+z/2$	4. $P[j\cdot r(o)] = \frac{2x+z}{2(1-w)}$
2. $P[or\cdot j] = w+x+z/2$	5. $P[or(j)] = \frac{2(w+x)+z}{2(1-y)}$
3. $P[oj\cdot r] = w+y+z/2$	6. $P[oj(r)] = \frac{2(w+y)+z}{2(1-x)}$

To illustrate how these equations are obtained, consider the orj games. In this class of games, one of the choices is dictated by all of the first three motives in Table 2. If S is in any of these states (with probability w + x + y) he will make this choice. He will also make this choice with probability 1/2 if he is in the indifferent state and since he will be in this state with probability z, the probability of making the dominant choice and being in the indifferent state is z/2. Thus, the probability that the dominant choice is made is w + x + y + z/2 as in Table 3.

The derivation of the expected choice probabilities for the last three dominance classes in Table 3 requires an additional assumption. In these cases, the two alternatives are equal for one of the criteria thereby preventing a choice from being made on the basis of that criterion.It is assumed that if S is in a state which does not allow a choice, he will shift to a new state which does permit a choice, and the conditional probabilities for the new states will be proportional to the probabilities in Table 2. With this assumption, the results for the three expressions in Table 3 are easily obtained.

Empirical Results: Study I

The first experiment in which this model of preference was evaluated has been described in detail by Messick and McClintock (1968). The Ss in this study were 180 female undergraduates at the University of California, Santa Barbara. They were run in pairs, subject to the constraint that they were not friends.

The dyads were randomly assigned to one of three experimental conditions which differed in terms of nature of the feedback received by the Ss. In all conditions the Ss were presented with a cumulative display which informed S of her cumulative score. This display was updated after every trial. For one third of the Ss this display presented S's accumulated own score. For the second third, the display presented the joint score for both Ss (i.e., the sum of their own cumulative scores). For the final third, the display presented the difference between S's cumulative score and that of the other S. All Ss were told that they would be given a monetary reward at the end of the experiment the size of which would depend only on her own score.

This experiment was not designed, unfortunately, to provide a test of the stochastic model. It is unfortunate because the sequence of 80 games which was employed contained widely differing numbers of games of the six different motivational dominance structures. There were 30 oj.r games, 16 j.r(o), 16 oj(r), 6 or.j, 6 orj, and 6 or(j) games, making 80 games in all.

The proportions of dominant choices in each of the six types of games were analyzed by analysis of variance treating motivational dominance structures and feedback conditions as factors. A main effect for games was found as well as a reliable interaction between feedback and game types. Consequently, the data from each of the three feedback groups were treated separately in evaluating the stochastic model.

The parameters of the model were estimated via the following equations.

(2) $$\hat{z} = 2[1-p(orj)],$$

(3) $$\hat{x} = p(orj) - p(oj.3),$$

(4) $$\hat{y} = p(orj) - p(or.j),$$

(5) and $$\hat{w} = 1-\hat{x}-\hat{y}-\hat{z}.$$

In these expressions, p( ) denotes the observed proportion of dominant choices in each of the game classes.

The estimated parameters for each of the three feedback conditions are presented in Table 4. It is encouraging to note that for each of the first three parameters (the fourth being a "noise" parameter), the estimate is largest in that group receiving the corresponding type of feedback. The own feedback group has the largest estimated $\hat{w}$; the relative feedback group has the largest estimated $\hat{x}$; and the joint feedback group has the largest $\hat{y}$.

Table 4: Estimated Parameters for Stochastic Choice Model (from Messick & McClintock, 1968)

	Display condition		
	Own	Joint	Relative
$\hat{w}$	.465	.435	.215
$\hat{x}$	.230	.265	.535
$\hat{y}$	.125	.200	.020
$\hat{z}$	.180	.100	.230

The choice proportions for only three of the game classes were used to estimate the four parameters (of which only three are independent, of course, since the sum must equal unity). To test the predictive adequacy of the model, therefore, the estimated parameters for each of the three experimental groups were substituted for the appropriate terms in the last three equations in Table 3 to generate predicted choice probabilities for these three game types for the three different groups. Thus, for each of these three game classes in each of the three experimental conditions, we can compare the predicted choice proportions to those which were obtained. The results of this comparison are presented in Table 5.

Table 5: Observed and Predicted Choice Proportions for or(j), oj(r), and r·j(o) Games for the Three Experimental Groups (from Messick & McClintock, 1968)

	Own		Joint		Relative	
	obs.	pred.	obs.	pred.	obs.	pred.
P[or(j)]	.865	.897	.865*	.938	.915	.883
P[oj(r)]	.840	.883	.865*	.932	.680*	.753
P[r·j(o)]	.600	.598	.556	.558	.895*	.828

*Significantly different ($p < .05$) by t test.

An examination of Table 5 reveals that the largest discrepancy between the observed and predicted values is .073, a value which is not intolerably large. T-tests were computed to test the hypothesis that the predicted values were the means of the distributions from which the observed proportions were drawn. This hypothesis can be rejected at the .05 level for only 4 of the 9 comparisons. (Under the assumption of the model, the more powerful binomial test was justified. However, independent evidence based on the variances of the distributions of proportions strongly suggested that the assumption of parameter constancy across Ss was in error. If so, the t-test is the appropriate statistical test).

The data in Table 5 must be considered only partially supportive of the model. There are no large discrepancies between the predicted and observed values, on the one hand, but four of the differences are large enough to be very unlikely to have occurred simply on the basis of sampling quirks. One possible explanation of these differences is that the model is incorrect in some fundamental way. There are, however, several other less radical possibilities which will be discussed in conjunction with the following study.

Empirical Results: Study II

The second experiment[2] we conducted to evaluate the stochastic model was designed in an effort to replicate the first study and to extend the model. The value of any mathematical model is a function both of its accuracy in predicting experimental results and also of the range of phenomena the model can predict. Consequently, in designing this replication we attempted to measure other behavioral variables which should relate to the choice process in decomposed games with the hope of being able to relate these variables to the model.

The Ss in this experiment were 54 female undergraduates enrolled in an introductory psychology course. The data from nine of these Ss was discarded either because of equipment failure (six Ss) or because their choices were entirely random (three Ss). Unlike the previous experiment, Ss were told that their payment at the end of the experiment would depend upon how "attentive" they were. This was done to avoid making any of the possible motives artificially salient and

---

1 Daniel Williams assumed the major responsibility for running this study.

the instruction was reinforced by a wire apparatus that was attached to each S's wrist.

A total of 36 games was employed. There were six of each game class, and each game class was represented exactly once in each block of six games. Within each block of six games, the games were randomized subject to the constraint that the last game in each block of six be different for the six blocks. The reason for this constraint will become apparent shortly. A total of 72 trials (games) was generated by repeating the first 36 games, changing the labeling of the two alternatives for each game.

Unlike the previous experiment feedback was not presented after each trial. Instead, at the end of each block of six trials, a feedback indicator light was turned on and S was allowed to select the type of feedback she received. S selected her feedback by pressing one of five buttons mounted circularly on a board present on the table in front of S. The buttons were labeled MINE, OTHER'S, TOGETHER, DIFFERENCE, and DON'T CARE. The cumulative scores which were displayed contingent on the feedback choice were, own score, other's score, joint score, relative score, and nothing, respectively. The constraint that each block of six trials end with different games was imposed to avoid the possibility that particular types of games occurring immediately before the feedback choice might bias Ss' feedback preferences.

Our expectations regarding the feedback choices were, first, that the choice of OTHER'S and DON'T CARE should occur very infrequently or not at all. Knowledge of the other S's score provides no information regarding any of the postulated motives. Moreover, if S is in the indifferent state when she is presented with the possibility for obtaining feedback, we assume that she will change to one of the three other motivational states with probabilities which are proportional to w, x, and y. This leads to the second prediction, namely, that the proportion of OWN, DIFFERENCE, and TOGETHER choices should be $\frac{w}{1-z}$, $\frac{x}{1-z}$, and $\frac{y}{1-z}$, respectively.

In addition to allowing Ss to select their feedback dimension, we measured two types of choice times in this study. For each game, we measured the time between the presentation of the game and S's choice of one of the two alternatives. The games were displayed via digital readouts in such a way that when the game was presented, a clock was started and the clock was stopped when S made her choice. These data will not be discussed in this paper except to admit that a model of choice times derived from the stochastic model by making some very simple temporal assumptions was clearly and strongly violated by the data.

The time required to make the feedback choice was also recorded. A clock was started with the onset of the feedback indicator light which was stopped when S made her feedback selection. While the stochastic model does not provide us with expectations concerning these choice times, it was felt that these data might shed further light on the nature of the choice process.

The basic choice data are presented in Table 6. The parameters were estimated as in the first study and the obtained estimates are given in the second column of Table 6. Clearly the predominant motive of the Ss in this study was competition with an estimated 63% of the choices being based on this dimension. That these Ss were even more competitive than those in the Relative Feedback group of the first study is probably attributable to the difference in the instructions used in the two studies. Ss in the first study were told that their payoff at the end of the experiment would depend on how many points they had accumulated which might have enhanced the individualistic motive at the expense of competition.

Table 6: Parameter Estimates and Observed and Predicted Proportions from Study II

State	Estimated probability	Game	Observed	Predicted	95% C.I
Individualism	.150	or(j)	.82	.90	.78 - .87
Competition	.635	oj(r)	.67	.73	.61 - .74
Cooperation	.019	j.r(o)	.80	.87	.74 - .86
Indifference	.196				

The predictive accuracy of the model was assessed by comparing the observed and predicted choice proportions for games in the or(j), oj(r), and j.r(o) cases. These quantities are given in the fourth and fifth columns of Table 6, respectively. In every case, the predicted values are larger by about 7% than the observed proportions. Ninety-five percent confidence intervals (displayed in the last column of Table 6) were constructed around the observed proportions and in two of the three games, or(j) and j.r(o), this interval excluded the predicted proportion.

While these discrepancies, along with those in the first study, may indicate a basic weakness in the model, there are two reasons for thinking that they do not. In the first place, the indifference parameter is estimated only from the orj game which is in some sense the simplest or easiest of all. This may result in an underestimate of z, the indifference parameter. If the indifference parameter were increased, all predicted values would regress toward .50. In all three cases in this study, and in three of the four significant discrepancies in the previous one, this change would reduce the discrepancy between the observed and predicted choice proportions.

The second possible explanation is more technical and somewhat more speculative. To the extent that there are differences among Ss in the choice probabilities, our method of estimating the predicted choice proportions (which assumes constancy across Ss) must be viewed as an approximation. This results from the fact that in computing the expected choice proportions for the last three games in Table 3 we compute, in effect, the ratio of two means, or, generally, the ratio of two expected values. It is a well-known statistical fact that the ratio of two expected values is not equal to the expected value of the ratio. If the variables are independent, the former quantity will be larger than the latter. In the present case, however, the numerator and denominator variables are not independent. They will be positively correlated, especially in the or(j) and oj(r) games. The consequence of this correlation might easily be to make the estimates obtained by taking the ratios of means larger than the value which would be obtained if the means of the ratios were used.

In view of these two possibilities and the fact that the discrepancies between observed and predicted values are numerically small, it would seem premature to reject the model.

Further supportive evidence is presented in Table 7 which displays the observed and predicted proportions of feedback choices along with the mean response time (in seconds) for each type of feedback choice. The agreement between the observed and predicted proportions is especially impressive in that the predicted values are derived from the game choices and do not require the estimation of any additional parameters. The inverse relationship between choice times and choice proportions evidenced in this table is not an uncommon finding in psychological research. There are a variety of explanations of such a relationship but it would take us too far afield to delve into these in this paper.

Table 7: Feedback Choice Proportions and Response Times

Feedback type	Observed	Predicted	Response Time
Difference	.80	.79	2.40
Own	.12	.19	2.85
Other	.04	*	3.07
Joint	.03	.02	3.20
Indifference	.006	*	3.43

To summarize to this point, the results of these first two studies have been generally supportive of the theory of preference we have described. A number of intriguing questions remain, however. Both studies so far discussed have employed only female Ss. Will the model also hold for males? We have confined the tasks in both studies to two choice games.

Is the success of the model restricted to this type of game or can it also be applied to three-choice games, for example? We have shown that the motives of individualism, competition, and cooperation are important in Ss choices, but we have not shown that other plausible motives are not important. In the following study, we attempt to deal with these issues.

Empirical Results: Study III

As was pointed out earlier, the construction of motivational dominance classes for decomposed games depends upon the specific set of motives or choice criteria one selects for analysis. In the study to be described in this section, it was decided to include the motive of minimization of other's gain (m) as a fourth possible state. Such a motive might be identified with an aggressive interpersonal orientation since its explicit goal is to reduce the outcomes of the other individual and hence to impede or hinder the other individual's goal attainment. (Such a motive presupposes that the other individual is striving to maximize his own gain, which may very well be untrue as the previous experiments have shown). The construction of the motivational dominance classes was further complicated by the fact that in this study, three choice games were utilized. Thus, in each game, S must select one of three alternatives, each of which specifies a payoff to S as well as a payoff to the other person. The problem of constructing motivational dominance structures consists of determining all the possible arrangements of the four criteria with the three choices. Eleven motivationally distinct classes of games emerge from this analysis. Since each game has three alternatives,

there are 33 possible choices which could be made. Expected choice probabilities were derived for each of these possible choices exactly as they were for the two-choice game.
Rather than writing out all of these expressions it should be sufficient to illustrate the procedure for one type of game. The game below is in the or.j.m class. This is to say that if S chooses on the basis of

	A	B	C
own payoff	50	20	40
other's payoff	10	0	30

either own gain or relative gain he will make the same choice, namely, A. If he chooses on the basis of joint gain maximization he will make a different choice (C). Finally, if he chooses so as to minimize the other's payoff he will make the third choice (B, in this case). The expected choice probabilities are derived directly from this analysis. The probability of an A choice equals the probability that S is in the individualistic state, plus the probability that he is in the competitive state, plus one third the probability that he is indifferent (since we assume that if S is in the indifferent state he will choose the three alternatives with equal probability). Letting v = P(Aggression), we can write the following expressions for this game.

$$P(A) = w + x + z/3,$$
$$P(B) = v + z/3,$$
and
$$P(C) = y + z/3.$$

Analogous expressions were derived for the remaining ten game classes.

Two independent factors were experimentally manipulated in this experiment. The first factor was the sex of the S. Forty males and 40 females, all enrolled in the introductory psychology course at the University of California, Santa Barbara served as Ss. The second factor which was manipulated relates to the manner in which the games were constructed. In a series of experiments dealing with competition, Messick and Thorngate (1967) demonstrated that the tendency to maximize relative gain was stronger when doing so prevented S from getting less than another, although S could not get more than the other, on the one hand, than when doing so allowed S to surpass the other although he could not fall behind, on the other hand. In an effort to attempt to replicate this finding, half of the games in each class were constructed in such a way that for all three alternatives, the payoff to S was at least as large as the payoff to the other (Case I). In the other half of the games, the payoff afforded the other was at least as large as that received by S (Case II). Thus the game used in the example above is a Case I game of the or·j·m type, while the one below is a game in the same class, but of the Case II variety.

	A	B	C
own payoff	60	70	40
other's payoff	100	80	70

In this experiment we employed 44 games (4 of each of the 11 classes, two in each Case) in a randomized sequence. The games were presented by slides and Ss were instructed, as in the first study, to attempt to attain as many points as possible for themselves. Ss were run in pairs, and were told their own cumulative score and that of the other S at the end of each five trials.

The parameters of the model were estimated separately for males and females, each for Case I and Case II games, giving four different sets of parameters. In addition, parameters were estimated from the pooled data, combining across sexes and cases.

The parameters of the model were estimated by equating the parametric equations for each choice with the observed choice proportions. This leads to a system of 33 equations in five (four independent) unknowns. Naturally such a system of equations is over-determined so an estimation technique was developed which permits rather stable estimation of the parameters.

The estimates of the parameters for the pooled data are presented in Table 8. The estimates in the first set in this table were made including the state of aggression. This estimate is very close to zero, however, and since it was close to zero in each of the four experimental groups as well, the parameters were re-estimated excluding aggression from the set of possible motives. The resulting estimates are presented in the second set in Table 8.

Table 8: Overall Parameter Estimates Including and Excluding "Aggression" from Study III.

State	Set 1	Set 2
Individualism	.315	.314
Competition	.326	.323
Cooperation	.230	.233
Aggression	-.008	--
Indifference	.144	.134

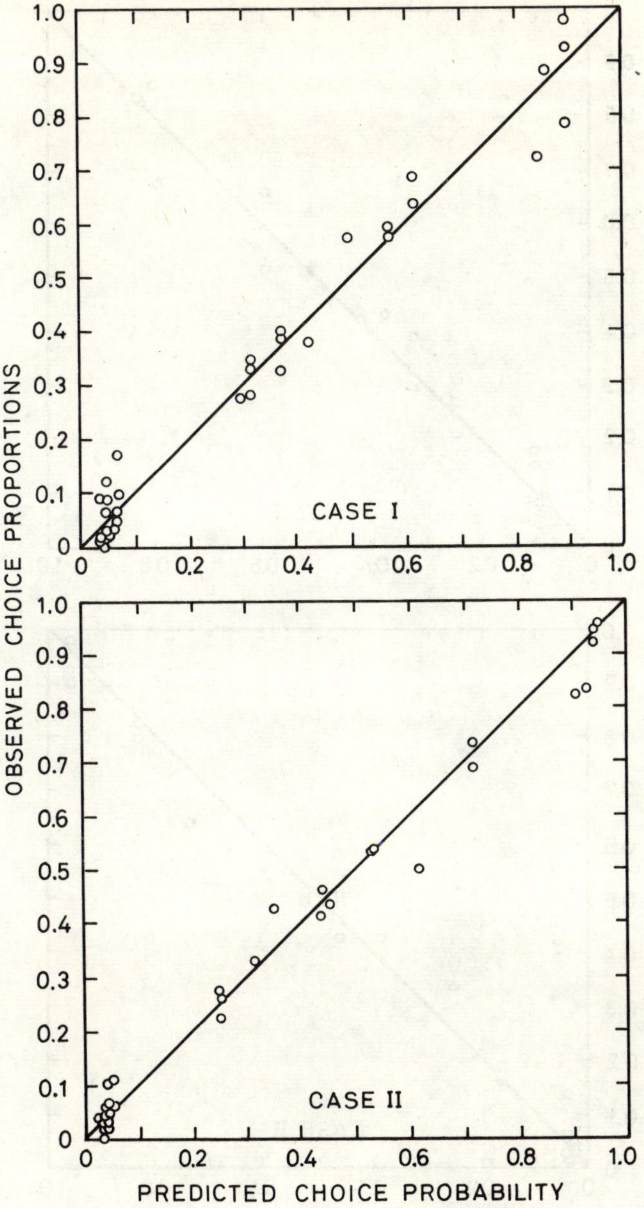

Figure 1: Observed and predicted choice proportions for males

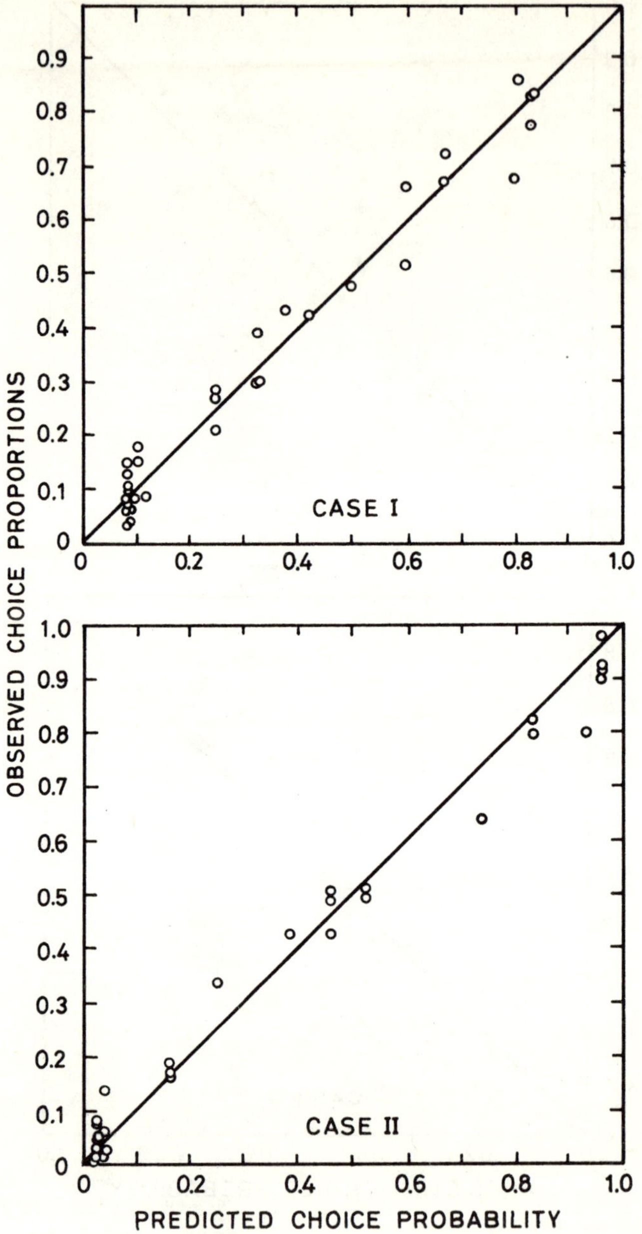

Figure 2: Observed and predicted choice proportions for females

Comparing these two sets of estimates leads to the obvious conclusion that tendencies to minimize the other's gain play a negligible role in this experiment. As a consequence, this motive was eliminated from all further analyses.
Within each of the experimental conditions (case by sex), the obtained proportions of choice in each class of game was plotted against the predicted choice probability. Parameter estimates were made separately for each of these four conditions. The results are graphed in Figures 1 and 2. It is immediately obvious from inspection of these figures that there is a very high correspondence between the predicted and observed choice proportions. The model, using only three of the 22 degrees of freedom in each set of data, clearly does an outstanding job of accounting for the variability in the observed choice proportions. The correlation coefficients between expected and observed values for the four groups are presented in Table 9.

Table 9: Correlation Coefficients Between Observed and Predicted Choice Proportions

	Case I	Case II
Males	.986	.993
Females	.986	.993

The correlation coefficients, however, do not tell the full story regarding the fit of the model to the data. Any linear transformation of the predicted values would fail to change the correlation coefficients, but such a transformation could clearly affect the fit of the model. Consequently, an additional analysis is called for.

For each of the eleven classes of games there are three observed proportions and three expected (predicted) proportions. Using these two sets of frequencies, a χ^2 goodness of fit was computed for each class. The obtained χ^2's were summed across game classes within experimental conditions to obtain an overall measure of goodness fit. Assuming the χ^2's within each sum to be independent, the total χ^2 will be based upon 19 degrees of freedom since there are a total of 22 degrees of freedom (two for each of the 11 classes) and three are used for parameter estimation.

The values of χ^2 for the four conditions are presented in Table 10. The observed choice frequencies are significantly different from the expected in two of the four conditions. The large χ^2 for Case I males can be attributed to two of the eleven game classes. The sum of the χ^2 for these two is 30.5 (for four degrees of freedom). In both games, the large χ^2 results from the fact that the expected proportions of two choices are very low, .046 and .069, while the obtained proportions were large relative to the expectation (i.e., .10 and .14 respectively). This result may reflect an underestimate of the indifference parameter, a problem which we have encountered previously in applying the model.

Table 10: χ^2 Goodness of Fit

	Case I	Case II
Males	48.8*	29.0
Females	27.7	53.4*

*Significantly different from expected. χ^2 (.05, df = .19) = 30.14.

Of the total χ^2 for the Case II females, 30.3 can be attributed to deviations in just two of the eleven games. Neither game was the same as those leading to large χ^2's for the Case I males. Again, the very large χ^2 can be attributed to very small expected proportions, .024 and .043 respectively. Despite the discrepancies between the predicted and observed values, however, it should be clear that the over-all correspondence between the model and the data is excellent.

Having validated the model for this experiment, it is now possible to examine the choice parameters for each of the experimental conditions in order to gain insight into possible differences between males and females with respect to their preferences and also to see if there are the expected differences between Case I and Case II games. The parameter estimates for each group are presented in Table 11.

The first feature of these data which becomes clear is that females tend to be more individualistic than males. This holds true for both Case I and Case II games. The likelihood of choosing on the basis of own gain, moreover, does not depend materially on whether the game is Case I or Case II.

This is not true with the likelihood of competition, however. Almost twice as many choices were competitive in Case II as in Case I games. These proportions are .410 as opposed to .213 respectively. There is clearly a higher incidence of competition in games in which S could not attain a higher outcome than the other. Overall, males are somewhat more competitive than females, although the difference between them washes out in Case II games.

Males are more cooperative than females. It is estimated that males make 28% of their choices on the basis of cooperative motives whereas the corresponding estimate for females is about 18%. This difference of ap-

Table 11: Estimated Parameters in Each of the Four Experimental Conditions.
The estimates are for the proportion of choices made on the basis of individualism, competition, cooperation, and indifference, respectively.

	Case I	Case II	Overall
Male	$\hat{w}$ = .259	$\hat{w}$ = .283	$\hat{w}$ = .271
	$\hat{x}$ = .273	$\hat{x}$ = .397	$\hat{x}$ = .335
	$\hat{y}$ = .342	$\hat{y}$ = .218	$\hat{y}$ = .280
	$\hat{z}$ = .139	$\hat{z}$ = .090	$\hat{z}$ = .114
Female	$\hat{w}$ = .349	$\hat{w}$ = .360	$\hat{w}$ = .354
	$\hat{x}$ = .153	$\hat{x}$ = .424	$\hat{x}$ = .288
	$\hat{y}$ = .252	$\hat{y}$ = .113	$\hat{y}$ = .182
	$\hat{z}$ = .236	$\hat{z}$ = .071	$\hat{z}$ = .154
Overall	$\hat{w}$ = .304	$\hat{w}$ = .322	$\hat{w}$ = .313
	$\hat{x}$ = .213	$\hat{x}$ = .410	$\hat{x}$ = .312
	$\hat{y}$ = .297	$\hat{y}$ = .165	$\hat{y}$ = .231
	$\hat{z}$ = .187	$\hat{z}$ = .081	$\hat{z}$ = .134

proximately 10% is constant across the case of the game.

The differences between Case I and Case II games are interesting. In the first place, there is no difference to speak of with respect to the estimated frequency of own gain choices. The likelihood of making a choice on the basis of own gain, a non-social motive, does not depend upon the opportunity afforded by the game to get more than the other (Case I) or to get less (Case II). Such is not the case with the estimated probability of competition. When S cannot get ahead (Case II) the frequency of competitive choices is more than 40% whereas the same figure is only about 20% when S cannot get behind. These data are nicely supportive of the finding by Messick and Thorngate (1967) that the tendency to avoid getting behind another is a stronger component of relative gain than is the desire to surpass another.

The fact that the incidence of competition increases in Case II games is interesting, but it is even more interesting to note that both for males and females, the increase entails a decrease in the proportions of cooperative and indifferent responses, but no corresponding decrease in individualistic responding. One interpretation of this pattern of results is that the effect of being in a situation in which one is at a disadvantage relative to another is to enhance social comparisons of outcomes and to weight relative standing more heavily in the evaluation of the outcomes. In other words, in a situation in which S cannot surpass the other, the stimuli associated with being behind are relatively salient and enhanced competition results.

An alternative explanation focuses on the fact that in Case II games, if S chooses to maximize relative gain he is simultaneously choosing that option which minimizes the absolute difference between his score and that of the other. Choosing on the basis of such a criterion might be denoted "equality." While in Case II games equality and competition are perfectly confounded, this is not so in Case I games. The equality criterion in Case I games tends to be most frequently associated with cooperation or indifference. Thus this interpretation of the difference between the choice proportions for Case I and Case II games suggests that there is an additional motive state, "equality," which is differentially correlated with other states in Case I as compared to Case II. This interpretation suggests, moreover, that the actual underlying probabilities are constant in Case 1 and Case II, and that the difference in the estimates results from the fact that no "equality" state is included in the model.

This possibility was investigated by rewriting the choice model to include an equality state. Naturally a separate estimate of the equality parameter can only be obtained in Case I since equality and competition are inseparable in Case II games. Two estimates of the probability of choosing on the basis of equality were obtained, one for males and one for females. The estimate for males was -.064 while that for females was -.066. The fact that both estimates are close to zero suggests that the equality interpretation of the Case I and II difference is incorrect.

Conclusions

The subjects in the experiments I have described are clearly not consistent money maximizers. One might take issue with this conclusion by arguing that if the amounts of money which were at stake had been larger, Ss might have been more attentive to this dimension of the payoffs. Such an objection, however, strikes me as irrelevant. Small amounts of money, when accumulated, make large amounts of money, a fact which renders the task of drawing a line between trivial and nontrivial quantities sticky at best. Moreover, even if it could be shown that people were more individualistic with larger payoffs, such a demonstration would not necessarily contradict the theory of the preference process which has been advanced here. Such data might only reflect an increase in the likelihood of individualistic choice in a manner similar to our finding of a difference in competition between Case I and Case II games in the last experiment.

It seems most fruitful to think of people as being local optimizers who can focus on any of a number of outcome dimensions. This is to say that when an S makes a choice, he does so with the goal of maximizing some aspect of the outcomes. The aspect being focused on may vary from person to person, or from time to time for the same person. The salience of different dimensions may change, moreover, as a function of situational or contextual changes. From this point of view it seems clear that the "value" or "utility" an individual associates with an outcome is best considered a manifestation of the individual's motivational or preference system rather than an attribute inherent in the outcome itself. Indeed, the ultimate significance of experimental economics as a scientific endeavor may depend in large measure upon its success in achieving an understanding of such preference systems.

Bibliography

Deutsch, M., The Effect of Motivational Orientation on Threat and Suspicion, Human Relations, 13, 1960, pp. 123-129.

Livingston, J.W., On the Measurement of Social Motivation in Decomposed Games, unpublished Ph.D. dissertation, 1971, University of California, Santa Barbara.

Messick, D.M., Some Thoughts on the Nature of Human Competition, Hypothese, 14, 1970, pp. 38-52.

Messick, D.M., and C.G. McClintock, Motivational Bases of Choice in Experimental Games, Journal of Experimental Social Psychology, 4, 1968, pp. 1-25.

Messick, D.M., and W. Thorngate, Relative Gain Maximization in Experimental Games, Journal of Experimental Social Psychology, 3, 1967, pp. 85-101.

Pruitt, D.G., Reward Structure and Cooperation: the Decomposed Prisoner's Dilemma Game, Journal of Personality and Social Psychology, 7, 1967, pp. 21-27.

Wyer, R.S., Prediction of Behavior in Two-person Games, Journal of Personality and Social Psychology, 13, 1967, pp. 222-238.

Wyer, R.S., Effects of Outcome Matrix and Partner's Behavior in Two-person Games, Journal of Experimental Social Psychology, 7, 1971, pp. 170-210.

15. TACIT COMMUNICATION AND COOPERATION IN A MIXED-MOTIVE GAME*

SAMUEL S. KOMORITA**

A general problem in bargaining and negotiation is the effects of concession-making. As Professor Bartos has described earlier, negotiators are frequently faced with a dilemma between maximizing the probability of reaching an agreement and maximizing the probability of obtaining an advantageous agreement. A yielding strategy - though it is more likely to result in an agreement - is also likely to result in a "bad" bargain. A tough strategy, on the other hand, is more likely to result in a "good" bargain, but it minimizes the probability of reaching an agreement.

It is plausible that in the initial stages of negotiations, both parties feel that the expected gains from obtaining an advantageous bargain outweigh the expected losses of not reaching an agreement. However, in subsequent encounters - if both parties have adopted a tough strategy - one or both parties may feel that the expected gains from an advantageous bargain would not compensate for the expected losses of not reaching an agreement. Thus, a more yielding strategy may be adopted in later stages of negotiation. In one of our earlier stu-

---

* This research was supported in part by the National Institute of Mental Health (Grant No. MH 18910).

** Indiana University.

dies (Komorita and Barnes, 1969), we found some evidence for this tendency, especially when the parties were under pressures to reach an agreement.

This change in expectations during the course of negotiation is implied by Stevens' proposal (1963) that the negotiation cycle involves a movement from the competitive aspects of negotiation at the early stages to an emphasis on coordination and cooperation at the later stages. Moreover, this formulation is consistent with the idea of expected outcome proposed by Professor Bartos and can be derived from the concept of "status quo point" proposed by bargaining theorists such as Nash and Shapley.

The provocative question is, "What are the relevant variables which evoke such changes in expectations?" One obvious factor is a stalemate or deadlock in the negotiations where neither party has conceded for an extended period of time. This is, I believe, the underlying basis of Osgood's GRIT strategy (Osgood, 1959; 1962). Osgood proposed that if negotiations are deadlocked, one side must make a small concession and wait for the other side to reciprocate the small concession. In subsequent negotiations, these reciprocated concessions are assumed to become progressively larger, until finally, the conflict is resolved.

Opposed to Osgood's proposal is the Level of Aspiration Theory of bargaining proposed by Siegel and Fouraker (1960). Their theory assumes that concessions by one party raises the aspiration level of the other party and evokes a firm, unyielding stance in subsequent negotiations. Their theory, therefore, implies that one should make very small concessions, if any.

Although there are some data supporting Osgood's proposal (e.g., Pilisuk and Skolnick, 1968; Crow, 1963), the bulk of the evidence seems to support Siegel and Fouraker's theory (for example, data presented by Bartos and Harnett at this conference). In my opinion, however, these studies supporting Siegel and Fouraker's theory do not necessarily imply a rejection of the Osgood proposal. Osgood's GRIT strategy was proposed in a context where the cost of not reaching agreement would be extremely high - namely, World War III. Moreover, his proposal assumed that there was a long history of competitive acts by both sides, and that the negotiations were deadlocked.

Accordingly, in my recent research, I have attempted to simulate the situation Osgood had in mind when he proposed his GRIT strategy, namely, a situation in which both parties believe that it pays to be tough, and both have adopted a tough, unyielding strategy. The negotiations, of course, are deadlocked. Such a situation is analogous to the game of "Chicken" where both parties believe or hope that the other person will eventually yield. In such a situation, a conciliatory act by one party is likely to be perceived as a sign of weakness and merely strengthens the other party's toughness. This outcome of course, is implied by Siegel and Fouraker's theory. One solution to this problem is for both parties to yield simultaneously so that neither loses "face" and receives an unfavorable outcome. In this context, recent studies on the effects of mediation by a third party is suggestive. A mediator seems to be effective to the extent that he can induce the parties to concede - unwillingly and simultaneously - so that neither party perceives such concessions to be a sign of weakness (Podell and Knapp, 1969; Pruitt and Johnson, 1970).

Given these considerations, the general research problem I wish to pose is as follows: assuming a stalemate in negotiations, under what conditions is a conciliatory act likely to be perceived as a sign of weakness and met with exploitation as implied by Siegel and Fouraker, and under what conditions is it likely to be perceived as "honest" or "fair" and reciprocated, as implied by Osgood? A basic assumption underlying our research is that the effects of concession-making - or more broadly, the effects of conciliatory acts - whether it is reciprocated as Osgood would predict, or met with firmness as Siegel and Fouraker would predict, depends upon the situational context in which the concession is made. For example, the results of one of our earlier studies (Komorita, Sheposh, and Braver; 1968) suggest that when a concession is made, it is likely to be perceived with trust and benevolent intent if the conceder is perceived to have done so willingly and was not compelled to do so. To the extent that this proposition is valid - and assuming that we wish to maximize the probability of reaching an agreement - this implies that a concession should be made when one's bargaining position is strong rather than weak. Concessions by a strong party is less likely to be perceived as a sign of weakness.

Now let me describe the experimental paradigm for testing these hypotheses. The situation I have just described typifies the behavior of subjects in the classic Prisoner's Dilemma game who have "locked-in" on the joint competitive outcome. One of the explanations for this seemingly irrational behavior is that in most experiments using this game, verbal communication is not permitted. If communication were permitted, one or both parties might communicate an intent to cooperate, and a mutually cooperative solution might be achieved. However, in many situations in the real-world, even when communication is possible, the parties have found it exceedingly difficult to reach a cooperative solution. Accordingly, Schelling (1960) has emphasized the role of tacit communication in bargaining when the credibility of the parties is suspect or when communication is not possible. In the context of the Prisoner's Dilemma game, credibility is a significant factor since some degree of mutual trust is required if cooperation is to occur.

Given that the parties are deadlocked in the jointly competitive outcome, how should they escape from this situation? One solution is for one of the parties to switch to a cooperative choice - sustaining a temporary loss - so as to induce the other to reciprocate the cooperative choice. Such a sacrifice has been called a "martyr" sequence by Rapoport and Chammah (1965), and would be consistent with Osgood's GRIT proposal. In some instances, the other person will reciprocate the martyr's behavior and reach a mutually cooperative solution. In most instances, however, his behavior is exploited and the martyr eventually returns to the competitive choice.

It is plausible that the conciliatory act by the martyr is ineffective in inducing reciprocity because it is not perceived as an intent to cooperate. For example, the sequence of choices leading to the deadlock and the length of the deadlock must be considered. A second possibility is that the conciliatory act is perceived with cooperative intent but is perceived as a sign of weakness and is exploited. Therefore, it was hypothesized that in order to tacitly communicate an intent to cooperate, it would be necessary to make a conciliatory move deliberately large and dramatic so that it would be salient and distinctive. Moreover, in order to discourage exploitation, the subject must be led to believe that the other person is competitive and that toughness will be met with toughness.

Accordingly, in order to vary these conditions systematically, we led pairs of subjects to believe that they were playing with each other, but in actuality, they played a simulated feedback program used by the experimenter. In the first study (Komorita and Koziej, 1970), this feedback program was as follows: (a) Extinction Phase: consecutive D-choices by the experimenter on the first 10 trials; (b) Repentance Phase: consecutive C-choices by the experimenter-matching the number of C-choices subject had made during the Extinction Phase; and (c) Reconciliation Phase: "tit-for-tat" strategy (imitate subject's response on previous trial) for 3 blocks of 20 trials.

The initial extinction phase was intended to simulate a deadlock or stalemate, and to communicate to the subject that the other person was competitive or tough; hence, exploitation would be difficult. We call it the Extinction Phase because we extinguish the subject's cooperative tendencies by making consecutive D-choices on the first 10 trials.

The Repentance Phase also served two purposes: first, it simulates conciliatory acts by the other person after a deadlock, and secondly, it permits the subject to retaliate against the other person for unreciprocated C-choices during the Extinction Phase. Since the program matches the number of C-choices made by the subject during the Extinction Phase, for subjects across the various experimental conditions, the cumulative outcomes after the Repentance Phase are also matched.

Finally, the Reconciliation Phase, as the name implies, was used to measure the extent to which subjects were able to reach a mutually cooperative solution. We used the proportion of C-choices on the last block of 20 trials as the main response measure.

The first variable we manipulated was the nature of the consequences for making conciliatory acts. We hypothesized that if it is costly to make a conciliatory overture, such a sacrifice would be salient and distinctive. Therefore, it should facilitate the communication of cooperative intent. In order to vary the magnitude of this sacrifice, we imposed a penalty for making a cooperative choice and used four different game matrices. These games are shown in Table 1. The 0-cost matrix (Game 1) was a control condition and represents a standard Prisoner's Dilemma game. In the Minus 1, Minus 2, and Minus 3 conditions, subjects were instructed that each time they pressed the Red button, (the C-choice) 1, 2,

Table 1. Game Matrices Imposing Cost For Cooperative Choice*

Game 1. 0-Cost (Control

	C(0)	D
C(0)	4, 4	-3, 10
D	10, -3	0, 0

Game 2. Minus 1 Condition

	C(-1)	D
C(-1)	5, 5	-2, 10
D	10, -2	0, 0

Game 3. Minus 2 Condition

	C(-2)	D
C(-2)	6, 6	-1, 10
D	10, -1	0, 0

Game 4. Minus 3 Condition

	C(-3)	D
C(-3)	7, 7	0, 10
D	10, 0	0, 0

*Left and right cell entries denote payoffs to row and column players, respectively. Numbers in parentheses after "C" choice indicate number of points subtracted from total score when C-choices were made.

or 3 points, depending upon the condition, would automatically be subtracted from their total score. They were also instructed to maximize their point-total in whatever way they wished, and that the total points they accumulated would be converted to money at the end of the experiment.

It can be seen that for each combination of choices, the outcomes are identical across the four conditions. In the Minus 1 condition, for example, if both made C-choices, the outcome would be 5, but subtracting 1 point for making a C-choice, the cumulative outcome would be 4. This is the same as in the 0-cost condition. If one person played C and the other D, the outcome would be -2 for the "Sucker's payoff;" however, there would be an additional loss of 1 point for making the C-choice, so that the cumulative "Sucker's payoff" would -3, the same as in the 0-cost condition. Similarly, for the Minus 2 and Minus 3 conditions, when the appropriate number of points are subtracted for making a C-choice, the outcomes are identical with the 0-cost, control condition.

In all four games, therefore, for any combination of C and D-choices, the cumulative outcomes are identical.

It should be pointed out that though the reward structure is identical, the four conditions differ in the contingency of the loss when a C-choice is made. In the 0-cost condition, a loss of 3 points is possible when a C-choice is made, but this loss is contingent on defection (D-choice) by the other. In the other three conditions, however, some loss is certain since the very act of making a C-choice penalizes the subject. In this sense, the sacrifice - when conciliatory overtures are made in the Repentance Phase - is not contingent upon the other person's choice.

The second variable we manipulated was the pre-programmed strategy of the experimenter during the 60 trials of the Reconciliation Phase. One condition was the "tit-for-tat" strategy described earlier. The second condition, the Martyr condition, was a modification of the "tit-for-tat" strategy such that whenever the subject made five consecutive D-choices, the experimenter played the role of a Martyr by making a C-choice. If the subject reciprocated the C-choice, another C-choice was made, but if the subject did not reciprocate, a D-choice was made. In both cases, the "tit-for-tat" strategy was resumed on subsequent trials, and the procedure was repeated each time the subject made 5 consecutive D-choices.

According to our hypothesis regarding the salience and distinctiveness of conciliatory acts, it was hypothesized that the level of cooperation on the last block of 20 trials would be an increasing function of Cost. It was also hypothesized that the Martyr condition would interact with the Cost variable such that it would evoke a higher level of cooperation under high cost than in the low cost conditions.

The subjects were undergraduate students, both males and females, and the results are shown in Table 2 . Since no

Table 2. Mean Proportion of Cooperative Choices on Last Block of 20 Trials (Data from Komorita and Koziej, 1970)

	Cost				
	0	-1	-2	-3	Total
Tit-for-tat	.54	.39	.57	.63	.53
Martyr	.51	.41	.48	.58	.49
Total	.52	.40	.51	.59	

sex differences were found, the data for males and females were combined, and each point in Table 2 represent data for about 24 subjects.

The main effect of strategy, "tit-for-tat" vs. Martyr, was not statistically significant. The hypothesized interaction was not significant either. The only significant result (5% level) was the effect of Cost. It can be seen, however, that the nature of this effect was not as hypothesized.

Our explanation of these results is that there are two opposing forces operating in this situation - one inhibiting and one facilitating reconciliation. On the one hand, subjects are motivated to avoid the cost of making a cooperative choice; this is reflected clearly in the -1 condition. On the other hand, deliberately taking a loss seems to be a mechanism for communicating one's intent - or trust in the other - and facilitates the reciprocation of a cooperative choice. It also seems to counterbalance the motive to avoid the costly cooperative choice.

With regard to the theoretical implications of this study, the results suggest a threshold for the magnitude of loss which effectively communicates an intent to cooperate. A significantly large or dramatic sacrifice may be necessary for a conciliatory act to be perceived as an inducement to reach a mutually cooperative settlement. This hypothesis, of course, has significant implications for Osgood's GRIT proposal and suggests that the magnitude of the initial concession, as proposed by Osgood, must be above some threshold value if it is to be effective. Indeed, under the conditions of this study, the results suggest that a concession involving a small sacrifice may arouse suspicion, and may actually be detrimental in inducing cooperation.

Now, let me turn to a second study using a similar procedure. The purpose of this study was to replicate the effects of Cost found in the previous study, and also to eliminate a confounding variable found in the earlier study. In the previous study, all subjects were exposed to 10 consecutive D-choices in the Extinction Phase. On the basis of pilot studies, we had assumed that all subjects would be making D-choices, thus, simulating a competitive stalemate. However, a sizeable proportion of the subjects were found to be making some C-choices at the end of the Extinction Phase.

To insure that subjects were making D-choices when conciliatory acts were initiated (in the Repentance Phase), we changed the extinction procedure. Instead of a constant number of D-choices as in the previous study, subjects were exposed to consecutive D-choices until they had reached an extinction criterion of 3 consecutive D-choices. Thus, we initiated conciliatory acts after each subject had experienced 3 consecutive DD outcomes (the stalemate). As in the previous study, in the Repentance Phase we matched the number of C-choices the subject hade made in the Extinction Phase, and then used a "tit-for-tat" strategy in the Reconciliation Phase (3 blocks of 20 trials).

In an attempt to replicate our previous results, we used three levels of Cost: 0-cost, Minus 1, and Minus 2. In addition, we also manipulated the length of the competitive stalemate prior to the conciliatory acts in the Repentance Phase. In one condition, the feedback program called for consecutive D-choices until the subject reached the extinction criterion of 3 consecutive D-choices, as described previously. This condition will be called the E(C) condition. In the second condition, we simply ran 5 additional D-choices after the subject had reached the extinction criterion. Thus, in this condition, hereafter called the E(C+5) condition, the Extinction Phase is 5 trials longer than in the E(C) condition, and should impress the subject that the other person is highly competitive and tough.

When conciliatory acts are made after a relatively long stalemate, it should be more distinctive and salient; hence, it might be predicted that subjects in the E(C+5) condition should reach a higher level of cooperation than in the E(C) condition. However, it is reasonable to assume that a long stalemate would arouse hostility toward the other - especially if the subject had made many unreciprocated C-choices. Moreover, in a previous study (Komorita and Mechling, 1967), we found that a long sequence of mutually cooperative choices prior to a betrayal faciliated subsequent reconciliation. Therefore, it was hypothesized that the mean level of C-choices in the E(C) condition would be higher than in the E(C+5) condition.

To summarize, there were 6 experimental conditions based on three levels of Cost and two levels of Extinction Length. All subjects were male undergraduate students with about 20 subjects in each of the 6 experimental conditions. As in the previous study, the main response measure was the proportion of C-choices on the last block of 20 trials.

Table 3 shows the mean proportion of C-choices for the various conditions. There seems to be an interaction between Cost and Extinction Length, but it is not significant at the 5% level. The main effect of Extinction Length also is not significant. The main effect of Cost- though it is significant at the 10% level - are equivocal with regard to the hypothesized effects. For the E(C) condition, the V-shaped function we found in the

Table 3. Mean Proportion of Cooperative Choices: Cost by Extinction Length

		Cost			
		0	-1	-2	Total
Extinction Length	E(C)	.64	.59	.68	.63
	E(C+5)	.52	.64	.73	.63
	Total	.59	.61	.71	

previous study was obtained; however, for the E(C+5) condition, there is a simple, monotonically increasing function.

In order to explain these results, we conducted some additional analyses of the data. First, we noticed that how the subject responded on the first trial seemed to be correlated with their subsequent responses. Consequently, we divided subjects in all conditions according to their response on the first trial, C or D, and reanalyzed the data using first trial response as a third independent variable. The results are shown in Tables 4 and 5. The main effect of First Choice is significant at the 1% level, but this variable interacts with the other two variables. The triple interaction between the 3 variables, however, is not significant.

Table 4. Mean Proportion of Cooperative Choices: First Choice by Extinction Length

		Extinction Length		
		E(C)	E(C+5)	Total
First Choice	C_1	.78	.63	.71
	D_1	.52	.64	.58
	Total	.63	.63	

Table 5. **Mean Proportion of Cooperative Choices: Cost by First Choice**

		Cost			
		0	-1	-2	Total
First Choice	C_1	.63	.70	.79	.71
	D_1	.56	.57	.61	.58
	Total	.59	.61	.71	

Table 4 shows the nature of the interaction between Extinction Length and First Choice. This interaction is significant at the 1% level and indicates that the long extinction length, E(C+5), relative to the short, E(C), inhibits cooperation for those who responded cooperatively on the first trial, but facilitates cooperation for those who responded competitively on the first trial. Though the main effect of First Choice is significant at the 1% level, it can be seen in Table 4 that the difference between C_1 and D_1 is negligible when Extinction Length is long, and very large when it is short.

Table 5 shows the nature of the interaction between Cost and First Choice. This interaction is only significant at the 10% level, so any interpretation or conclusions drawn from this data must be considered speculative. However, these results suggest that Cost has negligible effects for subjects who made a D-choice on the first trial, but has the hypothesized effect for subjects who made a C-choice on the first trial.

In addition to these analyses, we also noticed considerable variability in the rates of extinction. Consequently, we divided subjects into fast and slow extinguishers on the basis of those who reached the extinction criterion in 5 or fewer trials (Fast) vs. those who took more than 5 trials (Slow). The main effect of Extinction Rate was significant at the 5% level, and though none of the interactions was significant, Table 6 is presented to give you a better idea of this effect. It can be seen that Fast extinguishers reached a higher level of cooperation than Slow extinguishers.

Table 6. Mean Proportion of Cooperative Choices: Cost by Rate of Extinction

		Cost			
		0	-1	-2	Total
Rate of	Fast	.64	.66	.79	.69
Extinction	Slow	.51	.53	.65	.58
	Total	.59	.61	.71	

Now, let me summarize the significant findings and discuss their implications. First, subject's response on the first trial yielded the most significant effect - subjects who responded cooperatively on the first trial, reached a higher level of cooperation than those who had responded competitively. However, the effects of First Choice interacts with both Cost and with Extinction Length.

With regard to the effects of Cost, based on our previous findings, we had predicted a V-shaped function. Obviously, we failed to replicate our earlier study, though there is a slight tendency of this in the E(C) group (Table 3). One simple explanation is the difference in extinction procedures and the difference in extinction rates between the two groups. It is plausible that the V-shaped function is characteristic of subjects who continue to make C-choices during the Extinction Phase and are very slow to extinguish. With reference to the data in Table 6, showing the interaction between Cost and Extinction Rate, this conjecture is based on the fact that in our first attempt to analyze this data, we divided subjects into 3 groups: Fast, Medium, and Slow. The Fast group showed a linear trend, the Medium group showed a slight V-shaped function, while the Slow group revealed a well-defined V-shaped function. Thus, the V-shaped function may be characteristic of those who are extremely persistent in making cooperative overtures in the Extinction Phase. This interpretation is supported by the fact that 48% of the subjects were classified as Slow in the present study, but using the same criterion for subjects in the previous study, 67% of them were classified as Slow extinguishers. Thus a much higher proportion of subjects in the previous study were slow to extinguish than in the present study.

Our original hypothesis regarding the effect of cost was that a conciliatory act involving a deliberate sacrifice would facilitate the communication of cooperative intent, lead to reciprocated cooperation, and facilitate a mutually cooperative solution. The data in Table 5, showing the interaction between First Choice and Cost, indicate that our hypothesis was supported for those who cooperated on the first trial, but was not supported for those who competed on the first trial.

There is additional support for this Hypothesis from studies conducted by Evans and Crumbaugh (1966) and by Pruitt (1967; 1970), who restructured the PD game into several "decomposed" games. All of Pruitt's decomposed PD games (DPD) had equivalent reward structures, as in the present study, and he found significant differences in the level of cooperation between these equivalent games. Two of these DPD games are shown in Table 7. Compared with the standard PD game (Game 1),

Table 7. Pruitt's PD and Two Decomposed PD Games (DPD).*
From Journal of Personality and Social Psychology (1967; 1970)

Game I (PD)				Game II (DPD)				Game IV (DPD)	
	C	D		Your Gains	Other's Gains		Your Gains	Other's Gains
C	12, 12	0, 18	C	6	6	C	-6	18
D	18, 0	6, 6	D	12	-6	D	0	6

*In each game, subject is asked to make C or D-choice simultaneously. In DPD, the final outcome is based on the sum of payoffs resulting from the subject's choice and the other player's choice. DPD III not included.

he found a high level of cooperation in Game IV and a very low level in Game II. Pruitt interprets his results in terms of eliciting different motives in these games, and indicates that Game IV evokes a high level of cooperation because it provides an opportunity to help the other at some cost to oneself, and elicits the motive of mutual assistance.

Our interpretation of his results - though not inconsistent with his - is that when a subject makes a C-choice in Game IV, he effectively communicates cooperative intent because it is costly - a loss of 6 units. In terms of the present study based on costs for a cooperative choice, a C-choice is perceived as a conciliatory act which is salient and distinctive because it involves a deliberate loss.

It is plausible that both groups, C_1 and D_1, uniformly perceived the conciliatory gesture in the Repentance Phase, but they reacted in the opposite fashion. Those who responded competitively on the first trial may have perceived the conciliatory acts as a sign of weakness and exploited such acts, while those who had cooperated on the first trial may have reciprocated such acts. What I am suggesting is that there need not be a one-to-one correspondence between the perception of an act and the behavior it evokes. Indeed, there are data to suggest that an individual may perceive a conciliatory act to be an inducement to cooperate but exploit such an act; conversely, an individual may perceive a conciliatory act to be a sign of weakness and yet reciprocate such an act. A two stage research strategy, therefore, may be the most fruitful approach to eliminate this confounding. Consequently, the question I posed earlier might be rephrased as follows: (a) under what conditions is a conciliatory act perceived to be a sign of cooperative intent? and (b) given that the act is perceived with cooperative intent, under what conditions will such conciliatory acts be reciprocated or be exploited?

Another provocative question is, "What determines what an individual will do on the first trial? What characterizes individuals who cooperate or compete on the initial trial?" Others have found a similar effect of early trials, so this effect is not unique to this study. Terhune (1968), for example, also found in a PD game that those subjects who cooperated on the first trial reached the highest level of cooperation on subsequent trials. Similarly, Pilisuk, Potter, Rapoport, and Winter (1965) found a positive relation between responses on the first five trials and subsequent behavior. In both of these studies, personality variables were also administered to the subjects. Pilisuk, et al, using several paper and pencil scales - including the F-scale - found no significant relations between these measures and level of cooperative behavior. Terhune, on the other hand, used the Thematic Apperception Test (TAT), and measured three motivational orientations: (a) need for achievement; (b) need for affiliation; and (c) need for power. He found that subjects high in need-achievement cooperated the most, while those high in need for power cooperated the least. Moreover, he found an interaction between the effects of first trial experience and these motive types: those high in need-achievement who experienced mutual C-choices on the first trial reached the highest level of cooperation, while those high in need-power who experienced mutual D-choices on the first trial, cooperated the least. My interpretation of his results is that these motivational orientations determine how conciliatory acts are perceived - high need-achievement individuals are more likely to perceive conciliatory acts as an intent to cooperate and are likely to reciprocate such acts. High need-power individuals, on the other hand, are likely to perceive such acts as a sign of weakness and attempt to exploit such behavior.

It is plausible that subjects who make a C-choice on the first trial have a cooperative orientation, while those who make a D-choice on the first trial have a competitive orientation. The data in Table 4 suggest that a long competitive stalemate inhibits subsequent cooperation for those who have a cooperative orientation, but facilitates cooperation for those with a competitive orientation. These data therefore suggest that a long sequence of competitive trials may be necessary to communicate to a competitive person that one will not tolerate exploitation, while only a short sequence, if any, may be necessary to communicate this to a cooperative person. Thus, it may pay to be tough against a tough person, but not necessarily against a cooperative person - a tough strategy against a cooperative person may subsequently evoke a tough strategy in return.

With regard to the effects of Extinction Rate, the data in Table 6 indicate that those who extinguished quickly reached a higher level of cooperation than those who extinguished slowly. One explanation for this is that Slow extinguishers - since they made more C-choices in the Extinction Phase - were exposed to a longer sequence of conciliatory acts in the Repentance Phase. Thus, they may be more likely to perceive such acts as a sign of weakness and attempt to exploit such acts. If this interpretation is valid, it suggests that there is an optimal number of conciliatory acts which facilitates reconciliation on subsequent trials.

The most plausible explanation, however, is that Slow extinguishers were slow to extinguish because they made more cooperative overtures during the Extinction Phase. This is tautological, of course, but that's why they were slow to extinguish. With our extinction program, however, we continued to defect in spite of these cooperative overtures - and we did not reciprocate their conciliatory acts. What we attempted to do was to communicate our cooperative intent to the subject, but in the process, they attempted to communicate their intent and we did not perceive and respond to these overtures. The main implication of this result, if this interpretation is valid, is that when conciliatory acts are made, they should be reciprocated as soon as possible. If such acts are ignored and not reciprocated within a given period of time, it may be extremely difficult to reach a cooperative solution on subsequent encounters.

In closing, let me make a few statements about the theoretical implications of these data for the controversy between Siegel and Fouraker's theory and Osgood's GRIT proposal. I'm not sure if these data support one theory more than the other, but I think it provides a more valid test of Osgood's proposal in that the concessions are made subsequent to a competitive stalemate. The data suggest that the effects of concessions may depend on the history of competitive acts prior to concession-making, and it also depends on the competitive orientation of the parties. There are undoubtedly many other situational variables which influence the perception and reactions to concessions. My hypothesis is that the Siegel-Fouraker proposal is valid at the initial and intermediate stages of negotiation, while Osgood's proposal is valid in the later stages - when the negotiations are deadlocked for an extended period of time and when the expected losses are very high. I believe there is considerable support for this conjecture - not only from controlled empirical studies - but from an examination of bargaining behavior in a variety of real-world situations.

Bibliography

Evans, G.W., and C.M. Crumbaugh, "Effects of Prisoner's Dilemma Format on Cooperative Behavior," Journal of Personality and Social Psychology, 3, 1966, pp. 486-488.

Komorita, S.S., and J. Mechling, "Betrayal and Reconciliation in a Two-person Game," Journal of Personality and Social Psychology, 6, 1967, pp. 349-353.

Komorita, S.S., Sheposh, J.P., and L.S. Braver, "Power, the Use of Power, and Cooperative Choice in a Two-person Game," Journal of Personality and Social Psychology, 8, 1968, pp. 134-142.

Komorita, S.S., and M. Barnes, "Effects of Pressures to Reach Agreement in Bargaining," Journal of Personality and Social Psychology, 13, 1969, pp. 245-252.

Komorita, S.S., and R. Koziej, Tacit Communication in the Prisoner's Dilemma Game, Paper presented at the Midwestern Psychological Association Meetings; Chicago, Ill., 1970.

Osgood, C.E., "Suggestions for Winning the Real War With Communism," Journal of Conflict Resolution, 3, 1959, pp. 295-325.

Osgood, C.E., An Alternative to War or Surrender, Urbana, Ill.: University of Illinois Press, 1962.

Pilisuk, M., Potter, P., Rapoport, A., and J.A. Winter, "War Hawks and Peace Doves: Alternate Resolutions of Experimental Conflicts," Journal of Conflict Resolution, 9, 1965, pp. 491-508.

Podell, J.E., and W.M. Knapp, "The Effect of Mediation on the Perceived Firmness of the Opponent," Journal of Conflict Resolution, 13, No. 4, 1969, pp. 511-520.

Pruitt, D.G., "Reward Structure and Cooperation: the Decomposed Prisoner's Dilemma Game," Journal of Personality and Social Psychology 1, 1967, pp. 21-27.

Pruitt, D.G., "Motivational Processes in the Decomposed Prisoner's Dilemma Game," Journal of Personality and Social Psychology, 14, 1970, pp. 227-238.

Pruitt, D.G., and D.F. Johnson, "Mediation as an Aid to Face Saving in Negotiation," Journal of Personality and Social Psychology, 14, 1970, pp. 239-246.

Rapoport, A., and A. Chammah, Prisoner's Dilemma, Ann Arbor: University of Michigan Press, 1965.

Schelling, T.C., The Strategy of Conflict, Cambridge: Harvard University Press, 1960.

Siegel, S., and L.E. Fouraker, Bargaining and Group Decision Making: Experiments in Bilateral Monopoly, New York: McGraw-Hill, 1960.

Stevens, C.M., Strategy of Collective Bargaining Negotiation, New York: McGraw-Hill, 1963.

Terhune, K.W., "Motives, Situation, and Interpersonal Conflict within the Prisoner's Dilemma," Journal of Personality and Social Psychology, Monograph Supplement, 8, 1968, pp. 1-24.

16. ARE INVENTORY DECISIONS OPTIMAL?[1]

AMNON RAPOPORT* AND BOBBY J. CALDER**

A distinction has been made (Rapoport & Wallsten, in press) between single-stage and multistage decision processes, depending on the number of decisions the decision maker (DM) is assumed or required to make. A broad class of multistage decision processes may be characterized by a nonempty set S of states of some system, a nonempty set D of possible decisions or courses of action available to DM, a probability distribution on S, known as a transformation rule or a transition function, associated with each state-decision pair (s,d), $(s,d)\epsilon S\times D$, and a reward or payoff function associated with the transition from one state of the system to another. The state of the system, denoted by s, $s\epsilon S$, may be defined somewhat arbitrarily. It consists of those variables that are assumed to significantly affect DM's decisions. These

---

* University of North Carolina at Chapel Hill

** University of Illinois at Urbana-Champaign

1 This research was supported in part by a PHS Research Grant No. MH-10006 from the National Institute of Mental Health and in part by a University Sciences Development Program Grant No. NV-2059 from the National Science Foundation. We wish to thank Will Daland for developing the computer programs and helping to run subjects and Graham J. Burkheimer for his help in analyzing the data and for critically reading the paper.

variables almost always include some physical parameters, such as DM's stock in inventory control problems or DM's capital in gambling problems, but may also include subjective variables, such as the information that DM possesses about the history of the decision process or about the parameters of the system.

At the beginning of stage (trial) k of the multistage decision process the system is in state s. DM observes the current state and makes a decision d, the system then moves to state s' (which may or may not be identical to s), selected according to the transformation rule, and DM receives the reward associated with this transition. The new state at stage k+1 depends on the previous state at stage k, on DM's decision at stage k, and possibly on some stochastic variables. The process continues for N stages, and DM is assumed to maximize some specified criterion function, typically but not necessarily the total expected reward over all stages or the subjectively expected reward for the last stage only.

This formulation is quite general, encompassing many engineering, military, psychological, and economic decision processes (see, e.g., Roberts, 1964; Murphy, 1965; Beckmann, 1968) in which DM's decision affects the system and consequently his next decision, and in which implications of any decision may reach far into the future. Considerable attention has been recently devoted to the formulation and solution of multistage decision processes in operations research, management science, and mathematical statistics (see, e.g., DeGroot, 1970; Howard, 1971). Behavioral scientists interested in experimentally investigating decision behavior have also been showing interest in developing theories and conducting controlled experiments to better understand how people plan and organize segments of their behavior as a sequence of decisions.

The approach typically taken by behavioral scientists has differed from the one adopted by statisticians and applied mathematicians in at least one important respect. Whereas the latter have been mainly interested in prescribing optimal behavior by constructing normative models, the former, who rarely know which criterion function, if any, DMs attempt to optimize, have focused on describing actual behavior by developing and then testing descriptive models which incorporate psychological variables and principles. There may be alternative ways of approaching the formidable task of constructing, testing, and then modifying descriptive models of human multistage decision behavior.

The research methodology underlying this study is the "normative-descriptive" approach, proposed, discussed, or exemplified by Edwards (1962), Rapoport (1968), and Toda (1968).

The most important aspect of this methodology is its use of the optimal policy as the base line of investigation. It starts by defining an ideal DM, who consistently employs the optimal policy, and then compares him in action with real DMs. Discrepancies between optimal and actual decision behavior will obviously appear. It is assumed that they will not be so large and unsystematic as to render the comparison utterly meaningless. If not, and if the discrepancies are systematic across DMs, or for each DM across different decision tasks, or for each DM and each task across repeated experimental sessions, they may be interpreted in terms of limitations imposed upon DM's memory, planning capability, or information processing capacity. Once these limitations are introduced as mathematical constraints into the optimization model, one may derive, analytically or numerically, the constrained optimal policy, collect more data, test the new model with these data, and successively improve the model so that, hopefully, DM's decisions can be interpreted as optimal under perceptual, cognitive, or intellectual limitations.

Mathematically, this "normative-descriptive" approach yields constrained optimization models of behavior. Classical constrained optimization techniques and the dynamic programming approach (Bellman, 1957) have proved most useful in deriving the optimal policy. Psychologically, this research methodology may prove to be useful only if the constraints introduced into the optimization model are compatible with current psychological knowledge. If they are not, and since every discrepancy between optimal and actual behavior can be introduced as an additional constraint into the model, the results will amount to a tautology.

A variety of psychological, methodological, and practical considerations dictate the aspects of planning, organization, and control to be examined and, consequently, the multistage decision tasks to be experimentally investigated. There is an understandable interest in selecting decision tasks which are important and feasible to study in a controlled environment, and which most DMs find challenging. Moreover, the research methodology suggests a concentration on decision problems for which analytical solutions are derivable, "since the optimal solution itself is our starting point rather than our goal. Our next step is to revise the normative solution to make it more descriptive, and this can be done a lot easier with analytical solutions at hand than with just numerical solutions (Toda, 1968, p. 11)." One decision task satisfying these requirements is the multistage inventory problem described below.

The Inventory Model

An inventory is a stock of goods held or stored for the purpose of future sale or production. Ordering or production decisions replenish the stock whereas purchasing or consumption depletes it. Given knowledge of the cost structure, the nature of the demand, and the maximum number of ordering or production decisions, DM's problem is to decide upon an inventory policy. This policy is a set of rules that define the quantity of stock to be ordered or produced at the beginning of each stage as a function of whatever information about the process has been accumulated.

For our experimental task we have selected an inventory model which involves discrete time periods of equal duration, linear costs, and uncertain demands. This model has been studied extensively by Arrow, Karlin, and Scarf (1958), whose notation we employ, and by others (see, e.g., Scarf, 1963). It involves certain assumptions about the cost structure, the demand, delivery of stock, and failure to meet demands, which are motivated and described in detail below.

Assumptions

In stocking any commodity there is a cost $c(z)$ of ordering a given quantity z of the commodity. The simplest assumption to make about $c(z)$, and one which is most easily grasped by subjects, is that it is directly proportional to the amount ordered, i.e.,

$c(z) = cz$.

A second cost is associated with the cumulated excess of supply over demand. Storage costs may be typically incurred by actually maintaining the stock or may be a measure of spoilage or obsolescence (Arrow, Karlin, & Scarf, 1958). We assume that storage or holding cost, $h(\cdot)$, is directly proportional to the amount stored.

If demands are uncertain, there exists the possibility that available stock level will be insufficient to meet demands. Failure to meet demands generates costs, called shortage or penalty costs, denoted by $p(\cdot)$. The penalty cost may be measured by the difference between the cost of emergency shipment and the cost of routine production or may be the loss of the customers' goodwill, depending upon how shortages are treated by the model. The simplest assumption to make is that $p(\cdot)$ is directly proportional to the amount of shortage.

The last element in our cost structure is revenues, considered to be negative costs. Unlike ordering, storage, and shortage costs, revenues are assumed to be independent of DM's control. Denoting revenues by $r(\cdot)$, we assume that they are proportional to the amount purchased.

To produce and store goods, capital is removed for a while from immediate use. It could, instead, have been invested elsewhere, yielding a return of R% per stage. The quantity $\alpha=1/(1+R)$, $0<\alpha<1$, called the discount factor, is an important element in any multistage inventory model.

Another element in multistage inventory models is the lag in delivery of the commodity after an order is placed. The assumptions about delivery lag are important only when demands are uncertain, since only then will information about the quantity needed for ordering change with time. To simplify the experimental task we have assumed instantaneous delivery.

Various assumptions about the demand may be made, each of which may drastically affect the inventory policy. The one that appears in virtually all work in inventory theory is that demand is independent of DM's decisions. Under this assumption two cases are typically distinguished. The case where the demand in subsequent stages is regarded as completely known is referred to as the deterministic case. When this assumption is not made one encounters the stochastic case. In the latter case it is convenient to assume that the demand at each future stage is a random variable, ξ, with a known probability distribution. In designing our experiment we opted for the stochastic case and kept the same demand distribution for all stages.

Since demand may exceed supply, some assumptions about excess demand ought also to be made. Demand may be "backlogged," i.e., permitted to wait until adequate stock is available. The penalty cost in this case reflects failure to satisfy the demand immediately. In the non-backlog case, the one used in our experiment, stock is not allowed to be negative. Two assumptions may be made in the latter case about DM's behavior in dealing with shortage. One is to satisfy excess demand by emergency shipment and pay a premium over the usual price for this service. A second assumption is never to meet unsatisfied demand, letting penalty cost reflect the loss of customers' goodwill. We presented the latter interpretation of $p(\cdot)$ in instructing our subjects about the task.

To recapitulate, our subjects were presented with a single-item, multistage, non-backlog inventory problem, with linear costs, instantaneous delivery, a proper discount factor, and independent and identically distributed demands with a known density function, $\phi(\xi)$. The subjects were instructed to maximize their profit in each of a sequence of independent inventory problems, and were paid at the end of the experimental session according to their performance.

The Optimal Policy

The first step of the "normative-descriptive" approach is to derive the optimal inventory policy and then define the ideal inventory controller as one who employs such policy consistently. The optimal policy minimizes the expectation of the present value of the various costs. To obtain it, the dynamic programming approach was used (see, e.g., Bellman, Glicksberg, & Gross, 1955, and Bellman, 1957, for the first results of this kind; see also Arrow et al. Ch. 9, 1958, and Scarf, 1963). The dynamic programming approach proceeds in the following way. Consider an inventory problem that starts with x units of stock, $x \geq 0$, and lasts for infinitely many stages ($N=\infty$). Let f(x) denote the discounted expected cost, which will be incurred during an infinite sequence of stages starting with inventory of x units and assuming that the optimal policy is employed at each stage. f(x) consists of two distinct parts, the expected cost incurred in the current stage and expected future costs. If a decision is made by DM to raise the stock from x to y, $y = x+z$, there will be an ordering cost of size $c(y-x)=c(z)$ plus a single-stage cost L(y). L(y) represents the single-period storage, shortage, and revenue costs when y units of stock are available. It is given by (Arrow et al., 1958, Ch. 9)

$$L(y) = \int_0^y [h(y-\xi)-r\xi]\phi(\xi)d\xi + \int_y^\infty [p(\xi-y)-ry]\phi(\xi)d\xi.$$

If DM orders at the first stage up to the amount y, and thereafter follows the optimal policy, then the expected cost from the second stage on, discounted to the present value, is

$$\alpha[f(0)\int_y^\infty \phi(\xi)d\xi + \int_0^y f(y-\xi)\phi(\xi)d\xi],$$

where α denotes the discount factor, $0<\alpha<1$. The ordering decision y should be made so as to minimize expected cost, and we obtain the well-known functional equation of inventory theory

$$(1)\quad f(x)=\min_{y\geq x}\{c(y-x)+L(y)+\alpha[f(0)\int_y^\infty \phi(\xi)d\xi + \int_0^y f(y-\xi)\phi(\xi)d\xi]\}.$$

If all costs are linear, as in our experimental task, the optimal policy is characterized by a single critical number $x_m(\alpha)$, $(x_m(\alpha)>0)$, as follows:

If $x<x_m(\alpha)$, order $x_m(\alpha)-x$,

If $x\geq x_m(\alpha)$, do not order.

Arrow et al. (1958) have shown that the critical number $x_m(\alpha)$ is determined as the unique solution of the equation

$$(2)\quad \int_0^{x_m(\alpha)} \phi(\xi)d\xi = \frac{r+p-c}{h+r+p-\alpha c}$$

where $x_m(\alpha)$ is determined if $r+p>c$.
Consider now a single-stage inventory problem, starting with an initial inventory of x units of stock and satisfying the assumptions about the cost structure and

the demand distribution made above. One may be interested in this case if it is assumed that DM regards each multistage inventory problem as a sequence of independent, single-stage problems. The expected cost in this case is $c(y-x)+L(y)$, and the optimal policy is characterized by a single critical number x_s $(x_s>0)$. The critical number x_s is determined as the unique solution of the equation

$$\int_0^{x_s} \phi(\xi)d\xi = \frac{r+p-c}{h+r+p}.$$

Clearly, as $\alpha \to 0$, (2) $\to$ (3).

An intermediate case between the two discussed above is the inventory problem that begins with an initial inventory of x_N units of stock and lasts for N stages. Let stages be labelled in the reverse order of the temporal order and let x_n denote the inventory at the beginning of stage n, n=1,2,...N. If an optimal policy is used at each stage n, the minimum of the expected discounted costs, when there are n more stages before the problem terminates, will be a function of x_n and n, denoted by $f_n(x)$. Like $f(x)$, $f_n(x)$ consists of two distinct parts, the expected cost incurred at stage n, and expected future cost for the n-1 remaining stages. It can be shown (Arrow et al., 1958; Scarf, 1963) that when all costs are linear and the demand distribution remains unchanged over time, the optimal policy is defined by a sequence of critical numbers $x_1(\alpha)$, $x_2(\alpha)$,..., as follows:

If $x_n < x_n(\alpha)$, order $x_n(\alpha)-x_n$,

If $x_n \geq x_n(\alpha)$, do not order,

where $x_n(\alpha) \leq x_{n+1}(\alpha)$, so that the critical numbers are decreasing monotonically as DM passes temporally through the N-stage problem. Moreover, it can be shown (Scarf, 1963) that $f_n(x)$ converges to $f(x)$ and consequently $x_n(\alpha)$ converges to $x_m(\alpha)$ as n becomes very large, and that this convergence is geometric.

Constraints

The next steps in the "normative-descriptive" approach consist of collecting data, then comparing actual and predicted decisions, finding and interpreting discrepancies, and incorporating them as constraints into the optimal model. It is for this purpose that our experiment has been conducted. The present experiment is not the first, however. A preliminary study by Rapoport (1967) of decision behavior in a multistage inventory task, a reanalysis of Rapoport's results by Pierskalla (1969), and some pertinent findings from a variety of decision making experiments suggest certain discrepancies from the optimal policy (2) that will be looked for below.

One possible inadequacy may lie with the assumptions about the demands. Independence of demand from stage to stage is a restrictive assumption both in real life and in the laboratory. Subjects may not entirely believe in the independence assumption when demands are generated by a computer in psychological experiments. Recency effects, which have repeatedly appeared in a variety of sequential decision making experiments, e.g., probability learning and gambling experiments, suggest that unless subjects are effectively trained they may not regard consecutive demands as independent, even if they are so instructed.

Another possible inadequacy of the optimal model (2) may lie with the assumptions about the duration of the problem, i.e., the value of N. In the earlier experiment by Rapoport (1967), in which the value of N was not told to the subjects, the level of stock maintained by the subjects for most of the inventory problems was not constant but, rather, decreased slightly over stages. Pierskalla (1969) commented correctly that the optimal model (2) was inadequately applied to the data, and suggested a class of more appropriate models, which incorporate specific assumptions about the distribution of N. None of his models seems to dramatically improve the fit. Nevertheless, Pierskalla's reanalysis of Rapoport's data points out the importance of knowledge about N as a variable affecting actual decisions. Indeed, it was his reanalysis which motivated the present study, and suggested the use of knowledge of problem duration as one of the main independent variables.

Method

Subjects

Sixty graduate and undergraduate male and female students served as subjects. No subject had previous exposure to inventory theory. Subjects participated in small groups of four to seven each but made their decisions independently of one another.

Independent Variables

The main independent variable was knowledge of the number of trials (stages) in each inventory problem. Subjects were assigned randomly to one of three groups for between-subjects comparisons. The first group, Group NI, was provided no information about the number of trials in a problem. The second group, Group CI, was told the exact number of trials in each problem. The third group,

Group PI, was informed only of the distribution of the number of trials for each problem, a uniform distribution between 6 and 25.

The other independent variables concerned the cost parameters of the ten inventory problems. The number of stages, N, the initial inventory, x_1, and the costs for each problem are presented in Table 1. Except for the first problem, which was given for practice only, each problem had the same values for x_1, c, and r. The values of h and p, however, varied from one problem to another according to a 3x3, storage by shortage, factorial design. Each cell of the design is represented by the storage and shortage values given in Table 1.

Table 1

Parameters for the Ten Multistage Inventory Problems

	Problem									
	1	2	3	4	5	6	7	8	9	10
N	9	13	20	8	25	22	6	19	12	16
x_1	100	100	100	100	100	100	100	100	100	100
c	12	12	12	12	12	12	12	12	12	12
h	4	10	20	2	20	10	20	2	10	2
p	30	30	20	20	40	40	30	40	20	30
r	20	20	20	20	20	20	20	20	20	20

Procedure

The ten inventory problems were administered by a PDP-8 computer. (For a detailed description of this system for computer-controlled multistage inventory tasks see Daland & Rapoport, 1971). The experimental task was presented in terms of a business game called Supply and Demand. Subjects were told that they would make many decisions, one at a time, and would be paid according to their performance. Each subject was initially given written instructions as follows:

> Consider yourself a production manager for a factory that produces a certain type of item. You were placed in your job by a big corporation, which owns many similar factories in different parts of the country, and may move you from one factory to another. At the beginning of each month you have to make a decision as to how many items to produce. After completing production you are faced with a demand for these items from several stores. This demand has to be met within the same month. If your inventory is not large enough to meet this demand (i.e., demand is bigger than inventory), you lose customers (and pay a certain penalty). On the other hand, if you produce too much (i.e., inventory is bigger than demand), you must store the excess (and pay storage costs), which can be used in subsequent months.
> Your task, as a production manager of the factory, is to determine at the beginning of each month how many items to produce to meet the (unknown) demand for the month, which varies from one month to another, so as to reduce costs and thereby maximize profits. To do so, there are three different types of cost and one type of income that you should consider.

After explaining the cost structure in terms of the inventory game, the instructions differed according to how much information DM received about the number of trials (months). Subjects in Group NI were told: "Each problem can have a different (and unknown) number of trials." Group CI was told: "The number of trials will vary considerably from one problem to another, i.e., you may stay only a few months in one factory but many more months in another. You will be informed of the exact number of trials for each problem." Group PI was told: "The number of trials will vary considerably from one problem to another and will always be between 6 and 25. That is, you may stay no less than 6 months in one factory and no more than 25 months in another. For each problem, any number of trials between 6 and 25 will be determined with equal chances. This number will be selected randomly by the computer at the beginning of each problem."

The instructions then explained the nature of the uncertain demand, and the idea of random sampling from the stationary demand distribution. Subjects were assured that the demands were already stored in the computer, were independent of one another and of DM's previous decisions. Along with the written instructions, subjects also received a chart which they kept in front of them during the experiment. The chart presented 100 demands randomly sampled from $\phi(\xi)$ and summarized in the form of a histogram approximately normal in shape. Besides this graph, subjects were given a list of the demands on the last twenty stages to indicate the lack of any sequential dependencies in the demands.

Subsequent written instructions guided the subjects through a five trial example problem administered by the computer. The format and meaning of the items displayed on the teletype were explained in detail. The first problem in Table 1 was also treated as practice and omitted.

In terms of the experimental procedure, the computer initiated each problem by printing the appropriate parameters in Table 1, the number of the problem, 1-10, the number of trials in the problem (Group CI only), and the four cost parameters, r, c, h, and p. Within each problem, the computer started each trial by printing the number of the trial, i, and the level of stock on hand, x_i, $i=1,2,\ldots,N$. The subject then typed his decision, z_i, a number between 000 and 999, designating the number of items to be produced on trial i. After checking the subject's response for mistakes, the computer informed him of the demand for that trial. The demand was randomly sampled from a normal distribution $\phi(\xi)$ with mean $\mu=322$, and standard deviation $\sigma=103$. The computer then informed the subject of his gain (positive or negative) for the trial and of his accumulated gain (positive or negative) from the beginning of the problem to the current trial. This sequence was repeated until the problem terminated. Then, either the subject was presented with a new problem or the experiment ended.

Questions at any point were encouraged and carefully answered. Although there was no time limit, the subjects typically spent about an hour and a half on the task. At the end of the session they were paid a proportion of their total gain. The average payoff was $5.31.

Results

The effect of each production decision, z_i, for each subject and each trial i was to fix the level of stock, $y_i=x_i+z_i$, available to meet the demand for that trial. The level of stock for each of the 141 trials in the last nine problems (see Table 1) was taken as the main dependent variable. To compare the three groups to one another and to test the effects of varying storage and shortage costs across problems, the analysis of data proceeded in two steps. First the data were analyzed for each problem separately and then an overall analysis was performed. Only then were the mean stock levels compared to the predicted stock levels.

Within a problem, we first tested for possible trial effects. Such effects were reported for several of the problems in the first inventory study (Rapoport, 1967). They are also predicted for Group CI by the optimal model, and for Group PI by the class of models proposed by Pierskalla (1969). All of these models prescribe stock levels monotonically decreasing over trials. Hence, all of them would be rejected if trial effects for all three groups were nonsignificant. Given such a finding, the nine problems could be assigned equal weights in an overall analysis by letting the individual mean stock level for each problem serve as a meaningful index of performance on which further statistical tests could be performed.

In analyzing trial-to-trial changes in stock levels for each problem, the multivariate analysis of variance (MANOVA) approach to repeated measures experiments was utilized (see e.g., Bock, 1963, for a general discussion of this approach). For each of the nine problems a one-way MANOVA was performed on the mean stock level (for a between-subjects comparison) and on five variables for each subject formed by specific orthogonal contrasts involving the repeated measures over trials (for a within-subjects comparison). Since problem 7 contained only six trials (see Table 1), the highest trend that could be compared across problems is the quintic. Accordingly, five orthogonal polynomial contrasts were computed for each subject for each problem, yielding five measures of the linear, quadratic, cubic, quartic, and quintic trends in the stock levels across trials. The MANOVA was performed on six variables, the five measures of trend discussed above plus the mean stock level, thus allowing for each problem the determination of group effect, trial (trend) effect, and group by trial interaction.

The MANOVA results for each of the nine problems are summarized in Table 2. Column 2 of this table summarizes the tests of the group main effect. It shows that

Table 2

Repeated Measures MANOVA of Stock Level by Problem

Problem	Group Main Effect	Linear and Quadratic Trend Effect	Group by Linear and Quadratic Trend Effect	Higher Order Trend Effect*	Group by Higher Order Trend Effect*
2	N.S.	N.S.	N.S.	N.S.	N.S.
3	N.S.	p<.016	N.S.	N.S.	N.S.
4	N.S.	p<.001	N.S.	N.S.	N.S.
5	N.S.	N.S.	N.S.	p<.021	N.S.
6	p<.040	p<.001	N.S.	p<.014	N.S.
7	N.S.	N.S.	N.S.	p<.002	N.S.
8	p<.038	p<.001	N.S.	N.S.	N.S.
9	N.S.	N.S.	N.S.	N.S.	N.S.
10	p<.035	N.S.	p<.048	p<.008	N.S.

*Covarying linear and quadratic trial trends.

there were significant ($p < .05$) group differences in three out of the nine problems, i.e., problems 6, 8, and 10. The mean stock levels for each trial and each group are portrayed in Figures 1 through 9 for problems 2 through 10, respectively. Note that the figures are not plotted on the same scale. Inspection of Figures 5, 7, and 9 shows that the significant group effects for problems 6, 8, and 10, respectively, are mainly due to a difference between Group NI and the other two groups. For these three problems, and for problem 7 as well, the means for Group NI lie above those for the other two groups for almost all trials.

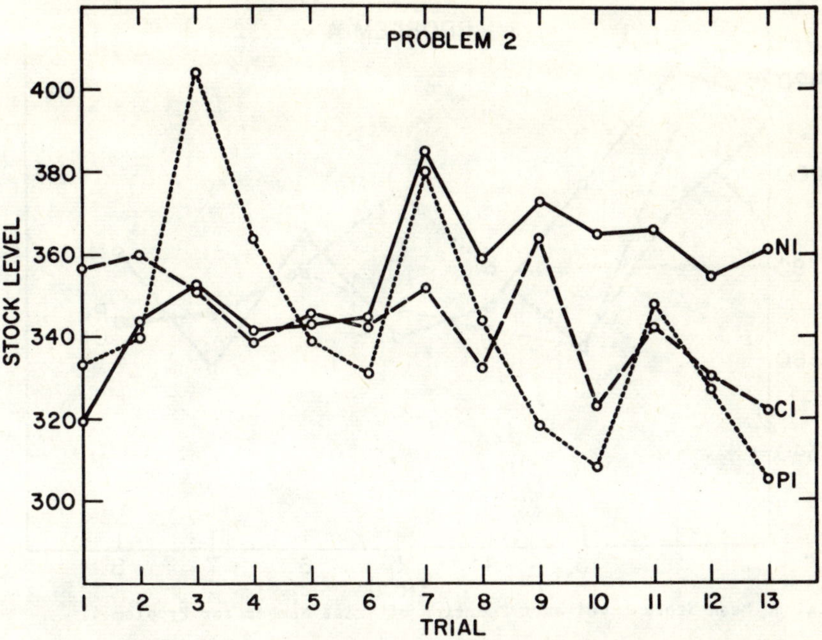

Fig. 1: Mean Stock Level as a Function of Trial Number for Problem 2.

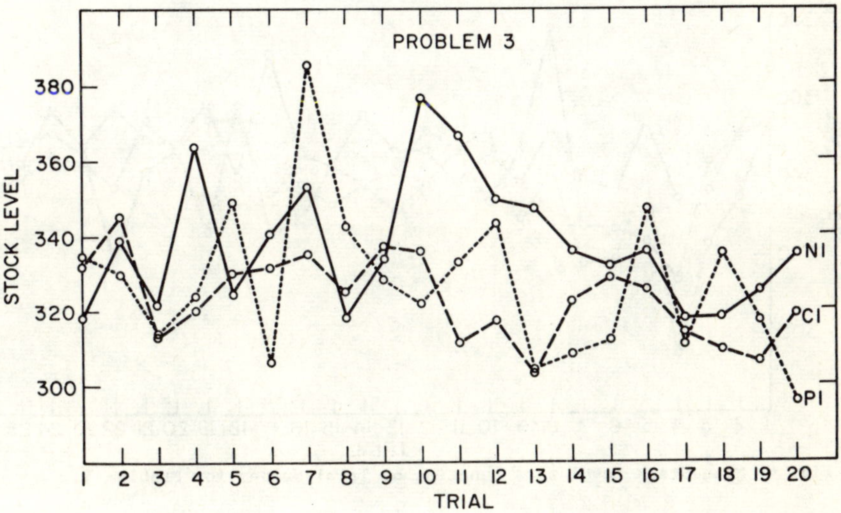

Fig. 2: Mean Stock Level as a Function of Trial Number for Problem 3.

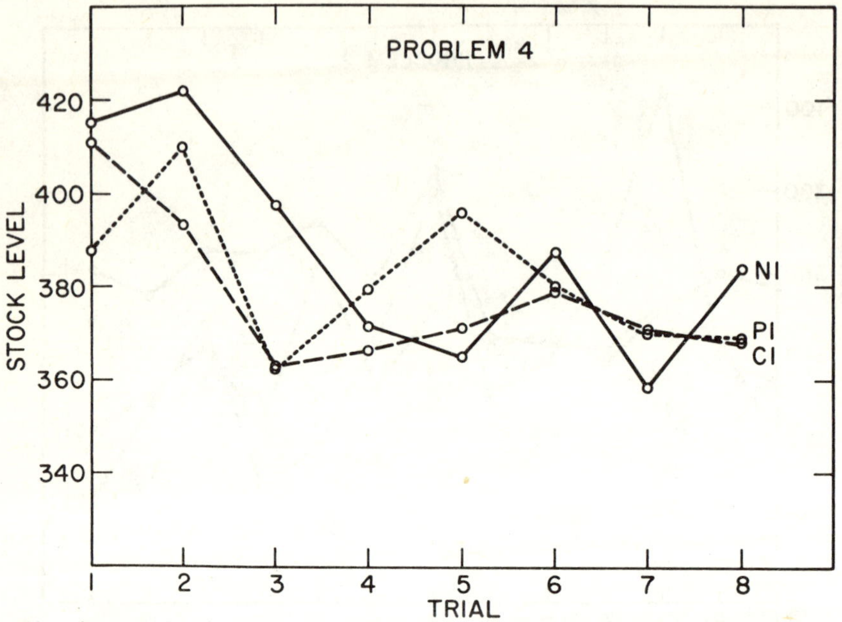

Fig. 3: Mean Stock Level as a Function of Trial Number for Problem 4.

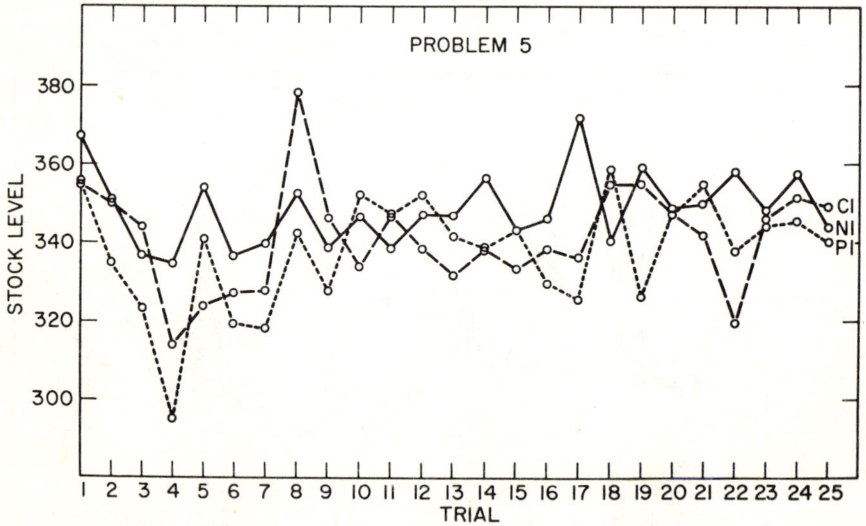

Fig. 4: Mean Stock Level as a Function of Trial Number for Problem 5.

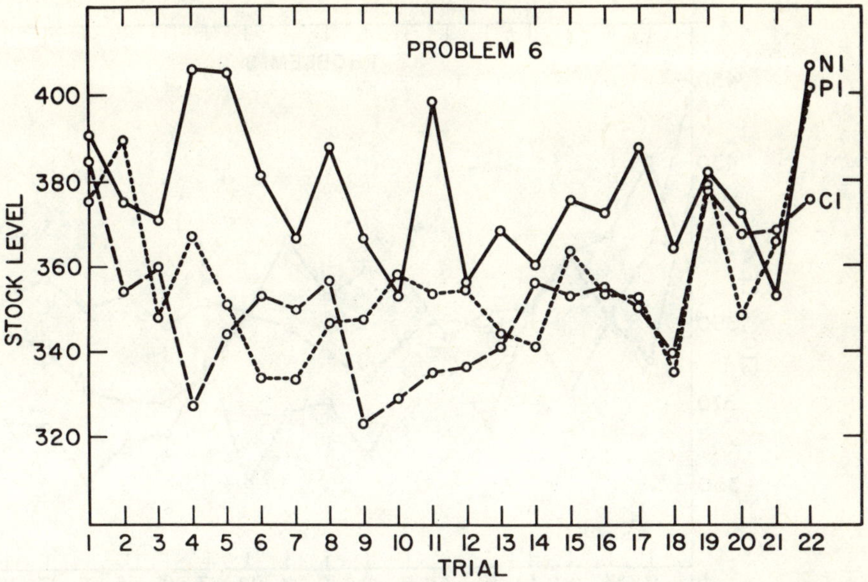

Fig. 5: Mean Stock Level as a Function of Trial Number for Problem 6.

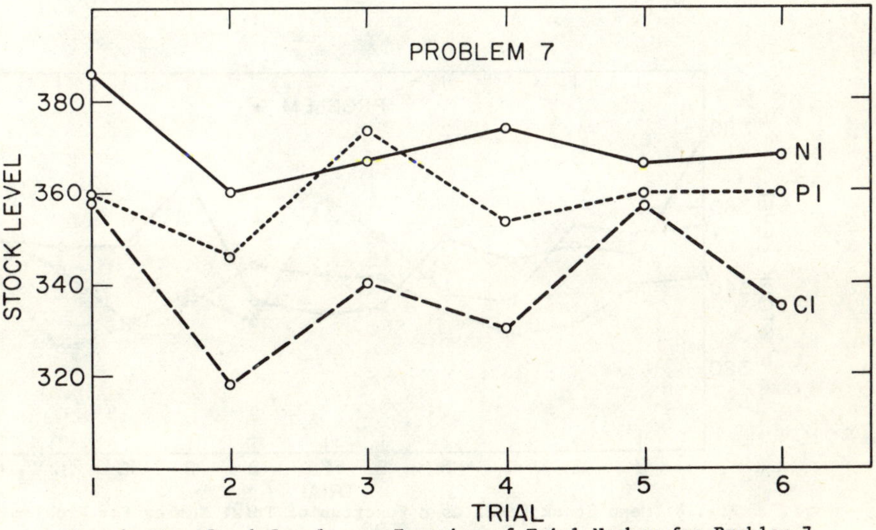

Fig. 6: Mean Stock Level as a Function of Trial Number for Problem 7.

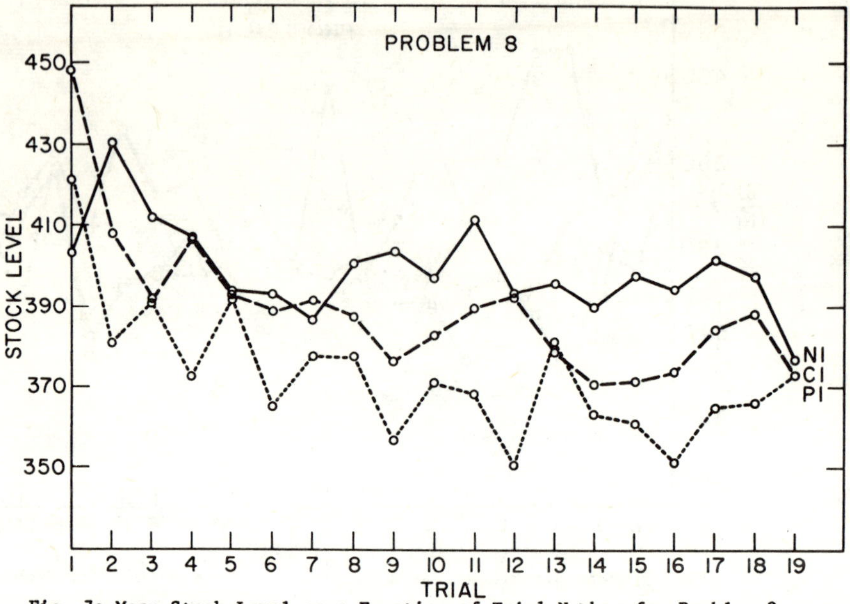

Fig. 7: Mean Stock Level as a Function of Trial Number for Problem 8.

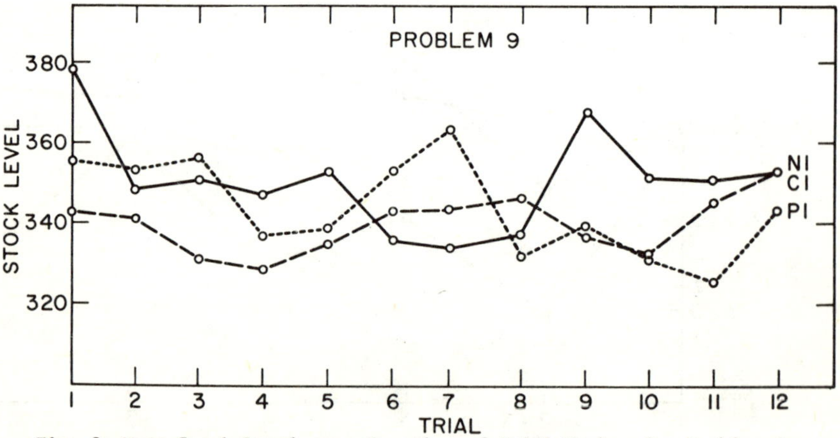

Fig. 8: Mean Stock Level as a Function of Trial Number for Problem 9.

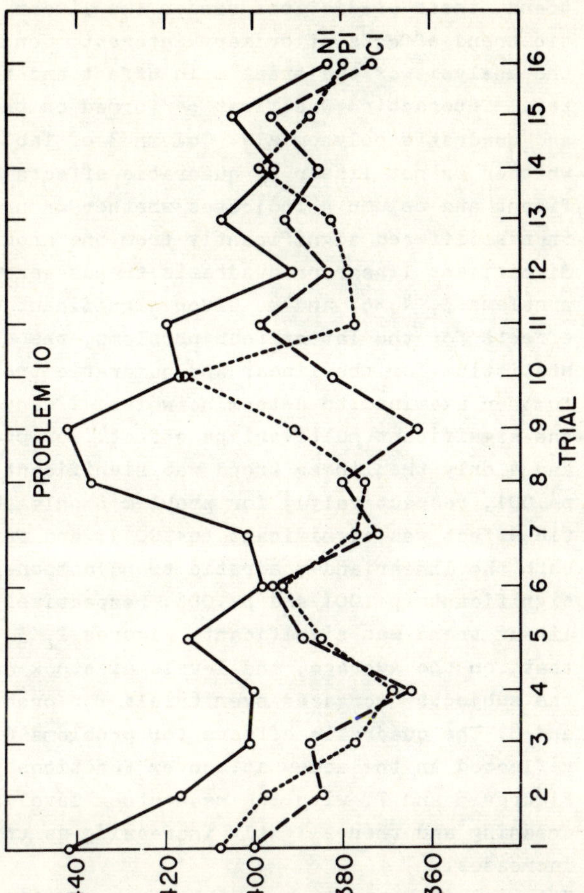

Fig. 9: Mean Stock Level as a Function of Trial Number for Problem 10

As mentioned above, the optimal model for the N-stage process, as well as the class of models studied by Pierskalla (1969), prescribe stock levels monotonically decreasing over trials. From our five measures of trend, these predictions render the linear and quadratic trend effects of primary interest. Consequently, the analysis of the trial main effect and the group by trial interaction was first performed on the linear and quadratic polynomials. Column 3 of Table 2 shows whether or not linear or quadratic effects were significant and column 4 indicates whether or not these trends differed significantly from one group to another. Significant linear or quadratic trends were found for problems 3, 4, 6, and 8. Given significant multivariate effects for the latter four problems, the univariate F statistics for the linear and quadratic trends were further examined to determine which, if any, produced the significant multivariate effect. For problems 3 and 4 only the linear trend was significant ($p<.046$ and $p<.001$, respectively), for problem 6 only the quadratic effect was significant ($p<.001$), and for problem 8 both the linear and quadratic trend components were significant ($p<.001$ and $p<.006$, respectively). When the linear trend was significant, Figures 2, 3, and 7 show that, on the average, the levels of stock maintained by the subjects decreased over trials for problems 3, 4, and 8. The quadratic effects for problems 6 and 8 are reflected in the somewhat convex functions plotted in Figures 5 and 7, with the mean stock level first decreasing and then slightly increasing as trial number increases.

Column 4 of Table 2 shows that the only linear or quadratic trend by group interaction occurred on problem 10. Even though the multivariate F was significant for this interaction, neither the linear by group interaction nor the quadratic by group interaction were individually significant at the .05 level. Since no interactions were reported for eight of nine problems, and since the multivariate F for problem 10 was marginally significant, a conclusion of no linear or quadratic trend by group interaction seems warranted.

To test for trial effects beyond those accounted for by the linear and quadratic trends, a higher order trend was examined, consisting of the lumped effects of the cubic, quartic, and quintic trends. For each of the nine problems, the orthogonal polynomial contrasts based on these three trends were subjected to the same MANOVA procedure, with the linear and quadratic trends used as covariates. Thus, any significant effects in this analysis are due to the residual terms of the higher order trends after the predictable linear and quadratic trend effects have been removed.

Indeed, for all nine problems there was a highly significant within cells regression of the higher order polynomial on the linear and quadratic polynomials, attesting to the appropriateness of the covariance analysis.

The MANOVA results for testing the higher order effect and the group by higher order interaction are presented in columns 5 and 6 of Table 2. Column 5 shows significant higher order trends for problems 5, 6, 7, and 10, none of which can be accounted for by the linear and quadratic trends. Column 6 indicates the presence of no significant interactions involving higher order trends.

The MANOVA results reported above show several trend effects in the stock level, the number of which is larger than expected by chance alone. These significant effects may reflect a conscious decision of the subjects to change their stock level as n decreases. Alternatively, or additionally, they may merely reflect trends in the particular sequence of the demand values that the subjects observed (see below for correlations between stock level and demand). Ideally each subject would have received a different sequence of demands, but, due to limitations of the computer system in the approach used for administering problems, this was not technically feasible. Instead, half the subjects in Groups NI and CI received one list of demands and the other half another list. All subjects in Group PI were given the same set of demands. The demand values presented to the subjects can be viewed as a concomitant variable. Specifically, the demand values may be utilized in determining whether trends in the demands influenced the levels of stock maintained by the subjects.

Along these lines, the analyses of trial effects reported in columns 3 through 6 of Table 2 were repeated, convarying orthogonal polynomials representing trends in the demand values. First the linear demand trend alone was covaried for all of the repeated measures MANOVA tests. Only two significant linear and quadratic trial main effects (problems 3 and 4) and one significant higher order trend main effect (problem 7) resulted from these analyses. All other trial effects and group by trial interactions were nonsignificant. To see whether higher order trends in the demands would further reduce the number of significant trial effects, the analyses were repeated, covarying the quadratic trend in the demands, for the three problems still containing significant effects. These analyses showed no significant trial effects for problems 3 and 4, which previously contained the significant linear and quadratic trial effects, but the higher order trial effect for problem 7 was still significant. Finally, another covariance analysis was performed on problem 7 using the cubic demand polynomial, which yielded no significant results. Thus, when the appropriate trends in the demand values were statistically removed from the subjects' decisions, there were no significant trial effects or group by trial interactions in the data.

Having ruled out trends across trials, or, when they exist, having explained them in terms of trends in the observed demands, the individual mean stock level for each problem may be used as a dependent variable in an overall analysis of problem and group effects. It may be recalled that the storage and shortage costs were assigned according to a 3x3 within-subjects factorial design. Hence, in the overall analysis, problem effects were determined both for the storage and the shortage factors. In addition, the three groups served as a between-subjects factor, making a Group x Storage x Shortage, 3x3x3, factorial design. This overall analysis also employed the MANOVA approach to repeated measures, although in this case independent difference contrasts were used instead of polynomial contrasts for the storage and shortage effects. Further, since this design is not balanced for the confounding with the serial order in which the problems were presented, one interaction contrast was constructed to represent the linear sequential effect of problem order.

Before performing the overall analysis, a prior analysis was conducted to see if any effects due to the order of presentation of the problems could be accounted for by the storage and shortage effects. A test of within cells regression between the linear sequential contrast and all of the remaining contrasts was significant ($p<.001$). Also, using the other contrasts as covariates in a repeated measures MANOVA of the linear sequential trend yielded a nonsignificant trend main effect ($F<1$) and a nonsignificant trend by group interaction ($F<1$). Hence, any order of presentation effect would appear to be explainable by the other effects, indicating that such an effect is not an important source of confounding.

As shown in Table 3, the overall repeated measures MANOVA performed on the mean stock levels revealed two significant main effects, a group effect, and a storage effect. Neither the shortage effect, nor any of the interactions were significant at the .05 level. The overall mean of the individual mean stock levels for each

Table 3

Overall Repeated Measures MANOVA of Mean Stock Levels

Source	df	F	p
Groups (G)	2, 56	3.60	<.05
Storage (St)	2, 53	31.84	<.001
Shortage (Sh)	2, 53	2.17	N.S.
G x St	4, 106	<1	N.S.
G x Sh	4, 106	1.68	N.S.
St x Sh	3, 50	<1	N.S.
G x St x Sh	6, 100	<1	N.S.

Note.-- Each effect has the sequential linear trend and the other appropriate contrasts covaried.

problem and each group is presented in Table 4. The corresponding standard deviations of the individual means appear in parentheses. Table 4 shows that the significant group effect resulted from the higher

Table 4

Predicted and Observed Mean Stock Levels for All Nine Problems

Problem	Observed			Predicted	
	Group NI	Group CI	Group PI	$x_m(1)$	x_s
2	354.8	343.3*	341.7*	406	357
	(54.9)	(21.3)	(29.7)		
3	337.4*	323.2*	327.1*	344	313
	(38.9)	(18.4)	(28.8)		
4	387.9	378.0	381.9	477	366
	(62.8)	(36.5)	(38.3)		
5	348.8	341.5	337.9*	378	348
	(17.5)	(22.0)	(17.8)		
6	377.2	351.8*	356.6*	419	372
	(46.7)	(20.1)	(25.3)		
7	370.3*	339.9	358.8*	363	333
	(55.3)	(27.0)	(34.0)		
8	399.5	389.5	373.1*	502	399
	(43.8)	(25.3)	(22.4)		
9	350.9*	340.2	344.3	387	338
	(25.6)	(26.7)	(26.9)		
10	411.0*	384.4	387.1	491	385
	(49.0)	(24.6)	(24.3)		

mean stock levels for Group NI. For each of the nine problems the overall mean stock level for Group NI is higher than the corresponding overall means for Groups PI and CI. The significant storage cost effect reflects a decrease in the mean stock level as the storage cost increases. Figure 10 shows that for a given shortage cost level, the overall mean stock level decreases as storage cost increases from 2 (problems 4, 8, and 10) to 10 (problems 2, 6, 9) to 20 (problems 3, 5, 7), and that for shortage costs 20 and 40 the decrease is approximately linear. The nonlinearity portrayed for shortage cost 30 could not be explained. Figure 10 as well as the nonsignificant shortage effect reported in Table 3 show that the stock levels maintained by the subjects were relatively insensitive to the variations in the shortage costs.

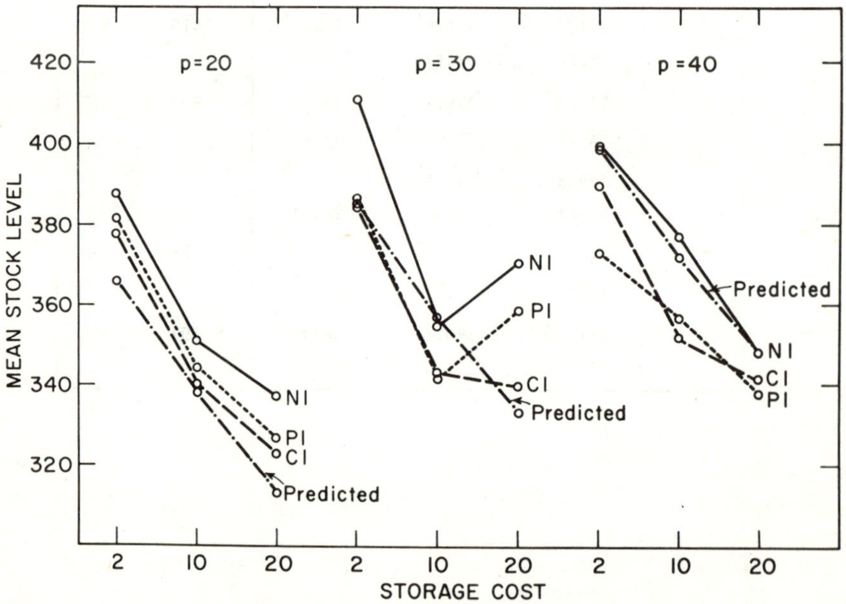

Fig. 10: Stock Level as a Function of Storage and Shortage Costs.

Beside the individual mean stock level, computed separately for each subject and each problem, the variability associated with each of these means is also of considerable interest. This variability might be affected by the experimental group treatment, by the shortage cost, by the storage cost, or by the sequential order of the problems. One would expect that, if the subjects are approaching optimality, variability around the mean stock level will decrease with practice. To investigate changes in variability, the standard deviations of the stock levels were computed separately for each subject and each problem. These standard deviations were transformed to logarithms, to account for skewness in their distributions, and then submitted to the same repeated measures MANOVA procedure used for the mean stock levels. None of the main effects or the interaction effects were significant at the .05 level. The linear sequential effect was also nonsignificant. Thus, the variability in stock level, which varied considerably from one subject to another, was not affected by the experimental manipulations, nor did it change over time. The geometric means of the standard deviations of the stock levels are presented in Table 5 for each group and problem separately. Although still large, they are seen to be considerably smaller than the standard deviation, σ, of the distribution of demands.

It was shown above that when trends in the demand sequence are covaried, significant trends in the stock level completely disappear. This dependence of stock level on trends in the demand may be more directly studied by correlating for each subject and each problem his stock level on trial i, y_i, and the demand observed on trial i-1, ξ_{i-1}, $i>1$. With 20 subjects and nine problems per group, 180 correlations were

Table 5

Geometric Means of Standard Deviations of Stock Level

Group	Problem 2	3	4	5	6	7	8	9	10
NI	46.7	38.5	34.0	36.7	30.0	20.5	31.1	28.9	31.8
CI	31.9	29.4	22.7	35.6	28.7	23.5	33.2	21.0	30.8
PI	58.4	45.0	41.3	42.3	43.7	31.5	32.7	26.3	33.8

computed for each group. Of a total of 540 correlations, 128 were significant at the .05 level, 41 for Group NI, 42 for Group CI, and 45 for Group PI. There was no evidence that this number changed significantly over problems. However, there was a difference between the number of positive and negative significant correlations. Whereas only 26 of the 128 significant correlations were negative, 102 were positive. To the extent that recency effects were significant, they were mainly positive. Perhaps because of the cover story, many subjects expected trends in the demands on some problems, consequently increasing their inventory above the mean stock level following a high demand on the immediately preceding trial and, conversely, decreasing their inventory following a low demand.

Covarying trends in the demand sequence, there was no evidence for significant trends in the stock level maintained by the subjects. Consequently, the infinite stage optimal model (2) and the single-stage model (3), as well as any other model prescribing constant stock level, are testable with the present data. Model (2) yields infinitely many predictions, depending on the value of α. Assuming no discounting of future costs, i.e., $\alpha=1$, the predicted stock levels $x_m(1)$ are presented in Table 4 for each problem. (We should have set $\alpha=1-\epsilon$, since $\alpha<1$, but when ϵ is set arbitrarily small the effect on $x_m(\alpha)$ is negligible). The predicted stock levels for models (3), x_s, are presented in the right-hand column on Table 4.

Table 4 clearly demonstrates the inadequacy of model (2) with $\alpha=1$. With only three exceptions, the values of $x_m(1)$ were significantly different from the observed mean stock levels for each problem and each group ($p<.05$ by a two-sided t test). Table 4 shows that, with only one exception, $x_m(1)$ is higher than the corresponding observed mean stock level, and that the discrepancy increases as $x_m(1)$ increases. Relative to model (2), model (3) provided a considerably better fit. Only 13 out of the 27 t tests that were performed yielded significant results. The significantly different mean stock levels are the starred entries in Table 4. The values of x_s presented in Table 4 are also plotted in Figure 10. It is seen that for the low shortage cost ($p=20$) x_s are always smaller than the corresponding mean stock levels, whereas when shortage cost is high ($p=40$), x_s lie above the mean stock levels of Groups CI and PI. For the intermediate shortage cost ($p=30$) x_s lie either above or below the mean stock levels, depending on the storage cost.

Discussion

The subjects were faced with a multistage inventory problem, in which the number of stages was fixed in advance. The subjects in Group CI knew the value of N for each problem. The appropriate model for the task they performed is the N-stage model yielding the critical stock levels $x_n(\alpha)$. This model, developed in a paper by Bellman et. al. (1955), is referred to as Model III by Pierskalla (1969). The numerical results presented by Pierskalla demonstrate that the critical stock levels $x_n(\alpha)$ very rapidly converge to the steady state stock levels $x_m(\alpha)$.

For the subjects of Group NI as well as for Rapoport's (1967) subjects the number of trials was selected randomly from a probability distribution. The appropriate model for analyzing the inventory decisions of these subjects is Pierskalla's Model IV, which assumes that N is a random variable with a known probability distribution. Like Modell III, Model IV possesses the same testable property that, regardless of the shape of the distribution of N, optimal stock levels decrease monotonically as the trial number increases. Model IV is applicable not only to Group NI, after parameters of the subjective probability distribution of N are estimated, but directly to Group PI, where the distribution of N is known.

The relationships between the mean stock levels of Group NI on one hand and Groups PI and CI on the other hand depend on the subjective probability distribution of N in Group NI, a distribution that may vary from one DM to another. Under certain assumptions about this distribution, e.g., a large mean, say 25, and a low variance, Group NI should maintain a higher stock level than Groups PI and CI, whereas under other assumptions the reverse relationship should hold. Hence, Models III and IV are neither confirmed nor rejected by the significant group effect yielded by the MANOVA of mean stock levels. Model IV and its special case Model III also predict a monotonically decreasing stock level over trials for each problem, with the main drop occurring toward the end of the problem. Whether Model IV accounts for the inventory decisions of Rapoport's subjects, as Pierskalla claims, or not, it certainly does not describe the inventory decisions in the present experiment. As the MANOVA of stock levels shows, and Figures 1 through 9 demonstrate, the subjects of all three groups maintained a constant stock level on most problems. To the extent that significant trend effects were found, they were explained in terms of trends in the randomly constructed demand sequences.

The subjects were significantly affected by two of the three variables manipulated in the experiment. The effect of deleting information about the value of N (Group NI) was to significantly increase the stock level on each of the nine problems. The effect of changing storage costs while keeping shortage cost constant was as expected: stock level decreased as storage cost increased. Subjects were not significantly affected by changes in the shortage cost since, as Table 4 shows, the differences among the three shortage costs, p=20, p=30, and p=40, were not sufficiently high. For a given storage cost the various shortage costs resulted in predicted stock levels, either $x_m(1)$ or x_s, which differed only slightly from one another. For example, when h=2, the predicted stock levels $x_m(1)$ are 477, 491, and 502, for p=20, p=30, and p=40, respectively. For the same shortage and storage costs, the predicted stock levels x_s are 366, 385, and 399, respectively. As Figure 10 shows, stock levels increased as shortage cost increased, but the change was too small and inter-subject variability was too high to yield statistically significant results.

One of the main difficulties in comparing alternative models for multistage decision tasks is that of sensitivity. Frequently, DMs may considerably deviate from the optimal policy incurring only a slight reduction in their expected gain. In the present experiment a DM employing the infinite-stage solution would have won \$9.26 for the entire experiment, whereas a DM using the single-stage solution would have gained \$8.15. There is a difference of \$1.11 between the two models. The mean gains were \$5.65, \$5.40, and \$4.88 for Groups NI, CI, and PI, respectively, with standard deviations of \$2.35, \$2.24, and \$1.97. Seventeen of the 60 subjects gained more than \$7.00, and seven of them won more than \$8.00.

Did the subjects perform optimally? Clearly not, though considering their lack of experience with inventory problems and insufficient knowledge of the demand distribution they did not do too badly. Can one specify under which conditions, if any, may inventory decisions be adequately described as constrained optimal? Only modest progress may be claimed in answering the latter question. By severely restricting DM's horizon, we have obtained the single-stage inventory model (3). This model prescribes a constant stock level for each problem, a prediction supported by the present results. It also asserts that when shortage cost increases from 2 to 10 to 20, while all other costs are held fixed, stock level should decrease almost linearly. As Figure 10 demonstrates, this prediction is weakly supported for two of the three shortage levels, with the observed and predicted curves being approximately parallel to each other. However, in 13 of the 27 t tests model (3) was rejected. Can it be modified to render it descriptive?

The results suggest three reasons for the inadequacy of the single-stage model. It might have failed because of a discrepancy between the objective and subjective probability distributions of demand, a discrepancy which might not have been completely removed by the instructions. Although the subjects were provided with a chart portraying the distribution of demands, as well as 20 demands randomly sampled from this distribution, they might have neglected this information, mistrusted it, or found it incomplete. Strictly speaking, the single-stage model is testable only when the subjective probability distribution of demands is known for each DM. Such distributions may be assessed directly or DMs may be provided with considerably more practice with the demand distribution to render the assumption of equality between objective and subjective distributions more tenable.

Another reason for the inadequacy of the single-stage model is that subjects did not regard consecutive demands as independent. Furthermore, this dependence, though reported to be weak, did not diminish with practice. There are several ways to account for this dependence. One approach is to assume that DM perceives the multistage inventory problem as a sequence of independent, single-stage problems, imposing a Markov process on the demands such that the demand on trial i determines probabilistically the demand on trial i+1. To implement the Markov model, the subjective probability distribution of the demands should be assessed and transition probabilities among consecutive demands or regions of this distribution ought to be estimated, a procedure which was not considered in the present study.

Another plausible reason for the inadequacy of the single-stage model lies with the tacit assumptions made about the cost structure. In testing the models we assumed that utilities are proportional to the various costs. This assumption would very likely prove incorrect, if tested, for the range of costs encountered in the present study. As Figure 10 shows, the single-stage model prescribes stock levels which lie below the observed mean stock levels for the low storage level (p=20) and above them for the high storage level (p=40). If a concave utility function were assumed, an assumption most readily adopted by most economists, the discrepancies between x_s and the observed mean stock levels might be considerably reduced. In the present study we have not engaged in measuring utility of money. To do so, and to implement and test the constraints suggested above, additional experiments should be conducted, shifting the emphasis from running many subjects for relatively short periods to running a smaller group of better trained subjects for longer periods.

Bibliography

Arrow, K.J., Karlin, S., and H. Scarf, Studies in the Mathematical Theory of Inventory and Production, Stanford: Stanford University Press, 1958.

Beckmann, M.J., Dynamic Programming of Economic Decisions, New York: Springer-Verlag, 1968.

Bellman, R., Dynamic Programming, Princeton: Princeton University Press, 1957.

Bellman, R., Glicksberg, I., and O. Gross, On the Optimal Inventory Equation, Management Science, 2, 1955, pp. 83-104.

Bock, R.D., Multivariate Analysis of Variance of Repeated Measurements, in C.W. Harris (Ed.) Problems in Measuring Change, Madison: University of Wiscons in Press, 1963, pp. 85-103.

Daland, W., and A. Rapoport, Inventory: A System of Programs for Computer-Controlled Multistage Inventory Tasks, Chapel Hill, N.C.: Psychometric Laboratory Research Memorandum No. 35, March, 1971.

DeGroot, M.H., Optimal Statistical Decisions, New York: McGraw-Hill, 1970.

Edwards, W., Dynamic Decision Theory and Probabilistic Information Processing, Human Factors, 4, 1962, pp. 59-73.

Howard, R.A., Dynamic Probabilistic Systems, New York: Wiley, 1971.

Murphy, R.E.Jr., Adaptive Processes in Economic Systems, New York: Academic Press, 1965.

Pierskalla, W.P., Analysis of a Multistage Inventory Task: Comments on a Paper by Amnon Rapoport, Behavioral Science, 14, 1969, pp. 378-389.

Rapoport, A., Variables Affecting Decisions in a Multistage Inventory Task, Behavioral Science, 12, 1967, pp. 194-204.

Rapoport, A., Choice Behavior in a Markovian Decision Task, Journal of Mathematical Psychology, 5, 1968, pp. 163-181.

Rapoport, A., and T.S. Wallsten, Individual Decision Behavior, Annual Review of Psychology, in Press.

Roberts, S.M., Dynamic Programming in Chemical Engineering and Process Control, New York: Academic Press, 1964.

Scarf, H.E., A Survey of Analytic Techniques in Inventory Theory, in H.E. Scarf, D.M. Gilford, and M.W. Shelly (Eds.) Multistage Inventory Models and Techniques, Stanford: Stanford University Press, 1963, pp. 185-225.

Toda, M., Algebraic Models in Dynamic Decision Theory, in C.A.J. Vlek (Ed.) Algebraic Models in Psychology, Leyden, The Netherlands: Psychological Institute of the University of Leyden, 1968, pp. 105-160.

17. THE ROLE OF EXPERIMENTAL METHODS IN A SOCIALIST ECONOMY

LADISLAV UNCOVSKY*

The problem of finding new forms of management in the national economy as well as in individual enterprises is very important in all of the socialist countries. After the theoretical analysis of a new method, it is very necessary to collect experiences which prove its effectiveness, before using it for the whole economy. The new methods, forms, or systems of management in some firms or other economic units, are introduced by means of experiments.

These types of experiments are fundamentally different from the notion of experiments as used in experimental economy. From the point of view of the theory of experimental methods, these experiments can be classified as field experiments of a special kind.

Several times in the last years, new systems of economic management or parts of it were examined in an experimental way, before they were approved for introduction into other enterprises; or, they were rejected. More complex systems of management, which concern the whole economy or a great part of it, exemplify experiments on the macroeconomic level. These types of experiments on a large scale are known especially from the Soviet Union.

---

* Institute of Economy, Bratislava, ČSSR.

Experiments of these kinds are executed in three steps:

1. Theoretical construction of the features of the new system,
2. testing of the system by experiment on chosen enterprises or other units,
3. transferal of the results of experiments to the remaining enterprises (units). Since the influence of new measures on enterprises was especially examined in the last years, it is possible to speak about experiments with enterprise management. Of course, in order to get information about the behaviour of enterprises under new circumstances, it is necessary to know a lot about the psychological and sociological aspects of experiments.

To illustrate the kind of experiments with enterprise management previously mentioned, an example in the Czechoslovak building industry may be presented. Its aim was to test a new system of payment for finished parts of a building, to replace payment for works made during a month, which had been the previous practice. This new type of invoicing and payment influenced very extensively all parts of the firms' activity. The system, which was intended to be introduced into the whole building industry, was examined in a few selected enterprises. The experimental enterprises were chosen partly on the basis of their ability to assure the representative character of the experiment, but also on the basis of their willingness to act as experimental enterprises.

Until the present the complete attention of specialists involved with experiments of this kind was focused on the problem of contents in an experiment. Very little attention was given to problems of methodology in experiments of this type.

It is evident that even in field experiments of this nature, methodological problems influence the results very strongly. From problems of this kind, the importance of which became clear in the above mentioned experiment, two may be mentioned:

1. the problem of choosing representative units (enterprises), and
2. the problem of controlling the experiment.

With regard to the first problem, it is obvious that many factors influence the functioning of an enterprise during the experiment. The problem is one of measuring or estimating the influence of these factors; the results may be biased by many circumstances. One of these may be the fact that experimental enterprises have advantages in some cases from the very fact that they are experimental ones. The influence of some factors may be different during the experimental period and after it, when the new system is introduced all over the economy. It so happened that experimental enterprises had, though not consciously, better conditions, i.e. in supply of materials, etc., than other enterprises. In such cases those enterprises chosen for experimental purposes may spoil the representative character of the sample. During the planning of the experiment, it is important to take measures which prevent a change in the functioning of experimental enterprises.

The problem of how to control the experiment is associated with the above mentioned fact. Thus far, only such methods as comparison with results of non-experimental enterprises or with that of other experimental enterprises, were considered.

As far as some considerations were made concerning the methodological aspect of these experiments. They had only qualitative character. The problem of finding more exact approaches to economic experiments of this kind is still a waiting solution. Statistical methodology may be especially useful in measuring the weight of different influencial factors and their comparison. Analysis of correlations and factor analysis seem to be useful for these purposes. It is probable that some methods found in experimental sociology and psychology may be applicable, too.

As to the objects of experiments, it seems to be important to focus greater attention on the psychological aspect of the problem. Until now the reaction of enterprises was measured more from the overall results of their work than from the analysis of individual behaviour of the managers and other members of the staff.

Up to the present time the methodology of field experiments of the above mentioned kind was not concerned with the use of mathematical models. The most important task of mathematical models, not only on a microeconomic but also on a macroeconomic level as well, is to find optimal solutions. Very often the problem of technological optimum is solved. In relation to this, the structural equations of the models are important, giving a detailed view of the technological possibilities of the firm. Matrix models and linear programming models represent this type.

One of the ways to analyse the behaviour of the enterprise in programming models is the sensitivity analysis and the analysis of the model with more objective functions. In several socialist countries results were published in this field.

In order to consider the reaction of enterprises in different situations and to different stimuli meaningfully, the models have to be extended by behavioural and institutional equations. Some tendency in this direction appears in the problem of macroeconomic activity. In this connection the use particularly of the econometric type of models for experimental solutions is being studied.

The problem of using models for experiments is closely associated with the use of business games. Interest in these games arose during the last years, especially in their application in the training of managers. In the beginning some games originating in Western countries were used, but the results of their use were not too promising. The majority of these games focus on problems of market behaviour of enterprises. For managers in socialist countries in the majority of industries the problem of production and of internal management of enterprises are much more important. Therefore, in several countries new games were developed or are being developed. Thus, in Prague, Czechoslovakia, the game "Management of Enterprises I" was developed. This game simulates the work of 3 - 3 enterprises, each producing 4 products. Demand is sensitive to prices and advertising costs. Players can change the number of workers, raise wages and use other stimuli. There are four selling areas which are chosen according to the corresponding sales situation.

Now a more complicated version of the game has been developed under the name "Management of Enterprises II." This game devotes more attention to problems of long-range management and to stochastic components of the algorithm.

In the Soviet Union in Leningrad the experimental business game "Reforma" was conceived. The aim of this game is to help train managers in a better way. In addition, it is a means of experimental statistical analysis of problems discussed in the methodology of planning, management and stimulation under conditions of the economic reform.

The game uses an economy divided into three sectors. Each sector is administrated by a minister and three vice-ministers. Each ministry has three enterprises with a director and three vice-directors. The last partner in the game is the bank, represented by four persons. The third sector is directly connected to the market (producers of consumer goods) and the demand is generated by the computer by means of a random number generator. All the participants act in the game under the same rules that are found in the real economy.
One of the possibilities of using the game for experimental purposes is to play the game with different goals for the enterprises and to examine the impact.

At the Computer Research Center, UNDP Program in Bratislava, tests were made as to the practicability of the SINTO Market Game. This game deals with the food industry and was especially adapted to the conditions of the market in socialist economies. The game was used as an instrument in advancing the education of managers in the food industry, and the results were very good. So far no attempt has been made to use the game for experimentation, but there are considerations for its use in the near future.

The last possible field of using economic experiments is the field of analysing behaviour of managers in enterprises and other economic units. One of these fields is the behaviour toward risk and uncertainty associated with investments. The decision about a part of the capital investments is, as a rule, in the hands of the enterprises and their managers. The behaviour of managers toward risk can therefore influence the process of investment.
Several experiments of this type show that conducting the experiments with persons other than the real mana-

gers has little meaning. Experiments with other persons, for example students, etc., have no great value due to the difficulties in formulation and creation of realistic conditions under which the decisions are to be made. This is the reason, why experiments of this kind have been based on questioning the managers.

There are several experiments of this type known. One of them was made by J. Kornai, who published it in his work [3]. The aim of this experiment was to estimate parameters in a problem of stochastic programming, which the author called "safety programming":

$$Ax = b \qquad (1)$$
$$x \geq 0 \qquad (2)$$
$$C(x) = \min! \qquad (3)$$

whereby C(x) is a stochastic objective function. The author shows how to transform the problem (1) - (3) into a problem of parametric programming:

$$Ax = b$$
$$x \geq 0$$
$$C_p(x) = \min!$$
$$0 \leqq P \leqq 1,$$

i.e. to find for all P in the given interval a minimal value of the objective function, which will not be exceeded by the real costs with the probability P. P is then the safety level. Thus if P = 0.8, the value of the objective function is $C_{0.8}(x)$, which will not be exceeded by the actual value with an 80% probability.

The value P can be interpreted as the attitude of the managers toward risk. The experiment consisted of asking the managers their opinion on different alternatives of investments, thus deriving their attitude toward risk.

Bibliography

[1]Machon, L., Podnikatelské hry (Business Games) in: Metódy simulácie a simulacné jazyky (Methods of Simulation and Simulation Languages), Bratislava 1970.

[2]Syrojeshin, M., V.V. Kolbin, Vozmozhnosti primenenija delovych igr v ekonomike na primere igry "Reforma" (Possibilities of applying business games on the example of the game "Reforma"), Primenenija matematiki v ekonomike, Izdatelstvo Leningradskovo univerziteta, Leningrad 1969, p. 122-135.

[3]Kornai, J., Mathematical Planning of Structural Decisions, Amsterdam 1967, p. 172-176.

18. INVESTMENT DECISIONS IN THE MANAGEMENT GAME SINTO-MARKET

OTWIN BECKER*

I.

The management game SINTO-market was developed by Dr. Selten and this author in 1967. SINTO-market is a three-person game, in which three firms compete in an oligopolistic market, using sales instruments such as prices, product differentiation and advertising expenditures. The model incorporated in this game has a remarkable degree of complexity so that the participants have to master very difficult decision situations. The players are confronted with a typical market situation, in which several brands of the same basic product can be offered, and product differentiation is one of the important sales instruments. If they make use of all brands which can be simultaneously introduced in the market, they have to determine up to 62 variables in each period, without having complete information about the consequences of their actions. This might prevent the players from discovering optimal strategies besides the fact that the game is played without the possibility of cooperation. The information given to the parti-

---

* Universität Graz.

Cf. Karl-Heinz Fischer, Advertising and Price Competition in the Management Game SINTO-Market, pp. 496-520 in this volume.
Manfred Reinfeldt, Product Differentiation in the Management Game SINTO-Market, pp. 521-559 in this volume.

cipants forces them to restrict themselves to more or less naive patterns of behavior; the general purpose of these experiments is to judge the quality of such decisions.

This paper is concerned with the investment decisions observed in a series of eleven games. Further contributions presented deal with prices, advertising expenditures and product differentiation. Although the variables studied in these contributions differ in many aspects, the general object is the same: to cast some light on the decision rules and policies adapted by the players.

II.

In order to describe the investment problems in the SINTO-MARKET, we shall give a brief outline of the relevant decision variables. Each firm possesses at the beginning of each period (t = 1,2...,15) a stock of productive assets with a book value A_t. According to n_t, the number of brands which the firms intend to produce in period t, their total capacity, C_t, is given by

$$(1) \qquad C_t = f(n_t) \cdot A_t$$

where

$$(2) \qquad f(n_t) = 0.002\ (1.03 - 0.03\ n_t)$$

The function $f(n_t)$ shows the maximum output being produced by one unit of the productive assets. Hence, with A_t constant, C_t decreases as n_t increases. With n_t constant over time, the capacity is proportional to the stock value of the productive assets. The development of A_t is determined by gross investment B_t, depreciation D_t, and sales of productive assets S_t, i.e.

(3) $$A_{t+1} = A_t - S_t + B_t - D_t$$

Selling of productive assets was permitted in the game but was a very costly policy, since the scrap value was only 50 % of the book value. The depreciation D_t amounts to 20 % of A_t. Hence, with $S_t = 0$, the sequence of the productive assets is given by

(4) $$A_{t+1} = 0.8\, A_t + B_t \qquad t = 1,2...,15$$

In order to change C_t the players have to decide on B_t. With $B_t = 0$, and n_t constant, they can reduce their firm's capacity of the next period by 20 %, i.e. capacity corrections are lagged only one period. According to the rules of the game, B_t may assume the value of any integer from 0 up to three times the value of owned capital. This latter condition was introduced as a financial investment restriction.

For any brand i introduced by the firm in the period t, the production Y_{it}, the sales X_{it}, and the quantities of finished products stored at the beginning of the period t, L_{it}, determine the magnitude of inventories, i.e.

(5) $$L_{i,t+1} = L_{it} + Y_{it} - X_{it} - R_{it}$$

If any quality component of the brand is changed, the quantity R_{it} in equation (5) represents finished products which have to be destroyed as unsaleable pro-

ducts, in this case $R_{it} = L_{it}$.
Finally, from the demand side, we introduce the variable Z_{it} as the demand for brand i in period t. The sales X_{it} are equal to Z_{it}, whenever $L_{it} + Y_{it}$ is not less than Z_{it}. Since the rules of the game do not allow the transfer of orders into the following periods and since the quantities to be produced have to be fixed without knowledge of the demand, the difference $Z_{it} - X_{it}$ shows the orders lost by insufficient inventories. According to these rules the relation between sales and demand can be expressed by

$$(6) \qquad X_{it} = \min (L_{it} + Y_{it}, Z_{it})$$

Our object now is to relate investment decisions to profits. In attempting to list the consequences of the decision problem, we first pick out a very simple case. Broadly, we assume here that the demand (Z_{it}, $i = 1,2...,10$; $t = 1,2...,15$) is known in advance and that the total demand Z_{it} does not decrease by more than 20 %. In this case, at least after some periods, a position can be reached in which capacity equals total demand in all preceding periods so that all orders can be executed and inventories can be avoided. This state can be maintained whenever the demand in the current period and in the next period are known and the sequence of total demand does not decrease.
Suppose now that capacity exceeds demand. In this case the firms can choose between two policies: they can either reduce the employment or produce at the capacity limit and store the excess of products. Inventory costs amount to 35 monetary units but the costs of unused capacity amount to at least 125 monetary units per unit of the products. Hence it is better to pro-

duce with maximum capacity and to reduce the capacity in the following period, if unavoidable, than to restrict the production in the current period.
Because the demand is not known in advance, another reason for holding inventories is to reduce the risk of offers which cannot be executed. The gross profit foregone in such a case depends on several decision parameters and differs from brand to brand, but is roughly 300 monetary units and is therefore greater than inventory costs. It stands to reason that the size of the inventory reserves, depends on the ability to forecast the relevant demand figures. When the inventories are held at a considerably high level, the problem of adjusting the capacity is very easily solved, because minor differences are meaningless. However, the consequences of this policy is high inventory costs, and it may be expected that a learning effect should lead the participants to better decisions.

III.

The investment decisions in the first period had to be done without information on the capacity needed at this phase of the game. In the written instructions given to the participants, the following informations was available:

Opening Balance			
Productive assets	500.000.	Owned capital	700.000.
Inventories	0.		
Claims against the mother company	200.000.		
	700.000.		700.000.

According to the rules of the game, gross investment is restricted to an integer value within the range $0 \leq B_1 \leq 1.700.000$. The players were told that the demand increases with time until the market reaches a saturation level, but they neither received information about the growth rates nor about the time when this saturation level would be reached. The fact that the development of demand follows this line of expansion is nevertheless an important hint for the players, because they could be sure that they would not be confronted with recessions.
Table 1 contains the decisions in the first period observed in our series of eleven games.

gross investment	frequency
0	6
100 000.	12
110 000.	1
150 000.	2
200 000.	2
250 000.	2
300 000.	5
350 000.	1
400 000.	1
850 000.	1
	33

Table 1: Investment decisions in the first period

The most frequent amount chosen was 100 000. This quantity equals the depreciation, and the policy implied is clearly to reinvest at this level. It is true that this alternative does not take care of growth aspects, but it is nevertheless based on arguments which are especially strong at the beginning of the game.

The second most frequent decision observed $B_1 = 0$, is far more naive and less strong. The participants knew that $B_1 = 0$ reduces the capacity by 20 %. Their arguments were to wait for the first results before deciding on investment, but it is just this argument which seems to be supported better by $B_1 = 100\,000$ than by $B_1 = 0$.

In 15 cases net investment was fixed to positive values. The quantity of 110 000, chosen by one firm, had a seemingly arbitrary preciseness. It is possible that this firm intended to expand its capacity by 10 % of depreciation, but this was only 2 % of the capacity at hand. In our opinion this solution is not very attractive. It is an unstable alternative, which might be rejected in a better organized decision process. The same might be true for other alternatives which are not based on convincing arguments.

The alternative 200 000 agrees with the positive balance on the account with the mother company. Even well below the financial restrictions, it may be desirable to avoid liabilities. The combination of two aspects, reinvestment at the level of depreciation and full use of the cash at hand, leads to a decision of 300 000 for gross investment; this was done by five players. Only three investment figures exceed this level. It is worth mentioning that 850 000, the highest quantity observed, equals 50 % of the maximum feasible amount.

A theoretical explanation of these decisions should be based on plausible objectives which lead per se to an attractive solution. In this way only a few figures might be selected. They suffer from the fact that the objectives are not justified by a convincing policy. It seems, therefore, that the attempt to rationalize decisions led to alternatives which were compromises; taking the mean of two proposals appears to be an attractive mechanism. It is our opinion that solutions like 150 000 and 250 000 - being chosen in four cases - resulted from such processes. According to this hypothesis the middle point between two basically attractive solutions can also be an attractive solution. An examination of Table 1 shows, however, that there is at least one important exception. Although 0 and 100 000 are the two most frequently selected quantities the mean of them was not chosen at all. The reason for this exception consists in the incompatibility of the arguments implied. Either the decision on investments is postponed to the next period ($B_1 = 0$) or it is carried, for instance, on the level B_1=100 000. The arguments for both cases contradict each other and cannot be logically combined.

With one exception previously mentioned all dispositions observed are quantities rounded off to multiples of at least 50 000 monetary units. Transformed into the capacity dimension, this was 100 units when one brand was to be produced. One might assume that investment-figures might be rounded off to some reasonable degree because of the uncertainty of their responses. We shall, however, show later that this rounding off is not always a merely technical result of uncertainty. When an argument which yields an investment-figure with seemingly great preciseness is accepted by the group, then they do not round off the figures.

The experiences of 30 firms at the end of the first period were similar: the production chosen exceeded the sales. Hence the players should have really reduced the capacity of their firms; but, as table 2 shows, only two

Firm	Period 1				Period 2			
	Net Investment	Capacity	Production	Sales	Net Investment	Capacity	Production	Sales
1	0	1000	1000	656	0	1000	1000	654
2	-100000	1000	1000	767	-80000	800	800	484
3	200000	1000	1000	441	200000	1358	1358	1817
4	0	1000	900	0	0	1000	900	640
5	0	1000	1000	874	100000	1000	1000	647
6	150000	1000	1000	1000	1462624	1261	1261	1261
7	100000	1000	800	800	900000	1200	1200	680
8	100000	1000	1000	716	80000	1200	1200	469
9	250000	970	700	700	250000	1455	1455	1348
10	-100000	1000	1000	953	1700000	800	800	634
11	10000	1000	900	645	78000	989	980	1111
12	50000	1000	1000	726	60000	1067	1060	1085
13	0	970	970	904	200000	970	970	1036
14	0	1000	1000	965	80000	1000	1000	1035
15	0	1000	1000	736	0	970	970	1135
16	150000	1000	1000	742	350000	1261	1261	1134
17	-100000	1000	660	565	280000	800	800	545
18	-100000	1000	1000	587	-80000	800	750	735
19	-100000	1000	1000	923	20000	800	800	863
20	200000	1000	1000	604	200000	1358	1358	1145
21	0	1000	800	410	0	940	940	1002
22	-100000	1000	1000	643	100000	752	750	1107
23	750000	1000	1000	722	500000	2425	2424	1123
24	0	1000	1000	917	150000	1000	1000	579
25	300000	1000	1000	790	100000	1600	1600	862
26	0	1000	1000	595	100000	970	970	1198
27	0	1000	1000	653	100000	940	938	1099
28	200000	1000	1000	925	200000	1400	1400	692
29	200000	1000	1000	582	100000	1358	1300	1415
30	0	1000	1000	624	0	970	970	837
31	0	1000	1000	555	50000	940	940	1148
32	50000	1000	1000	672	60000	1100	1100	649
33	200000	1000	1000	410	896000	1358	1358	969
		32940	31730	22802		36842	36613	31138

Table 2: Results in the first two periods

Period 1 \ Period 2	MIN	DES	STA	EXP	Σ
MIN	2	0	0	4	6
DES	0	0	0	0	0
STA	0	0	5	7	12
EXP	0	0	0	15	15
Σ	2	0	5	26	33

MIN : $B_t = 0$

DES : $0 < B_t < 0.2\ A_t$

STA : $B_t = 0.2\ A_t$

EXP : $B_t > 0.2\ A_t$

Table 3: Frequency of Investment Policies in the first two periods

firms actually did that. All the other firms expanded their capacity without a convincing motivation. In the instructions a market expansion is announced, but no data is given. Nevertheless, as is shown in table 3, all firms continued to pursue their policy or decided for expansion.

IV.

We shall continue at this point to explain the individual investment decisions of the first periods. Our object is to examine the cumulative results after a certain number of introductory periods. To do this we aggregate all magnitudes of the firms from period 3 to period 14. The average results are listed in table 4. The variable C^*_{t+1} is the capacity of the next period as the result of the investment of the current period,

Capacity	C^*_{t+1}	2239.5
	C_t	2133.3
Production	Y_t	2092.8
Sales	X_t	2038.4
	X_{t-1}	1898.8
	X_{t-2}	1741.3
Inventories	L_t	800.7
Products depreciated	R_t	22.9

Table 4: Average Results

during which the number of brands is assumed to be constant. With certain exceptions, the firms produced on full employment level. The average employment amounted to 98 %. About 97,5 % of the production was sold, about 1 % had to be depreciated as unsellable, so that the inventories at the end of period 14 were not significantly larger than those in period 3. The fact that production nearly equalled maximum capacity and had been almost completely sold suggests a simple theoretical explanation: it may be assumed, that on the average the players were able to forecast the sales of period t+1 and that they adjusted the capacity of their firms to this level. The expected demand, which we write $\hat{X}_t$, might be determined by the players using very different methods. On the average, however, it might be possible to explain X_t by a simple extrapolation formula based on the last difference of sales which were known to the players when they decided on

C^*_{t+1}. Hence $\hat{X}_{t+j}$ can be assumed to depend on X_{t-1} and $(X_{t-1} - X_{t-2})$ and we have as a linear approximation

$$(7) \qquad \hat{X}_{t+j} = X_{t-1} + j(X_{t-1} - X_{t-2})$$

Assume now that $C^{(1)}_{t+1} = \hat{X}_{t+1} = \hat{X}_{t+1}$, i.e.

$$(8) \qquad C^{(1)}_{t+1} = X_{t-1} + 2(X_{t-1} - X_{t-2})$$

expresses the planned capacity according to our first theory. From the figures in table 4 we get $C^{(1)}_{t+1}$ = 2213.8. The difference to C^*_{t+1} = 2239.5 is very small.

In order to provide a stronger test for equation (8) the differences between $C^{(1)}_{t+1}$ and C^*_{t+1} should be analysed in the individual periods. The results of this test are shown in table 5. Greater differences occur in at least 7 periods, i.e. the ability of $C^{(1)}_{t+1}$ to predict C^*_{t+1} is very small. In five periods even the signs of changes differ. Hence we conclude that the conformity between $C^{(1)}_{t+1}$ and C^*_{t+1} does not support our theory (1). This conformity merely expresses the fact that average sales and average capacities are equal asymptotically.

A better expansion is provided by theory (2), which can be constructed in the following way. When the players decide on capacity, they first look at the production figures of the current period because both decisions are to be made at the same time. Let $(X_{t-1} - X_{t-2})$ be an indicator for the market expansion as mentioned above. It may be expected that the production planned for the next period, say Y^*_{t+1}, is given by $Y^*_{t+1} = Y_t + (X_{t-1} - X_{t-2})$. Under the assumption that C^*_{t+1} is fixed on the level Y^*_{t+1} we get a second theoretical value,

Variable	Period 3	4	5	6	7	8
C^*_{t+1}	57971.0	62263.0	61283.0	59024.0	62668.0	66392.0
Y_t	50481.0	54475.0	59243.0	58767.0	56265.0	62629.0
X_{t-1}	31138.0	37101.0	44088.0	49750.0	56058.0	62188.0
ΔX_{t-2}	8336.0	5963.0	6987.0	5662.0	6308.0	6130.0
L_t	14403.0	27643.0	37299.0	45805.0	46463.0	37734.0
$C^{(1)}_{t+1}$	47810	49027	58062	61074	68674	74448
$C^*_{t+1}-C^{(1)}_{t+1}$	10161	13237	3221	-2050	-6006	-8056
$C^{(2)}_{t+1}$	58817	60438	66230	64429	62573	68759
$C^*_{t+1}-C^{(2)}_{t+1}$	-846	1826	-4947	-5405	95	-2367
$C^{(3)}_{t+1}$	59968.6	59684.8	61048.7	60232.7	61039.8	67983.3
$C^*_{t+1}-C^{(3)}_{t+1}$	-1997.6	2578.2	234.3	-1208.7	1628.2	-1591.3

Table 5: Period aggregates

Variable	Period 9	10	11	12	13	14
C^*_{t+1}	73178.0	81033.0	86760.0	92300.0	94512.0	89450.0
Y_t	63436.0	71039.0	81113.0	87105.0	91870.0	92339.0
X_{t-1}	70566.0	74172.0	76540.0	81659.0	83485.0	85189.0
ΔX_{t-2}	8378.0	3606.0	2368.0	5119.0	1826.0	1704.0
L_t	29488.0	18171.0	12328.0	11571.0	15191.0	20972.0
$C^{(1)}_{t+1}$	87322	81384	81276	91897	87137	88597
$C^*_{t+1}-C^{(1)}_{t+1}$	-14144	-351	5484	403	7375	853
$C^{(2)}_{t+1}$	71814	74645	83481	92224	93696	94043
$C^*_{t+1}-C^{(2)}_{t+1}$	1364	6388	3279	76	816	-4593
$C^{(3)}_{t+1}$	73286	80660	87076	91291	92738	91822
$C^*_{t+1}-C^{(3)}_{t+1}$	-108.2	372.1	-316.3	1008.3	1773.7	-2372.9

Table 5: Continued

(9) $C^{(2)}_{t+1} = Y_t + (X_{t-1} - X_{t-2})$

The average results (see table 4) give $C^{(2)}_{t+1} = 2250.3$, which matches C^{*}_{t+1} well. The differences in the individual periods are in most cases smaller than those of our first theory. It is striking that periods with the greatest differences in the first theory are somewhat better explained by the second theory and vice-versa. It should be noted, however, that both theories are incomplete, because they do not take into consideration changes in inventories. Eventhough some of the players may not have tried to adjust their inventories in the first periods, the inventories had reached in period 7 an amount of about 80 % of current production, and at this level they were without a doubt too high, even if large reserves had been planned. The decreasing inventories in the periods 8-12 are at least partly the result of a planned reduction. On the other hand the differences of theory (2) do not indicate this movement.
We now drop the assumption that the difference $(X_{t-1} - X_{t-2})$ is the single indicator of development. The difference $C^{*}_{t+1} - C_t$ can alternatively be assumed to depend on $(Y_t - Y_{t-1})$ and (with signs reserved) on $(L_t - L_{t-1})$. The reason for equating ΔC^{*}_t with ΔY_{t-1} is to continue the development of production. The reason for setting up $\Delta C^{*}_t = - \Delta L_{t-1}$ is to adjust the inventories to the previous level. According to these considerations, a convex linear combination, as expressed by

(10) $\Delta C^{(3)}_t = a_1 \, \Delta Y_{t-1} + a_2 \, \Delta X_{t-2} - a_3 \, \Delta L_{t-1}$,

whereas $a_1 + a_2 + a_3 = 1$,

should be a better explanation of the typical behavior. In order to test equation (10) we first estimate the regression equation

$$(11) \qquad C^{(3)}_{t+1} = a_o + a_1 Y_t + a_2 X_{t-1} + - a_3 L_t + a_4 (X_{t-1} - X_{t-2}) + u_t$$

without restrictions on the coefficients. By taking the figures from table 5 the results are:

$$\hat{a}_o = 34.131$$
$$\hat{a}_1 = 0.3982$$
$$\hat{a}_2 = 0.3155$$
$$\hat{a}_3 = 0.2836$$
$$\hat{a}_4 = 0.$$

The residuals are shown in the last row of table 5. It is very interesting that the coefficient of ΔX_{t-2} is insignificant, and that the sum of the remaining coefficients (0.9973) does not differ significantly from the theoretical value 1. By taking differences in equation (11), the constant can be eliminated, hence we have:

$$(12) \qquad \Delta C^{(3)}_{t+1} = 0.40 \, \Delta Y_{t-1} + 0.32 \, \Delta X_{t-2} - 0.28 \, \Delta L_{t-1}$$

The constants of this equation are averages of the individual capacity adjustment policies.

The theories (1) - (3) had overly large differences when compared with the individual data. Table 6 shows, that the average deviation between C_{t+1} and $C^{(j)}_{t+1}$

Variable	Firm 1	2	3	4	5	6	7	8	9	10	11
C^*_{t+1}	2556	1671	2970	1368	2660	3040	2311	1510	2453	2248	2196
C_t	2331	1537	2872	1301	2483	3162	2286	1429	2363	2360	2064
Y_t	2450	1542	2867	1184	2483	2845	2305	1426	2358	2100	2060
X_{t-1}	2150	1348	2480	1127	2262	2540	2140	1265	2225	1886	1948
ΔX_{t-2}	228	102	200	157	189	174	161	105	175	113	157
L_t	497	667	1118	1179	278	4351	1022	906	763	2086	322
$C^{(1)}_{t+1}$	2678	1645	3067	1341	2672	3019	2465	1531	2534	2213	2217
$C^*_{t+1}-C^{(1)}_{t+1}$	-121	26	-97	27	-12	21	-154	-21	-81	35	-21
$C^{(2)}_{t+1}$	2607	1553	2880	1442	2640	2888	2462	1474	2576	2112	2261
$C^*_{t+1}-C^{(2)}_{t+1}$	-50	118	90	-74	20	152	-150	36	-123	136	-65
$C^{(3)}_{t+1}$	2546	1884	2640	1527	2657	1735	2336	1744	2458	1874	2377
$C^*_{t+1}-C^{(3)}_{t+1}$	11	-213	329	-159	4	1305	-25	-234	-5	375	-181

Table 6: Firm averages

Variable	Firm 12	13	14	15	16	17	18	19	20	21	22
C^*_{t+1}	2673	3161	1439	1593	2534	2832	1843	1979	2205	1871	1524
C_t	2474	2943	1406	1504	2450	2658	1658	1834	2108	1737	1452
Y_t	2470	2942	1387	1502	2284	2658	1566	1847	2112	1737	1483
X_{t-1}	2310	2571	1349	1394	2056	2356	1269	1667	1970	1584	1296
ΔX_{t-2}	196	239	42	105	141	211	116	131	154	158	111
L_t	666	730	250	283	1361	475	785	301	568	318	966
$C^{(1)}_{t+1}$	2666	3181	1429	1607	2425	2869	1683	1977	2266	1894	1595
$C^*_{t+1}-C^{(1)}_{t+1}$	7	-20	10	-14	109	-37	161	2	-61	-24	-71
$C^{(2)}_{t+1}$	2702	3049	1433	1604	2338	2779	1501	1929	2278	1899	1519
$C^*_{t+1}-C^{(2)}_{t+1}$	-29	112	6	-11	196	53	343	51	-73	-28	4
$C^{(3)}_{t+1}$	2557	2808	1941	1991	2206	2700	1835	2209	2335	2135	1759
$C^*_{t+1}-C^{(3)}_{t+1}$	116	353	-502	-398	328	132	8	-230	-130	-264	-236

Table 6: Continued

Variable	Firm 23	24	25	26	27	28	29	30	31	32	33
C^*_{t+1}	2943	2145	2379	1906	2463	2449	2165	1753	2435	2510	2085
C_t	2946	2048	2239	1790	2236	2304	2053	1592	2231	2362	2186
Y_t	2805	2071	2253	1721	2232	2283	1981	1596	2256	2269	2071
X_{t-1}	2710	1881	2052	1523	2032	2112	1836	1443	1902	2098	1879
ΔX_{t-2}	198	135	196	110	200	167	159	120	191	195	160
L_t	1221	506	634	903	273	144	174	227	1016	401	1031
$C^{(1)}_{t+1}$	3003	2206	2448	1831	2431	2450	2141	1717	2446	2465	2231
$C^*_{t+1}-C^{(1)}_{t+1}$	-60	-61	-70	75	31	-1	24	36	-12	45	-146
$C^{(2)}_{t+1}$	3106	2151	2443	1744	2431	2446	2155	1684	2284	2489	2199
$C^*_{t+1}-C^{(2)}_{t+1}$	-163	-6	-65	162	31	3	9	70	151	21	-114
$C^{(3)}_{t+1}$	2659	2308	2398	1943	2485	2567	2352	2060	2244	2485	2159
$C^*_{t+1}-C^{(3)}_{t+1}$	284	-162	-19	-37	-23	-118	-187	-306	191	25	-74

Table 6: Continued

Variable	Actions: (35) MIN	(34) DES	(110) STA	(160) EXP	(57) MAX	(396) Total
C^*_{t+1}	1851.1	2418.1	2071.8	2208.7	2774.3	2239.5
C_t	2314.0	2651.1	2074.3	1870.5	2565.4	2133.3
Y_t	1972.8	2650.4	2040.2	1873.6	2568.5	2092.8
X_{t-1}	1742.0	2220.3	1690.9	1790.8	2507.8	1898.8
$X_{t-1}-X_{t-2}$	169.1	117.2	108.6	212.9	113.5	157.5
L_t	1950.8	987.0	901.3	495.3	646.4	800.7
R_t	37.2	20.9	43.5	12.2	5.3	22.9
$C^{(1)}_{t+1}$	2080.2	2454.7	1908.0	2216.6	2734.9	2213.8
$C^*_{t+1}-C^{(1)}_{t+1}$	-229.1	-36.6	+163.8	-7.9	+39.4	+25.7
$C^{(2)}_{t+1}$	2141.9	2767.6	2148.7	2086.5	2682.0	2250.3
$C^*_{t+1}-C^{(2)}_{t+1}$	-290.8	-349.5	-76.9	+122.2	+92.3	-10.8
$C^{(3)}_{t+1}$	1816.1	2509.2	2123.8	2281.9	2657.2	2239.5
$C^*_{t+1}-C^{(3)}_{t+1}$	+35.0	-91.1	-52.0	+74.1	+117.1	0.

Figures are averages; the number of cases is given in brackets at the top of the table.

Table 7: Adjustment of Capacity divided into actions.

(j = 1,2,3) is in many cases absolutely larger than the average difference between C_{t+1} and C_t. Hence the ability to explain the individual decisions is very poor.

The differences are not typically associated with the actions applied by the firms. This can be seen in table 7. The average deviations are of the same magnitude as those of table 6.

The fact that theory (3) shows large deviations among the firms might depend on individual differences in the coefficients of equation (12). In order to analyse the individual data the regression equation

$$(13) \qquad c^*_{t+1}=b_1c_t+b_2y_t+b_3x_{t-1}+b_4x_{t-2}+b_5l_t+b_6t+u_t$$

was estimated. The subscripts in equation (13) denote the values of the corresponding variables. The results of this regression analysis are reported in table 8. The signs of the coefficients agree in most cases with theoretical expectations. Large differences occur in the magnitudes of the coefficients and also in the basis of regressors, which minimizes the residual variances. The selection procedure applied excludes variables whose coefficients differ significantly from zero, according to a two-tailed t-test on the 5 % level.

Table 9 shows the average differences between actual and theoretical values. The suitability of this analysis is better than those of the theories (1) - (3).

Firm	Coefficients of						Multiple Correlation
	c_t	y_t	x_{t-1}	x_{t-2}	l_t	t	
	1	2	3	4	5	6	
1			0.977		-0.429		0.936
2	0.970						0.941
3					-0.990	1.302	0.952
4						0.948	0.899
5	0.523		0.414		-0.273		0.977
6		0.394				-0.673	0.926
7	-7.508	7.774	-0.525		-0.456	0.568	0.983
8		0.493	0.186		-0.374		0.985
9		0.732			-0.347		0.931
10	1.217		0.473				0.859
11			0.899	-0.298			0.900
12			-1.411			0.099	0.787
13		0.506			-0.640		0.879
14	-0.888	0.822	-0.625	0.307	-0.928		0.963
15					-0.426	0.743	0.922
16					-0.423	0.723	0.930
17	0.962						0.925
18			1.898		-1.266		0.818
19	0.858			0.216	-0.255		0.972
20		0.296			-0.416	0.385	0.981
21					-0.209	0.877	0.945
22			0.790				0.624
23		0.816					0.665
24	-0.846			0.340	-0.878	1.009	0.926
25			0.467		-0.578		0.929
26	0.755				-0.548		0.924
27		0.739			-0.382		0.889
28			0.275		0.269	0.942	0.992
29	-1.341	1.496	1.523		1.074		0.962
30						0.971	0.943
31			-0.657		-0.366	1.475	0.952
32	1.579	-0.513	-0.291	0.071	-0.456		0.998
33					-0.702		0.493

Table 8: Individual regression coefficients

Period	C_{t+1}	$C_{t+1}^{(4)}$	Differences
3	1756	1770	-14
4	1886	1865	21
5	1845	1855	-10
6	1789	1821	-32
7	1899	1892	7
8	2012	2048	-36
9	2218	2209	9
10	2455	2465	-10
11	2629	2647	-18
12	2797	2732	65
13	2864	2790	74
14	2711	2768	-57

Table 9: Average deviations of the individual regression equations ($C_{t+1}^{(4)}$).

V.

It is very interesting to see that the investment function (12) may be used in models of inventory cycles. The disequilibrium system in inventories which we propose is based on our empirical results. The model consists of the following equations:

$$(14)\quad C_t - C_{t-1} = a_1(Y_{t-1} - Y_{t-2}) + a_2(X_{t-2} - X_{t-3}) - a_3(L_{t-1} - L_{t-2})$$

$$(15)\quad Y_t = b_1 C_t$$

$$(16)\quad L_t = L_{t-1} + Y_t - X_t .$$

The coefficient b_1 in equation (15) is less than one. Using equations (15) and (16) to eliminate production and inventories in equation (14) we get the system:

$$(17)\quad C_t - (1+a_1 b_1)\, C_{t-1} + b_1(a_1+a_3)\, C_{t-2} = W_t, \quad \text{say,}$$

where

$$(18)\quad W_t = a_3\, X_{t-2} + a_2\, (X_{t-2} - X_{t-3})$$

expresses the influences of previous demand figures. We now have a linear difference equation in terms of C with well-known properties. It can be shown that the homogeneous part of equation (17) does not yield oscillations. The solutions of the characteristic function

$$(19)\quad \lambda^2 - (1+a_1 b_1)\, \lambda + b_1\, (a_1+a_3) = 0$$

are

$$\lambda = \frac{1 + a_1 b_1}{2} \pm \frac{1}{2} \sqrt{(1-a_1 b_1)^2 - a_3 b_1}.$$

With the coefficients observed, the condition

$$(1 - a_1 b_1)^2 > a_3 b_1$$

is satisfied, and the roots are $\lambda_1 = .85$ and $\lambda_2 = .54$. With $X_t = \bar{X}$ constant, the capacity would converge monotonously against $\bar{C} = \frac{1}{b_1} \bar{X}$. Fluctuations in capacity are generated by fluctuations in demand only, and not by inventory cycles. If, however, a_3 had a considerably larger value than observed, equation (17) would produce at least damped cycles.

VI.

It is very important to note that the regression analysis, especially if applied to the individual data, leads in some cases to large differences. This is for several reasons:

1. According to the structure of the game the action „MIN" ($B_t = 0$) restricts the reduction of capacity from below. As previously mentioned, selling the invested capital was possible but too expensive.
2. According to the rules of the game the action „MAX" is restricted from above. This was a strong restriction for firms which had made large losses during the game.
3. Compared with the theoretical values the investment figures selected by the firms are far more crude. First, because the policy „STA"

was often chosen instead of a small adjustment of capacity. Secondly, as a rule, the investment figures selected under the actions „DES" or „EXP" were rounded off. This was done partly to get a smoothed figure for gross investment, partly to get a smoothed figure for the book value of production assets.

As is shown in table 10 the frequency of the actions MIN, STA and MAX totals 257 cases, i.e. in more than 50 % of all cases the net-investment figures were either zero or coincided with one of the boundaries. The average investment formula (12) can not be expected to explain these decisions.

In the remaining 238 cases, in which the actions DES or EXP were selected, differences between theoretical and actual quantities might have been due, to a great extent, to the effect of rounding off the investment figures. Most of the participants preferred integer balance figures, which were smoothed in such a way that they showed only few non-zero characters. In table 11 these decisions are classified according to the "smoothness" of gross investment and productive assets. For simplicity the smoothness r(L) of an integer literal L is defined as the number of left point zeroes. For example, if L = ZZZ0000., with Z indicating a non-zero character, r(L) = 4.

Table 11 shows that in most cases investment figures with four or more left point zeroes were chosen. The smoothness of B_t depends on the smoothness of A_t. With $r(A_t)$ small, say $0 \leq r(A_t) \leq 3$, investment figures with a considerable degree of smoothness are preferred. If $r(A_t) \geq 4$ the largest frequencies were for the case $r(B_t) = r(A_t) - 1$. In these cases the players clearly intended to maintain the smoothness of the book value of the productive assets.

Period \ Actions	MIN	DES	STA	EXP	MAX	Σ
1	6	0	12	15	0	33
2	2	0	5	24	2	33
3	2	0	10	20	1	33
4	4	1	6	21	1	33
5	5	5	12	10	1	33
6	6	2	16	8	1	33
7	5	3	7	16	2	33
8	3	4	11	10	5	33
9	2	1	4	19	7	33
10	1	2	5	17	8	33
11	0	2	5	15	11	33
12	1	0	7	12	13	33
13	1	3	10	10	9	33
14	5	9	11	4	4	33
15	15	3	13	2	0	33
Σ	58	35	134	203	65	495

Table 10: Frequencies of investment actions.

r(B_t) \ r(A_t)	0	1	2	3	4	5	6	Σ
0	9	0	0	0	0	0	0	9
1	1	0	3	0	0	0	0	4
2	1	0	1	4	0	0	0	6
3	1	0	1	1	25	1	0	29
4	23	5	3	5	17	46	1	100
5	25	6	5	8	14	25	4	87
6	1	0	0	1	0	1	0	3
Σ	61	11	13	19	56	73	5	238

Table 11: Smoothness of investment and stock values

In order to prove this result we relate the observations of $r(A_{t+1})$ with $r(A_t)$ subject to $r(B_t) = r(A_t) - 1$. Table 12 contains the 82 cases in which this condition is fulfilled. If the characters of B_t were fixed independently from A_t, then nearly all cases with $r(B_t) = r(A_t) - 1$ would lead to $r(A_{t+1}) = r(A_t) - 1$. The probability that $r(A_{t+1})$ equals $r(A_t)$ at random amounts to 1/9. Table 12 shows, however, that only in 27 from 82 cases was the smoothness of A_t actually reduced.

$r(A_{t+1})$ \ $r(A_t)$	2	3	4	5	6	Σ
2	2	0	0	0	0	2
3	0	1	3	0	0	4
4	1	2	19	20	0	42
5	0	1	3	26	4	34
6	0	0	0	0	0	0
Σ	3	4	25	46	4	82

Table 12: Transition of smoothness in productive assets under $r(B_t)=r(A_t)-1$.

19. ADVERTISING AND PRICE COMPETITION IN THE MANAGEMENT GAME SINTO-MARKET

KARL-HEINZ FISCHER*

This paper is concerned with the investigation of the decision process in the SINTO-market with regard to price and advertising policy. The analysis is based on the information data of the players and their decisions; no data of the decision process are available. Thus, our Problem is one of enlightenment of this process.

The participants had only qualitative information about the influence of prices and advertising expenditures (in short: advertising) on total demand, such as:

a) Sales can be increased by higher advertising and lower prices - everything else equal.

b) Advertising does not only influence current sales but also future sales.

c) Changes in price have an adverse effect on the brand image; they reduce sales. For small changes these effects are small but for big changes far-reaching.[1]

---

* Universität Frankfurt/Main

1 Otwin Becker and Reinhard Selten, Experiences with the management game SINTO-Market, in: Contributions to Experimental Economics, Vol. 2, ed. by Heinz Sauermann, Tübingen 1970, pp. 136-150.
Otwin Becker and Reinhard Selten, Spielbeschreibung des Unternehmens-Spiels SINTO-Markt, Control Data GmbH, Frankfurt am Main, 1967.

I. The Development of Prices and Advertising Expenditures

The Development of the Averages

We distinguish between two different situations for price and advertising policy in the SINTO-market.

1. Price and advertising for an active brand, i.e. a brand which was introduced in former periods,
2. price and advertising for a new brand, i.e. a brand which is to be introduced in the decision period.

In the following we will give an overall view of the development of prices and advertising for the active brands only.

The average price in each period of all brands and all games tends to decline significantly in the course of the games. The Spearman rank correlation coefficients[1] between these averages and the time, i.e. the corresponding period number, are:

for period 1 to 15: $r_S = .98$, $\alpha < .001$
for period 1 to 5: $r_S = 1.00$, $\alpha < .01$
for period 6 to 15: $r_S = .92$, $\alpha < .01$

Only in two periods was the average price higher than the average price of the preceding period (Table 1).

From the corresponding average of the advertising expenditures we find that the averages decline from period 1 to 5 and then fluctuate within a small inter-

1 Speaking of rank correlation, we mean the Spearman rank correlation coefficient, r_S. The program RANG was written by: F. Gebhardt, Deutsches Rechenzentrum, Darmstadt.

Table 1: Averages

period	prices	advertising expenditures
1	898.1	100 657
2	895.4	78 367
3	885.1	69 489
4	873.8	78 625
5	863.9	66 237
6	857.6	56 121
7	841.3	57 695
8	836.7	53 944
9	836.7	54 970
10	839.5	52 789
11	833.0	54 090
12	835.9	52 636
13	833.5	54 125
14	828.6	57 552
15	813.3	56 623

val. The correlations between these averages and the time corroborates this statement:

for period 1 to 15: $r_S = .69$, $\alpha < .01$
for period 1 to 5: $r_S = .70$, $\alpha < .10$
for period 6 to 15: $r_S = .01$.

This indicates that the high correlation for period 1 to 15 is mainly influenced by the development of the averages in period 1 to 5.

Analysis of Variance

To find some hints of the characteristics of the development of prices and advertising expenditures we ran an analysis of variance.

The analysis of variance for the price data shows a reduction of variance. This assimilation of prices is mainly attributed to an assimilation within the games and not between the games. Separating the total price variance into the variance within the games and the variance between the games clearly confirms this statement. In Table 2 we have listed the coefficients of variation expressed as percentage. This table indicates that the reduction of total variance in the course of the game is essentially due to a reduction of the variance within the games.

Table 2: Prices: Coefficients of variation (expressed as percentage)

period	total	within the games	between the games
1	13.71	13.70	13.70
2	11.33	10.80	13.64
3	10.16	8.17	19.60
4	9.95	7.79	22.41
5	9.32	6.77	23.90
6	8.56	6.64	21.25
7	6.01	4.97	13.61
8	5.64	4.67	12.77
9	5.61	4.48	13.06
10	5.40	4.29	12.47
11	5.50	4.26	12.83
12	5.34	4.11	12.35
13	5.28	3.94	12.75
14	5.88	4.32	14.70
15	11.07	9.86	20.62

Disregarding the first two periods we can see that the variance within the games is significantly smaller than the variance between the games. From period 3 to 15 the F-quotient of these variances is significant with $\alpha < .01$. The increase in variance in period 14 and 15 probably indicates an "end effect". The rank correlation coefficients between the coefficients of variation of prices and time, i.e. the corresponding period number, for the three variances are listed in Table 3.

Table 3: Rank correlation coefficients between the coefficients of variation of prices and time

	total	within the games	between the games
period 1 to 15	$- .64, \alpha < .01$	$- .69, \alpha < .01$	$- .40, \alpha < .10$
period 1 to 13	$- .99, \alpha < .01$	$-1.00 \quad \alpha < .01$	$- .78, \alpha < .05$

An analysis of variance of the advertising expenditures also shows an assimilation effect (Table 4).

From period 3 to 15 the variance within the games is significantly smaller than the variance between the games. The F-quotient of these variances is also significant at the .01 level. The rank correlation between the coefficient of variation of advertising expenditures and time over 15 periods is:

for the total variance $r_S = - .55, \alpha < .05$

for the variance within the games $r_S = - .85, \alpha < .01$

for the variance between the games $r_S = + .23$.

Regarding period 1 to 13 the correlations are nearly the same.

Table 4: Advertising expenditures: Coefficients of variation (expressed as percentage)

period	total	within the games	between the games
1	49.50	53.72	37.45
2	55.16	49.76	76.26
3	65.30	54.64	118.75
4	60.00	45.90	138.85
5	61.77	49.69	140.33
6	57.47	50.48	114.51
7	53.91	41.19	136.48
8	57.11	42.77	148.42
9	49.71	33.65	137.14
10	55.43	45.35	122.32
11	44.47	29.22	120.22
12	39.63	22.80	113.17
13	46.87	30.13	127.47
14	51.60	37.96	128.80
15	49.68	33.56	135.76

From these results the average behavior of firms in the SINTO-market might be described as follows: after high advertising expenditures, which result from the introduction of brands at the beginning of the game, the average of the advertising expenditures fluctuates about a nearly stable mean, whereas the prices were lowered continuously. This shows the general tendency of aggressive price competition with nearly stable advertising expenditures.

The Development of Prices of the Individual Games

To verify also the tendency of decreasing average prices for the individual games, we computed the rank correlation coefficients between the average price and time. To eliminate the "start effects" and the "end effects" we examine only the periods 4 to 13. Table 5 shows the results.

Table 5: Rank correlation coefficients for average price and time and for average advertising expenditures and time

game	average* price-time	level of significance	average* adv. exp.-time	level of significance
1	- .997	.01	+ .782	.01
2	- .746	.01	+ .455	.10
3	+ .109	-	- .976	.01
4	- .032	-	- .177	-
5	- .969	.01	+ .194	-
6	- .988	.01	- .212	-
7	- .914	.01	- .243	-
8	+ .140	-	- .855	.01
9	- .924	.01	- .212	-
10	- .683	.05	- .924	.01
11	+ .529	.10	+ .442	.10

*period 4 to 13

Three positive correlations and eight negative correlations appeared. This shows that in the individual games the firms applied different price policies.

If we assume that the different policies lead to different average prices, we may take the average prices as an indicator for the competitiveness of the game. According to the theory of the firm, we formulate the hypothesis that the higher the collective success, the lower the competitiveness (or the higher the cooperative character of the game). The rank correlation between the average prices and the collective success, i.e. the sum over the objective variable (the final owned capital) of the three firms in a game, is $r_S = .49$ ($\alpha < .10$). It is not surprising that the level of significance is only .10, because extremely high average prices have a negative influence on the collective success. Our hypothesis is only valid within a reasonable range. This can be seen from game 10, which was the most successful. The average price of this game was nearly equal to the overall average price; the number of price changes was the lowest of all games since the prices were constant in the last eight periods.
The rank correlation coefficient $r_S = -.14$ between the total number of active brands, which is the sum of the active brands over 15 periods, and the average prices is not significant. This shows that the total number of active brands can not be used as an indicator of aggressive price competition in the games.

The Development of Advertising Expenditures of the Individual Games

We have come to the result that the average advertising expenditures over all games decreased from period 1 to 5 and then fluctuated within a small interval.
In Table 5 we have listed the correlation coefficients between the average advertising expenditures of period 4 to 13 and the time. There are three significant nega-

tive correlations and three significant positive correlations. The other five correlations are not significant. Table 5 shows that different advertising policies have been used.
In general the declining of the average advertising expenditures in the periods 1 to 5, which we described before, is verified for the individual games, but the fluctuations in period 6 - 15 do not reappear in all games.
We assume that there is a stronger competition in games with more advertising and therefore a tendency to lower collective success. The rank correlation $r_S = -.34$ between collective success and advertising expenditures is significant only on the .15 level. This result supports the assumption that advertising affects collective success. The low significance level shows the necessity of reasonably high advertising expenditures.
As we found no correlation between the average price and the average advertising expenditures in a game, we may suppose that the players combined the instruments of prices and advertising in different manners. These policies will be investigated later by means of factor analysis.

The Assimilation of Prices and of Advertising Expenditures in the Individual Games

As described before, there is a reduction of price variance in the course of the games. For the individual games we computed the rank correlation between time and the coefficient of variation of prices of period 4 to 13[1] (Table 6). This coefficient can be taken as a mea-

---

1 We eliminate the "start" and the "end effects."

sure of assimilation, i.e. the higher the negative correlation, the stronger the assimilation. Therefore we call this coefficient "assimilation coefficient."

Table 6: Assimilation coefficients

game	price	level of significance	advertising expenditures	level of significance
1	- .84	.01	- .86	.01
2	- .92	.01	- .90	.01
3	- .92	.01	+ .18	-
4	- .39	-	- .50	.10
5	- .80	.01	- .64	.05
6	- .10	-	- .37	-
7	- .02	-	+ .13	-
8	- .97	.01	- .26	-
9	- .69	.05	- .88	.01
10	- .70	.05	- .48	.10
11	- .99	.01	- .60	.05

The tendency of price assimilation is more or less obvious in all games.
Correlating the average prices to the assimilation coefficients, we find the tendency: the higher the assimilation of prices, the higher the average price (r_S = .42, α = .11).[1] This suggests that the assimilation of prices is higher in games with a more cooperative character.

---

1 The correlation between the average prices and the correlation coefficients of the standard deviation of prices and the time shows the same tendency.

One may assume that not only the strength of the competition influences the assimilation of prices, but also the total number of introduced brands and the discontinuance of active brands. Since both correlations are not significant we conclude that these influences are not effective.
Table 6 also shows an assimilation of advertising expenditures. but this assimilation is not quite as strong as the assimilation of prices.

II. Some Factoranalytical Results on the Applied Price and Advertising Policies

Our preceding investigation has shown that the development of prices and advertising expenditures was different in the individual games. One can expect that the firms applied different types of price and advertising policies. To find some hints for a general explanation of these policies we ran some factor analyses[1] on the data.
The first step of our evaluation was to factoranalyse the data of all games. Our basic-set of variables consists of three decision variables and ten information variables of the participants, two realization variables and two model variables. The ten information variables are the lagged values of the three decision variables and the two realization variables. The participants had only qualitative information about the

1 We used as method the principal component analysis with varimax rotation. The communalities were estimated by the squared multiple correlation with iteration by refactoring. The program PAFA was written by: P. Schnell and F. Gebhardt; Deutsches Rechenzentrum, Darmstadt.

two model variables. For this reason the participants could form expectations on these two variables. The basic-set of variables is listed in Table 7.

Table 7: The basic-set of variables

Variables \ Time	t	t - 1	t - 2
price (P)	P_t	P_{t-1}	P_{t-2}
advertising expenditures (W)	W_t	W_{t-1}	W_{t-2}
sales (X)	X_t	X_{t-1}	X_{t-2}
production (Y)	Y_t	Y_{t-1}	Y_{t-2}
inventories (L)	L_t	L_{t-1}	L_{t-2}
attractiveness (Z)	-	Z_{t-1}	-
trend (F)	-	F_{t-1}	-

All variables defined in Table 7 are the values for a brand. The decision variables are P_t, W_t, Y_t; the information variables are P_{t-1}, W_{t-1}, X_{t-1}, Y_{t-1}, L_{t-1}, P_{t-2}, W_{t-2}, X_{t-2}, Y_{t-2}, L_{t-2}; the realization variables are X_t and L_t; the model variables are Z_{t-1} and F_{t-1}. The variable Z_{t-1} is the attractiveness of a brand depending on the quality characteristics in period t-1[1] and the variable F_{t-1} is the demand expansion trend in period t-1.[2]

---

1 Otwin Becker and Reinhard Selten; Experiences..., op. cit, p. 139.

2 Otwin Becker and Reinhard Selten; Experiences..., op. cit, p. 138.

This basic-set of variables allows a systematic evaluation of the data for all games to find the best basis for the investigation of the individual games. At first we factoranalyzed all 17 variables. The next steps are systematic eliminations of subsets of this basic-set. The sample size for all games is N = 1456. Table 8 shows the factor patterns of all variables (1st analysis).[1] The first analysis indicates that the prices in period t (P_t) and the advertising expenditures in period t (W_t) are highly autocorrelated with their lagged values P_{t-1}, P_{t-2} and W_{t-1}, W_{t-2}, respectively. There is no connection with the other information variables. The correlation between prices and attractiveness (Z_{t-1}) and between prices and demand expansion (F_{t-1}) will be discussed later. Production (Y_t) and sales (X_t) are autocorrelated with their lagged values. We also see a high intercorrelation between sales and production.
If we eliminate the information variables of period t-2 we receive higher communalities for P_t and W_t (2nd analysis, Table 9). The above mentioned correlation structure between the decision and information variables is of the same nature as in the 1st analysis.
Next we eliminate the two model variables Z_{t-1} and F_{t-1} (3rd analysis, Table 10). The factor pattern of the remaining variables seems nearly steady in spite of this elimination. The communalities of P_t and W_t are higher than in the 2nd analysis. The analysis with the two model variables (Z_{t-1}, F_{t-1}), however, allows a better interpretation of the extracted factors. Especially the trend (F_{t-1}) in connection with one or more variables

1 In this analysis and in the following analyses factor loadings less than .20 were omitted.

Table 8: 1st Analysis

Factors / Contribution* / Variables	1	2	3	4	5	6	total reproduced communality
	19.5	18.7	17.8	16.4	14.2	13.4	
P_t		.72					.55
W_t					.67		.51
X_t	.78			.32			.80
Y_t	.88						.84
L_t			.80				.66
P_{t-1}		.91					.84
W_{t-1}					.83		.75
X_{t-1}	.49			.67		.34	.87
Y_{t-1}				.85			.84
L_{t-1}			.89				.86
P_{t-2}		.69				-.24	.55
W_{t-2}					.62	.27	.51
X_{t-2}	.37			.38		.73	.84
Y_{t-2}						.79	.71
L_{t-2}			.70				.62
Z_{t-1}		.37		.53			.52
F_{t-1}	.51	-.34	-.22				.52

* Contribution of the factor in percent of total reproduced communality; total original communality of total variance: 81 %; total reproduced communality of total variance: 73 %;

Table 9: 2nd Analysis

Factors / Contribution* / Variables	1	2	3	4	5	total reproduced communality
	23.4	22.7	20.1	18.6	15.2	
P_t			.78			.63
W_t					.73	.59
X_t	.45	.72				.79
Y_t	.29	.89				.88
L_t				.87		.78
P_{t-1}			.84			.73
W_{t-1}					.82	.72
X_{t-1}	.82	.42				.92
Y_{t-1}	.74	.23				.66
L_{t-1}		-.25		.83		.77
Z_{t-1}	.67		.40			.63
F_{t-1}		.50	-.37	-.26		.51

* Contribution of the factor in percent of total reproduced communality; total original communality of total variance: 81 %; total reproduced communality of total variance: 72 %;

Table 10: 3rd Analysis

Factors / Contribution* / Variables	1	2	3	4	5	total reproduced communality
	25.9	20.1	19.3	18.6	16.1	
P_t			.85			.73
W_t					.77	.66
X_t	.60			.60		.78
Y_t	.37			.89		.93
L_t		.87				.79
P_{t-1}			.84			.74
W_{t-1}					.77	.66
X_{t-1}	.88			.29		.89
Y_{t-1}	.80					.68
L_{t-1}		.83		-.27		.78

* Contribution of the factor in percent of total reproduced communality; total original communality of total variance: 81 %; total reproduced communality of total variance: 76 %;

gives a hint of the type of development in the course of the game, i.e. increasing, decreasing or constant values.

In the following 4th analysis we examine the three decision variables (P_t, W_t, Y_t), the two realization variables (X_t, L_t), and the two model variables (Z_{t-1}, F_{t-1}). From Table 11 we see, that the communalities of P_t and of W_t are very low in comparison with the former analyses. There is a weak connection between these two variables and the other five variables.

Table 11: 4th Analysis

Factors	1	2	3	total reproduced communality
Contribution* / Variables	55.6	23.8	20.6	
P_t		.46		.26
W_t			.45	.22
X_t	.94			.90
Y_t	.88		.30	.87
L_t			.56	.33
Z_{t-1}	.33	.73		.65
F_{t-1}	.53	-.40	-.39	.59

* Contribution of the factor in percent of total reproduced communality; total original communality of total variance: 62 %; total reproduced communality of total variance: 55 %;

If we eliminate Z_{t-1} and F_{t-1} from the last subset we observe a further strong reduction of the communalities of P_t and W_t (5th analysis, Table 12).
To summarize the results of the above analyses, we can state that prices (P_t) and advertising expenditures (W_t) were mainly explained by their lagged values P_{t-1} and W_{t-1}. This autocorrelation, however, hinders the disentangling of the influences from the information

Table 12: 5th Analysis

Factors / Contribution * / Variables	1	2	total reproduced communality
	71.8	28.2	
P_t	-.26		.08
W_t		.38	.15
X_t	.97		.94
Y_t	.78	.46	.81
L_t	-.20	.54	.33

* Contribution of the factor in percent of total reproduced communality; total original communality of total variance: 52 %; total reproduced communality of total variance: 46 %;

variables on the price and advertising decision. For this reason it seems to be appropriate to eliminate this connection, i.e. to examine only the decisions P_t and W_t and not their lagged values. Due to the high autocorrelation between X_t and X_{t-1} (sales), Y_t and Y_{t-1} (production) and L_t and L_{t-1} (inventories), it is also necessary to observe only one value of these variables in the further analysis. After the elimination of these autocorrelations, it is likely that we will find a better connection between prices, advertising expenditures and sales, production, inventories, respectively. Since Y_t is a decision variable like P_t and W_t we first choose these three variables for our analysis. On the other hand Y_{t-1}

might be influenced by the values of period t-2. The realization variables X_t and L_t should be eliminated, since we can assume that X_{t-1} and L_{t-1} were handled as information data by the participants and have had an influence on the decisions of P_t, W_t and Y_t. As mentioned above there are advantages for interpretation of the factors if the two model variables (Z_{t-1}, F_{t-1}) are included. For these reasons we regard in our 6th analysis of all games the following variables: P_t, W_t, Y_t, X_{t-1}, L_{t-1}, Z_{t-1}, F_{t-1} (Table 13). This variable set will then be factoranalyzed for the individual games.

Table 13: 6th Analysis

Factors	1	2	3	total reproduced communality
Contribution* / Variables	55.3	28.2	16.5	
P_t		.44		.20
W_t			.61	.37
Y_t	.75		.35	.71
X_{t-1}	.87			.79
L_{t-1}	-.34			.17
Z_{t-1}	.59	.68		.80
F_{t-1}	.49	-.61		.67

* Contribution of the factor in percent of total reproduced communality; total original communality of total variance: 62 %; total reproduced communality of total variance: 53 %;

In the 6th analysis we extracted three factors. The first factor, which we call general production-factor, shows the consequences of a general growth factor, i.e. with an increasing demand, the sales increased, the inventories decreased and the production increased. Another characteristic of the model structure can be seen by the influence of attractiveness of a brand on sales and production. A high attractiveness leads to high sales and production and vice versa.

The second factor, which we call general price-factor, is a general competition factor. The prices were positively connected with the attractiveness of a brand. Since a higher price can result a priori from a higher attractiveness, the firms apparently adopted this element of the model structure. The negative connection of prices with the demand expansion shows the observed decreasing tendency of prices in the course of the games. Furthermore it is interesting to see that no other variables are highly correlated with prices as could be assumed according to the model structure, with respect to inventories and sales.
The third factor (general advertising-factor) is an individual growth factor of the firm. The expansion of the market due to advertising expenditures is associated with increasing production.
Our next step was to compute factor patterns for the individual games. We used the variable set of the 6th analysis. The sample sizes were between N = 120 and N = 150. For each of the eleven games two or three factors were extracted; all together 29 factors. Because there are similar factors in some games, we were able to combine the 29 factors to a smaller number of typical factors. The distribution of the 12 typical factors over the individual games is listed in Table 14.

Table 14: Distribution of the typical factors

Game \ Factors	F_1	F_2	F_3	F_4	F_5	F_6	F_7	F_8	F_9	F_{10}	F_{11}	F_{12}
1		+				+						
2		+			+	+						
3				+						+		
4	+											+
5					+			+			+	
6		+	+		+							
7					+					+		+
8	+			+			+					
9	+		+		+							
10	+									+		
11						+			+			+

The first three factors (F_1, F_2, F_3) are similar to the above discussed general production-factor, general price-factor and general advertising-factor. We now make an attempt to interpret the nine factors F_4 to F_{12}. In Table 15 we characterized the factor patterns of these factors. High factor loadings are represented by x or -x

Table 15: Factor patterns of the typical factors

Variables \ Factors	F_1	F_2	F_3	F_4	F_5	F_6	F_7	F_8	F_9	F_{10}	F_{11}	F_{12}
P_t		x		x	-x			-x	x			
W_t			x			x	-x	x	x	x		
Y_t	x		x	x	x	x		x	x			x
X_{t-1}	x			x	x	x	-x		x		x	x
L_{t-1}	-x			-x			x			x	-x	
Z_{t-1}	x	x		x								x
F_{t-1}	x	-x		x	x	x	x	x	x		x	x

for an inverse loading. We considered only factor loadings greater or equal to .20. The factor patterns of the individual games can be grouped by means of Table 14 and Table 15.

Factor 4: non-aggressive price policy

Increasing production and sales and decreasing inventories were connected with increasing prices. This indicates that the firms try to increase their earnings by higher prices. Therefore it can be assumed that competition in the games 3 and 8 was relatively low.

Factor 5: aggressive price policy

Increasing production and sales were connected with decreasing prices. This typical quantity policy indicates a strong price competition.

Factor 6: aggressive advertising policy

Increasing sales were connected with increasing production and advertising expenditures. This indicates also a quantity policy.

Factor 7: non-aggressive advertising policy

Increasing sales and decreasing inventories were reasons for decreasing advertising expenditures. A relatively weak advertising competition can be assumed.

Factor 8: aggressive price and aggressive advertising policy

A combined price-advertising policy was used in game 5 where increasing production was connected with decreasing prices and increasing advertising expenditures. This indicates an aggressive price and advertising competition.

Factor 9: non-aggressive price and aggressive advertising policy

Game 11 shows a more conservative price policy combined with an aggressive advertising policy because increasing production and sales were connected with increasing prices and increasing advertising expenditures.

Factor 10: inventory policy

The advertising expenditures were mainly guided by the development of the inventories. Increases in the inventories led to increasing advertising expenditures and vice versa.

Factor 11: trend-factor

This factor shows that in the course of the game the sales increased and the inventories decreased.

Factor 12: attractiveness-factor

The above discussed connection between the attractiveness of a brand and production and sales is represented by this factor.

The interpretation of the factor patterns points out that different policies were applied in the games. We have not extracted a factor which indicates a price policy for game 4 and game 10. In game 4 the prices remained nearly constant in the course of the game. In game 10 the prices were constant in the last eight periods.
Regarding the individual games it is evident that the three firms made use of the same price and advertising policies. This suggests the idea that the firms adapted themselves to the policy of a "policy leader."

The adaptation can be observed especially for the price policies. In games with aggressive price competition one firm opens a price cutting process and the other firms imitate this policy two or three periods later. Reasons for beginning this policy are low sales and high inventories. Higher sales from the decreasing prices lower the inventories. The price cutting process stops when the inventories reach zero.[1] Periods of increasing prices then followed. This shows that in oligopolistic games in which inventories occur a low price policy loses its aggressiveness with decreasing inventories. During the periods of aggressive price competition no additional aggressive advertising policy could be observed, except for game 5.

In games with non-aggressive policies the prices remained constant or increased slightly. Only occasional adaptations of some high or low introduction prices have been observed at the beginning of the game. In these games the variance of prices is relatively low. The advertising expenditures were determined by the development of the inventories. Increasing inventories led to increasing advertising expenditures and vice versa. This shows that the advertising expenditures are a more flexible instrument in the SINTO-market than the price policy.

One of our main results was the assimilation of prices and advertising expenditures in the course of the games. Another assimilation phenomenon could be observed with respect to the policies applied. When one player starts an aggressive policy the other players are more or less obliged to increase their aggressiveness, too. This is true not only for the price policy, but also to a lower extent for the advertising policy.

---

1 The capacity was always fully employed.

Bearing in mind the influences from the average prices and the average advertising expenditures on collective success, we can conclude that there is a tendency such that the most aggressive player determines the collective success of all three firms due to oligopolistic interdependence.

20. PRODUCT DIFFERENTIATION IN THE MANAGEMENT GAME SINTO-MARKET

MANFRED REINFELDT*

Introduction

The theoretical problem of profit maximization in case of existing preferences on the buyers' side of the market is usually solved by product differentiation. On the seller's side this simply means disaggregating the expected total demand function, thus transforming the one-product problem into a multiproduct problem. Profit is then maximized for each market separately, taking into account the cost func-

---

* Universität Frankfurt/Main

tion. The model underlying this solution implies some restrictions which are important regarding the usefulness of the results. First of all, preferences are assumed to be known so that the individual demand functions can be derived. In the second place, the seller is assumed to act without regard to possible reactions of potential competitors in the market. Finally, preferences are assumed to depend on only one distinguishable characteristic, which may exist in reality or in the buyers' opinion only.
It should be interesting to do away with these restrictions in order to get a more realistic model for examining the quality problem. It is the purpose of this paper to discuss the parts of the SINTO-model concerning the quality problem, to analyse the decision situation in the model and to evaluate the results obtained in a series of 11 experiments.

I. The Quality Aspects of the Model

1. The Information Basis

SINTO is a synthetic product, various brands of which may be supplied by three oligopolists. The demand for each SINTO brand depends on its price, on advertising expenditures, and on three quality components called fine grainedness, tartness, and wrapping luxuriousness. Since the effects on demand of fixing these parameters are only qualitatively known to the participants in the market, the decision situation is that of incomplete information. With respect to the quality components this means that the firms must fix each of these parameters at one of ten levels numbered 0,1,...,9 without exact knowledge of the effects of

their decisions on sales.
The influence of the quality parameters on demand is known to be the following:[1]

- buyers prefer brands with the first and second components (taste characteristics) fixed at medium levels to those with extreme ones;
- within the medium levels there exists a tendency of fine-grained and tart products to be slightly preferred to coarse-grained and mild ones;
- the competitive effect of one brand on another one increases with increasing similarity of their taste characteristics;
- the taste characteristics are neutral with respect to production costs of a brand;
- the third quality component increases demand with increasing level; production costs rise proportionally to its level.

Among the quality components the taste characteristics are of particular theoretical interest. Usually, as in the case of the third quality component, differences in the characteristics by which two brands are to be compared will affect the competitive situation in different ways depending on the sign of the difference. In the case of the taste characteristics, however, the competitive influence of two brands does not depend on the direction of dissimilarity. This symmetry property of the taste characteristics together with their cost neutrality represents a plausible two-dimensional model for product differentiation which avoids the restrictions stated above.

---

1 No reference is made in this paper to those formal properties of the model which are not known to the players. For a discussion of the formal model see: Otwin Becker and Reinhard Selten, Experiences with the Management Game SINTO-Market, in: Heinz Sauermann (ed.), Contributions to Experimental Economics, Vol. II, Tübingen 1970, pp. 136-150.

To summarize the important quality aspects of the decision situation: demand is known to depend on two taste characteristics; all brands on the market are competing with respect to these components; neither is the exact demand or the competitive strength of similarity known, nor can it be reliably estimated because of the general oligopolistic interdependence of the market.

2. The Decision Basis

Since the quality problem is an essentially two-dimensional one it can be graphically represented in form of a 10 x 10 "brand map," in which the names of the brands supplied in one period can be listed according to their taste characteristics combination. As this map proves a powerful tool for decision making on the quality scene, it seems appropriate to express the information given about the quality model in terms of a plausible graphical meaning.

Demand may be conceived as a mountain covering the map with its peak slightly below and to the right of the central fields, sloping away to the edges of the map.

The competitive aspect of similarity may now be seen as a problem of distance between the fields where the brands are placed; competition decreases with increasing distance in the map.

The problem of maximizing profit with regard to the taste characteristics is now transformed into finding an optimal position on the map. The difficulties of decision making lie in the information gap regarding demand and regarding the decisions of the competitors. There is no chance to find an optimal solution analytically, so optimality can be approached only more or less closely by the use of auxiliary strategies to be developed by the firms.

In the inauguration period of the market, with the brand map still blank, a naive decision behavior that would not take into consideration the actions of the competitors would try to occupy the demand peak. Supposing, however, that all firms behave like this and decide in favour of the field (or the region around it) which they consider to be the right one, this would mean the maximization of competition about a much smaller part of demand than could have been acquired by placing the brands apart. Yet this behaviour seems likely because the information available about demand is less for any other area on the map than for the peak region. Besides, choosing different places in the first period would imply expectations or information about the fields the competitors would be likely to choose - information not available in a non-cooperative first period.

The normal decision situation is based on a brand map with some fields already occupied. Placing a new brand on the map, once its introduction into the market is decided upon, requires some considerations of the following kind. It would be desirable to place the brand in the area of highest demand. If, however, the field considered is already occupied, placing one's own brand there would mean sharing demand with the competing brand (which can be a brand of one's own firm, too). Moving away from this field in either direction will change demand as well as the competitive strength of the existing brand. The lack of knowledge about the extent to which demand changes and competition decreases, while moving away from all brands in the peak area in any direction, will lead to a decision based on subjective criteria about the

demand value of the fields on the brand map.
If the competitive aspect is to be emphasized, a good decision would be to occupy a vacant area, i.e. to place a new brand on a field that is as far as possible from the existing brands. If the competitive aspect is to be combined with general demand considerations, the vacant area strategy could be modified by valuating the area with the estimated part of the demand mountain covering it. If the competitive aspect is to be neglected, a strategy of imitating successful brands by placing a new brand on or near the field of a successful existing brand could be plausible. The basic ideas of these concepts require more exact definition and more detailed considerations about their significance, which will be given below.

3. The Evaluation Method

The strategies described above, i.e. the imitation strategy and the pure and weighted vacant area strategies, are expected to give a good explanation of the observed decision behavior. It is obvious that the employment of these strategies is exposed to the subjective interpretation of "vacant area" or "successful," and to the weights which are to be applied to vacant areas. Furthermore it cannot be expected that the players had operational definitions that would have permitted the exact computation of the strategy variables for each decision alternative (each of the 100 fields of the map). Rather it is likely that their ordering of alternatives followed the optical impression when regarding the brand map.

The task of evaluating the actual behaviour includes finding operational definitions of the perception the

brand map may bring about. In order to estimate the goodness of fit of an actual decision with respect to the various strategies, the actual values of the strategy variables have to be related to the best value that could have been achieved.
The map which the decisions are based upon is considered to be that of the previous period corrected for potential changes of one's own brands. By using this map in the decision process it is assumed that no change in the competitors' decisions will occur. Although this assumption may not be very realistic, it seems plausible because of the lack of a better alternative. The goodness of decisions as to this decision map is then to be tested in order to see whether it supports the hypothesis, that the strategies defined have been of importance to the decisions at all, and to which extent the individual actions can be clearly attributed to a particular strategy.

II. Product Differentiation Strategies

1. Imitating a Successful Brand

The most important measure for the success of a brand seems to be its sales figure, because the amount sold is the aggregate result of all influences on the demand side of the market. In situations where it is impossible to separate the respective influence of the decision parameters on demand, it is a plausible strategy to learn from the competitors "how they did it" with respect to their most successful brands, i.e. the brands with the highest sales figures. A simple consideration could be that imitating one (or more) of the successful brands reduces the risk of miscalculating the effects of one's own quality decision. According to the information available the expectation is justified, that the new brand, placed on or near the field of the one to be imitated, will participate in the success of the leading one. This does not, of course, mean that sales previously achieved in this field are equally divided, because success still depends on the other decision parameters (and here even a complete imitation of decisions does not guarantee equal results because of the dynamic aspects of decisions in preceding periods).

Imitation may have causes other than convenience of decision. Since placing a new brand on a field already occupied establishes the strongest competitive relations possible, an aggressive behavior will use this imitation strategy in order "to do harm" to a competitor. This motive cannot be clearly isolated; it should be assumed valid in all cases of complete imitation, whereas placing a new brand in the neighbourhood might indicate a friendly attitude towards the competitor. These distinctions seem arbitrary, particularly since the possibility of keeping at a distance from one brand, without getting too close to another one, diminishes with increasing occupation of the brand map.

Regardless of what may be the true motive of using the imitation strategy, a firm employing it must always be aware of the possibility that the competitor(s) concerned will react to the inevitable demand drain.

For computational purposes the strategy can be formalized as follows:

Let r,s denote the levels of the two taste characteristics, and r^*, s^* those of the most successful competing brand. Then (r^*, s^*) gives the reference field in the map for the imitation policy. For each of the

100 fields (r,s) with r,s = 0,1,...,9 the distance d^*_{rs} to the reference field can be measured by the length of the straight line between the two fields' central points

$$d^*_{rs} = \sqrt{(r-r^*)^2 + (s-s^*)^2}.$$

Clearly the pure imitation strategy with

$$\min_{r,s} d^*_{rs} = 0$$

would imply placing the new brand on the field (r^*, s^*), but there are reasons to regard decisions for nearby fields as realisations of this strategy as well.

2. Occupying a Vacant Area

Regarding the decision process mainly under competitive aspects requires a new brand to be placed on a field in the middle of a vacant area. Thus, by maximizing the average distance to the surrounding brands, it is assured that the negative effects of the new brand on the brands already existing are minimized, and inversely the negative effects of the existing brands on the new one are minimized as well.

Since a vacant area is bounded by the surrounding brands, to be called neighbouring brands, it is clear that the possible size of those areas depends on the number and distribution of existing brands in the map. In the beginning periods they can be expected to be large and to decrease with increasing number of brands which are added in the course of time. The exact shape

and size of a vacant area depend largely on the individual gestalt considerations of the players, i.e. on what area a player intuitively will conceive to be vacant when regarding the map. For analytical purposes, the general framework of these considerations is to be formalized in a way which permits the derivation of equivalent decisions without referring to the intuitive factors in the valuating process.
As seen from each possible position of a new brand, a separation line with respect to any existing brand can be introduced, by which the map is divided into two parts: the area beyond the separation line is assumed to be protected against the influence of the new brand, the area this side to be accessible. When all separation lines, thought to be crossing the respective positions of the competing brands, are constructed, the area which is accessible in relation to all competing brands is called the vacant area.

Figure 1: Separation Lines in the Brand Map

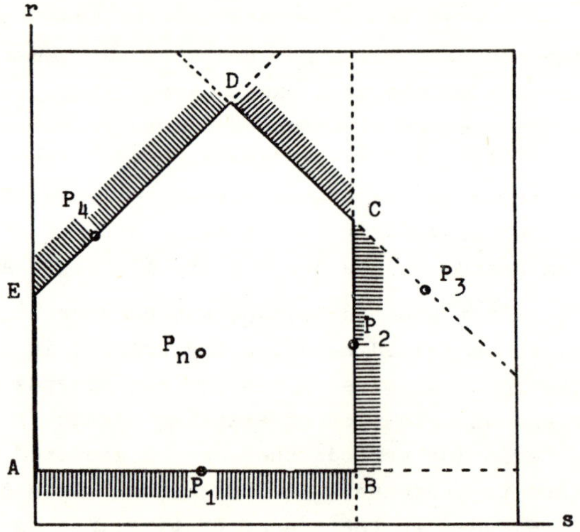

In Figure 1 the position of the new brand is denoted by P_n, the positions of the competing brands by $P_1,\ldots,P_4$. For P_n the map is divided in relation to P_1 by the separation line through A and B, in relation to P_4 by the line through E and D, etc. The shaded area is considered to be protected, the non-shaded area ABCDE is considered to be accessible as seen from P_n and thus represents the vacant area of position P_n. Let Z denote the set of all positions of the brand map

(1) $$Z = \{(r,s) | r \in N,\ s \in N\}$$

with

$$N = \{0,1,\ldots,9\} \ .$$

Let r_n and s_n be the taste characteristics of the new brand, n_c the number of competing brands existing, r_m and s_m the taste characteristics of the m-th competing brand ($m = 1,2,\ldots,n_c$). Then the set F_{mn} of points accessible for the new brand in relation to the m-th competing brand can be defined as

(2) $$F_{mn} = \{(r,s) \in Z | d_{sm}(s - s_m) \leq d_{rm}(r_m - r)\}$$

with

(3) $$d_{rm} = \operatorname{sgn}(r_m - r_n)$$
$$d_{sm} = \operatorname{sgn}(s_m - s_n)$$

and

$$\operatorname{sgn}(0) = 0 \ .$$

If for any m the relation

$$r_m - r_n = s_m - s_n = 0$$

holds, the set of accessible points is defined to be empty

$$(4) \qquad F_{mn} = \emptyset .$$

The intersection set V_n of the F_{mn} as defined by

$$(5) \qquad V_n = \bigcap_{m=1}^{n_c} F_{mn}$$

constitutes the set of points accessible for (r_n, s_n) in relation to all (r_m, s_m).
Since each point in the above definition is graphically represented by a field on the brand map, the corresponding area may be used to compute the vacant area measure. Since the separation lines are constructed as straight lines along the inner edges of the fields concerned, as shown in Figure 2, the measure is defined as the sum of

- the number of fields inside the separation lines,
- half the number of fields which are cut in halves by one diagonal separation line,
- one fourth the number of fields in which two diagonal separation lines intersect.

The simple computational procedure following from this definition is the consequence of the restrictions on the slope of the separation lines. By (2) a separation line is defined as

Figure 2: Brand Map*

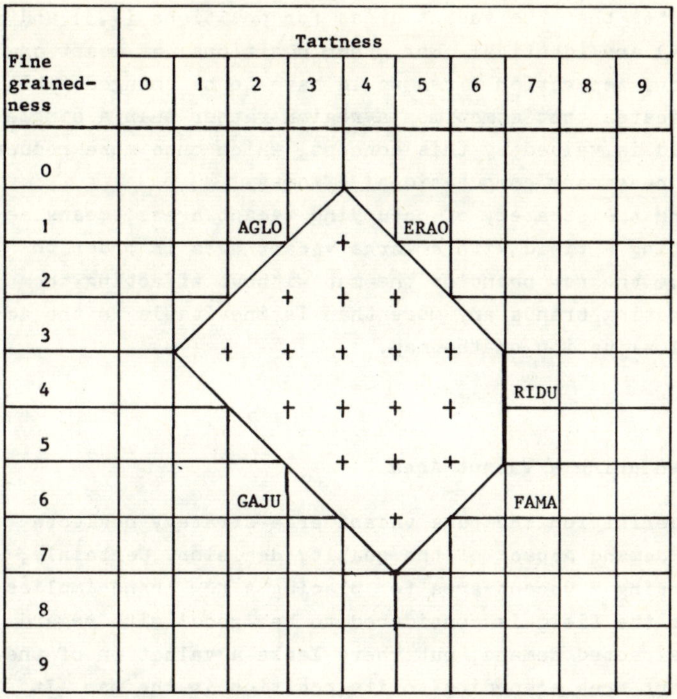

*Brand names are taken from a list of registered names for each firm; the final letters O, A and U denote firms 1 to 3, respectively.

(6) $$r = r_m + (s_m - s) \frac{d_{sm}}{d_{rm}},$$

the slope $-\frac{d_{sm}}{d_{rm}}$ being the negative ratio of two values of the sign function. Thus the separation lines are

drawn horizontally, vertically,[1] or with slope |1| only. The resulting convex polygon is sometimes not very sensitive to changes of the (r_n, s_n). Figure 2 demonstrates that the vacant areas for positions (4,3) and (4,4) are identical. For other positions, at least one of the separation lines would have to be changed. This indicates that sometimes a region rather than a single field is valued by this concept, which once more reduces the necessary computational efforts.
Using the strategy of occupying vacant areas, means selecting a field with a large vacant area in order to place the new brand on the map without affecting the competing brands any more than is inevitable in the actual situation on the map.

3. Weighing a Vacant Area

By definition the pure vacant area strategy neglects the demand aspect of the quality decision. Certainly, choosing a vacant area for placing a new brand implies that the field is considered to be 'good' with regard to expected demand, but there lacks a valuation of the vacant area according to its position in the map. It is obvious, that two areas of equal size and shape can be expected to represent different demand values when located in different regions of the demand mountain.

Valuation of the vacant areas in order to introduce the demand aspect into the strategy necessitates an estimation of the value of the demand mountain covering a vacant area. Since no information is given about the slope of the mountain it is natural to use the sales figures of the existing brands for estimation purposes.

---

1 For $d_{rm} = 0$ the definition $\frac{d_{sm}}{d_{rm}} = \infty$ is applied.

The demand satisfied by a brand can be interpreted as being partly drawn away from surrounding fields. Since, however, the competitive influence of a brand decreases with increasing distance from its position on the map, the shares gained from the other fields can be expected to be smaller, the more remote these fields. The observed sales figure therefore could possibly correspond to the volume of a mountain with its peak above the field occupied. For the purpose of constructing this mountain the actual sales figure of a brand can be spread out over the map, thus assigning a fictitious sales figure to each field. Since there are no hints given as to how far the influence of a brand extends, each field in the map should be assumed to be affected; inversely, this assumption requires the spreading procedure to be applied to all existing brands. By adding the fictitious sales figures of all brands falling to the share of each position on the map, an average sales mountain is constructed that can be considered an estimate of the true demand mountain.

Denoting by n_a the total number of brands existing, the definition of fictitious sales figures f_{mrs} of brand m accruing to field (r,s) according to the usual definition of potential models is given by

$$(7) \quad f_{mrs} = \operatorname{sgn}(\alpha)\, x_m\, d_{mrs}^{-\alpha} + c; \qquad \alpha \neq 0;\ m = 1,2,\ldots,n_a$$

with

$$d_{mrs} = 1 + \sqrt{(r_m - r)^2 + (s_m - s)^2}$$

The value of the parameter α depends on the players' expectations as to the extent to which the influence of a brand vanishes with increasing distance from its position; the sign of α reflects the player's opinions on the surface shape of the sales mountain. Figure 3 shows the different curvature types of the sales mountain surface with respect to α. The tent-shaped type of the curvature ($\alpha > -1$; $\alpha \neq 0$) implies the competitive influence quickly vanishing near the peak and then slowly exhausting itself, whereas the dome-shaped type ($\alpha < -1$) implies a relatively strong influence nearby which diminishes rapidly with increasing distance. The cone-shaped type ($\alpha = -1$) being the marginal case between the first two types deserves special interest because of its parametric prominence. Since it cannot be plausibly assumed that an operational strategy can be based on an intricate parametric structure, special values for α, such as -1 or +1, seem a priori to have the better chances to be proven valid. For these special cases relation (7) becomes

$$f_{mrs} = c - x_m \, d_{mrs}$$

and

$$f_{mrs} = c + x_m \frac{1}{d_{mrs}} ,$$

respectively, which seem manageable measures when time and computing capacity are limited.

The sums of the fictitious sales figures for each field constitute the weights to be applied to the fields contained in the vacant area. The weighted vacant area measure for the position of the new brand is finally defined by summing these weights for the fields included in the vacant area for (r_n, s_n)

Figure 3: Curvature Types of Sales Mountain Surface

$$f = sgn(\alpha) \times d^{-\alpha} + c \; ^{*}$$

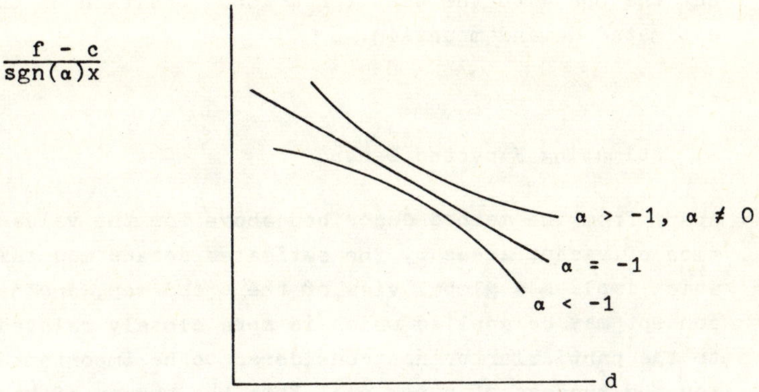

* The value of c should be chosen according to

$$c < sgn(-\alpha) x d_{max}^{-\alpha}$$

in order to make sure that the fictitious sales figures are positive for each position in the brand map (in the 10 x 10 case d_{max} is given by $1+9\sqrt{2}$). If, however, the sales figures are computed for ranking purposes only, c = 0 will do equally well.

---

(8) $$w_n = \sum_{(r,s)\in V_n} \sum_{m=1}^{n_a} f_{mrs} \; .^{1}$$

Employing this strategy by placing a new brand in a field with a high w_n implies a balanced behaviour with respect to the competitive and the demand aspects of

---

1 For fields divided by diagonal separation lines the corresponding shares of the fictitious sales figures have to be used.

the decision. It is a vacant area that is selected; however, this area is not necessarily the largest one, but the one with the best (or a good) position on the estimated demand mountain.

4. Estimating Expected Demand

Apart from the method described above for the valuation of vacant areas by the estimated demand mountain, which implies a global view of the brand map, another concept may be applied which is more closely related to the particular brands considered to be important for the success of a new one. From the theory of vacant area the brands are known, which by their positions define the separation lines valid in the area definition. These brands, to be called the neighbouring brands, are considered to 'protect' the area beyond the separation lines against the competitive influence of the new brand. Consequently it is a plausible hypothesis that the brands beyond these lines are not (or only to an inconsiderable extent) affected by new brands; competition can be assumed to be limited to the neighbouring brands.

By placing a new brand in the accessible area, the demand which so far accrued to the neighbouring brands can be considered to be redistributed so that the new brand also gets a share. For this share a simple definition can be given.

Let B_n denote the set of neighbouring brands for field (r_n, s_n)

(9a) $$B_n = \{m \mid (r_m, s_m) \in V_n\} \text{ ,}$$ [1]

B_n' the set of brands existing on field (r_n, s_n)

(9b) $$B_n' = \{m \mid (r_m, s_m) = (r_n, s_n)\} \text{ .}$$

Furthermore, let n_n denote the number of neighbouring brands situated around the vacant area, n_n' the number of brands on (r_n, s_n); then estimated sales x_n^* of a new brand are defined by

(10) $$x_n^* = \frac{\sum\limits_{m \in B_n} \frac{x_m}{2} + \sum\limits_{m \in B_n'} x_m}{\frac{n_n}{2} + n_n' + 1} \text{ .}$$

This definition is based on the assumption that the influence of a brand is equally spread in all directions, so that half the sales of a neighbouring brand are subject to the assumed redistribution. Since for competing brands on (r_n, s_n) the accessible area is equal to the vacant area, their total sales figures are added. The sum of all these sales is an estimate for the demand that can be distributed among the competing brands. Assuming that the new brand will absorb an average part

---

1 In the case of $V_n = \emptyset$ where at least one competing brand already exists on the field proposed for the new brand, a redefined V_n is to be used in the definition (9a). This new V_n is computed according to the normal procedure with all brands on field (r_n, s_n) considered non-existent.

of demand, the number of brands in the denominator must be augmented by one to provide for the new brand. For $B'_n = \emptyset$ relation (10) becomes

$$x^*_n = \frac{\sum_{m \in B_n} x_m}{n_n + 2} ,$$

which shows that the correction for the new brand in the denominator of (10) is relatively important, as long as there are only a few neighbouring brands on the map, but that the importance decreases with increasing number of neighbouring brands. This seems justified as the intense competition among a large number of brands is not strongly affected by the additional competitor.

This strategy is just another approach to the problem of valuing a field by its estimated competitive and demand aspects. Choosing the field with the highest possible (or a "good") x^* is a decision based on expectations and valuations which are only locally valid. Assuming that the effects of placing a new brand on the map are of minor importance to the brands beyond the neighbouring ones, and that the global effects cannot be reliably estimated, this strategy has computational advantages over the one defined in the previous chapter.

III. On the Use of the Strategies

The strategies described above are conceived as possible ways to cope with the decision situation, which is characterized by incomplete information about the slope of the demand mountain over the brand map, and about the strength of the competitive relation between a new brand and any one already existing. In the four strategies these two aspects are taken into consideration to different extents.

The imitation strategy (strategy I) is the most inactive strategy, as it requires the least computational efforts. The new brand is supposed to share the success of the brand imitated. Though the strongest competitive relation possible is established by placing a new brand on a field already occupied, this strategy should not be classified according to its competitive effects; rather it can be assumed that in spite of the consequences - possible reactions of the firms which interpret the use of this strategy by a competing firm as an act of aggression - this strategy is chosen because in the decision maker's opinion the alternatives cannot be properly valued. To avoid the risk of incorrectly estimating the demand on other fields, the field is chosen where high sales are evident.

The pure vacant area strategy (strategy II) emphasizes the competitive aspect by choosing a field which is located as far as possible away from the neighbouring competing brands. Since the shape of the vacant area, as conceived by the players, depends on their individual gestalt considerations, the problem arises as to how a measure can be defined, which on the one hand is suitable to the topological view of the map, but which on the other hand is not rendered implausible by its computational intricacy. The concept of separation lines is thought to comply with this demand, as it permits the vacant area to be measured by merely counting the whole, half, and quarter fields contained within the accessible area.

The field selected by strategy II is supposed to be least affected by competitive brands, although the question is left unanswered, what amount of demand can be expected there. In order to answer this question, estimation techniques have to be developed by using the sales figures of the competing brands. This may be done in two ways. One is to compute by means of a potential approach an estimate of the demand mountain which is used to weigh the fields contained in the vacant area. This method which is employed by strategy III implies the influence of a brand covering the whole map. As opposed to this view, strategy IV defines neighbouring brands which are thought to be the important ones with regard to the estimation procedure, because it is their sales that are directly and considerably affected. The new brand is considered to draw away as much demand from the neighbouring brands as is necessary to get an average share of the demand available in that area.

The application of these strategies implies that the decision makers explicitly or implicitly consider the basic assumptions underlying their construction to be valid. Since different degrees of reflection and experience are involved in the construction of the various measures, it could be assumed that in the beginning periods the simpler measures are preferred. Additionally, the map will most likely be occupied by only a few competing brands in these periods, so that the vacant area strategy especially is optically supported by regarding the map.

With the number of brands increasing, the amount of information necessary for an efficient use of the other strategies is growing. Since the absolute size of vacant areas necessarily decreases, the possibility arises that there are some vacant areas of quite similar size and shape which ask for additional criteria to find out which of them is to be preferred. These criteria are given by the demand estimates which can then be based on sufficient information. The selection problem can, however, produce the inverse effect, that instead of making use of additional criteria the easier way of imitating a successful brand is taken.

Since it cannot be taken for granted that the measures defined above can or will be computed exactly in an actual decision situation, the question arises, how to classify the goodness of a decision observed with respect to the strategy employed. In particular the assumption does not seem plausible that all possible fields are valued in order to find the absolutely best one for a strategy. Rather it can be assumed that the decision maker will try to find a fairly good decision by means of optically comparing alternative places on the map. At least a rough classification of the goodness of whole regions is possible without danger of largely incorrect estimation. The decision for a region decisively reduces the computational work left for the selection of a particular field. This again may be done more or less exactly, depending on the degree of accuracy with which the computational procedures are employed. It might probably prove sufficient to employ once more the technique of optical comparison, for the utmost accuracy in this second stage of the decision process would give rise to the impression of an accuracy of the whole process which does not, and is not even intented to, exist. Employing a decision procedure which follows the basic ideas of the strategies defined above without referring to their computational accuracy might prove to be a way which can be considered adequate to the actual decision situation in the model.

It follows from the previous considerations that, for the purpose of analyzing decisions actually observed, their goodness can only be ordinally defined. If, for example, a vacant area of a certain size is compared to another one of half this size, the second cannot be expected to have exactly half the expected demand of the first. Therefore the strategy measures can only be used as ordinal ones; for reasons of simplicity they are transformed into a ranking scale, numbering by 1 the best field, by 100 the poorest one.[1] Thus each case of placing a new brand on the map is characterized by four rank numbers, one for each of the strategies.

Since the decision makers are not supposed to have ranked all fields on the map but rather have compared whole regions in the first stage of the selecting process, the actual ordering scale cannot be expected to be equally detailed. Consequently a decision classified as good cannot on the average be expected to have a rank very close to the first rank of the detailed scale. Rather will it lie in a certain range around it, the extension of which depends on the number of ranks on the rough scale as compared to the complete one.

---

1 According to the definition of the strategies it is sometimes inevitable that tied ranks occur. In these cases the mean rank of the ties is assigned to each of the fields concerned.

*IV. Results**

It is the aim of the following tests to analyze whether at all and to what extent the statistic material supports the hypothesis that the strategies above have been used in the actual experimental decision making. The sample sizes - 35 for the initial period and 165 for the other periods - are the respective numbers of observed introductions of new brands in the map. The basic material consists of the frequency distribution of cases observed for the initial period, and of the frequency distributions of the ranks assigned to each of the other cases with respect to the four strategies. To specify the questions the statistical tests are to give an answer to:

- does the frequency distribution of the initial period show a concentration of cases in the peak region?
- do the frequency distributions of the other periods show an accumulation of cases with low ranks beyond the scope that could have randomly occurred?
- does it prove sufficient to explain each of these cases by the use of its dominant strategy?

In order to answer the first question, which is of the binomial type, the number of cases falling into the peak region has to be compared to the number of cases which do not. For the second question the means and frequency distributions observed for the strategy ranks have to be

* The author is indebted to Zentrales Recheninstitut der Johann Wolfgang Goethe-Universität, Frankfurt/Main, which provided for the computer capacity necessary for this evaluation program.

compared with the corresponding test distribution. For the third question a new frequency distribution is to be constructed by assigning the dominant strategy to each case as the only one to have been valid in the decision. The construction and properties of the test distributions are given in the appendix.

1. Testing the Initial Strategy

As was pointed out earlier, the decision situation in the first period is quite different from that in later periods. The strategies developed above are not applicable here, because they are meaningful only in relation to competing brands already existing. Because of the absence of brands, the strategy variables yield the same result for all 100 places of the map (the vacant area measure is 100, the other three measures 0, respectively). Therefore an ordering of alternatives is impossible which clearly rules out the usefulness of the strategies in this period.
The strategy to be used in this period can only be based on the initial information given to the decision maker about the position of the demand peak. Following the previous discussion in an earlier chapter, the decision makers are likely to have tried to occupy the peak region. Since this region has not been exactly specified as to position, size, and shape, the frequency distribution of the cases observed may be expected to show a cluster of cases below and to the right of the map's central point, deviations from the mode being due to the fact that expectations differed as to which field exactly represents the peak. A closer view of Figure 4 reveals that the square with the corner fields

Figure 4: Frequency Distribution of Initial Cases in the Brand Map*

	0	1	2	3	4	5	6	7	8	9
0										
1										
2									1^{++}	
3								1		
4					1^{+}		1			
5						2	1			
6						1	10^{+}	6		
7					1^{++}	1	5	2	1	
8									1	
9										

* The fields marked by + and ++ contain one case each which is part of a pair of brands introduced simultaneously by one firm.

(5,5), (5,7), (7,5), and (7,7), which constitutes 1/11 of the area of the map, contains 6/7 of the brands introduced in the first period. Disregarding the cases of the simultaneous introduction of two brands by one firm, where at least one brand has been placed apart in order to avoid competition between one's own brands, there are only two cases not below and none not to the right of the central point of the map. It is obvious that the assumption of a uniform distribution over the map does not hold. However, by means of a binomial test the null hypothesis, that the number of cases is equally divided into cases falling into the peak region and cases not doing so must be rejected at the .0005 level of significance in favor of the hypothesis, that the proportion of cases falling into the peak region is significantly higher.

2. Testing the Single Strategies

The null hypothesis to be stated for the test is that each of the rank numbers assigned to the 165 cases of the normal period has been randomly drawn from a uniformly distributed population of numbers
$r = 1,2,\ldots,100$ with mean $\bar{r} = 50.5$ and variance
$\sigma^2 = 833.25$.[1] Under the null hypothesis the mean of observed ranks should be expected to be within the range specified by the sampling distribution of the mean. Since the actual mean is expected to be below the expected value, one-tailed probabilities for the occurrence of the means observed must be computed. With a sample size of 165 the sampling distribution is considered to be approximately normally distributed with variance $\frac{\sigma^2}{165} = 5.05$. The following table shows the means observed for the strategies including some selected parametric variations for the estimate of the demand mountain in strategy III.
The exact probability as computed from the convolution of the uniform distribution for the mean to be 41.5 or less is given by .00025, so the null hypothesis can be rejected at this level for strategies I, II, IV and III with $\alpha > 0$. As to the strategies III with $\alpha \leq -1$ corresponding to the cone-shaped and dome-shaped types of the sales mountain surface they obviously show a majo-

1 See Appendix.

Strategy		Mean
I		40.0
II		41.4
III	α = -2	57.9
	α = -1	60.3
	α = 1	35.6
	α = 2	34.8
IV		38.6

rity of poor ranks. Thus the validity of the tent-shaped type of surface can be established. By comparing the two relevant means, no clear dominance of one of the parameters can be seen; it is, however, noteworthy that the result of the prominent α = 1 approach seems to support its theoretical importance. After the hypothesis of randomness of the rank means is rejected, a closer look at the frequency distributions is appropriate to discuss their formal properties. The distributions are supposed to be at least unimodal. Since low (good) ranks are supposed to prevail, they are expected to be skewed to the right. An exception can be expected for the vacant area strategy. By definition (4) a vacant area of size zero is given for each brand placed on a field which is already occupied; these cases which correspond to the imitation strategy whenever successful brands are concerned, will always be at the end of the ranking scale. The relation between imitation and vacant area grows weaker when the degree of imitation decreases; if, however, the imitation strategy is applied often enough, a second local mode is due to arise. This might be true, too, for the relation of the vacant area strategy to strategy III. Weighing the vacant area will sometimes lead to the selection of a field which has, as seen by the pure vacant area, only a medium position on the ranking scale. Therefore, in the centre, a third mode might possibly arise. Thus the pure vacant area frequency distribution might prove trimodal which makes this measure a fairly universal one for a general review of the strategy situation.

The modes and skewness of the distributions cannot be expected to arise purely in the detailed scale; rather, they should be subject to random deviations due to the fact that the actual decisions were guided by a rough scale which can only be approximated by combining the ranks of the detailed scale into a smaller number of groups. Figure 5 shows the bar charts of the four frequency distributions with ranks aggregated in groups of ten ranks each. The above expectations are approximately confirmed; although the aggregation has already smoothed some irregularities of a more detailed graphical representation, some minor modes still exist. Only the vacant area strategy is purely trimodal as was expected. For all strategies the skewness to the right is evident.

In order to test whether this skewness lies beyond the scope of randomness, the test value

$$T = \sum_{g=1}^{g_o} \frac{(n_g - e_g)^2}{e_g}$$

is computed, where g_o denotes the number of groups, n_g the number of cases falling into group g, and e_g the expected number of cases under the null hypothesis. Since the test is performed against the uniform distri-

Figure 5: Frequency Distributions of Single Strategies

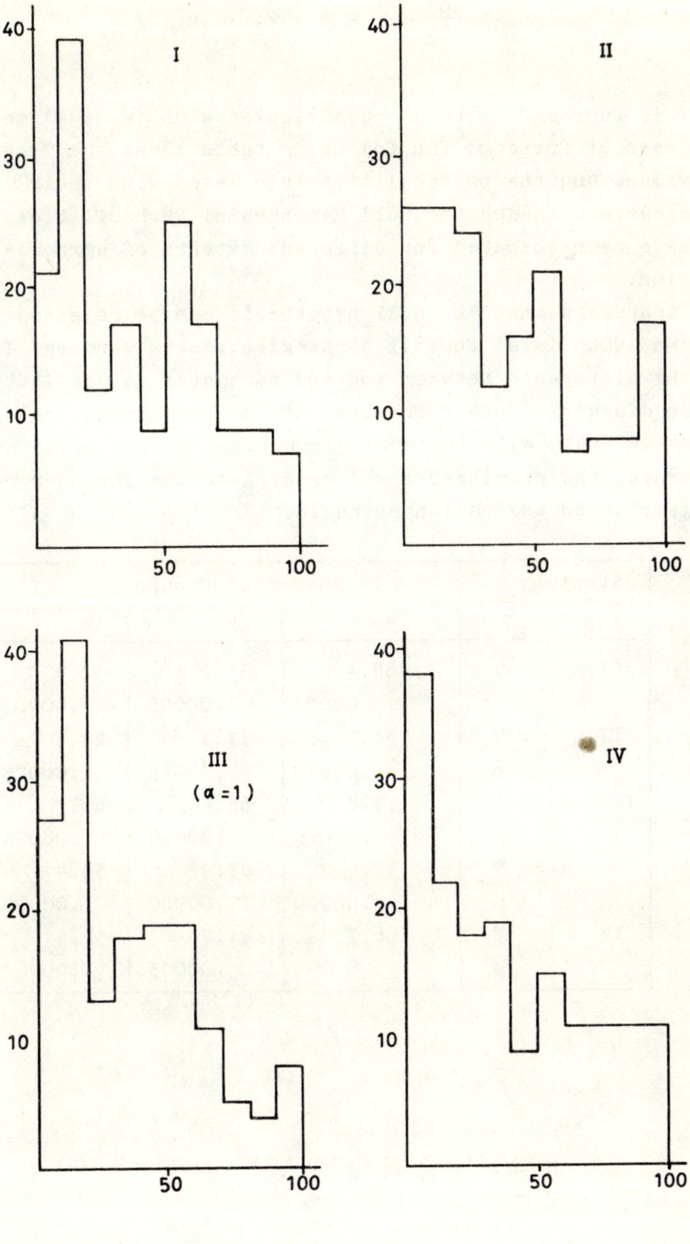

bution, e_g is defined by

$$e_g = \frac{165}{g_o} , \quad g = 1,2,\ldots,g_o \quad .$$

T is supposed to be χ^2 -distributed with (g_o - 1) degrees of freedom. The following table shows the T-values and the probabilities associated with their occurrence under the null hypothesis. Probabilities have been computed for different extents of aggregation.

It appears that the null hypothesis can be rejected at the .0005 level for all strategies. As to strategy III, the difference between the two parameter values left in discussion after the test of the rank means indicates that, with increasing roughness of the ordering scale, the prominent α = 1 case gives the stronger rejection to the null hypothesis.

Strategy			Number of Groups		
			20	10	5
I		T	65.4	53.2	32.8
		p	.00001	.00000	.00002
II		T	48.2	31.1	23.5
		p	.00040	.00049	.00025
III	α=1	T	77.8	68.4	60.1
		p	.00000	.00000	.00000
	α=2	T	82.9	67.9	54.4
		p	.00000	.00000	.00000
IV		T	56.7	41.2	32.4
		p	.00005	.00003	.00002

It may be concluded that all tests show a highly significant rejection of the hypothesis that the valuation by ranks of cases observed in relation to the strategies defined could have randomly occurred. As to the estimated parameters in strategy III it can be seen that the most simple one, $\alpha = 1$, which means a spreading of sales over the map inversely proportional to distance, gives the best result of the values tested.

3. Testing the Selected Strategies

The results of the tests for randomness of the frequency distributions for the four strategies support the hypothesis that these strategies have been of importance to the quality decisions. This does not, however, tell much about the share the basic considerations of each strategy might have had in the individual case.
By combining two adjacent bars of the frequency distributions given in Figure 5, five groups are established, each containing 20 ranks. This number of groups gives the roughest scaling of decisions appropriate, since reducing it further would eliminate the trimodal shape of the vacant area distribution. The group of best decisions contains about one third of the cases observed with the remaining two thirds spread among the other four groups. Since not all of them can be classified as poor, it may be stated that there exist brands which are good as to one strategy, and at the same time not poor as to others.
Here the question arises whether these cases are the result of the deliberate use of a strategy mix, or

whether decisions are based on one strategy without considering its goodness with respect to the other ones. The former assumption does not seem plausible. Taking into account that it is nearly impossible to reliably estimate the effects of a single strategy, this is all the more true for a strategy mix. Therefore it seems appropriate to assume that each decision is purely (mainly) based on one strategy, to be called the dominant strategy. All new brands introduced into the market can then be classified according to their dominant strategy.
This strategy is defined to be the one with regard to which the lowest of all ranks is valid. By assigning the best rank achieved to each case observed[1] a new frequency distribution arises. This can be used for testing the hypothesis that the decision behavior observed can be explained by the selection of a single strategy according to which a good field on the map is then to be decided upon.
The null hypothesis to be stated for the test is that the selected rank numbers assigned to the 165 cases have been randomly drawn from a population of numbers $r = 1,2,\ldots,100$. The probability distribution of r is given by the distribution of the minimum of four uniformly distributed numbers $r_i (i=1,\ldots,4)$ with mean $\bar{r}(4) \approx 20.5$ and variance $\sigma^2(4) \approx 266.6$.[2] Since the actual mean is expected to be below the expected value, the one-tailed probability for the occurrence of a value as small as the actual 17.9 must be computed. The convolution of the minimum distribution shows that the null hypothesis is to be rejected at the .025 level, which is a much weaker rejection than that used in the

1 For strategy III the $\alpha = 1$ type is chosen.

2 See Appendix.

case of the single strategies.
In order to support the rejection decision, a closer view of the frequency distribution as given in Figure 6 is necessary. The theoretical distribution being skewed to the right, the empirical distribution is expected to show even more of the good ranks.

Figure 6: Frequency Distribution of Selected Strategies

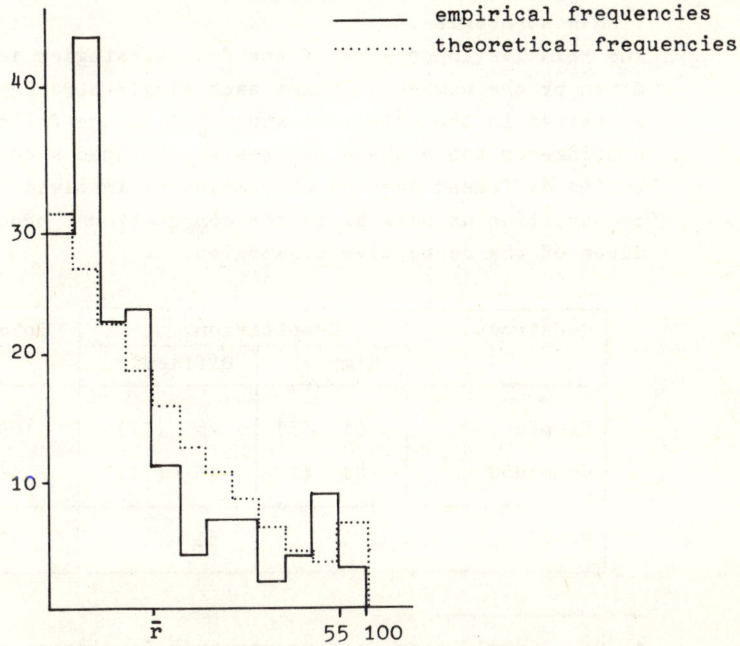

With the minor exception of the first bar, this assumption holds below the mean of the distribution, while beyond it actual frequencies are below the theoretical ones with exception of the group containing ranks 51-55; the poorest ranks have been combined in one group in order to meet the minimum requirements of the χ^2-test for the expected frequencies.[1] The T-value, as defined in the previous chapter, is 35.1; the probability of its occurrence under the null hypothesis as given by the χ^2-distribution with 11 degrees of freedom is .0004. This permits the rejection of the null hypothesis at the same level as was used for the single strategies.

The relative importance of the four strategies is given by the number of times each single strategy is contained in the selection strategy. In the following contingency table these numbers are grouped according to the different degrees of complexity involved in the construction as well as in the computational procedures of the respective strategies.

Construction	Computation		Total
	Simple	Difficult	
Simple	61 (I)	48 (II)	109
Compound	41 (IV)	15 (III)	56
Total	102	63	165

1 Cf. Siegel, Sidney: Nonparametric Statistics for the Behavioral Sciences, New York, Toronto, London 1966, p. 46.

The table shows that the pure strategies, classified as simple because they refer to only one aspect of the decision problem, have been selected nearly twice as much as the two-aspect strategies. On the other hand the strategies, which can be computed in a simple way, are preferred to the more difficult ones. By means of the two-sample-χ^2-test this preference can be shown to be significantly stronger for the compound strategies at the .05 level.

Conclusions

It has been the purpose of this paper to analyze the quality decisions in the SINTO game. The model being characterized by incomplete information, oligopolistic interdependence, and two-dimensionality as to the taste characteristics - the main factors influencing demand preferences - the exact relations of the model are not known to the decision makers. The strategies they are supposed to have used in order to make good decisions are stated in terms of a brand map which permits the introduction of a plausible topological meaning to the strategies.

The strategies are classified according to the extent to which they refer to the demand and competitive aspects of the quality problem as well as to the amount of computational efforts required for their employment. After assigning a measure of goodness to each decision observed, some tests are performed in order to analyze whether the observed goodness could be random. This hypothesis can generally be rejected at a high level of significance so as to permit the following conclusions:

- all strategies defined are of importance in the decisions observed,
- it is sufficient to assume each decision to be based on its dominant strategy only,
- simple strategies are preferred to complex ones.

Appendix: Probability Distribution of the Minimum of n Uniformly Distributed Random Numbers

Let r be a uniformly distributed random number with possible realisations $1,2,\dots,r_o$ and probabilities $\frac{1}{r_o}$ each.
Drawing a random number n times the probability that r will be the minimum value achieved is given by the difference of the probabilities for achieving at least r and achieving at least r+1

$$p(r:r=\min_i r_i;\ i=1,2,\dots,n) = \frac{1}{r_o^n}\,[(r_o+1-r)^n-(r_o-r)^n].$$

The expected value as defined by

$$\bar{r}(n) = E(r) = \frac{1}{r_o^n}\sum_r r\,[(r_o+1-r)^n - (r_o-r)^n]$$

can easily be seen to be

$$\bar{r}(n) = \frac{1}{r_o^n}\sum_r r^n\ .$$

The variance as defined by

$$\sigma^2(n) = E[r-E(r)]^2 = \sum_r p(r)\,r^2 - E^2(r) =$$

$$= \frac{1}{r_o^n} \sum_r r^2[(r_o+1-r)^n - (r_o-r)^n] - \bar{r}^2(n) =$$

$$= \frac{1}{r_o^n} \sum_r [r^2-(r-1)^2] [r_o+1-r]^n - \bar{r}^2(n) =$$

$$= (r_o+1) \frac{2}{r_o^n} \sum_r r^n - \frac{2}{r_o^n} \sum_r r^{n+1} - \frac{1}{r_o^n} \sum_r r^n - \bar{r}^2(n)$$

can be shown to depend on the two means $\bar{r}(n)$ and $\bar{r}(n+1)$, i.e.

$$\sigma^2(n) = 2r_o[\bar{r}(n) - \bar{r}(n+1)] + \bar{r}(n)[1-\bar{r}(n)] .$$

From these relations simple formulae for mean and variance can easily be given for small n, e.g.

$$\bar{r}(1) = \tfrac{1}{2}(r_o+1) \; ; \; \sigma^2(1) = \tfrac{1}{12}(r_o^2-1) .$$

For the computation of $\sigma^2(4)$ the two means

$$\bar{r}(4) = \frac{(r_o+1)(2r_o+1)}{30r_o^3} (3r_o^2 + 3r_o - 1)$$

and

$$\bar{r}(5) = \frac{(r_o+1)^2}{12r_o^3} (2r_o^2 + 2r_o - 1)$$

may be inserted into the formula above.

21. THE EFFICIENT DETERMINATION OF TRUE PREFERENCE EQUIVALENCES*

MASANAO TODA*** AND KENNETH R. MACCRIMMON**

1. Equivalences in Studies of Preference

In studies of preference in economics and psychology we need to know equivalences for various sure or risky prospects. Consumer demand theory in economics is based upon the map of equivalences among commodity bundles, i.e., the indifference map. Expected utility theory requires the certainty equivalences for lotteries. Unfortunately, many experimental techniques for ascertaining equivalences are either inefficient or non-motivating. In addition, there has been both theoretical and experimental confusion about the type of equivalence determined, due to a disregard of the decision maker's existing state. In this paper we distinguish between the various kinds of equivalences and provide an efficient general method for ascertaining them, which we prove induces true equivalences.

Existing methods for obtaining equivalences can be characterized as either "direct" or "indirect". With direct methods we attempt to get the equivalence with

---

* This paper appeared earlier as: Working Paper 85-69-7, April 1970, Graduate School of Industrial Administration, Carnegie-Mellon University, Pittsburgh, Pa. 15213.

** University of British Columbia.

*** Hokkaido University.

a single response, in that the decision maker is asked to choose from a list, or to construct for himself, an alternative (i.e., the equivalence) indifferent to a given alternative (see, for example, Grayson |1960| and Swalm |1966|). With indirect methods we usually ask the decision maker to choose his more preferred alternative from a number of pairs presented to him. Each choice yields an inequality and from the system of inequalities, one can infer equality or indifference (see, for example, Davidson, Suppes, with Siegel |1957| and Becker |1962|). This distinction is similar to the direct preference implied by Marshall |1890|, Pareto |1906| and others, and the indirect "revealed preference" approach of Samuelson |1938|. It is also similar to the method of adjustment and the method of constant stimuli in psychophysics. There is a big difference, however, from the form of the alternative presented to the subject in psychophysical experiments. In such contexts the subject is usually given an alternative varying along a single dimension, such as apparent brightness or size, and is readily perceived as a single gestalt. In decision theoretic experiments, consisting of bundles of wagers, a great amount of effort must usually be devoted to the formation of a single gestalt. Conscientious choice of decision theoretic alternatives, then, imposes cognitive strains on a subject. This is particularly true of the indirect method which requires more choices than the direct, and so is at more of a relative disadvantage than its psychophysical counterpart, the method of constant stimuli. Even the direct method is more demanding than its counterpart, the method of adjustment, because of the more complex alternatives. Consequently, we do not want to solely rely on the response-contingent payoff in most psychophysical experiments, the subject's self-satisfaction from being conscientious. The indirect method has the relative advantage of making it easier to compensate the subject, by making his payoff dependent on his choices in some of the pairs.

It should be apparent that a particularly useful procedure in decision theoretic experiments would be one that used the lesser number of judgments of the direct method while incorporating a payoff mechanism such as used with indirect methods. In this paper we shall study such a procedure. We call it the "equivalence dominance" procedure (ED) since its principal characteristics are to form the payoffs in such a way as to make the subject's true equivalence dominate any other possible response and to do this with the efficiency of the direct methods. A simpler form of this procedure was used in utility experiments by Becker, DeGroot, and Marschak |1964|.

Confusion and incorrect conclusions can arise when the types of equivalences being measured are not clearly specified. In the simpliest case, if we think of a decision maker with a stock of one commodity (perhaps lotteries) and a stock of cash, we can distinguish between his cash equivalence for buying another unit of the commodity and his cash equivalence for selling a unit he holds. Beyond this, however, if he is offered a unit of the commodity as a gift, we might ascertain the equivalent cash amount he would take in lieu of the commodity gift. In describing the ED procedure, we shall initially restrict our attention to the buying equivalence, and then later will show that the results also hold for selling and gift equivalences, and also for combinations of all three. Obviously, we do not have to restrict ourselves to the determination of cash equivalences for a commodity (or lottery), we could equally well obtain the commodity (or lottery) equivalence for some unit amount of cash - or even some other commodity. For descriptive ease, we shall confine our discussion to cash equivalences but the reader should be aware of the generality of the procedures.

The ED - Buying (ED - B) procedure is as follows: The subject is offered the option of buying a fixed amount of a certain commodity for a particular price. The price, however, is a random variable and its value will be randomly selected from a fixed domain according to a particular probability distribution. Before the price is selected the subject is asked to state a maximum buying price. After the price has been selected it is compared with the announced maximum buying price. If the price is less than or equal to the maximum buying price a deal is made, namely, the subject obtains the commodity for the price selected. If the price is greater than the subject's maximum buying price no deal is made, and the subject retains his status quo. This procedure is described to the subject, he is told that it will only be performed one time and that no bargaining is allowed.

In section 3 we shall prove that in order to maximize expected utility the subject should give his true buying equivalence as the "maximum buying price." First, however, in section 2 we shall present a brief survey of the expected utility theory we need, making use of notation that explicitly accounts for the subject's existing state. In sections 4 and 5 we shall consider some extensions of the basic procedure.

2. Personal State Form of Expected Utility

In an expected utility approach to decision problems the basic elements are actions, events and consequences. The <u>actions</u> are under the control of the decision maker (i.e., the subject), while the <u>events</u> are uncontrollable by him (and in experiments are often controlled by the experimenter). The <u>consequence</u> of the decision to the decision maker is jointly determined by the action he takes and by the event that occurs. For example, the events may be a head or a tail occuring on the toss of a coin, while the actions may be wagers such as "receive a pastry if head, receive nothing if tail" or "receive $1.00 if head, pay $1.00 if tail." The consequence of choosing the first wager and a head occuring is "receiving a pastry", the other consequences are specified in a similar manner.
The decision maker's personal valuation for "receiving a pastry", and thus the correctness of our predictions of his choices, may depend to a considerable extent on how hungry he is at the time of choice. Similarly his utility for money gain or loss may depend on his current financial status. In general, then, we should consider those aspects of the decision maker's <u>personal state</u> that can be expected to influence the utility he attaches to particular consequences he may receive.

When personal states are explicitly noted, then it should be clear that a consequence has the effect of moving the decision maker from a prior state to a posterior state. For example, "receiving a pastry" moves a subject from a state of "being hungry" to a state of "possessing a pastry when hungry." Thus, the utility of the consequence is determined by the change in utility from the prior to the posterior state. This emphasis on the importance of a particular origin is not unique to this study, being in the spirit of the origin based on current or customary wealth in the studies by Friedman and Savage |1948, 1952| and Markowitz |1952|. Here, though, we also would want to consider physiological, emotional and other factors in addition to financial position. In any case, the utility function itself is of the usual form, i.e., unique up to a positive linear transformation.

Let us set these notions forth in notation we shall use in the remaining sections. Let $A \equiv \{a\}$ be the set of actions available to the decision maker, $E \equiv \{e\}$ be the set of events relevant to, but not controllable by him, and $C \equiv \{c\}$ be the set of consequences, where $c = \rho(a,e)$. That is, the selection of a particular action and the occurrence of a particular event leads, under the consequence function ρ, to a particular consequence. Let S_i be his personal state (defined in terms of the relevant aspects) at time i, then receiving a consequence c while in state S_i leads to a new state S_{i+1}. That is, $S_{i+1} = \tau(c, S_i)$ where τ is the state transformation function. Clearly, the new state can be written in an extended fashion as $S_{i+1} = \tau(\rho(a,e), S_i)$. A utility function, u, is defined mapping from the set of personal states to the real line. The utility of state S_i is written as $u(S_i)$ while the net utility gain in going from S_i to S_{i+1} is $u(S_{i+1}) - u(S_i)$. This net gain can be attributed to the consequence that occured and so it is natural to speak of the utility of consequence c (leading from S_i to S_{i+1}) as $u(S_{i+1}) - u(S_i)$ and to write it as $u(c|S_i)$. The conditionality on S_i must be included since the same apparent consequence connecting two distinct states might have a quite different utility.

In a similar way we can derive an expected utility for an action by valuing it according to expected net utility gain from the posterior states it yields. If action a from state S_i leads to states S_{i+1}^j due to the respective events e_j, which have subjective probability $p(e_j)$, then for the discrete case we write

$$(1)\quad EU(a|S_i) = \sum_j \rho(e_j)\left[u(S_{i+1}^j) - u(S_i)\right].$$

Here also the conditionality on prior state S_i must be explicitly recognized. Expression (1) may be rewritten in terms of utility of consequences as

$$(2)\quad EU(a|S_i) = \sum_j p(e_j) \cdot u(c_j|S_i)$$

where $c_j = (a, e_j)$. When the probability distribution is continuous this may be written as

$$(3)\quad EU(a|S_i) = \int_E p(e)\ u(c|S_i)de = \int_E p(e)\ u(\rho(a,e)|S_i)de$$

We assume that in any given state the decision maker maximizes expected utility. That is, he selects that a^* such that

$$(4)\quad EU(a^*|S_i) = \max_a \int_E p(e)\ u(\rho(a,e)|S_i)de$$

In experiments, the experimenter would specify {a}, the set of available actions, and {e}, the set of events influencing payoffs. The subject's own value system specifies the function u, while his set of beliefs specifies p. While the experimenter by providing or withholding information may be able to affect u and p somewhat, his main control comes from his discretion in choosing particular individuals as subjects in his experiments. For example, the typical use of college sophomores might imply some restricted set of u's and p's to be observed. Similarly, selection procedures can be used to get particular values of the subject's prior personal state S_0. In addition, though, the experimenter can influence the prior state more directly by specifying conditions on participating in the experiment. For example, by requesting that the subject not eat before the experiment he may be able to assure the state "being hungry", or by providing the subject with a particular number of units of some commodity the experimenter may establish a desired stock of the commodity to be initially held by the subject.

3. *The Equivalence Dominance Procedure - Buying*

In this section we shall show that the equivalence dominance procedure -buying induces a true equivalence that maximizes expected utility. Let us restate the ED-B procedure as follows:

> The subject is offered the option of buying a fixed amount, y, of a particular commodity for a price, x. The price x is a random variable selected from $|\underline{x}, \bar{x}|$ according to distribution $f(\cdot)$. Before the price selection, the subject names his maximum buying price x_b. If $x \leq x_b$, the subject obtains y and gives up x. If $x > x_b$, the subject retains his status quo.

Let us denote the prior state as S_0, consisting of initial holdings of the commodity, y_0, and initial holdings of cash x_0, and the remaining aspects r_0 which we assume stay unchanged over the course of the exchange dealings.

The events over which the person has no control are the values of x in the interval $|\underline{x}, \bar{x}|$. Let us initially assume that the subjective probability density, $p(\cdot)$, over $|\underline{x}, \bar{x}|$ is continuous. The subjective probability density, $p(\cdot)$, need not be identical to the "objective" probability density, $f(\cdot)$, used to generate the asking price.

The possible actions are the possible levels at which the maximum buying price, x_b, may be set. These levels may be any non-negative number not exceeding x_0. The consequences for setting a maximum buying price, x_b, are:

$$(5) \qquad \rho(x_b, x) = \begin{cases} (-x, y) & \text{if } x \leq x_b \\ (0,0) & \text{if } x > x_b \end{cases}$$

The utility for the consequences is written as $u(-x, y|S_0)$ and $u(0,0|S_0)$, respectively. By a cash equivalent for a commodity amount, y, we mean a cash value x_b^* such that:

$$(6) \qquad u(-x_b^*, y|S_0) = u(0, 0|S_0).$$

We wish to show that the optimal choice for a maximum buying price is the value for which $x_b = x_b^*$ in that it is for only this action that expected utility is maximized. Thus we state,

Theorem 1:

Given (1) $u(-x_b, y|S_0)$ is monotone decreasing in x_b,

(2) $u(-x_b, y|S_0) = u(0,0|S_0)$ has a solution in the domain of x_b,

(3) $p(\cdot)$ is positive in a finite neighborhood of x_b^*,

$$EU(x_b = x_b^*|S_0) = \max_{x_b} \int_{\underline{x}}^{\bar{x}} p(x)\, u(\rho(x_b, x)|S_0)dx \tag{7}$$

if, and only if, $u(-x_b^*, y|S_0) = u(0,0|S_0)$.

Proof:

For any x_b such that $\underline{x} \leq x_b < x_b^*$,

$$EU(x_b|S_0)=\int_{\underline{x}}^{x_b} p(x)u(-x,y|S_0)dx+\int_{x_b}^{x_b^*} p(x)u(0,0|S_0)dx + \int_{x_b^*}^{\bar{x}} p(x)u(0,0|S_0)dx \tag{8}$$

Likewise,

$$EU(x_b^*|S_0)=\int_{\underline{x}}^{x_b} p(x)u(-x,y|S_0)dx+\int_{x_b}^{x_b^*} p(x)u(-x,y|S_0)dx + \int_{x_b^*}^{\bar{x}} p(x)u(0,0|S_0)dx$$

Then,

$$EU(x_b^*|S_0)-EU(x_b|S_0)=\int_{x_b}^{x_b^*} p(x)[u(-x,y|S_0)-u(0,0|S_0)]dx \tag{9}$$

Within this integral domain the integrand is non-negative by assumption (1), and the integral itself is positive by assumption (3).
Analogously, for any x_b such that $x_b^* < x_b \le \bar{x}$,

$$(10)\quad EU(x_b^*|S_0)-EU(x_b|S_0)=\int_{x_b^*}^{x_b} p(x)|u(0,0|S_0)-u(-x,y|S_0)|dx$$

is positive.
Therefore, $x_b = x_b^*$ gives the unique maximum of

$EU(x_b|S_0)$. QED.

The proof indicates why the method is called the equivalence <u>dominance</u> procedure. Consider the conditional utilities reproduced in Table 1. The equality and inequality signs between the lines indicate the size of the relative utility values. Note that $x_b = x_b^*$ <u>strictly dominates</u> any $x_b < x_b^*$ and any $x_b > x_b^*$, and thus the "equivalent" response is the dominant one.

Table 1. Conditional utilities

Actions \ Events	$\underline{x}\le x\le x_{b,low}$	$x_{b,low}<x<x_b^*$	$x = x_b^*$	$x_b^*<x\le x_{b,high}$	$x_{b,high}<x\le\bar{x}$
$x_{b,low}$: $x_b<x^*$	$u(-x,y\|S_0)$	$u(0,0\|S_0)$	$u(0,0\|S_0)$	$u(0,0\|S_0)$	$u(0,0\|S_0)$
	$\|\|$	$\wedge$	$\|\|$	$\|\|$	$\|\|$
$x_b = x_b^*$	$u(-x,y\|S_0)$	$u(-x,y\|S_0)$	$u(-x,y\|S_0)$	$u(0,0\|S_0)$	$u(0,0\|S_0)$
	$\|\|$	$\|\|$	$\|\|$	$\vee$	$\|\|$
$x_{b,high}$: $x_b>x^*$	$u(-x,y\|S_0)$	$u(-x,y\|S_0)$	$u(-x,y\|S_0)$	$u(-x,y\|S_0)$	$u(0,0\|S_0)$

Let us now examine the conditions stated in Theorem 1 and show that they are not as restrictive as they might seem:

<u>Condition (1)</u>:

The purpose of condition (1) is to force a unique solution. If the utility function was just monotone non-increasing then we would have a multiple point or band solution. Any point in this solution band satisfies expressions (6) and (7). In experiments we would expect to observe examples of such "imperfect discrimination" but would hope that the subject would learn to discriminate more finely with practice.

<u>Condition (2)</u>:

We must be assured that a solution to $u(-x,y|S_0) = u(0,0|S_0)$ exists. This will be satisfied when $u(-x_b,y|S_0)$ is continuous. Further the solution must satisfy $0 \leq x_b \leq x_0$. As long as the commodity is desirable and a saturation level has not been reached we can be sure $x_b > 0$. This can be controlled in experiments by the choice of commodities and the level allowed to the subject. It might be more difficult to assure that $x_b \leq x_0$ since the subject may feel that the amount y is worth more to him than his current cash holdings, x_0. In this case also, the experimenter, by considering the subject's level of cash and roughly estimating an appropriate valuation of units of commodity, has control by either raising the level of x_0 or lowering the level, y.

<u>Condition (3)</u>:

The assumption of finite density $p(x_b^*)$ may be violated when x_b^* is in the interval $[\underline{x}, \bar{x}]$ or when x_b^* is outside this interval. In the first case, by choosing a density $f(\cdot)$ spread over the whole interval the experimenter can reasonably expect that the subject's personal probability density $p(\cdot)$ will have finite probability around any value in the interval. For this reason, a uniform distribution is a good, although not required, choice. In the case where the true equivalence is outside $[\underline{x}, \bar{x}]$, the subject would give either $\underline{x}$ or $\bar{x}$ as his maximum buying price. Again the experimenter has control over the interval chosen, and so should choose an interval $[\underline{x}, \bar{x}]$ which he is relatively certain will contain x_b^*. Making the domain too large, however, will reduce the penalty of a sub-optimal response as we shall now show.

In order to gain further insight into our equivalence determining procedure, let us examine the loss function for setting $x_b \neq x_b^*$. Let $d \equiv x_b^* - x_b$ and note the loss $L(d|S_0)$ is

$$(11) \qquad L(d|S_0) = EU(x_b^*\ S_0) - EU(x_b|S_0)$$

Let us assume that $d \geq 0$ (i.e., $x_b^* > x_b$) without loss of generality. Then from Table 1 we have

$$(12) \quad L(d|S_0)=\int_{x_b}^{x_b^*} p(x)u(-x,y|S_0)dx \ \int_{x_b}^{x_b^*} p(x)u(0,0|S_0)dx$$

For simplicity, let us select the status quo as the origin of the utility function, that is

$$(13) \qquad u(0,0|S_0) = 0$$

Then the loss can be expressed as

$$(14) \qquad L(d|S_0) = \int_{x_b}^{x_b^*} p(x)\ u(-x,y|S_0)dx$$

An interesting special case occurs when the subjective probability density is uniform, i.e.,

(15) $p(x) = \frac{1}{r}$ where $r = \bar{x} - \underline{x}$,

and the utility $u(-x,y|S_0)$ is linear in money. We state the latter assumption as $u(-x,y|S_0) = -ax + b$ where a and b are functions of y and S_0, and $a > 0$. Furthermore, if we note

(16) $u(-x_b^*, y|S_0) = 0$

by (6) and (13), then we have

(17) $u(-x,y|S_0) = a(x_b^* - x)$

By substituting (15) and (17) into (14) we have, for the present special case

(18) $L(d|S_0) = \int_{x_b}^{x_b^*} \frac{1}{r}a(x_b^*-x)dx = \frac{-a}{2r}(x_b^*-x)^2 \Big|_{x_b}^{x_b^*} = \frac{ad^2}{2r}$

Thus, if the subject has a uniform subjective probability density and a linear utility for money in the domain we are dealing with, then the method has a quadratic loss function. Note that the loss is inversely proportional to the range, r, and so, as mentioned earlier, making the range too large will cut down the loss accruing to non-optimal responses.

The ED-B procedure discussed above ascertains only one equivalence at a time. That is, a commodity amount, y, is specified and its cash equivalence, x_b^*, is obtained. The procedure can be easily generalized, however, to simultaneously measure multiple equivalences. Let $y_1,y_2,\ldots,y_n$

be different amounts of the commodity, where without loss of generality $y_1 < y_2 < \ldots < y_n$. The commodity will be sold to the subject in one of these n alternative amounts. The exact amount to be offered will be determined by some random procedure. Before learning the exact amount for sale, the subject is asked to give his maximum buying price for each possible amount, with the terms of the deal to be determined as previously. Clearly, as long as only one amount will be offered for sale, the simultaneous choices will have no cumulative effect, and the maximum buying price for each possible amount can readily be shown to be the true cash equivalence for that amount. In this manner we obtain the multiple equivalence relations

$$(19)\quad u(0,0|S_0) = u(-x^*_{1b},y,|S_0) = u(-x^*_{2b},y_2|S_0) = \ldots$$
$$= u(-x^*_{nb},y_n|S_0)$$

We can represent these equivalences by a single indifference curve through the prior state $S_0 = (x_0,y_0)$, as in Figure 1. As long as we confine our attention to buying (positive) amounts of the commodity we will only get points on the indifference curve above (x_0, y_0). In order to obtain points below this prior state, we need a "selling" version of the ED procedure, and this will be described in the next section. Still other versions with indifference curves that do not go through the prior state will be examined in section 5.

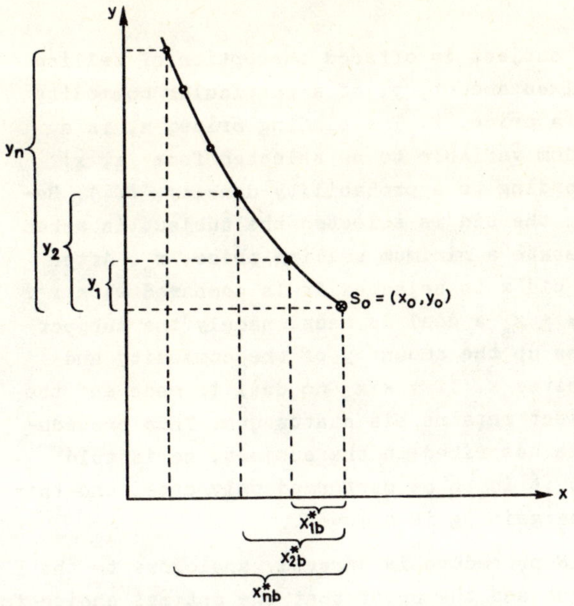

Figure 1: Indifference curve obtained from the ED-B procedure

4. Combined Buying and Selling Equivalences, and Their Graphical Representation

In order to obtain the part of the indifference curve below S_0, we need to change the signs of x and y. This results in a different interpretation of the procedure in that buying a negative amount of commodity for a negative price actually means that the subject is selling a positive amount of the commodity from his current holdings. Accordingly, this version is called the ED-Selling (ED-S) and can be stated as follows:

> The subject is offered the option of selling a fixed amount, y, of a particular commodity for a price, x. The bidding price, x, is a random variable to be selected from $|\underline{x}, \bar{x}|$ according to a probability density, f(·). Before the bid is selected the subject is asked to state a minimum selling price, x_s. After the bid x is selected it is compared with x_s. If $x \geq x_s$ a deal is made, namely the subject gives up the amount y of the commodity and receives x. If $x < x_s$ no deal is made and the subject retains his status quo. This procedure is described to the subject, he is told that it is to be performed only once, and that no bargaining is allowed.

The ED-S procedure is directly analogous to the ED-B procedure and the proof that the optimal choice for minimum selling price is the value for which $x_s = x_s^*$ in that it is for only that action that expected utility is maximized follows directly, <u>mutatis</u> <u>mutandis</u>. Similarly, for the special case in which p(·) is uniform and $u(x, -y|S_0)$ is linear in x, the loss function will be quadratic.
In addition, we can also get simultaneous selling equivalences for different amounts of commodity to be bid for, and we will obtain, parallel to (19)

$$(20)\quad u(0,0|S_0) = u(x_{1s}^*,-y_1|S_0) = u(x_{2s}^*,-y_2|S_0) = \ldots = u(x_{ms}^*,-y_m|S_0)$$

where x_{js}^* is the minimum selling price (and true selling equivalence) for the amount of commodity, y_j out of his current holdings.

The next step obviously is to combine the multiple ED-B and ED-S procedures to simultaneously obtain (19) and (20). In this case the subject does not know if he is going to buy or sell the commodity. The experimenter is somewhat like a whimsical customer-supplier, and the subject does not know ahead of time whether he will receive an offer of commodities for sale or a cash bid for commodities he holds. Thus, he must specify his maximum buying prices for possible commodity amounts offered, and his minimum selling prices for possible bids on various levels of his current commodity holdings. From these price-equivalences and amounts we can draw the whole indifference curve shown in Figure 2. The solid circles represent the subject's maximum buying prices for the respective amounts of the commodity and the hollow circles represent his minimum selling prices for respective amounts of the commodity.

In this graphical representation we can see that the experimenter randomly selects a y value, indicating that the subject is buying if $y > y_0$ and selling if $y < y_0$, and then the experimenter randomly selects an x value, indicating his asking price or his bid, respectively. If this (x,y) point is to the right of the indifference curve, the subject, by his placement of the curve, has indicated that he would accept such an offer. If the selected (x,y) point is to the left of the indifference curve the subject has indicated that he would reject it.

This latter interpretation suggests a direct graphical procedure for obtaining the indifference curve. The subject is given a sheet of paper on which a rectangle with X - Y axes is drawn. The X axis is scaled from $\underline{x}$ to $\bar{x}$ and the y axis is scaled from $\underline{y}$ to $\bar{y}$ (see Figure 3). The subject's status quo is depicted by a point

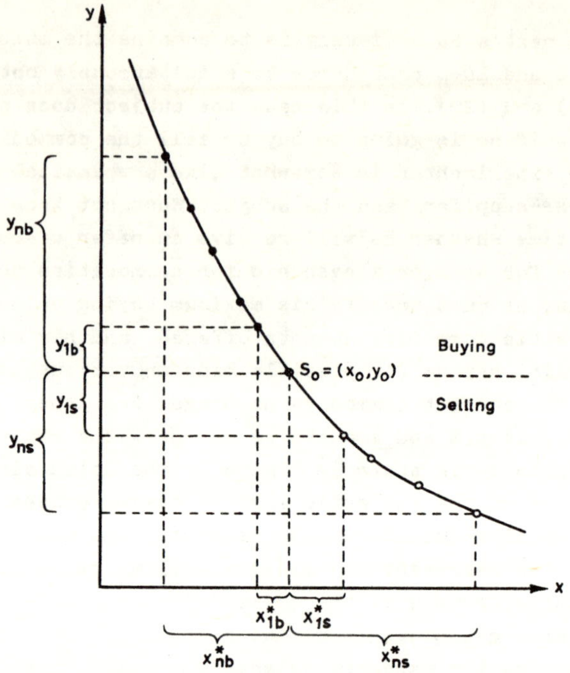

Figure 2: Complete indifference curve from the combined ED-B and ED-S procedures

(x_0, y_0). A point (x,y) in this space represents the experimenter's possible offer of making the appropriate transaction to move the subject from (x_0, y_0) to (x,y). The experimenter will choose a point at random as his non-negotiable, standing offer. Before knowing this value the subject must divide the whole rectangle into two regions, an acceptance region and a rejection region. If the point (x_1, y_1) selected by the experimenter is in the acceptance region the subject must conduct the transaction moving him from (x_0, y_0) to (x_1, y_1), but if the point selected (x_2, y_2) is in the rejection region the subject will retain his status quo (x_0, y_0). The curve thus drawn will pass through (x_0, y_0) and points on the curve above (x_0, y_0) will represent maximum buying prices, while points below (x_0, y_0) will represent minimum selling prices. The proof for optimality is again analogous to that given for the simple ED-B case.

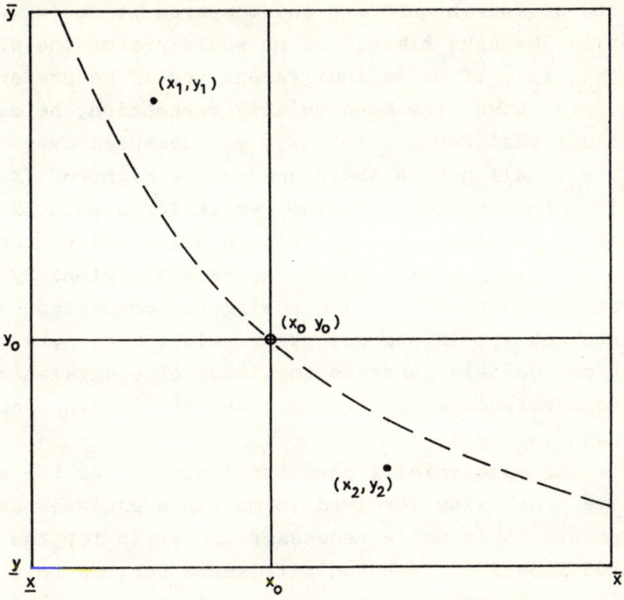

Figure 3: Obtaining equivalences graphically

The experimenter may strengthen the power of the loss function by removing the first and third quadrants from the outcome space if he is sure that, for the subject, $u(x,y|S_0)$ is monotone non-decreasing in both x and y. Note that if this monotonicity condition holds, a point in the first quadrant offers both more x and more y than (x_0, y_0) and thus would not be on the indifference curve passing through (x_0, y_0), while a point in the third quadrant offers both less x and less y and similarly would not be on the indifference curve. In addition to increasing the power of the loss function, we can also use this property to help the subject simplify his mental labor in making equivalence judgments. Suppose he arbitrarily selects a point in the second or fourth quadrant and compares it to (x_0, y_0). That is, he asks himself if he would prefer the point to (x_0, y_0), if he is indifferent, or if he prefers (x_0, y_0). Given the monotonicity assumption, he can conclude that for a point (x_1, y_1) accepted over (x_0, y_0), all points above and to the right of (x_1, y_1) will be in the accept region, while for a point (x_2, y_2) rejected for (x_0, y_0), all points below and to the left of (x_2, y_2) will be in the reject region. By proceeding sequentially and choosing for comparison only points not yet in the accept or reject region, a subject can quickly generate the locus of equivalences to some reference point, i.e., the indifference curve through (x_0, y_0).

While the monotonicity assumption simplifies the cognitive processing involved in multiple equivalence judgments it is not a necessary condition for the method itself. If monotonicity seems dubious in a particular case then we allow the subject to partition the rectangle into an accept region and a reject region of arbitrary shape. Note, then, that we can dispense with the monotonicity condition in the discussion of ED-B in section 3.

5. *Equivalences for Gifts and Forced Deals*

In the preceding sections we have only considered the ascertainment of equivalences to the decision maker's prior state. Other equivalences, however, can be determined by a slight extension of the procedure. In utility experiments, for example, it is common to offer the subject a gift of a lottery or a commodity and to ask for the cash (or commodity) equivalence of this gift. That is, if the subject is offered an amount y' of a commodity, he is asked the minimum amount of x he would take in lieu of y'. Note that this "gift" equivalence is conceptually different from the selling equivalence because if the experimenter's offer falls in the rejection region, in the selling case the subject retains his status quo (x_0, y_0) while in the gift case he gets $(x_0, y_0 + y')$. So in one case we are obtaining the indifference curve through (x_0, y_0) while in the other case we get the indifference curve through $(x_0, y_0 + y')$. Not only are these equivalences conceptually different but there is no practical reason to expect the values of equivalent x, for a particular y, to be the same in different equivalence contexts. Further discussion of these aspects along with a study of confusion over these differences in the existing literature will be deferred to another paper.

The concept of offering a gift to create a new status quo is obviously not restricted to an amount y' of the commodity, we could as easily offer a gift of cash (or some second commodity) x', or even both x' and y'. In these latter two cases we could be determining the indifference curves through $(x_0 + x', y_0)$ and $(x_0 + x', y_0 + y')$, respectively. Although it is natural to think of x' and y' as being positive and thus being gifts, they could equally well be negative or one negative and one positive. For example, when y' is positive and x' is negative, after the subject gives his equivalences, if the selected point falls in the rejection region he does not retain his original status quo but is forced in effect, to buy the amount y' of the commodity for a price x'. The experimenter, then, will be able to ascertain indifference curves through all the possible gift points he is prepared to offer, and through all the "forced deal" points he can make the subject comply with.

The only departure of this extended version of the procedure from the ED-B case discussed in section 3 is that, in the consequence vector, (x', y') replaces (0,0) as the outcome when $x_b < x$. By making this replacement throughout the theorem and proof, it is easy to see that the desired result $u(-x_b^*, y|S_0) = u(x', y'|S_0)$ holds.
The incorporation of the extended version into the graphical method given earlier is the most effective way of obtaining the whole indifference map. The experimenter can choose a set of forced deals (x', y'), for example $(x_1', 0)$, $(x_2', 0)$, ..., $(x_n', 0)$, and for each of the forced deals ask the subject to partition the rectangle into an acceptance and a rejection region. Then one (x',y') deal is chosen at random, the corresponding offer (x,y) is then chosen and the subject is paid off according to the acceptance and rejection regions he has drawn. This method was used in experiments of MacCrimmon and Toda |1969|.

6. *Summary*

In this paper we have presented a procedure for obtaining preference equivalences for commodities or lotteries. Although, to simplify the discussion, we have emphasized cash equivalences, the procedure is as readily used in obtaining commodity or lottery equivalences. The procedure described is useful because it induces true equivalences, in that any other possible responses are dominated. This property was proved and a quadratic loss function for non-optimal responses was shown for a particular case. The concept of equivalence was clarified not only for buying and selling contexts but also in situations where the status quo might change due to a gift or a forced deal. Efficient methods were discussed for obtaining a whole indifferent map (i.e., loci of equivalences) by direct graphical construction.

Bibliography

Becker, G.M., |1962|, Decision Making: Objective Measures of Subjective Probability and Utility, Psychological Review, vol. 69, no. 2, pp. 136-148.

Becker, G.M., M.H. DeGroot, and J. Marschak, |1964|, Measuring Utility by a Single-response Sequential Method, Behavioral Science, vol. 9, no. 3, pp. 226-232.

Davidson, D., P. Suppes, and S. Siegel, |1957|, Decision-making: an Experimental Approach, Stanford University Press.

Grayson, C.J.Jr., |1960|, Decisions under Uncertainty: Drilling Decisions by Gas and Oil Operators, Harvard University Division of Research.

Friedman, M., and L.J. Savage, |1948|, The Utility Analysis of Choices Involving Risk, Journal of Political Economy, vol. 56, no. 4, pp. 279-304.

Friedman, M., and L.J. Savage, |1952|, The Expected Utility Hypothesis and the Measurability of Utility, Journal of Political Economy, vol. 60, no. 6, pp. 463-474.

MacCrimmon, K.R., and M. Toda, |1969|, The Experimental Determination of Indifference Curves, Review of Economic Studies, vol. 36, no. 4, pp. 433-451.

Markowitz, H., |1952|, The Utility of Wealth, Journal of Political Economy, vol. 60, no. 2, pp. 151-158.

Marshall, A., |1890|, Principles of Economics.

Pareto, V., |1906|, Manuale di Economia Politica.

Samuelson, P.A., |1938|, A Note on the Pure Theory of Consumer's Behavior, Economica, vol. 5, pp. 61-71, 353-354.

Swalm, R.O., |1966|, Utility Theory: Insights into Risk Taking, Harvard Business Review, pp. 123-136.

22. TECHNIQUE AND METHODS OF EVALUATION OF FIELD EXPERIMENTS IN DECISION-MAKING

JOSEF HESSELBACH*

I. Introduction and Motivation for the Experiment

The experiment I am refering to here must be seen in the overall context underlying a complex research project. In our department we want to investigate the behavior of farm managers in decision-making. The potential applications of such research findings are obvious: Our primary interest is to develop decision-making tools that are of relevance and validity to decision-making situations, but applications can also be seen in education and for agrarian policy making.

Drastic price changes in traditional economic theory would lead to a change in resource allocation and resource use resulting in a different production plan under a market of perfect competition and with firms having alternatives in producing different commodities.

In agriculture we have a market situation with near-perfect competition and each farm firm has a rather great number of production alternatives. The most important resources, as there are labor, land and capital, normally have definite restrictions for a certain firm so that drastic price changes would effect in a change of the optimal allocation of resources to dif-

* Max Planck-Institut für Landarbeit und Landtechnik, Bad Kreuznach.

ferent enterprises within a farm firm.
At the time - in 1963 - when we planned to start the experiment, the authorities for the European Common Market made important decisions about the timing of introducing common market situation which for German Agriculture meant drastic price changes at least for some commodities, especially grain crops and milk. Papers and farmer's magazines were full of reports about these decisions and the future price situation. Therefore it was very easy to sell this kind of experiments to farmers to have them cooperate with us. Without too much explanation which would have had the danger of revealing the true background of the experiment it was possible to find enough farmers to start an experiment which nevertheless was considered to be a pilot study to develop an experimental technique and a method of evaluating such experiments.
It is our hope that after full evaluation of the now completed experiment we will have a chance to repeat similar experiments in a much broader style with the experience of that pilot study.

II. *Experimental Technique*

To achieve drastic price changes for agricultural commodities apart from normal market prices we, the experimenter could have made ourselves the market partner of the cooperating farmers and could have bought their commodities according to our own price system rather than normal market prices. This is in fact what we have done, only instead of actually taking the products under our own control and selling them to the market like a trader or using them in our own farms we let the products of the farmers under the experiment go their normal market channels and asked only the buyers - having their consent - to settle the deal with us and send us the money for the products. We then used the physical records of such a deal, changed only the prices per unit and on that base settled up with the farmer and sent him the money according to our price system.

With the same farmer we had a system of price increases and reductions which has been kept stable over the whole period of five years (1964 to 1969). The increases and reductions were fixed at a percentage base of what the dealer did pay us. Therefore any bargaining or treatment of the products by the farmer which influenced the price positively or negatively did come through to the farmer.

The percentage rates of increases or reductions were varying up to 20 percent of the actual market price, so that increasing one commodity by 20% and decreasing another one for the same farmer by 20% should make a great difference in competing about scarce resources.

Six farmers have been contracted to cooperate in this experiment. Only two out of the six (neighbors) had the same pricing system (percentage rates of increases or reductions). The treatment over a period of five years can be considered to represent a long range influence, especially because at the beginning of the period the duration of the experiment has not been fixed. The contract with the farmer was an agreement for an indefinite number of years. The contract could be terminated by each partner with an advance notice of six months to the end of a calendar year. We gave the impression of an at least five to seven year's interest on our side. The contracts have been terminated after four and a half year to the end

of the fifth year.
Table 1 gives the percentage changes of the first-hand prices to the experimental prices.

Table 1: Percentage Increases and Reductions of Actual Market Prices for Six Farmers

Commodities	Experimental Farm No.				
	1	2	3	4	5 and 6
Milk	+ 20	-	+ 10	+ 10	- 10
Beef cattle	-	+ 10	- 5	-	-
Swine	+ 10	-	-	+ 5	+ 7,5
Feeder pigs	-	+ 15	+ 5	-	-
Grain	- 10	- 10	- 10	-	-
Potatoes	+ 20	- 10	- 20	-	-
Sugar beets	- 20	+ 10	+ 10	- 10	-

The rates in table 1 were not a matter of the contract or discussion with the farmers. If they did care they could have noticed it the first time we settled their account with us which however was at least seven month after we started the procedure since we used the first six month as a kind of introductory period where we did not make any price changes at all. Also not in all cases are the prices of commodities sold fixed and known to the farmer at the time of delivering the product. The only purpose of this period was to make farmers and their partners acquainted with the new system of settling their selling and buying products and distract attention from the experimental situation in general.

None of the five different sets of price changes corresponds closely to what were the expected price changes through the realization of the Common Market. The increases or reductions by the price changes on the income are true changes of the income situation of each farmer. We have tried, by choosing the percentage increases and reductions, to compensate the influence on the overall income situation at least for the beginning of the experimental period. As a safety feature it has been guaranteed to the farmers that in case of an overall reduction of the income the difference would be refunded, since there should not be a penalty for participating in the experiment. In total an amount of DM 20.000 has been given to the six farmers over the five year period through higher prices or through adaptation of their production program to the experimental price situation. This amounts to an average of about 3.300 DM per farmer during the five year period or to less than 600 DM per year which is in no case more than 4 % of their annual net income. Another 500 DM per year and farmer were given for providing labor records and as a compensation for a delay of their incoming cash flow by an average of one month.

Instead of undergoing all the detailed procedure with the cash flow going from the dealers to us and a changed flow from us to the farmers, we could have asked the farmers to keep records about their business and we could have settled our percentage increases and reductions on a monthly, quarterly or yearly base directly with the farmers. Such a short-cut way would have brought in too much aura of an experiment. We tried to make the price changes as realistic as they really were for the experimental period and did hope that the "new prices" would become realistic variables in the mind of the farmers and their decision-making.

To distract attention from the real background of the experiment we also masked our experiment with some features only of minor interest in the experimental context. We established a more complete book keeping system than was previously kept on the farm and we laid special emphasis on a labor diary. The control and data transfer of the established records system was put foreward to be the reason of a monthly visit on the farm, whose main purpose was to register the decisions and all the considerations of the farmer to develop and change the farm production program.

III. Methods of Evaluation

1. Equilibrium with Respect to the Value of the Objective Function

As already hypothesized the experimental treatment should change the equilibrium of a production plan or at least lead to different tensions within a stable production plan. The change in equilibrium must be quantified and used as a yardstick for the challenge to the farmer to develop his farm firm and production plan over time in order to give a realistic framework for interpreting the farmer's behavior in decisions and the decision itself he takes during the experimental period.

To determine what is an equilibrium situation we used linear programming for each individual farm firm using the true resource situation, the input-output coefficients, and production alternatives available to each farm.

There are a number of states of equilibrium to define for each farm.

Let M_1 be the equilibrium under the actual market prices and E_1 respectively under the experimental price situation at the time t_1 (the beginning of the period under consideration), then M_i and E_i would be equilibria at any discrete point over the time (t_i) with i going from 0 to n, n being the horizon of the period under consideration. R_1 and respectively R_n would be the actual farm organization at the beginning and end of the experimental period. R_o then would be the actual farm organization right before the beginning of the experimental period and as the time increment from t_o to t_1 would be very short, it would be the same farm organization however the respective objective function would be calculated using the actual market prices. Likewise R_{n+1} would be a farm organization identical to R_n however the objective function would be calculated under the actual market prices right after the experimental period, whereas R_1 and R_n would be calculated with the experimental prices at the beginning and at the end of the experimental period respectively. Having defined these different states of the actual farm situation and the equilibria under market and experimental price situations the following fields of tensions can be drawn (fig. 1 to fig. 4).

Starting with a normal (non-experimental) business situation in general we cannot assume the firm to be in congruence with the equilibrium (fig. 1). The manager of the firm might make mistakes and therefore be more or less far off the equilibrium or optimal solution for his business situation. Also we cannot exclude the case that in defining the equilibrium by misjudging some circumstances we have not found the true equilibrium. The true equilibrium may be different from what we think and in the extreme case the actual firm may have the optimal solution where

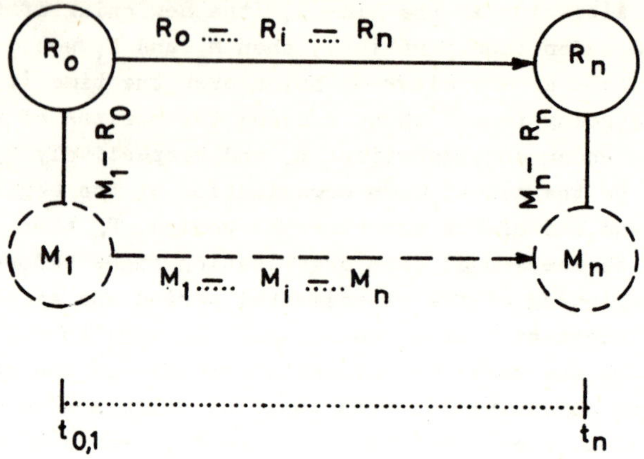

Figure 1: Field of Tension in a Normal (Non-Experimental) Market Price Situation (General Case)

we think the optimal solution to be different from the actual situation. Therefore great care must be exercised in analyzing a situation if the conclusions we draw from such an analysis shall be relevant.

If however we have a true equilibrium which is different from the actual situation, we have a tension between M_1 and R_o and likewise between M_i and R_i which means at any point over time. The tension over time might increase or decrease depending upon the development of M_i and R_i relatively to each other. Dealing with such a situation as a research worker (in business world a firm consultant would be in the same situation as a research worker) we however have to differentiate between two tensions:

a. the tension felt by the firm manager or the gap between the actual and optimal firm organization as it is recognized by the management itself (subjective tension)

b. the tension found by comparing the true equilibrium with the actual firm organization (objective tension).

Starting from these two different situations simply by empirical investigation still we can focus our research on two aspects:

a. what are the obstacles, how are they removed, how long does it take, which information and decision process can be observed in overcoming subjective tensions

b. assuming that the research worker (firm consultant) has demonstrated the objective tension to the management of the firm: to what degree, with which tools does the manager accept the objective tension which then becomes identical with subjective tension and then again which processes can be observed.

So far we can handle our research goals by pure empirical investigation. Where does the experiment come in?

If we want to learn more about the processes of management in order to be able to design better tools for management, good educational programs but especially to reveal knowledge about the influence of policy measures (action-response pairs) we should for a first approach exclude the role of a consultant within the management process since this would be a disturbing factor. Having done this we very often will find that there is no subjective tension in a firm at any point in time. We can only observe $R_i - R_{i+1}$ response due to and identical with $M_i - M_{i+1}$ tensions and the fac-

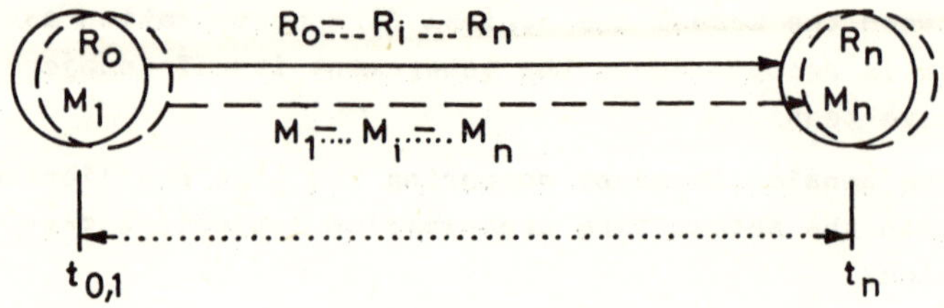

Figure 2: Development of Actual Firm Organizations in Congruence with Equilibria over Time (Ideal Case)

tors causing these tensions are out of our control and may be manyfold and even compensating or competing with each other. We find ourselves in the situation demonstrated in fig. 2. Moreover normally tensions over time very seldom will build up suddenly, but rather will sneak in and will be neutralized in small pieces or will built up to a certain level until they will be neutralized by a package of actions. To wait for drastic changes in tension in empirical research situations might be an expensive gamble.
With experimenting in this area we can create small or great tensions whatever we want to look at and we do control the amount and direction of the tensions by our experimental treatment. The general case would be represented by fig. 3, here we assume objective tensions also before the experimental treatment starts. It should be possible to find out before starting the experimental treatment whether a subjective tension exists whether it is equal to or how it compares with objective tension and what measures and preparations are already considered and started to overcome subjec-

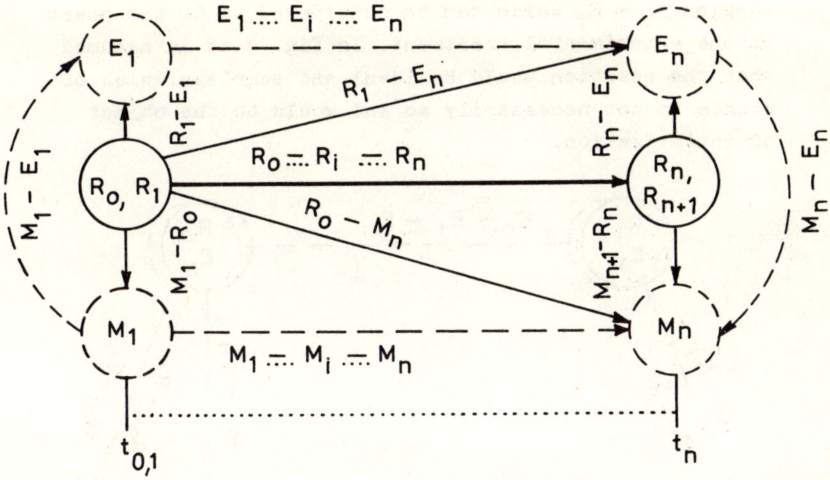

Figure 3: Field of Tensions in an Experimental vs. a Market Price Situation (General Case)

tive tension. To know these facts would be of great importance at least for the behavior in the beginning phase of an experimental treatment working differently from what the original tensions right before the experiment were. Assuming the existence of at least objective tension as a general case, then fig. 3 could be used to represent such a situation. Whether such an enrichment of the field of tensions is wanted by the experimenter would depend upon the research objective. Without subjective tension involved which means identifying the actual situation with an optimal solution under the conditions before the experimental treatment starts, fig. 4 can be used to model the experimental situation, where then full control exists about the tension $M_1 - E_1$ which can be considered to be the power of the experimental treatment. In fig. 4 it is assumed that the reaction would be ideal and complete which of course is not necessarily so and would be the object of investigation.

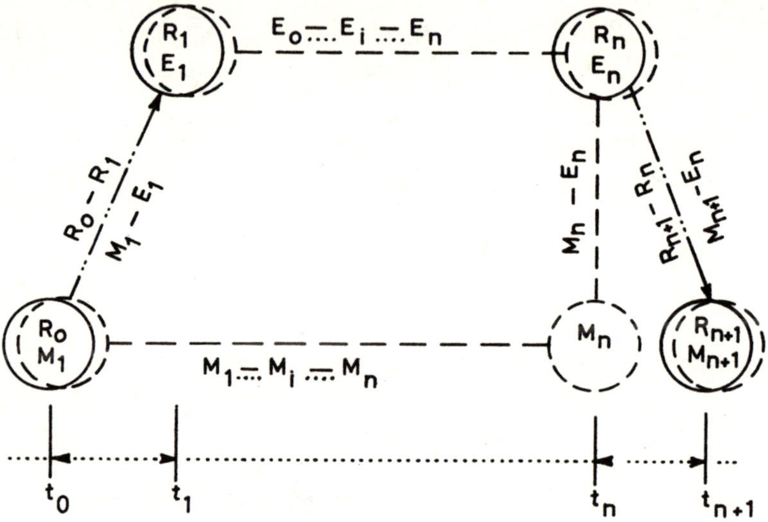

Figure 4: Ideal Adaptation of Actual Firm Organization to Changing Equilibrium caused by Experimental Treatment (Ideal Case)

Having laid out a field of possible tensions in an experimental situation we have to look for yardsticks to survey our fields. Our dotted circles indicate hypothetical situations in our case calculated by linear programming, the solid circles represent actual situations of the farm firm. Assuming maximum income or net worth

growth as a goal in farming the return over variable costs of an operation could be a yardstick to compare different farm organizations. The difference in return over variable costs between any two farm organizations would be the validness of the existing tension between these two organizations.
Using the field of fig. 3 the following pairs of tension can be singled out:

I	M_1-R_o	VIII	R_i-E_i
II	R_1-E_1	IX	M_i-E_i
III	M_1-E_1	X	R_1-E_i
IV	E_1-E_i	XI	R_o-M_i
Va	R_o-R_{n+1}	XII	R_o-R_1
Vb	R_1-R_n	XIII	R_n-R_{n+1}
VI	M_1-M_i		
VII	M_i-R_i		

For pair I to XI except pair V the real situation R is either linked to a hypothetical situation under market prices (M) or under experimental prices (E). For those pairs R is calculated either with market prices or with experimental prices depending upon to which hypothetical situation R is linked. For pair V either market or experimental prices could be used. If in using experimental prices (Vb) the difference in the objective function would have a higher value than with using market prices (Va), two reasons could be found:

a. the conditions of the experimental situations favored development over time more than the actual market price situation

b. a good response to the experimental price situation can be observed.

If Va would be greater than Vb the opposite conclusions can be drawn, however in any case the two components could work against each other rather than the same direction. So would it be possible with a good response to the experimental situation that the difference between Va and Vb is low or in favor of Va because of unfavorable conditions for firm development in general with the experimental situation (By the way: this would be a situation not very useful for an experiment, because with the experimental technique chosen the probability of immotivated compensation would be very high and firms would be punished for their willingness to cooperate).

Assuming that t_o is the point in time just before the experiment starts and t_1 right after the start or in other words: the same farm organization is calculated with two different price systems. Likewise if R_n is the farm organization at the end of the experimental period and the objective function for R_n is calculated with experimental prices whereas R_{n+1} still is the same farm organization however the objective function is calculated at market prices right after the experiment (assuming that the prices also were valid in the last accounting period of the experimental phase):

Pair XII would then be the expected increase or decrease in the objective function for the first accounting period caused by the experimental prices assuming that within the first accounting period still no reaction to the new situation can be taken. It therefore would be the "subsidy" payment by the experimenter, which we have tried to keep at a minimum. Pair XIII likewise would be the "subsidy" payment for the last accounting period of the experimental phase. Since farmers had five years time to react to the experimental price situation this pair gives a yardstick of how the chance of reorganization and increasing the objective function has been used: the higher the difference between pair XII and XIII the better the adaptation.

In close connection with pair XIII attention should be given to pair VII, VIII and IX. One would in the ideal case expect pair VIII to be zero or to be in equilibrium. Pair IX would have a certain tension (if both, it and pair I were also zero then the experimental treatment would have no challenging power except for the fact of an experiment itself and the pretended circumstances that could mislead a decision maker). Comparing pair IX and pair XIII, pair IX would be the objective yardstick to judge pair XIII. To the degree pair XIII reaches the tension of pair IX the decision maker did adapt his firm to the experimental situation.

The tension for pair IX would be the sum of pair VII and VIII, if the deviation of R_i from M_i or E_i would necessarily be on a straight line between M_i and E_i that is in a two-dimensional response surface. Since we are dealing with multi-dimensional response possibility R_i could be far off M_i and E_i as well, so that the decision maker would miss the optimal solution under either pricing system much more than M_i and E_i differ from each other.

In comparing VII and VIII with each other we could conclude that the decision maker did react better to the experimental situation if VIII is smaller than VII and vice versa. The latter case could indicate that the decision maker does not take the experimental treatment no matter how realistic it is for the period itself as the true situation but rather based his decision on the actual market situation bearing in mind that some day the experiment will expire and normal market prices will be valid again.

Pair IV, VI, X and XI must be looked at together. Pair IV and VI are yardsticks for the dynamics under the two price systems. Since with the experimental treatment we offset the actual market prices, pair IV is more important than pair VI for our evaluation although pair VI cannot be neglected as explaining variable for the decisions observed.
Comparing pair V to VI and IV gives an indicator for the observed dynamic process of change compared to the dynamics challenged by either one situation itself.
Pair X then is challenged dynamics of the experimental treatment taking the actual situation R_1 into account. The challenge (pair X) may be greater than dynamics of the experimental price system (pair IV) in itself since R_1 may be "behind" E_1, the opposite case may also be true since R_1 not being in equilibrium with E_1 may be already ahead of E_1 on the way to E_n. Looking at the dynamics of R_o - M_n (pair XI), the offset situation, may help explain actual behavior especially if the decision maker cannot refrain from experiencing the experimental treatment as kind of an unrealistic and exceptional situation.
Finally pair I, II and III marks the starting position of the experimental treatment compared with the situation right before the experiment. Whereas the dynamics of IV and VI may be out of control (as in our experiment) of the experimenter, the tensions in I, II and III can be manipulated to a high degree by the experimental treatment choosen. As special cases the tension in I and II might be zero, even pair III could have zero tension for the experiment to start with if in the course the treatment is changed. In our case the pre-experimental period to test the experimental technique can be looked at as a situation with pair III at zero tension.

It is not intended to give the results of the first experiment in great detail. Moreover I will not try to put foreward any theory or hypothesis drawn from that first experiment. First of all the experiment has been designed to develop and test an experimental technique and not to test a theory or hypothesis. The small number of cases would not permit it.
But to illustrate the proposed instruments for evaluation, the effect of the experimental treatment and the development over time is demonstrated for a few cases.

In Table 2 the results of the experiment for four farms out of the six cooperating are given: In the first line (R_o) the gross income situation at the beginning of the experimental period is given. There is a considerable variation between the four farms all of which are of the type of family size farms. The much higher potential of farm 4 compared to the others is due to the fact that farm 4 has wine production as an alternative which is a very attractive enterprise under our market conditions.
However looking at pair I we can see that exactly this farmer seems to be far off his equilibrium situation assuming profit maximization as the objective. Farmer 1 could increase his profit by about 50 percent, farmer 2 by about 25 percent whereas only farmer 3 seems to be in equilibrium. Having changed the prices, the tension of pair II would now be relevant at the beginning of the experiment. Here we can see, that the tension stays about the same for farm 2 and 4 whereas for farm 1 it is stronger and the highest change can be experienced by farmer 3 who was in equilibrium.
Pair III at the same time gives an indication of how different the equilibria under the two different sets of circumstances are. It also gives a yardstick of the conflict that might arise if a farmer would be in

Table 2: Evaluation of the Field of Tensions (Figures given in the upper part indicate gross income above variable costs)

		Farm No. 1	2	3	4
	R_o	16480	25365	26420	36400
	R_1	17200	25290	25630	36900
	M_1	25170	31270	26485	67098
	E_1	27867	31116	29350	65580
	R_{n+1}	31540	33770	58760	57970
	R_n	32570	35220	58160	58320
	M_n	35034	35309	58760	78524
	E_n	37145	35353	58160	80593
I	M_1-R_o	8690	5905	65	30698
II	R_1-E_1	10667	5826	3720	28680
III	M_1-E_1	2697	-154	2865	-1518
IV	E_1-E_n	9278	4237	28810	15013
Va	R_o-R_{n+1}	15060	8405	32340	21570
Vb	R_1-R_n	15370	9930	32530	21420
VI	M_1-M_n	9864	4039	32275	11426
VII	M_n-R_n	3494	1539	0	20554
VIII	R_n-E_n	4575	133	0	22273
IX	M_n-E_n	2111	44	-600	2069
X	R_1-E_n	19945	10063	32530	43693
XI	R_o-M_n	18554	9944	32340	42124
XII	R_o-R_1	720	-75	-790	500
XIII	R_n-R_{n+1}	1030	1450	-600	350

danger of a schizophrenic attitude towards the experiment that is if he would not accept the experimental situation to be the true world for him and act as if no experimental treatment is taking place. In one case (farm 2) out the four the equilibrium is (almost) the same under either set of conditions and this situation continues through the total period (see pair IX). This farmer having the lowest growth potential over time (see pair V) however did make full use of his chances. The same applies for farmer 3 with a much higher growth potential. Also farmer 1 and 4 have a considerable growth to report, but could not fully bridge the gap between the optimum and their actual situation (see VIII) during the experimental period. The biggest gap remains for farmer 4 who on the other hand has a high income, he might not be a profit maximizer contrary to farmer 3 who evidently had the highest growth potential and did use it fully. Unfortunately for farmer 3 the optimum at the end of the period is the same under either conditions or in other words our experimental treatment in the course of time became ineffective so that no conclusions can be drawn about the possible adaptation to the experimental conditions and the deviation from an optimum under real market prices.

2. Opportunity Costs, Shadow Prices, Cost Ranges, and Change in Shares as Explaining Variables

So far we were only concerned with the influence of the experimental treatment on the objective function and how to measure the dynamics of the situation. The objective function however is only an aggregate result of different elements that bring together the objective function value. In dealing with the motivation and pressure for decisions after an experimental treatment we also have three more sets of variables to take into account:

a. the opportunity costs for scarce resources

b. the shadow prices for production alternatives not included in the optimal solution and the cost ranges for those included in the optimal solution

c. the change of the shares of single products on the total value of the objective function.

The opportunity costs would give us the direction for the development of a firm over time. By our experimental treatment we would probably change the opportunity costs even more than the use of the available resources at the beginning of a treatment. The amount of change would be a hidden incentive and yardstick for the pressure to develop (expand) the resource in a certain direction.

The shadow prices for production alternatives not included in the optimal solution but found in a firm again are a yardstick to judge the decision to keep or expand or even start with a production alternative not found in the optimal solution. Low shadow prices would prove the instability of a production plan as far as the enterprises and their shares are concerned and at the same would indicate a rather stable situation as far as the value of the objective function is concerned depending upon different production plans. High shadow prices would mark us such activities that are not profitable to take up or that should be stopped in case they are in the actual production plan. Again by experimental treatment it is possible to change the shadow prices for commodities. As any change can be considered to bring resistance and difficulties whether true or imaginative the change in the objective function as an incentive has to be seen together with the proportion of change in the enterprise mix. A small change in the objective function might require a complete reversal of a production program. In such a case we expect that a manager will avoid the trouble of change for only a small increase in profits. The change of production shares therefore will be a hindering factor in the process. Again it is possible by the kind of experimental treatment to construct different situations as to the optimal shares of enterprises before and after the treatment.

3. Equilibrium With Respect to Product Quantities

Finally a simple tabulation of the direction of the price changes (experimental treatment), the resulting change in the equilibrium, the reaction by the experimental subjects and the position according to the new equilibrium can be made for the sample, any subset of it or for each individual unit, where each commodity under control of the experimenter is counted as a item. In table 3 the 81 different possibilities are laid out and at the same the figures in the various cells are a summary of all the commodities observed in six farms. It is evident from the table that 90 % of the equilibria remained unchanged by the changes in prices although about half of them were directly affected by price changes. One can find examples of "rather unrational" behavior as in the case where the optimal quantity increased but we observed a decrease below the equilibrium quantity, or at the other end of the scale: where despite of a higher price the optimal quantity went down, however we observe an increase above the optimal quantity.

IV. Research Implications

It seems that we succeeded in developing an experimental technique to handle field experiments with small firms under a market of perfect competition and also that despite the complex structure of field experiments it seems possible to exercise control and have methods of evaluation. However an experiment on a broad scale which may enable us to make statistical analysis formulate and test hypothesis and theories yet has to be carried out. Because of the amount of research funds involved in such experimentation and the still unfriendly atmosphere towards experimentation in the social sciences it seems necessary at the same time to develop laboratory experiments which will be less expensive and yield results much quicker since the main advantage of laboratory experiments as I visualize them is the quick motion of dynamic processes. I still believe that laboratory experiments ought to be as realistic - or dirty as some may call it - as they possibly can be. Even then field experiments to me seem necessary to check certain features and findings of laboratory experimentation (calibration) if we want to be sure that the behavior in laboratory experiments is not influenced by the experimental situation itself and if the inferences we draw from experimental results to real world situations shall hold.

Table 3: Change of Product Quantities and Position Against Equilibrium Status

Situation after 5 years of experiment		The Equilibrium changed at the beginning of the experiment: decrease			no change			increase			no. of cases	
change comparing 69 vs. 64	position against equilibrium status 1969	Experiment changed prices										
		−	±	+	−	±	+	−	±	+		
decrease	−				2	5	3		1		11	
	±				1	2	1				4	26
	+		1		3	2	5				11	
no change	−					4					4	
	±				2	3					5	13
	+				1	2	1				4	
increase	−					2	5			1	8	
	±				1	1	1				3	37
	+	1		1	6	11	3	1		3	26	
No. of Cases		1	1	1	16	32	19	1	1	4		
		3			67			6			76	

23. PRAGMATIC DECISIONS ON AN EXPERIMENTAL MARKET

HORST TODT*

I. Introduction

Game experiments are an instrument to close the gap between purely theoretical research on model markets with strictly rational acting competitors and purely empirical research on real markets with human beings making decisions. The mixture of both types of structures, i.e. a model market with human beings making decisions, is a domain of experimental economic research. We use this technique in tackling some problems that have emerged from preceding investigations into the structure of West German tourist markets. Although similar configurations may be found on other markets as well, we stick to this very context for explanatory purposes. Hence we base our experimental set-up not on a model of a completely fictive market but rather try to cast some of the essential traits of certain competitive situations of tourism in model form. In this sense we speak of an idealized touristic market. One of the general characteristics of touristic markets is the concatination of common and conflicting interests of competing firms, resulting in a most complex interrelationship among them. Consider the idealized case of two vacation resorts consisting of three hotels each. The hotels, of course,

---

* Universität Hamburg

compete by means of the classic instruments "price" and "advertising." Furthermore they have control on their individual standard by qualifying themselves for a definitive "category," which runs to "product variation." In addition to these familiar market operations the three hotels of a resort may influence demand by common action. Any vacation resort is largely dependent not only on natural and artificial attractions but also on numerous amenities and aesthetical improvement of the site that cannot always be provided for on a commercial basis. In order to survive, the hotels have to take care of this kind of "face-lifting" with respect to the vacation resort as a whole whatever style the place may represent and whatever organisation they choose (or are forced to choose) for this purpose.

Face-lifting has proven to be most effective on real markets both as a means to create new demand and as a competitive instrument of resorts taken as a whole. Nevertheless, it is difficult to assess its effects on any individual resort, and even more difficult to get an idea of how much common policy might have contributed to the success of a single hotel. This point will become apparent by discussing how face-lifting leads to growing demand. Usually this year's visitors of a resort will tell their friends at home what they ought to think of the place. In case of effective face-lifting these reports induce a band-wagon-effect. Therefore during the next vacation time, i.e. the following year, a larger number of visitors will stay at the resort considered and the whole process is repeated with the result of further increasing demand, and so on. The lag between cause (face-lifting) and full effect (largest number of visitors) may be of considerable length, e.g. five or even ten years. Meanwhile the market situation may have changed completely in any other respect, thus excluding reliable measurement of just one factor. On the other hand it has been shown by interviews in a number of West German vacation areas that 80 - 95 % (depending on the type of resort) of all visitors staying there for the first time had chosen the very trip on recommendation of friends.

Now suppose that the hotels are perfectly informed about the nature of their competitive instruments, i.e. "price," "advertising," "category," and "face-lifting." Furthermore, they are able to draw quite a few plausible qualitative conclusions and have some vague idea of scale. But they have no precise knowledge of any detail. Therefore they are not in a position to consider a theoretically-founded strategy; they will not even seriously try to develop any relevant elements of such a strategy. These considerations lead us to the central question of our experiments: Is there any common sense rule governing market action of the hotels under these conditions?

II. The Model Market

The idealized market situation already described is the background of the actual experiments. They are based on a formal model, which we do not intend to discuss here. We need, however, a thorough description of the economic situation and the technical set-up of the experiments.

Each game experiment lasts 20 periods. A period represents one year with a touristic season of exactly 200 days, such that there are at most 200 visitors (or more precise: overnight accomodations) per bed and period. In every period the 6 hotels have to make up their mind about exactly the same type of decisions. For the sake of simplicity we assume that each hotel is run by an entrepreneur (which may be a group of individual persons) who gets the building and its inventory from a leasing corporation that keeps everything in good repair. At the beginning of each period the entrepreneur has to decide whether he wishes to change capacity (number of beds offered) and/or category for the next period (1st decision phase). Capacity may be changed by full tens in both directions. As to category, entrepreneurs have only an option to choose a lower or an upper standard for the whole hotel. The leasing corporation takes care of everything and charges the hotels for their services depending on category and capacity irrespective of actual use (see Table 1).

	Current charge		Extraordinary charge	
	lower standard	upper standard	change of category (concerns all beds)	change of capacity (concerns beds added or returned, category does not matter)
Charge per bed	1400	2400	1000	2000

Table 1

After considering capacity and category of the following period, common policy of the current period has to be decided upon in a next step (2nd decision phase). There is, of course, a great variety of ideas and actions that enter into face-lifting. We assume, however, that there is no problem of choosing optimal actions because unfailing experts show the way; yet there is a problem of spending the right amount of money. It is a problem which the hotels of a resort have to solve by negotiation. Notice that there is only qualitative information in the model market so that entrepreneurs do not really know the result for which they are aiming. Hence, the whole set-up cannot add anything to the bargaining problem. But players are forced to talk to one another and to be conscious of being linked together. The high degree of uncertainty was chosen with respect to the very similar situation in reality. If entrepreneurs do not agree eventually, the majority decides. In this case the voting power of a hotel is proportional to its capacity. Thus a hotel of 100 beds may autonomously decide upon common expenditures for face lifting, if its competitors in the same resort have only for example, 40 and 50 beds respectively, at their disposal. Cost, however, is distributed on a different ratio. Irrespective of category, the actual number of visitors determines how much a hotel is charged for face-lifting. For the sake of simplicity we have the entrepreneur decide at once about the amount per visitor instead of total expenditures. We further require the hotels to determine an integer amount (e.g. DM 1,--, 2,--, ...). Face-lifting is internally treated as a capital stock which is depreciated by a fixed percentage and increased by current expenditures at the end of every period. The last step of the decision process encompasses simultaneous determination of price and advertising (3rd phase). In measuring advertisement we choose the amount spent, thus following the traditional line. Advertising cost may vary by multiples of DM 1000,--. One cost factor has not been mentioned so far, i.e. current cost other than charges of the leasing corporation and the amount required for the common instrument (face-lifting). Current cost contains all the rest of cost, mainly caused by wages and catering (DM 8,-- and DM 13,-- per visitor for lower and upper category). It depends on the category and cannot be influenced by entrepreneurial decisions.

The relevant data have to be filled in an account form during the game experiment. A period 0 is preplayed, not only for explanatory purposes, but also to give an idea of scale. All hotels are in exactly the same position (i.e. lower category; capacity: 60 beds; price: DM 25,--). The experiment starts with period 1. At the end of each period the hotels are told how large their demand is, i.e. the number of visitors. Now they are in a position to compute their gains (losses). The surplus of period 0 (60.000,-- DM) is left to the firms as starting capital. If cumulative gains become less than zero, the hotel closes down. We interpret this case of illiquidity as bankruptcy. It is plausible that illiquidity occurs more frequently during the first few periods of an experiment, since cumulative gains are low. Game participants receive information of all these details; furthermore, a few nearly obvious facts are explicitly added:

(a) The success (demand) of any hotel depends on the actual use of the instruments of all hotels.
(b) The kind of interdependence is "normal," which means, for example, that price reduction tends to increase demand for the own offer and to decrease demand for the competitors' offer and so on.
(c) The division of the market into two vacation resorts and (possibly) two categories creates four market segments.

> It is plausible that hotels of the same category have more directly conflicting interests than hotels of a different category. A similar consideration is valid for the two locations.

One of the major intentions is to create a completely free model market. Such a free market can be realized only if there is sufficient information about almost everything. The hotels have to tell one another all details of their competitive situation, such as prices, advertisement, capacity and even gains. There is, however, one important restraint: Information about current data is not disclosed before all other competitors have made their corresponding decisions. Otherwise, one hotel might choose for example its price dependent on its competitors' price decisions during the same period. Such an advantage conflicts with the idea of symmetry. On the other hand, further freedom is admitted to the entrepreneurs. For example, they are allowed to form coalitions and to agree on side payments.

The final objective for the game participants is to reach a cumulative gain as large as possible by the end of the experiment. Participants of game experiments of competitive character, however, are inclined to consider their relative rather than their absolute position. Hence it may happen that a hotel will accept poor gains or even losses whenever more successful competitors may be overtaken. To avoid such an attitude, a prize was given depending on cumulative gains surmounting a certain threshold (DM 2.000.000,--) by the end of the experiment.

III. The Experiments

1. Technical Remarks

For each game experiment we needed at least 12 participants and at most 18, since the management of a hotel may consist of two or three persons. Nine of the ten game experiments were arranged with the help of students of Frankfurt University. One experiment was part of a course for employees in the field of tourism.

An experiment takes about nine hours, including the instruction of the participants. The model market reacts on three individual parameters (category, price, advertisement) of six hotels and on two common parameters of the two resorts, i.e. 20 parameters all together. The resulting demand for six firms could be found by the help of a mechanical desk computer. An electronic check showed, fortunately, that there was no relevant error in any game experiment.

2. General Observations

During the game experiment quite a lot of observations could be made which contributed to our understanding of the action of the participants. Further suggestions came from the comments that every hotel had put on paper. We shall now try to use this sort of information relating it to common sense arguments in order to explain a few remarkable facts and finally to formulate a hypothesis of actual economic decision.

The situation at the beginning: Because of the decisions of period 0, all hotels are in the category u

(lower category) during period 1. The very first decision of the participants of an experiment is whether the hotels will change category in the following second period. A change, no doubt, reduces competition, and hence increases the chances for gain. Although uncertainty prevails in the early stages of every game, the hotels are very well aware of this fact after the proceeding instructions. Moreover, if an upper category makes sense then it would certainly be profitable to use this option. This is a more psychological than logical argument, nevertheless it has some weight in a game situation. But is it necessary to change at once? Choosing the upper category implies the loss of all liquidity, thus provoking considerable risk. On the other hand, the chance to be the first hotel in the upper category and the advantage of a quasi-monopolistic position stand against risk. The usual vote, however, is for safety. Among the 60 hotels in exactly the same situation (6 times 10 hotels in all experiments) only four preferred immediate change. One of the four hotels was at once bankrupt because it overestimated the advantages of the quasi-monopoly, and hence asked the very high price of DM 50,--. It would have survived on a price of DM 49,--. The other three hotels reached the end of the game as the best in their vacation resort.
Our description of the risky situation at the beginning of a game has not been complete so far. If just one hotel changes at once, it can deliberatly be pushed into bankruptcy by the other two competitors of the same resort. At the beginning the two competitors have a capacity of 120 beds as compared to 60 beds of the hotel that changes category; hence they may dictate the expenditures for face-lifting. The gain per visitor is DM 5,-- in period zero. Assume

that expenditures for face-lifting are enlarged by an amount well above DM 5,--, say DM 10,-- per visitor, while everything else is left as it has been. In this case every hotel at the resort considered will have a loss, but only the hotel which changed category will become illiquid because of the lack of financial reserves. Bankruptcy is actually inevitable in the case described. There is no strategy for the changing hotel to escape its self-made trap. Furthermore it is a considerable advantage to get rid of a competitor. It may be questioned, however, whether the hotels intending a bankrupt coalition can be perfectly sure that the plan works. They cannot! There could be a chance for the changing hotel to attain larger gross gains, e.g. by means of higher prices. It is not certain that the plan works, but it is plausible. What else should the warning of bankruptcy mean!

The remarkable point about bankrupt coalitions is that they have never been discussed. Nobody seems to have even had the idea to make competition from the cost side. We must admit that it is a rather unusual, far-fetched idea; therefore, we think it was obviously non-existent for the participants of the game. Even if the idea had come under discussion, there is an argument against realizing it. The risk of illiquidity is a general danger in the first periods. Therefore, the partners of a bankrupt coalition accept some risk themselves, and they cannot be sure whether chance and risk will remain in a sensible relation.

The other decision of the first phase concerns capacity of the second period. Here, again, risk is involved. The consequences of errors, however, are by far less serious, provided the hotels act cautiously. Expanding or shrinking capacity by 10 beds requires a unique payment of DM 20.000,-- leaving DM 40.000,-- to the hotel. A hotel changing category for the second period cannot change capacity at the same time because it may spend DM 60.000,-- (i.e. gains of period zero) at most. Among the 56 firms that did not change category, 33 expanded, two reduced capacity.

The standard of knowledge at the beginning does not allow a firm opinion as to capacity. Nevertheless there is some argument for a preliminary constant capacity. The hotels may agree to keep the situation of the first and perhaps one or two further periods strictly comparable in order to improve information. Imagine one hotel increases price by DM 1,--, another hotel reduces the amount spent for advertising by DM 1.000,--, while the rest of the parameters, especially that of the third hotel, remain the same as in period 0. This sort of "information coalition" was actually tried in two cases without success. It seems to be extremely difficult to unify attitudes under conditions of uncertainty. Ideas of a far-reaching agreement,e.g. joint profit maximization, proved completely unrealistic.

After all, one can understand that the hotels are inclined to change capacity. They want to do something and hence begin a process of trial and error. Obviously hotels regularly start this process in a positive direction, i.e. by increasing capacity. This tendency prevailed in all experiments from the beginning to the end.

The course of the experiments: Sound reasons prevent the hotels from changing category at once. Similar arguments may be used to postpone such a change even during the following periods; but the arguments quickly lose weight. Eventually, however, some of the hotels will change category. We call the distribution of hotels on categories "competitive structure." Bankruptcies touch the market position of the surviving hotels in a similar way, like changes of category, though even more deeply. Therefore we consider bankrupts as a "third category." Table 2 attributes empirical changes of category and bankruptcies to periods.

Period	1	2	3	4	5	6	7	8	9	10	11	12
Number of changes into the upper category (Period of decision)	4	6	10	3	5	3	1			1		1
Number of bankrupts	2	1	1		3			1				1

Table 2

There were no changes after the 12th period. We may qualify the changes of the competitive structure as an adaptation process of mainly the first five or six periods.

We may characterize the competitive structure by a sequence of letters u (lower category), o (upper category) and k (bankrupt). For a single vacation resort we have the following n = 10 distinguishable competitive structures, where the order of o's, u's and k's is meaningless:

(ooo), (oou), (uuo), (uuu), (ook), (ouk),
(uuk), (kko), (kku), (kkk).

The two places together possibly take on $\frac{1}{2}(n-1)n = 45$ genuinely different competitive structures. Now we are in a position to compare (1) the definitely best with

(2) the common sense and (3) the actually realized structures. The best structure to be achieved by rationally acting, completely informed entrepreneurs is (oou) (oou).[1] Common sense would prefer a structure (oou) (uuo) since it is most natural to suppose that both hotel categories will have equal chances in an otherwise symmetric model; the structure (oou) (uuo) shows an equal number of both categories most evenly distributed among locations. In the course of an experiment it may be recognized, however, that the upper standard hotels do better than the other. Therefore the best structure could possibly be attained by learning and pure common sense as well. In any case, we are allowed to delete structures with a k, because bankruptcy may be avoided by sufficient care. But common sense does not always govern human action and so we expect cases of illiquidity in the structures actually realized. Table 3 shows the final competitive structures of the ten games in chronological order.

game	structure
1	(oou) (uuo)
2	(uuo) (ouk)
3	(oou) (ouk)
4	(oou) (ouk)
5	(oou) (uuo)
6	(uuo) (okk)
7	(uuo) (ouk)
8	(ook) (ouk)
9	(oou) (ouk)
10	(oou) (oou)

Table 3

1 This statement follows from the discussion of the formal model and cannot be proven here.

Bankruptcy did not occur in only three of the ten experiments. We wonder whether this result may be accepted as the consequence of common sense policy combined with occasional errors. Certainly the nine cases of illiquidity are examples of errors. They are furthermore errors of a definite character. On the other hand, the illiquid hotels neither intended their present state, as the o-and u-hotels actually did, nor was their failure caused mainly be decisions as to category. Therefore we just cancel the k's in our mind and remember the arguments for a common sense distribution of the o's and u's. Again we suggest most evenly distributed categories as an objective. For six hotels this means a structure:

(oou) (uuo);

(as mentioned above)

for five hotels: (oou) (ouk) or (uuo) (ouk);

for four hotels:

(a) one k in each place: (ouk) (ouk)

(b) two k's in one place: (oou) (ukk) or (uuo) (okk).

A comparison with table 3 shows that eight of ten games have one of these common sense competitive structures. The other two games (games eight and ten) show a shift to "o." But such an o-shift is still compatible with common sense, as experience modifies the initial rule in this direction. Hence we assert that competitive structure is determined by common sense considerations independent of the other competitive instruments, i.e. price, advertising, face-lifting and capacity, as well.

Face-lifting: The idea of an instrument to be commonly applied by competing firms is most unfamiliar to nearly everybody. Although the participants of a game at once realize the fundamental importance of the instrument, they do not know to what intensity it should be used. Roughly speaking, the general level of face-lifting varies with average expenditures of several, say five, periods. Neglecting face-lifting for five periods, however, will usually imply a serious handicap; hence, experience accumulates too slowly, as to be fruitfully used. The resulting uncertainty is one of the difficulties of real hotels in vacation resorts, too.

A general decision rule for the common policy cannot be determined, but two major regularities may be observed.

(a) Some places try to strengthen their market position by an intensive common policy, thus forcing the opponent into a similarly intensive common policy.

Number of periods during which face-lifting is charged according to head row and column							
place 1 \ place 2	charge per visitor						
	0-2	3-5	6-8	9-11	12-14	15-17	18-20
0-2	1		1				
3-5	5	26	10	2	3	1	
6-8		13	24	10	7	4	
9-11		1	19	13	11	2	5
12-14		1	7	2	2	2	
15-17			2	3	3	5	
18-20			1	3		1	

Table 4

Table 4 is a contingency table disclosing the mutual dependence of face-lifting.
(b) After a few periods of high expenditures for face-lifting, the hotels usually realize how much of their possible gains they give away. They therefore reduce expenditures for common policy. Sometimes this tendency is reversed again some periods later because of the expected negative, long-run consequences.
Price, advertisement, capacity: Price, advertising and capacity stay in a very close context. Although capacity is not a competitive instrument in the proper sense, it must be planned with respect to the level of price and advertising. Price and advertising are instruments to influence demand while capacity represents offer. It is actually impossible for the players to combine the three parameters (price, advertising, and capacity) in an optimal manner. Hence any individual opinion or other rule-of-thumb may be followed. Two contradictory lines of individual market policy - apparently the most important ones - may roughly be described as:

(a) Large capacity with the consequence of low price and high advertising costs keeps gain per visitor small but guarantees large total gains, or
(b) small capacity allows a high price, requires no high advertising costs, and is therefore more profitable.

A common prejudice favours alternative (a) while attitude (b) seems to be more efficient, if it is not exaggerated. Not only a common prejudice, but also some other circumstances make alternative (a) the more realistic one. Remember that capacity for the next period is to be decided upon before price and advertising of the current period. Now a natural optimism seems to support the hope that a possibly wrong capacity in this period might be correct next period because the market is growing. Furthermore, the charge for any change of capacity makes entrepreneurs less prone to reduction, since they must pay in this case to get rid of something which they have received for money. Hence capacity proved a more rigid parameter with a bias to expansion.

Price and advertisement are the more flexible instruments with immediately visible effects - as far as the effects of a single instrument become visible at all. In quite a number of cases they have been used to outweigh the rigid attitude with respect to capacity.

Number of changes in ten game experiments																	
Period / Parameter	2	3	4	5	6	7	8	9	10	11	12	13	14	15	16	17	Total
Capacity	2	5	4	5	14	5	6	1	5	3		1					332
Advertising expenditure		1	1		1	2	2	1	2	12	6	9	9	2	2	1	598
Price				1	1	2	2	5	3	6	6	5	12	3	3	2	614

Table 5

A hypothesis of actual economic decision: We have described experimental decision behaviour so far by simple common sense arguments and direct observations. On this discussion we may distinguish two kinds of decision situations:

(1) Entrepreneurs are able to decide on perfect knowledge or at least on plausible and sound suppositions;

(2) there are essentially different decision alternatives none of which may be selected on convincing or at least sensible a priori reasons.

The final competitive structure is an example of decision situations of the first kind, most other decision situations are of the second kind. If there are essentially different decision alternatives,entrepreneurs may act at random and learn from the result, thus introducing a process of trial and error. But as soon as it is plausible that a certain decision will improve the position of the hotel, this decision ought to be realized. Hence we are looking for a simple pragmatic rule of behaviour that obeys these requirements. There is such a simple pragmatic rule, namely the principle of imitation of more successful competitors. Hence the most successful firm should proceed by trial and error while the less successful firms ought to choose the more straightforward method of imitation. This concept needs a more concise definition in order to be submitted to a statistical test.
We confine the notion "pragmatic rule of behaviour" to such a special definition of the principle of imitation.

3. The Pragmatic Rule of Behaviour

The observed competitive structure has been explained by common sense arguments. Face-lifting is not to be decided upon just by one hotel, though elements of imitation are obvious. Nevertheless the principle of imitation is mainly confined to the individual parameters price, advertisement, and capacity. These parameters have thus far been only very superficially described.

The principle of imitation simply means that a firm uses not only its own experience but also the experience of its competitors. Since we have free information, there is a solid ground on which imitation may proceed. We shall see, however, that an appropriate imitation is more difficult to perform than it seems at first glance.

The principle of kinship: A hotel investigating into chances of imitation will not simply compare gains of the last period. At the same time it will be necessary to get an idea as to how far the market position of a competitor is comparable at all. A hotel in the other vacation resort and in the other category possibly favoured by bankruptcy of a third hotel can be compared with utmost caution only. On the other hand, a hotel in the same resort and in the same category operates under strictly equal conditions. Between both extremes there are two intermediate cases, i.e. the cases "same category - different place" and "same place - different category." Now it seems to be intuitively clear to all participants of the game experiments that category is to be considered as the dominating characteristic. This impression becomes an almost obvious fact for all participants in the course of any game. It is difficult to say why this impression prevails; it is a fact, however. Hence we may establish a hierarchy of more or less comparable hotels. We say for brevity's sake that hotels are more or less "akin" and classify this sort of relationship as "kinship." For technical reasons we add as a fifth relationship that of illiquidity, i.e. the relationship of an actually no longer existent hotel to any other. We assume that they are least akin. Now we are in a position to define a degree of kinship by the following scheme:

Degree of kinship of two hotels	Category	Place
1	identical	identical
2	identical	different
3	different	identical
4	different	different
5	one or both hotels bankrupt	

By the "principle of kinship" we mean that common sense requires current and thorough observation solely of the most akin hotels, i.e. of the hotels with lowest degree of kinship relative to the hotel under consideration. Less akin hotels may be observed with less attention. Only fundamental events such as change of category, bankruptcies and perhaps remarkable changes of capacity need be noticed. The principle of kinship reduces current market observation considerably and keeps work within reasonable limits.

Notice that the relationship between two hotels of the same degree of kinship and that between a hotel and its most akin competitor is formally quite different. Especially a hotel is not necessarily most akin to its most akin competitor. Within a market operating on the principle of kinship, there are usually isolated groups of firms that do not care much about outside competitors. Nevertheless the situation can not be described in an appropriate manner by a clean partition of the whole market into groups of mutually influencing competitors. A self-explanatory diagram with arrows designating the direction of influence shows the complex relationship for the competitive structure appealing most to common sense:

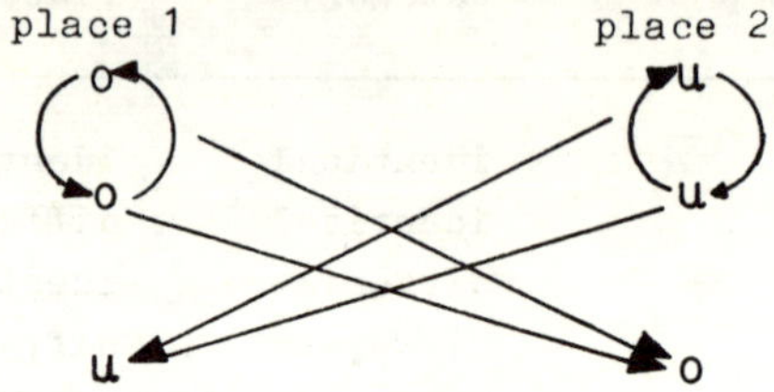

We now see the implications of the principle of kinship. It contradicts the elementary economic idea of a general, unrestricted interdependence.

Pragmatic behaviour - a first definition

Pragmatic behaviour requires both finding the most akin competitor and selecting the parameter to be adapted to the more successful hotel. Imitation is usually not perfect. Suppose an entrepreneur accounts a high price for his competitor's success. Now he may be led to the opinion that a still higher price will raise his gains above that of his competitor's. In order to be cautious, however, he increases his expenditures for advertising at the same time, though his competitor operates on a lower level. We think this is an example of imitation, but we also see how difficult it is to decide merely upon the basis of visible reaction, whether imitation was intended or not. Fortunately, we know from the comments of the firms that there has been a vivid feeling for the weight of the instruments to be applied. As already mentioned, capacity is not easily varied. Next to a change of category, it is considered to be the most far-reaching decision; therefore, we attach the number 1 to it. Price and advertising expenditures are not distinguished that clearly. As a rule, however, we may assume preponderance of price, though a few participants might have thought otherwise. Hence the order is:

Hierarchical Position	Instrument
1	capacity
2	price
3	advertising

Now we may proceed to define "imitation" according to the rules of pragmatic behaviour. First we assume that one of the most akin competitors has had a larger gain during the last period. Now we look for the instrument of lowest hierarchical position actually varied during the current period. Irrespective of the change of any other parameter, we assume imitation if and only if the instrument considered is adapted (including imperfect adaptation and overadaptation) in the direction of the corresponding instrument of the most successful among the most akin competitors. We hope to cover most cases of intended imitation by this rule. There are, however, counter-examples. The example above, for instance, may easily be modified with this effect. Imagine a hotel which considers advertising as the most important instrument. It will certainly adapt (or over-adapt) advertising cost to the level of its competitor and perhaps change price at the same time in the wrong direction. Although imitation is intended, this case would be deleted by our rule.

Pragmatic behaviour - a second definition

A more serious defect of our first rule of pragmatic behaviour is to be discussed here. The rule does not take into account that a hotel may have strong reasons not to imitate a successful competitor. Imagine that the hotel considered has a considerably larger capacity than its more successful most akin competitor, but little demand. It expects an increasing demand for the future and wishes not to reduce capacity. Suppose further that the price is below that of the competitor, which is most likely because of the large capacity. An adaptation to the higher price, however, contradicts common sense. On the contrary, the hotel will be forced to further reduce the price; hence, it does not imitate a successful competitor according to our rule.

A more adequate rule should not judge cases like this as contradictory to pragmatic behaviour. On the other hand, these considerations are valid only for clear cases of poorly used capacity. We do not want, however, to include nearly exhausted capacities into these considerations. Nearly exhausted capacity indicates a realistically adapted set of parameters. As to the question what "nearly exhausted" should mean we choose deliberately a value of 90 % or more. If, therefore, capacity is used less than 90 %, any behaviour that tends to improve the situation, i.e. reduction of capacity, or price, or an increase of advertising expenditures (ranked according to the same hierarchical rule as before) will be qualified as compatible with pragmatic behaviour. The original rule of pragmatic behaviour is valid otherwise.

A Test: A natural way to test statistical significance of both versions of the pragmatic rule of behaviour is offered by the sign test. We have just to find out for every hotel and every period who is the most akin competitor (who always exists). If the hotel considered itself as most successful, then the rule is not applicable. We attach a 0 to this case. Otherwise, we have alternatively to decide on the basis of the two rules, whether the pragmatic rules was followed, or not, symbolizing the situations by +1 and -1 respectively. We have carried out a sign test for all 51 hotels that reached the end of the experiment, as far as it was possible.

Table 6 and table 7 attribute for both versions of the pragmatic rule, number of hotels to number of sign $\neq 0$.

First Version of the Pragmatic Rule of Behaviour														
Number of signs $\neq 0$	<5	5	6	7	8	9	10	11	12	13	14	15	16	17
Number of Hotels	10	7	3	6	4	5	6	4	1	2	2		1	

Table 6

Second Version of the Pragmatic Rule of Behaviour														
Number of signs $\neq 0$	<5	5	6	7	8	9	10	11	12	13	14	15	16	17
Number of Hotels	4	4	2	2	8	5	4	5	9	3	3	1		1

Table 7

First Version of the Pragmatic Rule of Behaviour[1]										
w	.0-.1	.1-.2	.2-.3	.3-.4	.4-.5	.5-.6	.6-.7	.7-.8	.8-.9	.9-.10
Number of Hotels	2	1	-	2	2	-	2	8	4	20

Table 8

Second Version of the Pragmatic Rule of Behaviour[1]										
w	.0-.1	.1-.2	.2-.3	.3-.4	.4-.5	.5-.6	.6-.7	.7-.8	.8-.9	.9-.10
Number of Hotels	-	3	1	1	2	-	1	6	10	23

Table 9

1 Intervals follow the inequalities: lower limit $< w \leq$ upper limit. 0 belongs to the first interval.

If the behaviour of the hotels is not influenced by one of the versions of our pragmatic rule we should expect an equal number of "plus" and "minus." This is our null hypothesis for either version. Let 1-w ($0<w<1$) be the probability that on the null hypothesis more pluses will occur than have actually been observed. For low values of 1-w, say 0.05 or 0.10, and for high values, say 0.95 or 0.90, we will reject the null hypothesis since they indicate predominating pragmatic behaviour or the opposite of it, respectively. Correspondingly we are inclined to associate a high value of w, say w = .9, with a high probability of the pragmatic rule of behaviour. If the null hypothesis should be valid we expect a value of w (or 1-w) near 1/2.[1] Table 8 and table 9 give an empirical distribution of hotels on 10 intervals of w. Although the results suggest that not every firm follows one of the alternative pragmatic rules, there is evidence for a strong tendency in this direction. The results displayed here are neither based on evident regularities of the empirical outcome (there are no such regularities), nor are they the last step of a sequence of trials to explain data. More sophisticated alternative rules of pragmatic behaviour are possible. The rigid schemes used here certainly fail to exhibit the complex truth. A further refined scheme developed on many trials, however, might disclose spurious improvements due to chance.

IV. Conclusion

Our empirical results show a strong tendency to imitate the most successful competitor. The most successful firm, however, has nobody to imitate. Other firms that do not wish to follow a more successful competitor because they are nearly as good (or for some other reason) are in a similar situation. They will proceed along a line of trial and error. If they succeed to improve their position beyond that of their competitors, they will be imitated. This picture of development apparently fits observations made on real West German tourist markets. Moreover, it is a further ar-

---

1 We have computed w-values based on a comparison with a hotel different from the most successful, most akin competitor and actually received a distribution close to 1/2.

gument for the concept of J. Schumpeter, who formulated a process very similar to that described above as a general law of economic development.

24. INDETERMINACY OF OUTCOME AND THE PRISONER'S DILEMMA GAME[1]

PHILIP S. GALLO JR. AND JOHN P. SHEPOSH*

Introduction

A good deal of research that has been conducted with the Prisoner's Dilemma game has been done with the hope that results from these studies could eventually be generalized to real life conflict situations. A number of researchers have felt that the development of such generalizations has been impeded by the rather limited structure of the Prisoner's Dilemma game, involving as it does two players, two choices for each player, no communication, and strictly determined outcomes. As a consequence, studies have appeared in which the structure of the game has been enriched in order to make it more similar to the more complex conflicts found in the real world.
By and large, these studies have indicated that the rather stereotyped behavior encountered in the standard Prisoner's Dilemma game can be broken down by the introduction of a wider range of behavioral possibilities to the subjects. Fortunately or unfortunately, as the case may be, they have also indicated

---

* San Diego State College

1 This research supported by NSF Grant GS-2332 to the senior author.

that experimental conflict situations are far more complex and are influenced by far more variables than we might have otherwise believed. For example, although a number of studies indicate that cooperation is enhanced by the opportunity to communicate (Loomis, 1959; Scodel, Minas, Ratoosh, & Lipetz, 1959; Daniels, 1967), still other conflict studies (Deutsch & Krauss, 1962; Pilisuk & Skolnik, 1968) report no effect or a reduction in cooperation as a function of communicative possibilities. Apparently, the effects of communication are mediated by mutual trust or distrust, which in turn is mediated by other experimental and personality variables. Seemingly minor changes in format can have profound and significant effects upon behavior. Evans and Crumbaugh (1966) have developed a non-matrix presentation of the Prisoner's Dilemma game which in every way retains the strategic properties of the original game. Yet, the subjects are considerably more cooperative when presented with the non-matrix version. Pruitt (1967), utilizing the "decomposed" version of the Prisoner's Dilemma game which he developed, has shown that the same parent Prisoner's Dilemma game can elicit widely differing amounts of cooperative behavior, depending upon the form of the particular "decomposed" game that is used. Researchers who have attempted to expand the number of choices available in the game have also turned up some rather strange and contradictory results. Komorita, Sheposh, and Braver (1968) added a third, somewhat punishing strategy choice to the basic game. Two experiments were conducted, both utilizing contingent strategies programmed by the experimenter. In one experiment, only the experimenter had the third choice available, in the second experiment, the subjects also had the option to use it. In general, the results indicated that programmed strategies were effective in manipulating the subjects' choices in the three-choice games to an extent not generally found in two-choice games. However, when the subjects had the option to use the third choice, they did so with considerable frequency, even though such a choice was clearly "irrational" in the game theory sense of the word. Pilisuk and Skolnik (1968), using a six-choice game, also found that programmed strategies were effective and evoked more cooperation than when natural pairs played. Gallo, Funk, and Levine (1969) compared two-choice, six-choice, and eleven-choice non-matrix Prisoner's Dilemma games under conditions of real and imaginary money. The most interesting finding was a strong interaction between the two variables. Real and imaginary money had little or no effect on the two-choice game. Subjects in the six-choice game were highly cooperative when real money was at stake and highly uncooperative when playing for imaginary money. This effect tended to dissipate when the subjects were allowed 11 choices. The results of studies that have expanded the format of the Prisoner's Dilemma game are both encouraging and discouraging. They are encouraging in that they indicate that the rather inflexible pattern of competition that is found in most Prisoner's Dilemma studies may be a function of the limited behavioral and communicative possibilities of the game, rather than being a function of the nature of the underlying conflict. They are discouraging in that no consistent patterns tend to emerge to help us better understand real life conflicts. Furthermore, although it is not terribly difficult to expand the format of the Prisoner's Dilemma game, it is often much more difficult to identify the real world analog of the experimental variable that has been manipulated. Thus, although it may be possible to state with some confidence that the manipulation of a certain experimental variable will have a predictable effect upon an experimental conflict, it may be nearly impossible to determine what variable to introduce into a real world conflict in order to obtain a similar effect. Concern over external validity is not limited to the question of the kinds of variables, but also whether and to what extent chance or indeterminacy effects outcomes.

It is therefore somewhat surprising that little or no research has been conducted to determine the effect of indeterminacy of outcome on behavior in the Prisoner's Dilemma game. The only uncertainty facing the players has to do with the choice that will be made by one's opponent. Once the two choices have been made, the payoffs are strictly determined by the payoff matrix. This seems to be in sharp contrast with most real life conflicts in which payoffs are often vague and unspecified and in which certain other factors, such as chance or intervention by a third party, may conspire to alter the payoffs once the choices are made.

Examples come to mind quite readily. A general may be faced with the decision to attack or not attack a particular enemy outpost. Information concerning the size of the enemy garrison and the weaponry available to it as compared to the size and weaponry of his own command may indicate certain gains and losses depending upon the enemy's decision to retreat or to defend the outpost. At the same time, changes in

weather conditions, unknown enemy reinforcements, or advance knowledge of the attack leaked to the enemy may dictate an outcome completely different from the expected one. Thus, the general must not only attempt to anticipate the enemy's response but must also gauge the probability that certain other factors will occur which could drastically change the outcome.
Similarly, labor and management negotiators may have to weigh the probability that certain presumably favorable outcomes may be overturned. Although the union may be able to negotiate shrewdly enough to obtain a highly favorable outcome, if government believes that the solution is inflationary, it may intervence and impose a settlement that would be less acceptable than if the union had agreed to a more modest solution initially. It would appear that many real world bargainers must not only assess the probability of various strategy choices that might be made by their opponents but must also assess the probability that they will achieve the hoped for outcome. In the laboratory, the introduction of chance factors into a strategy game could affect game behavior and in certain instances could even change the nature of the game.

The present experiment was designed to explore the effects of introducing indeterminacy of outcome into the Prisoner's Dilemma game. Since the payoffs are equal when the two players jointly compete or jointly cooperate, indeterminacy was introduced only on trials in which one player cooperated and the other competed. When this outcome occurred, the players exchanged payoffs with 25%, 50%, or 75% probability, depending upon the particular experimental condition. Other groups of subjects played on expected value matrices derived from the above three conditions. That is, the subjects in the 25% exchange expected value group played on a matrix which displayed the average payoff per trial that would be expected if off-axis payoffs were exchanged 25 % of the time, etc. Thus, some subjects saw a standard Prisoner's Dilemma matrix and knew that payoffs would be exchanged on a certain percentage of the trials while other subjects played on a matrix in which this chance factor had already been taken into account.

It is logical to expect that as the probability of exchanging outcomes increased, the subjects would be less and less likely to choose the competitive response. Despite the fact that most predictions based on logic have not been supported by the results of Prisoner's Dilemma research, it was predicted that the greater the probability of exchanging payoffs, the greater the amount of cooperation that would be produced. It was further predicted that subjects who played on the expected value matrix and could see the actual effects of exchanging payoffs would be more cooperative than subjects who played in the condition in which chance dictated the exchange. It was reasoned that subjects in the condition in which chance dictated the exchange would underestimate the effect of chance on outcomes, that is, they would not extract all of the certainty from the information provided.

One additional point of interest in the study was to determine whether subjects' perceived locus of control would differentiate behavior in a game situation in which outcomes were dictated by chance. Locus of control was measured by the Internal-External Control Scale (Rotter, 1966). Since Low-External subjects perceive events as being a consequence of one's own actions it was expected that they would tend to take into account indeterminacy and thereby regulate their behavior to a greater extent, i.e., show a greater degree of cooperation than High-External subjects.

Method

Subjects

Seventy male and seventy female students enrolled in introductory psychology classes at San Diego State College served as subjects in the experiment. All subjects received credit toward an experimental participation requirement. Ten male and ten female subjects were randomly assigned to one of seven experimental conditions. All subjects were run in likesexed pairs.

Apparatus

The experimental apparatus for each subject was a response box which consisted of a 2 x 2 matrix of payoff values with lights in each cell to indicate the subjects' joint choice, two push buttons corresponding to the two available choices, and a red warning light used to signal the beginning of a trial. The subjects' responses were recorded on a master panel which could be seen by the experimenter but not by the subjects.

Subjects in four of the experimental conditions played on Matrix A, shown in Figure 1. These conditions were the control group and the 25%, 50%, and 75% probability of exchange groups. Subjects in the control group played under standard Prisoner's Dilemma rules. An additional piece of equipment was introduced for subjects in the other three groups. It consisted of a circular plywood disc, 12 inches in diameter, which was mounted on a plywood base. A plexiglas spinner was mounted in

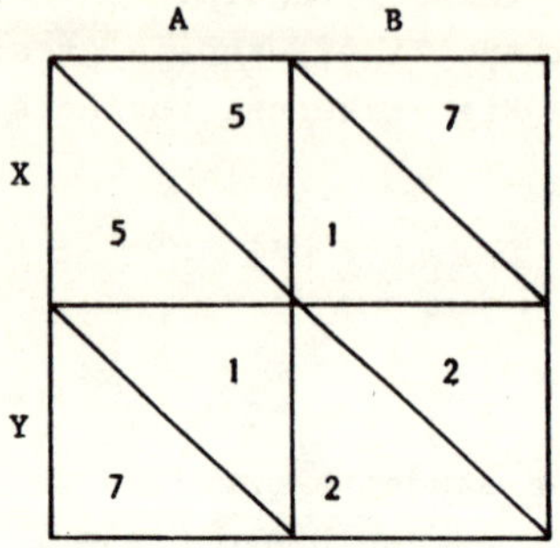

Matrix A - The Parent Matrix, used for Control & Spinner Groups.

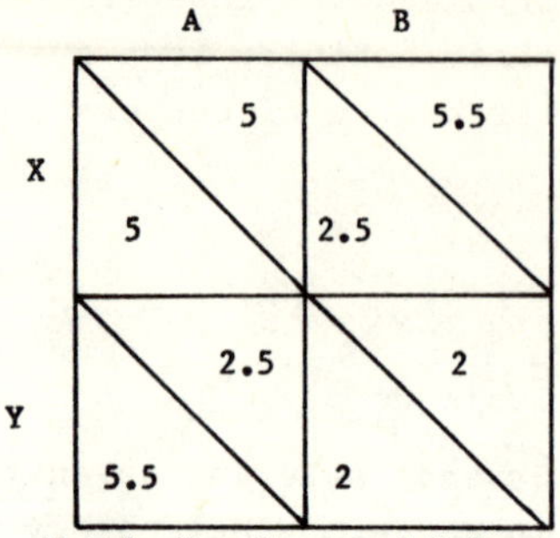

Matrix B - Expected Value, 25% Probability of Exchange.

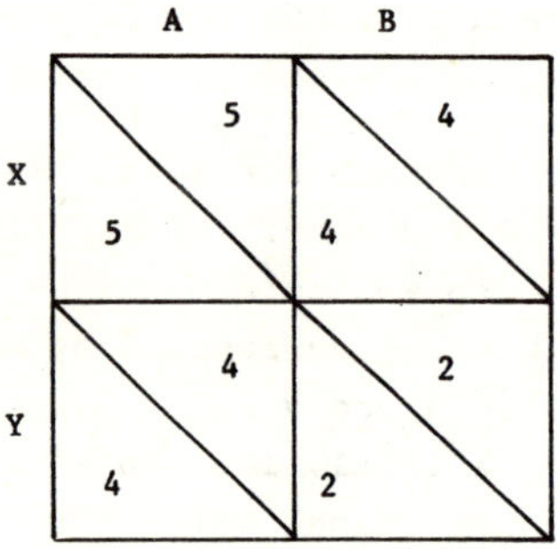

Matrix C - Expected Value, 50% Probability of Exchange.

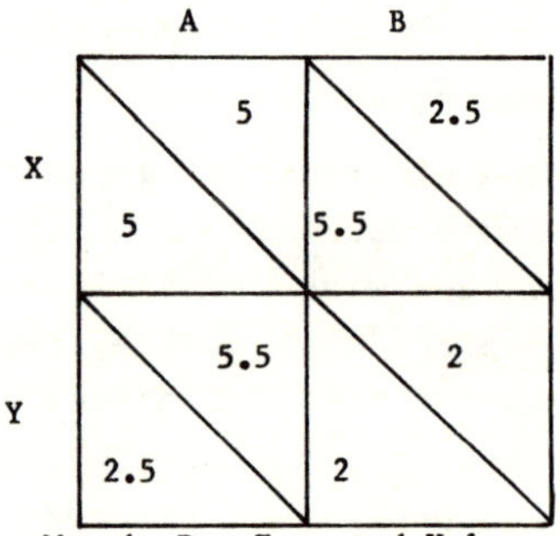

Matrix D - Expected Value, 75% Probability of Exchange.

Fig. 1. The Matrices Used in the Experiment.

the center of the circle. Beneath the spinner was affixed a cardboard disc which was partitioned into two areas, one marked "keep" and the other marked "exchange." In the 25% exchange group, 25% of the area of the disc was marked "exchange" and 75% was marked "keep." In the 50% exchange condition, 50% of the area of the disc was marked "exchange" and 50% was marked "keep." In the 75% exchange condition, 75% of the area of the disc was marked "exchange" and 25% was marked "keep." The discs are illustrated in Figure 2.

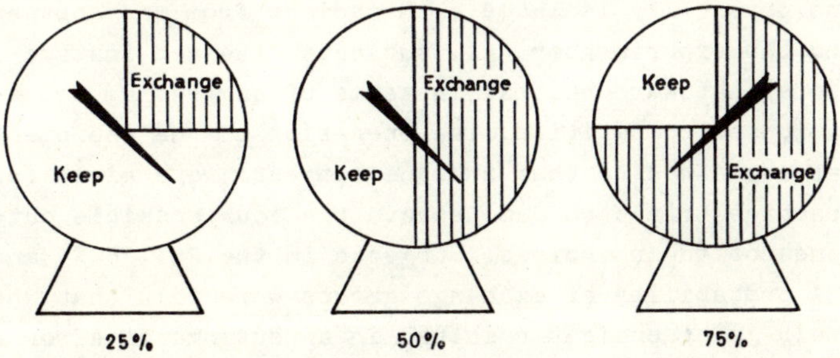

Figure 2: The Probability of Exchange Spinners

The spinner was finely balanced to assure that the appropriate proportions would be generated.
The remaining three groups played on Matrices B, C, and D, shown in Figure 1. Matrix B represents the expected payoffs from Matrix A if off-axis payoffs are exchanged 25% of the time. The payoffs were obtained by multiplying the value of the payoff by the probability that the subject would obtain it. Thus, for Cell BX, Player 1 has .75 pro-

bability of obtaining 7 plus .25 probability of obtaining 1 = 5.5. Similarly for Cell BX, Player 2 has .25 probability of obtaining 7 and .75 probability of obtaining 1 = 2.5. The values in Cell AY were computed in the same manner. The payoff values in Matrices C and D were also computed in the same fashion, using .50 probability of exchange for Matrix C and .75 probability for Matrix D.

Procedure

The subjects were brought into the experimental room together and seated at a table in front of their individual game equipment. A wooden barrier visually and physically isolated each subject from one another and the experimenter. All subjects received instructions that were neutral in terms of suggesting cooperation or competition. The operation of the equipment was explained to them and the subjects were given four practice trials to demonstrate the four possible outcomes of their choices. Subjects in the 25%, 50%, and 75% probability of exchange groups were told that when their joint choices resulted in an outcome of AY or BX, there was a chance that they would have to exchange payoffs with the other person. The spinner apparatus was demonstrated to them and the probabilities explained.

Since previous research in this laboratory had convinced us that the presence or absence of real money as payoffs can be a potent variable in game playing research, all subjects played for real money. At the end of the experiment, the subjects received 1¢ for each point that they had earned. This fact was carefully explained to each subject prior to the first trial. All subjects played for 50 trials. One hundred percent joint cooperation would thus have paid each subject a total of $2.50.

Twenty subjects were randomly assigned to a control group. These subjects played on Matrix A and the payoffs were strictly determined by the matrix. The remaining 120 subjects were randomly assigned to one cell of a 2 x 3 design. These subjects had either a 25%, 50%, or 75% chance of exchanging payoffs when the outcome was AY or BX. Half of these subjects played on Matrix A and utilized the spinner apparatus to determine probability of exchange. The other half of the subjects played on either Matrix B, C, or D. Thus, each probability group was matched to a group playing on a comparable expected value matrix.
At the termination of the game all subjects completed the Internal-External Control Scale (Rotter, 1966). They were then debriefed and paid the amount that they had earned. All subjects signed a receipt for the money which also pledged them to secrey about the experiment. As far as could be determined, no subject divulged information about the experiment.

Results

All analyses were performed on the number of cooperative (A or X) responses per dyad. Although every cell had equal numbers of male and female subjects, no breakdown was made on the basis of sex since no previous study run in this laboratory had yielded a sex difference in behavior. The first analysis compared the four groups of subjects that had been run on Matrix A - the control group (0 probability of exchange), 25% probability of exchange, 50% probability of exchange, and 75% probability of exchange. The data, based upon number of cooperative choices over 5 blocks of 10 trials were analyzed using a 5 blocks x 4 experimental conditions analysis of variance. The percentages of cooperative responses for the treatment groups were, respectively, 40%, 42.9%, 67.7%, and 81%. The analysis indicated that the treatment groups were significantly different ($\underline{F}_{3,36}$ = 12.36, $\underline{p}$ < .001). Trend analysis was also applied to these data. The linear component was highly significant ($\underline{F}_{1,36}$ = 34.19, $\underline{p}$ < .001) whereas

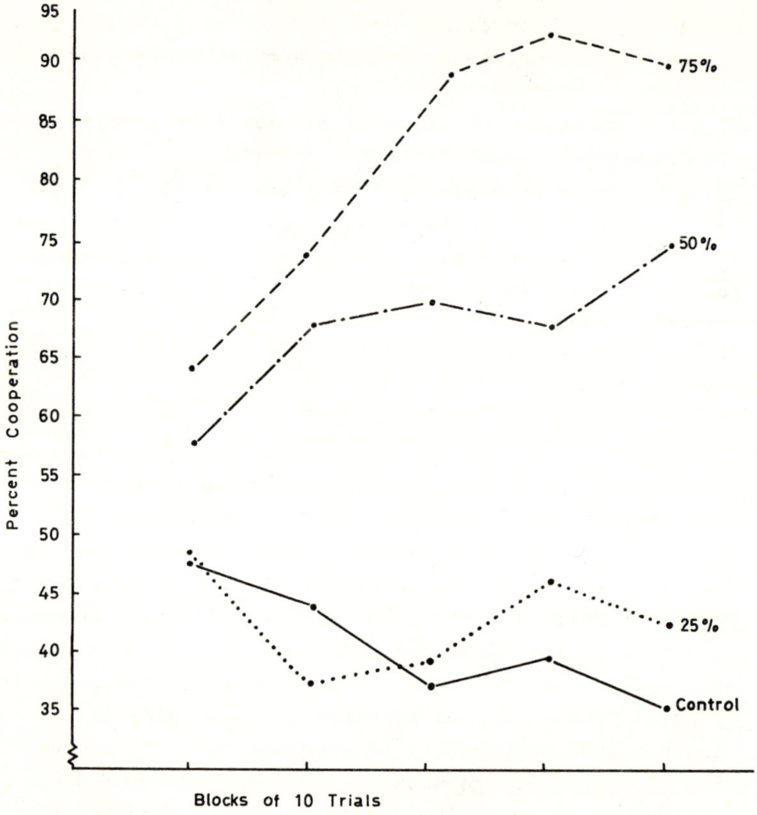

Figure 3: Mean Percent Cooperation for the Four Probability of Exchange Groups

the quadratic and quartic components both yielded F ratios below one. The analysis also yielded a significant condition x blocks interaction ($F_{12,144} = 3.93$, $p < .01$). Figure 3 illustrates the nature of the interaction. As can be readily seen, the control condition (0 probability of exchange) and the 25% probability of exchange condition showed a slight decrease in level of cooperation while the reverse trend is evident for the 50% and 75% probability of exchange conditions.

The main analysis was performed on the data from the 2 x 3 factorial design. This analysis compared the various probability groups (25% vs. 50% vs. 75%) and the method of effecting the exchange (spinner vs. expected value matrices). In addition, the 50 trials were again blocked into 5 groups of 10 trials each. A 2 x 3 x 5 mixed design analysis of variance was used to analyze the data. The mean percentages of cooperative responses for the between-subjects portion of the analysis are shown in Table 1.

Table I

Mean Percent Cooperative Responses per Dyad

Method of Exchange	Probability of Exchange: 25%	50%	75%	Total
Spinner	42.9	67.8	81.7	64.1
Expected Value	45.2	96.9	94.7	78.9
Total	44.1	82.3	88.2	

The results of this analysis indicated that subjects who played on the expected value matrices were more cooperative than those who played with the spinner ($F_{1,54}$ = 17.19, $p < .001$), that increasing probabilities of exchanging payoffs resulted in greater cooperative behavior ($F_{2,54}$ = 60.18, $p < .001$), and that there was a significant interaction between the two variables ($F_{2,54}$ = 4.76, $p < .005$). The interaction indicated that difference in cooperativeness between the subjects who played with the expected value matrix and those that had the spinner were smaller at 25% and 75% probability of exchange and reached a peak at 50% probability of exchange.

The within-subjects portion of the analysis indicated two significant effects. Contrary to the findings of most studies, the subjects became more cooperative as the game progressed ($F_{4,216}$ = 6.35, $p < .001$). However, this finding must be interpreted cautiously because of a significant interaction between trial blocks and probability of exchange ($F_{8,216}$ = 6.46, $p < .001$). The subjects in the 25% probability of exchange group actually became less cooperative as the game went on whereas subjects in the 50% probability group increased somewhat and subjects in the 75% probability group increased quite a bit. Figure 4 presents the level of cooperation obtained for each of the six conditions across blocks of trials. Both 25% probability of exchange conditions showed similar patterns of cooperation over the run of the game. Differences between the expected value matrix conditions and spinner conditions are evident for the 50% and 75% probability of exchange levels. For both expected value matrix conditions, a high degree of cooperation occurs asymptotically on the first block of 20 trials. By contrast, the level of cooperation in the spinner conditions increased gradually.

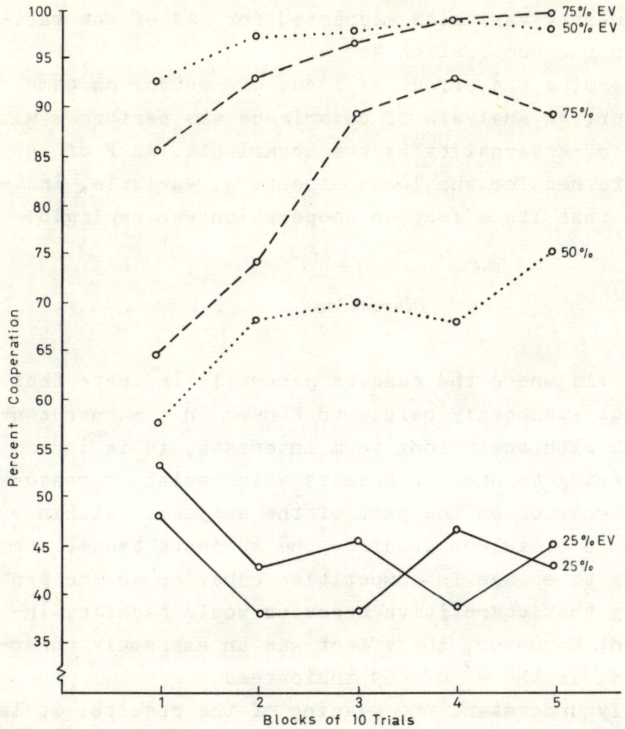

Figure 4: Mean Percent Cooperation for the 25%, 50%, & 75% Probability of Exchange Groups and the Corresponding Expected Value Matrix Groups

An assumption was made that the between-subjects part of the analysis represented a fixed effect model analysis of variance, and the statistic w^2, as proposed by Hays (1963), was computed for each of the $\underline{F}$ ratios. These computations yielded an w^2 of .59 for probability of exchange, .08 for method of exchange, and .04 for the interaction of the two variables. Combined, the experimental variables accounted for 71% of the variance in the cooperation scores.

To determine the effect of locus of control on game behavior, an analysis of covariance was performed with degree of Externality as the covariable. An $\underline{F}$ of .45 was obtained for the locus of control variable, indicating that its effect on cooperation was negligible.

Discussion

In a field where the results generally indicate that subjects stubbornly refuse to behave in a manner consistent with their long-term interests, it is indeed encouraging to uncover results which point to reasonable behavior on the part of the subjects. Within the range of values studied, the subjects became less willing to engage in competitive behavior as the probability that competitive behavior would backfire increased. Moreover, the effect was an extremely powerful one, as the w^2 of .59 indicates.

To fully understand the meaning of the results, it is necessary to examine the expected value matrices that were used in this study. As previously mentioned, matrices B, C, and D represent the long term expected payoffs for subjects playing on Matrix A with 25%, 50%, and 75% probability of exchanging payoffs. Thus, each expected value group was matched with a group of subjects who played on the parent matrix with a certain probability of exchange. However, the subjects in the expected value conditions had no way of knowing that they were so matched, and thus their behavior was directed at the specific payoff matrix that was in front of them.

It is obvious from an inspection of the matrices that only the subjects in the control condition were actually playing on a Prisoner's Dilemma matrix. The subjects who played on Matrix B were in fact playing on a weak form of "chicken" matrix, whereas subjects who played on matrices C and D were in fact playing a strategically "trivial" game in which the cooperative response dominated the competitive response. Using Rapaport and Guyer's Taxonomy of 2 x 2 Games (1966), Matrix C is representative of an absolutely stable equilibrium and Matrix D is a strongly stable equilibrium game. In Matrix C, the largest individual payoff was for joint cooperation. In Matrix D, the largest individual payoff occurred for the cooperator when the other player competed. Thus, it is not surprising that the number of A and X responses increased linearly over the four matrices, approaching 100% on matrices C and D. While the latter two matrices offer little or no theoretical interest, it should not be overlooked that the injection of indeterminacy changes the nature of the game profoundly. The implication for contingency planning is rather apparent.

It is also not surprising that the amount of cooperative behavior increased as the game progressed. As the interaction of trial blocks with probability of exchange indicates, this effect is largely accounted for by the subjects in the 50% and 75% conditions. The subjects who played on the "chicken" matrix did in fact become less cooperative over time. Only subjects who played on what were in effect trivial matrices became more cooperative. Since most of the non-cooperative behavior in the 50% and 75% groups occurred early in the game, it is probable that this behavior represents merely initial unfamiliarity with the game.

The most interesting findings of the study have to do with the significant difference between the expected value groups and the spinner groups and the significant interaction of this variable with method of exchange. In the groups utilizing the spinner to effect exchanges, cooperative behavior increased as probability of exchange increased. However, when the probability reached as high as 50%, rational behavior would dictate that the subjects should have become close to 100% cooperative. Yet, the subjects in the 50% group attained only 67.8% cooperation and the subjects in the 75% group reached 81.7%. It would seem apparent that when faced with probabilities, rather than expected values, the subjects rather consistently overestimated their chances of successful competition. This effect was strongest at the 50% probability of exchange level. An alternative interpretation to that of perceived invulnerability is that information processing and utilization was more difficult in the condition in which exchange was dictated by chance. Therefore a lag in the increase of cooperative behavior over time would be expected. This would obtain particularly for the 50% probability of exchange condition. In the 25% probability of exchange condition, subjects would tend to disregard the prospect of exchange whereas in the 75% probability of exchange condition the prospect of exchange was highly probable and therefore regarded as a given.

Using the expected value groups as a baseline, the subjects perception of their chances of successful competition were more closely veridical when the probability of exchange was low (25%) or high (75%) and least veridical when the probability was intermediate (50%).

We had included the Internal-External Control Scale in the eventuality perceived locus of control differentiated game behavior of subjects under conditions where exchange was dictated by chance, According to the theory, Low-Externals should come to terms with an uncertain environment more readily than High-Externals. This expectation was not borne out by the data. It appears that this construct has little effect in this type of situation. This conclusion is based on a statistical analysis. A more rigorous test would be to run homogeneous dyads: High-Externals vs. High-Internals, etc.

Overall, the results indicate that decision makers are able to modify their behavior to take into account changes in the probability of successful competition. They are most successful in behaving in a manner calculated to further their long-term interests when the results of chance factors are clearly spelled out for them, as in the expected value matrices. When information is presented in probability form, there is a tendency to behave as though the probabilities are more in their favor than they actually are. In view of studies on gambling behavior, these results are not particularly unexpected. Moreover, this form of wishful thinking seems most pronounced when the probabilities of successful competition are in some intermediate range. It would appear that decision makers can be aided in making rational decisions by having the consequences of their behavior spelled out to them in the clearest form possible.

In the present experiment, indeterminacy was introduced in a rather simple and straightforward manner. A more interesting variation of the expected value matrix condition would be to provide the subjects with a shifting sequence of matrices which would allow for a more dynamic interaction. Similarly, the probability of exchange could be varied from trial to trial in a random fashion, averaging to some certain prespecified values.

It would also be interesting to explore the effects of providing subjects with incomplete information about the probability of successful competition. Hopefully, such variations would increase our knowledge of the role of indeterminacy in determining behavior in real life conflict situations.

Bibliography

Daniels, V., Communication, Incentive, and Structural Variables in Interpersonal Exchange and Negotiation, Journal of Experimental Social Psychology, 3, 1967, pp. 47-74.

Deutsch, M., and R.M. Krauss, Studies of Interpersonal Bargaining, Journal of Conflict Resolution, 6, 1962, pp. 52-76.

Evans, G.W., and C.M. Crumbaugh, Effects of Prisoner's Dilemma Format on Cooperative Behavior, Journal of Personality and Social Psychology, 3, 1966, pp. 486-488.

Gallo, P.S., Funk, S.G., and J.R. Levine, Reward Size, Method of Presentation, and Number of Alternatives in a Prisoner's Dilemma Game, Journal of Personality and Social Psychology, 13, 1969, pp. 239-244.

Hays, W., Statistics for Psychologists. New York: Holt, Rinehart & Winston, 1963.

Komorita, S.S., Sheposh, J.P., and S.L. Braver, Power, the Use of Power, and Cooperative Choice in a Two-person Game, Journal of Personality and Social Psychology, 8, 1968, pp. 134-142.

Loomis, J.L., Communication, the Development of Trust and Cooperative Behavior, Human Relations, 12, 1959, pp. 305-315.

Pilisuk, M., and P. Skolnik, Inducing Trust: A Test of the Osgood Proposal, Journal of Personality and Social Psychology, 8, 1968, pp. 121-133.

Pruitt, D.G., Reward Structure and Cooperation: The Decomposed Prisoner's Dilemma Game, Journal of Personality and Social Psychology, 7, 1967, pp. 21-27.

Rotter, J.B., Generalized Expectancies for Internal vs. External Control of Reinforcement, Psychological Monographs, 80, 1966, pp. 1-28.

Scodel, A., Minas, J.S., Ratoosh, P., and M. Lipetz, Some Descriptive Aspects of Two-person non-zero-sum Games, Journal of Conflict Resolution, 3, 1959, pp. 114-119.

25. AN EXPERIMENT WITH TEN DUOPOLY GAMES AND BEAT-THE-AVERAGE BEHAVIOR*)****

MARTIN SHUBIK** AND MARTIN RIESE***

1. Introduction

This is a report on an experiment combined with the teaching of a seminar on competition, oligopoly and the theory of games during May and June 1970 at the Institute for Advanced Studies in Vienna. Ten teams, each with two players, played for sixteen periods in the identical oligopolistic market. No player was informed of either the market structure or of any of the parameters of the market before the play.
The players were informed of their costs, production limits, and inventory carrying costs. A small money prize (100 Austrian schillings) was offered to the player who managed to achieve the highest score (profits) relative to his competitor. This briefing had

---

* This work was performed partially with the support of the Institute for Advanced Studies, Vienna, Research Memorandum No. 52, March 1971, and partially with the support of NSF grant GS-2840.

** Yale University.

*** Institute for Advanced Studies, Vienna. Computation by Marianne Preyer, Institute for Advanced Studies, Vienna.

**** The authors wish to thank Prof. G. Bruckmann for his valuable comments, especially his observations on the dynamic optimal advertising policy.

the effect of converting a nonconstant sum two-person game into a two-person zero-sum game where the goals of the players on a team could be described in terms of:

$$\max_{s_1} \min_{s_2} \{P_1(s_1,s_2) - P_2(s_1,s_2)\}$$

where P_1 and P_2 are the payoff functions of each player and s_1 and s_2 stand for their strategies.

2. *The Game*

2.1. The Structure of the Game

The experiment was based on a business game constructed by Shubik and Levitan [1]. A short sketch of the main features of this game is given below.

2.1.1. Scenario

The game described here is an "environment poor" game in the sense that all rules are formal and well described for the actual playing of the game. The firms and their market are completely specified by the structure of the model and the information resulting from their interplay is presented in form of balance sheets and industry statistics.

2.1.2. Number of Players

The number of players can be varied from one to twelve; in our experiment there were two. There is only one product per player and one market. A team consisted of a single player.

2.1.3. Demand Conditions

The overall demand leaving out the effect of advertising and assuming that the prices charged by all firms are identical is linear. When the prices charged by the firms are not the same, there is a rationing scheme which computes the contingent demand schedules. Lost sales are also recorded.

The demand equation for the product of the ith firm is given by

$$F_i(p,a) = \frac{1}{n}\left|\alpha-\beta(p_i+\gamma(p_i-\bar{p}))\right| f_i(\theta,a)(1+\eta\sqrt{\Sigma a_j})$$

where

$$f_i(\theta,a) = \begin{cases} \theta+(1-\theta)\dfrac{na_i}{\Sigma a_j} & \text{if } \sum_{j=1}^{n} a_j > 0 \\ 1 \text{ if } \sum_{j=1}^{n} a_j = 0. \end{cases}$$

p_i = price charged by player i,

a_i = advertising expenditure by player i,

$\bar{p} = \sum_{i=1}^{n} p_i/n$

α = the size of the market when all $p_i = 0$,

β = price sensitivity of overall demand,

γ = inter-firm price sensitivity coefficient,

η = cooperative advertising coefficient,

θ = competitive advertising coefficient.

There are three major components of the formula: The first deals with the effects of price and price relationship in the market; the second and third account for, respectively, the competitive and overall institutional effects of advertising on firm and industry demand. A fourth term representing trend, cycle and random elements was ommitted in the version under consideration.

2.1.4. Cost Conditions

Production is an independent variable. Production costs are linear. There is an upper bound specified on the size of production during any quarter. There are costs attached to changing the level of production. The overheads are specified as parameters of the program. Depreciation depends in a linear manner upon the amount of capacity of the firm. It was constant in this experiment because capacity was not changed. There are constant unit inventory carrying costs.

Advertising costs are merely the direct expenditures for advertising.

2.1.5. Random Variables

The introduction of random variables is optional. One may be introduced to influence overall demand and others to effect individual advertising. (Not used in this experiment).

2.1.6. Financing

Bank loans are made automatically as the cash needs of the firm call for them. A rate of interest on loans has to be specified.

2.1.7. Ruin Conditions

The game is designed to allow the study of ruin and entry of new firms in the market. In this experiment credit lines, up to which borrowing is automatic, were set so high that no ruin was possible. Also entry of new firms was avoided.

2.1.8. Revenue Function

The following symbols are defined:

Π_i = before tax net revenue for the ith firm,

σ_i = actual sales for the ith firm,

c = unit cost of production,

K_i = fixed costs of the ith firm,

c_I = unit inventory carrying cost per period,

I_i = average inventory level of the ith firm,

a_i = advertising expenditures of the ith firm.

The profit of the firm before tax is:

$$\Pi_i = p_i\sigma_i - c\sigma_i - c_I I_i - a_i - K_i$$

A tax is imposed on net profits. The tax rate is known by the players.

2.1.9. Decision Variables

There are seven possible decision variables under the control of the individual firm: price
advertising
production level
quantity offered for sale
dividends
investment
exit

Only the first three were used in the experiment described here. Every quarter the firms have an opportunity to select a new price for their product. As can be seen from the demand-equation, this version does not have any time lag effect of price. Demand is independent of previous fluctuations.

Advertising appears as an independent decision variable: Competitive and cooperative effects of advertising are

controlled by different parameters. The impact of advertising may be cumulatively lagged over several periods.
The firms are required to select a production rate during each quarter. Production scheduling appears in only a rudimentary form, in the sense that there are inventory carrying costs for finished goods and there are costs associated with changing the levels of production in either direction. Half of the current production plus initial inventories are available for sale in each period.

2.1.10. Payoff and Objective Function

The players were instructed to maximize their cumulated profit differences, i.e. the largest positive difference of current net worth at the end of play. The players were also instructed not to communicate with their competitors (although the game does not provide an opportunity for cooperation even with communication).

2.1.11. Information Conditions and Briefing

The players did not know the functional forms which provide the basic structure of the game. The parameters, which they did know, are displayed in Exhibit 1. Briefing was done verbally in class, stating only the goal of the game and some general rules of playing.
The players were informed after each period about the specific actions and the complete balance sheet of their competitor, as well as obtaining their own balance sheets and market information. At the beginning, the information for one identical sample period was given to all players. These initial values served to give them some insight into the mechanism of the game.

Exhibit 1

Institute for Advanced Studies

B u s i n e s s G a m e

May 1970

List of Parameters

	P1	
Unit cost of production (variable Stückkosten)	150	
Unit inventory carrying cost (Lagerkosten pro Stück)	10	
Unit cost of change of production (zusätzl. Stückkosten bei Änderung d. Produktion)	20	
Administrative costs (Fixkosten, administrativ)	500,000	per period
Depreciation (Abschreibung)	250,000	per period
Income tax (Steuer)	50 %	per period
Rate of interest on loans (Zins für Darlehen)	3 %	per period

You do not know the parameters for market demand.

2.1.12. Frequency of Play

The game was played at the rate of one period a day for 16 periods. Time spent for decision could be varied by the players, as they could turn in their decisions any time before the deadline for the computer run.

2.1.13. Termination

The end of the game was decided by a random process that gave a probability of 1/2 to termination (respectively continuance) after period 15. The players were not informed about that in advance.

2.2. Parameters

2.2.1. Market Parameters

α	"size of the market" was set to	1.04×10^6
β	price sensitivity of overall market to average price	0.266×10^4
γ	inter-firm price sensitivity coefficient	0.3×10^1
η	cooperative advertising coefficient	1.212×10^{-4}
θ	competitive advertising coefficient	1.

That means that there is no competitive advertising effect and the best advertising strategy is a let-your-competitor advertise-for-you policy.* This was done to stress the beat-the-average features of the game and to simplify them.

2.2.2. Cost Parameters

c_I	Finished goods unit inventory carrying cost	10
c	average unit production cost	150
Δ_q	unit cost of change of production	20
ρ	discount rate	3 %
K	fixed costs or overheads (administrative only	500,000
	depreciation	250,000
	maximum permitted production per quarter	500,000

* This is not quite accurate. See 3.1.1. for further discussion.

2.2.3. Advertising Parameters

Effectiveness weights for previous and current advertising:

3 periods ago	0
2 periods ago	0
1 period ago	.5
current	.5

2.3. Initial Conditions

Initial cash	$.2 \times 10^8$
initial inventory	200,000
advertising expenditures	
3 periods ago	6,000,000
2 periods ago	6,000,000
1 period ago	6,000,000
last production rate	250,000

2.4. Initial Decisions

The decisions for the sample period were made by the referee in the following way:

	Price	Advertising	Production
Player 1	240	6,000,000	250,000
Player 2	240	6,000,000	250,000

All parameters, initial conditions and initial decisions were identical for all players.

2.5. Theoretical Solutions

In this section the computation of the joint-maximization, non-cooperative and beat-the-average solutions for the symmetric game, as played in the experiment are given. Detailed development of the pertaining formulae is given in [1].

These three solutions serve to provide a reasonable upper boundary for cooperative behaviour (jm), a lower boundary (ba) and a solution which may be regarded as a measure of "inner direction" (nc).

2.5.1. Joint Maximization

If each firm takes a highly cooperative attitude towards all the others, we may consider that each firm acts to maximize the sum of the profits of all firms. By symmetry we may assume all prices and advertising budgets equal and maximize the profit of one firm. The optimal solution gives:

Price	=	277.5
Advertising	=	2,517,768
Production	=	154,080
Net Profit	=	7,803,487

2.5.2. Non-Cooperative Equilibrium

This solution describes an individual being concerned solely with his own payoffs to the exclusion of the welfare of all others.

Price	=	225
Advertising	=	486,372
Production	=	222,630
Net Profit	=	7,173,855

2.5.3. Beat-the-Average

A beat-the-average solution is an equilibrium solution of the transformed game with payoffs

$$P_i = \Pi_i - \frac{1}{n-1} \sum_{j \neq i} \Pi_j$$

In the case of a duopoly this amounts to

$$P_i = \Pi_i - \Pi_j$$

Price	=	204
Advertising	=	0
Production	=	248,000
Net Profit	=	5,700,999

2.5.1. The Efficient Point or Competitive Equilibrium

If the firms were run by a central agency using marginal cost pricing, then:

Price	=	155	
Advertising	=	0	?
Production	=	308,160	
Net Profit	=	-750,000	

There are several conceptual problems with this solution. If advertising influences overall demand, as it does here, should the central agency advertise for the public benefit? We will assume zero advertising, but note that this is merely avoiding a deep conceptual difficulty, and is not a solution to it.

The net profit when p = 155 is negative. In a steady state the administrative costs and overheads must be paid. In the long run they too could be regarded as variable costs. For a steady state "breakeven point" price must be set at approximately p = 157.34.

2.5.5. The Starting Point

From the above calculations we see that the starting point for a player was such that his price was above the noncooperative equilibrium, but below the joint maximum. His advertising was far above the joint maximum. His production and inventory were too large for even the "beat-the-average" steady state. These are illustrated in Figure 1.

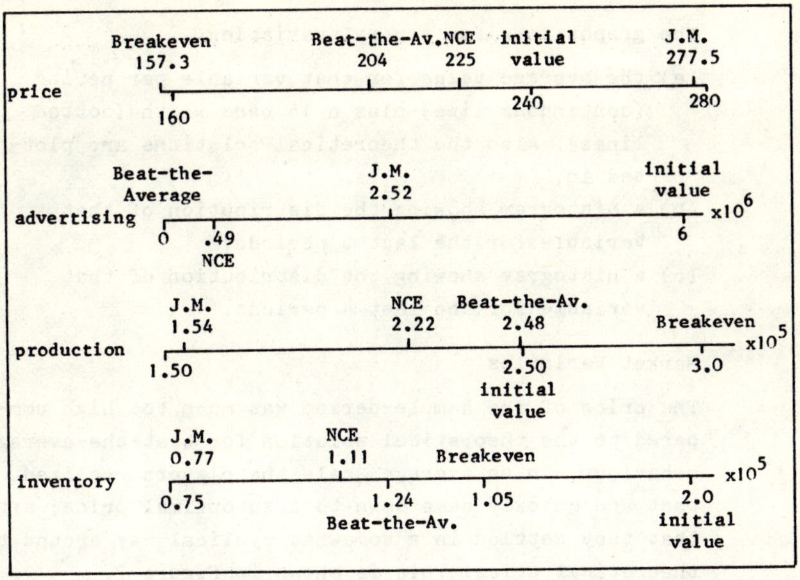

Figure 1

3. Description of Experiment

3.1. Overall Performance

This section is devoted to the description of the players' behaviour in total. This is done by observing how aggregate variables changed from period to period and whether they had a tendency towards the theoretical solutions. The distribution of the variables at different times is examined in order to see if there is a reduction in variance towards the end. Then from the aggregate data something like an idealized player is constructed; the behaviour of which is described.

3.1.1. Aggregation

The graphs show for several variables

(a) the average value for that variable per period (continuous line) plus a 1б band width (dotted lines). Also the theoretical solutions are plotted in,

(b) a histogram showing the distribution of that variable for the last 8 periods,

(c) a histogram showing the distribution of that variable for the last 4 periods.

Market Variables

The price of the sample-period was much too high compared to the theoretical solution for beat-the-average behaviour. On an average scale the players realized that and quickly came down to a suboptimal price; after that they settled in a somewhat cyclical way around the theoretical price. This is shown in Figure 2.
From the distribution it can be seen that the variance decreased towards the end. The mode still represents a suboptimal price indicating that most players did not fully recover from the strong fall in price at the beginning. But the long upper tails show that digression from the optimum to the right more frequently occurred than to the left.
Corresponding cycles in the opposite direction of aggregate sales can be observed. See Figure 3.
The optimal steady state solution of advertising expenditures was soon guessed by the players. In the last quarter of the play advertising virtually ceased.*

* However G. Bruckmann observed if one's opponent has stopped advertising and is charging a higher price than yourself, it pays to advertise a small amount to take advantage of this situation. An example shows this:

Figure 2

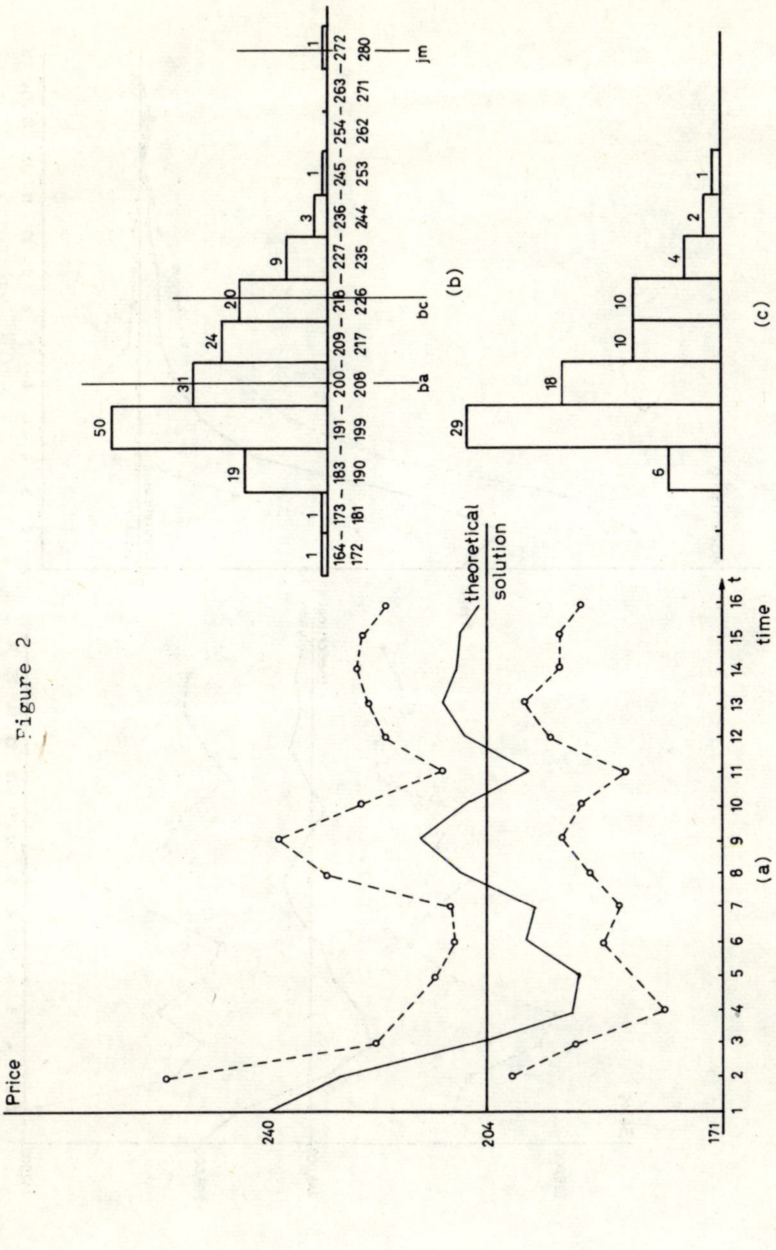

Price
240
204
171
theoretical solution
time
t
(a)
164 – 173 – 183 – 191 – 200 – 209 – 218 – 227 – 236 – 245 – 254 – 263 – 272
172 181 190 199 208 217 226 235 244 253 262 271 280
ba
bc
jm
(b)
(c)

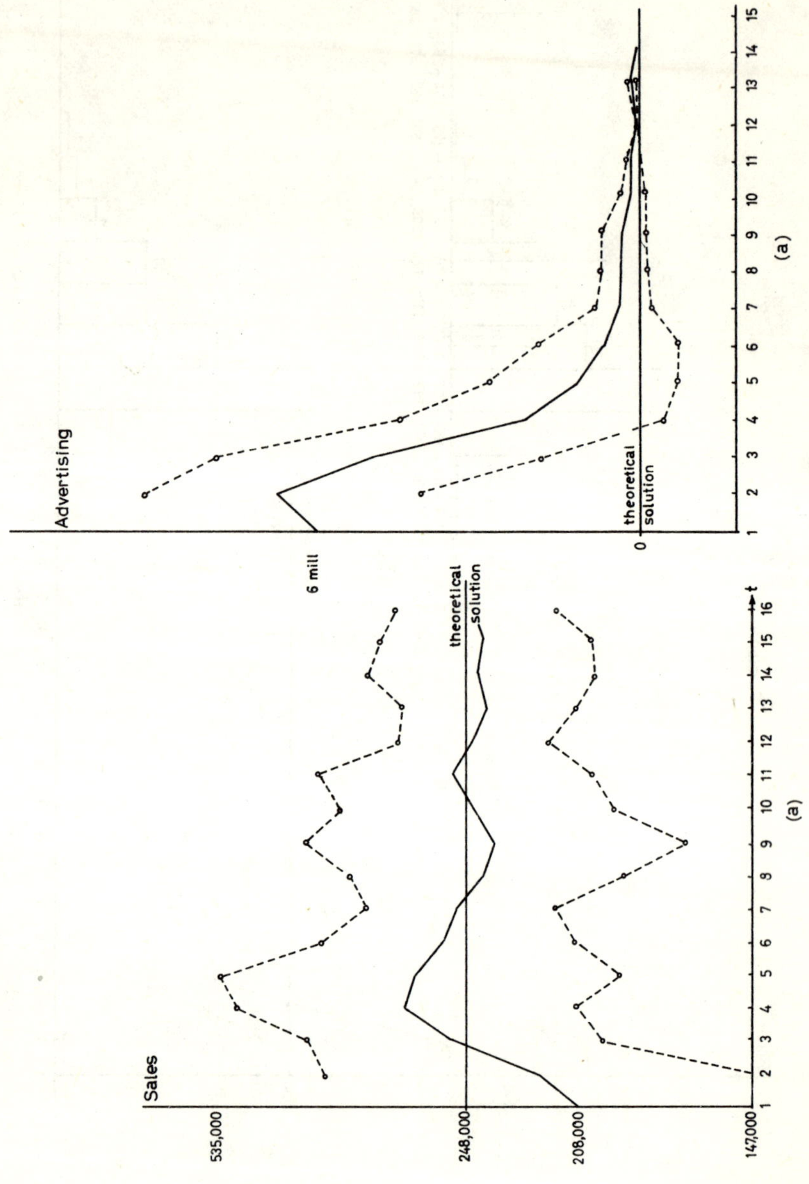
Advertising
6 mill
0
theoretical solution
(a)
Sales
535,000
248,000
208,000
147,000
theoretical solution
t
(a)

Internal Variables of the Firm

In a steady-state the theoretical solution requires production to be equal to sales and inventory to half of production. From the diagrams it can be seen that aggregate production fluctuated moderately around the theoretical value; inventory on the other hand was considerably higher (see Figure 4).

The main feature is the rise in production at the beginning. The hope of the players, that by rising production and lowering price they were on the right way, was not fulfilled. The decrease in price was too small. The players found themselves stuck with an inventory even higher than sales and had to try to reduce their inventory-holdings by curbing production and heading for higher sales. (In another related experiment inventory levels were found to be far higher than expected [2]).

$$\Pi_1-\Pi_2=(1+\eta)\sqrt{(a_1+a_2)}\left[S_1(p_1-150)-S_2(p_2-150)\right]-a_1+a_2,$$

where S_i = the sales of the ith firm.

For a_1 to be optimal, given a_2 we have:

$$\frac{\partial(\Pi_1-\Pi_2)}{\partial a_1}=(1+\eta)\frac{S_1(p_1-150)-S_2(p_2-150)}{2\sqrt{a_1+a_2}}-1=0 \quad \text{or}$$

$$a_1=\left\{\frac{(1+\eta)}{2}\left[S_1(p_1-150)-S_2(p_2-150)\right]\right\}^2-a_2$$

This was the reason given for his team maintaining a small amount of advertising when he expected to charge a lower price than his competitor.

Coordination

To reflect the degree of coordination between the market decisions and the internal decisions of the firm three further variables were constructed. These are shown in Figure 5.

EX_t = (Inventory$_{t-1}$ + 1/2 Production$_t$) - Sales$_t$

This is the excess available stock in each period. In a steady state the optimal solution is, of course, zero.

LOST SALES This is the deficiency of stock in each period. In a steady state the optimal solution is again zero.

These two variables show the deviation of inventory-holdings and production scheduling from optimal in either direction. To have a handy combined measure a third variable is introduced.

$$IP_t = \begin{cases} EX_t & \\ \text{LOST SALES}_t & \text{if } EX_t = 0 \end{cases}$$

From the diagrams it can be seen that the magnitude of excess stock is by far greater than of LOST SALES. This can be explained by the fact that incurring LOST SALES affects profit (let alone profit difference) much more seriously than carrying excess stock. In the second half of the play a convenient balance between risks and costs seems to have been reached.

Profit Variables

Two markedly opposite trends in level of profits and profit differences can be observed. After some periods

Figure 4

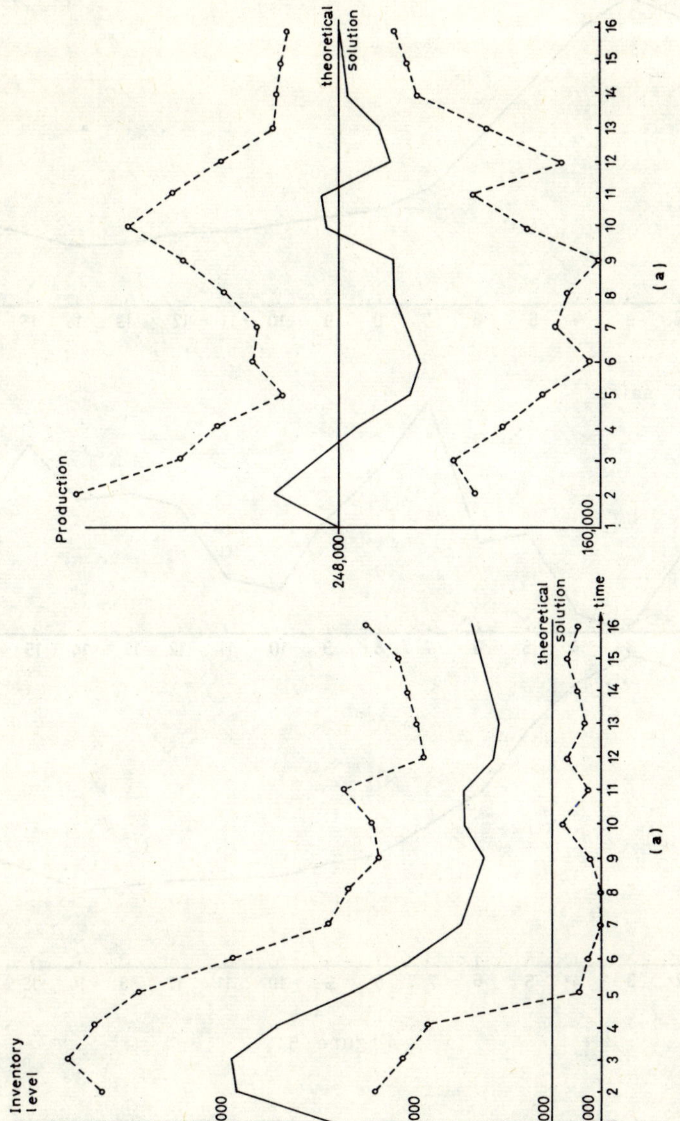
Production
theoretical solution
248,000
160,000
(a)
Inventory level
300,000
200,000
124,000
98,000
theoretical solution
time
(a)

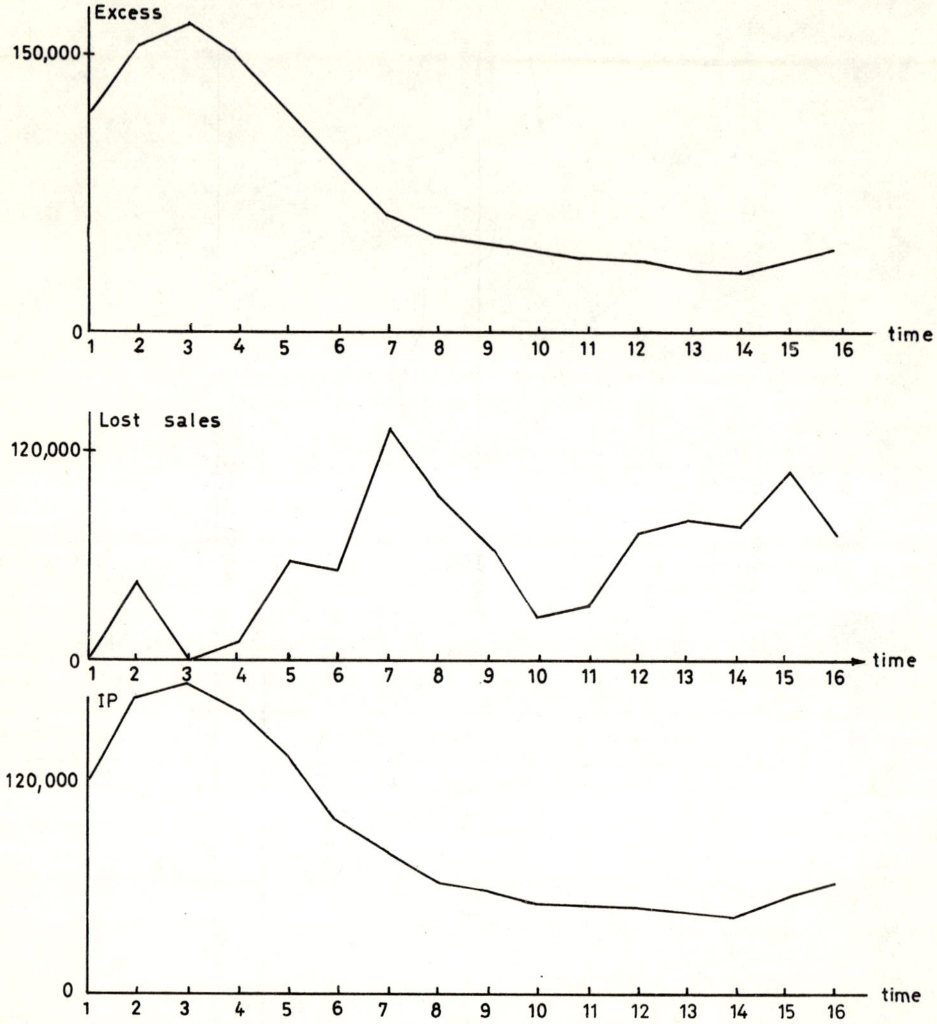
Excess
150,000
0
1 2 3 4 5 6 7 8 9 10 11 12 13 14 15 16
time
Lost sales
120,000
0
1 2 3 4 5 6 7 8 9 10 11 12 13 14 15 16
time
IP
120,000
0
1 2 3 4 5 6 7 8 9 10 11 12 13 14 15 16
time

Figure 5

of experimentation profit level showed an upward trend. Players learned how to make higher profit but so did their competitors, as can be seen from the decreasing variance. Great differences of profits were achieved at the beginning, due to ignorance of the game and of the behaviour of the competitor. After discovering some of the mechanism of the game, the players were able to employ better, though not optimal, strategies.

To neutralize the effect of advertising on profits adjusted, profit variables were constructed in the following way: advertising expenditures per period of each player were added to the net profit in that period, thereby approximating the profit he would have obtained, if he had outguessed the optimal advertising expenditure. Adjusted profits and profit differences are plotted in broken lines.

It can be seen that the influence of the ignorance about advertising on profit differences is negligible because the negative effect is canceled. Profit levels on the other hand are strongly influenced. The effects are shown in Figures 6 and 7.

3.1.2. A Macro-Model

On the aggregate data as described in 3.1.1. the standard linear regression model was applied. This can serve as an explanation for the behaviour of the typical player in this experiment. The resulting equations can easily be interpreted in a causal way, as if the mass itself or its representative acted according to a specific behavioral pattern.

The equations were estimated in relative differences of the first order, thereby stressing the dynamic features of the game.

The reaction equations for the two main decision variables are given below. The standard deviation as a percentage is

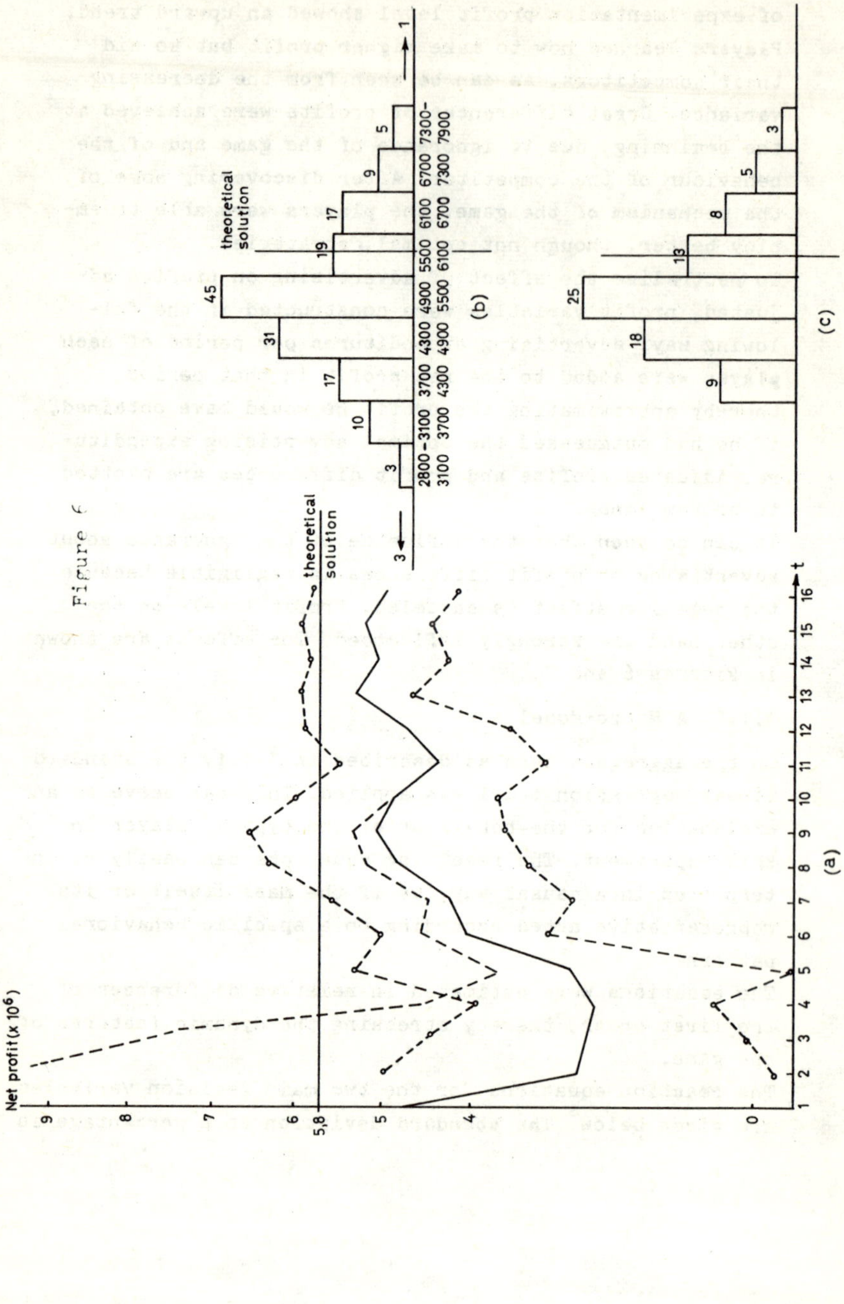
Net profit (x 10^6)
theoretical solution
t
(a)
theoretical solution
2800–3100 3100–3700 3700–4300 4300–4900 4900–5500 5500–6100 6100–6700 6700–7300 7300–7900
(b)
(c)

Figure 6

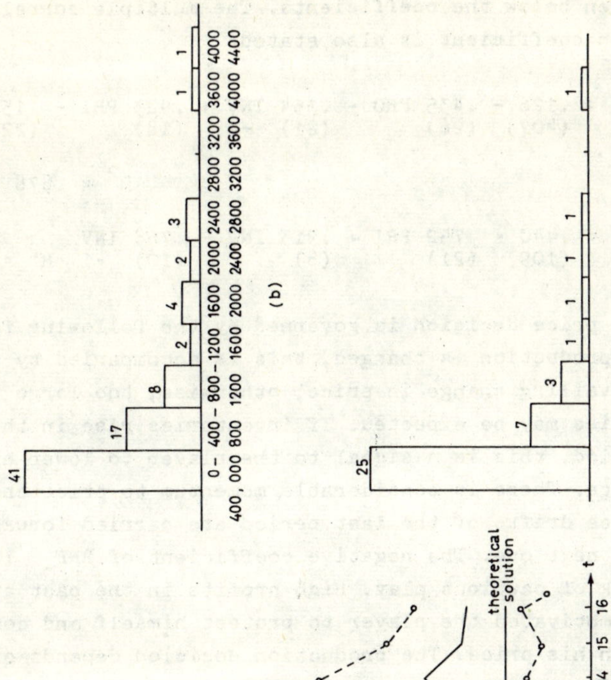
Profit difference (x10^6)
3 mill
2
1
0
theoretical solution
t
(a)
41
17
8
2
4
2
3
1
1
0- 400- 800- 1200 1600 2000 2400 2800 3200 3600 4000
400 000 800 1200 1600 2000 2400 2800 3200 3600 4000 4400
(b)
25
7
3
1
1
1
1
1
(c)

Figure 7

given below the coefficients. The multiple correlation coefficient is also stated.

$$PRI = \underset{(407)}{.126} - \underset{(26)}{.435}\,PRO - \underset{(21)}{.354}\,INV_{-1} + \underset{(18)}{.923}\,PRI - \underset{(22)}{.158}\,PRF_{-1}$$

$$R^2 = .878$$

$$PRO = \underset{(109)}{.440} - \underset{(21)}{.752}\,PRI + \underset{(8)}{.913}\,INV - \underset{(10)}{.768}\,INV_{-1} \qquad R^2 = .935$$

The price decision is governed by the following factors. If production is changed, this is accompanied by a countervailing change in price; otherwise, too large inventories may be expected. If inventories rise in the last period, this is a signal to the player to lower his price. There is considerable momentum to price changes. Price drifts of the last period are carried forward to the next one. The negative coefficient of PRF_{-1} is a mark of cautious play. High profits in the past apparently motivated the player to protect himself and come down with his price. The production decision depends on the simultaneously made price decision and changes in the opposite direction. The wish to build up or reduce inventories is the second component in the production-decision. The change of inventories in the previous period enters negatively. If the player accumulated inventory in the previous period, he will decrease production in the current period as expected.

Heuristics and Game Theory

This particular experiment was so designed that from the game theoretical point of view it can be regarded as a set of two-person zero-sum games, each with a pure strategy solution, given the goal set for the players. The (static) game theory solutions serve to provide standards against which we can compare actual behavior. The two "macro" or behavioral equations can be regarded as heuristics or rules of thumb which could be used to construct an artificial player for this game. Using the two equations above combined with the structural equations for sales and profits, it is possible to calculate the steady state predicted by this type of behavior.

The game theoretic approach, by its assumption of full knowledge, ability to compute, and no learning or change in values and perception during the course of the game, provides a contrast to a behavioral approach and provides several clues to measurement. For example, we would expect that inventories would be higher than the game theoretical solution, and that lost sales would appear because they are called for by virtually any dynamic process of adjustment, where the players have to experiment to learn more about both the market structure and each other's behavior.

3.2. Individual Performance

3.2.1. Decision Variables

The distribution of average price per player, average production per player and average advertising per player are shown in Figure 8, 9, and 10. Also the theoretical solutions are plotted in. The players can be identified by the numbers in the histogram. Players 1/11, 2/12 etc. from a team. The appearance of numbers within the same class indicates the ranking (increasing order).

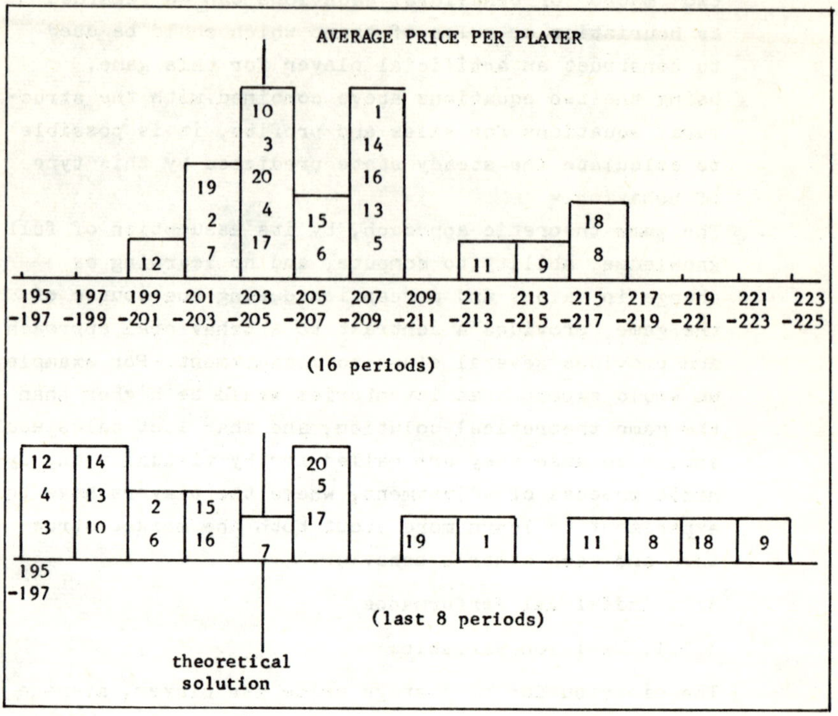

Figure 8

Two types of players can be distinguished:

high production - low price
low production - high price

(KENDALL-rank correlation coefficient -.530 between average price per player and average production per player for 16 periods.
-.379 for 8 periods.

Significance level: .317 (95 %)).

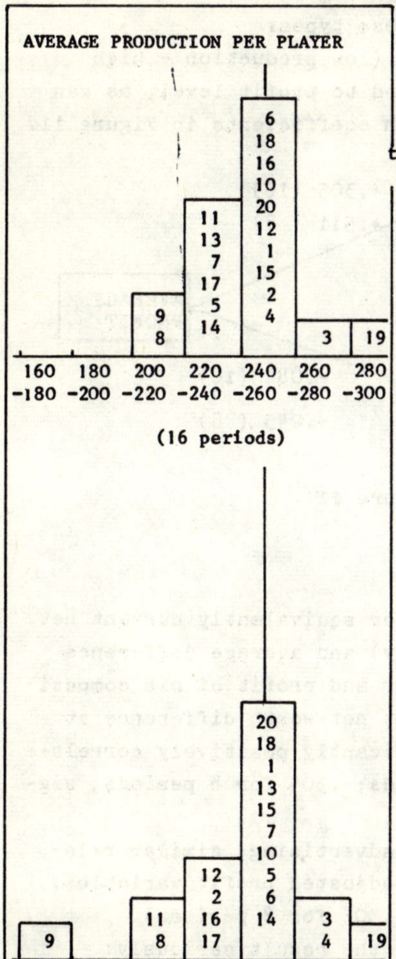

Figure 9

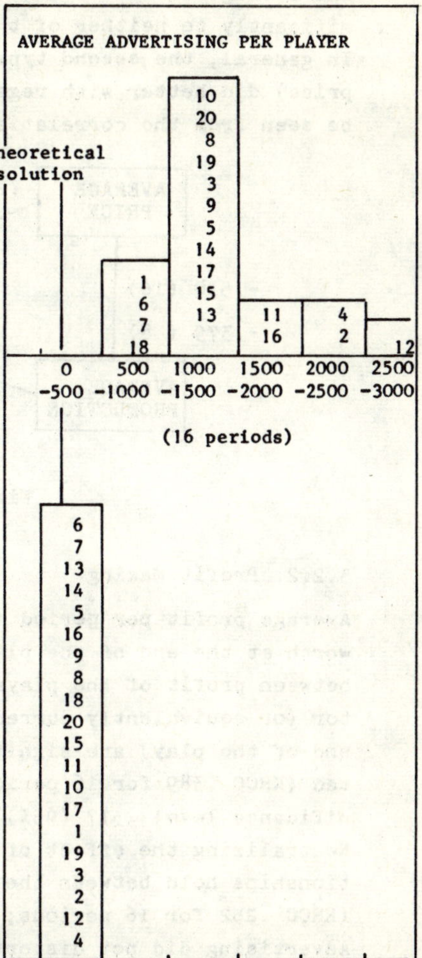

Figure 10

The average amount of advertising is correlated significantly to neither of these types.
In general, the second type (low production - high price) did better with regard to profit level, as can be seen from the correlation coefficients in Figure 11.

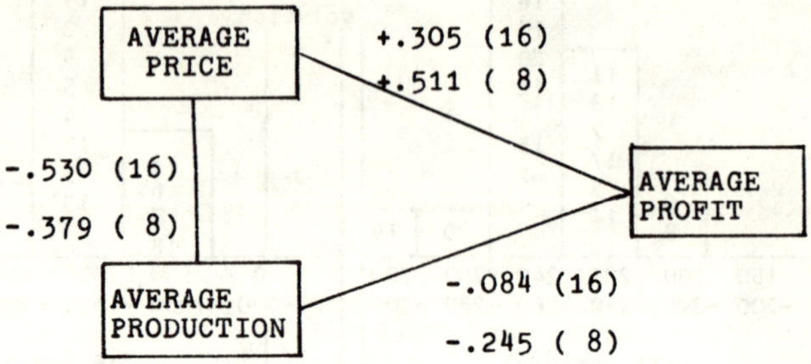

Figure 11

3.2.2. Profit Making

Average profit per period (or equivalently current net worth at the end of the play) and average difference between profit of the player and profit of his competitor (or equivalently current net worth difference at end of the play) are significantly positively correlated (KRCC .389 for 16 periods; .305 for 8 periods; significance level .317 (95%)).
Neutralizing the effect of advertising, similar relationships hold between the adjusted profit variables: (KRCC .252 for 16 periods; .305 for 8 periods).
Advertising did not distort the result seriously:
KRCC .447 between unadjusted and adjusted profit level
.421 between unadjusted and adjusted profit difference.
To track the influence of stability of each player on

profits the coefficient of variation was calculated for some variables. In Figure 12 one can see the following relationships:

VP	coefficient of variation in price
VPR	coefficient of variation in profit level
VINV	coefficient of variation in inventory
AVPR	average profit per player
AVPRD	average profit difference per player

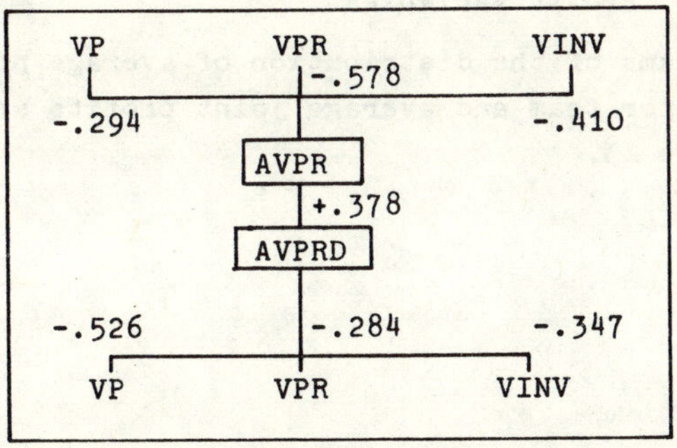

Figure 12

The accumulation of high profits was associated with stable accumulation. Great variations of profits per period were a mark of unsuccessfull play. The correlation between fluctuation of inventory holdings and profits indicates that deviation from a steady state, not only from the optimal one, did not pay. Wild fluctuations in price-level affected profits negatively. Because of the positive correlation between profit and profit difference, similar relationships hold for the accumulation of profit differences.

3.2.3. Individual Differences

No test for individual differences in the players prior to playing was made. Were these to be performed, a fruitful interlink between the economic (and game-theoretic) experimentation and socio-psychological experimentation might be forged by an investigation of the distribution of individual behavior in relation to the tests.

3.3. Team Performance

3.3.1. Profit Variables

Diagrams of the distribution of average profit difference per team and average joint profits are given in Figure 13.

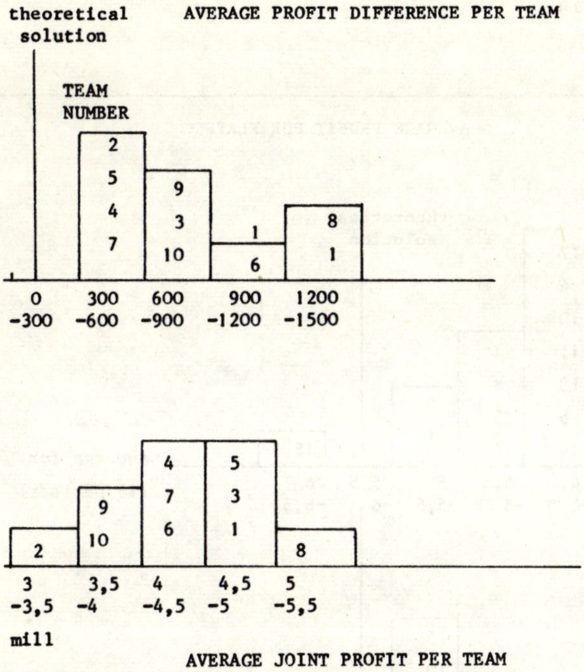

Figure 13

Difference of net profits and joint profits are correlated positively (KENDALL rank correlation coefficient .466, significance level .486 (95 %)). That means that small differences of profits did not occur because both duopolists played brilliantly but could not outdo each other; this indicates also poor performance of both competitors.

The distribution of average profit per player is given in Figure 14.

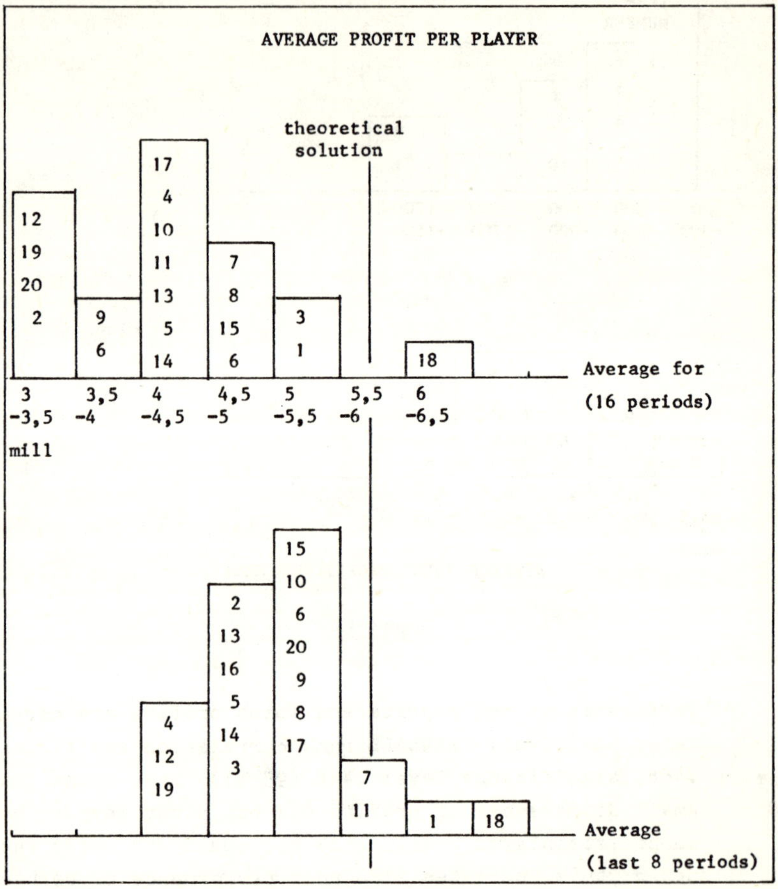

Figure 14

3.3.2. A Sign Test

The sign of the difference of net profits per period was computed for all teams. Six teams show a random distribution. The remaining four are those that came first, second, third, and fifth with respect to the maximization of difference of cumulated net profits. Adjusting for advertising only two of these teams remain, in the other two, dominance was due to the wrong advertising policy of the competitor.

This shows that in the winning teams one player was systematically outdoing his competitor. A similar result is this: Considering only the second half of the play, and thereby eliminating the effects of ignorance at the beginning, in all teams but one the same player managed to accumulate a positive difference of profit as in the complete game.

4. *Concluding Remarks*

Compared with a matrix game, this business game is quite rich, complicated and has a complex environment. By the device of briefing the players to try to maximize the difference in their scores, the game is turned into a two-person zero-sum game with a saddle point. The strategy space is multidimensional. An extremely strong Prisoner's Dilemma game is built in on advertising and the evidence obtained was, that this was reflected in the actual play. In previous experiments 3/ where the players were trying to maximize individual payoffs and the game was truly non-constant sum, this effect was also observed. The economic solution predictions were quite good in predicting the range to which price and advertising proceeded. Profits were lower than the steady state prediction. This could be explained by the dynamic aspects of the game which were manifested in the learning and control problems of the players. Inventories were in general too high. It took time to work out the implications of advertising. The value of production scheduling and its relationship to management of prices was probably not appreciated by many of the players.

Bibliography

[1] Levitan, R., and M. Shubik, "A Business Game for Teaching and Research Purposes," Part 1, CFDP No. 115, Cowles Foundation of Research in Economics at Yale University May 16, 1961.

---, Part 2a, CFDP No. 115, June 2, 1961.

---, Part 3, CFDP No. 115, September 6, 1961.

---, Part 4, "Mathematical Structure and Analysis of the Nonsymmetric Game," CFDP No. 219, March 2, 1967.

[2] Feder, P., and G. Wolf, Data Analysis in a Business Game. Report 40, Department of Administrative Sciences, Yale University, 1971.

[3] Shubik, M., Wolf, G., and H. Eisenberg, An Experimental Oligopoly Business Game: Part I, Some Experiments. Technical Report 33, Department of Administrative Sciences, Yale University, 1970.

Journal Articles

Albach, Horst / Gabelin, Thomas: Effiziente Entscheidungen in Gruppen
Zeitschrift für Betriebswirtschaft 40 (1970), Ergänzungsheft, pp. 37-52

Alpert, Bernard: Non-Businessmen as Surrogates for Businessmen in Behavioral Experiments
The Journal of Business 40 (1967), pp. 203-207

Anderson, Norman H. / Shanteau, James C.: Information Integration in Risky Decision Making
Journal of Experimental Psychology 84 (1970), pp. 441-451

Beach, Lee Roy / Wise, James A.: Subjective Probability and Decision Strategy
Journal of Experimental Psychology 79 (1969), pp. 133-138

Bonacich, Phillip: Putting the Dilemma back into Prisoner's Dilemma
Journal of Conflict Resolution 14 (1970), pp. 379-387

Brown, Bert R.: The Effects of Need to Maintain Face on Interpersonal Bargaining
Journal of Experimental Social Psychology 4 (1968), pp. 107-122

* This compilation of literature is meant to be supplementary to the bibliography in the first and second volumes of "Contributions to Experimental Economics" and therefore contains essentially only literature from the years 1969-1971. Again only works which reported on experiments and their results were accepted. The compilation does not contain the contributions of the third volume.

Chertkoff, Jerome M.: The Effects of Probability of Future Success on Coalition Formation Journal of Experimental Social Psychology 2 (1966), pp. 265-277

Chertkoff, Jerome M.: Coalition Formation as a Function of Differences in Resources Journal of Conflict Resolution 15 (1971), pp. 371-388

Chertkoff, Jerome M. / Conley, Melinda: Opening Offer and Frequency of Concession as Bargaining Strategies Journal of Personality and Social Psychology 7 (1967), pp. 181-185

Cohen, John / Hansel, C.E.M.: The Nature of Decisions in Gambling Acta Psychologica 13 (1957), pp. 357-370

Conrath, David W.: Experience as a Factor in Experimental Gaming Behavior Journal of Conflict Resolution 14 (1970), pp. 195-202

Coombs, C.H. / Bezembinder, T.G. / Good, F.M.: Testing Expectation Theories of Decision Making without Measuring Utility or Subjective Probability Journal of Mathematical Psychology 4 (1967), pp. 72-103

Coombs, C.H. / Komorita, S.S.: Measuring Utility of Money Through Decisions The American Journal of Psychology 71 (1958), pp. 383-389

Coombs, C.H. / Pruitt, D.G.: Components of Risk in Decision Making: Probability and Variance Preferences Journal of Experimental Psychology 60 (1960), pp. 265-277

Daniels, Victor: Communication, Incentive, and Structural Variables in Interpersonal Exchange and Negotiation Journal of Experimental Social Psychology 3 (1967), pp. 47-74

Davis, James H. / Hornik, John A. / Hornseth, John P.: Group Decision Schemes and Strategy Preferences in a Sequential Response Task Journal of Personality and Social Psychology 15 (1970), pp. 397-408

Deutsch, Morton / Lewicki, Roy J.: "Locking - In" Effects During a Game of Chicken Journal of Conflict Resolution 14 (1970), pp. 367-378

Dolbear, Jr., F. Trenery / Lave, Lester B.: Inconsistent Behavior in Lottery Choice Experiments
Behavioral Science 12 (1967), pp. 14-23

Druckman, Daniel: Prenegotiation Experience and Dyadic Conflict Resolution in a Bargaining Situation
Journal of Experimental Social Psychology 4 (1968), pp. 367-383

Edwards, Ward: Variance Preferences in Gambling
The American Journal of Psychology 67 (1954), pp. 441-452

Emerson, Richard M.: Power-Dependence Relations: Two Experiments
Sociometry 27 (1964), pp. 282-298

Emshoff, James R.: A Computer Simulation Model of Prisoner's Dilemma
Behavioral Science 15 (1970), pp. 304-317

Faley, Thomas / Tedeschi, James T.: Status and Reactions to Threats
Journal of Personality and Social Psychology 17 (1971), pp. 192-199

Fiornia, Morris P.: A Note on Probability Matching and Rational Choice
Behavioral Science 16 (1971), pp. 158-166

Froman, Lewis A. jr. / Cohen, Michael D.: Compromise and Logroll: Comparing the Efficiency of Two Bargaining Processes
Behavioral Science 15 (1970), pp. 180-183

Gallo, Philip S. / Funk, Sandra G. / Levine, Joseph R.: Reward Size, Method of Presentation, and Number of Alternatives in a Prisoner's Dilemma Game
Journal of Personality and Social Psychology 13 (1969), pp. 239-244

Gamson, W.A.: An Experimental Test of a Theory of Coalition Formation
American Sociological Review 26 (1961), pp. 565-573

Gillis, John S. / Woods, George T.: The 16PF as an Indicator of Performance in the Prisoner's Dilemma Game
Journal of Conflict Resolution 15 (1971), pp. 393-402

Gordon, M.J. / Paradis, G.E. / Rorke, C.H.: Experimental Evidence on Alternative Portfolio Decision Rules
The American Economic Review 62 (1972), No. 1, pp. 107-118

Gruder, Charles L.: Relationships with Opponent and Partner in Mixed-Motive Bargaining
Journal of Conflict Resolution 15 (1971), pp. 403-416

Guyer, Melvin / Rapoport, Anatol: Information Effects in two Mixed-Motive Games
Behavioral Science 14 (1969), pp. 467-482

Halpin, Stanley M. / Pilisuk, Marc: Prediction and Choice in the Prisoner's Dilemma
Behavioral Science 15 (1970), pp. 141-153

Hardin, Russell: Collective Action as an Agreeable n-Prisoner's Dilemma
Behavioral Science 16 (1971), pp. 472-481

Harnett, Donald L. / Hughes, David G. / Cummings, Larry L.: Bilateral Monopolistic Bargaining Through an Intermediary
The Journal of Business 41 (1968), pp. 251-259

Harris, Richard J.: Note on "Optimal Policies for the Prisoner's Dilemma"
Psychological Review 76 (1969), pp. 363-375

Hesselbach, J.: Verhaltensforschung bei unternehmerischen Entscheidungen
Zeitschrift für Betriebswirtschaft 40 (1970), pp. 647-664

Kelley, Herold H. / Beckman, Linda Linden / Fischer, Claude S.: Negotiating the Division of a Reward Under Incomplete Information
Journal of Experimental Social Psychology 3 (1967), pp. 361-398

Kleinke, Chris L. / Pohlen, Paul D.: Affective and Emotional Responses as a Function of Other Person's Gaze and Cooperativeness in a Two-Person Game
Journal of Personality and Social Psychology 17 (1971), pp. 308-313

Kogan, Nathan / Wallach, Michael A.: Risky - Shift Phenomenon in Small Decision Making Groups: A Test of the Information-Exchange Hypothesis
Journal of Experimental Social Psychology 3 (1967), pp. 75-84

Komorita, S.S.: A Model for Decision-Making Under Risk
The American Journal of Psychology 77 (1964), pp. 429-436

Komorita, S.S. / Barnes, Marc: Effects of Pressures to Reach Agreement in Bargaining
Journal of Personality and Social Psychology 13 (1969), pp. 245-252

Krauss, Robert M.: Structural and Arbitudinal Factors in Interpersonal Bargaining
Journal of Experimental Social Psychology 2 (1966), pp. 42-55

Lichtenstein, Sarah / Slovic, Paul / Zink, Donald: Effects of Instruction in Expected Value on Optimality of Gambling Decisions
Journal of Experimental Psychology 79 (1969), pp. 236-240

Lieberman, Bernhardt: Not an Artifact
Journal of Conflict Resolution 15 (1971), pp. 113-120

Liebert, Robert M. / Smith, William P. / Hill, J.H.: The Effects of Information and Magnitude of Initial Offer on Interpersonal Negotiation
Journal of Experimental Social Psychology 4 (1968), pp. 431-441

Littig, Lawrence W.: Effects of Skill and Chance Orientations on Probability Preferences
Psychological Reports 10 (1962), pp. 67-70

Lupfer, Michael / Jones, Mark / Spaulding, Lionel / Archer, Richard: Risk-Taking in Cooperative and Competitive Dyads
Journal of Conflict Resolution 15 (1971), pp. 385-392

Mackenzie, Kenneth D. / Barron, Hutton F.: Analysis of a Decision Making Investigation
Management Science 17 (1970), pp. B-226 - B-241

Marwell, Gerald / Ratcliff, Kathryn / Schmitt, David R.: Minimizing Differences in a Maximizing Difference Game
Journal of Personality and Social Psychology 12 (1969), pp. 158-163

Marwell, Gerald / Schmitt, David R. / Shotola, Robert: Sex Differences in a Cooperative Task
Behavioral Science 15 (1970), pp. 184-186

McClintock, Charles G. / Nuttin, Josef M. jr. / McNeel, Steven P.: Sociometric Choice, Visual Presence, and Game-Playing Behavior
Behavioral Science 15 (1970), pp. 124-131

McConnell, J. Douglas: An Experimental Examination of the Price-Quality Relationship
The Journal of Business 41 (1968), pp. 439-444

Meeker, Robert J. / Shure, Gerald H.: Pacifist Bargaining Tactics: Some "Outsider" Influences
Journal of Conflict Resolution 13 (1969), pp. 487-493

Messé, Lawrence A.: Equity in Bilateral Bargaining
Journal of Personality and Social Psychology 17 (1971), pp. 287-291

Messick, David M. / McClintock, Charles G.: Motivational Bases of Choice in Experimental Games
Journal of Experimental Social Psychology 4 (1968), pp. 1-25

Miller, Louis / Meyer, David Edward / Lanzetta, John T.: Choice among Equal Expected Value Alternatives: Sequential Effects of Winning Probability Level on Risk Preferences
Journal of Experimental Psychology 79 (1969), pp. 419-423

Morgenstern, Oskar: Experiment und Berechnung großen Umfangs in der Wirtschaftswissenschaft
Weltwirtschaftliches Archiv 76 (1956), pp. 179-237

Ofshe, Richard / Ofshe, Lynne S.: Choice Behavior in Coalition Games
Behavioral Science 15 (1970), pp. 337-349

Oshikawa, Sadaomi: Consumer Pre-Decision Conflict and Post-Decision Dissonance
Behavioral Science 15 (1970), pp. 132-140

Pallak, Michael S. / Heller, Jack F.: Interactive Effects of Commitment to Future Interaction and Threat to Arbitudinal Freedom
Journal of Personality and Social Psychology 17 (1971), pp. 325-331

Payne, John W. / Braunstein, Myron L.: Preferences among Gambles with Equal Underlying Distributions
Journal of Experimental Psychology 87 (1971), pp. 13-18

Pilisuk, Marc / Kiritz, Stewart / Clampitt, Stuart: Undoing Deadlocks of Distrust: Hip Berkeley Students and the ROTC
Journal of Conflict Resolution 15 (1971), pp. 81-95

Podell, Jerome E. / Knapp, William M.: The Effect of Mediation on the Perceived Firmness of the Opponent
Journal of Conflict Resolution 13 (1969), pp. 511-520

Pruitt, Dean G. / Drews, J.L.: The Effect of Time Pressure, Time Elapsed and the Opponent's Concession Rate on Behavior in Negotiation
Journal of Experimental Social Psychology 5 (1969), pp. 43-60

Pruitt, Dean G.: Motivational Processes in the Decomposed Prisoner's Dilemma
Journal of Personality and Social Psychology 14 (1970), pp. 227-238

Pruitt, Dean G. / Johnson, Douglas F.: Mediation as an Aid to Face Saving in Negotiation
Journal of Personality and Social Psychology 14 (1970), pp. 239-246

Rapoport, Anatol / Dale, Philip: Models to Prisoner's Dilemma
Journal of Mathematical Psychology 3 (1966), pp. 269-286

Rapoport, Anatol / Guyer, Melvin / Gordon, David: A Comparison of Performances of Danish and American Students in a "Threat Game"
Behavioral Science 16 (1971), pp. 456-466

Rapoport, Anatol: Optimal and Suboptimal Decisions in Perceptual Problem-Solving Tasks
Behavioral Science 14 (1969), pp. 453-466

Riker, William H.: Bargaining in a Three-Person Game
American Political Science Review 61 (1967), pp. 642-656

Riker, William H. / Niemi, Richard G.: Anonymity and Rationality in the Essential Three-Person Game
Human Relations 17 (1964), pp. 131-140

Rosen, Sydney: The Comparative Roles of Informational and Material Commodities in Interpersonal Transactions
Journal of Experimental Social Psychology 2 (1966), pp. 211-226

Ross, Robert T.: Optimum Orders for the Presentation of Pairs in the Method of Paired Comparisons
Journal of Educational Psychology 25 (1934), pp. 375-382

Royden, Halsey L. / Suppes, Patrick / Walsh, Karol: A Model for the Experimental Measurement of the Utility of Gambling
Behavioral Science 4 (1959), pp. 11-18

Runzheimer, Bodo: Die Situationskontrolle im Experiment
Zeitschrift für Betriebswirtschaft 38 (1968), 1. Ergänzungsheft, pp. 59-74

Shaban, Janet / Jecker, Jon: Risk Preference in Choosing an Evaluater: An Extension of Atkinson's Achievement-Motivation Model
Journal of Experimental Social Psychology 4 (1968), pp. 35-45

Shimp, Charles P.: Optimal Behavior in Free-Operant Experiments
Psychological Review 76 (1969), pp. 97-112

Shubik, Martin: The Dollar Auction Game: A Paradox in Non-cooperative Behavior and Escalation
Journal of Conflict Resolution 15 (1971), pp. 109-111

Sjöberg, Lennart: Studies of the Rated Favorableness of Offers to Gamble
Scandinavian Journal of Psychology 9 (1968), pp. 257-273

Slovic, Paul: Manipulating the Attractiveness of a Gamble without Changing its Expected Value
Journal of Experimental Psychology 79 (1969), pp. 139-145

Smith, Vernon L.: Experimental Studies of Discrimination Versus Competition in Sealed-Bid Auction Markets
The Journal of Business 40 (1967), pp. 56-84

Smith, William P.: Reward Structure and Information in the Development of Cooperation
Journal of Experimental Social Psychology 4 (1968), pp. 199-223

Starbuck, W.H. / Bass, F.M.: An Experimental Study of Risk-Taking and the Value of Information in a New Product Context
The Journal of Business 40 (1967), pp. 155-165

Stech, Frank J. / McClintock, Charles G.: Cooperative and Competitive Price Bidding in a Duopoly Game
Behavioral Science 16 (1971), pp. 545-557

Swinth, Robert L.: Artifacts in the Siegel-Fouraker Study of Bargaining and Group Decision Making
Management Science 16 (1969), pp. 85-92

Tedeschi, James T. / Bonoma, Thomas / Lindskold, Svenn: Threatener's Reactions to Prior Announcement of Behavioral Compliance or Defiance
Behavioral Science 15 (1970), pp. 171-179

Tversky, A.: Utility Theory and Additivity Analysis of Risky Choices
Journal of Experimental Psychology 75 (1967), pp. 27-36

Vidmar, Neil / McGrath, Joseph E.: Forces Affecting Success in Negotiation Groups
Behavioral Science 15 (1970), pp. 154-163

Vidmar, Neil: Effects of Representational Roles and Mediators on Negotiation Effectiveness
Journal of Personality and Social Psychology 17 (1971), pp. 48-58

Vincent, Jack E. / Tindell, James O.: Alternative Cooperative Strategies in a Bargaining Game Journal of Conflict Resolution 13 (1969), pp. 494-510

Wallace, Donnel / Rothaus, Paul: Communication, Group Loyality, and Trust in the Prisoner's Dilemma Game Journal of Conflict Resolution 13 (1969), pp. 370-380

Wendt, Dirk: Value of Information for Decisions Journal of Mathematical Psychology 6 (1969), pp. 430-443

Wyer, Robert S.: Prediction of Behavior in Two-Person Games Journal of Personality and Social Psychology 13 (1969), pp. 222-238

Zajonc, Robert B. / Wolosin, Robert J. / Wolosin, Myrna A. / Sherman, Steven J.: Individual and Group Risk-Taking in a Two-Choice Situation Journal of Experimental Social Psychology 4 (1968), pp. 89-106

Contributions in Collected Works

Becker, Otwin / Selten, Reinhard: Experiences with the Management Game SINTO-Market in: H. Sauermann, ed., Beiträge zur experimentellen Wirtschaftsforschung, Vol. II, Tübingen 1970, pp. 136-150

Berg, Claus C. / Selten, Reinhard: Ein Gerät zur optischen und akustischen Anzeige von Entscheidungszeitpunkten in Oligopolexperimenten mit kontinuierlicher Zeit in: H. Sauermann, ed., Beiträge zur experimentellen Wirtschaftsforschung, Vol. II, Tübingen 1970, pp. 222-229

Coombs, C.H. / Beardslee, David: On Decision-Making Under Uncertainty in: R.M. Thrall/C.H. Coombs/R.L. Davis, eds., Decision Processes, London 1954, pp. 255-285

Friedman, James W.: Equal Profits as a Fair Division in: H. Sauermann, ed., Beiträge zur experimentellen Wirtschaftsforschung, Vol. II, Tübingen 1970, pp. 19-32

Gamson, W.A.: Experimental Studies of Coalition Formation in: L. Berkowitz, ed., Advances in Experimental Social Psychology, Vol. I, New York 1964

Häselbarth, Volker: Preisträgheit in Geldmarktexperimenten
in: H. Sauermann, ed., Beiträge zur experimentellen Wirtschaftsforschung, Vol. II,
Tübingen 1970, pp. 151-161

Sauermann, Heinz: Die experimentelle Wirtschaftsforschung an der Universität Frankfurt am Main
in: H. Sauermann, ed., Beiträge zur experimentellen Wirtschaftsforschung, Vol. II,
Tübingen 1970, pp. 1-18

Selten, Reinhard: Ein Marktexperiment
in: H. Sauermann, ed., Beiträge zur experimentellen Wirtschaftsforschung, Vol. II,
Tübingen 1970, pp. 33-98

Selten, Reinhard / Berg, Claus C.: Drei experimentelle Oligopolspielserien mit kontinuierlichem Zeitablauf
in: H. Sauermann, ed., Beiträge zur experimentellen Wirtschaftsforschung, Vol. II,
Tübingen 1970, pp. 162-221

Selten, Reinhard / Schuster, Klaus G.: Psychologische Faktoren bei Koalitionsverhandlungen
in: H. Sauermann, ed., Beiträge zur experimentellen Wirtschaftsforschung, Vol. II,
Tübingen 1970, pp. 99-135

Mimeographed Papers

Knox, R.E. / Douglas, R.D.: Low Payoffs and Marginal Comprehension: Possible Constraints upon Behavior in the Prisoner's Dilemma
Paper presented at the Western Psychological Association Meeting,
San Diego 1968

Messé, L.A. / Sawayer, J.: Unexpected Cooperation: The Prisoner's Dilemma resolved?
Unpublished Paper,
University of Chicago 1966

Moore, O.K. / Berkowitz, M.I.: Game Theory and Social Interaction
Office of Naval Research, Technical Report, Contract No. SAR/NONR-609 (16),
New Haven 1956

Beiträge zur experimentellen Wirtschaftsforschung

Herausgegeben von Heinz Sauermann

1967. VII, 276 Seiten.
Brosch. DM 57.--, Lw. DM 62.--

Langsam gewinnt die deutsche Wirtschaftswissenschaft Anschluß an die internationale Forschung. Hier gilt es, von einem Unternehmen zu berichten, das sich selbst im internationalen Vergleich als bahnbrechend ausnimmt: Seit 1957 arbeitet in Frankfurt eine Forschungsgruppe unter Leitung von Prof. Sauermann an experimentellen Untersuchungen ökonomischer Probleme.

Schmollers Jahrbuch 3/1969

Die Arbeit der Gruppe stellt ohne Zweifel eine Pionierleistung moderner Wirtschaftsforschung dar. Sie dürfte sich anregend auch auf andere Gebiete der Sozialwissenschaften auswirken, zumal, wenn Ergebnisse der weiteren Experimente, etwa zur Erwartungsbildung, veröffentlicht werden.

Zeitschrift für die gesamte Staatswissenschaft 3/1969

Beiträge zur experimentellen Wirtschaftsforschung

Contributions to Experimental Economics

Band II/Volume II

Herausgegeben von Heinz Sauermann

1970. VII, 252 Seiten, 1 Bild
Brosch. DM 56.--, Lw. DM 62.--

Es ist wertvolles zusätzliches Material. Es wird noch mehr folgen müssen (Sauermann ermutigt in seinem Vorwort zu dieser Hoffnung), ehe allgemeinere Ergebnisse vorliegen. Das kann nicht anders sein. Die experimentelle Wirtschaftsforschung arbeitet "bausteinmäßig", und eines ihrer Ziele ist es gerade, die allgemeinen Aussagen der allumfassenden analytischen Theorien zu prüfen. Dafür bietet diese wichtige Veröffentlichung dann auch gute Beispiele.

Schmollers Jahrbuch 6/1970